The Relevance
of Charles Peirce

The Relevance of Charles Peirce

edited by Eugene Freeman

Series editor: Eugene Freeman
Editor of The Monist: *John Hospers*
Managing Editor: Sherwood J. B. Sugden

The Hegeler Institute

Monist Library of Philosophy
La Salle, Illinois
1983

First Edition

ISBN: 0-914417-00-2

The Hegeler Institute
publishers of *The Monist*, an International Quarterly Journal
of General Philosophical Inquiry
and of the Monist Library of Philosophy
Box 600, La Salle, Illinois 61301

To M. Elisabeth Carus
for her lifelong devotion to philosophy
and to The Monist.

CONTENTS

Foreword 7

Preface 9

MAX H. FISCH
The Range of Peirce's Relevance 11

JOHN E. SMITH
Community and Reality 38

EUGENE FREEMAN
C. S. Peirce and Objectivity in Philosophy 59

KARL POPPER
Freeman on Peirce's Anticipations of Popper 78

CHARLES HARTSHORNE
A Revision of Peirce's Categories 80

JOHN BOLER
Peirce, Ockham and Scholastic Realism 93

JAAKKO HINTIKKA
C. S. Peirce's "First Real Discovery"
and Its Contemporary Relevance 107

T. L. SHORT
Peirce and the Incommensurability of Theories 119

JAMES F. HARRIS & KEVIN HOOVER
Abduction and the New Riddle of Induction 132

WILLIAM J. GAVIN
Peirce and "The Will to Believe" 145

MIHAI NADIN
The Logic of Vagueness and the Category of Synechism . . . 154

CHARLES J. DOUGHERTY
Peirce's Phenomenological Defense of Deduction 167

BERTRAND P. HELM
The Nature and Modes of Time 178

THE RELEVANCE OF CHARLES PEIRCE

KARL-OTTO APEL
C. S. Peirce and Post-Tarskian Truth 189

E. F. KAELIN
Reflections on Peirce's Aesthetics 224

SUSAN HAACK
Descartes, Peirce and the Cognitive Community 238

RISTO HILPINEN
On C. S. Peirce's Theory of the Proposition:
Peirce as a Precursor of Game-Theoretical Semantics 264

DAVID GRUENDER
Pragmatism, Science, and Metaphysics 271

J. JAY ZEMAN
Peirce on Abstraction 293

SANDRA B. ROSENTHAL
Meaning as Habit: Some Systematic
Implications of Peirce's Pragmatism 312

ROBERT ALMEDER
Peirce on Meaning 328

PETER SKAGESTAD
C. S. Peirce on Biological Evolution
and Scientific Progress 348

CHRISTIAN J. W. KLOESEL
Bibliography of Charles Peirce, 1976 through 1981 373

Index 407

FOREWORD

Charles Peirce, now universally acclaimed as America's greatest philosopher, and considered by many to be one of the great philosophers of all time, was virtually unrecognized and unpublished during his lifetime. However, one of the few of his contemporaries who did appreciate his genius was Dr. Paul Carus, editor of *The Monist* from 1890 to 1919. The now classic series of papers that Peirce wrote for *The Monist* is today a landmark in the history of American philosophy. It is thus fitting that the historic ties between Peirce and *The Monist* should be commemorated by the publication of the present volume on *The Relevance of Charles Peirce* as a volume in "The Monist Library of Philosophy."

The Monist is an international quarterly journal of philosophy, founded in 1888 by Edward C. Hegeler as a journal of the philosophy of science. In 1961, under the editorship of its present editor, Eugene Freeman, its scope was broadened to include the entire range of philosophical inquiry, including problems arising in related disciplines. The scope of each issue of *The Monist* is specifically limited to a single general topic, selected and defined in advance by its Editorial Board. Accordingly, this monographic format gives each issue of *The Monist* the advantage of a unity and coherence not customarily found in scholarly journals in which the articles may range over a number of relatively unrelated topics.

A single issue of *The Monist*, however, is not intended to offer more than a preliminary study of the topic it deals with. "The "The Monist Library of Philosophy" series has been established to provide on occasion a more rounded and complete treatment in book form of a topic or theme than can be given in a single issue of *The Monist*. The first three volumes in this series were published by The Open Court Publishing Co., formerly publishers of *The Monist*. These were: *Kant Studies Today*, edited by Lewis White Beck; *Basic Issues in the Philosophy of Time*, edited by Eugene Freeman and

Wilfrid Sellars; and *The Philosophy of Spinoza*, edited by Eugene Freeman and Maurice Mandelbaum. We are indebted to M. Blouke Carus, Director of The Hegeler Institute, for a grant to make possible the continued publication of "The Monist Library of Philosophy" series.

ACKNOWLEDGMENTS

The essays in this book were published in *The Monist*, Vol. 63, No. 3 and Vol. 65., No. 2, with the exception of the following: The paper by John E. Smith was first published in *Perspectives on Peirce*, edited by Richard J. Bernstein and appears here with the kind permission of the Yale University Press. The paper by Eugene Freeman and the Reply to it by Karl Popper first appeared in *The Philosophy of Karl Popper* and is printed here with the kind permission of The Library of Living Philosophers, Inc. and Sir Karl. The second half of the paper by Karl-Otto Apel was first published in *The Transactions of the Charles S. Peirce Society*, Vol. XVIII, No. 1, and appears here with the kind permission of its editors, Richard S. Robin and Peter H. Hare. The papers by Robert Almeder and by Peter Skagestad were first published in *Synthese* Vol. 41, No. 1, and appears here with the kind permission of its editors, Risto Hilpinen, Ilkka Niniluoto, and Esa Saarinen, and the D. Reidel Publishing Co. We are also indebted to the Edgar Henderson Memorial Symposium on the Philosophy of Charles Peirce, held at Florida State University in May, 1980, where drafts of the papers by Rosenthal, Kaelin, Hilpinen, Gruender and Haack were read.

Eugene Freeman

PREFACE

"I don't think it extravagant praise to say that of late years there has been no intellect in Cambridge of such general powers and originality." These words were written over a century ago by William James in a letter to President Gilman of the Johns Hopkins University recommending Peirce for a Professorship. In the same letter James went on to point out that Peirce's "purely philosophical activity was known to comparatively few," a circumstance that, unfortunately, continued to hold true for some time to come. Things began to change when in 1923 Morris R. Cohen published *Chance, Love and Logic* containing such important writings as the "Illustrations of the Logic of Science" and Peirce's papers in *The Monist*, 1891–1893. A decade later the devoted work of Charles Hartshorne and Paul Weiss led to the publication in six volumes of *The Collected Papers of Charles Sanders Peirce* (1931–1935), to which were added in 1958 two more volumes edited by Arthur W. Burks. Peirce's "philosophical activity" was gradually becoming more widely known and appreciated for its originality and breadth of insight. Thirty years ago there appeared *Studies in the Philosophy of Charles Sanders Peirce*, edited by Philip P. Wiener and Frederic H. Young, the first among numerous ensuing volumes of essays dealing with the many aspects of Peirce's thought. I mention these few details merely to point out that, while at the present time Peirce has been so thoroughly discovered that the study of his thought approaches the magnitude of an industry, it was not always so. The recognition of Peirce commensurate with his philosophical genius was slow in coming; the full story is told by Max H. Fisch with his characteristic thoroughness in the opening article of this volume, "The Range of Peirce's Relevance."

The full spectrum of Peirce's interests and competence is truly remarkable. While the greater volume of his writing is to be found in the areas of logic, the philosophy of mathematics and of natural science, and the theory of signs, no one can afford to ignore his inquiries into the issues of metaphysics, ethics, religion, esthetics and history. The extent of Peirce's concern to attain a synoptic vision of things is easily underestimated if one is interested in what he had to say only in some particular area. But Peirce himself was bent on laying hold of the interconnectedness of all things. He was, to take but one example, convinced that the history of science manifests intelligible patterns of development, but he was not content to leave the matter there. Instead, he insisted that a theory of reality is needed to account for these patterns through an understanding of the relations between the cosmos and the human mind.

The essays in this volume provide ample evidence of the breadth, originality and vitality of Peirce's thought, and at the same time highlight the power of his basic notions for illuminating current philosophical issues. As these essays make clear, it is a matter of the utmost importance that Peirce has finally emerged from the shadows to assume his rightful place not only in the development of American philosophy but also in that wider dialectic of human thought which knows no geographical boundaries.

I wish to acknowledge the special debt owed to the Editor of *The Monist*, Eugene Freeman, since the initial proposal to have two issues devoted to the current significance of Peirce was his.

John E. Smith

New Haven, Connecticut
July, 1982

THE RANGE OF PEIRCE'S RELEVANCE

"Arisbe," the Peirce home near Milford, Pennsylvania, belongs to the National Park Service, and the Delaware Water Gap National Recreation Area is responsible for its care. In 1979 a geodetic triangulation station was installed in the front yard and named the "C. S. Peirce Station."[1] This was intended, at least in part, as a recognition of the fact that Peirce's scientific career was in the service of the Coast and Geodetic Survey, and that the first of his more than thirty years in its service was spent with triangulating parties along the coasts of Maine and of the Gulf states. It offers a suggestive metaphor for the present occasion. If the questions, methods, answers and reasons of another thinker, or of a whole movement of thought, whether earlier or later than Peirce, are illuminated by locating them, directly or indirectly, positively or negatively, in relation to those of the C. S. Peirce station, we may count that as part of the range of Peirce's relevance. In the case of an earlier thinker or movement, the relevance does not depend on Peirce's awareness or acknowledgment; in the case of a later thinker or movement, it does not depend on awareness or acknowledgment by that thinker or by one or more representatives of that movement. If the thinker is oneself, the triangulating will of course require a certain detachment. At least within limits, and perhaps even without limit, degrees of nearness or remoteness, likeness or difference, do not as such constitute degrees of relevance. And even if our interest is primarily in philosophical relevance, mathematical or scientific relevance may entail philosophical, and so be counted.

What follows is the first part of a planned longer study, the second and third parts of which will appear in a later paper. The first part works backward from 1980 to the last year of Peirce's life (1913–14), sampling claims, recognitions and acknowledgments along the way; the second surveys the present range of acknowledged relevance; and the third looks forward to recognitions of relevance still to come.[2]

1. A Backward Glance

In August 1980, at the Joint Mathematics Meetings, the Mathematical Association of America is sponsoring a "minicourse on *Teaching calculus using infinitesimals*," the way to which has been opened by Abraham Robinson's *Non-standard Analysis* (1966) and H. Jerome Keisler's *Elementary Calculus* (1976). Neither Robinson nor Keisler mentions Peirce, and he may not be mentioned in the minicourse, but Carolyn Eisele sees in nonstandard analysis a vindication of Peirce's almost single-handed advocacy of infinitesimals against the long dominant method and doctrine of limits.[3] The philosophical relevance in this case lies in the proof that we *can* reason logically and mathematically about infinity, and therefore about continuity.

The May 1979 issue of *Synthese* ("An International Journal for Epistemology, Methodology and Philosophy of Science" published in Holland since 1936) consisted of five "Essays on the Philosophy of Charles Peirce" and might itself have been called "The Relevance of Peirce" if *The Monist* had not already announced its present issue as in preparation.

At the annual meeting of the Semiotic Society of America in 1978 there was a plenary session on methodology. One of the five papers was by Thomas A. Sebeok and Jean Umiker-Sebeok, entitled " 'You Know my Method': A Juxtaposition of Charles S. Peirce and Sherlock Holmes." This was published in 1979.[4] It began with two epigraphs: Holmes's "I never guess" and Peirce's "But we must conquer the truth by guessing, or not at all." In March 1980 it appeared in book form.[5] This is the first book in which Peirce appears as a working detective and in which his philosophy of science is interpreted as a theory of detection.

At the International Congress for the History of Science in Edinburgh in August 1977, Carolyn Eisele presented a paper on "Peirce as a Precursor in Mathematics and Science" which is noteworthy not only for its own substance but also as representative of what is probably the most frequent type of relevance claim.[6]

When the C. S. Peirce Bicentennial International Congress was held in Amsterdam in June 1976, it was remarked in the presidential address that Peirce himself had been in Europe in 1876 on the second of five European sojourns in the service of the U. S. Coast and Geodetic Survey; that he represented the Survey at meetings of the International Geodetic Association; that that was the first international scientific association, and that Peirce was the first American participant in the meetings of such an association. It was also remarked that it was Vening Meinesz's gravity survey of Holland in 1913–1921 that first proved the practicability of a method proposed by Faye in 1877 and shown by Peirce in 1879 to be theoretically sound, for avoiding the flexure or swaying of the pendulum stands then used in determinations of gravity.[7] One of the hosts of the Congress remarked that recognition of Peirce's importance had been more continuous in the Netherlands than elsewhere in Europe because of the "significs" movement going back to Gerrit Mannoury and L. E. J. Brouwer. (Mannoury had followed Schröder in recognizing Peirce's priority over Dedekind in analyzing the distinction between a finite and an infinite collection.)

A Bicentennial Conference on the History of Geology was held at the University of New Hampshire in October 1976, and its proceedings were published in 1979 under the title *Two Hundred Years of Geology in America*.[8] In the latter half of the nineteenth century geology became an—indeed *the*—American science. Several of the twenty-eight papers trace its emergence from the earth sciences as a complex whole. Institutionally, it was the Coast Survey that, when Peirce began his more than thirty years in its service, had become "the center of the American scientific community."[9] Val Dusek's paper on "Geodesy and the Earth Sciences in the Philosophy of C. S. Peirce" assumes that he was "America's greatest philosopher" and "perhaps the one truly universal mind that nineteenth-century America produced," and argues that both the wide range and the main focuses of his work for the Survey gave him a "background in the observational and experimental sciences" and thereby "a balanced view of science" such as few philosophers have ever had. Dusek acknowledges that Peirce concluded a review of his acquaintance with the sciences by saying that he was more completely ignorant of geology than of any other, but remarks that "this was *comparative* ignorance, not absolute." He mentions that Peirce "studied classification with Louis Agassiz for six months," but does not mention that one of the tasks Agassiz set him was sorting fossil brachiopods, and that fifty years later he was still drawing illustrations from paleontology. Nor does Dusek mention that Peirce's father in the 1850s was one of the early theorists of the formation of continents and of "continental drift," or that Peirce himself in 1897 was chosen by the Director of the Geological Survey to adjudicate a controversy between two of the leading geologists, Becker and Van Hise, concerning slaty cleavage; that the founder and editor of the *Journal of Geology* wished to publish a paper by Peirce detaching the positive general substance of his report from the details of the controversy; and that Peirce agreed to write such a paper but never found time for it.[10]

The Johns Hopkins University celebrated its centennial by holding a series of symposia extending throughout the academic year 1975–76, beginning with "The Charles Sanders Peirce Symposium on Semiotics and the Arts" on September 25–26, 1975. The five contributors included Thomas A. Sebeok on "Iconicity," Umberto Eco on "Peirce's Notion of Interpretant," and Roman Jakobson in "A Few Remarks on Peirce, Pathfinder in the Science of Language." The papers were published in *Modern Language Notes*, and Jakobson's illuminating "Remarks" have just made a prominent reappearance in his *The Framework of Language*, inaugurating the Michigan Studies in the Humanities.[11]

In 1974 *The Philosophy of Karl Popper* appeared in The Library of Living Philosophers. It contained a three-part paper by Eugene Freeman and

Henryk Skolimowski on "The Search for Objectivity in Peirce and Popper."
In the first part Freeman found the germ of Popper's notion of falsification in
Peirce's remark that "the best hypothesis, in the sense of the one most recommending itself to the inquirer, is the one which can be the most readily refuted
if it is false."[12]

At the semi-centennial meeting of the History of Science Society in 1974
a morning session was devoted to "Charles Sanders Peirce: Scientist,
Mathematician and Historian of Science."[13]

At the 80th annual meeting of the American Psychological Association
in 1972, Thomas C. and Joyce V. Cadwallader presented the first of a series
of papers leading gradually to the conclusion that Peirce was the first modern
experimental psychologist in the Americas.[14] (One of these papers was
presented to the History of Science Society's Peirce session in 1974.)

In 1970 Kathleen Nott in her *Philosophy and Human Nature* gave
greater prominence to Peirce than to any other of the philosophers she found
most helpful.

At a time in 1970 when IBM's great "Computer Perspective" exhibit
was in preparation, Preston Tuttle was examining the Allan Marquand
papers at Princeton University. He came upon a letter from Peirce dated "18-
86 Dec. 30" containing the first known design for an electric switching circuit
machine for performing logical and mathematical operations. The letter
became a feature of the exhibit and was published in the book that grew out
of it.[15]

In 1968 W. J. Baumol and S. M. Goldfeld included Peirce among their
Precursors in Mathematical Economics on the basis of correspondence
between him and Simon Newcomb in 1871 which Carolyn Eisele had
published in 1957.

Also in 1968, on page 5 of *The Origins of Pragmatism*, A. J. Ayer wrote:
"We shall indeed find that the theory of scientific method for which Professor
Popper has become justly celebrated in our own times was very largely an-
ticipated by Peirce."

When Rosser and Turquette published their *Many-valued Logics* in
1952, the first known system of three-valued logic was that of Post in 1921.
When Peirce's system of 1909 was discovered in his logic notebook in 1965,
Turquette collaborated with me in an article on "Peirce's Triadic Logic,"[16]
and he then went on in three further articles, and in two papers presented at
professional meetings, to develop Peirce's system in greater detail.

When Karl Popper published his *Logik der Forschung* in 1934 he knew
nothing of Peirce. When he published its English translation in 1959 and *Conjectures and Refutations* in 1962, his first-hand acquaintance with Peirce's
work was still very slight. But in his 1965 Compton Memorial Lecture *Of*

Clouds and Clocks he was ready to say:

> Among the few dissenters [to physical determinism—the doctrine that all clouds
> are clocks] was Charles Sanders Peirce, the great American mathematician and
> physicist and, I believe, one of the greatest philosophers of all time. . . . So far as I
> know Peirce was the first post-Newtonian physicist and philosopher who thus
> dared to adopt the view that to some degree *all clocks are clouds*; or in other
> words, that *only clouds exist*, though clouds of very different degrees of
> cloudiness. . . . I further believe that Peirce was right in holding that this view was
> compatible with the classical physics of Newton. I believe that this view is even
> more clearly compatible with Einstein's (special) relativity theory, and it is still
> more clearly compatible with the new quantum theory. In other words, I am an
> indeterminist—like Peirce, Compton, and most other contemporary physicists;
> and I believe, with most of them, that Einstein was mistaken in trying to hold fast
> to determinism. (I may perhaps say that I discussed this matter with him, and
> that I did not find him adamant.)[17]

In 1964 the Yale department of philosophy commemorated the fiftieth
anniversary of Peirce's death by holding a series of lectures which was
published in 1965 under the title *Perspectives on Peirce*.[18] Among them was
Norwood Russell Hanson's "Notes Toward a Logic of Discovery." This was
one of several papers by Hanson developing further the argument of his *Patterns of Discovery*.[19] In these, as in the book, though he referred incidentally
to Aristotle, Whewell, and F. C. S. Schiller, it was chiefly on Peirce that he
built.

In 1962 the Coast and Geodetic Survey launched a research vessel
named for Peirce. It was commissioned in 1963 and is still in the service of the
National Oceanic and Atmospheric Administration, which makes frequent
reports of its findings. A ceremony honoring Peirce, with an address by
Carolyn Eisele, was held aboard the vessel at Washington on May 4, 1980.

In 1958 (the year in which volumes VII and VIII of the *Collected Papers*
appeared, edited by Arthur W. Burks), the *Journal of Public Law* published a
symposium of three papers on Peirce, followed by a republication of his 1892
paper "Dmesis," introduced as "one of the very few writings in which this
philosopher deals directly with law."

During World War II the charting of air routes became of increasing
strategic as well as scientific importance, and the Coast and Geodetic Survey
published a new and enlarged edition of Peirce's 1879 quincuncial map of the
earth, with the major international air routes now charted upon it. After the
war an edition without the air routes was published for more purely
educational purposes. Not only did the quincuncial projection yield the best
map for the charting of air routes, but

> An added advantage in the use of a projection on which the whole sphere can be
> repeated in a transposed position is to provide peoples residing in either the

Eastern or Western Hemispheres with a world pattern in accordance with their inherent geographical conception. A citizen of the United States using the map is able to observe the relationship of world land areas from his point of view as occupying a central geographical position; likewise a resident of Asia, by means of the repeated world image, is able to visualize the relationship of continents with Asia as the geographical center.[20]

When Dewey in 1938 published his *Logic: The Theory of Inquiry*, the first six volumes of the *Collected Papers* had appeared (1931–1935) and he had reviewed them. In the book he wrote that, as far as he was aware, Peirce was "the first writer on logic to make inquiry and its methods the primary and ultimate source of logical subject-matter,"[21] and that, "with the outstanding exception of Peirce," he had learned most from writers with whose positions he had in the end been compelled to disagree.[22]

Of the many eminently publishable papers that Peirce had not succeeded in publishing, *The Hound & Horn* in 1929, at a time when the *Collected Papers* were already in preparation, was permitted to publish his 1907 paper entitled "Guessing."[23] In some respects it remains the best introduction to Peirce. It puts into more colloquial terms such as "guessing" what elsewhere he had called hypothesis, abduction, or retroduction. Excerpts from it reappeared in 1958 in volume VII of the *Collected Papers*, but the detective episode was omitted.[24] That episode became the chief single Peircean source for the 1980 book by the Sebeoks.

When Russell and Whitehead published the second edition of *Principia Mathematica* in 1927, the most relevant things were Henry Sheffer's stroke function and his "General Theory of Notational Relativity." From that we may infer that, had they known of it, one of the most relevant things when they were preparing the first edition would have been Peirce's anticipation of the stroke function about 1880.

In 1923 two books of major importance for extending the awareness of Peirce's relevance appeared in the International Library of Psychology, Philosophy, and Scientific Method. One was *Chance, Love and Logic*, edited by Morris R. Cohen. It contained two of Peirce's most important series of papers—the "Illustrations of the Logic of Science" of 1877–78 and the *Monist* series of 1891–93—along with the most thematic paragraphs of the *Journal of Speculative Philosophy* series of 1868–69. The other book was *The Meaning of Meaning*, by Ogden and Richards, containing in Appendix D relevant extracts from papers published by Peirce from 1867 through 1906, and also from his unpublished letters to Victoria Lady Welby.

The *first* journal issue devoted to Peirce was that of the *Journal of Philosophy* in December 1916, nearly sixty-four years ago. It began with an article by Royce and his student Kernan on Peirce's leading ideas—his evolutionism, his insurance theory of induction, his tychism, his objective idealism—and on his unpublished manuscripts, which, at Royce's urging, had been acquired by Harvard University from Peirce's widow just two years earlier. It ended with a bibliography of Peirce's published writings by Morris R. Cohen. In between there were an article by Dewey on "The Pragmatism of Peirce" and articles by two of Peirce's ablest students, Joseph Jastrow and Christine Ladd-Franklin.[25]

In May 1913, early in the last year of Peirce's life, Royce sent him the two volumes of *The Problem of Christianity*, for the solution of which, in lectures at the Lowell Institute in Boston and at Oxford University, he had gone back to the theory of signs in four of Peirce's earliest published papers: "On a New List of Categories" (1867) and the three papers of the *Journal of Speculative Philosophy* series of 1868–69. Royce later said that he had received "a very kind letter of acknowledgment which I deeply prize, and which showed . . . that my interpretation of him gained on the whole, his approval."[26] Peirce had written to Victoria Lady Welby in December 1908, nearly six years earlier, that he had been "entirely absorbed" in the theory of signs "since 1863, without meeting, before I made your acquaintance, a single mind to whom it did not seem very like bosh."[27] In 1911 she wrote him that she thought she had found a disciple for him in C. K. Ogden, then still a student at Cambridge University.[28] Royce, in this last major work of his, was the third. Their number now is legion.

The above are of course but a few samples of the claims and acknowledgments of Peirce's relevance that have been made—or, in a few cases, that might have been made—from the last year of his life to the present time. Every student of his work will think of others more important than many of mine. I shall mention still others in parts 2 and 3 of the present essay (forthcoming). But I trust the above have served their immediate purpose, that of affording a first impression of the *range* of Peirce's relevance. Part 2 will offer a more systematic survey of the *present* range, and part 3 will venture predictions of recognitions still to come. Those that came during his active lifetime are matter for his biography.

2. The Present Range

A survey of the fields in which Peirce's relevance is now recognized may best begin with that in which such recognition is most nearly universal. The commonest English form of the name of that field is now semiotics. As a field of systematic study, it is still so young that there are as yet few if any university departments bearing its name; but there are several interdisciplinary programs and research centers, and several national societies and journals;

and there is an International Association for Semiotic Studies, which was founded at Paris in 1969; which publishes the most voluminous journal in the field, *Semiotica*; and which held its first congress at Milan in 1974 and its second at Vienna in 1979. At the latter there were three "working sessions" devoted to "Investigations into Peirce's Theory of Signs."

The Charles S. Peirce Society holds its regular single-session annual meeting in conjunction with the annual meeting of the Eastern Division of the American Philosophical Association; but, by invitation, it has been holding two- or even three-session meetings in conjunction with the annual meetings of the Semiotic Society of America. Moreover, the latter Society frequently has one or more Peirce sessions in its own program. Papers on Peirce are increasingly frequent in the semiotic societies of other countries also. It may soon be the case, if it is not so already, that more papers on Peirce are presented to semiotic societies and published in semiotic journals than to all other professional societies and in all other professional journals taken together.

Though the history of semiotics may be traced back to the ancient Greeks, and though Peirce and Saussure had modern predecessors, it has become common to recognize them as the modern founders of semiotics. (Saussure's term *"sémiologie"* is already obsolete, and so, apparently, is Peirce's preferred spelling "semeiotic.") Peirce's most fundamental published papers go back to 1867-1871, a decade before Saussure's *Mémoire* and half a century before his *Cours*. Those early papers of Peirce were first *re*published, and much of his relevant later work was first published, in 1931-1935, in the first six volumes of his *Collected Papers,* one of whose two editors was Charles Hartshorne, an older colleague of Charles Morris at the University of Chicago. Morris acquired and annotated those six volumes as they came out, and drew upon them in his own major works in the field, *Foundations of the Theory of Signs* (1938) and *Signs, Language, and Behavior* (1946). In the former he said that Peirce's work was "second to none in the history of semiotic." If by semiotics we mean the *general* theory of signs, then there is certainly one respect in which Peirce's work still is (and will almost certainly remain) second to none; namely, in the *degree* of its generality. Morris had become more focally conscious of this by the time of his second work, in the appendix to which he explained his preference for beginning and remaining at a lower level. It may safely be predicted that in this field at least Peirce will long remain relevant as providing a framework within which semioticians can locate the more limited ranges of their own researches.

More scholars have come to semiotics from cultural anthropology and from linguistics or philology than from any other single field. (It is to an anthropologist, Margaret Mead, that we owe the prevalence of the form "semiotics.")

Saussure was himself a linguist. Peirce was a chemist and his first professional publication was in chemistry, but his second was on the pronunciation of Shakespearian English, and he was a lifelong student of comparative linguistics. In 1870, during the first of his five European sojourns,[29] he wrote home that he had heard eighteen distinct languages spoken, seventeen of them (including Basque) in places where they were the languages of everyday speech. His escape from the provincialism of the Indo-European family had begun.

For forty years the most distinguished linguist in the United States has been Roman Jakobson. He came to us from the Moscow and Prague linguistic circles, and to Peirce from Husserl and Saussure. I have already mentioned his Johns Hopkins remarks on Peirce as "Pathfinder in the Science of Language." In his 1971 foreword to the second volume of his own *Selected Writings,* Jakobson says it is Peirce who in this country has been for him "the most powerful source of inspiration." Besides the thirty indexed passages on Peirce in the volume, there are several unindexed ones. In one of these he refers to Peirce as "the deepest inquirer into the essence of signs," and in another he says that Peirce's statement that "a symbol may have an icon or an index incorporated into it" "opens new, urgent tasks and far-reaching vistas to the science of language."[30]

To the *Scientific American's* September 1972 issue on communication Jakobson contributed the article on "Verbal Communication." He quotes Peirce in the first paragraph and in two later ones, the first of which speaks of him as "the initiator of semiotics." One of Jakobson's three illustrations is from Peirce's rendering of Poe's "The Raven" in "art chirography." Jakobson says "He intended to show how ties between sound and meaning. . . can be transmuted into autonomous interplay of letter and meaning."

In his inaugural address, in French, at the first congress of the International Association for Semiotic Studies, at Milan in 1974, Jakobson gave great prominence to Peirce, "the most inventive and the most universal among American thinkers," and called attention both to his three earliest relevant publications, of 1867 and 1868, and to an "amazing" still earlier Lowell Institute Lecture of 1866 on consciousness and language, which had remained unpublished until 1958.[31]

Noam Chomsky, of generative and transformational grammar fame, has a narrower Peircean range, focusing on a collection of passages on abduction brought together in chapter 13 of Vincent Tomas's 1957 anthology of Peirce's *Essays in the Philosophy of Science.*[32] In 1976, when his conversations with the French linguist Mitsou Ronat moved into the philosophy of language, and she asked him to which philosophy he felt closest, he replied: "In relation to the questions we have just been discussing, the philosopher to whom I feel closest and whom I'm almost paraphrasing is Charles Sanders Peirce."[33]

Among still younger linguists, one of the most productive and influential is Michael Shapiro. He specializes in Russian and other Slavic languages and in Japanese, and thinks of himself as continuing Jakobson's work, with amplifications and revisions. In a recent article on "Poetry and Language, 'Considered as Semiotic,' " he says that "Linguistics and poetics as disciplines have yet to undergo what must eventually become a full-blown Peircean revolution in the humanities and social sciences."[34] Partly as a means of hastening that revolution, he thinks it is not too soon to begin preparing for a sesquicentennial Peirce conference, preferably in Cambridge, and ideally to climax on Sunday, September 10, 1989, the 150th anniversary of Peirce's birth there in 1839.

One of the most striking features of the last quarter of a century has been the high frequency of articles, chapters, journal issues, and entire books on metaphor, many of them by philosophers.[35] No single article is more often referred to than Paul Henle's, whose approach is by way of Aristotle's definition of metaphor and Peirce's distinction between symbols and icons as kinds of signs.[36] There is a more recent and more comprehensive brochure by Michael and Marianne Shapiro, entitled *Hierarchy and the Structure of Tropes*, the last of whose five parts is on "Tropes in the Framework of Peircean Semiotic." In the first, called "Background," we read: "What has been insufficiently apperceived, to echo Henning Andersen's phrase (following C. S. Peirce), is the fact that all figures of speech are a particular kind of 'abductive innovation.' "[37]

Developments in linguistics often lead to developments in cultural anthropology, in sociology, and in other social sciences. It should not surprise us, therefore, if advances in semiotics, as a field more general than and embracing linguistics, should likewise lead to advances in the social sciences, directly as well as by way of linguistics. Claude Lévi-Strauss's *Structural Anthropology* acknowledges its debt to the structural linguistics of Saussure and Jakobson. If it owes anything to Peirce, it may be only indirectly, through Jakobson and other post-Saussurean linguists.[38]

In 1978, the Chicago anthropologist Milton Singer, in "For a Semiotic Anthropology," gave an account of "the tilt of culture theory to semiotics and semiology in the 1960s," compared Saussure's language-centered dyadic semiology with Peirce's logic-centered triadic semeiotic, gave reasons for preferring the latter to the former, and intimated that Lévi-Strauss and other anthropologists who had adopted the former had done so without really examining the latter.[39]

Singer was the American Anthropological Association's "Distinguished Lecturer" for 1978. His lecture, published in 1980 under the title "Signs of the Self: An Exploration in Semiotic Anthropology,"[40] was devoted entirely to Peirce. Its first section, headed "Man's Glassy Essence," was a detailed examination of Peirce's concluding Lowell Lecture of 1866, which had so amazed Jakobson. Singer went on to explore "the thesis that an application of Peirce's general theory of signs will produce a semiotic conception of the self that is also a phenomenological and a pragmatic conception."[41]

Singer has continued his argument in "Personal and Social Identity in Dialogue"[42] and in his book, *Man's Glassy Essence: Explorations in Semiotic Anthropology*.[43] The latter is now the most comprehensive and persuasive argument for a Peircean anthropology.

In sociology and social psychology one of the liveliest movements is called symbolic interactionism. Back in 1938, in a volume edited by Emerson P. Schmidt and entitled *Man and Society: A Substantive Introduction to the Social Sciences*, Herbert Blumer contributed the chapter on social psychology. He distinguished three schools, proposed the name "symbolic interactionists" for the third, to which he himself belonged, and cited George Herbert Mead's *Mind, Self, and Society* as "the most illuminating treatment of the self" from its point of view. In 1969 Blumer published a book called *Symbolic Interactionism: Perspective and Method,* with a chapter on "Sociological Implications of the Thought of George Herbert Mead." To the philosophers who had contributed to it he now added Dewey and James, but said he relied chiefly on Mead, "who, above all others, laid the foundations of the symbolic interactionist approach."

In 1973 John M. Lincourt and Peter H. Hare published an article on "Neglected American Philosophers in the History of Symbolic Interactionism"[44] in which they called attention to Chauncey Wright, Peirce, and Royce as other philosophers not yet recognized in this connection but deserving recognition along with Mead, Dewey, and James.

In 1942 C. Wright Mills took his Ph. D. degree at the University of Wisconsin with a thesis entitled "A Sociological Account of Some Aspects of Pragmatism." In 1964, two years after his death, his thesis was published by Irving Louis Horowitz under the title *Sociology and Pragmatism: The Higher Learning in America*.[45] Long chapters on Peirce, James and Dewey are preceded by an introductory chapter whose longest section is on the "Biographical Composition of the Metaphysical Club" in which pragmatism was born. At the end of the book there is a postscript of 1943 in which Mills traced most of the faults of his thesis to its not including a chapter on Mead.

And now comes a book of 1980 by two young sociologists, J. David Lewis and Richard L. Smith, entitled *American Sociology and Pragmatism:*

Mead, Chicago Sociology, and Symbolic Interaction.[46] They take off from
Mills's postscript, and supply not only the deficiencies he acknowledged but
others of which he was unaware. In the first half of their book, to their
chapters on Peirce, James and Dewey, they add one on Mead. But in the latter half they supply the materials for "an intellectual history of Chicago
sociology." Mills had remarked on Peirce's realism and James's nominalism.
Lewis and Smith go on to associate Mead and Peirce as realists, James and
Dewey as nominalists; they present evidence that Mead's influence on
Chicago sociology has been greatly exaggerated; they reject Blumer's
nominalistic interpretation of him; and they argue that by adopting their own
interpretation of him, and thus by associating him with Peirce rather than
with James and Dewey, we shall greatly enhance his claim to sociological
recognition.

From anthropology, sociology and social psychology it is a natural next
step to psychiatry, and more particularly to the interpersonal psychiatry of
Harry Stack Sullivan and of his journal *Psychiatry*. Though Peirce was the
first modern experimental psychologist in the Americas, he was scarcely a
psychiatrist. (Some of his critics, and even some of his admirers, think he
could have used one.) But at least three Peircean articles have appeared in
that journal. By far the longest and most substantial article in the first issue,
in February 1938, was Albert M. Dunham's Chicago Ph. D. thesis of 1933,
written under the direction of Charles Hartshorne, on "The Concept of Tension in Philosophy." Dunham began with Peirce in his introduction, devoted
by far the longest chapter to him, entitled "Peirce and the Aesthetic of
Events," and returned to him in the conclusion. (The other philosophers to
whom he paid most attention in chapters I-IV were Whitehead and Santayana.)

The second Peircean article was Walker Percy's "Toward a Triadic
Theory of Meaning" in the issue for February 1972, and the third was "C. S.
Peirce and H. S. Sullivan on the Human Self," by John M. Lincourt and
Paul V. Olczak, in that for February 1974.[47]

The other chief American journal in the field is *Psychiatric Quarterly*.
The psychiatrist Maurice R. Green at the 1958 meeting of the American
Psychiatric Association presented a paper on "The Roots of Sullivan's
Concept of the Self" which traced those roots through Mead and James to
Peirce. In the following year Green presented to the Harry Stack Sullivan
Society a paper on "Prelogical Processes and Participant Communication"
in which he went back to one of the great classics of experimental psychology,
the memoir on subliminal perception which Peirce and his student Jastrow
presented to the National Academy of Sciences in 1883. Both of Green's
papers were published in the *Quarterly*.[48] In both he compared Sullivan's

pretaxic, protaxic and parataxic modes of experience with Peirce's three categories.

So much for Peirce's relevance to American psychiatry. But what of Freud? I am not aware that Peirce knew anything of Freud, or Freud of Peirce, though each might have heard of the other through G. Stanley Hall. But Svend Erik Larsen has recently published an essay on Freud and Peirce in which he first outlines the generative structure of jokes, as analyzed by Freud in his 1905 book on *Jokes and Their Relation to the Unconscious*; then outlines the generative structure of semiosis, as analyzed by Peirce; and then finds a close relation between the triadicity of the one and that of the other.[49] His paper should encourage some student of Freud and Peirce to bring Freud's Ego, Id, and Superego into comparison with Peirce's I, It, and Thou.

There is an extensive and growing literature on perception—philosophical, psychological, physiological, model-theoretic, and computer-theoretic. One of the most comprehensive and interesting anthologies was edited in 1966 by the psychologist and computer scientist Leonard Uhr under the title *Pattern Recognition*.[50] Its five parts range from "Conceptual Framework" through "Computer Simulations of Complex Models." The first begins with three selections from Peirce, a short one from his Harvard Lectures of 1903 on pragmatism (CP 5.115-119) and two long ones from his 1868 article on "Some Consequences of Four Incapacities" (CP 5.283-287, 295-317). All the other selections in the volume are of much more recent date. None is as fundamental.

Passing now to recognitions of Peirce's relevance by professional philosophers, I remark first that the present issue of *The Monist* and that for July 1980 supply their readers with ample materials for making their own preliminary surveys.[51] I shall assume that they have done so, and limit myself to some supplementary remarks, the first of which is that he has contributed more than any other American philosopher to the vocabulary of philosophy—and inspired others to such coinages as Wilfrid Sellars's "Peirceish" and his use of Peirce's initials CSP for "conceptual structure Peirceish."[52]

As late as 1905 Peirce could say that his "one contribution to philosophy" was his 1867 "New List of Categories" (CP 8.213). Many philosophers (as well as semioticians) have asked: "But what of his theory of signs?" The answer to that is: "Not only does the 'New List' contain the first published exposition of his theory of signs, but the categories of the new list were and remained the very foundation of the theory of signs." Some philosophers have gone on to ask: "But what of his pragmatism?" The answer to that is: "His pragmatism is a theorem of his theory of signs." Some of the philosophers ask next, "What is the proof of that theorem?"; others, "But what of his synechism?" The answer to those questions is: "Peirce in 'What Pragmatism Is' in *The Monist* in 1905 wrote that the proof of pragmatism was 'the one contribution of value' that he had *still* to make to philosophy, 'For it would essentially involve the establishment of the truth of synechism' " (CP 5.415).

If some of the philosophers go on to ask, "Is there anything in Peirce's later philosophy that does *not* depend upon the 'New List'? His realism, say, his tychism, or his fallibilism?", the answer is "No." So a philosopher who finds relevance in anything else in Peirce should find it in the "New List" too.

But most of the philosophers who have read "On a New List of Categories" have read it not in the *Proceedings* of the American Academy for 1867, in which it appeared as the third of five papers on logic, and not in the collective offprint of the first three entitled *Three Papers on Logic,* but in volume I of the *Collected Papers* where it appears toward the end of Book III, which is entitled "Phenomenology" (CP 1.284-572 at 545-559). How did that much of what was logic in 1867 become phenomenology in 1931?

Locke at the end of his *Essay* had identified logic with semeiotic, the general theory of signs. Peirce in the "New List" distinguished three kinds of signs: likenesses (which he later called icons), indexes, and symbols. He then confined logic to symbols and went on to exclude from logic such studies even of symbols as belonged to formal grammar and to formal rhetoric, so that logic was but a third part of a third part—that is, a ninth part—of semeiotic (CP 1.559). And even before the "New List" he had rejected the notion that logic is a normative science.[53]

But well along in his five-year Lectureship in Logic at The Johns Hopkins University (1879-1884) Peirce discovered, with some help from his student Mitchell, that logic cannot do business without icons and indexes (CP 3.363). And at least as early as 1882 he had begun conceiving logic as "the method of methods" (CP 7.59). In the 1890's if not earlier he began distinguishing a narrow sense of logic in which it *ex*cluded and a broad sense in which it *in*cluded what he now called Speculative Grammar and Speculative Rhetoric or Methodeutic, and he inclined more and more to the broad sense. But a logic that included Methodeutic would be in some sense a normative science. Around the turn of the century, moreover, Peirce was inclining more and more toward including ethics and even aesthetics among the research sciences. A normative logic would presuppose a normative ethics, and a normative ethics would presuppose a normative aesthetics. But aesthetics and ethics and therefore also logic would then presuppose the theory of categories, which must therefore be assigned to a nonnormative philosophical science antecedent to aesthetics. Peirce at first called that prior science High Philosophy, Categories or Categorics (NE 4:17); but by the time of his

Minute Logic of 1902 he was at least trying out Phenomenology (CP 1.280). These new developments were all reflected in his Harvard Lectures on Pragmatism in the spring of 1903 and in his Lowell Lectures that fall. Their first printed presentation was in the *Syllabus* which he distributed at the latter (CP 1.183-192). The choice of the name Phenomenology was a bow toward Hegel (CP 5.37 f.); but Peirce had misgivings about it almost from the beginning, lest it should suggest too close a relation. In 1903 he was already trying out Phaneroscopy; in 1904 Phenoscopy; in 1905 Phanerology and Phanerochemy. From 1905 onward his most frequent name is Phaneroscopy; and, for the object it analyzes, Phaneron.

Why, then, did the editors of the *Collected Papers* choose "Phenomenology" as the title of Book III of Volume I? Because that was the name to which Peirce had given greatest publicity; because he had used it in several of his major unpublished writings; and because they had become acquainted with Husserl at Freiburg and thought it important not only to associate Peirce retrospectively with Hegel but also to associate him prospectively with the leading phenomenologist of the 1930's, when the *Collected Papers* were appearing. (Weiss would later call Hegel, Husserl and Peirce "the three great phenomenologists."[54]) Perhaps they were also struck by the fact that Husserl first gave prominence to the term "phenomenology" in the title of the second volume of his *Logische Untersuchungen* in 1901, the year before that in which Peirce's most frequent use of it began.

The first book on Peirce's categories was written under Hartshorne's direction by our editor, Eugene Freeman, and published in 1934.[55] It is still an excellent introduction, and it raises objections to which no adequate reply has yet been made.[56] Chief of these is that, though phenomenology may be competent to prove that there are three categories, it is incompetent to prove that there are not more; so that, if there is such a proof, it must be the work of that first branch of metaphysics which Peirce calls ontology. I suggest rather that it is the work of logic; more exactly, of the logic of relations. Though Peirce frequently claimed to have a proof and to have presented it, nobody has so far found it in his surviving writings, and until 1981 nobody had even published a plausible reconstruction of it. But now we have Hans G. Herzberger making use of the resources of "bonding algebra" to construct a proof of "Peirce's Remarkable Theorem" which is certainly neither phenomenological nor ontological but logical.[57] We may fairly infer that when Peirce inserted phenomenology in his classification of the sciences, he did not move up into it the whole of that part of his categoriology that had previously been assigned to logic. But we may also hope that readers who are in position to shed further light on these matters will seize the early occasion for doing so that is offered by *The Monist*'s July 1983 issue on Categories.

Two further remarks about phenomenology. (1) In his pioneering article of 1957 Herbert Spiegelberg concluded that while there is no evidence of any historical interaction, and there are deep-seated differences, "there are enough parallels between Husserl's and Peirce's phenomenologies to justify the question about a common root for them both."[58] Charles J. Dougherty has recently pursued that question and proposed a positive answer.[59] (2) Sandra Rosenthal and Patrick Bourgeois have recently published a book extending the comparison by including pragmatists other than Peirce and phenomenologists other than Husserl.[60] They do not mention that Heidegger in the last months of his life was intently reading the recent two-volume German translation of Peirce by Gerd Wartenberg, with long introductions by Apel.[61]

The range of Peirce's relevance in logic, both acknowledged and unacknowledged, both in the narrow sense of logic with which he began and in the broad sense with which he ended, is so much greater than that of any other logician that we very much need a comprehensive and critical guidebook. A few examples: (1) Don Roberts, Kenneth Ketner, and others have found Peirce's existential graphs ideally suited for beginning courses in logic. (2) A. R. Turquette has published a series of articles on Peirce as pioneer in triadic or three-valued logic. (3) Though the Boole-Peirce-Schröder line in logic was partially eclipsed for a time by the Frege-Peano-Russell/Whitehead line, it has emerged from the eclipse, and Hilary Putnam and others have given strong reasons for preferring it. (4) There is an extensive and growing literature on Peirce's contributions to mathematics itself, to the history of mathematics, to "the logic of mathematics" as including methodeutic and more particularly heuretic, and to mathematical pedagogy. For better measures of this range of his relevance, we very much need a comprehensive, well organized and critical survey of this literature. (5) Of all the great logicians, Peirce has most to offer to students of tense logic, speech act logic, erotetic logic, game-theoretic logic, general systems theory, and the logic of vagueness. (6) In inductive logic, and more particularly in probability theory, I. J. Good, responding recently to criticisms of his "probabilistic causality," explained that it involves the concept of "weight of evidence" "as used by C. S. Peirce (1878), and by myself in over forty publications."[62] (7) Philosophers of law have often remarked that there were several distinguished lawyers in the Metaphysical Club in which pragmatism was born, and have traced connections between pragmatism and "legal realism"; but more recently Roberta Kevelson and others have found relevance to legal reasoning in a much wider range of Peirce's work in logic.

On two further points of relevance I take space to enlarge somewhat.

(A) No other logician compares with Peirce in attention to systems of notation and to sign-*creation*. For the psychologist and logician Shea Zellweger, as to the neurophysiologist Warren McCulloch before him, the most relevant part of Peirce's *Minute Logic* of 1902 is in the eleven pages of manuscript omitted by the editors (at the end of CP 4.261) in which he introduces two notations for the sixteen binary connectives of the two-valued propositional calculus. One of these may be called his box-X, the other his cursive notation. He says it was his Johns Hopkins student Christine Ladd-Franklin "who first proposed to put the same character into four positions in order to represent the relationship between logical copulas, and . . . it was a part of her proposal that when the relation signified was symmetrical, the sign should have a right and left symmetry" (NE 3:272n). Peirce's own notations simply carry out that proposal in a particular way.

Zellweger has recently patented a new notation for the same connectives, which he calls "the logic alphabet," the essentials of which he had worked out over a period of several years before he saw or even heard of those pages of Peirce. He accepts four of Peirce's criteria for a good notation, and follows Peirce in calling two of them *iconicity* and *cursiveness*. The other two, in substance contained in Peirce's box-X, he calls *frame consistency* and *eusymmetry*. Although his logic alphabet differs from Peirce's notations, he conceives his own notation as directly continuing Peirce's work. He has also invented and has recently patented a number of extremely simple and novel devices (such as a logic bug, a flipstick, and a logical garnet) for displaying the sixteen binary connectives as a single system, and especially for performing the logical operation of negation when it acts upon the symbols for these connectives. There is probably no other contribution to formal logic whose fullest exposition so far in print is in the *Official Gazette of the United States Patent and Trademark Office*[63] and contains a paragraph on Peirce's relevance.[64]

(B) Peirce's first discovery in logic was that, besides deduction and induction, which he associated with the first and third figures of the syllogism, there is a third kind of inference which he associated with the second figure, and which he at first called hypothesis, later abduction or retroduction. (Closely linked with this discovery was his discovery in 1866 that "no syllogism of the second or third figure can be reduced to the first, without taking for granted an inference which can only be expressed syllogistically in that figure from which it has been reduced" [CP 2.807].) Deduction was "the logic of mathematics"; hypothesis and induction were "the logic of science." Peirce later shifted focus from the classification of arguments to the stages of inquiry; the order then became abduction, deduction, induction; and the stages in mathematics paralleled those in the sciences.

K. T. Fann's book on *Peirce's Theory of Abduction*, written in 1963, published in 1970,[65] and favorably reviewed by F. Michael Walsh in *Philosophy* in 1972,[66] begins with the questions: "Is there a logic of dis-

covery? If so, what is the nature of such a logic?" The questions go back, if
not to Aristotle, at least to Bacon and Whewell, Gore and Carmichael. (Carmichael's book grew out of articles in *The Monist* and was published by its
publisher.[67]) At the time Fann wrote, the chief proponent of a logic of discovery was Norwood Russell Hanson, and he found his chief support in
Peirce's theory of abduction. That was the occasion for Fann's book. The
questions are still very much alive. As late as 1978 there was a Conference on
Scientific Discovery at the University of Nevada which resulted in two
volumes edited by Thomas Nickles: *Scientific Discovery, Logic, and
Rationality,* and *Scientific Discovery: Case Studies.*[68] Peirce is prominent in
Nickles's introduction and in the papers by Laudan, Curd and Gutting in the
first volume, and in that by Schaffner in the second. It seems likely that
Peirce's relevance will be recognized as long as the questions are discussed.

   Turning briefly to rhetoric, I note that there is something that calls itself
"the new rhetoric." Its most representative work is a treatise bearing that title by Ch. Perelman and L. Olbrechts-Tyteca. In the United States, one of its
chief representatives is Henry W. Johnstone of Pennsylvania State University, where the journal *Philosophy and Rhetoric* is published. When the
editors of that journal heard that Peirce had drafted an essay on the rhetoric
of scientific writing, they were glad to be its first publishers.[69] Another range
of rhetoric is represented by a manuscript apparently intended to be the first
of six lessons for Episcopalian rectors on the reading of the order of worship
at morning and evening prayer. This first lesson focuses on the address to the
congregation (Ms 1570). It has not yet been published, but several
Episcopalian rectors have read it with great interest.

   I shall assume that our readers have made their own surveys of the range
of Peirce's acknowledged relevance in metaphysics. I mention it again only to
remark that the principal papers he published appeared in *The Monist*; and I
move on now to another range of relevance: that of suitability for inclusion in
collections of "the great books," in dictionaries of quotations, and in other
anthologies.

   When Mortimer Adler in 1940 included a "purist" list of the great books
in his *How To Read a Book*, volumes I-VI of the *Collected Papers* had appeared and he included them along with *Chance, Love, and Logic* (1923). But
the only book that Peirce himself had published was *Photometric Researches*,
and that was quite properly thought not suitable for inclusion in the *Great
Books of the Western World* in 1952. In the *Syntopicon*, however, which constituted volumes 2 and 3 of the set, there were 102 chapters each devoted to
one of "the great ideas." Additional readings were recommended at the end
of each chapter, and readings from Peirce were recommended in the following 37: Being, Cause, Chance, Dialectic, Evolution, Form, God, Good and

Evil, Habit, Hypothesis, Idea, Induction, Infinity, Logic, Love, Man, Mathematics, Matter, Mechanics, Memory and Imagination, Metaphysics, Mind, Nature, Necessity and Contingency, One and Many, Opinion, Opposition, Philosophy, Quality, Quantity, Reasoning, Relation, Religion, Science, Sign and Symbol, Truth, and World.

There were several selections from Peirce in James R. Newman's four-volume anthology *The World of Mathematics* in 1956, and one of these, to which Newman had given the title "The Essence of Mathematics," was repeated in the 1975 volume of *The Great Ideas Today*.

Charles P. Curtis and Ferris Greenslet in 1945 included several passages from Peirce in a one-volume "thinker's anthology" called *The Practical Cogitator* (after Bowditch's *Practical Navigator*). It has gone through several editions and is still in print.

The first dictionary of quotations to contain numerous ones from Peirce was Edward F. Murphy's *The Crown Treasury of Relevant Quotations* in 1978. Though known from the age of five to John Bartlett, he was not admitted to the latter's *Familiar Quotations* until the "Fifteenth and 125th Anniversary Edition" in 1980, seventy-five years after the compiler's death. This tardiness may be explained in part by the fact that his style was rather dialogical than aphoristic or epigrammatic. We may recall his saying that for him every language, including his native English, had been a foreign language; that he thought in diagrams and in experiments on diagrams rather than in words. Or we may recall his frequently saying that all thought is dialogic in form, as Socrates in the *Theaetetus* and the Stranger in the *Sophist* had said. Even in what we might at first describe as private thought, the self of one moment appeals to the oncoming self of the next moment for confirmation or correction or further development. (Peirce's own career was chiefly that of a research scientist in the service of the Coast and Geodetic Survey; and he extended the dialogic model of thought to scientific research as the business of putting questions to Nature and getting answers. Considerations of economy were much more prominent there than in mathematics or philosophy, and he found the dialogic model of the economy of research in the game of Twenty Questions.)

This suggests a different sort of anthology. Scattered through Peirce's writings are a number of passages in explicitly dialogic form. It would be worth collecting these. But there are much more numerous passages in which, without the obvious form of a dialogue, assigning names to the participants, Peirce is anticipating objections to the position he is taking, and meeting those objections. The same anthology might include several of these.

On the other hand, with a view to better representation of Peirce in dictionaries of quotations of the traditional kind, it would help if some Peirce scholar with a sense for style would compile an anthology of single sentences and short paragraphs which are specimens of Peirce at his best within such limits.

I now conclude part 2 by citing one example of recognized relevance of a kind quite different from any of the above. When the Royal Irish Academy in Dublin thought to take some notice of the Bicentennial of American Independence in 1976, it adopted the proposal of its Committee for Philosophy to have a lecture on an outstanding American philosopher, and invited Professor J. A. Faris of Queen's University, Belfast, to give it. His lecture on "Charles Sanders Peirce, Philosopher and Logician" was delivered on December 13, 1976, and a shortened version was published in the Academy's *Proceedings* in the following year.[70]

3. Something Peirce Himself Found Relevant—and a Glance Forward

There are no more pervasive themes in Peirce's work, from early until late, than that all thought is in signs and is dialogic in nature, and that even at its most private and silent it is none the less dialogue between the self of one moment and the oncoming self of the next. And he found relevance from the beginning, not only in the vernacular "I says to myself, says I," and in Socrates's arguments in the *Theaetetus* and the Stranger's in the *Sophist*, but also in the fact that one major philosopher had put so nearly his entire thought-life into the written *form* of dialogues.

For Peirce it was a theorem of semeiotic that "the entire thought-life of any one person is a sign."[71] In the case of Plato, however, on the assumption that his dialogues contain an approximately complete and accurate record of his thought-life, the first problem becomes that of arranging his dialogues in chronological order, determining the time-spans between them, and reading them in that order. Steps in that direction were taken by Lewis Campbell in the introductions to his editions of the *Theaetetus* (1861; 2d ed. 1883) and of the *Sophist* and *Statesman* (1867). Then, in 1897, Wincenty Lutoslawski, in *The Origin and Growth of Plato's Logic*, which he dedicated to Campbell, applied the "stylometric method" as well as content analysis to determine the chronological order of about twenty of Plato's most important dialogues.

Peirce was a frequent reviewer for, and a regular reader of, *The Nation*, in which Lutoslawski's book was listed under "Books of the Week" on January 13, 1898, and Paul Shorey's review of it appeared on September 1, 1898. Peirce wrote Lutoslawski on November 20 a letter which has not yet been found. Lutoslawski made a preliminary reply to Peirce's criticisms on a postal card from Leipzig on December 3 and promised to reply at length later.[72] If he did so, his letter has not been found.

Peirce's annotated copy of Lutoslawski's book is preserved in The Houghton Library at Harvard University. On page 376, where Lutoslawski quotes Plato's Socrates as defining thought at *Theaetetus* 189E as "a conversation of the soul with itself," Peirce writes in the margin: "This is, I think, Plato's greatest contribution to thought."

In 1901 Peirce presented to the National Academy of Sciences a paper "On the Logic of drawing History from Ancient Documents." After developing his general theory, he applied it to three illustrations: the nature and history of the Aristotelian corpus, the chronology of Plato's dialogues, and the life of Pythagoras. In the second of these, which runs to forty-four pages, he assumes "that Lutoslawski's treatment of the facts has been judicious up to the point when the matter becomes a question for the mathematician."[73]

In 1902 Peirce drafted four preliminary chapters of a treatise to be called *Minute Logic*.

> I. Intended Characters of this Treatise
> II. Prelogical Notions
>> Section I. Classification of the Sciences
>> Section II. Why Study Logic?
> III. The Simplest Mathematics
> IV. Ethics

By that time, logic had become for Peirce a normative science, connected through ethics with aesthetics. In Chapter IV he first reviews the pre-Platonic theories of the supreme good, and then says:

> As to Plato, unless we are content to treat the only complete collection of the works of any Greek philosopher that we possess as a mere repertory of gems of thought, as most readers are content to do; but wish to view them as they are so superlatively worthy of being viewed as the record of the entire development of thought of a great thinker, then everything depends upon the chronology of the dialogues. I have critically examined the data brought together by Lutoslawski, and have applied to them all the refinements of the theory of probabilities, with the result of being firmly convinced of the correctness, in the main, of that writer's conclusions. It is necessary that an entirely new study of Plato's philosophy should be founded upon that view of the chronology.
>
> I will endeavor briefly to do this for the single point of what is ultimately good.[74]

And Peirce proceeds to devote more than two hundred pages to that single point, without reaching the end.

Our survey of the range of Peirce's recognized relevance is sufficient evidence that his writings, both those he published and those he left unpublished, are a "repertory of gems of thought." But suppose we were now to try the hypothesis that they are also "worthy of being viewed as the record of the entire development of thought of a great thinker," and the further hypothesis that much, if not everything, depends upon their chronology. The writings he published would pose few difficulties, as their dates of publication are sufficiently close to their dates of composition; but he dated less than a fourth of the writings he left unpublished. Our first task, then, would be, from all the surviving evidence, to assign at least approximate dates to the undated ones. We could then arrange all his known writings in a single chronological order. We might find reason to treat each series of papers as a unit, and place it as of the date of publication or composition of the first paper of the series. Unpublished papers datable only within a year or two might be placed next to the dated papers within that period to which they seem most closely related in content. We would then be in position to begin preparing a chronological edition of his writings. No such edition exists. A nearly complete edition might run to eighty volumes. A selective twenty-volume chronological edition is just beginning to come from the Indiana University Press. It will be more comprehensive than all previous letterpress editions taken together. More than a third of the writings it contains will be appearing in print for the first time. Each volume will contain a chronological list which will guide the reader to everything it omits that Peirce published or wrote within the span of years the volume covers, an historical introduction that will give the reader some idea of Peirce's occasions for what he wrote and what he published within that span, and an index that includes the introduction as well as the Peirce texts.

What bearing will such an edition have on the range of Peirce's relevance? For readers who are already students of the development of thought, concerning particular questions if not in general, the labor of bringing Peirce within the scope of their studies will be immeasurably reduced. For readers for whom every idea of Peirce's has so far been a "detached idea"— detached not only from his ideas on *other* questions but also from his earlier and later thoughts on the *same* question—it will become relevant at least to justify preferring a particular detached idea of his to any of his later or earlier thoughts on the same subject.

Here in conclusion are a few of the questions concerning the development of Peirce's thought that the new edition should put us in position to resolve, and thereby to move his later thoughts to higher levels of relevance.

Who were the thinkers whose writings he studied most intensively after the first three, which were Whately's *Elements of Logic* in 1851, Schiller's *Aesthetic Letters* in 1855–56, and Kant's *Critique of Pure Reason* from 1856 onward? In what order, and at what stages of the development of his own thought? What were the questions with which he began? What others did he take up, in what order, and when? To what questions did he return again and again? To which of them did his answers change, and what was the sequence of changes? To which did his answers remain the same? Were there significant changes in his arguments for those answers? To what extent were his philosophic views modified from time to time by his own original researches in mathematics and in the sciences, and by the major scientific discoveries and controversies of his time?

In each distinguishable period, to what degree did he bring his thought to systematic completeness? Did he have a single system from beginning to end, with only minor internal adjustments from period to period, or were the changes so great that we may fairly describe the development of his thought as a succession of three or four incompatible systems?

If he was above all a logician, and if he conceived logic from the beginning as a branch of semeiotic, the general theory of signs, but moved gradually in the direction of making it coextensive with semeiotic, then what was the place of semeiotic itself within his thought as a whole at each stage of its development?

Is it the case, as it seems to be, that he was a declared nominalist throughout the period of volume 1 of the new edition (1857–1866), that he took his first steps toward realism in that of volume 2 (1867–1871), and that he continued to move in that direction on the whole, but with occasional lapses back toward his original nominalism? Or is the story of the development of his thought in that respect much more complicated than it has so far been made out to be? And in any case what were his reasons for each step that he took?

Beginning with his earliest study of Kant at the age of seventeen, he attached more importance to categories than any other post-Kantian philosopher has done; perhaps than any other philosopher has *ever* done. We very much need a chronological and critical study of his categoriology from beginning to end. When he finally recognized (perhaps created?) a philosophical science (antecedent to the normative sciences and to metaphysics) which for a time he called phenomenology, just how much of his categoriology was moved into it, and how was the rest distributed? How would he respond to the criticisms of Freeman, Hartshorne, Schneider and others, and what should our own conclusions be?

Though he was always extremely modest about his competence in aesthetics, he never ceased to value highly his early study of Schiller.[75] Several students of aesthetics have found more illumination in his incidental remarks here and there than in the books of professional aestheticians. The new edition should open the way to a more consecutive and complete study of his thoughts on aesthetics (and on ethics) than has so far been feasible.[76]

Philosophers will readily think of other questions equally worth pursuing, and now, like those above, about to become more readily pursuable. So also will inquirers coming to Peirce from mathematics, from the natural and social sciences, and from humanistic studies—say, for examples, from chemistry and physics, astronomy and geodesy, cartography and metrology; from anthropology and psychology, economics, history, and literature; from folklore, linguistics, and lexicography. The amazing range of his relevance we are only beginning to guess at. A decade from now we may have begun to measure and comprehend it.

Max H. Fisch

Peirce Edition Project,
Indiana University/Purdue University at Indianapolis

NOTES

1. *Studies in the Scientific and Mathematical Philosophy of Charles S. Peirce: Essays by Carolyn Eisele*, edited by R. M. Martin (The Hague: Mouton Publishers, 1979), p. 376n. Hereafter SSMP.

2. This first installment contains only part 1. The second installment will contain parts 2 and 3.

3. SSMP pp. 61–69, 166, 204, 215n., 240, 246–48, 269f., 285–88, 297f., 353–55.

4. *Semiotica* 26–3/4, 203–50.

5. Gaslight Publications, 112 East Second, Bloomington, Indiana 47401. (Since then the paper has made a third appearance in Thomas A. Sebeok, *The Play of Musement*, Indiana University Press, 1981, pp. 17–52.)

6. SSMP 292–99.

7. *Proceedings of the C. S. Peirce Bicentennial International Congress*, Texas Tech Press, Lubbock, Texas 79409 (forthcoming).

8. Cecil J. Schneer, editor. University Press of New England, Hanover, New Hampshire 03755.

9. P. 147.

10. The sixty-five documents I have collected for this episode come chiefly from the Becker papers in the Library of Congress, the Geological Survey files in National Archives, the Van Hise papers at the Wisconsin Historical Society, and the Chamberlin papers in the University of Chicago archives.

11. Horace H. Rackham School of Graduate Studies, University of Michigan, 1980. Pp. 31–38. See also pp. ix, 3, 7–12, 14, 15, 19, 22, 23f., 45, 50, 76, 87f., 90, 98f.

12. Open Court Publishing Co. Ed. Paul A. Schilpp. Pp. 464–519, at 479.

13. The papers were published in the *Transactions of the Charles S. Peirce Society* 11: 145–94, 1975.

14. *Proceedings of the 80th Annual Convention, American Psychological Association*, 1972, pp. 773–74.

15. *A Computer Perspective*, by the office of Charles & Ray Eames, with an introduction by I. Bernard Cohen. Harvard University Press, 1973. P. 33. (See also p. 53.)

16. *Transactions of the Charles S. Peirce Society* 2:71–85, 1966.

17. *Of Clouds and Clocks* (St. Louis, Mo.: Washington Univ. Press, 1966), pp. 5f.

18. Edited by Richard J. Bernstein. Yale University Press.

19. Cambridge University Press, 1958.

20. Albert A. Stanley, "A Quincuncial Projection of the World," *Surveying and Mapping* 61: 19, 1946. Cf. SSMP 145–59. (Peirce was a student of balloon, glider and other flying machines, reviewed books about flight, and in the 1890s thought of his Arisbe farm as "an admirable place for experiments in flying" and claimed to have "a very convenient method of experimenting." Cf. SSMP 42.)

21. P. 9 n1.

22. P. iv.

23. *The Hound & Horn*, vol. 2 no. 3 (April-June 1929), pp. 267–282.

24. CP 7.36–48.

25. *Journal of Philosophy* 13: 701–37, 1916.

26. J. H. Cotton, *Royce on the Human Self* (Harvard University Press, 1954), p. 218.

27. CP 8.376.

28. *Semiotic and Significs: The Correspondence Between Charles S. Peirce and Victoria Lady Welby,* ed. Charles S. Hardwick (Indiana Univ. Press, 1977), pp. 138f.

29. Max H. Fisch, "Peirce as Scientist, Mathematician, Historian, Logician, and Philosopher," *Proceedings of the C. S. Peirce Bicentennial International Congress* (Graduate Studies, Texas Tech University, No. 23, September 1981), pp. 13–34, at 13–16.

30. Pp. V, 261, 357.

31. See the English translation in *The Framework of Language* (n11 above) 1–29 at 7–12. The part of Peirce's lecture first published in 1958 is in CP 7.579–96; the whole of it is in *Writings of Charles S. Peirce: A Chronological Edition,* vol. I, 1857 –1866 (Bloomington, IN: Indiana University Press, 1982), 490–504.

32. See especially Chomsky's *Language and Mind* (New York: Harcourt, Brace & World, 1968), 78–79.

33. *Language and Responsibility* (New York: Pantheon Books, 1979), 71.

34. *Transactions of the Charles S. Peirce Society,* 16 (1980): 97–117. This particular article is noteworthy as drawing nearly all its Peirce quotations from *The New Elements of Mathematics* (hereafter NE) rather than from the *Collected Papers*.

35. There is even a book entitled *Science as Metaphor,* edited by Richard Olson (Belmont, CA: Wadsworth Publishing Co., 1971).

36. *Language, Thought, & Culture,* edited by Paul Henle (Ann Arbor, MI: University of Michigan Press, 1958), 173–95.

37. *Studies in Semiotics,* vol. 8 (Research Center for Language and Semiotic Studies, Indiana University, 1976), p. 2.

38. There are two indexed references to Peirce in his *The Savage Mind,* one appreciative, the other critical.

39. In: *Sight, Sound, and Sense,* ed. Thomas A. Sebeok (Bloomington, IN: Indiana University Press, 1978), pp. 202–31.

40. *American Anthropologist,* 82: 485–507.

41. P. 486.

42. Forthcoming in: *New Approaches to the Development of the Self,* ed. Benjamin Lee (New York: Plenum Press).

43. Forthcoming from Indiana University Press. See also his "On the Semiotics of Indian Identity," *American Journal of Semiotics,* 1 (1981): 85–126, at 85, 88–91, 96, 113–119, and "Emblems of Identity," which is forthcoming in *On Symbols in*

Anthropology: Essays in Honor of Harry Hoijer, ed. Jacques Maquet (Malibu: Undena Publications, 1981).

44. *Journal of the History of the Behavioral Sciences*, 9 (1973): 333–38.

45. New York: Oxford University Press (Third printing, 1969).

46. University of Chicago Press, 1980.

47. See also Lincourt and Olczak, "H. S. Sullivan and the Phenomenology of Human Cognition," *The International Journal of Social Psychiatry*, 25 (1979): 10–16.

48. 36: 271–82, 1962; 35: 726–40, 1961.

49. "La structure productrice du mot d'esprit et de la semiosis: essai sur Freud et Peirce," *Degrés* 8:21 (1980), d1–18.

50. New York: John Wiley & Sons, 1966.

51. Four other wide-ranging collections: *Proceedings of the C. S. Peirce Bicentennial International Congress* (see n29 above). *Pragmatism and Purpose: Essays Presented to Thomas A. Goudge* (Toronto: University of Toronto Press, 1981), Part One: The Thought of C. S. Peirce (pp. 3–148). *Studies in the Philosophy of Charles Sanders Peirce*, ed. Philip P. Wiener and Frederic H. Young (Cambridge, MA: Harvard University Press, 1952); *Second Series,* ed. Edward C. Moore and Richard S. Robin (Amherst, MA: University of Massachusetts Press, 1964).

52. *Science and Metaphysics* (London: Routledge & Kegan Paul, 1968), 140ff.

53. Frederick and Emily Michael ("Peirce on the Nature of Logic," *Notre Dame Journal of Formal Logic*, 20 (1979): 84–88) argue that, despite the disclaimer, his logic was normative from the beginning.

54. *Beyond All Appearances* (Carbondale, IL: Southern Illinois University Press, 1974), pp. 21, 24.

55. *The Categories of Charles Peirce* (Chicago, IL: Open Court Publishing Co., 1934).

56. Pp. iii, 5–6, 10–11, 20, 29–30, 47, 56.

57. In: *Pragmatism and Purpose* (see n51 above), pp. 41–58.

58. "Husserl's and Peirce's Phenomenologies: Coincidence or Interaction," *Philosophy and Phenomenological Research*, 17 (1957): 164–85, at 185.

59. "The Common Root of Husserl's and Peirce's Phenomenologies," *The New Scholasticism*, 54 (1980): 305–25.

60. *Pragmatism and Phenomenology: A Philosophic Encounter* (Amsterdam: B. R. Grüner, 1980).

61. J. Glenn Gray, "Heidegger on Remembering and Remembering Heidegger," *Man and World*, 10 (1977): 62–79, at 77.

62. *Pacific Philosophical Quarterly*, 61 (1980): 301.

63. Vol. 1007, No. 3, June 16, 1981, Patent No. 4,273,542.

64. Col. 2. Of Zellweger's forthcoming papers see especially "Sign-Creation and Man-Sign Engineering" in *Semiotica*.

65. The Hague: Martinus Nijhoff.

66. Vol. 47, pp. 377–79.

67. Is it the case that R. D. Carmichael's article in *The Monist* for October 1922 was the first article, that his book published by The Open Court Publishing Company in 1930 was the first book, and that the first chapter of the book was the first chapter, to bear the title "The Logic of Discovery"? *The New York Times*'s Arno Press reprinted the book in 1975 in its History, Philosophy & Sociology of Science Series.

68. *Boston Studies in the Philosophy of Science*, vols. 56 and 60 (Dordrecht, Holland: D. Reidel Publishing Co., 1980). See also the articles by Gutting, Blackwell and Kisiel in *Revue Internationale de Philosophie* No. 131–132, 1980.

69. Vol. 11, no. 3, Summer 1978, pp. 147–55 (with a bibliographical note by John Michael Krois).

70. Vol. 77, Section C, pp. 279–300 (1977).

71. Ms 1476, page numbered Nichols 5½, c. 1904, continuing from a point corresponding roughly to CP 8.191 in the final draft.

72. Ms L 259.

73. Ms 690 p. 200; typewritten transcript p. (125).

74. Ms 434, pages numbered Logic 1/IV. 33 and 34.

75. Friedrich Schiller, *On the Aesthetic Education of Man*, edited by Elizabeth M. Wilkinson and L. A. Willoughby (Oxford: Clarendon Press, 1967), pp. clxxxviiif.

76. See for example his 1857 college theme on Ruskin's criticism of Schiller (vol. 1, pp. 10–12).

COMMUNITY AND REALITY

Charles Sanders Peirce was at once a genuine and a disturbing philosopher. He was genuine because he dealt directly with the difficult problems of philosophy: the nature of truth, the theory of reality, the problems of mind and of God. In his approach there was none of the modern or advanced tendency in thought that anticipates speculative problems merely in order to avoid them or to dissolve them into the misadventures of human speech. Peirce is disturbing because he forces us to confront experience afresh, and if need be to revise our categories so that they will accord with the real world. If you study Peirce you have to be prepared for surprises; you have to be tough-minded enough to consider the possibility that things may in fact prove to be very different from the way you have long since decided that they *must* be.

The secret of Peirce's greatness as a philosopher—a greatness we are only now beginning to appreciate—lies in the skill with which he combined openness to experience with logical acumen and the ability to develop a comprehensive and coherent system. His empiricism has long been understood; his ability and his success as a systematic, speculative philosopher have been underestimated. In an earlier paper on Peirce[1] I quite mistakenly described him as *not* being a systematic philosopher after the fashion of Hegel. In this I was deceived. While I never underestimated the metaphysical and even theological bent of his thought, I did confound the form in which his writings have come to us with the logical structure of his thought. I took the fact that in order to discover Peirce's theory on a given topic one has to plow through volumes of papers, drafts and revisions of drafts, reviews, and partially completed manuscripts, to mean a lack of system. It is now clear to me that this was an error. Peirce has a metaphysical system of remarkable scope, and on any given topic there is a clear drift to his thought even if he did not make it easy for us to find it out. In view of this fact, I want to treat his view of reality in systematic fashion and as a matter of principle. I shall not undertake to trace his intellectual odyssey through the customary early, middle, and late writings. This task may be left to intellectual historians and to the guardians of Peirce's papers. Instead I shall treat Peirce's theory of reality as an integral position sufficiently clear and unified to form a distinctive alternative to other philosophical outlooks.[2]

My chief aim is twofold: first, to present Peirce's theory of reality, involving as it does the idea of a community of inquirers or knowers, and second, to offer some critical appraisal of its consistency and adequacy. In seeking to achieve the first aim it will be necessary to mark out the distinctively realistic, idealistic, and pragmatic strains in the theory and then to show how he synthesized these strains in an original way. In seeking to achieve the second aim, I shall adapt a device used by Peirce himself. Just after the turn of the century, Peirce wrote several reviews of Josiah Royce's Gifford Lectures, *The World and the Individual*, and it is evident that he regarded Royce's view as the most serious rival of his own. Without becoming too deeply involved in academic discussion, I shall seek to evolve a final appraisal of Peirce's view from a crucial comparison with that of Royce.

The General Theory of Reality

In Peirce's manuscripts and notes for his projected work on logic of 1873, we find a discussion of the concept of reality that will serve as a start. This discussion nicely brings out the several strands in the theory and it is largeldy in agreement with the many other characterizations he offered of the meaning of reality. He starts by asking how a variety of observations and processes of thought can lead ultimately to a settled conclusion that is accepted by all who understand what is meant. The fact that diverse thinkers agree in a common result is not to be taken simply as a brute fact; on the contrary, the convergence of many observations, ideas, views in a common object stands in need of explanation. At the outset Peirce freely admits that the theory according to which external realities *cause* the common result and belief in one identical object can serve as an explanation. The causal theory, he says, is "convenient for certain purposes" (7.335) and is without internal logical flaw. But he has a philosophical objection to that theory; what needs to be explained, he says, is not an ordinary event among others in the world, and it cannot be put in the same class with such events. The fact that investigation leads to a fixed result concerns the theory of truth; the logic of investigation and its outcome, though related to fact, is itself a matter of principle not to be treated after the fashion of singular occurrences in the course of nature. The point is an important one, for while Peirce was vigorous in his insistence that reality has force, power, resistance (what he called Secondness) over against ideas and representations, he still refused to accept a simple, causal theory of knowledge and truth.

If a causal theory will not suffice, some further explanation is required. This is furnished by Peirce's theory of reality as the ulimate result of inquiry. It is best to begin with a summary statement of Peirce's view and then seek to unfold its meaning in more detail by elucidating its constituent aspects. Since Peirce gave expression to his theory in so many places it will be necessary to select several quotations as standard. I believe that Peirce was not entirely consistent in the statement of the theory, but we must be careful not to take a difference in accent for a difference in viewpoint. "The real is that which is not whatever we happen to think it, but is unaffected by what we may think of it" (8.12). Or again, the real is "that whose characters are independent of what anybody may think them to be" (5.405). Still further, Peirce speaks of reality as what a community of investigators is destined to discover if they have the proper method of inquiry and persist far enough in its application: "the opinion which is fated to be ultimately agreed to by all who investigate, is what we mean by the truth, and the object represented in this opinion is the real" (5.407). Finally, "reality is independent, not necessarily of thought in general, but only of what you or I or any finite number of men may think about it . . . though the object of the final opinion depends on what that opinion is, yet what that opinion is does not depend on what you or I or any man thinks" (5.408).

These passages give expression to the essentials of Perice's theory, although, as we shall see, they must be supplemented by others. Three ideas are dominant in the passages we have cited: first, the idea that reality has some sort of *independence* of being thought or represented; second, the idea that reality is related to thought and ideas in some essential way; and third, the idea that reality is the ultimate result of a process of inquiry and is in some sense to be identified with the fact that those who conduct the inquiry come to believe or accept this result. Those acquainted with the development of modern philosophy will see at once that Peirce was deliberately trying to combine elements and characteristics that have generally been regarded as mutually exclusive. Using the labels of philosophical schools, it seems that Peirce wanted to be at once a realist, an idealist, and a pragmatist. And indeed this is the case. The problem is to see whether Peirce was able to construct a coherent theory from such normally divergent tendencies. We must consider in more detail each of the three ideas in question, and then we shall be in a position to grasp the full scope of Peirce's view.

1. Reality and Independence

In many passages Peirce claims that being real means that a thing retains its characters regardless of what particular men may think (1.578; 3.161; 5.405, 5.408, 5.503; 6.495; 7.339; 8.12). That this independence of thought does not mean independence of thought in general, but only of particular thoughts, is a point to which we shall return. For the present we may concentrate on independence because that aspect marks the realistic strain in Peirce's thought. Unlike Hegel, who emphasized the utter transparance of all reality to reason, Peirce was insistent on the *forcefulness* or otherness of things as a mark of reality. In Peirce's terminology, reality belongs with Secondness, or the domain of fact. ("The reality of things consists in their persistent forcing themselves upon our recognition") (1.175); or again, "In the idea of reality, Secondness is predominant; for the real is that which insists upon forcing its way to recognition as something *other* than the mind's creation")(1.325). The real is what demands our attention, and on more than one occasion Peirce interpreted the human phenomenon of *willing* as our response to the insistence of what stands over against us (1.381; cf. 1.358, 1.325; 3.337, 3.613).

In order to avoid confusion it is essential to notice the difference between reality and the real. This is not a pedantic distinction, but rather a mark of Peirce's subtlety. The real in the sense of the thing, the idea, the feeling, has the status of fact; it is what reveals itself in action and reaction with other things. Sometimes Peirce says that the real thing is what exists, but we must be careful in using this formulation because Peirce generally refused to identify reality with what is existent or actual. The important point is that *what* is real is itself a something or other that has forcefulness and insistence. On the other hand, we do not entirely answer the question of what it means to be real merely by pointing to real things. Reality is the status enjoyed by real things, and, as such, its meaning cannot be grasped apart from a theory. We may summarize by saying that the real thing is marked by Secondness or forcefulness and power, whereas the theory of reality is a matter of Thirdness or of thought, and this involves something more than the ability to react with other things.

There are at least two other ways in which Peirce expresses what we have called the realistic pole or the independence of the real thing over against thought. One is his concept of the index or indexical sign, and the other is the doctrine of the dynamical object. Time and again Peirce argued that it is impossible to distinguish between the real world and a fictitious or imaginary one by means of a general description (2.337; 3.363; 8.39 ff.). Expressed in terms of the theory of signs, this means that every assertion must contain at least one index designating the real subject matter about which assertions are made. Armed with predicates alone, or universals, we are unable to reach the real world; unless we begin with a designated real subject no dialectic of inquiry will produce such a subject. As Peirce says, no language contains a general indicator telling us that we are now talking about the real world; we either know already that our discussion is about such a world or we must be content to talk about fictions or merely to play games with words. In our conversations we may succeed in commanding attention to realities by our tone of voice or the seriousness of our demeanor, but unless it is thus understood at the outset that we mean to refer to a real subject matter there is no purely logical movement within the sphere of thought that will suffice to distinguish talk about an imaginary world from talk about the only real world there is.

Peirce used this line of argument against Royce in his review of Royce's early book, *The Religious Aspect of Philosophy*. There Royce had claimed that we reach the individual, the real subject, only at the point where full and perfect knowledge—complete determination—has been achieved. For reasons not germane to our purpose, Royce was bound to hold that, as long as we have nothing more than partial knowledge, we are unable to identify the individual or real subject of our assertions. Peirce objected vigorously, claiming that this view entirely ignores the function of the index[3] in providing a real subject at the outset of inquiry, although Peirce betrays the idealist flavor of his position by taking this index to mean the *will* that forces attention. It may, of course, be objected to Peirce's view in turn that, in continuing to define the real object through the manner in which it is indicated, he fails to sustain a realist position. On the other hand, it is clear that Peirce refuses (at least in this argument) to identify the real by means of any description, not even a complete or final one. We have yet to see whether this refusal is consistent with his theory of reality as the ultimate opinion destined to be arrived at by the community of investigators.

One further expression of the realistic pole is found in the concept of the dynamical object. We normally think of an idea or sign as representing an object to be of a certain character, and we say that when the idea is adequate the object is as the idea determines it to be. Peirce accepts this, but he distinguishes between the object as thought or the *immediate* object and the object that exerts itself in relation to other objects or the *dynamical* object. The immediate object is dependent on the sign, but the dynamical object reverses the relationship, because "[the dynamical object] is the Reality which by some means contrives to determine the Sign to its Representation" (4.536). The dynamical object is thus no mere object of thought, but rather a source of effects; it is a dynamic center which has constraining power over the sign that is to represent it. The stubborn character of the dynamical object is one of the factors that enter into the process of inquiry and help to justify the claim that the process will arrive at a stable result independent of particular thoughts (cf. 5.503).

Thus far nothing has been said about Peirce's famous Scotistic, or scholastic, realism. The reason for the omission may be explained. The philosophical realism, which Peirce frequently attributed to Duns Scotus and sometimes to the scholastic tradition, generally embraces two theses:[4] (1) reality includes what is general, and (2) reality includes the vague and real possibilities. The former thesis is intended to be a denial of the claim that reality is exhausted by wholly actual individuals entirely contained in a present moment of time, and the latter is intended to be a denial of the view that mere possibility is a blank nothingness. Now while it is certainly true that these realistic theses are relevant to and indeed form part of Peirce's theory of reality, it is not correct to identify what I have been calling the realistic pole in Peirce's theory with the so-called Scotistic realism. For the realistic pole concerns primarily the matter of the independence of the real as over against thought and representation, whereas the Scotistic realism is concerned chiefly with the reality of the general, and the denial of the modern view that reality is made up entirely of sensible particulars. Scotistic realism figures most prominently in Peirce's general theory of reality at the point where it becomes necessary to defend the real possibility that attaches to possible or future experience. As we shall see, the status of the ultimate opinion that "would be" discovered by the community of inquirers upon fulfillment of the relevant conditions depends upon Peirce's doctrine of real possibility, which is the heart of the Scotistic realism.

2. Reality and Thought in General

That there is a strong idealistic strain in Peirce's philosophy cannot be denied; whether his theory of reality as such is to be described as thoroughly idealistic is a question more difficult to answer. We may postpone this question and concentrate on the idealistic element. Three considerations are essential. The first, and most obvious, is Peirce's own description of his thought as idealistic. Secondly, there is the close connection to be found in every phase of Peirce's thought between signs and representation—in his terminology, Thirdness—and the real object. Finally, there is the definition of reality in terms of opinion and belief, together with the claim that the real is not external to or independent of thought in general.

As regards the first point, Peirce associated his view with a form of Hegelianism (1.42), and described objective idealism as "the one intelligible theory of the universe" (6.25, cf. 6.102). In several places (e.g., 5.358n.) Peirce referred to Royce's *World and the Individual* as generally correct, and in a letter to William James (8.284) he called his own pragmaticism the "true idealism." Although we must not depend too heavily on self-conscious interpretation of this sort, the fact remains that Peirce was extraordinarily circumspect in the expression of his views, and, as should now be clear, he was at least as reliable a commentator on Peirce as any member of the Charles Peirce Society!

With regard to the status of signs, thought, and representation, it is clear that Peirce viewed them as belonging to the nature of the real.[5] Thirdness in the sense of law and meaning (including both the *meaning* of terms and *meaning* to do some act or other) has its own reality and cannot be reduced to Firstness and Secondness. Thirdness, moreover, cannot be derived from the relation between Firstness (quality) and Secondness (fact), or indeed from any dyadic relation. The relation, however, between Thirdness and the real object is not so clear, and Peirce has made statements about that relationship that are certainly paradoxical, and in the end inconsistent with each other. The idealistic element predominates on most occasions.

There is, Peirce says, nothing that is incognizable in principle. There is no "thing in itself," and while it is not the case that everything is in fact known, everything real is knowable, and there is no transcendence of the object of knowledge. Peirce says (8.13) that the view of reality to which he is sympathetic is one that is "fatal to the idea of . . . a thing existing independent of all relation to the mind's conception of it" (cf. 5.311). Or again, in criticizing Royce, he says, "We do not aim at anything quite beyond experience, but only at the limiting result toward which all experience will approximate" (8.112). Peirce goes on to characterize the view as one that "eliminates any non-notional correlate of knowledge" (8.112). This all sounds like philosophical idealism, a conclusion that is reinforced by Peirce's definition of reality in terms of belief or opinion.

Over against what has just been said, however, stand Peirce's most puzzling attacks upon idealism. It is as if, in the development of his own pragmaticism, Peirce felt free to express the idealism in it without apology, but that in the face of a thoroughgoing idealist like Royce he felt constrained to advance realism as if its truth were a foregone conclusion. One cannot but acknowledge the extreme tension in Peirce's thought at this point. On the one hand, we find him saying that without thought there can be no opinion, and hence no final opinion such as would serve to identify reality. Hence the real cannot be external to mind. On the other hand, we find him attacking Royce in the most vigorous terms for failing to see that *to be* and *to be represented* are not the same. In one place (8.130) we even find Peirce arguing that realism as a philosophical position is a matter of fact, and that it neither can nor need be made a matter of demonstration. "The question of realism," he says, "is a question of hard fact, if ever there was a hard fact," so that the realist escapes the need to establish his position by the sort of dialectic illustrated in Royce's *World and the Individual*. Peirce was no doubt goaded by the polemical intent. Royce had attempted to fasten upon realism the extreme thesis that "to be is to be independent of an idea"—where "independent" is taken as symmetrical—so that if the thing is independent of the idea or representation, the idea or representation is equally independent of the thing. The result is that the idea may vary in any way or to any extent you please without ceasing to be a representation of the intended object. Peirce took this consequence to be absurd. We need not settle the question of the correctness of Royce's interpretation of realism to see that his rejection of it in such extreme form led Peirce to bring out all the realistic elements in his own position. I am inclined to think that Peirce's position was in fact determined to a greater extent by dialectical relation to other views than he was willing to allow (cf. 8.126).

We turn now to the third outcropping of Peirce's idealism as expressed in the fundamental doctrine that reality is to be defined in terms of an opinion or belief. The pragmatistic aspects of this doctrine—the nature of inquiry, the community of investigators, and the probabilistic intepretation of synthetic reasoning—will be considered in the next section. Here emphasis will fall upon the fact that reality is said to coincide with an opinion, a belief, a system of propositions that represent the ultimate outcome of inquiry. Our question here concerns the extent to which the real is dependent upon thought or representation, and whether reality has transcendence over being known. It is well to bear in mind that, while Peirce explicitly denied the identification of being with being represented, the question of the precise relation between the two remains open. The denial of identity all by itself means no more than that the two items in question are "other than" each other in at least one specifiable respect. But while being and being represented may be other and not identical, it may be the case that one is dependent on the other so that the relation is asymmetrical. In short, the denial of identity does not tell us enough, for, as will become apparent, Peirce believed that he could deny the identity of being and being represented without also holding that the real is entirely independent of representation.

Whatever inconsistencies there may be in Peirce's theory, one idea is expressed repeatedly, namely, that reality is independent of what is thought by this, that, or the other individual, and even of any finite collection of individuals, but that it is not independent of thought in general. Peirce's position, that is to say, ultimately takes shape as an *objective* idealism in which the rational pole is purged of any hint of subjectivism or privacy in belief by the rigorous control of the method of inquiry. I would regard as atypical the well-known statement in Peirce's exposistion of the "social theory of logic" in which he refers to the "ideal perfection of knowledge" as that by which "reality is constituted" (5.356). The reason why this assertion cannot be taken at face value is found in the many points at which Peirce himself finds it necessary to distinguish the object represented from the opinion that represents it, and even from the ultimate opinion that can be only in the future (see 8.103 ff.). It is not consistent with all the realistic passages in Peirce's writings to say that for him knowledge *constitutes* reality. The identification is too strong, and would mean that Secondness, in the sense of the dynamic element that is not cognitional, had been eliminated and everything reduced to Thirdness; this is precisely the error with which Peirce charged Hegel. On the other hand, reality is defined through opinion and thought; there is no modifying that fact and no valid way of explaining it away. The fact is, and this is the crux of Peirce's entire philosophy, that he believed it defensible to connect reality essentially with thought as long as the thought in question is of a certain ultimate character that does not depend upon finite thinkers who, taken singly, are fallible and without final authority (see especially 8.14). The thought or opinion that defines reality must therefore belong to a *community* of knowers, and this community must be structured and disciplined in accordance with super-individual principles. Moreover, it is not possible to minimize the idealism implicit in this conclusion by attempting to interpret thought, opinion, belief in a behavioristic way. For an opinion is thought, and thought means Thirdness; Thirdness has its own being and is never identical with any action, any fact or finite collection of facts. The final estimation of Peirce's position must be one that takes his idealism seriously and interprets it as such. Whatever shortcomings there may be in Peirce's theory cannot be overcome by the device of translating thought into something other than itself.

3. Reality and Community

Here the chief aim is to complete Peirce's theory of reality by developing the pragmatistic elements in it; in so doing we must also indicate how he believed it possible to combine the realistic and idealistic poles in his thought. The real is what is disclosed through the application of empirical method; it is also called the stable belief expressed in that ultimate opinion resulting, in the long run, from the persistent following of the method of science. The doctrine is a complex one and contains several distinct ideas, each of which forms a topic in its own right. We may cite a few typical statements: "When we busy ourselves to find the answer to a question, we are going upon the hope that there is an answer, which can be called *the* answer, that is, the final answer . . . which sufficient inquiry will compel us to accept" (4.61); "the real is the idea in which the community ultimately settles down" (6.610); "The opinion which is fated to be ultimately agreed to by all who investigate, is what we mean by the truth, and the object represented in this opinion is the real" (5.407); "the validity of an inductive argument consists, then, in the fact that it pursues a method which, if duly persisted in, must, in the very nature of things, lead to a result indefinitely approximating to the truth in the long run" (2.781); "the real, then, is that which, sooner or later, information and reasoning would finally result in, and which is therefore independent of the vagaries of me and you . . . the very origin of the conception of reality shows

that this conception essentially involves the notion of a COMMUNITY"
(5.311); and finally, "in addition to actuality and possibility, a *third* mode of
reality must be recognized in that which, as the gipsy fortunetellers express it,
is 'sure to come true', or, as we may say, is *destined*" (4.547); "anything may
fairly be said to be *destined* which is sure to come about although there is no
necessitating reason for it" (4.547n.1).[6]

From the above statements of the community theory of reality we must
extract, for more detailed scrutiny, the following notions: (1) belief or opinion
as a goal of inquiry; (2) serious inquiry governed by the form of synthetic
reasoning; (3) the community of inquirers; (4) convergence of belief destined
in the long run; and (5) the mode of real possibility, or the "would-be." It is
obvious that each of these topics demands extended treatment that is out of
the question in the present context, and yet the main subject—Peirce's theory
of reality—cannot be understood apart from these topics. Attention,
therefore, must be confined to absolute essentials.

(1) Belief or opinion as the goal of inquiry. For Peirce, the human mind
is neither fixed nor static; it is a most complex set of powers and capacities
that stand related to a unified person seeking to live a purposeful life in an
evolving universe. The mind moves between the poles of doubt and belief. The
former is marked by uneasiness, restlessness, and hesitation in overt action;
when we are in doubt we are not sure how to move. Belief, on the other hand,
means confidence, resolution, and that sort of adjustment or ease in behavior
or response that we all recognize in our habitual actions. Between doubt and
belief stands inquiry. Doubt is not a resting place; we seek to move away from
the uneasiness of doubt to the stability of belief. Inquiry, investigation,
testing, experience, experiment are all names for the middle term, the means
or bridge over which we are to pass from doubt to belief.

Peirce was well aware that in actual fact men often believe what is not
true or warranted and often refuse to believe what is true. He was, moreover,
too steeped in his own empiricist cast of mind not to know that men have
ways of arriving at and maintaining their beliefs that are not in accord with
the way of experience and the scientific temper he recommended. Peirce
never maintained that in fact everyone does fix his belief as a result of
disciplined inquiry based on objective evidence and careful reasoning. But
Peirce did believe that, unless a man succeeded in remaining isolated, utterly
independent, prejudiced, and confined to his own private opinion, he would in
the long run come to believe the warranted results of objective inquiry. Peirce
was, in short, a hopeless idealist in this regard; for him the course of the
universe guarantees this happy dissemination of the truth.

Peirce, as we have seen, identifies reality by means of a certain type of
belief. The real is that which is represented through and meant by a

warranted opinion. What is must be represented in an opinion or belief before we can speak about truth. Things might be, to be sure, without ever being said to be true in our human sense, but we could not know this to be the case. Knowledge, in short, introduces belief, ideas, and opinions. But the opinion that defines the real must have an extra-human character about it.

For our purpose it is not necessary to settle the matter of the full meaning Peirce attached to belief, its relation to action, to habit, and to concepts or intellectual purport. Whatever belief may turn out to mean in Peirce's view, it is still essentially connected with reality. That belief is not identical with action or behavior in his view is now generally admitted. Peirce did not dissolve reality into human functionings as pragmatism is generally supposed to have done. But he does hold that reality cannot be utterly independent of the objective conditions according to which warranted opinion comes about. This is his pragmatic idealism.

(2) Serious inquiry governed by the form of synthetic reasoning. It is obvious that if we are to have a warranted belief going beyond the mere fact that some opinion is believed, there must be a basis for the warrant. This basis is supplied by the *method* of inquiry and the theory of induction or synthetic reasoning, or the process of extending knowledge of real things as "the lock upon the door of philosophy" (5.348). The problem of understanding science is at one with the problem of finding some law or pattern in the development of new belief from old belief and fresh experience. That form of reasoning is justified that tends on the whole and in the long run to lead to "certain predestinate conclusions which are the same for all men" (3.161). For Peirce, science in the sense of a method for arriving at conclusions rather than in the sense of a systematic form of presenting them is the embodiment of inductive procedure.

It is clear from the many discussions of induction and the nature of science offered by Peirce at every stage of his development that the ground or warrant for a concluding opinion is always the *method* by which it has been reached. Inquiry, that is to say, has a logical structure so that any proposed result of inquiry finds its ultimate justification in its relation to that structure. Serious inquiry aimed at acquiring knowledge of the real world as distinct from fictitious or imaginary universes starts with the assumption that there is an answer, *the* answer to the question that directs the process. Moreover, there is the further assumption that this answer would be found if the inquiry persisted. Empirical inquiry means the application of synthetic reasoning or induction. Without becoming deeply involved in Peirce's account of probability, we may say that such justification as induction receives at his hands takes the form of a large circle of explanation. On the one hand, he holds that the principle of induction[7] cannot be given a deductive foundation (2.693) and cannot be based on the celebrated "uniformity of nature." This view is in accord with his claim (5.341 ff.) that we need no logical ground for logicality itself beyond a large proportion of successes in actual inquiry. On the other hand, he says:

> that the rule of induction will hold good in the long run may be deduced from the principle that reality is only the object of the final opinion to which sufficient investigation would lead. That belief gradually tends to fix itself under the influence of inquiry is, indeed, one of the facts with which logic sets out (2.693).

Whether Peirce's solution of the problem of induction is successful or not is a matter of lesser importance for our purpose than the fact that in his view the warrant for belief resides in the *form* of inquiry and not in the predilections, interests, or other beliefs that can be ascribed to those who accept the results of inquiry. It would therefore be more in accord with Peirce's intention to say that reality, insofar as it is identified through the ultimate belief resulting from inquiry, is defined by a *form* of rationality rather than by the fact of a belief's being held. And even if Peirce did on occasion regard the fact that the result of inquiry compels belief as the pragmatic way of understanding reality, it still remains true that it is the *logical warrant* for the belief, and not the fact of believing, that is the important factor. In short, his pragmaticism, despite the emphasis on practice, is quite rationalistic.

(3) The community of inquirers. Enough has already been said to make it clear that—for Peirce—the process of knowledge is no merely individual affair. The idea that scientific inquiry requires many individuals and is a cooperative undertaking stems from two sources. One is to be found in Peirce's rejection of absolutely immediate cognition or intuition, and the other is in his extensive knowledge of natural science.

From a logical point of view, the claim that every cognition is fallible means that every cognition is subject to review, confirmation, correction, or rejection by some subsequent cognition. The heart of the experimental approach is found in critical testing of hypotheses so that no idea or opinion taken in isolation and apart from an experimental process can be accepted as expressing the truth. In order to criticize a given perception or theory, we must appeal to another. In rejecting the tradition of intuitive rationalism initiated in modern philosophy by Descartes, Peirce allied himself with the Hegelian approach, according to which truth can be attained only through an organic process that is dialectical in the sense that it involves a gradual criticism of what is merely private or subjective, and the preservation of the objective and universal. The process is too vast to be confined to the experience and thought of any single individual, and in any case each individual must be subject to a standard transcending his own ideas. Moreover, the individual himself is a microcosm of the community since his own personal experience and thought involve him in a continual dialogue and dialectic of ideas. To obtain a critical result it is necessary to compare, contrast, and correct our ideas, and especially to test them in the stream of experience. No one of these operations of thought is immediate or intuitive, but each requires a *series* of ideas and logical operations that takes us continually beyond the boundary of any single or isolated idea. It is important to notice that the community principle means both a community of inquirers or knowers and a community or system of ideas.

Peirce regarded the idea of the community as essential for the understanding of science. This fact throws further light on the theory of reality, because that theory may be interpreted as an extension and analogy of the convergence of opinion that Peirce found to be characteristic of scientific inquiry. The use of natural science as a model is readily understood as soon as we recall that Peirce had an extensive knowledge of actual scientific procedure and was engaged throughout his life in scientific work of his own. Peirce was in touch with science in the making, and that is precisely the feature he continually emphasized in his many writings on science and scientific method. For Peirce, science is primarily an activity or actual process of inquiry; it is only secondarily a systematic body of results. Although Peirce was second to none in the ability to analyze what is sometimes called the logical structure of science, he would not agree that science can be understood apart from the actual process of inquiry. Science, as he saw it, means an actual attack by a community of actual investigators on an actual problem posed by some actual subject matter. Progress depends on communication, comparison, and criticism of results. The work of science is not achieved by any individual or group alone, but only by the cooperation of many individuals and groups.

The emphasis on cooperative endeavor naturally raises the question of the nature of the community. For Peirce, the attainment of critical conclusions requires that each individual investigator be capable of transcending his private interests and opinions. The community of investigators purporting to be scientific is defined by the willingness of each individual member to sacrifice what is personal and private to him alone in order to follow the dictates of an interpersonal method that involves free exchange of views and results. "In storming the stronghold of truth, one mounts upon the shoulders of another who has to ordinary apprehension failed, but has in truth succeeded by virtue of the lessons of his failure." (7.51). The comulative results of investigation are preserved by the community. The community idea is not a mere metaphor, nor does it stand as but a piece of rhetoric in praise of science; the idea belongs to the logical structure of scientific activity. Not everyone who investigates is a scientific inquirer, but only those who are cognizant of and willing to bind themselves to empirical method. In this way alone can there come into being knowledge of a real world that is "independent of the vagaries of me and you" (5.311).

The idea of science as an activity engaged in by a community of inquirers, and the conception of reality as an ultimate opinion reached by this process of inquiry, are reciprocal notions. On one side we have the idea of the real as an ultimate opinion which is, though not external to thought in general, still independent of what this, that, or the other individual thinker may happen to think. On the other side we have the idea of the method for reaching such an opinion that requires individual inquirers to constitute themselves as members of the community of science through their willingness to sacrifice their privacy and bind themselves by the rules of an interpersonal method.

(4) Convergence of belief destined in the long run. In the foregoing account of science and empirical method two features have been omitted; each is vital and in some ways both are more important than all the rest. One is the idea that processes of inquiry tend to converge to a limit or stable and ultimate belief; the other concerns the mode of real possibility through which Peirce interprets what "would be" the result of a process extended in the "long run."

Peirce believed that every controlled process of inquiry if persisted in tends to issue in a stable result that establishes itself as *the* answer to the question of the inquiry. This stable result means at the same time the exclusion of all other views on the matter. Peirce offers two reasons for this conclusion. On the empirical side he cites the evidence of the history of science: persistent inquiry actually produces a limiting opinion or narrowing interval within which belief never ceases to oscillate. On the logical side there is the theory of probability and Peirce's evolutionary metaphysics according to which the entire universe exhibits a drift toward rationality or order in habits.[8] The history of science shows that questions actually do get answered, and the logic of inquiry shows that in the long run all questions would be answered.

What are we to understand by Peirce's repeated claim that the ultimate stable belief defining the reality of this or that is *destined* to come about, and what empirical meaning are we to attach to the concept of the long run? The community of inquirers is said to be constrained in some way to reach a final belief that is destined, but this is to happen only if favorable conditions continue to prevail and the inquiry persists in the "long run." To say that a belief is destined to result is to say that a certain opinion *would be* arrived at in the long run. The claim assumes that the method of inductive inquiry is reliable, that it is "a method which, if duly persisted in, must, in the very nature of things, lead to a result indefinitely approximating to the truth in the long run" (2.781). The constraining element implied in the term "destiny" Peirce elucidates through the example of throwing a pair of dice. If we throw the dice often enough sixes will be sure to turn up, although there is no necessitating reason that they should. By analogy this means that the real universe in which inquiry takes place is such that the ultimate opinion is sure to come about at some time, although there is no necessitating reason for this and there is no certainty that in fact the opinion has been reached at this or that particular time (see especially 4.547n.).

Peirce is pointing to a state of affairs that falls somewhere between the extremes of accident and mechanical necessity. What is destined to come has *some* constraining or rational form in it so that it is neither haphazard nor wholly fortuitous, and yet on the other hand what is destined does not come about with the brute necessity of a self-repeating system. The element of rationality behind the destiny resides in the *method* that determines the activity of the community of investigators. In speaking of the active work of scientists, Peirce says:

> the progress of investigation carries them by a force outside themselves to one and the same conclusion . . . This activity of thought by which we are carried, not where we wish, but to a fore-ordained goal, is like the operation of destiny. No modification of the point of view taken, no selection of other facts for study, no natural bent of mind even, can enable a man to escape the predestinate opinion (5.407).

This Calvinistic logic means apparently that the outcome is inevitable but not necessary! Peirce was, of course, aware of the need to suppose the continuation of favorable conditions. The reaching of the predestinate opinion is favored both by the nature of the universe and the form of inquiry, but neither would suffice unless there were also a dedicated community of inquirers loyal to the spirit of science. If the race were to be extinguished or if interest in inquiry no longer existed or if empirical method were abandoned, the predestinate opinion would remain undiscovered.

In addition to what has already been said about the goal of inquiry, there is the fact that it is a result to be reached only in the "long run." The idea of the long run was a happy hunting ground for Royce, and it caused the pragmatists much trouble. When Peirce speaks of a certain ratio having a certain value in the "long run," he means that an endless succession of fractions has a probability limit, and this is a value, as he says, "about which the values of the endless succession will never cease to oscillate" (2.758). The long run, that is, means an endless series, and only if we have an endless series are we able to ascribe to it a finite character. There is no contradiction, Peirce holds, in the idea of an endless series of finite terms having a finite *sum*. And yet he was willing to admit that the endless succession as such cannot be experienced (see 5.528) "but involves a first dose of ideality, or generality." The entire conception of the long run is not without a certain ambiguity. Sometimes it clearly means the endlessness itself of the series and the denial that any finite number of terms adequately expresses the "would-be." Sometimes it means what was referred to above as the probability limit, in which emphasis falls not on the endlessness of the series but on its convergence to a stable result. Happily we may leave the problem of the actual infinite, which is precisely the problem to which this discussion points, to other papers on Peirce. For our purpose it is sufficient to note that for Peirce the appeal to the long run is to an endless succession required for exhibiting a finite character and to a succession which cannot be experienced as such.

(5) *The mode of real possibility, or the "would-be."* This topic is so central to Peirce's system that it might be used as a basis for unifying the whole. We can be concerned with it only insofar as it figures in the theory of reality. The real has been identified as an ultimate opinion that would be reached under certain circumstances. An opinion expressing the result of inquiry takes conceptual form and, according to Peirce's pragmaticism, conceptual meaning is understood in terms of the way things would behave in the long run. Real possibility, therefore, figures twice over in the definition of reality; on the one hand it concerns the process of inquiry and the opinion that would result if the process were pushed to the limit; on the other hand the "would-be" concerns the nature of an opinion and the proper interpretation of what Peirce called "intellectual purport." We shall consider only the latter.

The nature of a thing means a totality of behavior including all that the thing has done and all that it would do in an endless series of relevant occasions. The "would-be" of a die, for example, could be expressed only in a series of conditional propositions stating the behavior of the die throughout an endless series of relevant events. Peirce compares this to a habit in the case of man. The nature of a man defined through habits means understanding him through real possibilities of behavior. The "would-be" or reality of the man is not identical with the behavior, either in the sense of a given act or a finite collection of them. If we may paraphrase the expression of John Stuart Mill, the "would-be" in Peirce's scheme is a permanent possibility of behavior. The key to the discovery of the "would-be," Peirce says, is what actually happens, but this is only a small part of the totality.[9] The ultimate or stable opinion is supposed to express the "would-be" in its totality. That opinion is not a mere recital of a series of events, but the expression of the habit or the power of the thing to behave in that way. How the "would-be" is a totality Peirce has not explained.

The pragmatistic theory of reality—the defining of the real through inquiry, stable belief, and the "would-be" of real possibility—is supposed to do justice to realism and idealism at the same time. Peirce believed that it was legitimate to take the idealist line and connect reality essentially with thought and opinion as long as tthe thought involved was independent of the finite and fallible thinker, and as long as it was not conceived in a "mentalistic" way. The interpretation of conceptual meaning in terms of habit and behavior rather than intuited, immediate ideas is intended to satisfy the latter demand, and the community of inquirers following an interpersonal method is supposed to satisfy the former demand. The realism, that is to say, is a realism of the dynamical nature of the object and objective thought; the idealism is that of a rationalism according to which the real is defined as the result of a process of knowledge. The two elements or emphases find their proper place within a wider matrix of inquiry, understood, to be sure, in the most concrete of terms, that is, as the controlled process of fixing belief and of moving from doubt and hesitation to belief and confident action.

The question that remains, however, is whether the entire system does not stand or fall with the validity of Peirce's special version of what we may call the "possible experience" doctrine. For it is in the doctrine of real possibility that the realistic and idealistic elements are combined. Realism demands an object that is always "all there," and in no way in need of an idea to represent it; instead Peirce offers a realism of Secondness, objective thought, and the "would-be" of behavior. Idealism demands actual presence of reality to thought or to mind; instead Peirce offers an idealism of eventual belief or stable opinion as the "would-be" of inquiry. It may be that Peirce was right in his reinterpretation of both realism and idealism, but wrong in his belief that a theory of reality can be founded on a theory of possibility, even so subtle a theory as that of the Scotistic realism.

Critical Comments

There are three major difficulties with the theory of reality outlined above. All stem from a common source: the defining of the real through the context of knowledge. Peirce, that is to say, for all of his understanding of the need for an ontological theory, still belonged to that modern tradition in philosophy according to which the key to *being* is found through *being known*. I want to suggest three critical points at which Peirce's theory shows the limitations of that approach. First, there is the problem of saying precisely what sort of reality is enjoyed by an ultimate *opinion* that would be, but in fact is not, apprehended by any finite community of knowers; second, there is the well-known problem of the futurism involved in pragmaticism and in what sense it can allow for *presence* of the total or unified person or thing; third, there is the problem of the reality of the several dimensions of things—esthetic, moral, religious, political—that seem to be excluded when the real is defined through the differential and highly abstract medium of theoretical science.

We can best see the point of the first criticism if we turn to Peirce's encounter with Royce. In his reviews of *The World and he Individual* (8.100 ff.), Peirce attempted to meet Royce's charge that reality cannot be identified with an intellectual result or opinion unless that opinion is actual and not merely possible. Royce claimed that possible experience is inadequate for defining the real, and that if we think in terms of reality as a final or critical judgment there must be a mind or form of experience capable of having that judgment as actual experience. Royce, of course, in holding to the reality of the Absolute experience, could define the real object as beyond finite thought by identifying it with the truth about it already possessed by the Absolute knowledge. Thus what the community of investigators *would* arrive at is precisely what the Absolute has as actual experience. In having a point of actual experience beyond finite experience, Royce has a ground for an actual object that is to be known by the finite community but is not dependent on that human knowledge. He has a real object beyond human thought, even if there are problems connected with the Absolute experience. Peirce saw one aspect of the difficulty, and admitted that the object at which the inquirers aim cannot be a future idea or opinion, for if the object of the ultimate opinion is another opinion in the future an infinite progress breaks out, and the result can only be the substitution of an abstraction for the real. Peirce's acknowledgment of the point is clear and unequivocal: "There is no escaping the admission that the ultimate end of inquiry—the essential, not ulterior end—the mould to which we endeavor to shape our opinions, cannot itself be of the nature of an opinion" (8.104). Instead of following out the consequences of this line and questioning the adequacy of identifying the real with an opinion in the first place, Peirce turned instead to dialectical criticism and attacked Royce's claim that the possible experience is no more than a "bare" or "mere" possibility. What makes this polemical comedy of genuine philosophical interest is that Peirce did lay hold of a genuine difficulty in Royce's theory, and indeed Royce later tried to correct it, ironically enough with help from Peirce, by moving away from the Absolute and on to the community of interpretation theory developed in *The Problem of Christianity*. Peirce, on the other hand, went back to a defense of the theory of real possibility armed with the insight—which is true—that Royce failed to appreciate the problem of real possibility, being content, as Peirce acutely said, with no mode of reality poorer than that of actuality.

What we have here is a case of failure to develop one's own theory adequately because of the temptation to correct the mistakes of others. Peirce was right, and Royce later attempted to correct his own omission, but the fact remains that Peirce did not see the consequences of his own admission. If the ultimate aim of inquiry is an object and not an opinion, how can the reality of that object be defined in terms of an opinion that would be found if inquiry were pushed to its ultimate end in the long run? Royce, being a wholehearted idealist, could accept the identification of the real with knowledge because he could always answer the question as to who gets the ultimate insight as an actual possession by appealing either to the Absolute experience or, as in the later philosophy, to the reality of the Cause to which the community of inquirers is dedicated. But Peirce was not a wholehearted idealist, and was even a Scotistic realist to boot: he had no way both of allowing that reality is an opinion or intellectual result and of giving to that opinion more support than it receives from the theory of real possibility. Royce saw that if to have a real object means a process of inquiry then that process must have an actual issue or fulfillment, and if it does not, we are left with an abstraction.

The defenders of Peirce will want at this point to call up the realistic reserves and claim that by the ultimate *opinion* Peirce does not mean a finite thought and he certainly does not mean anything mental. True, the opinion that expresses the total "would-be" of the object must be understood in terms of behavior and of power to continue in the pattern of the habit. Thus it might be said that since the opinion in question is not the sort of reality that needs to be actual in a mind, Royce's charge fails to be conclusive. But even allowing for the most completely non-idealistic interpretation of real possibility and the "would-be," whether you can identify the real with any ultimate state of affairs that is not actual, and can be reached only in the long run, remains a problem. Peirce no doubt believed that, to use the language of James, the "cash value" of the long run can be supplied by the theory of real possibility, but even so it remains true that, on Peirce's own admission, the long run has a large dose of ideality or generality in it. My conclusion is this: pile possibility on possibility, even real possibility on real possibility, and the result is not the real, but the really possible. Reality in the end for Peirce is future experience, and this is not enough.

The second difficulty may be treated shortly since it points to a criticism of the pragmatic approach that has often been made. To identify the real with the future, even the rich and full-bodied future of Peirce's realism, is to lose the totality of an object or a person within *present* experience. It is not necessary to transform the world into a timeless, pure actuality to view it as having an integral unity and totality *at each present moment* in time. I may confront another person and be aware that he is still growing and developing and yet also be aware that, although incomplete, he confronts me as a unity and total self in every present encounter. Another way of putting the point is to say that the other self does not become a real individual unity *only* at the point where the final opinion about him is reached. The fact is that Peirce was well aware of this point, and as we have seen he used the idea of the indexical sign that denotes the real individual at the beginning of inquiry against Royce's claim that only perfect knowledge serves to individuate. But Peirce seems to have overlooked the fact that the present integrity of the real individual is lost if that reality is identified with an opinion or type of experience that never manages to establish itself in the present. The unity and totality of the individual both transcend and are ingredient in every stage of the process of development; they do not wait to be constituted by the limit of a process of experience that can be reached only in the future.[10]

My final point concerns the limitation of the standpoint marked out by scientific inquiry. Peirce seems to have underestimated the differential character of the controlled, theoretical inquiry that is to issue in the real truth about things. The question may fairly be raised as to whether the knowing relation is the only relation in which we stand to the world and to the things in it. Ethics, esthetics, and religion point to dimensions of things that are excluded from the highly precise, and therefore abstract, considerations that alone are relevant for scientific inquiry. This is not to say that Peirce neglected these other dimensions in his thought; it is rather to say that they cannot easily be included by a theory of reality in which the ultimate truth comes from scientific inquiry alone. The reality of things is not exhausted in their being material for knowledge. This is the great error of much modern philosophy; Peirce was not free from it.

John E. Smith

Yale University

NOTES

1. "Religion and Theology in Peirce," *Studies in the Philosophy of Charles Sanders Peirce*, ed. P. P. Wiener and F. H. Young (Cambridge, MA., 1952), pp. 251–67.

2. Peirce was a meticulous thinker and never one to omit detail. This means that there are subtleties and qualifications in his view on every topic; they make it especially difficult to consider any of his ideas in brief compass. Tributes to Peirce,

however, must be limited even if Peirce's attention to detail and the number of his papers were not.

3. See 8.39ff.; in view of Royce's great debt to Kant, it is ironical that Peirce should accuse him of passing over Kant's view of space and time as forms of intuition guaranteeing individuality as distinct from categories that function as predicates and are thus insufficient for providing a real subject.

4. See 5.543 for a succinct statement; the Scotistic realism is mentioned in many places where it is invariably contrasted with nominalism.

5. Peirce upheld an essentially idealistic interpretation of signs and the function of representation. While it is not true that all instances of Thirdness require the notion of mind (see, for example, 1.366), Peirce almost invariably mentioned intention and the ability to represent as a mental activity in his discussions of signs and triadic relations (1.420, 1.475; 5.292, 5.287). The various attempts that have been made to reduce Peirce's theory to a form of behaviorism remain unsuccessful because genuine Thirdness and intellectual purport are never identical with actual behavior. Thirdness, in the sense of sign and law connecting phenomena, is indeed related to public fact, overt act, and external events, but there is always generality in Thirdness, and generality—a form of intellectual purport—cannot be exhausted in any fact or finite collection of facts. Moreover, the attempt to equate Thirdness with habit raises the same difficulty. For while Peirce did connect Thirdness intimately with habit, and thus did not confine himself to a narrow, "mentalistic" conception of mind as merely immediate consciousness, habit itself cannot be understood apart from generality or general tendency to continue in a certain pattern. Like intellectual purport, habit is never adequately analyzed into actual behavior.

6. I purposely omit from the list of passages cited those (such as 5.351–52) that raise, or seem to raise, the question as to whether there is anything real at all. Peirce's entire philosophy is oriented to the problem of coming to know and to justify our knowledge of what there is; he is not primarily concerned with the question: Is there anything to know? That is to say that Peirce does not belong to that school of philosophers who start with language, thoughts, sensory data, and then go on to ask *whether* there is an external world.

7. In most cases Peirce takes this principle to be the inference from a known part or sample of a class to all other members not yet experienced. In 5.341 an alternative formulation of the principle of induction is: How is it that when some facts are true, other facts standing in a special relation to them are also true?

8. One of the liabilities of treating a comprehensive topic in a brief paper is found in the need to omit what should not be left out of account. Peirce's evolutionary cosmology as expressed in the doctrines of Tychism (Chance), Synechism (Continuity) and Agapism (Evolutionary Love) should be brought in as part of his general theory of reality. Morever, a thorough consideration of his theory of habit is also needed for the proper understanding of the "would-be," or mode of reality that stands between actual fact and logical possibility.

9. The most important passages for understanding the theory of real possibility are: 1.420; 2.661–68; 4.580; 5.453, 5.467, 5.528; 6.327.

10. I do not overlook the fact that Peirce (see 7.340 ff.) sought to respond to the difficulty cited by claiming that the reality does not *begin* to be the way it is said to be in the idea or belief when the belief first comes into being. He attempts to disconnect the being of the object from the idea, while claiming that the only *meaning* we can give to the descriptive term or idea is by pointing to the actual behavior.

CHARLES PEIRCE AND OBJECTIVITY IN PHILOSOPHY

The Meaning of Objectivity

I make a distinction between what I call *factual objectivity* and what I call *rule objectivity*. The former is ontological and involves *conformity to reality* or facts. The latter is epistemological and involves *conformity to rules* which establish objectivity by fiat and social agreement. Factual objectivity is closely related to the ordinary language sense of objectivity, which presupposes the (uncritical) realistic distinction between mutually exclusive 'subjects' (or selves) and 'objects' (or not-selves). If we disregard for the moment the practical difficulties of reaching ontological and epistemological agreement as to where the demarcation line between the self and the not-self is to be drawn, we find the ordinary language meaning of 'objectivity', as given for example in Webster's unabridged dictionary, quite instructive. 'Object' is defined in one context as "The totality of external phenomena consituting the not-self"; 'objectivity' is defined derivatively as "the quality, state, or relation of being objective"; and objective, in turn, is defined as "something that is external to the mind." Here 'subject' (or self, or mind) is the basic undefined term, in terms of which we can define objectivity as non-subjectivity, in polar contrast to 'subjective', which means 'that which is part of or inside of the self '. To be objective thus means to be other than the self, or external to the self (we do not raise here, of course, the interesting problems of the possible differences between the self and the mind, but merely include the latter as part of the former). The test of objectivity and subjectivity, on this view, is whether something is inside or outside of the self, i.e., part of the self or not. This ordinary language notion of objects and subjects presupposes the (uncritical) realistic view that we perceive *chairs,* not *percepts* of chairs, and that chairs are outside of our minds and thus our selves, even though the percepts of the chairs we perceive are not.

We cannot, however, be satisfied with a distinction between subject and object which is unambiguous only to the extent that it remains purely formal without empirical content. In order for objectivity to be factual objectivity, i.e., to have factual content, the demarcation between the self and the not-self must be ontologically correct—the line must be drawn between them in what as a matter of fact is the *right* place. It must also meet whatever epistemological requirements are necessary to give us the requisite assurance that we *know* that it is correct. But, whereas philosophers are able to agree that what is 'inside' the self is subjective and what is 'outside' is objective, they are not always able to agree on where the line of demarcation between the self and the not-self is to be drawn, because of the enormous variation in their ontological and epistemological presuppositions and assumptions. Thus what is objective for one philosopher may be a mere figment for another.

This account places high demands on what is expected of objectivity for it to be factual objectivity. Perhaps the demands are too high. What we expect of objectivity for it to be factual is that it should be genuine—that it should be veridical—we might almost say that it should be factually factual, or objectively objective, that it should attain absolute verisimilitude.

But of course it should be apparent that terms like genuine objectivity, or objective objectivity, and even the very term factual objectivity, beg the question of genuineness in much the same almost desperate table-pounding fashion as is involved in referring to perception as veridical, that is, as not merely true, but *truly* true. Such verbal devices only show the absurdity of trying to express ourselves by using old words whose meanings have become too blurred and ambiguous to fit our needs, to say nothing of the futility of raising our voices or repeating ourselves in frustration when our words carry no conviction, as is so often the case when we try to express the inexpressible—the absolute that is forever beyond the reach of our knowledge—the truth that is truly true, the reality that is really real, the objectivity that is objectively objective.

What I call 'rule objectivity', on the other hand, makes much less pretentious claims, as it is concerned only with the practical questions relating to *the rules of what constitutes acceptable evidence* on the basis of which claims for objectivity are validated. Validation of a claim to objectivity begins with individual replications by independent observers of the crucial observations (and arguments) on which a particular claim to objectivity depends. Each such replication is insofar a test of the *factual* objectivity of the original claim, a test in which negative results are categorical refutations, whereas positive results yield confirmations which are only tentative.

It is well known that positive confirmation in science is hardly more than an unattainable ideal limit. However, when replications are pooled, whereas in a strict logical sense they still do not categorically furnish absolute confirmation, they become in James's term, "practical absolutes" which furnish us with sufficient confirmation to permit us to continue our investigation as though (*als ob*) the confirmations were *absolute.* Thus pooled replications on which there is intersubjective agreement furnish a collective confirmation which has *rule* objectivity. The individual observers who replicate the appropriate tests and arguments are like a collective jury, or a collective umpire, and wherever questions of fact or judgment are decided by juries or umpires, whatever they are able to agree upon as *being in their opinion* objectively valid is defined *by the rules under which they operate* as *being* objectively valid, i.e., as rule objective validity. It is evident that rule objectivity is thoroughly pragmatic—it is objectivity as it affects human behavior. In a word, we behave toward that which has rule objectivity as though (*als ob*) it were true in fact instead of by agreement, and 'intersubjective agreement' is seen to be the translation into pragmatic or operational language of the term 'objectivity'.

The rules of science, by a similar fiat, grant rule objectivity to a claim for objectivity which is confirmed by the pooled replications of *competent,* independent observers. Science does not claim factual objectivity for its claims of the moment—to do so would in a sense reduce the method of science to the absurdity of making an endless series of factual claims which are always fated to be contradicted by new evidence. Rule objectivity, on the other hand, does not directly claim to be factual, but only that there is adequate intersubjective agreement to prove that the claim has not yet been falsified. Accordingly, a claim validated by rule objectivity can be revoked without contradicting the previous validation, which did not claim factuality, but only that all the replications made up to that date were in agreement as confirmatory of the claim. Should subsequent replications fail to agree, then the claim that the replications agree can be withdrawn without the embarrassment of confessing that what I claimed yesterday as the truth today I admit as false. In a word, rule objectivity testifies to social agreement, not to factuality. Furthermore,

not only is a claim which has gained its validation on the basis of rule objectivity treated *as though* it had gained its validation on the basis of factual objectivity, but this fiction (and that it is a fiction is never denied) is carried still
further in behaving toward all claims which are granted rule objective validity
as though they were all *equal* in their factuality, even when we are convinced
on other grounds that this is not the case.[1]

Science ostensibly accepts, in the absence of any immediate evidence to
the contrary, all rule objective validations as equally valid, and treats them as
though they had been equally validated *factually*. However, it does not accept
its own verdict as final, but continues to make a vigorous and sustained
search to find the very evidence to the contrary which would refute its own
validation. This is because even though all rule objective validations are
equally valid as rule validations, they may each have a different degree of
truth content. Accordingly, our conviction about the reliability of a
hypothesis is increased by three factors (of which the least powerful is the
first), namely:

1. the competence and skill of the persons involved in proposing and
   testing the hypothesis on the basis of whose agreement rule objective
   validity is granted;
2. the total number of replications made; and
3. the total number of tentatively confirmed but independently established claims which mutually support each other.

It is obvious that on all three counts rule objective validity has a far greater
probability of being factually valid in science than in any other enterprise.
The almost limitless opportunity for continued replication and retesting in
science persuades Peirce that in the long run science is *predestined* to hit on
the truth (5.407).[2] This is one of the fundamental disagreements between
Peirce and Popper. For Peirce seems on some occasions,[3] but not on others
(5.590-604), to adhere to the "manifest theory of truth," as Popper calls it: it
is the nature of truth that it will hit us sooner or later, given enough time.
Popper, on the other hand, emphatically denies this: we may never hit on the
truth, it is very hard to come by—and even if we were to hit upon it, we can
never know with certainty that we have done so. Hence the greatest emphasis
is placed on error elimination. The more successful we are in purging error,
the closer we can hope to approach the truth.[4]

The Problem of Objectivity in Peirce's Philosophy

The problem of objectivity in Peirce's philosophy was the problem of establishing the objective validity in experience of the categories which Peirce
had proposed as the fundamental categories of logic. The apparently formal

and empty names which Peirce uses to identify his categories are not merely numerical labels. Rather, they are *descriptive* names[5] for various fundamental categories of logic which at the same time are ontological categories. In their pure form, as abstract ideal limits, *Firstness* is the category, for which the prototype in logic is the monad, of those entities which are what they are in and of themselves alone—thus they are *originals*. *Secondness* is the category of those things which would not be what they are if they were not *constitutively* related to one other thing—e.g., causes or effects. *Thirdness* is the category of those things which would not be what they are if they were not *constitutively* related to two other things—e.g., a mediator, or an interpreter. The essential claim of Peirce's logic of relations was that there are three unique and irreducible kinds of relations, monadic, dyadic, and triadic (or polyadic). He then argued that they must have been derived from three irreducibly different kinds of logical thought processes, and thus by some stretch of logic, they are fundamental categories of being.

> . . . When the notation which suffices for exhibiting one inference is found inadequate for explaining another, it is clear that the latter involves an inferential element not present to the former. Accordingly, the procedure contemplated [that of discovering the irreducible types of notation] should result in a list of categories of reasoning, the interest of which is not dependent upon the algebraic way of considering the subject. [3.428]

However, even if we grant that Peirce, through his logic of relations has discovered the ultimate categories of reasoning, it seems to me that we are still far from having demonstrated how or why these categories are transformed into objective categories of all being. Where does the objectivity of Peirce's categories come from? As nearly as I can make out, through the affirmation of a purely metaphysical presupposition which in an earlier study (in 1934) I called Peirce's *Ontological Postulate*, namely, "that the principles of formal logic and epistemology are directly related to the principles of Being, that the structure of logic is the key to the structure of Reality."[6] This postulate was the foundation of Peirce's ontology, which was "simply the hypostatization of a logic into a categorial system without argument" (*CCP*, p. 1). Peirce defines the categories as "a table of conceptions drawn from the logical analysis of thought and regarded as applicable to being" (1.300). "I shall not here inquire," Peirce writes, "how far it is justifiable to apply the conceptions of logic to metaphysics. For I hold the importance of that question, great as it is, to be perhaps secondary, . . ." (1.301).

But a set of categories derived from formal abstract principles of logic must also be formal and abstract. In order to get to categories which have factual objective validity, we must start from concrete factual experience, rather than from an abstract logic. However, concrete experience is always particular, and categories to be adequate must be universal, not merely particular. Some happy combination of the universality, afforded only by abstract logical principles, and the applicability to nature, afforded only by concrete particular experience, is required as the minimum necessary attribute of categories in order for them to be at the same time, as Whitehead would have required,[7] sufficiently factual to be "applicable" and sufficiently general (universal) to be "adequate" for the understanding and the explanation of human experience.

Peirce's Method: Mathematical Empiricism

Peirce's concern to ensure for his categories both the universality of mathematics and the applicability of empirical science led him to formulate a method which Charles Hartshorne has termed 'mathematical empiricism' (*CCP*, p. 3n.). This method is the philosophical counterpart of the method of empirical science. The latter consists essentially of the proposing of a speculative hypothesis (which Popper aptly refers to as a conjecture) to solve a problem which has meaningful consequences in human experience—i.e., one which is testable (or as Popper aptly puts it, is falsifiable) by observation. Testable predicted consequences of the hypothesis are then checked by making appropriate observations and the hypothesis is thereby either refuted or tentatively retained.

Perhaps the greatest similarity in the methods of Peirce and Popper appears in their accounts of the nature and origin of the hypothesis. For both men, the hypothesis is a conjecture, and for both, it is the outcome of a shower of wild imaginative guesses, one of which survives. For Peirce the process whereby the thinker is led from the examination of unexplained facts to a theory which explains them is called 'retroduction' or 'abduction'. For Popper, the examination of a knowledge situation suggests *problems*, which we attempt to solve by putting forth tentative theories (imaginative guesses). The procedures of testing hypotheses or solving problems may start as logical exercises when we test them for coherence, congruence, and noncontradiction, but must always terminate in empirical testing. Popper points out that we always place our problems into what he calls a "third world background" (i.e., a background of objective ideas which are neither physical things nor merely subjective mental entities but independent knowables—like Plato's ideas—thus *objects* for knowledge).[8] This third world background, Popper adds, "consists of at least a *language*, which always incorporates many theories in the very structure of its usages . . . and many other theoretical assumptions, unchallenged at least for the time being" ("Obj. Mind," pp. 22-32).

Nor does Peirce, any more than Popper, challenge the theoretical assumptions on which he rests his philosophy. One of Peirce's most memorable remarks is his eloquent "let us not pretend to doubt in our philosophies what we do not doubt in our hearts." Peirce followed this advice devotedly, even to the point of letting his heart make his eyes see things that were not there, such as the observations he fancied were made by philosophers by virtue of which philosophy becomes a positive (i.e., an empirical) science.

> Mathematics . . . makes no external observations, nor asserts anything as real fact. . . . Philosophy is not quite so abstract. For though it makes no *special* observations, as every other positive science does, yet it does deal with reality. It confines itself, however, to the universal phenomena of experience; and these are, generally speaking, sufficiently revealed in the ordinary observations of every-day life. [3.428]

Like the disappointed father who gives his new-born daughter the name of the son he had longed for, Peirce cannot accept the fact that philosophy is not an empirical science, so he gives it the name he had hoped it would bear. He grants, and then attempts to brush away, the crucial objection that philosophers do not make special observations as all other empirical scientists do, and that without specific empirical content philosophy could hardly claim to be a positive science. Peirce contends that philosophers *do* deal with empirical reality, but that their observations are limited to "the universal phenomena of experience," as "revealed in the ordinary observations of every-day life" (3.428).

A similar contention is found in Popper, who writes that ". . . scientific knowledge is merely a development of ordinary knowledge or common sense knowledge . . . " (*L.Sc.D.*, p. 18). At this point, however, it seems to me that Peirce has stretched the meaning of either the term 'observation' or 'universal' beyond recognition. 'Observations', in the ordinary language sense in which the term refers to the results of a crucial procedure in empirical science, are, of course, *sensory* observations, i.e., observations mediated by one or more of the special sense organs. Whereas 'universal' means 'infinitely boundless' and infinite boundlessness is obviously beyond the reach of ordinary observations, which cannot extend outside of the limited confines of the space and time in which they are made. I know of no kinds of "ordinary observations of every-day life" which will disclose anything but particular phenomena. If by chance an observer were actually to observe phenomena which were indeed manifestations or instantiations of something or some things which were indeed universal, the observer could not know their universality, if all he knew about them came from his ordinary observations of them. The knowledge of their universality would have to come to him from some other way of knowing.

I do not quarrel with Peirce's contention that his categories are objective—rather, I share his heartfelt conviction on this. What I do question is Peirce's paradoxical claim about the universality of what can be known through *observation*, thus, about the objectivity of Thirdness as given directly in *perception*. That Thirdness is "perceived" is the basic contention of Peirce's strikingly original and subtle Phenomenology, which he invents in the vain hope that it will furnish him with an epistemological tool powerful enough to give the abstractions of logic the concrete content required to transform them into objective principles applicable to all being. The Phenomenology "treats of the Universal Qualities of phenomena in their immediate phenomenal character"[9] (5.122).

In some ways Peirce's Phenomenology reminds me of the 'nail soup' made in the old folk tale by stirring a pot of boiling water with a magic nail. The gypsy who owned the nail would persuade a housewife to let him demonstrate his magic in return for his dinner. They would go to the kitchen and a pot of water would soon be boiling briskly on the stove. The gypsy would then stir the pot slowly with his magic nail, while the housewife watched him carefully. After a while he would say, "Plain nail soup is very good. But it is even better with a pinch of salt." The housewife would nod her head, and add some salt. The stirring and the watching would be resumed. Then the gypsy would mention another way to improve nail soup. In due course the soup would be finished, and the housewife would be surprised to discover that the soup made by using the magic nail tasted exactly like the soup she made herself without it.

It happens that I do think that Peirce's categories are genuinely objective and universal, just as I think that nail soup would be genuinely nutritious. But I am no more conviced that the universality which I grant I find in the categories comes from perception than I am convinced that the nutriments in the soup come from the nail. Murray Murphey, who holds a similar view, puts it this way: "It is impossible to regard Peirce's phenomenological treatment of the categories as anything more than a quite unsuccessful sleight of hand."[10] But even though Peirce is unsuccessful here in what he set out to do, I think Murphey's metaphor is hardly appropriate. Sleight of hand implies deliberate deception by a kind of skilled trickery, and Peirce was not trying to trick his reader into accepting something that Peirce himself knew was not true. On the contrary, although Peirce's arguments may not have been correct, nevertheless he believed in them with all his heart. Thus the deception was not sleight of hand, but self-deception, like nail soup made by a cook who believed in the magic of the nail.

Murphey points out that it is essential to Peirce's position that in order to avoid subjectivism, and at the same time to account for orderly experience, it is necessary for Peirce to maintain that Thirdness is directly perceived, since he accepts the empirical axiom that nothing can be in the intellect which was not first known through the senses, from which it follows that unless generality is given in perception, it can never be known at all (*DPP*, pp. 376

ff.). I think that Peirce is right in holding, as Kant does, that we are able to account for orderly experience through our knowledge of universals, but as I have already stated, I think that Peirce was mistaken in his contention that such universals are given in perception.

Peirce's nail soup, which he calls his phenomenology, instead of containing nothing but sensory observation, is enriched by the addition of *illicitly added ontological ingredients which give the phenomenology all the universality and generality that perception can never give it.* Peirce is able to add the illicit ingredients to his nail soup by using the word 'observation' in four different senses, three of which are specialized whereas the fourth is general, combining the other three ambiguously and vaguely. These four senses of the term 'observation', which may be symbolized as O_s, O_i, O_H, and O_g, are the following:

1. O_s is observation in the narrow literal sense where it means sense perception.
2. O_i is observation in its broader metaphorical sense where it means rational insight or intuition.
3. O_H is observation in an intriguing Hegel-like synthesis of the preceding two senses, where it designates the simultaneous observation (O_s) of icons of abstract entities and the observation (O_i) of the entities themselves as mirrored in their icons.
4. O_g is observation in the conveniently ambiguous general sense which includes the foregoing three senses without distinguishing between them.

It is O_H which adds the ontological richness to observation which O_s can never bring. Formal mathematical and logical entities and relationships are on my view forever beyond the grasp of O_s. But they are within easy reach of O_H, which begins with a genuinely phenomenological step in which icons of abstract entities are observed by O_s. This is followed by a wholly ontological step required for the validation of O_H. This consists of the acceptance of a presupposition or postulate the truth of which guarantees the correctness of the procedure of knowing abstract entities by observing their icons. This presupposed postulate is not put into words by Peirce. As I would reconstruct it, the postulate might be expressed as follows:

Whatever is true of an icon as observed by O_s, is true of the abstract entity for which the icon is a visible sign.

The postulate is seen to be true by intuition or rational insight, i.e., O_i, whereas the abstract entity is known 'observationally' through the complex synthesis of empirical and rational observation which I have called O_H.

In summary, the abstract entities are not directly observable (O_s), but the icons which are constructed to mirror them are directly observable (O_s).

However, the abstract entities are observable in a sort of indirect fashion through O_H. Accordingly, the paradoxical claim can be made that we can observe the 'unobservable', by observing the icons which mirror the unobservable—very much as Perseus, by looking at the reflection mirrored in his shield, was able to view with impunity the forbidden sight of the face of Medusa.

Another subtle variation from ordinary language notions of perception is Peirce's important distinction between a perception and a perceptual judgment. This distinction affords Peirce the grounds for introducing an additional amount of interpretation into the essence of perception (he had already pointed out that some degree of interpretation is involved from the outset in perception). Like the perception itself, the perceptual judgment, on Peirce's view, retains its objectivity despite its being to some extent an interpretation by the subject, inasmuch as the subject has no control over the process, any more than he has over the prior process of perceiving (2.140-41).

Peirce defines a perceptual judgment as "a judgment absolutely forced upon my acceptance, and that by a process which I am utterly unable to control and consequently am unable to criticize" (5.157). This is very much like Descartes's notion of ideas which are so clear and simple that we cannot resist them. A critical case of the kind of perceptual judgments involved in Peirce's so-called perception of universals is afforded by the perception of the relationship between events which are apparently successive in time, i.e., the relationship of apparent subsequence. As difficult as the notion can be from a logical point of view, Peirce found it quite acceptable to assume that "Thirdness pours in upon us through every avenue of sense" (5.157).

> Now consider the judgment that one event C *appears to be* subsequent to another event A. Certainly, I may have inferred this; because I may have remarked that C was subsequent to a third event B which was itself subsequent to A. But then these premises are judgments of the same description. It does not seem possible that I can have performed an infinite series of acts of criticism each of which must require a distinct effort. The case is quite different from that of Achilles and the tortoise because Achilles does not require to make an infinite series of distinct efforts. It therefore appears that I must have made some judgment that one event *appeared to be* subsequent to another without that judgment having been inferred from any premiss [i.e.] without any *controlled* and *criticized* action of reasoning. If this be so, it is a perceptual judgment in the only sense that the logician can recognize.

The crucial claim here is Peirce's identification of 'perceptual judgment' and perception.

> But from that proposition that one event, Z, is subsequent to another event, J, I can at once deduce by necessary reasoning a universal proposition. Namely, the definition of the relation of apparent subsequence is well known, or sufficiently so for our purpose. Z will appear to be subsequent to Y if and only if A appears

to stand in a peculiar relation, R, to Y such that nothing can stand in the relation R to itself, and if, furthermore, whatever event, X, there may be to which Y stands in the relation R, to that same X, Z also stands in the relation R. [Cf. 3.562B] This being implied in the meaning of subsequence, concerning which there is no room for doubt, it easily follows that whatever is subsequent to C is subsequent to anything, A, to which C is subsequent—which is a universal proposition.

Thus my assertion at the end of the last lecture appears to be most amply justified. Thirdness pours in upon us through every avenue of sense. [5.157]

What Peirce does here is illicitly to include intuition and deduction along with perception as being necessarily involved in the so-called perceptual procedure, from which Peirce "can at once deduce by necessary reasoning a universal proposition." But a procedure which involves as an essential step "deduction by necessary reasoning" can hardly be asserted to be sense perception. And that Peirce intended us to interpret his words as referring to some kind of perception other than sense perception is hardly consistent with his proclamation at the end of the paragraph just quoted in which he writes that "Thirdness pours in upon us through every avenue of sense" (5.157).

The exact place where Peirce goes wrong is in his defintion of perceptual judgment (5.157) quoted above, in which he defines perceptual judgment in terms of necessary but not sufficient characteristics. That perceptual judgments are forced upon us, that we have no control over them, and thus cannot criticize them, I grant is quite true. But I would say that this is equally true of many of the judgments we make in logic and mathematics through 'insight' or 'rational intuition', where we 'see' that a proposition is true, but only in a metaphorical and not in the perceptual sense of seeing, O_i and not O_s.

In a word, Peirce's basic mistake is to use the metaphorical sense of 'perceiving' or 'seeing' as though it were the literal sense. In the metaphorical sense of seeing, we 'see' that something is true by insight or intuition (cf. 6.493). In the literal sense of seeing, we see by looking at something with our eyes and perceiving it. If we broaden the term 'perception' to include the metaphorical sense, which of course includes 'rational insight', there is no difficulty in agreeing with Peirce's contention that we can know universals (Thirdness) through 'perception'. But, although this dissolves the difficulties which would confront us if we were to have used the term perception in its literal sense, it also dissolves that part of the claim that Thirdness is objective which rests on Thirdness being perceived. Things which are *perceived* have a prima facie claim to objectivity, but only if they are perceived through sensory perception (O_s). If they are known through some way other than through sensory perception, the claim that they are objective because they are *perceived* is a misrepresentation, unless it is explicitly made clear that the term 'perception' is not being used in its ordinary sense of 'sense perception', but as a figure of speech.

Thus we have gone full circle, and we return to Peirce's starting point, the Ontological Postulate, that the ultimate categories of logic *must be* the objective categories of being.[11] This postulate is the foundation on which the *objectivity* of Peirce's categories rests, and I cannot accept his claim that he is able to validate the objectivity of his categories by means of perception. It is only by rational intuition that we can know this postulate. By pooling the efforts of independent competent observers who are able to replicate the act of seeing by their own rational intuition that the postulate is self-evident for them, their agreement grants rule objective validity to the postulate, to the extent that they can agree.

Objectivity in Philosophy on Peirce's Terms: His Sign Theory

Peirce, who was typically a scientist in his rejection of absolutistic claims in philosophy, makes no pretense of offering us absolute truth or absolute factual objectivity. For those who are content with rule objectivity and degrees of truth content, Peirce's philosophy, when accepted on his own terms, is extraordinarily successful.

The principles and criteria for objectivity in philosophy which can be developed from Peirce's philosophy rest ultimately on two presuppositions[12] which are basic to his theory of the categories:

1. Peirce's Ontological Postulate—that the structure of logic is the mirror of the structure of reality;
2. That Peirce's three categories of logic are ultimate categories of metaphysics and of reality.

From the monad, dyad, and triad of Peirce's logic are derived not only his categories of Firstness, Secondness, and Thirdness, but his theory of signs as well. For Peirce there are three basic types of signs, the icon, the index, and the token (or symbol), and these are not merely variations on the theme of his three categories, but, to use the same figure, the categories themselves played in a different key.

In Peirce's theory of signs, the monad, or Firstness, is present in the form of the *icon*; the dyad, or Secondness, as the *index*; and the triad, or Thirdness, as the *token* (or symbol). An icon is a monadic sign which stands for something else, its object, by resembling it—thus by being itself, it is also (figuratively) its object. For example, an iconic sign of whiteness is a patch of white chalk on a blackboard, which stands for whiteness by (figuratively) being whiteness. Or a diagram of a relationship, such as the inclusion of one class within another, is an iconic sign of the relationship, which stands for the relationship by (figuratively) being the relationship.

An index is a dyadic sign which stands for its object by pointing to it, through some connection with its object that denotes it without describing it—e.g., demonstrative and relative pronouns, pointing fingers, weather-vanes, indicators on instruments, etc.

Peirce has one of the most clear-headed and convincing accounts of the factual objectivity and existential reality of the 'external' world in the entire history of philosophy. For Peirce as an empirical scientist as well as a philosopher, objectivity meant replication by an independent observer of the testimony on the basis of which a claim for objectivity is made. But here the critical first step is to communicate successfully to the would-be replicator *where and how he is to look* if he is to see what the subject sees. This is done by demonstration, and while not infallible, there is no better method of demonstration than the directing of the attention by means of a pointing finger and an indexical pronoun, or by a 'pointer reading' on a scientific instrument. If no replicator is able to see anything at the end of the pointing finger, e.g., the pink elephants to which the victim of delirium tremens points, we know that the subject is describing a world of fiction and not fact. Peirce points out that *the only way* that we can distinguish the real world from the world of fiction is by using indexes (2.337, 3.363, 8.39 ff.).[13]

Peirce uses Duns Scotus's term "haecceities" to designate the *thisness* to which attention is directed by a gesture accompanied by a demonstrative (or indexical) pronoun, e.g., "Look at *this*." 'This' names a something for which objective reality is claimed, a claim which can be confirmed by intersubjective testing. Thus from the category of Secondness, from which Peirce's indexical signs are derived, Peirce is able to establish the factual objectivity of the external world by *denotation.*

A token or symbol is a triadic sign, which stands for its object through the intervention of a mind or interpreter which connects sign and object through its own fiat, e.g., "let the word 'dog' stand for dog in the English language." All conventional 'symbols' (in the ordinary language sense) are triadic signs (or tokens), thus all meaning is triadic.

Peirce's clarification of the nature of signs, and of meaning in general led directly to his doctrine of pragmatism, which for him was essentially a theory of meaning rather than an epistemology or metaphysics. This theory throws a flood of new light on traditional epistemological and metaphysical problems. By defining the meaning of any concept as 'the conceivable consequences in experience which the affirmation or denial of that concept implies', Peirce excludes as without meaning all claims which are beyond the theoretically possible reach of intersubjective testing, and thus limits the bounds of the objective world to the bounds of the *rule objective* world. By setting attainable limits for his goals, Peirce is thus able to achieve them admirably well—perhaps as well as any philosopher who ever lived.

General Requirements for Objectivity

A set of three general requirements for objectivity can be formulated on the basis of Peirce's theory of signs:

1. all reasoning is diagrammatic;
2. the ultimate test of objectivity is denotation;
3. meaning must be defined pragmatically.

(1) From the category of Firstness, as expressed in the icon, we can formulate the following requirement. As Peirce himself stipulated, since reasoning consists of experimentation upon relations expressed by icons, ultimately *all reasoning must be diagrammatic*. "For reasoning," in Peirce's words, "consists in the observation that where certain relations subsist certain others are found, and it accordingly requires the exhibition of the relations reasoned within an icon" (3.363). When the relations involved in a piece of reasoning are expressed by means of diagrams or icons, such as, e.g., mathematical formulae or diagrams, the formulae of symbolic logic or logical diagrams such as those of Euler or Venn, the reasoning can accurately be replicated by intersubjective testing, and is thus objective.

(2) From the category of Secondness, as expressed in the index, we can formulate the requirement that the *ultimate test of reality consists of denotative procedures*, the final links of which are ostensive identifications by means of *indexes* (thus, demonstrative pronouns) and *gestures*. This is hardheaded realism. We attempt to establish correspondence between our descriptions and haecceities, and we identify the haecceities by pointing to them. When astronomers first pointed their telescopes at exactly the place indicated by the calculations of Leverrier and Adams, they transformed a theoretical Neptune into an 'objectively real' *haecceity*.

(3) From the category of Thirdness, as expressed in the token, we can formulate the requirement that *meaning must be defined pragmatically*. That is to say, meaning is the relating of a sign to its referent by an interpreter.

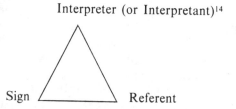

Interpreter (or Interpretant)[14]

Sign   Referent

A sign is *something* that stands for *something else* for an *interpreter*. Meaning is always triadic and always involves the *purposes of the interpreter*, who attaches the referent to the sign as its meaning *for him*. Thus, meaning is essentially pragmatic, that is, in the sense that it involves human purposes. It is only when we introduce the third element, the interpreter, who relates the referent and the sign vehicle as constituting meaning for him, that meaning arises.

Built into the criterion which defines meaning triadically, in terms of the fiat of the interpreter (which of course is determined by his purposes) is the famous restriction that the interpreter must be a radical empiricist. Meaning can be found only in "conceivable consequences in human experience."

Secondness is the acknowledgment of a brute external reality which is in no way dependent on the thinking of the knower for its existence. The objectively real is the "that" or "this" pointed to by the index. On the level of Secondness it is known only as a brute fact without meaning—an "other" or an "object" as distinguished from the subject who knows it. But what it *means* is known only through Thirdness, through its *pragmatic meaning*, as defined by the fiat of the interpreter, who limits its meaning entirely to the conceivable consequences it can have in human experience, and thus to human purposes.

Thus Peirce's theory of pragmatism, conceived as a *theory of meaning*, developed from the logical implications of the category of Thirdness. *The essence of pragmatism is identical with the category of Thirdness*, namely the recognition that meaning and purpose are inseparable, that meaning must be interpreted in terms of human purposes and conduct.[15]

The general requirements for objectivity discussed above enable us to draw the following conclusions from what we can term the pragmatic criterion of objectivity (pragmatic in the sense just stipulated).

1. The criterion rules out as meaningless any purported aspects of meaning which are not "confirmable" by sensory observation of empirical phenomena. It thus eliminates all supranatural metaphysics and all absolutes from science, and insofar as philosophers follow suit, from philosophy as well.

2. It ensures that the independent observers who participate in the intersubjective testing will all agree on what crucial observations need to be made to replicate a claim for objectivity, since each of the observations to be made is precisely specified beforehand, and thus the testimony of the participants will be uniformly precise in its relevance.

3. It ensures that the skills required of the participants will be well within the reach of each of them, since only basic perceptual skills, and no highly specialized qualities of intelligence or good judgment are called upon. Thus this ensures that the rule objective validity established by the pooled judgment of the participants has the highest possible reliability.

Popper's criterion of falsifiability is congruent with the above three consequences of the pragmatic criterion for objectivity. So much so that at first glance Popper's criterion of falsifiability may seem to be equivalent to the pragmatic criterion of meaning, differing only in that it is expressed in its logically equivalent negative rather than positive form. However, even though the principles are logical equivalents, an enormous conceptual advance is made by Popper in this deceptively simple but brilliantly original turn from the positive to the negative form of the pragmatic principle. It is to Popper, and to Popper alone, to whom we are indebted for recognizing the importance of the negative form of the principle as expressing most adequately what (rule) objectivity means in science; and once this has been pointed out, simple as it may seem, we can never go back to the positive principle without seeing that it does not quite capture the essence of scientific objectivity.

The germ of the Popperian notion of falsification is actually expressed by Peirce—"the best hypothesis, in the sense of the one most recommending itself to the inquirer, is the one which can be the most readily refuted if it is false" (1.120). But the idea remained a relatively dormant seed until it reached full flower in Popper's philosophy of science.

I am reminded here not only of Columbus and the egg, but of the brilliant and paradoxical reversal of Occam's principle of parsimony by Karl Menger, who points out[16] that the simplicity which is so prized in science and mathematics is sometimes a pseudosimplicity, and that we should be as ready to use what he calls his "prism" to disperse an oversimplified complexity (like the concept of function) into its individually important consitituent concepts, as we are ready to use Occam's razor to prune away an overcomplicated simplicity.

Methodology and Metaphysics: Tychism and Platonic Realism

Peirce is a resolute champion of the doctrine of fallibilism and indeterminism in science and philosophy. In a famous remark, Peirce observes that

> the most refined comparisons of masses, lengths, and angles, far surpassing in precision all other measurements, . . . fall behind the accuracy of bank accounts, and . . . the ordinary determinations of physical constants, such as appear from month to month in the journals, are about on a par with an upholsterer's measurements of carpets and curtains. . . . [6.44]

Similarly, as Skolimowski has noted in volume I of *The Philosophy of Karl Popper* (LLP, p. 488), Popper holds that there is no secure foundation for knowledge—that we can build only on piles driven into the swamp.

Popper reaches this conclusion from his insistence that to be scientific means to be falsifiable—to be falsifiable means that we can never have absolute truth (which of course could not be falsified). Popper's argument is primarily methodological or epistemological.

Tychism

From similar grounds, Peirce derives a similar conclusion—but he continues beyond science to spin out a metaphysical doctrine which, although it is consistent with fallibilism in the sense in which the term is used above, is neither a necessary nor the only plausible one which would be consistent with it: namely, his doctrine of *Tychism*, or the doctrine that in the world, there is to be found freedom, originality, creativity, indeterminism—which are not dependent on our thinking, and are thus real. These are manifestations, or schemata, of Peirce's important category of Firstness—for which these terms are each in a sense question-begging affirmations of Peirce's faith in their objectivity—a faith which is as cardiac as it is cortical, and which, in the best of company, e.g., Bergson, Whitehead, Boutroux, William James, Hartshorne, and others, I share with Peirce.

Peirce's Tychism is a fully developed metaphysical position which affirms his personal conviction that there are certain manifestations of Firstness in nature, such as real chance, real possiblity, real freedom, real creativity—thus real indeterminism, which would be logically impossible and thus could not even be conceived unless the laws of nature wiggled. And, on Peirce's terms, the conclusion that the laws of nature do in fact wiggle, even if the amount of wiggling is less than we could actually observe, is inescapable; if they did not, there would be no Firstness in the world, no originality, no freedom, no indeterminism, nothing but events inexorably fated to occur, through laws that were absolutely uniform, and thus permitted no exceptions to wiggle out from under their rule.

Accordingly, Peirce *begins* his argument with his metaphysical conclusion, his affirmation of the reality of freedom, spontaneity, creativity, possibility, chance (thus indeterminism), to which he fits the only premise that could support such a conclusion, namely, that the laws of nature are sufficiently irregular to provide for freedom and spontaneity, i.e., that they wiggle.

This despite the fact that (for me) his premise appears to be counterintuitive in at least two respects:

1. The complexity required of laws which could wiggle is so enormous as to make them counterintuitive in their complexity alone, in contrast to the intuitive clarity and simplicity of laws which are perfectly regular and do not wiggle; and

2. Even on the wiggle theory, a certain amount of extrapolation and smoothing of the imperfections of the data is mandatory—some of the discrepancies between our predictions and our results still need to be attributed to imperfections in our measurements.

But for anyone with a cardiac faith in a tychistic metaphysics which affirms the reality of freedom, chance, creativity, indeterminism, counterintuitive though it may be to hold that the laws of nature wiggle—even a minute (unobservable) amount—the counterintuitivity must be ignored and the wiggling of the laws must be postulated as a premise. Otherwise there can be no freedom, chance, spontaneity, creativity, etc. in the universe. Or the argument can be reversed, as I think was the case with Peirce, with the elements of a tychistic indeterminism being postulated as the premises from which it follows, necessarily, that the laws do wiggle.

The major difference between Peirce and Popper here is that Popper remains consistent in his denial of the possibility of ever reaching or knowing absolute laws on strictly methodological and epistemological grounds, and thus does not, as far as I can tell, commit himself to any statement which affirms or denies that the laws wiggle. What his conclusion comes to is that *we can never know, on scientific grounds, that they do not.*

Platonic Realism

What is in some respects the most striking similarity in the metaphysics of both Peirce and Popper is their realistic ontology. For Peirce, whose original formulations of his position were nominalistic, it took many years of sustained reflection and revision for him to move to a consistently realistic ontology. In a recent issue of *The Monist,* Max Fisch points out, in a definitive study of Peirce's progress towards realism,[17] that it was not until 1897 that Peirce can be said to have been successful in moving from nominalism to realism on the important issue of the reality of *possibility.* As late as 1902, Paul Carus, then editor of *The Monist,* charged that Peirce was extremely nominalistic in his views on *necessity,* but in his reply Peirce showed clearly that his ontology was on the contrary thoroughly realistic. The last doubts were dispelled, however, in Peirce's third series of *Monist* articles, which began in 1905. Here Peirce finally purged his pragmatism of the "nominalistic dross" which had tainted its earlier forms by unequivocally rejecting the nominalistic error that "the potential, or possible, is nothing but what the actual makes it to be" (1.422), and affirming instead the objective reality of "real modality, including real necessity and real possibility" (5.457), the objective reality of "real *vagues,* and especially real possibilities" (5.453).

With his fully matured realistic insight, Peirce was then able to solve the famous question about the hardness of the diamond which was kept in a wad of cotton and then burnt in a furnace before it had ever been tested for hardness. His solution, which is implied by his ontology, was that the meaning of 'hardness' is to be understood in terms of the *possible* test that *might have been* made rather than the actual test that never was made. Thus by defining pragmatic meaning in terms of conceivable consequences in experience, rather than by merely actual ones, Peirce was able to make a basic contribution to modal logic which unfortunately seems to have been overlooked by the contemporary logicians who are currently investigating conditional definitions, reduction sentences, and dispositional concepts (cf., the essay by Pap, and Carnap's replies to Pap, in the Schilpp volume on Carnap's philosophy).[18]

Popper's realistic ontology, although it is fundamentally in agreement with Peirce's in accepting the objective reality of the Platonic Forms (which Popper designates as "third world entities" or "intelligibles") contains a striking variation from orthodox forms of Platonism, in his contention that

> the third world is (together with human language) the product of men, just as honey is the product of bees. *Like Language* (and like honey) *it is an unintended and thus an unplanned product of human action.* . . . even the natural numbers are the work of men, the products of human language and of human thought. Yet there is an infinity of such numbers, more than will ever be pronounced by men, or used by computers. And there is an infinite number of true equations between such numbers, and of false equations; more than we can ever pronounce as true, or as false. . . . unexpected new problems arise as an unintended by-product of the sequence of natural numbers; for instance the unsolved problems of the theory of prime numbers. . . . These problems are *autonomous.* They are in no sense made by us; they are discovered by us; and in this sense they exist, undiscovered, prior to their discovery. ["Obj. Mind," pp. 29-30]

Thus in much the same fashion as there was a paradoxical nominalistic ingredient in Peirce's early avowedly realistic ontology, so there is presently a paradoxical subjectivistic ingredient in Popper's avowedly realistic ontology. That the Platonic forms are *man made* is a fascinating conjecture which glows with a spark of plausibility until the question is raised as to how man-made forms differ (except for the accident of their birth) from either (a) forms made by the Deity or (b) forms that never were made but always were. For myself, I can see no difference between them—if there is no trace of subjectivity in the forms after they have come into being, then how they came into being has no operational significance and their subjectivity is vacuous. Thus Popper's interesting variation from orthodoxy seems to me to be provocative and paradoxical but in the end much more in agreement with Peirce's position than different from it. Perhaps as Popper continues to develop his ontology a new shower of Popperian conjectures will produce a new speculation about the Forms that will be less paradoxical and less vacuous—I will wait for it with great interest.

Eugene Freeman

San Jose State University

Notes

[1] Thus, even though we know that some innocent men are hanged and some guilty men are set free by our courts, all verdicts of 'guilty' are equally (rule) objectively valid and all verdicts of 'innocent' are equally (rule) objectively valid. But we know that they are not equally (factually) objectively valid. On occasion, for example, an appeal and a new trial will disclose evidence which will prove that the previous verdict distorted the facts and was a miscarriage of justice. Or a photograph will belatedly show that an umpire was mistaken when he ruled that a runner was out because he did not touch second base, or that the judges of a race called the wrong winner. Juries and umpires and referees, in short, are fallible, and, although some of their mistakes can be corrected, the machinery available for correcting mistakes is sharply limited and quickly exhausted in contrast to the almost endless opportunity for correction and revision in science.

[2] All references to Peirce in this paper follow the standard practice of designating volume and paragraph in the *Collected Papers of Charles Sanders Peirce*, edited by Charles Hartshorne and Paul Weiss (Cambridge: Harvard University Press, 1931-58).

[3] Actually, Peirce himself denied his own 'manifest theory of truth' in his more fundamental metaphysics of 'Tychism' and his generally fallibilistic philosophy of science.

[4] Recently Popper has proposed a schema for the acquisition of knowledge as follows:

$$P_1 \rightarrow TT \rightarrow EE \rightarrow P_2$$

Here P_1 is the *problem* from which we start, TT (the 'tentative theory') is the imaginative conjectural solution which we first reach, for example our first *tentative interpretation*. *EE* ('*error elimination*') consists of a severe critical examination of our conjecture, our tentative interpretation: it consists, for example, of the critical use of documentary evidence and, if we have at this early stage more than one conjecture at our disposal, it will also consist of a discussion and comparative evaluation of the competing conjectures. P_2 is the problem situation as it emerges from our first attempt to solve our problem. It leads up to our second attempt (*and so on*). A satisfactory understanding (to say nothing of finality) will be reached if the interpretation, the conjectural theory, finds support in the fact that it can throw new light on new problems—on more problems than we expected; or if it finds support in the fact that it explains many subproblems, some of which were not seen to start with. Thus we may say that we can gauge the progress made by comparing P_1 with one of our later problems (Pn, say). Karl Popper, "On the Theory of the Objective Mind," in *Proceedings of the Fourteenth International Congress for Philosophy* (Vienna, 1968), p. 32. Hereinafter cited as "Obj. Mind."

[5] They are *descriptive* names inasmuch as the essence of the number 'one' is constitutively involved in 'Firstness'; the essence of the number 'two' is constitutively involved in 'Secondness'; the essence of the number three is constitutively involved in 'Thirdness'.

[6] Eugene Freeman, *The Categories of Charles Peirce* (La Salle, Ill.: The Open Court Publishing Co., 1934), p. 1. Hereinafter cited as *CCP*.

[7] Alfred North Whitehead, *Process and Reality* (New York: Macmillan and Co., 1929), p. 4.

[8] This is one of Popper's most recent doctrines, and is not to be found in the treatises of his classical period (*The Logic of Scientific Discovery* and *Conjectures and Refutations*). It is considered at some length by Skolimowski in Part II of the present paper.

[9] Here Peirce puts himself into a predicament from which he cannot easily (if at all) escape.

[10] Murray G. Murphey, *The Development of Peirce's Philosophy* (Cambridge: Harvard University Press, 1961), p. 368. Hereinafter cited as *DPP*.

[11] Cf. p. 468 above.

[12] For myself, I am quite ready to accept without reservations both of these presuppositions, and to reserve for discussion elsewhere the question I raised in a previous study as to whether or not there are alternative categories (*CCP*, p. 20). To this question Father W. P. Haas has responded by pointing out that Peirce described many other categories which were "more or less variations on the theme of the basic three": William Paul Haas, O.P., *The Conception of Law and the Unity of Peirce's Philosophy* (Notre Dame, Indiana: The University of Notre Dame Press, 1964), p. 33. This does not answer my question, which was concerned with the possibility that there may be other ultimate categories which are *not* variations on Peirce's basic three. However, I do not think that it would be required of Peirce's categories that they be the *only* categories of philosophy (ultimate or otherwise) for them to be of first rank in their importance (as I am convinced that they are), and for them to serve as the foundations for a philosophy that will offer us rule objectivity.

[13] This claim is echoed in Bridgman's doctrine of operationalism.

[14] Peirce uses the term interpretant as a broader term than interpreter to designate the context in which interpretation occurs—as e.g., the rules and usages of a language—but for the present purpose the simpler notion of interpreter will suffice.

[15] *CCP*, p. 41.

[16] Karl Menger, "A Counterpart of Occam's Razor in Pure and Applied Mathematics—Ontological Uses," *Synthese*, **12**, No. 4 (1960), 415-29.

[17] Max Fisch, "Peirce's Progress from Nominalism Toward Realism," *The Monist*, **51**, No. 2 (April, 1967), 159-78.

[18] *The Philosophy of Rudolf Carnap*, ed. by Paul A. Schilpp (La Salle, Ill.: The Open Court Publishing Co., 1963).

FREEMAN ON PEIRCE'S ANTICIPATIONS OF POPPER

Professor Freeman justly assesses my more radical fallibilism as "one of the fundamental disagreements between Peirce and Popper"; Peirce believes (at least sometimes) that "it is the nature of truth that it will hit us sooner or later, given enough time. Popper, on the other hand, . . . denies this" (see the text to their n. 2). This is a very fair remark. But what is the reason for this great divergence? The Einsteinian revolution. Peirce wrote before Einstein shattered our belief in Newton's most wonderful and most successful theory. Newton's theory had been, it is true, criticized by Mach; but his philosophical arguments, originally due to Berkeley,* impressed few physicists, especially as Berkeley and Mach rightly accepted Newtonian theory as the best in existence. To be a fallibilist at all in those days was no mean achievement; and it is greatly to Peirce's credit that he was one. My more far-reaching fallibilism, on the other hand, is the direct result of Einstein's revolution.

Freeman also points out another basic difference: Peirce "accepts the empirical axiom that nothing can be in the intellect which was not first known through the senses, from which it follows that unless generality is given in perception, it can never be known at all". Freeman, like myself, does not believe that universals are given in perception. But my disagreement with Peirce goes somewhat deeper: I think that *nothing* is "first known through the senses". The senses themselves interpret and theorize, they are fallible: they are, literally, only the feelers of the central nervous system, which is a problem solver. However the gap between Peirce and myself is narrowed by Freeman's remark that "perceptual judgement" is "on Peirce's view, . . . to some extent an interpretation by the subject". But it is also "a process which [we are] utterly unable to control and consequently . . . unable to criticize". (This is Freeman quoting Peirce 5.157.) This I do not agree with; as soon as a "judgement" (a term I rarely use) is linguistically formulated, it becomes part of world 3 and can be criticized. Perhaps Peirce's "judgement" is the unformulated "impression" or "belief" which (according to my view) is indeed part of myself and out of my critical control; just as the expectation of an animal is out of its control. But I do not think so, since Peirce (5.157; quoted by Freeman) indicates that a perceptual judgement, though not "inferred from any premise", is like one of those things which may be inferred. If this is so, then it widens the gulf between his "no control thesis" and my thesis of our critical control of world 3 objects.

Another big gulf between Peirce and myself is his thesis (quoted by Freeman) that "all reasoning is diagrammatic", while I am inclined to say "all reasoning is critical". (But see Bernays's contribution, and my reply to him in section 28.)

This brings me to Freeman's generous—too generous—remarks about my principle of falsifiability. I am greatly indebted to Freeman for pointing out what a difference my negative formulation makes. I could only wish he had emphasized that my criterion, though it may be called a "pragmatic criterion for objectivity" (as he does call it), is one of demarcation; and though perhaps one of "meaning" in Peirce's sense, it is not a criterion of "meaningfulness" in the positivists' sense. Professor Freeman then quotes Peirce (1.120) as saying that "the best hypothesis, in the sense of the one most recommending itself to the inquirer, is the one which can be the most readily refuted if it is false".

Professor Freeman's last comparison but one is devoted to Peirce's "Tychism", which indeed is more similar than Freeman could possibly have known to the "Metaphysical Epilogue" which I developed fifteen years ago in the last chapter of my as yet unpublished *Postscript*. As for the similarities and dissimilarities of Peirce's realistic position and my own—my theory of world 3—I should only like to stress that my realism is not (like Plato's) one of essences—of concepts or natures which neither are in need of, nor permit, any further explanation; nor are all the denizens of my (man-made) world 3 man-made: the theories usually are, and so are the world 3 mistakes, but not the world 3 problems: they are internally generated, and perhaps discovered.

Karl Popper

NOTE

* See my "A Note on Berkeley as Precursor of Mach," *The British Journal for the Philosophy of Science*, vol. 4 (1953–54), no. 13 (May, 1953), pp. 26–36; now ch. 6 of *Conjectures and Refutations: The Growth of Scientific Knowledge* (London: Routledge & Kegan Paul; New York: Basic Books, 1963).

A REVISION OF PEIRCE'S CATEGORIES

Peirce's three "Neo-Pythagorean" categories have not given his students any complete satisfaction, but I cannot doubt that, though partly misconceived, they can, when freed of certain errors, be of great value.

1. The Numerical Clue

Early in his career Peirce set out to revise Kant's categories—and they needed revision. I have tried, through most of my long career, to revise Peirce's categories—and again, revision was needed. I believe that, at last, I have had some success. My two previous attempts were not acclaimed by Peirce scholars, and I was myself somewhat dissatisfied with them.[1] The present version is in part substantially different.

Instead of seeking a wholly "presuppositionless" stance from which to inspect the given—a search I distrusted when, before I had read Peirce, I encountered Husserl in 1923–24—Peirce tried to limit his explicit presuppositions to some elementary formal mathematical insights. He did not try to completely "bracket" the physical world, an attempt which, as Husserl goes at it, presupposes that the physical world is not genuinely given, but rather is only intended or postulated. In other words Husserl assumes that an experience is logically self-sufficient, independent of any world of realities other than itself. Not only is this a presupposition, it is one in conflict with the given. Our being "in the world" is an irreducible though more or less vague datum. To anticipate, this is what Peirce's Secondness (also Whitehead's prehension) comes to.

Let me state some points of agreement with Peirce. (1) He was right to consult *phenomena* from the outset in philosophy. (2) He did well to look to *relations* among phenomena as crucial, since all analysis must employ them. (3) He did well also to see both *dependence* and *non-dependence* as equally basic forms of relatedness. Without dependence there can be no inference from one phenomenon to others; without independence anything would in principle be inferrable from anything else, which is illogical. In logic P→Q is significant only because it does not hold universally. It is the same with dependence and independence among phenomena. (4) Peirce was brilliantly original in seeing in the process of *counting* some formal clues to dependence and independence. To say "first" is not to imply any definite or actual second, but to say "second" is to imply a definite first. The first person to make a certain statement could be the last and only person to make it, but the second person could not be the only one. Firstness thus does model independence and Secondness, dependence.

True, the second person might not know or be observably influenced by the first, but in that case, and insofar as the apparent non-influence can be taken as absolute, the secondness is extrinsic, or relative to spectators or historians of the sequence. It is also obvious that in counting there may be arbitrariness in the order of items considered, as in counting votes. But even in such cases there is real dependence; for the conscious or felt *act* of assigning Secondness presupposes and depends on the act of assigning Firstness. And Peirce is seeking relations among experiences.

Peirce did once put the question, "Is the *basic* Secondness or dependence the form in which the dependence is one-way only or the form in which it is mutual?[2] Most oddly he failed to give a sharp answer to his question. Clearly "x second to y" is the principle while "x second to y *and* y second to x" is the special and indeed degenerate case, since it destroys the distinctiveness of the dependent and the independent factors as such. And in a clearly analogous case Peirce saw this, the case of propositional implication. Equivalence is not the principle of which one-way implication is a special form. P→Q is basic, P↔Q a complication derivative from the other. So with one-way and two-way Secondness.

What misled so fine a logician here? It was some apparent phenomenon of interaction, such as two persons trying to push a door in opposite directions. The symmetry appears a given fact, each man's force opposing, second to, that of the other. Perhaps the physics of today, better than prerelativity and prequantum physics, helps to clear up this confusion. In any case, it was not wise to trust an example involving two minds and two bodies, not to mention the door, to establish an elementary categorial point.

Far safer is Peirce's example of immediate memory, or the experience of surprise as dependent on a previous expectation (or lack of it). Present awareness feels the contrast with previous awareness that was innocent of the contrast. The innocence is essential to the previousness. Had Peirce only seen—or did he see it?—that in perception as well as memory it is always *independent* and *previous* events on which present experience depends, he would have almost reached Whitehead's concept of prehension, which by definition is one-way. Peirce does say that feelings tend to "spread" and, unless this spreading is instantaneous, Whitehead's concept, "feeling of (past) feeling," is implied.

Another question that Peirce seems not quite to put and answer clearly and convincingly is this: Is the basic idea modelled by Secondness that of dependence on one and only one other thing, or is it that of dependence on other things, regardless of how many or few others? Peirce regards the single other as definitive of Secondness and dependence on two others ("Thirdness") as essentially different, while dependence on more than two can, he holds, be reduced to cases of Thirdness. Thus he *counts the number of items* on which a phenomenon depends, defining Firstness as dependence on zero others, Secondness on one other, Thirdness on two others, and dismissing all higher numbers as reducible.

My suggestion is that Peirce here misapplied the numerical model and thereby got into needless trouble. No actual phenomenon, and he virtually admits this, depends on nothing else.[3] God, as classical theism defined God, would depend on nothing else; similarly, Whitehead's primordial nature of God (or my "abstract eternal essence" of God); but are these abstractions actual phenomena? Peirce says Firsts are not actual feelings but only qualities of feelings, or pure possibilities. This brings them close to Whitehead's eternal objects. What an actual feeling, a real phenomenon can be is independent of *some* other things while also dependent on some. The number of items of which the phenomenon is independent or on which it is dependent, is, I suggest, categorially irrelevant. What counts are the *kinds of relations* of dependence or independence. Thus in a visual experience countless stimuli condition the experience in essentially the same way. But the stimuli come from the near or immediate past, not from the future.[4] Of all future events the experience is independent. Peirce's own view of time ("the indeterminate future," "the irrevocable past") fits this, as indeed does his whole basic philosophy except when he is explaining his categories.[5] Counting the number of past items on which an experience depends, or future items on which it does not depend, is idle. Why not an infinite or indefinite number in both cases?

But now we seem to have only two categories, Firstness or independence (of some things) and Secondness or dependence (on some things). And Peirce insists there are three and only three categories in the set. Moreover, in this he is right. Sheer dependence (in relation to some) and sheer independence (in relation to some) do not exhaust the forms of dependence and independence. As we shall see, Peirce's own philosophy, more than any previous one, makes this clear. But the third category is not found by adding one more item on which a phenomenon depends. It is found by noting a *third relation* in which a phenomenon can stand to others (no matter how many others) besides simple dependence and simple independence. This third relation in which things can stand is also modelled by the process of counting, but not in the way Peirce has in mind. To say "first" is not to imply a definite, actual second, but it is to imply one or more *conceivable* further members of the class in question. We do not count wholly unclassified items.

Moreover, relations of an experience to past or future experiences or events are not adequately described by saying simply that particular past events are implied as conditions of the experience, while particular future events (Peirce being an indeterminist) are simply not implied. Were that the whole story, we could foresee nothing of the future and there would be no causal laws at all, however statistical or approximate. Future events in their full particularity are indeed unpredictable and matters of chance, as Peirce says, but the approximate *kinds* or *classes* of such events are predictable and determined. Like countable items, events later than a given event are not unclassified; they all share the relational property of having that event in their past as among their necessary conditions. Peirce rightly insists that, while the past is the "sum of accomplished (meaning fully particularized) facts," the future can only be conceived in more or less "general" terms, through laws or "real thirds." The past is what happened, the future is what (within certain limits of probability) *may* happen. Thus there really is a third relation among events besides or intermediate between simple dependence and simple independence, and this third relation is real possibility, probability, or law. Here precisely is where nominalists, whom Peirce likes to scold, are most wrong; they have no proper view of the future.

Before Bergson, Whitehead, and others, but helped by Aristotle, Peirce saw sharply and profoundly the categorial distinctiveness of futurity. "Time is a species of objective modality" is one expression of his insight. Given a particular past, all later events are, in their full concreteness, arbitrary additions to that past, but certain abstract, more or less general features of these additions are settled in advance. Because of the reality of chance and (the same thing from a different aspect) the partial openness of the future, no event is a necessary successor to its predecessors, which are thus Firsts with respect to all their successors. But there is nevertheless a positive relation of an event to the intensive class of its possible successors.

Thirdness, then, is neither sheer dependence nor sheer independence but an *intermediate* relation: nondependence with respect to definite particulars, dependence with respect to more or less general outlines. Futurity, or real possibility (causality in the forward direction), contrasts alike to sheer necessity and pure possibility. Analogously, abductive arguments introduce hypotheses not strictly required by, but implying, the available evidence, somewhat as events are not required by but imply their predecessors to which they are second. Deductive arguments require—are second to—the truth of their conclusions as events require their antecedent conditions.

It is time to ask how the necessity relating premises to conclusions differs from that relating experiences to predecessors. To say that the one necessity is logical, the other causal or ontological, labels but hardly analyzes the differences. The difference is in *degree of concreteness*. Premises are abstract, simplified outlines, and so are conclusions, while experiences are concrete and completely particularized. Hence, while our knowledge of a premise can be quite clear and adequate, so far as its relation to a deductive conclusion is concerned, this is never the case with our knowledge of experiences as requiring their necessary conditions. Concrete events, which actual states of experience are, exceed our powers of clear intuition. For example, we may seem, in an experience, to remember such and such a feature of previous experience, and if we remember it, then necessarily it occurred. But the line between remembering and imagining or guessing is more or less hazy for introspection. The same sort of difference occurs with perceiving and imagining, and many aspects of an experience are not definitely introspected at all, even incorrectly. Experience is incomparably richer than our understanding can clearly grasp. Leibniz and Democritus knew this; Peirce, also Whitehead, assert it. (Husserl is uncritical here.)

If logical necessity is only between propositions, then causal or ontological necessity is not logical. However, propositions are significant only as elements in awareness. The ontological necessities of a state of awareness, an experience, are those whose detection more and more adequate introspection approaches as a limit. The Firstness of an experience is what ideal awareness, say that which God has of the experience, would disclose as its independence of (some) other experiences; the Secondness is what ideal awareness would disclose as its dependence on (some) other experiences. The common aspect of logical and ontological modalities is, then, awareness or experience.

The foregoing is in partial agreement with Leibniz, according to whom each monad (individual sequence of experiences) mirrors or expresses every other, but only God can grasp the vast or infinite complexity involved. Our Peircean version is: each momentary experience expresses and has as necessary condition all previous moments but no subsequent ones. It also expresses certain limitations on its possible successors. Somewhat as Leibniz thought, only God can distinctly intuit the necessary (or the contingent-probabilistic, qualifiedly necessary) relationships.

Mahayana Buddhism (Fa Tsang in 7th–8th Century China) had a view like that of Leibniz with a similar (though possibly less complete) neglect of the asymmetry between strict dependence on past and partial dependence on future becoming. Delightfully relevant to our topic is Fa Tsang's declaration that, not only can there not be a second without a first, or a third without a second, there also cannot be a first without a second or a second without a third. He here neglects the distinction between definite actual terms and indefinite or possible ones. Here Peirce is right and Mahayana Buddhism is infected with sophistry. Hegel (in the *Logik*) and Blanshard repeat much the same error. They miss the openness of the future, apparent even in the abstract matter of counting.

Fa Tsang lacks Leibniz's artificial distinction between real dependence and mere correspondence via divinely preestablished harmony. The Chinese philosopher stressed dependence on past states of other monads almost equally with that on states of the same monad. Mahayana Buddhism was more monistic with respect to spatial plurality in contrast to temporal than Leibniz. But adequately clear and explicit grasp of futurity as qualified dependence or Thirdness was lacking in both philosophies.

It was always mysterious to me how Peirce got the idea of generality simply by adding a third relatum to the relational situation. I now see that he did not actually get it in this way. His real point was that one-way independence or Firstness is unqualifiedly so only with respect to future *details*. Although there are no particular successors which an event must have, it does have to have successors, and some general features of these are settled in advance.

I submit that my generalizations of Firstness (sheer independence of at least something), Secondness (dependence on at least something), and Thirdness (qualified, partial, or probabilistic dependence on at least something) are in Peirce's spirit. He liked to stress "the way mathematicians generalize," and clearly for Peirce the independence of events from their successors does not mean that any sort of event could follow a given event, any more than we count totally unclassified entities. A world in which the future was completely unforeseeable and without even probabilistic or approximate laws is not what he would have regarded as more than verbally conceivable. Its existence would be entirely "unknowable," a notion Peirce (rightly) took to be a non-concept. It follows that there are indeed three forms of dependence: (1) the positive form, strict dependence; (2) the negative form, strict independence (both holding asymmetrically among definite particulars); and (3) dependence that leaves the final particularity open and can be stated only in more or less general terms.

With the above revisions Peirce's scheme achieves far greater clarity. His Secondness is then equivalent to Whitehead's prehension, or feeling of (previous) feeling, or sensing of (previous) sensing. His Firstness is any such feeling as bound to be felt by suitable subsequent subjects or feelers. His Thirdness includes Whitehead's "symbolic reference" or, more generally, "mentality." Whitehad is is some respects clearer than Peirce, in others less clear.

The central role of asymmetrical dependence is better seen using Firstness and Secondness as models than Whitehead's language consistently suggests. On the other hand it was Whitehead who clearly asserted the asymmetry of perception and the perceived, the data of which are never strictly contemporary with or influenced by the perceiving. Whitehead thus brings out the common temporal structure of perception and memory. He was aided here by relativity physics. Whitehead also, thanks probably to quantum physics, avoids Peirce's confusion between continuity as order of possibility and continuity as (allegedly) the order of actual becoming. Thus the excesses of Synechism are escaped, with the advantage that we can speak of events in the singular as well as in the plural, of definite actual entities that become, rather than continuously change without ever achieving singular definiteness. Synechism confuses pure geometry with physics or psychology. Quantum physics supports a nonsynechistic ontology, but as Von Wright has shown, logical analysis should have led philosophers to reject synechism.[6] Here Peirce erred.

Peirce's uses of his categories in the theory of signs are not diminished in value by the proposed revisions. Thus *indices* are signs insofar as dependent upon, second to, their object(s), hence yielding knowledge of the latter's existence: *icons* are signs insofar as they are independent of, or first with respect to, their possible objects. They give knowledge not of existence but of quality, whether or not any other instance than the sign of the quality exists. By what they are, simply in themselves, they stand for whatever may or could resemble them. *Symbols* are signs insofar as they give information through some probability, law, rule, conviction, or habit—some real Third—governing behavior. Symbols are terms, propositions, or arguments. Terms—e.g., 'human'—are symbols standing for what there may be, thus analogous to icons; propositions are symbols standing for what there actually is; and arguments stand for certain relations of symbolized meanings and thus are symbolic on a higher level. Terms must be understood through perceived or imagined icons, and propositions through both icons and indices. A photograph with a proper name is a "decisign," a proposition saying what a certain existing person, place, or thing looks like. An argument is a proposition relating propositions. All signs as such are more than merely iconic or indexical, since neither similarity nor dependence suffice to make an object a sign; some interpreter of the object must so use or intend it, and this requires *purpose*, of which reference to the future as partially indeterminate is an essential aspect.

In such ways it appears that my tinkering with the three categories has not deprived them of their relevance. Another confirmation of the relevance of my revision is that it strengthens Peirce's use of categories to test philosophies. Hume, Berkeley, and Russell lack genuine Secondness and indeed so does Hegel, who also has no really clear form of Firstness. Extreme nominalism has no clear distinctions between Firstness, Secondness, and Thirdness; extreme monism also lacks such distinctions. Classical determinism makes causal requirement symmetrical, analogous to a logic limiting implication or logical dependence to equivalence. Many a philosophical error is avoided if the distinctiveness and ultimacy of the three modes of dependence is adequately realized. Peirce pointed the way to a great discovery without altogether arriving at it.

Peirce called his categorial theory "my one contribution to philosophy," and the inquiry which led to it phaneroscopy, also phenomenology. His use of the second term did not, so far as I know, precede his reading of Husserl and may have been suggested by this reading. But the idea and practice of basing all philosophy on an inquiry into the given, the phenomena, was Peirce's before it was Husserl's.

2. The Logical Clue

As I said at the beginning of this essay, Peirce's phenomenology explicitly presupposed mathematics, including mathematical aspects of logic. Peirce was one of the chief inventors of the mathematico-logical theory of relations, or as he termed it, with penetration, the "logic of relatives." This superseded for him the old "subject-predicate logic," as Russell and Whitehead later called it, and which they regarded as the source of some traditional errors. Whitehead spoke disparagingly of "the urge to say, 'S is P'." Not that there are no entities with properties to which logically correspond subjects with predicates. The point rather, as Peirce saw clearly, is that what describes an entity is not simply its predicates. Thus, *S is surprised.* The description is incomplete, surprised by what? Or, *S perceives*—perceives what? We must divide predicates into those which seem complete in themselves and those requiring one or more particular entities besides the one being described. The essential predicates are relative ones, and imply dependence or relativity. There are relations because there are relative or dependent things. An elementary proposition of the most important kind refers to *more than one subject*, if that means concrete entity; it is the predicate that is single.

Yet there is in a sense (in an elementary proposition) but one primary subject, the one that is being described; and the other entities that the proposition refers to are not being described but are merely used in the description of the primary subject. In medieval logic the entities forming part of the description (e.g., the entities a perceiving subject perceives) are termed objects, in contrast to the subject, of the relation. This usage, which seems to me appropriate, I very likely acquired from Peirce. Anyway, he certainly was aware of the distinction it expresses. It means that the Aristotelian ideal of a subject that requires no other comparably concrete entities for its description but only repeatable forms, predicates, is not an ideal at all but a basic mistake. There can be no such subjects or substances. Predicates ostensibly complete in themselves as descriptive of the primary objects are pure Firsts, monadic predicates. They are mere possibilities, as Peirce says, abstractions from the actual properties of things, which are always (with respect to previous events) relativities, examples of Secondness or Thirdness.

Russell took over the logic of relatives, largely from Peirce, and neatly missed its ontological point. For him the subjects of relations were not relative but absolute. Logically they required only themselves and their private predicates. For Russell, as for Hume, reality consists in an array or succession of momentary states each of which is what it is in logical independence of the others. Thus Aristotle's supposed ideal is taken literally once more. True, there are relations among the states; but the relations are "among" or "between" states, belonging to none of them in themselves. Given two states, S^2 following S^1, it is only the pair that really has the relation of following. The pair thus is a third entity or pseudo-entity, and it alone is genuinely relational. S^1 and S^2 are logical absolutes. Each is first to the other, but there is no Secondness. Moreover, to pair items is to relate them. Thus in the Hume-Russell view relatedness is not accounted for ontologically, is given no proper place in reality.

Secondness, taken as primarily asymmetrical, excludes two contrary extreme doctrines: absolute pluralism, as in Hume, Russell, and many others, and absolute monism, as in Bradley or Sankara. Granted Secondness and Firstness, there must be many actualities, but each actuality is a unity of itself with others (its predecessors). There is no actuality inclusive once for all, since no actuality is the last, Thirdness being the requirement that there shall be *some* suitable successors to any given actuality. The non-inclusiveness of actuality with respect to successors is Firstness. A first has no definite future second, but is destined to be seconded—as one may put it. There are no future seconds which definitely *will be*; what will be is that the "indeterminate" future will be progressively replaced by additional constituents of a partly new determinate or "irrevocable" past. Thus the three categories do imply ontological consequences. They really have the importance that Peirce ascribed to them.

It seems close to obvious that without Secondness there can be no understanding of what it is distinctively to be a caused or conditioned phenomenon, that without Firstness there can be no understanding of what it is distinctively to be a cause or condition, and that without a third and intermediate relation between sheer dependence and sheer independence there can be no understanding of time's arrow, the contrast between the already settled, decided past, and the not yet decided, needing-to-be-decided—yet not merely indeterminate—future. The past is the sum of accomplished facts; the future is the set of real or limited possibilities for future accomplishment, a determinable seeking further determination. The nominalistic error is not to see that futurity and generality are inseparable, as are pastness and particularity. Time is indeed "objective modality." Of the critics of nominalism I regard Peirce as second to none. But he should not have been so fascinated, almost hypnotized, by the idea of counting "One, two, three."

The other basic source of confusion (already referred to) in Peirce is also a fascination, that with continuity. He expressed this feeling candidly, and one finds it in Benjamin Peirce, his father. Neither father nor son seriously considered the reasons, implicit even in Charles's own doctrines, for taking unqualified continuity as the order, not of actualities but of possibilities, not of events but of thinkable ideas. He did see that possibilities form continua, thus all possible hues and shades of color, or all possible sizes or shapes. But actual colors or sizes or shapes are a selection, involving discontinuities. All the animals that have lived on earth, being finite in number, could not form a continuum of size, shape, color, or anything else. Only all thinkable creatures, being infinite or indefinite in number, may be conceived as forming continua with respect to various properties. Yet although Peirce saw how possibility and continuity belong together, he wanted actuality also to be continuous. This was his "synechism." He held that when we experience first red and then blue we pass through a continuum of intermediate colors, each present for infinitesimal time.

Peirce rationalized his overindulgence in the admiration of continuity by the specious argument: since continuity is a totality of possibilities, we should approach phenomena with the hypothesis that they are continuous, since in that way we avoid excluding anything a priori. Not so, we are excluding any and every one of the infinite forms of possible discontinuity, in spite of the a priori truth which Peirce himself discovered and made clear that continuity is the order of possibilities, a meaningless truth if it is also the order of actualities. Our initial hypothesis should be that actuality is discrete, but with our minds open among the unlimited conceptual, but mutually incompatible, possibilities for discontinuity. The totality of ways in which a continuum of possibility can be broken up into discrete actualities—what is that but the continuum over again? So I think Peirce really missed the target here.

The consequences of his uncritical love for continuity were substantial and not fortunate. It immediately meant that though he had an ontology of relations in the idea of relative actualities, he lacked any definite terms or subjects for the relations. There seems to be a succession of experiences, but (if the succession is a continuum) there are no single experiences. In any fraction of a second, however small, we have an experience, but this experience is not really "an" experience, since it has parts each of which is an experience. In any fraction of a second, Peirce held, we have infinitely many successive experiences. Hence his denial of direct intuition (or what Whitehead calls prehension).[7] Some have praised this Peircean doctrine. I think it was a mess. There are, to be sure, no intuitions both entirely distinct and infallible, but there are direct intuitions. They are the key to relations of dependency or secondness, and to all causality.

Another consequence was that, though Peirce talked about the "logic of events," and saw what the physicists have been seeing lately, that science deals with relations of events, not (in last analysis) with relations of things or persons, he could not, in the continuum of becoming which he posited, give meaning to the idea of a definite single event. Hence he failed to clearly transcend the old Aristotelian pattern of reality as a set of things and persons, individuals, taken as ultimate terms of analysis. Even James came closer to anticipating our present recognition of quanta, objectively single happenings. Moreover, it was Peirce who wanted to guide the future development of physics. That he never dreamt of something like quantum theory is a defeat for him. He did anticipate the idea of indeterminacy, or real possibilities, and of laws as statistical. But the idea of discreteness which we tend now to see as essential (though Einstein struggled against it to the end) did not occur to him, except that he once admitted (perhaps thinking of James's "drops of experience") that our experiencing *may* occur in discrete units, saying only that we do not know this to be so.

Peirce did say that individuals can hardly be regarded as entirely definite. After all, each moment they receive new determinations not prescribed by causal laws and initial conditions but coming to them by chance. The secret lesson of Leibniz's theory of genetic identity, an open secret since Whitehead, is that only the past (not the future) careers of individuals are wholly definite. Aristotle knew this, Leibniz denied it and thereby got into paradoxes; Peirce agreed with Aristotle not Leibniz, but with Aristotle failed to clearly draw the conclusion, which is that each moment there is a new determinate actuality, the individual-now. It is a continuation of the individual career as it has previously been, but, since the less cannot contain the more, the indeterminate the determinate, if we are looking for concrete or definite unitary wholes of reality, we should recognize that the individual-now is always a new such whole. The Buddhists, whom Peirce admired, saw this. But the assertion of the continuity of becoming makes it impossible to conceive a definite single whole in the succession of such wholes constituting an individual career.

I shall never forget what Bochenski once said to me, apropos of the thesis that reality consists of events: "Aristotle said so. He did not dot all the i's and cross all the t's, but . . ." So when I encounter writers who defend

Aristotelian substances against Whitehead, who did dot the i's and cross the t's, I am not immensely impressed. They all fail to see what Bochenski did see, that Whitehead's "societies" are nicely tailored to do what "substance" was primarily intended to do, which is to furnish identifiable features of reality sufficiently definite for ordinary purposes, but not necessarily so for science or metaphysics. To suppose them entirely definite is to commit oneself implicitly to the paradoxes of Leibnizian laws of succession unique to each individual and equally determinate for past and future.

How right Bochenski was, in comparison to extreme opponents of Whitehead who yet appeal to Aristotle, may be seen by considering how Aristotle explained the identity of an individual through change as the actualization of potentialities inherent in the individual all along. Aristotle's point is translatable into process terms. Of course an individual event-sequence or career, once begun, has the potentiality for its later prolongations. But the actualization of a potency is not contained in the potency, rather the potency is contained in the actualization. The present is more than the past, there is a new whole of determinations. This is the creationist view of reality. Events are capable of being superseded by what is more than they are. An infant "self" does not contain the adult phase of "itself." There is a numerically new concrete reality with each new determination.

Andrew Reck complains that such a view makes things much too fragile. The reply is that it leaves them exactly as fragile as they are and not a whit more. All individuals are destructible (except God), for all Reck can show, and if he wonders why they last as long and well as they do, I remind him that calling something a "substance" tells us nothing as to what enables it, for a limited time, to maintain the "defining characteristic" of its career. The explanation of causal stability, of which individual endurance is only a special case, by self-identity is merely verbal since the criterion for being a substance is precisely the kind of causal stability in question. The explanation is circular, as Buddhism realized long ago.

That self-identity is a special case of causality is obvious enough; for causal influence relates members of two careers as truly as members of one and the same career. Buddhism generalized the problem of causality far better than Aristotle did, and came much closer to modern physics in this respect. Process philosophy has a definite theory of causality, not adequately taken into account by some critics.[8]

As for Peirce, his admiration for Aristotle was extreme ("by many lengths the greatest intellect") and this admiration, coupled with his fondness for continuity, probably helped to prevent him from dotting the i's and crossing the t's, from anticipating quanta, and process metaphysics. Yet his three categories, freed of one-sided synechism and a kind of numerology, harmonize happily with those twentieth-century doctrines. I agree with several writers who have said that Peirce could have been an even better thinker had he not spent so much of his life in solitude, far from colleagues and students who could have forced him to see the limits of certain of his convictions. As it was, he did wonderfully well. And only from Whitehead have I, for one, perhaps learned more. Peirce started ontology on the track indicated as the right one by the logic of relatives. Russell and many other famous logicians never got on that track at all.

Charles Hartshorne

Emeritus Professor,
The University of Texas at Austin

NOTES

1. "The Relativity of Nonrelativity: Some Reflections on Firstness," in *Studies in the Philosophy of Charles Sanders Peirce*, ed. Philip P. Wiener and Frederic H. Young (Cambridge: Harvard University Press, 1952), pp. 215–24. "Charles Peirce's 'One Contribution to Philosophy' and his most Serious Mistake," *op. cit.*, Second Series, ed. Edward G. Moore and Richard S. Robin. Amherst: University of Massachusetts Press, 1964, 455–74.

2. On the symmetry or nonsymmetry of Secondness see *The Collected Papers of Charles Sanders Peirce*, ed. Charles Hartshorne, Paul Weiss, and A. C. Burks, (Cambridge: Harvard University Press, 1931, 1934, 1958), paragraphs 1.322, 324, 327; 5.45; 7.531; 8.330.

3. For Peirce's attempts to illustrate his definition of Firstness as zero dependence on anything else see his *Collected Papers* (hereafter *CP*), 1.302–313, 357; 5.44.

4. According to some physicists, quantum theory implies that events may be dependent upon particular future events, but this interpretation of quantum experiments my metaphysics forces me to reject. See John Archibald Wheeler, "Genesis and Observership," in *Proceedings, University of Western Ontario Series in the Philosophy of Science*, ed. Robert Butts and Jaakko Hintikka (Dordrecht and Boston: Reidel Publishing Co., 1977). There is also a problem about contemporary events, which relativity physics takes to be mutually independent, whereas quantum theory casts serious doubt upon this. See my essay "Bell's Theorem and Stapp's Revised View of Space-Time," also essays by Henry P. Stapp and Wm. B. Jones, in *Process Studies* vol. 7, no. 3 (Fall, 1977).

5. For Peirce's view of futurity see *CP*, 2.86; 5.458–461.

6. G. H. von Wright, *Time, Change, and Contradiction* [The Twenty-second Eddington Memorial Lecture, Delivered 1968] (Cambridge University Press, 1969).

7. For Peirce's denial of direct intuitions see *CP*, 5.258–263, 265; 7.536, 674f.

8. See my "Creativity and the Deductive Logic of Causality," *Review of Metaphysics* vol. 27, no. 1 (Sept., 1973): 62–74.

PEIRCE, OCKHAM AND SCHOLASTIC REALISM

Peirce's references to Ockham are less frequent and less fulsome both in detail and in praise than his references to Scotus. And if one expects a critique of "the greatest nominalist that ever lived" (1.29) to be especially revealing, they are also somewhat disappointing. Nevertheless, the comparison and contrast with Ockham offers another occasion to examine the "question of nominalism and realism" which Peirce thought to be so important.

To begin with, I shall examine some interesting similarities—within dissimilarity—in the positions of Peirce and Ockham. In the second and third sections, I shall try to set the medieval and Peirce's own discussion of universals in the context of a broader concern about explanation and intelligibility. Finally, I shall use that context in order to show the relevance of Peirce's "Scotistic realism" to his analysis of the ideas of truth and reality.

I

The most striking similarity between Peirce and Ockham is their readiness to describe thinking in terms of signs. For Ockham this serves a special purpose. Among instances of the "most pernicious" fallacy (*Expositio In Librum Perihermenias Aristotelis*, Bk. I, *Proem.*, 8) of attributing to things the properties of signs, Ockham singles out for special attention the issue of a ground for predication (*Summa Logicae* II, ch. 2). That x is predicated of y, Ockham insists, requires no matching composition in things but is only a function of what 'x' and 'y' signify. (The "signification" of a term, for Ockham, is not a synonym for its meaning but is closer to an abbreviation for "the way something is a sign of something.") If predication is a function of signification, then, like universality, it is a property of the sign-system and not a property of things signified.

By way of contrast, consider the following remarks from Peirce's review of *The Works of George Berkeley* (1873):

> . . . there are many objects of thought which, if they are independent of that thinking whereby they are thought (that is, if they are real), are indisputably independent of all *other* thoughts and feelings. (8.13)
>
> It is plain that this view of reality is inevitably realistic; because general conceptions enter into all judgments, and therefore into true opinions. Consequently a thing in the general is as real as in the concrete. . . . since it is true that real things possess whiteness, whiteness is real. It is a real which only exists by virtue

of an act of thought knowing it, but that thought is not an arbitrary or accidental one dependent on any idiosyncrasies, but is one which will hold in the final opinion. (8.14)

And from the 1903 Harvard Lectures on pragmatism:

The general is essentially predicative and therefore of the nature of a representamen. (5.102)

The whole passage (8.12–17) deserves study; but one might well acknowledge an initial rhetorical advantage in Ockham's account. A natural model for the workings of signs and objects takes them to be individuals. The idea that reality (as an ultimate object) should consist in thoughts or judgments seems almost perverse; I shall discuss below some of the reasons Peirce has for putting his case in just this way. His objections to an individualistic (or atomistic) account of signs are, I hope, more familiar.

Although Ockham's views on the nature of the concept underwent changes, his final position is not unexpected (cf. Adams, 1977). The concept is a mental occurrence which is a natural (rather than conventional) sign. The process of thought consists in the having (or habitual having) of such mental signs. The definition of a sign which Ockham takes over from Augustine is actually very close to the explicitly triadic analysis that Peirce proposes: a sign is something that brings something else to mind (*Summa Logicae* I, ch. 1). But Ockham seems to find no inconsistency in treating concepts as dyadic: The having of the concept is an individual mental event and constitutes "cognizing" an object (which in turn consists of an individual or individuals).

Ockham's emphasis on the directness of natural signification is meant to bring out a contrast with the way conventional signs are parasitic on previous signs. Peirce's interest in the triadicity of signs is more radical. He is willing to allow that there are individual mental occurrences that may function as signs: in fact, thinking takes place by means of signs. But "having the concept of something" is not the occurrence or even the potential occurrence of some mental individual (event or whatever). An individual mental event is actually a sign only inasmuch as it can or would enter into a triadic relation with an object and an interpretant.

While Ockham does introduce the notion of habit in his analysis of concepts, he does not do so to establish their triadic or non-individual character. And his theory of the concept as an individual has provoked the criticism of writers other than Peirce. (Putnam, 1978, pp. 126f.)

The atomism of Ockham's account of mental processes has another feature which conflicts with Peirce's analysis: for Ockham holds a theory of intuition in pretty much the form to which Peirce objects (5.262). (The theory is discussed in Boler, 1973, and Scott, 1969.) Since the anti-intuition articles (5.213–357) appear while Peirce was still carrying out his research into medieval logic (i.e., in 1868–69), it is probably not significant that Ockham's theory of intuitive cognition is not mentioned there. But cases of real continuity are, for Peirce, relevant to realism (5.102–4). His denial of a privileged first cognition does not mean that the process of cognition cannot begin; it means that it must begin as a process. The fact that process cannot be resolved into discrete individual components is used by Peirce to show that a commitment to any objective process is a commitment to real or objective non-individuality.

His own realism, Peirce insists, is a more developed position than scholastic realism because the generality represented by a universal is only a limiting case of non-individuality (6.172; 5.436). The generality of scholastic realism reflected in the manner in which 'horse' ranges over many individual horses is only the simplest form of being "of many." Multiple-place predicates (including the sign triad) introduce a more complex form, not for being true of many sets of individuals but because the predicate's holding of some one set is not reducible to that set of individuals alone. (Cf., Boler, 1963, ch. III.)

That the link between generals and relations was in Peirce's mind when thinking about Ockham is clear (8.20; 5.312). But had he pressed the issue, Peirce might have discovered a more precise antithesis to his own position. For Ockham does hold that connotativity—a feature of relational terms on his account—is, like universality, a property of the way individual things are signified and not a property of the things signified. I shall try to explain this briefly.

Ockham divides categorematic terms into absolute and connotative. (See Peirce's account at 2.393.) Connotative terms "signify one thing in virtue of something else." Propositions that contain connotative terms can be "expounded" into a concatenation of propositions at least one of which contains a multiple place predicate. (The anachronism and partial misrepresentation of Ockham's logical scheme is justifiable, I think, in the service of brevity.) For example, "*x* is white" is expounded as "*x* is a *body* and a *whiteness* is in *x*." (Whiteness, for Ockham, are individual inherent accidents.) "*x* is a parent" becomes "*x* is an *animal* and *x* begat *y*." (Cf. *Summa Logicae* II, ch. 11.)

There is some dispute about the exact nature of Ockham's position on relations, and some commentators would say that Peirce's characterization of Ockham is too reductionist. The issue is complicated, moreover, because any application of a notation with multiple-place predicates to Ockham's remarks is itself an interpretation. But it is at least a plausible reading of

Ockham that he thinks that the ordered sets of things signified by multiple-place predicates stand to that predicate in the way that the many things signified by a universal terms stand to it. In short, Ockham as much as Peirce thinks that generality and relationality are to be treated along similar lines. For Peirce they are both real; for Ockham they are both to be resolved into the individual things signified and the concept signifying them. Ockham's conceptualism is supposed to be less severe than nominalism; but as Peirce notes (1.27), there is some question as to whether it provides a workable alternative.

But is the opposition of Peirce and Ockham that of nominalism and realism? Of course, Peirce says that it is; but that only points up the difficulty in relating his position to both realists and nominalists among the scholastics. For example, to a large extent, Ockham's reaction to allowing relations as independent entities derives from his concern that there be no commitment to a reality which cannot be explained by appeal to the existence, modification or agency of substances. It is the same with his suspicion of the reification of motion of change—or even of its nominalization (cf., Shapiro, 1957, pp. 24ff., 137, 141–4)—for, he says, things are said to be in motion rather than motion being said to be in them (*ibid.*, p. 151). The contrast in Peirce is striking:

> Accordingly, just as we say that a body is in motion, and not that motion is in a body, we ought to say that we are in thought and not that thoughts are in us. (5.289)
>
> Thought is more without us than within. It is we that are in it rather than it in any of us. Only one must not take a nominalistic view of thought as if it were something that man had in his consciousness. (8.256)

Though Ockham's statement of the problems about motion and relation would likely have struck his realist confreres as extreme, Peirce's way of expressing the criticism would not be more readily accepted. Not only were medieval Aristotelians, in their varying ways, dualists when it comes to basic kinds of explanatory laws—for Peirce, see 6.25—but even the realists among them would have been sympathetic with Ockham's defense of the primacy of substance. In fact, the "moderateness" of medieval realists is reflected in their refusal to allow universals a causal status. Form may have a causal influence on matter, but that takes place, so to speak, "within" substance. Scotus may appear to be an exception for according to "common natures" a real but less-than- numerical unity and, therefore, a reality of sorts. But even he insists that in any actual individual, the common nature is "contracted" (by haecceity); it exists only as individualized and as common has no effect. As with all the scholastic Aristotelians, Scotus takes substance as the primary causal agent. Of course, its moderateness is not what attracts Peirce to

Scotus' analysis: Scotus is "too nominalistic" for insisting upon contraction (8.208).

Peirce's own position on real generality is no mere adjustment of Scotus'. But to deal with the incommensurability of Peirce's position with those of medieval Aristotelians—both realists and nominalists—the issues must be located in a somewhat broader context. In this first section, my main purpose has been only to indicate two (perhaps unexpected) cases of similarity in the approaches of Peirce and Ockham: the account of thinking in terms of signs and the assimilation of the phenomena of universality and relation.

II

To some extent, the parochial and peculiar aura of medieval controversies about universals can be dispelled if they are taken to be part of a general inquiry into the issue of the intelligibility of things (or of "the world"). Medieval realists—especially Aquinas and Scotus—recognize two vices which, so to speak, bracket epistemic virtue. On the one hand there is the foolishly cluttered ontology that results from insisting on a one-for-one correspondence between things in the world and the elements of a representational system (thought or language). And on the other, there is the scandal—anachronistically put—of the unknowable thing-in-itself.

An assessment of the one-for-one theory had been made explicit in the maxim: Do not confuse the properties of signs with the properties of things signified. Both terms (as early as Anselm) and universals (as early as Abailard) were recognized to have a "mode of signification" which was not matched by any "mode of being" on the part of things so signified. That Ockham greatly extended the application of the maxim (e.g., to the categories including relation) should not be allowed to obscure the fact that it was common property for medieval realists and nominalists alike. To ignore the maxim, it was generally recognized, was to risk a double confusion: a commitment to bizarre (unnecessary or even impossible) entities and ignorance of the subtleties of different modes of signification.

The risk of making things in themselves unintelligible was not so explicitly recognized. Ockham, for example, had no intention of denying that things can be known in themselves (cf., Moody, pp. 48n1, 53 and 280). But while he would surely have rejected Peirce's charge—"The nominalist by isolating his reality so entirely from mental influence as he has done has made it something which the mind cannot conceive . . . ." (8.31)—Ockham seems to think no defense is needed. His attention is absorbed in the criticism of what he takes to be an insufficiently sharp distinction between thought and thing; and he is, in the process, sometimes insensitive (Henry, 1972, pp. 88–95).

Without minimizing the importance of the differences between them, it is fair to say that both Aquinas and Scotus maintain that the only way we can characterize what the world is "really like" is in terms of potential intelligibility—that is, in terms of what can be understood through the constructs of the human mind. Consider Aquinas' claim that, apart from the activity of the intellect, the world is not actually intelligible (e.g., *Summa Theologiae* I, q.79, a.3 with replies). The contrast is with sensation where the potentially sensible can become actually sensible in a non-cognitive process (e.g., colored objects become actually visible in the daylight). The immediate object of the understanding, according to Aquinas, consists in what things are, that they are, and so on: that is, in something predicative or propositional in nature. And (*pace* Plato) the world does not contain such actually intelligible things. The world of individual things is known (about) in understanding "what's" and "that's" fitted to sensory data.

Scotus' handling of the issue is not altogether (though it is very) different. In the "metaphysical mode"—in contrast to the approach of physics or logic—individual things in the world are taken as composites of "formalities": of what a truly knowing mind would conceive (Grajewski, 1944, p. 931). These components are not distinguished as "*res et res*" but as "*realitas et realitas*." It is pretty clearly this doctrine to which Peirce refers when he says that he got the term "reality" from Scotus. And though the substantive claim does not thereby become transparent, one can recognize an historically justified terminology in Peirce's claim that reality, as the object of belief, is predicative in nature. (Peirce sometimes contrasts "two views of reality"— e.g., at 8.17. On the "nominalistic" one, reality is the unknown cause that sets the process of sensation and understanding in motion. For the other, reality is the outcome of a process that arrives at true belief.) Peirce's account of reality will come up again in the last section. For the moment, I want to follow up on the differences from the scholastics in Peirce's account of epistemic virtue and its attendant vices.

The keystone, for Peirce, is the identification of being and intelligibility (5.257, 313, 352; 6.270, 339; 7.561, 564): what there is independently of any thought about it can only be described in terms of being potentially understood. The false conclusion that things are therefore unknowable in themselves results from denying that something's being known to be such-and-such and knowing something to be such are but two ways of expressing the same fact (6.339). The point, I believe, is this. "Brutus kills Caesar" and "Caesar is killed by Brutus" are but two ways of expressing the same fact; similarly, "The world is known by the mind" and "the mind knows the world." What knowledge we have of the mind and the world independent of this fact is only in terms of potential intelligibility (active and passive).

That Peirce labels the doctrine of an unknowable thing-in-itself 'nominalistic' (5.312, 5.316, 6.492, 8.31) shows that he thinks (correctly, I believe) he shares the overall view on intelligibility with medieval realists. What he does not mention, however, is the scholastics' preoccupation—in Ockham's case almost a fixation—with the correlative error of the one-for-one model of representative knowledge. In Peirce's analysis, the alternative vice to the incognizable is a false idealism he attributes to Berkeley and which he thinks Kant has successfully refuted (e.g., 1.36 ff., 6.95, 8.30). This perverted idealism concludes from the fact that we cannot think of anything without thinking about it to the false belief that we can have knowledge only of our own states of consciousness (5.85).

I do not want to follow Peirce into his dispute with Berkeley (or his interpretation of Kant). Here, I want only to emphasize how the doctrine of being as intelligibility is located, for him, in an explicitly idealist context. The point is not that all comparison and contrast with the scholastics is thereby discredited. But the incommensurability must be respected. That Ockham's position is both anti-realist and anti-idealist does not simply intensify his opposition to Peirce; that Scotus "agrees" with Peirce in espousing realism does not simply put him in the middle.

III

Peirce's claim to the title of "scholastic realist" derives in his own eyes from his sharing with certain medievals a belief in objective generality. That belief, in its natural setting in Peirce apart from any comparison or contrast, is expressed in terms of the reality of Thirdness as a separate and objective category. (In order not to complicate matters, I am ignoring Firstness throughout my account.) Before taking up any details of comparison or contrast with scholastic realists, I want to set out briefly Peirce's view on the relation of Thirdness and Secondness as it pertains to what I will call "basic" Seconds.

According to Peirce, the data of our experience as something which is factual occurs as individual "reaction-events" (my terms). These basic Seconds are not events after the fashion of birthday parties or movie premieres but rather are the contentless "occurrings" which are the residue of, say, striking a blow or running into a ladder, where the kind of action is no part of the Second itself. Peirce adopts this category from a view he shares with the most hardheaded empiricists (or positivists) of his time. Far from abandoning it as his "realist" consciousness developed, Peirce uses this primitive, bare occurring of Secondness as the first step in his argument to show the reality of Thirdness. For no physical fact, no physical process or physical object of the sort we normally take as real, can be adequately exhibited as constituted by reaction-events alone.

Physical objects and processes, of course, are actual and individual; and Peirce does identify them at times as Seconds. But they are not basic Seconds. It is the reaction-events which mark their histories that explain why physical objects are individual and actual; but it is the peculiar continuity of each history that explains them as objects (animals, plants or whatever). In any physical object or process, then, Thirdness is as real as Secondness.

For Peirce, I think, there is only one realm of basic Seconds: the reaction-events of past, present and future. Any thirdness of whatever level is actual and real only for its effect (however indirect) on some actual event. Even though Peirce comes to allow that an unscratched diamond can be properly said to be hard, he does not withdraw his criticism of Hegelian idealism for disregarding the category of Secondness. That is to say, while Peirce emphasizes the independence of a "would be" from any actual set of Seconds, the potency of a Third that has no manifestation in past, present or future Seconds could not be distinguished from mere possibility.

The relation of ordered Thirds is another matter. To use Peirce's geometrical analogy: physical objects stand to basic Seconds as segments of a line to points; but they are embedded in higher level Thirds as segments in larger segments which share, so so speak, the same points or Seconds. It is the irreducibility of Thirdness (of any order) to Secondness which is characteristic of Peirce's realism. When he says that he holds an extreme realism of the Scotist sort, it would be misleading to take as Peirce's main concern the relation of physical objects and higher level Thirdness. In fact, he appeals to the adapted Scotistic model in order to represent the relation of Second and Third; and that relationship is exhibited primarily in the case of basic Seconds and Thirdness. Of course, Peirce holds to the reality (and agency) of higher level Thirds; and he is an avowed panpsychist. No doubt his peculiar "realism" makes it easier for him to do that than it would have been for Scotus. But those idealist positions are not a simple consequence or essential feature of Peirce's "realism."

The position of Aquinas—though Peirce has less interest in him than in either Scotus or Ockham—offers a helpful focus for comparing and contrasting Peirce's theory of real generality with the medievals. Form, Aquinas says, stands to matter as intellectual insight to sensory presentation—or in modern terms, as organizing hypothesis to data in need of explanation (cf. Lonergan, 1967, p. 144 and passim). Form makes sense of matter as of a kind of thing; or in metaphysical terms, forms explains why matter is a thing of a kind. To answer such questions as "What makes this bronze a statue? What makes this flesh and these bones an animal?" is to cite the form of something.

Consider Peirce's Secondness and Thirdness as analogues of Aquinas's matter and form. For example: form has a causal influence on matter but while a thing is the product of the two, form does not become matter. Similarly, Thirdness and Secondness are not separable in any real object, but Thirdness does not become Secondness. And we might say that Thirdness "makes" Secondness to be a thing of a kind while Secondness "makes" a thing to be actual and individual.

One obvious disanalogy, of course, is that the "stuff" which is matter on Aquinas' account is different from the reaction-events which are basic Seconds in Peirce's scheme. The difference reflects a different approach to the "data" of inquiry. For Peirce, both the results of modern science and problems in modern theory of knowledge require that basic data must be event-like. And in keeping with this, Thirdness functions by collecting or ranging over reaction-events in the life history of any individual physical object. This, I think, is what lies behind Peirce's claim that the generality of form in scholastic accounts is only a limiting case of the continuity of Thirdness in his own.

The idea of a Third—a law of potency or force—that governs the appearance of reaction-events is more suitable to an idealist metaphysics than is the traditional hylomorphism. The defining characteristic of Secondness is not materiality but resistance; a material thing, like any other thing, is a projection from the lawlike interrelationship of Seconds. The distinction between materialism and idealism, then, depends solely on the kinds of laws one must adopt to explain the relevant correlations.

It is, of course, appropriate to use dispositional propositions to describe Aristotelian forms. To say of something that it is living or rational is to indicate that a certain range of predicates is appropriate; and that can be expressed in terms of the sorts of operations of which the thing is capable. Operative potencies (sight, for example) are defined in terms of their operations; and even substantial forms (the psyche of animals, for example) are discovered or postulated as integrating functions of the various operations of things.

Peirce's "would-be" according to his most developed accounts, is obviously a close analogue to operative potencies. But it could be misleading to describe his position there as "extreme scholastic dispositionalism." Dispositions, for the Aristotelian, are grounded in forms, eventually in a substantial form (which is something actual). Their agency is ultimately attributed to the subject or substance; any unities of a "higher order" than substances are treated as functions of substances and are not located in a transcendent form or power. For Peirce, on the other hand, higher level agencies can be projected from higher level "would-be's." A thing, after all, is a particular, organized set of Seconds—its organization manifesting Thirdness (and Firstness). And one thing can be embedded in a higher order thing where the relevant Thirds both govern the same Seconds in a hieratically organized way. It is not necessary that matter be able to become something like con- rete reasonableness, for the base of the projection is not matter but reaction events; and a "would-be" manifested in such Seconds can constitute a "thing." It is a form of *hubris* associated with the ego to think that the con- geries of powers that we call an individual human being is a privileged limit to the agency of Thirdness (cf., "Man's Glassy Essence," 6.238–271).

Would Peirce have been better advised to ground the analogy for his scholastic realism in the form/matter analysis of Aquinas? The disanalogies, I think, are more severe than the possibly misleading aspect of his denial of contraction. On Aquinas' account, the forms of material things do not ex- haust the potentialities of the matter of those things; that is, the matter now constituting this horse can become something else or has potentialities to other forms (*Summa Theologiae* I, q.55, a.2; q.84, a.3, *ad* 1). But for Peirce, the reaction events that constitute the Seconds of the actual life history of a physical object are not potential to anything else; Secondness has no poten- tiality. Peirce's Seconds are "in" Thirds; Aquinas' forms are "in" matter. In fact the reversal is complete: form for Aquinas is in the order of act, while its analogues in Peirce (the "would-be" or Thirdness) is objective nonactuality. Consequently, to use the matter/form analysis as a model for the relation of Thirdness and Secondness would require standing it on its head in a most un- becoming way.

Of course there is no contradiction in Peirce's calling a "real possibility" what a medieval Aristotelian puts in the order of act. But it will be confusing rather than enlightening if one's understanding of Peirce's position is based on the wrong model.

IV

While there is evidently more to be said about the differences in the scholastic and Peircean accounts of potentiality, I should like to turn in this last section to the approach Peirce shares with certain medieval realists on be- ing and intelligibility in order to try to shed some light on Peirce's analysis of truth and reality. Allowing for a certain vagueness in terminology which I shall mark by using capitals, and using a scheme that goes beyond Peirce's terminology but allows the rest of us to express our unidealist worries, we can say that both the Mind and the World are revealed in instances of knowledge (or true belief) having Reality for their "object".

"The Mind knows the World" and "The World is known by the Mind" are but two ways of expressing one fact. And as entities independent of that fact, Mind and World can only be characterized as potencies (passive and active) that are realized in it. Reality is not a third thing in this picture but is a result of making it precise. If we are willing to give up a theory of knowledge based on intuition—that is, a theory in which intellectual cognition is like vision or sensation where "The Mind knows the World" develops from the structure of "I see/touch a tree"—then we shall have to make explicit the propositional (or predicative) character of the object of our knowing. (The appropriateness of using 'know' with a noun object is only a distraction here.) The object of knowing (or understanding) has as its form "that such-and-such" or "what such-and-such is" and the like. The World—if we take that to consist of all the (individual) things there are—is "known in" or becomes intelligible in the proper object of knowledge. The latter, since it is the object of knowing and not the activity, is something objective and its technical name is Reality.

When Peirce says that thoughts (as what thinking is about) are real but should not be construed "nominalistically" as items of consciousness, I think it is the model of knowing that I have just described which he has in mind. Whatever Peirce might say about what I am calling the World, one can at least be clear about the technical sense he gives (following Scotus) to the notion of Reality. The position is anti-intuitionist and anti-nominalist (in Peirce's sense) but it is not necessarily idealist. Idealism, I should think—that is, once beyond the false idealism Peirce attributes to Berkeley—has to do with the characterization not of Reality but of the World. And even characterized as potential intelligibility, the World does not have to be propositional or thought-like in itself.

That Peirce is an idealist is not in doubt. Just how to characterize his idealism and how to understand how he arrived at or justified it is not so clear (to me). The problem comes out more starkly in the context of Peirce's sign theory. The technical use of 'Reality' fits well enough in the role of interpretant. Peirce seems to have held all along that:

(a) The interpretant of an idea must be an idea.

And we can take that as the precise meaning of:

(a') An idea can resemble only an idea.

As it happens, (a') is often taken for an exclusively idealist position, but I think the account I have given of the technical sense of 'Reality' shows that this need not be the case.

Things stand differently with:

(b) The object of an idea must be an idea.

And:

(b') An idea can represent only an idea.

This claim appears in Peirce's unpublished writings quite prominently at one time (cf., Altshuler) and it strikes me as both idealist and puzzling. While

Reality (in its technical sense in Peirce) can be propositional (or predicative) in nature and the object of belief, I find it hard to conceive of it as a terminal object—that is, it seems to me to be only a sign of the World. And I am not at all sure just what arguments or considerations Peirce thinks would show me wrong. The resolution of this problem, I think, lies in unraveling the full mystery of the role of the ultimate opinion in Peirce's scheme. (Reality is the object of the ultimate opinion (6.393); and Truth is the approximation or concordance of a belief with that opinion (5.407).)

Some of Peirce's remarks indicate that he thinks one must adopt the conclusion that everything is of the nature of mind because of the advantages it has in the area of explanation. The hypothesis that there is one basic kind of law is simpler, and the facts are (Peirce claims) more easily explained by a single psychical law than by a single materialistic one. I can understand this claim without having to agree to it. But the argument for idealism which I was considering before was not that we could have ideas only of ideas simply because ideas are all there is. Rather, it claimed that something about the representative process necessitated an idealist conclusion. And that is what I do not understand.

One line of reconstruction is to suppose that Peirce was working towards a position proposed by such writers as Quine and Putnam who, in their differing ways, might be said to question the plausibility of drawing a distinction between Reality and the World (Perhaps something of this sort lies behind the analysis sketched out in Rorty, 1961. See also the suggestions of Føllesdal, 1973, and Hintikka, 1976.) Another approach would be to examine the presuppositions and/or consequences of Peirce's theory of signs; for example, the system may require the ultimate identity of sign, object and interpretant. But, as with the former alternative, one would have to spell out just what is involved in the identity of Reality (as something predicative and thought-like) with the World. Otherwise, it will not be clear whether Peirce is here engaging in revisionist metaphysics or whether this is one of those cases where "propositions . . . that sound absurd sometimes express plain facts" (6.182).

Finally, among alternatives that seem plausible to me now, one might be able to show that Peirce's use of "would-be" is the key factor. As I suggested in an earlier section, Peirce's substitution of Seconds for "matter" in the traditional hylomorphic scheme might so diminish the role of matter as to make idealism a natural result of his explanatory scheme. Of course, this would be another instance of an argument for idealism through the theory of explanation and not through the representative schema itself. But there still would be a significant gain if our reasonable expectations about the independence of the World could be shown to resolve into the would-be of Peirce's definition of truth and reality in terms of the ultimate opinion.

There is one troublesome factor about the "would-be" relative to the ultimate opinion which I have been suppressing. Contrary to the medievals, Peirce does not think that there is any actual case of knowledge that can be identified as such (3.460, 5.316); consequently, we can pick no actual case to ground the potencies of Mind and World. Instead, for Peirce, we have to talk of what *would be* thought in an Ultimate Opinion to have a point of reference for identifying Reality (and thereby Mind and World). This introduces a type of potentiality that is different from the operative potencies underlying the dispositions Peirce usually appeals to. It is the "terminating potentiality" one finds with, say, acorns and oaks.

I would like to have it work out that the intersection of the operative potencies (derived as Mind and World from the case of Reality) with the terminating potentiality that constitutes Reality itself is the source of the complication that accounts for an awkward formulation of otherwise "plain facts" in Peirce' theory. As things stand at the moment, however, I would not want to mislead an innocent inquirer about what might lie in wait at the center of that maze.

John Boler

University of Washington

BIBLIOGRAPHY

M. M. Adams, "Ockham's Nominalism and Unreal Entities," *Philosophical Review* 86 (1977): 144–76.

B. Altshuler, "Peirce's Theory of Truth and his Early Idealism," *Transactions of the C. S. Peirce Society* (forthcoming).

J. Boler, *Charles Peirce and Scholastic Realism* (Seattle: University of Washington Press, 1963).

———, "Ockham on Intuition," *Journal of the History of Philosophy* 11 (1973): 95–106.

D. Føllesdal, "Indeterminacy of Translation and Underdetermination of the Theory of Nature," *Dialectica* 27 (1973): 289–302.

M. Grajewski, *The Formal Distinction of Duns Scotus* (Washington: Catholic University of America Press, 1944).

D. P. Henry, *Medieval Logic and Metaphysics* (London: Hutchinson, 1972).

J. Hintikka, "Quine versus Peirce?" *Dialectica* 30 (1976): 7–8.

B. Lonergan, *Verbum: Word and Idea in Aquinas* (Notre Dame: University of Notre Dame Press, 1967).

E. A. Moody, *The Logic of William of Ockham* (London: Sheed and Ward, 1935).

H. Putnam, *Meaning and the Moral Sciences* (Boston: Routledge, Keegan Paul, 1978).

R. Rorty, "Pragmatism, Categories and Language,"*Philosophical Review* 70 (1961): 197–223.

T. K. Scott, "Ockham on Evidence, Necessity and Intuition," *Journal of the History of Philosophy* 7 (1969): 27–49.

H. Shapiro, *Motion, Time and Place according to William Ockham* (St. Bonaventure: The Franciscan Institute, 1957).

C. S. PEIRCE'S "FIRST REAL DISCOVERY"
AND ITS CONTEMPORARY RELEVANCE

Like Leibniz, C. S. Peirce drew much of the inspiration for his philosophical work from a close study of logical and mathematical reasoning. Now what insights did this study reveal to Peirce?[1] His own answer is formulated as follows: "My first real discovery about mathematical procedure was that there are two kinds of necessary reasoning, which I call the Corollarial and the Theorematic . . . ."[2] The import of this discovery was lost on philosophers for a long time. The purpose of the present paper is to show what Peirce's insight amounts to, to point out some of its applications, relate it to certain recent developments in the philosophy of logic, and thereby vindicate Peirce's distinction. This undoubtedly will also help to show its present day relevance.

Peirce attributed tremendous importance to his distinction. Its importance was not restricted by him to mathematical reasoning, either. Rather, a study of mathematical thought serves here as a guide to necessary reasoning in general. "The examination of the methods of mathematical demonstration sheds extraordinary light upon logic, such as I, for my part, never dreamt of in advance," Peirce writes by way of introducing his discovery. (Eisele, vol. 4, p. 47.) After having presented it, he says: "I show that no considerable advance can be made in thought of any kind without theorematic reasoning." (Eisele, vol. 4, p. 49.) Small wonder, therefore, that Peirce thinks of the distinction as "a matter of extreme importance for the theory of cognition." (Eisele, vol. 4, p. 56.)

What, then, is this remarkable distinction between corollarial and theorematic reasoning? One explanation Peirce offers is as follows

> *Corollarial deduction* is where it is only necessary to imagine any case in which the premisses are true in order to perceive immediately that the conclusion holds in that case. . . . *Theorematic deduction* is deduction in which it is necessary to experiment in imagination upon the image of the premiss in order for the result of such experiment to make corollarial deductions to the truth of the conclusion. (Eisele, vol. 4, p. 38.)

A similar explanation goes as follows:

> Any *Corollary* (as I shall use the term) would be a proposition deduced directly from propositions already established without the use of any other construction than one necessarily suggested in apprehending the enunciation of the proposition. . . .

Any *Theorem* (as I shall use the term) would be a proposition pronouncing, in effect, that were a general condition which it describes fulfilled, a certain result which it describes in a general way . . . will be impossible, this proposition being capable of demonstration from propositions previously established, but not without imagining something more than what the condition supposes to exist . . . . (Eisele, vol. 4, pp. 288–89.)

The main difference between these two explanations is that in the former a distinction is made between two different kinds of deduction whereas in the latter a parallel distinction is made between the respective conclusions of the two different kinds of deduction.

Both the import of Peirce's distinction and its significance have been overlooked almost completely by later philosophers and logicians. The fact that his thoughts about the distinction remained largely unpublished (and possibly unwritten) by Peirce himself and underemphasized by his subsequent editors (cf. Eisele, vol. 4, p. 56) explains this neglect only to a very small extent. The main reason, I am afraid, is that the precise nature of Peirce's distinction has not been understood by later logicians and philosophers. I shall approach it here genetically, through its historical antecedents.

Peirce's choice of the terms "theorematic" and "corollarial" points to the salient paradigm on which his distinction is modelled. It is the division of a proposition into parts in Euclid. This is explained by Peirce himself as follows:

Euclid always begins his presentation of a theorem by a statement of it in *general terms*. . . . This was called the πρότασις or *proposition*. To this he invariably appends, by a λέγω, 'I say,' a translation of it into *singular terms*, each general subject being replaced by a Greek letter that serves as the proper name for a single one of the objects denoted by that general subject. . . . This second statement was called the ἔκθεσις, or *exposition*. . . . The principal theoric step of the demonstration is, however, taken in what immediately follows; namely in 'preparation' for the demonstration, the παρασκευή, usually translated 'the construction' . . . . Euclid's παρασκευή consists of precise directions for drawing certain lines, rarely for spreading out surfaces. . . . Those lines, which are drawn in the παρασκευή are not only all that are referred to in the condition of the proposition, but also all the additional lines which he is about to consider in order to facilitate the demonstration of which this παρασκευή is thus the soul, since in it the principal theoric step is taken. But . . . sometimes the text does not very sharply separate some parts of the παρασκευή from the next step, the ἀπόδειξις, or demonstration. This latter contains mere corollarial reasoning, though . . . this corollarial reasoning will sometimes be a little puzzling to a student who has not so thoroughly assimilated what went before . . . . After this, a sentence . . . repeats the πρότασις . . . . This is called συμπέρασμα, the 'conclusion' . . . . (*Collected Papers* 4.616.)

The basis of Peirce's generalization in Euclid is clearly indicated by himself. The locus of merely corollarial reasoning in Euclid is the *apodeixis*, which is called by Peirce *demonstration*. The whole argument is corollarial if and only if the *apodeixis* alone suffices to establish it, in other words, if and only if no subsidiary construction, often known under the alias auxiliary construction, is needed. Peirce is assuming that the *ekthesis* is always carried out. Making this assumption, we can say that geometrical reasoning is corollarial if no constructions (no further or auxiliary constructions) are needed in it, and theorematic if they are indispensable.

This distinction was not original with Peirce, however, insofar as it is applied merely to geometrical arguments. On the contrary, it was something of a commonplace in Peirce's time. Corollarial consequences were sometimes called by geometers "logical consequences," as distinguished from "geometrical consequences," which correspond to Peirce's theorematic deductions. In many other ways, too, the crucial role of constructions in nontrivial geometrical reasoning was emphasized in traditional discussion. For instance, in one passage Aristotle seems to go as far as to say that after the necessary auxiliary constructions have been carried out, a geometrical theorem is obvious. (See *Metaphysics IX*, 9, 1051a21 ff.)

Peirce's brilliant insight is that this geometrical distinction can be generalized to *all deductive reasoning*.[3] This is a much more formidable achievement than might appear *prima facie*. In order to appreciate what Peirce did, it is useful to recall that there is a strong tradition in the philosophy of logic and mathematics which denies the possibility of any general logical distinction which like Peirce's turns on the concept of construction. Peirce sometimes connects his insight with the development of modern logic, especially the logic of relations. (See e.g., Eisele, vol. 4, p. 59; *Collected Papers* 3.641.) There is a much better known view than Peirce's, however, which sees one main upshot of modern logic in showing that the concept of construction (on which Peirce relies in making his distinction) is completely dispensable in geometrical and other valid deductive arguments. The figures of earlier geometry are unnecessary, according to this line of thought, because valid geometrical reasoning can be completely formalized. The reason why figures were thought of as indispensable by earlier philosophers and mathematicians was simply the incompleteness of earlier axiomatizations (according to this view). This incompleteness made it necessary for geometers to go beyond their own explicit assumptions and to appeal tacitly to geometrical intuition. For this purpose (it is alleged) geometrical figures had to be used.

It follows (according to the view I am discussing) that even in elementary geometry the Peircean distinction is really dispensable. It was due merely to Euclid's particular manner of presentation of his arguments with the help of figures. It was not (the defenders of this view will say) really a distinction between different kinds of deductive arguments in geometry, for it referred to the idea of construction which (it is alleged) is foreign to the real deductive logical argumentation which is going on in geometry.

The best known latter-day representative of views of this type was undoubtedly Bertrand Russell. The views under scrutiny are mistaken, however, and the sharpness of Peirce's insight is demonstrated by the fact that he realized this mistake. The generalization which Peirce saw is indicated by his second explanation quoted above. What makes a deduction theorematic according to Peirce is that in it we must envisage other individuals than those needed to instantiate the premise of the argument. The new individuals do not have to be visualized, as the geometrical objects introduced by an Euclidean construction are. They have to be mentioned and considered in the argument, however.

How are such new individuals introduced? An example is obtained by converting the arguments used in elementary geometry into arguments using modern symbolic logic, especially quantification theory. Then each new layer of quantifiers adds a new individual (geometrical object) to the configurations of individuals we are considering. After all, each quantifier invites us to consider one individual, however indefinite. (The existential quantifier "$(\exists x)$" can be read "there is at least one individual, call it x, such that"; and correspondingly for the universal quantifier.) Hence we obtain a good reconstruction of Peirce's theorematic-corollarial distinction for deductions using the tools of modern quantification theory: a valid deductive step is theorematic if it increases the number of layers of quantifiers in the propositions in question. This is, apart from the possibility of a minor sharpening of the definition, precisely my distinction between non-trivial and trivial logical arguments (surface tautologies and depth tautologies). Hence Peirce's intended distinction is to all practical purposes the same as the one which is introduced, studied, and applied in my 1973 book.[4]

This observation nevertheless leaves a large number of further questions open. First, the generalization of the geometrical distinction just mentioned works only in formulations of quantification theory which, like Quine's,[5] employ bound variables only. When free singular terms are used, it is steps of instantiation that increase the complexity of the configurations considered in the proof. They become then the hallmarks of theorematicity. In some ways, this is clearly most immediate generalization of the geometrical distinction.

This does not exhaust all the apparently different ways in which new individuals can be introduced into a deductive argument. Another way is through functional application. This is perhaps the closest rational reconstruction of those explanations of Peirce's which are couched in terms of the need "to experiment in imagination upon the image of the premiss" in a theorematic deduction or in similar terms. (Cf. here also *Collected Papers* 4. 323.) This way of introducing new individuals can nevertheless be thought of as reducing to the other ones. For we all know from elementary logic how function symbols can be eliminated in favor of predicate symbols and quantifiers.

Since I have shown that all these different ways of introducing new individuals are equivalent, we can see that the distinction Peirce intends coincides with mine. Peirce's understanding of the logical situation is shown in several other ways, too. For instance, his comments strongly suggest that according to him theorematic reasoning is possible only in the logic of relatives. (Cf. Eisele, vol. 4, p. 58.) What distinguishes this part of logic from Boolean algebra is precisely the fact that more than one individual is there considered at one and the same time (*Collected Papers* 3.392), thus opening the possibility for introducing auxiliary individuals.

More generally, to have seen the possibility of generalizing the geometrical distinction to all deductive reasoning is an achievement which justifies the pride Peirce takes in his "first real discovery." At the same time, Peirce does not seem to reach complete clarity concerning the nature of his own distinction. This failure is perhaps excusable and explainable through the state of the art of logic in Peirce's time. Concerning the main point, viz., the generalizability of the geometrical distinction, Peirce was absolutely right.

To put the same point in slightly different terms, what Peirce realized was in effect that the geometrical distinction does not disappear even when geometrical arguments are "formalized," that is, presented as explicit logical inferences. This presupposes a keen insight into the logical structure of the arguments in question and into logical inferences in general. It is for this reason that Peirce attributes his "first real discovery about mathematical procedure" to his logical acumen.

Peirce's crucial insight was what happens when a traditional semi-formal geometrical argument which employs figures is converted into an explicit logical argument. Figures actually displayed of course become redundant, but the letters (or letter combinations) referring to them will become free variables (or other free singular terms, such as dummy names, depending on how the underlying logic is set up and what terminology is used in it in connection with instantiations), used in the formal argument. (Cf. the quotation above from *Collected Papers* 4.616, where Peirce speaks of Euclid's use of Greek letters as proper names for geometrical objects.) Each time a new geometrical object was introduced into the old semi-formal argument, a new free singular term is introduced in the formal argument, typically through a step of instantiation. Hence the complexity of the configurations of individuals considered in the semi-formal and the formal argument is the same.

Furthermore, the distinction between theorematic and corollarial reasoning which was made in the original semi-formal geometrical arguments in terms of this complexity immediately carried over to the corresponding formal arguments.

This possibility of recognizing some of the key concepts and distinctions that used to be made concerning traditional geometrical propositions in a new garb even after all arguments of elementary geometry are completely formalized (logicized) is in fact quite interesting, especially historically. The possibility of finding accurate counterparts to Euclidean steps of construction even in the most completely formalized logical proofs is not the only nor perhaps the deepest insight into this useful analogy between traditional geometrical arguments and logical proofs. Conversely, we can use the analogy to find anticipations of modern logical concepts and even results in the traditional philosophy and methodology of mathematics. For instance, one of the messiest problem areas in old geometry was the order of the different parts of argument, that is, the relative order of steps of construction and steps of *apodeixis*.[6] Precisely the same problem of commuting different kinds of steps of deduction lies in the heart of the most interesting conceptualizations and results of modern proof theory.[7] Hence the analogy I am calling attention to shows where the deeper problems of proof theory for the first time in history began to catch the eye of mathematicians, logicians, and philosophers.

In spite of the sharpness of Peirce's insight, he does not reach a completely satisfactory formulation of his distinction, as was already indicated. This failure seems to be due to a more general failure to understand fully the nature of the distinction and its implications. A symptom of this is Peirce's uncertainty whether the distinction can meaningfully be made in all cases. "Perhaps when any branch of mathematics is worked up into its most perfect form all its theorems will be converted into corollaries," Peirce muses (Eisele, vol. 4, p. 289). Here modern logic again offers some help. The question as to whether a class of theorems can be converted into corollaries depends of course on the rules of inference used. I have shown that if these rules are restricted to "natural" ones in a sense that can be easily defined, not all theorems of an undecidable theory can be converted into corollaries (in what seems to be precisely Peirce's sense). (See *op. cit.*, note 4 above, pp. 178–182.) Hence the contingency Peirce envisaged cannot arise in general, even though it could in principle come about in sufficiently simple theories.

Peirce also expresses his puzzlement whether the distinction perhaps is "inherently impossible in some cases" (Eisele, vol. 4, p. 290). The answer is that the distinction is relative to a system of rules. Given a set of rules, the distinction is of course applicable in all cases.

Peirce realized himself that his intuitive insight in generalizing the geometrical notion of construction to all deductive reasoning was not backed up by a definitive analysis of the logical situation. "There is still some question how far the observation of imaginary, or artificial constructions, with experimentation upon them is logically essential to the procedure of mathematics, as to some extent it certainly is, even in the strictest Weierstrassian method, and how far it is merely a psychological convenience" (Eisele, vol. 4, p. 158). Peirce would have been reassured by such recent developments as the definition of explicit measures of deductive information and its semantical backing in the form of Rantala's urn models.[8] These recent developments vindicate strikingly the objectivity of Peirce's distinction.

The sharper modern characterization of Peirce's distinction also offers an important advantage. If a theorematic inference is characterized by the introduction of auxiliary individuals into the argument, we can turn theorematicity into a matter of degree. An argument is the more theorematic the more new individuals (the more "constructions") are used in it. This yields a rough measure of the nontriviality of an argument, a measure that can be sharpened still further. Peirce does not envisage such a quantification of his distinction. Instead, he indicates that he wants to make "subdivisions of theorematic deduction" and that he considers these subdivisions "of very high theoretical importance" (Eisele, vol. 4, p. 38). These subdivisions seem to be in an entirely different direction from my degrees of nontriviality, however.

In general, it is thus eminently clear that Peirce's explanations of the theorematic vs. corollarial distinction are supposed to spell out the very same distinction between arguments in which it suffices merely to have a good look at old objects (of the kind which happen to be under scrutiny in the argument in question) and those in which new entities are introduced into our reasoning which I was explicating (and discussing) in my 1973 book. (See note 4 above.) The main difference is that Peirce's explanations remained completely informal, while my formulations of the distinction rely on such formal (syntactical) notions as the number of layers of quantifiers in a proposition at its deepest. The reason for this difference is not that Peirce did not appreciate the role of quantifiers in introducing individuals into our arguments. What he did not understand, to the same extent as for instance Frege, was the systematic situation. He did not realize to what large extent first-order reasoning (quantificational reasoning) captures the inferences we perform in logic and mathematics. He was one of the first two logicians—the other one was Frege—to formulate an explicit notion of a quantifier. However, unlike Frege he did not realize what an extensive traffic this notion can be made to bear. In Peirce's own work, quantifiers are merely one of the many tools in his incredibly rich bag of tricks as a logician. Here he missed an important insight, however. Even if quantificational reasoning does not capture all of the modes of reasoning actually employed in the different kinds of deduction we perform, it comes close enough to allow at least an interim formulation of the theorematic-corollarial distinction in terms of the number of layers of quantifiers in the propositions involved, along the lines adumbrated above. Even though Peirce had all the ingredients of such a definition available to him, he did not avail himself of it because he did not realize how much could be accomplished by means of such an explication.

It seems to me that Peirce's distinction, explicated along the lines I have indicated, is fully as important as he thought. Peirce himself seems to have considered a vindication of the concept of abstraction as the most important application of his discovery. (Cf. e.g., Eisele, vol. 4, pp. 49–50, 159–162.) I shall not discuss this application here, however. Several philosophically and historically important applications are discussed in my book *Logic, Language-Games, and Information.*[9] I do not have enough space here to consider more than a couple of such applications. One of them is the greatest common denominator in several problems, each of them interesting in its own right. This common problem is the question: How can anyone fail to see all the logical consequences of premises one is aware of? This problem goes back all the way to Aristotle, as I have shown elsewhere.[10] Indeed, this problem of "logical incontinence," as I have called it, is the crucial problem (and one which ultimately remained unsolved by Aristotle) vitiating his systematization of logical truths (valid syllogisms). In our time, the very same problem of "logical omniscience" has constituted the main objection which has been levelled against informational ("possible-worlds") treatments of the logic of such epistemic concepts as knowledge, belief, and memory. These problems are all solved by the Peirce-Hintikka distinction. There may indeed be a problem as to how anyone can fail to carry out a corollarial deduction. After all, all that is apparently needed for such a deduction is a good look at what is given in the conditions of the conclusion to be proved. But there is not even a problem as to how one can fail to draw a theorematic conclusion. Since such a conclusion is characterized by the need of introducing the right auxiliary individuals into the argument, it can fail not only because of a wrong choice of auxiliary individuals but more importantly by a simple failure to consider the more complicated configurations of individuals obtainable by introducing auxiliaries. Thus, to think of the premise of a theorematic inference is not *ipso facto* to think of its conclusion, because an additional *factum* (in its etymological sense) is needed for the latter, viz., the carrying out of suitable auxiliary constructions.

If there is any further problem left here, it is to make genuine semantical (model-theoretical) sense of the idea of the number of individuals considered in an argument on which the theorematic-corollarial distinction is based.

Such backing is provided by game-theoretical semantics as spelled out by Rantala in terms of his urn models,[11] and elaborated in my 1975 paper.[12]

An application of the distinction which I partly share with Peirce is to Kant's famous distinction between analytic and synthetic judgements. (For this subject in Peirce, see especially Eisele, vol. 4, pp. 57–59, 84; *Collected Papers* 3.641; 4.52 etc.) As Peirce in effect points out, the distinction he makes turns Kant's contrast into an ambiguous one. Analytic inferences according to Kant may be interpreted so as to include only corollarial deductions, or else both corollarial and theorematic deductions. As Peirce also points out, Kant's failure to distinguish between these two interpretations can be viewed as being due to Kant's ignorance of the logic of relations. (As was pointed out above and as Peirce was fully aware of, the corollarial-theorematic distinction comes alive only when we move from Boolean inferences to relational ones.) What Peirce fails to point out, however, is that there is excellent evidence to the effect that Kant had in mind something very much like corollarial deductions only when he characterized analytical inferences. This evidence is marshalled in my *Logic, Language-Games and Information*.[13] Basically, it can be seen that Kant recognized geometrical and other mathematical inferences as being fully necessary without any appeal to anything like geometrical imagination or intuition (in the present-day sense of the latter term). Yet they are synthetic according to Kant, because they involve constructions, that is, introductions of new individuals to instantiate general concepts.

This does not by any means exhaust the applications of Peirce's distinction. For instance, Peirce's comments on the experimentation in imagination and on the observation involved in it which is needed in theorematic deduction (see above, quote from Eisele, vol. 4, p. 38; cf. also *Collected Papers* 3. 641; 4.233) constitutes an interesting anticipation of Erik Stenius's views on the synthetic character of numerical statements.[14] But even without a presentation of any further applications we can see that the importance Peirce associated with his "first real discovery" is fully justified.

In view of the importance of the Peircean distinction, illustrated by these applications, why was it neglected so completely for so long? An important part of the answer is that Peirce's distinction was based on ideas which were by-passed by the mainstream of modern logic during the whole crucial period from Frege to Herbrand or perhaps even to Beth and Hintikka.[15] Peirce's distinction depends on recognizing certain *iconic* elements in our logical symbolism and logical inferences, to use Peirce's own term. (By an iconic sign, he means, roughly, a non-symbolic picture-like sign, a sign that refers to its significandum virtue of qualities it shares with the entity signified, e.g., in virtue of the structure which they share.) In contrast, the emphasis in modern

logic was for a long time on its symbolic, non-iconic character. This is witnes-
sed not only by Hilbert's formalism but also by Frege, who consistently
denied the role of what he called "intuitions" (*Anschauungen*) and what
Peirce would have called iconic signs in logic and arithmetic. For instance we
read in *Grundlagen*, §60:

> Time and again we are led by our thought beyond the scope of our imagination,
> without thereby forfeiting the support we need for our inferences.

And even when the iconic elements were occasionally emphasized, the
emphasis was almost always on the pictorial qualities of individual sentences
or sets of sentences, not on the iconic aspects of logical inferences. For instance, Wittgenstein's famous picture theory of language is quite wrongly
so-called. Its pictorial element is restricted to atomic propositions only.
Truth-functional operations were never really absorbed into Wittgenstein's
picture theory, which hence is at best a picture theory of atomic sentences,
nor were logical inferences.

Likewise, whatever iconic elements there are revealed in contemporary
model theory (logical semantics) are restricted to what one can say of individual sentences. In general, model-theoretic considerations apparently
have nothing to contribute to our understanding of actual proof procedures.

In contrast to what we thus find in the onetime mainstream of symbolic
logic, Peirce himself stressed the iconic element in his actual work in logic.
His actual working methods involve prominently such iconic concepts as "existential graphs." We can now see that this emphasis on the iconic aspects of
logical inference was a necessary condition for Peirce's recognition of the
theorematic-corollarial distinction. Ironically, the same emphasis served to
alienate most of Peirce's contemporaries among logicians, with their
predilection for the purely symbolic aspects of modern "symbolic" logic,
from his insights.

It is not accidental that Peirce's distinction should have been
rediscovered by logicians who have independently been emphasizing the pictorial (model-theoretical) elements of logical inferences and other logical
operations. We can perhaps see a tradition here in modern logic different
from the symbolic, proof-theoretical tradition of Frege and Hilbert. An
ultimate vindication of the Peircean tradition would be a "model theory of
proof theory," that is, a systematic model-theoretic interpretation of the
basic proof-theoretic concepts and results. It seems to me that Rantala's urn
models have opened to us the possibility of developing such a theory.[16]

Jaakko Hintikka

The Florida State University

NOTES

*The writing of this paper was made possible by a Fellowship from John Simon Guggenheim Memorial Foundation for 1979–80. It was read at the Edgar Henderson Memorial Symposium on the Philosophy of Charles S. Peirce held at the Florida State University on May 17–18, 1980. An early version of my paper was presented also to the Florida Philosophical Association at its 1979 meeting in Gainesville, Florida. I have profited from the discussions which my paper prompted on those two occasions, especially from the comments by Jay Zeman in Gainesville. I have also enjoyed the stimulation of discussions with Merrill B. Hintikka and Risto Hilpinen while working on this paper.

1. My references to Peirce are all either to *The Collected Papers of Charles Sanders Peirce*, vols. 1–6, eds. Charles Hartshorne and Paul Weiss, vols. 7–8, ed. Arthur W. Burks (Cambridge, Mass.: Harvard University Press, 1931–1958) (in short, *Collected Papers*), or to Charles S. Peirce, *The New Elements of Mathematics*, ed. Carolyn Eisele, vols. 1–4 (The Hague: Mouton, 1976) (in short, Eisele).

2. Eisele, vol. 4, p. 49.

3. The distinction can in fact be extended in a most interesting way to certain types of nondeductive reasoning. Even though the generalization is not pointed out explicitly there, its possibility can be seen from my paper, "Sherlock Holmes Confronts Modern Logic," forthcoming in the proceedings of the 1978 Groningen meeting on the theory of argumentation. There is no trace of such a generalization in Peirce, however.

4. Jaakko Hintikka, *Logic, Language-Games, and Information: Kantian Themes in the Philosophy of Logic* (Oxford: Clarendon Press, 1973). (See especially pp. 136–43 and 173–78.)

5. See W. V. Quine, *Mathematical Logic* (rev. ed., Cambridge, Mass.: Harvard University Press, 1961).

6. Cf. Jaakko Hintikka and Unto Remes, *The Method of Analysis* (Dordrecht and Boston: D. Reidel, 1974), especially chs. 5–6.

7. See e.g., Dag Prawitz, *Natural Deduction: A Proof-Theretical Study*, Stockholm Studies in Philosophy, vol. 3, (Stockholm: Almqvist & Wiksell, 1965).

8. Veikko Rantala, "Urn Models: A New Kind of Non-Standard Model for First-Order Logic," *The Journal of Philosophical Logic*, vol. 4, no. 4 (1975): 455–74.

9. See note 4 above.

10. See my paper, "Aristotle's Incontinent Logician," *Ajatus*, vol. 37 (1978): 48–65.

11. See note 8 above.

12. Jaakko Hintikka, "Impossible Possible Worlds Vindicated," *The Journal of Philosophical Logic*, vol. 4, no. 4 (1975): 475–84.

13. See note 4 above.

14. See Erik Stenius, "Are True Numerical Statements Analytic or Synthetic?," *The Philosophical Review*, vol. 74 (1965): 357–72. For Peirce, see his frequent references to observation in connection with theorematic reasoning, for instance in *Collected Papers* 2.267 and 4.233.

15. See. E. W. Beth, "Semantic Entailment and Formal Derivability," *Mededelingen der oninklijke Nederlandse Akademie van Wetenschappen, Afd. Letterkunde*, M. R. 18, no. 13 (1955): 309–42, reprinted in *Philosophy of*

Mathematics, ed. Jaakko Hintikka (London: Oxford University Press, 1970), pp. 9–41; Jaakko Hintikka, "Form and Content in Quantification Theory," *Acta Philosophica Fennica*, vol. 8 (1955): 11–55.

　16. See note 8 above.

PEIRCE AND THE INCOMMENSURABILITY OF THEORIES

1. Introduction: The Problem of Incommensurability

Once upon a time a version of positivism prevailed in the philosophy of science. A key assumption made in positivism is that there is a class of observations—I will call them 'basic observations'—that are independent of theory. Basic observations are expressed in a non-theoretical or purely descriptive language: they refer to no postulated entities and presuppose no explanatory hypotheses or other logically contingent propositions. Theories, according to this philosophy, are admissable in science only if they are capable of yielding some implications about the basic observations that would be made under various conditions (where these conditions are also specified in the language of basic observation). Theories that provide entirely different accounts of the physical world can be compared by comparing their implications for basic observation. And they are tested by comparing these implications to the basic observations that are actually made. As a general rule, if one theory is replaced by another, then all basic observations that confirmed the first must also confirm the second, but not conversely. Thus, despite revolutions even in our most fundamental theoretical conceptions, there is or can be a cumulative growth of our strictly empirical knowledge.

In the late 1950's and early 60's the assumption that there is a class of theory-independent observations was successfully attacked, particularly by Wilfrid Sellars, N. R. Hanson and P. K. Feyerabend.[1] According to these authors, all observations, or at least those of any relevance to scientific investigation, are already "laden" with theory. Each observation refers to and describes entities postulated in one or more theories. Observation requires sensory stimulation, but what one reports on the occasion of given stimuli will depend upon the theories or general beliefs about the world that he holds. There is no direct reporting of the stimuli themselves; their existence, too, is postulated (i.e., in theories that seek to explain perception). Nor is there any direct observation of sensory images or feelings; or, if there is, that is something we learn to do only after we have learned how to describe what we take to be physical realities. Thus, observations must be rejected if and when the theories they presuppose turn out to be false.

Of course, most observations, and even many of those made in scientific investigations, are independent of all *scientific* theory. But the "conceptual framework" provided by common sense, no matter how naturally and unselfconsciously it was developed, is a theory in several important respects. First, ordinary concepts of things, their properties, potentialities, and relations, etc. form a network or system: they cannot be understood in separation from one another. Second, common sense includes many very general yet logically contingent propositions, such as that our eyes, ears, and so on are affected in various more-or-less regular ways by processes taking place outside of our bodies. Third, in employing common sense concepts in observation we assume some or all of the contingent propositions just mentioned. Hence, if those propositions should turn out to be false, then the ordinary observations presupposing them must be rejected. In fact, Feyerabend has argued that common sense is inconsistent with the theories of modern science and has been refuted by critical comparison to them. If we nevertheless continue to speak in ordinary ways, it is with the realization that what we say we see— e.g., the sun rising—is not exactly what we say it is.

It would seem to follow, and many have in fact drawn this conclusion, that there can be no cumulative growth in our empirical knowledge; for even our most fundamental theories are subject to refutation and replacement, and with their rejection we lose all the seeming observations they had made possible. Further, there is now an obvious problem about how theories are to be tested. For, even if some theories can be tested against observations made possible by more fundamental theories, against what observations will the most fundamental theories be tested? Feyerabend suggests that in order to avoid dogmatism we must develop alternative fundamental theories, thereby enlarging the stock of potential observations against which they can all be tested.[2] However, since each of these theories, save at most one, must be false, it is difficult to see how the "observations" they make possible provide any genuine test.

And then there is the problem of incommensurability. Two theories developed in the framework of the same more fundamental theory might share some of the same concepts, even if they are rivals. For example, "mass" seems to be used in the same sense in the caloric and the kinetic theories of heat, since each of these theories are, or were originally, formulated in the context of Newtonian mechanics. But in the case of fundamental theories, every term appears to be definable only in relation to other terms of the same theory; for there is no deeper theory nor any theory-neutral body of data in relation to which the meanings of these terms might be fixed. Thus, even if the same term occurs in different fundamental theories, e.g., "mass" in Newtonian mechanics and in relativity theory, it will not be with exactly the same meaning. But, if so, then the assertions of one fundamental theory cannot be expressed nor, hence, denied in the language of an opposing theory. And since there is no observation language neutral between and common to alternative fundamental theories, there is no possibility of specifying, in a language acceptable to both points of view, the subject about which they are supposed to disagree. Each fundamental theory will posit its own ontology or world. But if we cannot give body to the claim that alternative fundamental theories are theories about the same thing, and if there is no language in which contradictions between these theories can be expressed, then we must relinquish the claim that they are alternatives. Some authors have considered this to be a *reductio ad absurdum* of the train of thought I have just sketched.[3]

Curiously, the contemporary rejection of positivism was anticipated over 100 years ago by C. S. Peirce. On Peirce's view, as on that of Sellars, Hanson, and Feyerabend, we can observe only that of which we have some conception, and the concepts we employ in the observations relevant to science are of postulated entities. For *what* we observe or think we observe is the postulated entity, though the observation is occasioned by sensation and informed by theory. Therefore, the observation is mediated by sensation and by theory, though of neither of these are we particularly, if at all, aware. Were we aware of the sensation and aware of it antecedently to our observation of the postulated entity, we could analyze the observation as a conjecture (an "abductive inference") that seeks to explain the sensation by postulating some physical cause of it. For that is in effect what the observation does do. But since observation, or, in Peirce's terms, the perceptual judgment, is the *first* judgment we form (in any inferential chain), it is not under our control and is not an inference nor a deliberate conjecture. Peirce once described it as "the extreme case" of abductive inference (5.181).[4] Therefore, though informed by the concepts and associated beliefs we already hold, the perceptual judgment is uncontrolled and, in that sense, indubitable: it is what we are *at the time* incapable of doubting. Nevertheless, precisely because it is mediated by beliefs that might be false—precisely because it is in some sense conjectural—every perceptual judgment or observation is fallible; it is conceivable that on some *future* occasion we will find reason to doubt it.[5]

In a series of three papers published in 1868, Peirce denied, not only the doctrine of direct or infallible observation, but *every* form of what he called "intuitive cognition"—that is, every form of direct and infallible knowing. Thus, there is for Peirce no infallible knowledge of values, of aims, or of the methods appropriate to achieving our aims. Our beliefs about what is valuable, about what we are really groping toward, and about the methods proper to our search are all conjectural and subject to revision in the light of experience. This leads us to a second major source of theoretical incommensurability—one that I have not yet mentioned. T. S. Kuhn, largely on the basis of historical examples, has suggested very powerfully that when there are fundamental changes in theory these are also changes in techniques of investigation, in the *kinds* of explanation or theory sought, in the criteria of success, and so on.[6] In short, it appears that not even the aims and methods of inquiry have been fixed once and for all from the beginning. Nor could they have been if Peirce is right that there is no intuitive cognition either of an empirical or of a rational kind, whether of facts or of values and methods. But if fundamental differences in theory involve differences also in aim and method, that will throw another difficulty in the way of comparing theories. And not only that, but it will also raise another doubt about whether the critical comparison of theories can be objective.

Peirce, however, continued to conceive of science as an objective and progressive inquiry. Denial of all forms of intuitive cognition and affirmation of the objectivity of inquiry remained twin themes in Peirce's philosophy for nearly fifty years. It would seem, therefore, that Peirce must have shown how alternative theories can be compared and objectively (if not conclusively) tested. Such an account, so far as he developed it, is to be found primarily in Peirce's theory of critical common-sensism. But in fact Peirce never did develop this theory in great detail. Nor, needless to say, did he present it as resolving exactly those issues which the writings of Feyerabend and Kuhn made notorious a half-century after Peirce's death. Therefore, to see how the problems of incommensurability are avoided or solved in Peirce's philosophy, we must go beyond exegesis. In what follows I shall try to show how Peirce's philosophy can be used to solve these problems, without our having to turn back down the straight and narrow but empty road of positivism.

2. Vagueness and Hypostatic Abstraction: How Theories are Compared

Opposing theories, even if they are not fundamental, are often incommensurable in this sense: they introduce or at least employ different concepts and, hence, not all the assertions made in the one will be expressible in the language of the other. But it does not follow from this alone that opposing theories—even those that are fundamental—are incommensurable in the sense that the subject of dispute cannot be identified in a manner that is acceptable from both points of view. This idea is nevertheless resisted by philosophers for a powerful reason: it does not seem possible for two persons to share a concept of x and yet to entertain other concepts of x which differ so radically from one another as to place x in entirely different categories. If one person thinks of heat as a substance (caloric) and another thinks of it as the kinetic energy of molecules, how could they share any concept of heat specific enough to distinguish it from everything else? For nothing could be both a substance and a quantity of motion, and it is hard to think of any identifying description that would be neutral between these two categories.[7]

I suggest that it is the ordinary conception of heat which plays this role, and that, in general, the initial subjects of inquiry are those apprehended by common sense. (Further subjects are introduced in the course of inquiry; e.g., theoriests can debate the nature of genes, which they agree in conceiving of as the bearers of hereditary characteristics.) But the existence of such a neutral conception seems to be rejected with the rejection of the positivist assumption of theory-independent observation. If common sense concepts already belong to the level of explanation, then how could they be compatible with each of two opposing explanations of the same thing? Thus we find Feyerabend claiming that common sense has been refuted by modern science.

Peirce, however, held that the trouble with common sense is not that it is false but that it is vague. "No words are so well understood as vernacular words, in one way; yet they are invariably vague . . . ." (6.494). The concepts which these words express import their vagueness to the common sense beliefs in which they occur. These beliefs, which are "of the general nature of instincts" (5.445), being founded "on the totality of everyday experience of many generations of multitudinous populations" (5.522), are consequently "more trustworthy than the best established results of science" (6.496) and change little from generation to generation (5.444; cf. 5.509). Indeed, they are indubitable in the sense that we cannot doubt, criticize, or control them, at least for some time, though they are fallible in the sense that it is conceivable that further experience could falsify them (5.440–442, 445, 451). And their indubitability is due in part to their vagueness: "By all odds, the most distinctive character of the Critical Common-sensist, in contrast to the old Scotch philosopher, lies in his insistence that the acritically indubitable is invariably vague" (5.446). "It is easy to speak with precision on a general theme. Only, one must surrender all ambition to be certain. It is equally easy to be certain. One has only to be sufficiently vague" (42.37). But no belief is perfectly vague, and so we find that common sense beliefs can be relied upon only in relation to the kind of experience on the basis of which they were formed: ". . . one thing the Scotch failed to recognize is that the original beliefs only remain indubitable in their application to affairs that resemble those of a primitive mode of life" (5.445). Thus, however secure, common sense fails to satisfy scientific curiosity: the experience on which common sense rests is "worthless for distinctively scientific purposes, because it does not make the minute distinctions with which science is chiefly concerned; nor does it relate to the recondite subjects of science . . . ." (5.522). Nevertheless, unsatisfactory as vague beliefs are, ". . . all science without being aware of it, virtually supposes the truth of the vague results of uncontrolled thought upon such experiences [i.e., the ordinary sort just referred to], cannot help doing so, and would have to shut up shop if she could manage to escape accepting them" (5.522). In the next section we will consider the role in the development and test of theories that Peirce accorded to common sense. For our present purpose it is necessary to obtain a more exact understanding of what Peirce meant by "vague."

In ordinary usage the word 'vague' has several senses. In one sense, the vagueness of a concept consists in its having fuzzy borders, as when there exists a borderline case to which the concept neither clearly applies nor clearly fails to apply or when there is no sharp line where an instance to which the concept does apply (e.g., a mountain) ends and something else (a valley) begins. This type of vagueness has monopolized the attention of analytic philosophers for fifty years.[8] Peirce draws our attention to an entirely different type of vagueness:

> A subject is *determinate* in respect to any character which inheres in it or is (universally and affirmatively) predicated of it, as well as in respect to the negative of such character . . . In all other respects it is indeterminate . . . . A sign that is objectively *indeterminate* in any respect is objectively *vague* in so far as it reserves further determination to be made in some other conceivable sign . . . Example: "A man I could mention seems to be a little conceited." (5.447)

At 5.505 Peirce gave the same definition, but in place of "conceivable sign" wrote "further sign or experience." Applying this general definition to theories we obtain this result: a theory is vague in Peirce's sense if and only if it implies that there is *some* more detailed (precise, informative, specific) account of exactly the same things but does not imply what this account would be. Thus, if I maintain the view that the American robin forms a species, then, given our concept of a zoological species, I imply that there is some true account of the anatomy common to all robins, of their common phylogenetic history, etc. (It does not follow that I or anyone else can provide this account now.) But no one such account is implied in my belief and, therefore, that belief is vague.

Similarly, to conceive of robins simply as a species of red-breasted, dark-backed birds is to have a vague conception of them. For if they really do form a species, then there are more specific concepts (e.g., which specify the anatomy and phylogeny of robins) that could be found which would apply to exactly the same individuals. More precisely: a concept is vague in this sense if and only if it is logically necessary that, if the concept is true (i.e., predicable with truth) of anything at all, then there is some more detailed (precise, informative, specific) concept that would be true of exactly the same things.

More than one relatively specific theory or concept might be suggested as an improvement on a vague theory or concept. Each of these will be introduced in the belief or hope that they hold true of the same thing or things the vaguer theory or concept is presumed to be true of. But not all of these more specific variants will be mutually compatible. Those that are not, are rival theories or concepts of that of which the vaguer theory or concept is presumed to be true. We might differ in the precise biological definitions we propose for a species and yet agree that it is *the* (presumed) species consisting of the red-breasted, dark-backed birds called 'robins' which is at issue.

Introducing the notion of a species of bird on the basis of a perceived coincidence of similarities among certain birds, is an example of what Peirce calls "hypostatic abstraction."[9] In a hypostatic abstraction an entity not hitherto contemplated is postulated, and it is identified only by its presumed relation to something else with which we are already familiar. In the robin example, a species is postulated which would explain the similarity of those birds called "robins." If we conceive of heat as *that which* explains certain phenomena, such as sensations of warmth, expansion and contraction, etc., or as *that which* flows from what we call "hot" to what we call "cold," then that concept is formed by hypostatic abstraction. And in one of his papers on critical common-sensism, Peirce wrote as follows of the introduction of a "dormitive virtue" to explain the tendency of people who take opium to fall asleep: ". . . this operation of hypostatic abstraction is not utterly futile. For it does say that there is *some* peculiarity in the opium to which the sleep must be due . . . ." (5.534).

Notice that a concept introduced by hypostatic abstraction can have no possible application unless a certain corresponding assumption is true. The idea of opium's dormitive virtue applies to nothing if there is not something in opium that accounts for the sleepiness of opium takers. But if the corresponding assumption is true, then the idea introduced by hypostatic abstraction must apply to something. And all that to which it applies will be of the same nature; for that is part of what is assumed. Thus, if there is a dormitive virtue in opium, then it is basically the same in all instances of opium. But a concept formed by such an hypostatic abstraction does not specify the nature of its presumed object. It follows that if a concept is formed by this type of hypostatic abstraction, then there must be more specific concepts that would apply to all that it applies to, if it applies to anything at all. Therefore, concepts formed by such hypostatic abstractions are necessarily vague. I suggest that there is no concept that is vague, in Peirce's sense of that term, that does not involve hypostatic abstraction.

Hypostatic abstraction may seem to presuppose a prior, independent description of the phenomena from which abstraction is made. But in fact even our most primitive descriptive concepts involve hypostatic abstractions, though of an implicit, pre-conscious sort. Peirce pointed out that a visual image or other "percept" "is the product of mental processes, or at all events of processes for all intents and purposes mental, except that we are not aware of them . . ." (7.624). For a percept is not a mere sensation or sense datum: it is a three dimensional complex of objects, their qualities, etc. that one's nervous system constructs out of the stimuli it receives. And even this is not yet an observation or perceptual judgment: the latter is a description and, hence, analysis of the percept (7.626), which, therefore, introduces an element of generality (5.150–157, 7.630–633), thus permitting deductions of universal propositions (5.181), including those that will ground predictions (7.644). And that is how perceptual judgments are open to correction by subsequent perceptual judgments.

Thus, even our first judgments—those which cannot be derived from any awareness of antecedent data—are conjectural in nature (5.181, 7.646—647). From the fact that perceptual judgments are open to subsequent correction, it is clear that they do not profess to describe only what is immediately before one's eyes (whatever that would mean). Take an extreme example. If others insist that it is green, then I will begin to doubt whether what I thought was red really is red. Implicitly, then, we think of something's being red as being *such* as to make observers of its color judge that it is red. Our ordinary concept of redness (i.e., a property ascribable to physical objects) is that of an explanatory principle, but it is an extremely vague concept of that principle. We know only that there is *something* about red objects that accounts for our ability to agree about which objects *are* red.

And in general, what we ordinarily observe we conceive of as being such as to explain not only our observation of it but also the agreement of other observations with that observation. Since these concepts contain no or few specifics about the presumed explanatory entities, they are all vague. Thus it is that ordinary language, and the common sense assumptions made in speaking it, impel inquiry, since the vagueness of our ideas leads some of us to seek more detailed and precise knowledge. But these concepts also provide identification of the initial subjects of inquiry (further subjects will be postulated as inquiry advances). For vagueness, as Peirce pointed out (5.505, 5.447), is not the same as generality. A vague (or hypostatically abstractive) concept identifies its object indirectly, in terms of its presumed causal (or other) relation to something else. Hence, it can identify its object narrowly while still leaving its nature largely unspecified. That is why, if we agree in conceiving of heat, for example, as *that which* causes such and so phenomena, we can go on to conceive of heat more specifically in such different ways as even to place it in different ontological categories. Our most primitive descriptive concepts provide a means of identifying the subjects common to rival theories, not because these concepts are phenomenalistic, but because they are explanatory as well as descriptive, only very vaguely so.

3. Peirce's Realism: How Theories Are Tested

We have noted that every hypostatic abstraction introduces an assumption. In cases germane to inquiry in the natural sciences, these assumptions are of a causal or explanatory nature. It is logically possible for them to be false, and if they are, then the concepts that presuppose them cannot apply to anything. In this sense, these concepts are theory-laden. Since our most primitive descriptive concepts are hypostatically abstractive, they, too, are theory-laden; but the theory with which they are laden is the very vague one that we call "common sense." Since it is logically possible for common sense to be mistaken, it is necessary for us to consider how observations that presuppose common sense beliefs may nevertheless be relied upon in the test of the more specific, deliberately constructed theories that we call "scientific."

Peirce, as we have seen, held that the vague beliefs of common sense have been confirmed by an overwhelming amount of "everyday" experience. But this experience is in the form of perceptual judgments which in fact presuppose the truth of common sense beliefs. How is it possible for judgments to confirm that which they also presuppose? So far as I know, Peirce did not answer this question; yet the answer is not hard to find once we look for it.

Consider an example. The ordinary person conceives of weight as that which is felt in hefting an object, as that which is relatively greater or lesser in different objects (as may be determined by balancing the two), and as that which may be measured by the degree to which an object depresses a spring scale. In this it is assumed that what is felt to have weight by one person will be felt to have weight by another, that if x is shown to be much heavier than y by balancing them, then the measurable weight of x will be greater than that of y, and so on. Now these propositions can be tested—and can only be tested—in making the very observations that presuppose their truth. Thus, if what felt heavy to one person regularly failed to have any perceivable weight to others, or if observations and measurements made by balancing and by spring scales ceased any longer to agree, then we would begin to doubt our common sense assumptions about weight. And although in that case we could no longer claim that our observations are observations of any such quantity as weight, still, their failure to agree will stand as evidence against common sense. Conversely, it is just because our observations of weight do so largely agree (especially when apparent exceptions yield to explanation), that we are so entirely and justifiably confident that there is such a thing as weight which is detected and measured in just these ways. Common sense, then, has been highly confirmed by the observations which it itself makes possible.

Common sense is not only highly confirmed, it is, Peirce said (*vide supra*), more certain, because vaguer, than scientific theories. But he must have meant this only with respect to that body of evidence—familiar experience—which confirms common sense. For this experience also confirms scientific theories, since they presuppose the truth of common sense beliefs. Yet it confirms them only to a very low degree, since they go so far beyond common sense and familiar experience. The observations which presuppose common sense only are, then, quite secure relatively to scientific theories (at least initially).

Now, although scientific theories imply more than common sense does about what would be observed under certain, perhaps unusual, conditions, many of these implications pertain to ordinary sorts of observation. For example, while the Aristotelians and Galileo conceived of the phenomenon of falling in mutually inconsistent ways, each supposed that his concept applied to what is ordinarily called "falling." Hence, what either theory implies about falling, as falling is conceived of in that theory, it also implies about falling, as falling is more vaguely conceived of in ordinary life. From the Aristotelian theory it follows that an object dropped from the top of a mast of a moving ship would strike the deck some distance behind the mast, while from the Galilean theory it follows that the object would fall at the foot of the mast; but in either case what actually happens can be observed in quite ordinary terms, without having to suppose either theory. Therefore, at least some scientific theories can be tested against observations that are laden only with the theory called "common sense." And common sense, as we have seen, is highly confirmed and relatively more certain than the theory at issue. Hence, these observations provide good (though not conclusive) evidence for or against the theories tested. Other, more advanced scientific theories, e.g., different theories about atomic structure, will in a similar way presuppose less sophisticated but better confirmed theories, e.g., the atomic theory of chemical combination. And in terms of the latter there can be observations confirming or disconfirming the former. In conclusion, while there are no observations that are not theory-laden, there are no theories that cannot be tested against observations.

Because they imply so much more, the more specific theories of science are in the long run more highly testable than the vaguer beliefs of common sense. Yet, progress in inquiry is itself further confirmation of common sense. For the vague belief that there is something that explains an agreement that exists among observations of a given type will be confirmed by the progress that is made in developing a more specific explanation of that phenomenon. Now, as is well known, Peirce identified reality with that which would be represented in the final opinion, if any, toward which inquiry is tending. But this reality is not a mere creation of inquiry; it is not itself the final opinion. And it is not a mere phenomenal unity. Instead, it is that which, by existing independently of inquiry but exerting an influence (through observation) on inquirers, explains the progress of inquiry toward its own representation. Hence, it is not necessary that inquiry actually arrive at a final opinion in order for there to be a reality; yet the common sense assumption that there is a reality remains an hypothesis which is partially confirmed or partially disconfirmed by the apparent progress or apparent lack of progress, respectively, of inquiry itself.

4. Peirce's Archetectonic: The Discovery of Methods and of Aims

The concept of final causation is central to Peirce's entire philosophy, but his most careful discussions of it occur in his classification of the sciences.[10] Peirce refers to this classification as an archetectonic which, while it is to organize work yet to be done, must grow out of actual inquiry as it has so far developed (1.179, 180, 203, 226–227). Therefore, this classification must be real or natural rather than conventional (1.204); that is, the organization of the sciences must not be imposed on it by any arbitrary will, but must be that organization to which inquiry itself seems naturally to tend. A real or natural class is one "of which the members owe their existence as members . . . to a common final cause" (1.204; cf. 1.211, 213–214, 220). "All natural classification is then, essentially, we may almost say, an attempt to find out the true genesis of the objects classified. . . . A science is defined by its problem; and its problem is clearly formulated on the basis of an abstracter [vaguer?] science" (1.227).

Organizing inquiry requires determining methods and goals. Peirce's teleological view of their determination is the only possible way to maintain the claim that methods and goals are objective, while denying that we have any intuitive cognition of them. The real aims of inquiry, and its proper methods, are those to which continued inquiry would eventually lead us; hence, on the basis of the history of inquiry to date, we can only form tentative but nevertheless guiding hypotheses about what these aims and methods are. Consider, for example, the transition from Aristotelian to modern physics or from purely taxonomic to evolutionary biology. In both cases the new forms of explanation proved, first, to work, and, second, to satisfy our curiosity better than did the older forms of explanation. We *discovered* that the vague goal of knowledge, explanation, or understanding more specifically includes, in physics, quantitative theories having predictive power and, in biology, genetic accounts. (Of course, what would better satisfy our desire to comprehend the world need not always turn out also to be possible; the determinist ideal in Newtonian physics might be an example of this.) The point is that *after* a few individuals of genius and daring developed these new forms of explanation—and did so without any prior guarantee that they would succeed—*then* the community of inquirers in general could see not only that explanations of these types are possible but also that they satisfy our intellectual desires better than could any explanation of the preceding types.

Whether there is any ultimate, single, coherent set of aims and methods that are objectively *the* aims and methods of disinterested inquiry must remain an hypothesis, just as there being a reality independent of inquiry remains an hypothesis. But in the one case as in the other, the progress of inquiry, or its lack of progress, is the test of the hypothesis. In fact, the history of science exhibits many apparently irreversible developments in aim and method. And, subsequently, it has been understood how these developments satisfy our vague desire to know better than did earlier forms of science. Therefore, we have some reason to suppose that the forms inquiry takes are not wholly arbitrary.

The two metascientific (or, if you will, metaphysical) hypotheses referred to here are mutually dependent. For we cannot properly define reality to be the object represented in a supposed final opinion, if the methods and aims of inquiry are themselves endlessly subject to personal whim or historical accident. Conversely, no methods or aims will prove satisfactory, unless there is an "external permanency" (as Peirce once called it) which answers to those methods and enables us, by their means, to fulfill those aims.

T. L. Short

Kenyon College

NOTES

1. Wilfrid Sellars, "Empiricism and the Philosophy of Mind," in Feigl and Scriven, eds., *Minnesota Studies in the Philosophy of Science*, vol. I (Minneapolis: Minnesota Univ. Press, 1956). N.R. Hanson, *Patterns of Discovery* (Cambridge: Cambridge Univ. Press, 1958). P.K. Feyerabend, "An Attempt at a Realistic Interpretation of Experience," *Proceedings of the Aristotelian Society*, N.S. 58, (1958); "Explanation, Reduction, and Empiricism," in Feigl and Maxwell, eds., *Minnesota Studies in the Philosophy of Science*, vol. III, (Minneapolis: Minnesota Univ. Press, 1962); and many related articles in succeeding years.
2. Feyerabend, "How to Be a Good Empiricist—A Pleas for Tolerance in Matters Epistemological," in Baumrin, ed., *Philosophy of Science: the Delaware Seminar*, vol. II (New York: Interscience, 1963).
3. Peter Achinstein, "On the Meaning of Scientific Terms," *Journal of Philosophy*, 61 (1964): 475–510. Dudley Shapere, "Meaning and Scientific Change," in Colodny, ed., *Mind and Cosmos: Explorations in the Philosophy of Science* (Pittsburg: Univ. of Pittsburgh Press, 1966).
4. In the usual fashion, references of the form *m.n* are to paragraph *n* of volume *m* of the *Collected Papers of Charles Sanders Peirce*, Hartshorne, Weiss and Burks, eds. (Cambridge, MA: Harvard Univ. Press, 1931–1958).
5. Documentation for this account of Peirce's view may be found below, in the penultimate and preceding paragraphs of Section 2. See also Richard Bernstein,

"Peirce's Theory of Perception," in Moore and Robin, eds., *Studies in the Philosophy of Charles Sanders Peirce*, 2nd Series (Amherst: Univ. of Massachusetts Press, 1964).

6. Thomas S. Kuhn, *The Structure of Scientific Revolutions* (Chicago: Univ. of Chicago Press, 1962 [revised ed. 1970]).

7. Recently, some authors, notably Hilary Putnam, have argued that mutually incompatible concepts may *refer* to the same things and, therefore, that it is not necessary for opposing theorists to share any concept of the disputed subject. I attempt to show that this view is inadequate, and I develop some of the ideas presented in this section in more detail, in "An Analysis of Conceptual Change," forthcoming in the *American Philosophical Quarterly*, October 1980.

8. That is, ever since articles on vagueness published by Bertrand Russell and Max Black in 1923 and 1932 respectively. Their attention to but one kind of vagueness (among the several that may be found in the O.E.D. entry for 'vague') still determines the pattern today: see e.g., § 23, "Vagueness," in W.V.O. Quine, *Word and Object* (Cambridge, MA: The M.I.T. Press, 1960). Peirce took account of this variety of vagueness also; for both, see Jarrett Brock, "Principle Themes in Peirce's Logic of Vagueness," *Peirce Studies*, vol I, 1979. .

9. Peirce discusses hypostatic abstraction in several places, but usually in relation to mathematical thinking or to explain that kind of reflection on one's own thought which the highest type of self-control requires. See especially 4.235 and 5.534. These other types of hypostatic abstraction do not have all the characteristics which, in the text, I attribute to those hypostatic abstractions that are formed in physical inquiry.

10. See also my "Peirce's Concept of Final Causation," forthcoming in *The Transactions of the Charles S. Peirce Society*.

ABDUCTION AND THE NEW RIDDLE OF INDUCTION

Although the relevance and importance of his work has been recognized only belatedly, Charles Sanders Peirce was, throughout his life, a careful student and significant contributor to the development of logic, scientific theory, and philosophy generally. Occasionally, complete appreciation of Peirce's efforts has been hampered because his work is often unique and, at times, highly idiosyncratic. Yet, we hope to show in this paper that for one aspect of his work in logic Peirce did not abandon the ordinary without purpose. Only relatively recently have philosophers of science become interested in the logic of discovery—that is, in the logic of the *selection* of hypotheses to be tested rather than simply in the ways of testing hypotheses which have already been selected.

We intend to show that there are logical problems in the selection of hypotheses, that Peirce was very clear-headed about what these problems are, and that he provided us with some of the best suggestions yet available on how to deal with these problems.

It is well known that Peirce eschews the traditional division of inference into deductive and inductive. Instead, he divides all inference into explicative and ampliative. While the former is simply equivalent to deduction, he subdivides the latter into abduction (also called hypothesis, retroduction, and presumption) and induction, giving three kinds of inference in all. Peirce's view of deduction is traditional in that it includes mathematics and formal logic;[1] however, in the case of *abduction*, Peirce singles out as an independent form of inference the formulation of hypotheses for inductive testing. All this is well known, but, we fear, too much ignored outside the constricted space of Peirce scholarship. Unfortunately, the notion of abductive inference, which is peculiarly Peirce's, has not exerted an influence proportionate to the significance of its insight.

Peirce, however, leaves no doubt about what he thinks of the importance of his distinction. He writes,

> Nothing has so much contributed to present chaotic or erroneous ideas in the logic of science as failure to distinguish the essentially different characters of different elements of scientific reasoning; and one of the worst of these confusions, as well as one of the commonest, consists in regarding abduction and induction taken together . . . as a simple argument (7.218).

Nevertheless, most current discussions of the problem of induction proceed without reference to Peirce's critical distinction—all to their loss, we believe.

We hope to take a small step toward rectifying this state of affairs by demonstrating the relevance of Peirce's analysis of inference to a significant problem in contemporary philosophy of science—specifically, to Nelson Goodman's "new riddle of induction." However, before proceeding to the central part of our discussion, a brief summary of the relevant features of Peirce's analysis of inference may prove helpful.

I

Unlike many philosophers of science, Peirce was a scientist by training and vocation. Perhaps, for this reason his investigations often take a broader, less rarefied view of the actual processes of scientific inquiry. While not simply formal, Peirce's analysis is grounded in general considerations of epistemology—especially in a prior analysis of the role of belief and doubt in the reasoning process. In fact, Peirce defines inference as "the process by which one belief determines another." "A belief," he continues, "is itself a habit of mind by virtue of which one idea gives rise to another" (7.354). A habit is a general rule or disposition; therefore, not only is a belief a certain disposition; but beliefs can also be determined by a general rule or habit (*CP*, 5.411). Peirce designates those general rules which determine inferences "leading" or "guiding" principles. Critical logic is largely an examination of these principles.

Belief, which plays a crucial role in his theory of inference, has, Peirce observes, the important property that it appeases doubt relative to the same matter. While the fact that feelings and states of mind are not necessary to the analysis of belief, it does suggest that what is necessary and distinctive is that belief leads to action given the appropriate circumstances, while doubt inhibits it (2.242). This suggests that the logical relationships of belief and doubt are the important aspects for Peirce.

Doubt exists only relative to belief. The source of doubt for Peirce is surprise (5.512, 5.543). Generally, however, Peirce reduces doubt to an awareness of any inconsistency in one's beliefs. Inconsistencies are characterized by the following logical conditions of doubting: A person A doubts p (a proposition expressing a belief) if, and only if, A is led to believe p and some other proposition q and A is aware of an inconsistency between p and q.[2] That is, that taken with the set of one's other beliefs such inconsistencies would lead to contradictory expectations or anticipated actions. Hence doubt exists only if there is belief.

"Logic," Peirce writes, is "the theory of the conditions which determine reasonings to be secure" (2.1). Inferences "fix belief" in that their conclusions are secure against doubt. As already observed, Peirce distinguishes three varieties of inference—deduction, abduction and induction. Let us now consider in detail the latter two sorts.

Abduction is the process of initially setting up or entertaining a hypothesis likely in itself (7.202). The form of an abductive inference is as follows: "The surprising fact, C, is observed; but if A were true, C would be a matter of course. Hence, there is reason to suspect A is true" (5.189, also cf. 2.624). Abductions carry no guarantee of their truth; they must be tested before anyone is justified in accepting them. Except for two considerations, they should hardly seem to deserve the name "inference."

Most relevant to our present purpose, Peirce holds that there is an *icon relationship* between the facts of the hypothesis and the facts observed. He cites as an example the likeness between the hypothesis of an elliptical orbit and the data about Mars which led Kepler to adopt the elliptical orbit in his theory of planetary motion. Peirce writes that "Presumption (i.e., abduction) is the only kind of reasoning which supplies new ideas" (2.777). Not only then is abduction fundamental to any increase in our knowledge, but it also has definite relational structures and leading principles which can be treated by critical logic.[3]

The third type of inference which Peirce identifies is induction. He holds that induction is nothing more than the testing of a hypothesis or theory by checking the occurence of lack thereof of a prediction deduced from it.[4] Although Peirce claims that conflating abduction and induction is the greatest source of confusion in science (7.218), neither he nor his commentators are completely free of this confusion themselves (e.g., cf. 2.759 and 5.170). The reason is not difficult to find.

The process, at first glance, is straightforward enough. An *abduction* yields a hypothesis; various consequences are derived from it by deduction; and these expected consequences are tested through *induction*. The three types of inference are most easily confused when the hypothesis is contradicted by induction, but only small modifications in the hypothesis are required to adjust it to account for new evidence. Peirce clearly believes that this process of adjustment is abductive, although it is often mistaken for induction (7.114). In scientific inquiry, the three types of inference are closely integrated (though distinct nonetheless) into one unified process. It is, therefore, understandable if occasionally the two are confused, especially when the question is not simply the validity of each type of inference, but rather the justification of the whole of scientific inquiry.

As an inference, induction has the psychological effect of fixing belief in a certain hypothesis. It becomes ever more difficult to doubt the truth of a hypothesis that is confirmed in ever more instances (2.96, 7.218). Logically, on the other hand, induction has a less powerful role. Every induction tests the conclusion of some abduction, and provides the grounds for supporting it. Because abduction suggests a hypothesis only in response to some surprising fact, there is, for any properly drawn hypothesis, already some positive support. The lack of any positive support, then, provides grounds *ipso facto* on which to doubt the hypothesis. Nevertheless, the role of induction is only to give an opportunity for nature to refute or falsify a hypothesis. No number of positive instances can demonstrably prove that a hypothesis is true (2.663).

II

Unfortunately, inference in scientific theory and ampliative inference generally have not often been discussed in Peirce's terms. The practice of treating all amplicative inferences as induction, which has dominated philosophical discussion of scientific theory to date, is particularly fraught with problems which, we suggest, Peirce's theory goes some way towards resolving.

The "traditional" problem of induction is usually described as the attempt to justify inferences concerning *un*observed events or phenomena on the basis of observed events or phenomena. What justification is there in inferring that what we have found to be true in observed cases will continue to be true in yet unobserved cases? This query is usually traced to David Hume and his claim that inductive reasoning cannot be justified. Various philosophers have tried to defend induction against Hume's skeptical attack; however, none of these attempts to defend induction has gained universal approval by the philosophical community, and the Humean stigma has remained with induction.

There, matters have stood until relatively recently when Nelson Goodman raised what he calls "the new riddle of induction."[5] Hume's analysis rules out certainty in ampliative inference and also any notions of truth or knowledge which require such certainty. Goodman expresses agreement with this consequence: "If the problem is to *find* some way of distinguishing antecedently between true and false predictions, we are asking for prevision rather than philosophical explanation" (*FFF*, p. 62). Hume was on the right tract but did not go far enough. He overlooked the fact, according to Goodman, that not *all* regularities produce beliefs or habits. For Hume, the problem of induction involved trying to justify how any set of observations *ever* justifies a claim about unobserved events. Goodman's new riddle of induction recasts the problem with the even more disturbing results that *every* claim about unobserved events based on *any* set of observations is *equally justified*.

Let us now examine Goodman's argument. The problem of "justification" for Goodman is really a problem of determining which inferences are valid and which ones are not. According to Goodman, a deductive argument is justified "by showing that it conforms to the general rules of deductive inference" (*FFF*, p. 63). Analogously, he suggests, the problem of justifying an inductive argument really amounts to showing that it conforms to the general rules of inductive inference (*FFF*, p. 63). The general rules, in turn, are "justified" because they yield "acceptable" inferences. The circularity, Goodman claims, is virtuous rather than vicious.

Such an approach dissolves Hume's way of putting the problem because we will no longer be concerned with attempting to answer such spurious questions as how a certain kind of knowledge is possible. The "new" problem becomes one of distinguishing between valid and invalid predictions and of *defining* the difference between them (*FFF*, p. 65). Such a task will amount to explicitly stating the principles and canons of induction which will define the confirmation relation in an analogous manner to the way in which the laws of deduction define the consequence relation (*FFF*, p. 67).

Goodman's argument is illustrated by his well known "grue paradox." Consider a new predicate, 'grue', which is defined as applying to "all things examined before [some specified time] t just in the case that they are green and to other things just in the case they are blue" (*FFF*, 74).[6] 'Green' and 'blue' are completely inter-definable with 'grue' and 'bleen' (blue before t or green thereafter). Thus, 'green' is whatever is grue before t and bleen afterwards (*FFF*, 79,80). The problem, says Goodman, is that if certain emeralds are examined before t they are both green and grue. Why should the hypothesis 'all emeralds are green' be chosen over the hypothesis 'all emeralds are grue'? Why should an emerald after t be expected to be green rather than grue (and, therefore, blue)? Both predications cannot be correct because they lead to contradictory expectations. The problem is why the one hypothesis is *lawlike* and the other not, or to put it in other terms, why the one is projectible and the other not.

The way out of the paradox according to Goodman is one of distinguishing "lawlike" hypotheses from others, because only "lawlike" hypothese are confirmed by their positive instances and hence justify projection. In order to define "lawlikeness" and resolve the "new riddle," Goodman offers the theory of entrenchment. He begins by defining *actual projection*. A hypothesis is actually projected if it is adopted after some of its instances have been determined true and the rest are yet to be determined (*FFF*, 87). Positive instances constitute the evidence class; undetermined instances, the projected class. A hypothesis with some positive instances is supported; with some negative instances violated; and with no undetermined instances, exhausted. Adoption of a hypothesis is actual projection when the hypothesis is supported, unviolated and unexhausted (*FFF*, 90).

On this account it is possible that two hypotheses could both be actually projected, conflicting in their prediction, but both supported and unviolated. For example, any evidence t which supports "all emeralds are green" also supports "all emeralds are grue." In order to decide between them, Goodman suggests that the one with the better entrenched predicates be projected. A predicate becomes better entrenched than another by having been used in the past in more actually projected hypotheses. Green is the "veteran" of many past projections and grue of very few, if any; hence, "all emeralds are green" should be projected (*FFF*, 95).

By its very nature, projection must be made without regard to the truth of the prediction. Goodman observes: "The criterion for the legitimacy of projection cannot be truth that is yet undetermined. Failure to recognize this was responsible . . . for some of the worst misconceptions of the problem of induction" (*FFF*, 99). The projected class consists of instances whose truth is undetermined, otherwise there would be no call for projection at all.

Entrenchment, then, is not a matter of truth, but of linguistic practice. Goodman writes: "The reason why only the right predicates happen so luckily to have become well entrenched is just that the well entrenched predicates have thereby become the right ones" (*FFF*, 98). His claim here only expresses one side of a circular notion. On the other side, if hypotheses using a particular predicate are continually violated, then that predicate loses entrenchment relative to others. So it is equally true that the right predicates (in the sense of those conforming to experience) become the entrenched ones or, at least, the wrong predicates do not become entrenched.

In posing his new riddle of induction, Goodman has conflated the two very distinct processes of scientific theory which Peirce was so intent upon distinguishing—namely, the formulation of hypotheses (i.e., abduction), and their testing (i.e., induction). We hope in the following section to demonstrate that Peirce's theory of inference anticipates Goodman's "new riddle," analyzes it more adequately, and resolves it more completely. We intend to show that the "new riddle of induction" is neither new nor a riddle of induction.

III

Considering Goodman's account of induction from Peirce's point of view, it seems obvious that Goodman confuses induction with abduction and also confuses the logical and psychological aspects of confirmation and testing. Nevertheless, there are points of contact between Goodman's and Peirce's accounts: Goodman's notion of projectibility involves the same problems as Peirce's account of abduction.

It is obvious that if Peirce's division of inference is accepted, the problem of selecting between competing hypotheses (e.g., the predication of 'green' or 'grue' to emeralds) or of projecting or not projecting a single hypothesis (e.g., "all men in this room are third sons") is a question of abduction—not of induction. Induction involves only the testing of hypotheses once projected, while abduction is the first setting up or entertaining of any hypothesis as likely in itself. Let us use Peirce's analysis of inference (especially of induction), to examine Goodman's theory.

Goodman's approach emphasizes language. Entrenchment accrues against the entire background of linguistic practice. In contrast, Peirce emphasizes belief in his pragmatic approach to inference, but the difference is really more one of vantage point than of substance. Just as Goodman recognizes that we intuitively avoid projection of 'grue', Peirce notes that our instinctive logical practice mitigates the need for critical logic in ordinary affairs (5.368). This instinctive logical practice is part of that important body of indubitable (i.e., never actually criticized) beliefs, which, he says, are indubitable only insofar as they apply to the primitive mode of life (5.445). These beliefs have withstood numerous potentially doubt inducing experiences and have not yielded to them. So long as present experience resembles this past experience, there will be no cause to doubt these beliefs. But when inference in science or any non-ordinary situation goes beyond common experience, the beliefs are no longer indubitable and critical logic is required (5.511, and 5.368). The process of continual adjustment between beliefs, inference and experience in Peirce's presentation parallels that in Goodman's treatment of the entrenchment of predicates. Using Peirce, Goodman's analysis of entrenchment can be reformulated: The right predicates have become entrenched because they are the ones which reflect our beliefs about the world.

In his theory of entrenchment, Goodman provides for the possibility of change in the relative entrenchment of predicates in the face of greater experience (*FFF*, 64, 98, 106ff). This parallels closely Peirce's suggestion that one's indubitable beliefs change as one's mode of life becomes more sophisticated (5.545). These same observations apply equally to the general requirements for validity. Goodman states: "A rule is amended if it yields an inference we are unwilling to accept; an inference is rejected if it violated a rule we are unwilling to amend (*FFF*, 64). Such recalcitrance can be expressed in Peirce's terms as the conflict between a belief that something is the case and a belief in the inference process, on the one hand, and a belief in the validity of the rule of inference and in the truth of the prediction, on the other.

Other, more detailed parallels between projection and abduction arise from Goodman's definition of "actual projection." According to Goodman, a hypothesis can be actually projected only if it is supported, unviolated and unexhausted. The requirement that the hypothesis must have some support prior to its projection is exactly the same as Peirce's requirement that an abduction explain some surprising fact.

Goodman's other requirements—that the hypothesis be unviolated and unexhausted—are very similar to Peirce's claim that predictions of a theory be designated in advance of testing (2.790, and *FFF*, 90). Both claims are based on the fact that the truth of any genuine ampliative inference is not yet determined (5.584). A hypothesis should pose a question to nature, not merely a catechism.

As already observed, Goodman accuses Hume of having overlooked the fact that not all regularities produce belief or habits. Similarly, Peirce observes that ". . . any two things resemble one another just as strongly as any two others, if recondite resemblances are admitted" (2.634). Both Peirce and Goodman hold, then, that not only must the existence of regularity be asserted, but also the relevant regularity must be specified (*FFF*, 77, 2.790, also cf. *FFF*, 61). This is Peirce's rule of predesignation, and it is what makes it possible in Goodman's theory to speak of support, violation and exhaustion.

A rule of predesignation, however, is no more than the claim that, for Peirce, an *abduction* must precede an induction. The failure to recognize this produces the same confusion which Goodman recognizes with the grue paradox. Peirce uses the following example:

> A chemist notices a surprising phenomenon. Now if he has a high admiration of Mill's *Logic*, as many chemists have, he will remember that Mill tells him that he must work on the principle that, under precisely the same circumstances, like phenomena are produced. Why does he then not note that this phenomenon was produced on such a day of the week, the planets presenting a certain configuration, his daughter having on a blue dress, the milkman being late that morning and so on?

But Peirce's solution makes no formal mechanistic appeal to entrenchment indexes; rather he writes:

> The answer will be that in early days chemists did use to attend to some such circumstances, but that they have learned better (6.413).

As the alchemists's abductions were falsified by formal or informal inductions, the more current beliefs of today—upon which the modern chemist's abductions are based—have replaced them.

That ampliative inference is best thought of in terms of abduction (hypothesis) and induction (testing) rather than under a single rubric of induction is never explicitly admitted by Goodman. Yet, it suits his theory: The old riddle of induction is truly a question about induction; but the "new riddle" is better understood as a problem of abduction. Goodman does admit—indeed emphasizes—that the "traditional" theory of induction cannot solve the grue paradox. This failure of induction to handle the paradox is the reason for Goodman's theory of projectibility. However, the whole theory of projectibility and the choice between a grue theory and a green theory all boils down to a choice between hypotheses. Here, it seems, we have a clearly identifiable issue in the logic of discovery. That Goodman does not separate projection as part of an abductive stage from confirmation as part of an inductive stage of inquiry has its roots in his confusion of the psychology and the logic of belief. In this regard, Peirce's analysis aids in understanding the deficiencies of Goodman's account.

The primary area in which Goodman makes this crucial confusion is his notion of confirmation. His view is explicitly stated when he writes: ". . . affirmation [of a hypothesis] as certainly true is not demanded, but rather something like affirmation as sufficiently more *credible* than alternative hypotheses" (*FFF*, 88, our emphasis). The role of credibility in the process of projection is reflected in three claims which Goodman makes: First, that a greater number of positive instances makes a projectible hypothesis more likely; secondly, that entrenchment can theoretically be quantified and used as an efficacious tool for the selection of hypotheses; and finally, that confirmation like consequence is a logical relation (*FFF*, 67–72, 84, 108, 118, 119).

The credibility of a hypothesis is a subjective psychological standard which may or may not be correlated with the future facts predicted by it. As Goodman himself noted, absolute certainty in prediction would be prevision not hypothesis. Peirce objects that not only is the likelihood or plausibility of a hypothesis not a certain indicator of its truth, it is also not possible to give it a valid numerical measure (2.662, 2.663). "Likelihood" is merely an indicator of the agreement or disagreement of preconceived ideas with the hypothesis (7.220). As such, it may serve to guide research but not to determine precisely which hypotheses ought to be projected.[7] Validity for Peirce is a logical not a psychological matter. Since positive instances impart no logical necessity that an inference will turn out true, it is only negative instances in the class of available evidence which affect the logical question of validity. A rule of inference is not necessarily true simply because it is supported, but it is certainly false if it is violated. It is disappointed expectation which provides the logical grounds to doubt an accepted inference.

The confusion of the psychology and logic of belief and the emphasis of positive over negative instances leads Goodman to believe that theoretically, a mechanical procedure would permit selection between rival hypotheses. Each hypothesis could be given, in theory, a comparative index of projectibility based upon the entrenchment of the predicates it employs and the comparative projectibility of hypotheses related to it heirarchically (e.g., "all bagfuls of marbles in Utah are uniform in color," if it is otherwise "actually projectible" contributes to the comparative projectibility of "all bagfuls of marbles in stacks S are uniformly of some warm color," if S is in Utah [*FFF*, 111]). The hypothesis with the highest comparative projectibility would be projected over its rivals supported by the same evidence. That this cannot be done in practice, requires that actually projectible hypotheses be distinguished by the following rule: "A hypothesis is *projectible* if all conflicting hypotheses are overridden, *unprojectible* if overridden, and *nonprojectible* if in conflict with another hypothesis and neither is overridden."[8] A hypothesis is overridden by a contrary overhypothesis which employs better entrenched predicates (*FFF*, 110–18, esp. 117).

Peirce does not see the simple collection of ever more positive instances as increasing the likelihood of the hypothesis. In fact, he observes that inductive certainty may be very similar to deductive certainty. One test may establish a qualitative result for a chemist, just as one proof is enough for a mathematician. On the other hand, even with a deduction a student may check his work several times (5.580). The degree of belief in an inference does not follow from any simple mechanical procedure. So it is unlikely that even with more careful development that an exact, quantified index of entrenchment could be usefully assigned to predicates (cf. *FFF*, 119). Rather, it is economy of money, time, thought and energy instead of formal rules or entrenchment indexes which should guide the abductive/inductive procedure, says Peirce (5.6000, 2.780).

Projection of a hypothesis, for Peirce, could only mean taking it up for inductive testing. Not only, then, is it possible on Peirce's account to be unconcerned about fine distinctions of entrenchment, but it may be the wisest procedure. Using Peirce's method, a scientist would check only those hypotheses which were consistent with his current beliefs which could be tested in a reasonable time, within his means, and so forth. Since within the scientific community, other scientists would be working on the same problem from various perspectives and under differing circumstances, a greater range of possible hypotheses would be examined. This is true in the forefront of science, where no body of shared beliefs is commonly agreed upon. It is even more true in a situation in which many unaccountable results have led one or more mavericks to suggest that some agreed upon beliefs be reexamined—the situation of Copernicus, Newton, Darwin or Einstein.

Goodman does not claim that a projected hypothesis must be correct. Although he often seems to forget it, a hypothesis must be subjected to some testing to be even logically acceptable and probably to a great deal of testing to be psychologically satisfying (5.599). Yet, if Goodman's rules were followed, each scientist would test the most projectible hypothesis and move on to the next one only if it were violated. In an ideal scientific community, in which every member had complete information on the operations of the other members, exact indexes of entrenchment and projectibility would suggest that the same hypothesis be projected and tested by each investigator at a given time. Such a conservative procedure would militate against radical changes of belief that have often advanced science, as well as restrict normal scientific progress. Even in a real scientific community such a procedure would severely restrict the scope of investigation.

Suppose a scientist faces a choice between two otherwise actually projectible hypotheses, H_1 and H_2, where H_1 overrides H_2 (i.e., H_1 employs better entrenched predicates than H_2), then according to Goodman, the scientist should project and proceed to test H_1. But suppose also that H_1 is of the nature that it will take a long time, say ten years, and a great deal of expense to test whereas H_2 is of the nature that it will take a relatively much shorter time, say a few days, and much less expense to test. Peirce's dominating concern with economy would require that H_2 be tested first even though it is overridden.

Similarly, if a particular hypothesis, e.g., H_2, accounts for more of a greater variety of phenomena than another hypothesis, H_1, then again economy in the scientific process requires us to test H_2 first to "save repetitious work" (7.221). In place of Goodman's mechanical procedure for choosing hypotheses for inductive testing Peirce suggests a much looser alternative. His dictum is, "Don't block the path of research." (1.135).

Goodman's "new riddle of induction" has justifiably provoked as much excitement and critical response from philosophers of science and epistemologists as any other single development in theory construction in the last quarter of a century. It is a measure of Peirce's greatness that he anticipated, in a very general way, Goodman's problem and dealt with it in a more illuminating way by clearly separating Goodman's question of the selection of hypotheses (abduction) from Hume's problem of the confirmation of hypotheses (induction). Once Goodman's riddle is properly understood as a problem of abduction, theory construction and the logic of scientific discovery, its significance becomes clear. What Goodman has valuably demonstrated is that abduction is, as Peirce had claimed, a different form of reasoning. The important result is to shift our out attention from problems of confirmation, induction, and David Hume to problems of theory construction, abduction and Charles Sanders Peirce.

James F. Harris,

College of William and Mary

and

Kevin D. Hoover,

Balliol College, Oxford

NOTES

1. References are to Charles S. Peirce, *Collected Papers*, Volumes I–VIII, edited by Charles Hartsborne, Paul Weiss and Arthur Burks, (Cambridge: Harvard University Press, 1931–58). All references to the *Collected Papers* are in the standard form, citing only the volume number, decimal point and paragraph number. Peirce also includes the categories of necessary inference, probable and statistical deductions. These are simply necessary deductions with probabilities as their subject matter (2.785, 2.694).

2. Formulated this way by Robert G. Meyers, "Peirce on Cartesian Doubt," *Transactions of the Charles S. Peirce Society*, 3 (Spring 1967): 16–17.

3. A second reason for treating abduction as a type of inference is that it has a degree of determinate force over our beliefs. This is especially true when it operates in the guise of sense perception which Peirce classifies as a limiting case of abduction.

4. This is Peirce's fully developed view. In earlier writings, he held that induction has a different but equally creative role as abduction (cf. 2.263, 2.264, 2.640, 6.709). We cannot trace here the development of Peirce's thought. For reference, see Arthur Burks, "Peirce's Theory of Abduction," *Philosophy of Science*, 12 (1946); Harry Frankfurt, "Peirce's Notion of Abduction," *Journal of Philosophy*, 45, 1958; and K. T. Fann, *Peirce's Theory of Abduction*, (The Hague: Martinus Nijhoff, 1970), pp. 20ff.

5. Nelson Goodman, *Fact, Fiction and Forecast*, Second Edition, (New York: Bobbs-Merrill, 1965). Chapter III. Hereafter *FFF* followed by page number.

6. Most of Goodman's critics have used various restatements of this definition. Many of them have unwittingly employed definitions which alter the meaning of 'grue,' Because the grue paradox is but an illustration of the new riddle of induction (of which other illustrations can be constructed), this issue is of relatively minor interest in the present context. Whether or not the supposed untoward results follow if Goodman's definition is taken strictly is debatable. On both points, see Frank Jackson, "Grue," *Journal of Philosophy*, 62 (March, 1975).

7. In 1878, Peirce claimed that probability ought to be connected with the psychological feeling of belief in a hypothesis (2.676). In 1902, however, he pointed

out that probability has only a doubly indirect relation to the validity of abduction (2.102).

8. Nelson Goodman, Robert Schwartz **and Israel Scheffler,** "An Improvement in the Theory of Projectibility," in Nelson Goodman, *Problems and Projects* (New York: Bobbs-Merrill, 1972), p. 390. This is Goodman's latest revision of what had been three rules in the first and two rules in the second edition of *FFF*. Each revision, he claims, only removes redundancy and adds clarity.

PEIRCE AND "THE WILL TO BELIEVE"

The multi-dimensionality of the term 'pragmatism' is by now a well-known phenomenon. Much has been made of the Peircean pragmatic theory of meaning vis-à-vis the Jamesian pragmatic theory of truth. Sometimes the contrast is made too quickly. This results in the undervaluing of important similarities between the two thinkers.

It is often said that the Jamesian position appealed to the affective dimension in life, in the sense of our having the "right to believe" in a hypothesis when the situation is unsolvable, yet forced, living, and momentous. Going further, James's metaphysics of "pure experience" involves more than just theoretical knowledge. He held the position that the human being is capable of experiencing dimensions of reality not completely reducible to the knowable, in the strong sense of that term. "Pure experience" is not an objective ground which can be demonstrated with certainty. In this sense, Jamesian metaphysics demands an element of "commitment."

In this paper, I want to suggest that these same elements, the affective and/or the will to believe play an important role in Peirce's position. More specifically, as Peirce begins to refine his pragmatic method, he reacts against two things: nominalism and personalism. Both of these have one thing in common: they emphasize the "foreground" of experience. Peirce reacts by emphasizing the "background" of experience. Science is the study of the "useless"; pragmatism defines meaning in terms of conceivable effects "in the long run." The *ongoing* scientific community becomes the basic unit of reference, etc. However, the two elements of nominalism and personalism are not collapsible. In reacting to these two different degrees of individualism, Peirce sets the stage for the question: "What is the relationship between realism and meaning?" Differently put, Peirce moved from a narrow to a broad definition of pragmatism. So much is well known. But Peirce's broader definition, which is *not* metaphysically neutral, contains an element of conviction or commitment. The relationship between meaning and realism is actually that of the relationship between epistemology and metaphysics. How does this relation function for Peirce? In my opinion, the possibilities are two: if one tries to justify Peirce's metaphysics via his pragmatic epistemology, the latter must be widened *still further*, to *include* an affective dimension or preference. If one tries to justify Peirce's epistemology via his metaphysics, here, too, an element of commitment is involved, in so far as Peirce's entire cosmological outlook is not capable of verification. Let us see how this comes about.

Peirce's pragmatism is developed within the doubt-inquiry-belief-action matrix made famous in the article "How to Make Our Ideas Clear." The Cartesian approach is rejected as insufficient. So is any claim to direct, intuitive knowledge. For Peirce, if two beliefs alleviate the same doubt content by producing the same habit of action, then they are identical; here is pragmatism being born. ". . . what a thing means is simply the habits it involves."[1] However, in the well-known example of the meaning of calling something "hard," Peirce initially gives a very positivistic description of the situation. "There is absolutely no difference between a hard thing and a soft thing as long as they are not brought to the test." This stance, if consistently maintained, would commit Peirce to strict operational definitions and, furthermore, to nominalism. "Generals" would be viewed as abstractions; disposition terms could not be properly defined. Ultimately, laws in science would be seen as mere duplications of physical phenomena. As such they would be expendable on *pragmatic* grounds as superfluous.[2] The scope of the difficulty becomes more obvious when one applies the pragmatic method to a term like "reality" and asks "What does it mean to say that 'x' is real?" Peirce defined real things in terms of their effect, which was to cause belief.[3] But he wanted to hold the position that ultimately some shared opinion would come about. Such a position is best stated in terms of the contrary-to-fact conditional, as indeed are the laws of science in general. Peirce, of course, realized all this and later on indicated that pragmatism was *not* to be taken in a neutral positivistic sense:

> . . . the question is, not what *did* happen, but whether it would have been well to engage in any line of conduct whose successful issue depended upon whether that diamond *would* resist an attempt to scratch it, or whether all other logical means of determining how it ought to be classed *would* lead to the conclusion which, to quote the very words of the article, would be "the belief which alone could be the result of the investigation carried *sufficiently far*."[4]

The above text is important because it clearly indicates Peirce's emphasis upon the subjunctive; pragmatism is not neutral; it is to be associated with a metaphysical stance of scholastic realism, which advocates the reality of generals; ". . . possibility is sometimes of a real kind."[5] This broader view of pragmatism avoids the problems of operational definitions,[6] but his new nonneutral metaphysical position raises the question of whether or not it can be justified by his epistemology.[7]

It is clear that Peirce did not want to merely conflate truth and reality, as in some form of idealism. But is is also clear that he rejected the position wherein "the really real" is completely independent of all thought, forever and ever. For Peirce, such a view would "block the way of inquiry."[8] Rather does Peirce define reality as independent of what you or I or any finite group of people might think about it, but not as necessarily independent of thought in general.[9] Going further, Peirce asserts that the opinion ultimately fated to be agreed upon by the community of scientific investigators is what is meant by truth, and "the object represented in this opinion is the real."[10] From this perspective then, individual beliefs are clearly "constrained"; also present or future opinions held in a communal fashion are subject to constraint—at this very moment. Only in the ultimate case limit where a completely shared opinion is arrived at do we have co-extension of knowledge and reality. Such a position raises the question: "how do we get from here to there?" Peirce's reply is normative: we ought to get from here to there by employing the pragmatic method.[11]

But which version? Clearly the broader of the two definitions is needed. Only by employing a version of the method which allows for the reality of generals can Peirce say that, even now we are subject to constraint by a reality which exhibits independence in some sense. But can one employ the pragmatic method itself to establish that there is some conceivable difference between nominalism and realism? Can the epistemology be used to justify the metaphysical stance? Arthur Burks, in an insightful introduction to Peirce's thought, argues that it cannot.

> The sole difference between the nominalist's and the realist's conception of law has to do with potentialities; and there can be a genuine dispute between the two only if propositions involving potentialities alone have practical consequences. But clearly they do not. It can make no practical difference to say of a diamond that has not been and never will be tested whether it would or would not have been scratched if it had been tested. So long as we agree to the law "All diamonds are hard" and its practical consequence that "If this diamond *is* tested it will not be scratched," then it can make no practical difference what we hold of a diamond that is *never* tested. An untested diamond is beyond practical interest. Another way of putting the matter is to say that action is based on actualities, not on potentialities, and that potentialities cannot affect conduct.[12]

In a footnote, Burks goes on to say that we do act on potentialities in the sense that "feelings of regret" are possible. For example, one might regret having made a particular speech, because had I not, I would have won the election. He (Burks) asserts, however, that such feelings of regret are not part of the conceivable effects of a belief. Such effects are "not consequences of the belief itself . . . but rather are consequences of holding the belief,"[13] i.e., they are emotional associations of the belief. Now it is undoubtedly true that Peirce often argued in this fashion, viz., against the sentient, the private, the merely satisfying, etc., particularly when he was reacting to James's position, which he considered too individualistic and conduct-orientated. But there also seems to be at least one instance where Peirce cannot make this distinction clearly, namely, the belief by the members of a scientific community that they are slowly and correctly arriving at a shared belief. Peirce held that the members of a (the) scientific community were driven by a "cheerful hope"[14] that their investigations would ultimately terminate in truth, if only they utilized the correct method, namely pragmatism. "We all hope that the different scientific inquiries in which we are severally engaged are going ultimately to lead to some definitely established conclusion we endeavor to anticipate in some measure."[15] Pragmatism was seen as the required method—not because it was self-justifying in an apodictic sense, but because it was self-criticizing. The "proof" of the method itself involves an application of the method. And Peirce appealed to the "facticity" of the history of scientific achievement as inductive proof that the method worked. Furthermore, if pragmatism did not actually prove a realism once and for all, it was at least compatible with the thesis that "There are real things existing independently of us." The method of pragmatism, taken in the broader sense of implying the reality of generals, was supposed to avoid the possibility of a group of scientific investigations "fixing by convention" what the truth would be, because the method forced the individuals to be constrained by experience, by independent reals. But the argument ultimately rests upon the cheerful hope that scientists will act in the manner described and prescribed by Peirce. There is nothing in the argument which would logically prohibit investigators deciding to hold some belief as paradigmatic in a Kuhnian sense. Indeed, it is at this level that Peirce's "Popperian" philosophy of science comes to the fore. Peirce believed that the "best hypothesis, in the sense of the one most recommending itself to the inquirer, is the one which can be the most readily refuted if it is false."[16] Whereas confirmation makes a hypothesis more likely, which is to say more in alignment with our preconceptions, Peirce did believe that hypotheses could be falsified. Peirce has an implicit faith in scientific method as honest, a faith capable of inductive justification, but a faith, nevertheless. Karl Popper argues in the same fashion, admitting that at any given moment "we are prisoners caught in the framework of our theories; our expectations; our past experiences; our language. But we are prisoners in a Pickwickean sense: if we try we can break out of our framework at any time. Admittedly, we shall find ourselves again in a framework, but it will be a better and roomier one, and we can at any moment break out of it again."[17] But as Kuhn has shown so well, if that were so, "there ought to be no very special difficulties about stepping into someone else's framework in order to evaluate it."[18] Kuhn's conclusion is that Popper "has characterized the entire scientific enterprise in terms that apply only to its occasional revolutionary parts",[19] and, further, that when a transfer *does* take place between paradigms, it is a "conversion experience that cannot be forced".[20] We need not take a position here on the Kuhn-Popper debate. The point is rather that Peirce himself made an act of faith in scientific method. While he believed that "the perversity of thought of whole generations may cause the postponement of the ultimate fixation"[21] of belief, ultimately, he would not accept a Kuhnian analysis. On this he was adamant. Also, the issue here cannot be dealt with merely by pointing to the history of science. It is precisely what that history is that is at issue.

We might sum the discussion up in a negative fashion by saying that Peirce's distinction between the four methods—tenacity, authority, a priori, and scientific[22]—is overdrawn. Peirce, himself, is *tenacious* in advocating the scientific method of pragmatism over all others, and he becomes more tenacious as James develops his own position. This does *not* mean that Peirce could not give good reasons for his position. His reasons were numerous, brilliant, and well-articulated. However, positively summarized, in the last analysis, Peirce's "cheerful hope" involves a Jamesian "will to believe" in a *situation* that is forced, living, and momentous.

What is the situation? Ultimately, it concerns "the really real," the known and the knowable. Peirce was willing to admit that the really real is not coextensive with the known, but *not* that "the really real" was not knowable. To take such a stance would be, in his opinion, to "block the road to inquiry." James might respond that *only* such a stance (really real—greater than knowable) keeps our theoretical concepts honest. In a vague, unfinished universe, one can avoid self-deception only if one admits the essential tentativeness of all hypotheses. This, on a meta-theoretical level, is a strategem, an attitude taken on James' part toward "the really real."

Peirce assumes the opposite strategem, or attitude, though "pragmatically" they may come to the same thing.[23] For him, it is "better" to assume the stance or hope that "the really real" is knowable—at least that this is possible. But this stance is a Peircean "will to believe." Furthermore, part of the meaning of adopting it *is* the consequences of holding it, on the part of the members of the scientific community. The "cheerful hope" cannot be expressed solely in terms of conceivable effects which would occur. Part of the "meaning" of the cheerful hope is its function as a catalyst. Otherwise an infinite regress is the result.

What then has this to do with the possibility of justifying Peirce's metaphysics in terms of his epistemology? Simply this: if one tries to make the distinction between nominalism and realism simply in terms of conceivable effects, i.e., *meaning*, such a distinction can be made if pragmatism is broadened still further, if the affective dimension is included, or better if, at least in some instances, the "consequences of belief" vs. "consequences of holding that belief" dichotomy is rejected. To do so flies in the teeth of Peirce's admitted emphasis upon the conceptual vis-a-vis the affective. But I am suggesting that at a meta-theoretical level, Peirce has no other choice. He chooses a different "belief" than James, but his choice is made ultimately in the same way. In short, Peirce's pragmatic epistemology can make room for or justify his metaphysical realism only if it is admitted that an extra-logical dimension is involved.

But this is only half the question. If Peirce's epistemology cannot justify his metaphysics without a "belief factor" can his metaphysics justify his epistemology? Here the issue is more obvious, and we can be briefer. However, the outcome is the same: an extra-logical dimension is involved.

Metaphysically, Peirce developed an objective idealism, to account for his "realist" approach to laws in science. Mind is viewed as basic and as capable of associating, of taking on habits. ". . . ideas tend to spread continuously and to affect certain others which stand to them in a peculiar relation of affectability."[24] The habits are the laws of nature. Matter from this perspective is viewed as frozen mind, as hidebound. Peirce viewed the universe as containing both a tychistic dimension and an anancastic aspect. But neither was a sufficient explanation of how things evolve. Peirce's evolutionary cosmology is "agapastic." The universe is moving from chance toward order, though at any given moment one can find aspects of both. Habits tend to spread and connect with others, in accordance with Peirce's principle of "synechism." Finally, the universe is viewed by Peirce as ". . . a vast representamen, a great sqmbol of God's purpose, working out its conclusions in living realities."[25] Such an outlook is remarkable for its richness and detail; yet it clearly involves an extra-logical dimension. Peirce himself viewed metaphysical outlooks as "guesses" based on current scientific facts. But his own exposition is clearly anthropomorphic. While Peirce, indeed, would have been the first to admit this,[26] it does raise questions about the self-sufficiency of a metaphysical position. But there is a bigger problem: Peirce asserted that his evolutionary outlook "constitutes a hypothesis capable of being tested by experiment."[27] Yet it is highly questionable whether the thesis that we are moving from firstness through thirdness toward secondness in accordance with the principle of cosmic love constitutes a verifiable, or better, falsifiable proposition—or ever could do so. Peirce espoused a belief in God and advocated reverie as a "base" (i.e., the humble argument) which might be partially justified by the more logical neglected argument. But as he himself held, the base is "abductive," and there is no complete logic of abduction. Finally, Peirce's agapastic evolutionary position is vehemently opposed to the

"gospel of greed" and is, in his words, his "own passionate predilection . . . .
Yet the strong feeling is in itself, I think, an argument of some weight in favor
of the agapastic theory of evolution,—so far as it may be presumed to
bespeak the normal judgment of the Sensible Heart."[28] Such references to
feeling and the sensible heart seem clearly to indicate that aspects at least of
Peirce's metaphysical cosmology are value-laden. To be sure, Peirce's contribution here is not a small one. But on this level also, an element of "conviction" or "commitment" is involved.

Conclusion

The predominant approach to Peirce is to divorce his epistemology and
his metaphysics, or at least his cosmology. The latter is "generally regarded
by contemporary philosophers as the black sheep or white element of his
philosophical progeny."[29] By way of contrast, in his recent book *Purpose and
Thought: The Meaning of Pragmatism*, John Smith has argued against any
such dichotomy: ". . . The theory of science and of truth cannot, in Peirce's
view, be elaborated without reference to a larger context embracing the
nature of the real and its relation to the inquirer who seeks to grasp it in the
form of truth."[30] In this sense, for Smith, the very success of science must be
viewed in a larger context, one of ontological dimensions. The achievements
of "scientific inquiry are not left in their immediacy at the level of brute fact
but must be understood as manifestations of patterns of development underlying the evolution of the entire universe."[31] The purpose of this paper was
to indicate, in one way, why Smith's "wholistic" approach is more adequate.[32] Specifically, the distinction between Peirce's epistemology and his
metaphysics is often made in terms of the logical vs. the psychological, the
objective vs. the subjective. I have tried to show that it is a mistake to employ
this distinction, because on *both* the level of epistemology and that of
metaphysical cosmology a so-called "psychological" element, a belief factor,
is involved. In reacting to nominalism and personalism—both foreground
experiences—Peirce under-estimated important differences between the two.
In arguing against nominalism and for realism, Peirce espouses a position
wherein *actual* possibility exists. But in reacting against the personal, the affective Peirce argues for the meaningful, and ultimately advocates a position
wherein possibility can exist only as logical possibility—as *possible* possibility. This ultimately sets up the question of the relation of Peirce's theory
of meaning to his theory of reality. In a sense, Peirce's theory of meaning
evolves into a theory of truth, since it points toward a reality which is *not*
completely "meaningful." In sum, whether one grounds Peirce's metaphysics

in his epistemology or his epistemology in his metaphysics, a version of James's "will to believe" seems to be a *necessary* ingredient.

William J. Gavin

University of Southern Maine

NOTES

1. *Collected Papers of Charles Sanders Peirce*, vols. 1–6, edited by Charles Hartshorne and Paul Weiss; vols. 7–8 edited by Arthur Burks (Cambridge: Harvard University Press, 1931–57). Vol. 5, paragraph 5.400. All paragraph references are to this edition.

2. See Carl Hempel, "The Theoretician's Dilemma," *Minnesota Studies in the Philosophy of Science: Vol. II: Concepts, Theories, and the Mind-Body Problem*, ed. H. Feigl, M. Scriven, and G. Maxwell (Minneapolis: University of Minnesota Press, 1958), pp. 37–98.

3. 5.406

4. 5.453

5. Ibid., *loc. cit.*

6. For an analysis of the problems here, see Rudolf Carnap, "Testability and Meaning," *Philosophy of Science*, III (1936) pp. 420–68 and IV (1937) pp. 1–40.

7. This same issue arises in other areas in Peirce's writings; e.g., in "critical common sense inquiry" vis-à-vis "scientific inquiry"; and in "existential doubt" vis-à-vis "hypothetical doubt." See 1.75–76; 5.394.

8. 1.135ff.

9. See 5.408

10. 5.407

11. For an excellent analysis of this issue in Peirce, see John Smith, "Charles S. Peirce: Community and Reality," in *Themes in American Philosophy* (New York: Harper Torchbooks, 1976), pp. 80–108.

12. Arthur Burks, "Charles Sanders Peirce: Introduction," in *Classic American Philosophers*, ed. Max Fisch (New York: Appleton-Century-Crofts, Inc., 1951), p. 51.

13. Ibid., *loc. cit.,* footnote

14. 5.407

15. 7.187

16. 1.120

17. Karl Popper, "Normal Science and Its Dangers," in *Criticism and the Growth of Knowledge*, ed. I. Lakatos and A. Musgrave (Cambridge: Cambridge University Press, 1970), p. 56.

18. Thomas Kuhn, "Reflections on My Critics," in *Criticism and the Growth of Knowledge*, p. 232.

19. Kuhn, "Logic of Discovery or Psychology of Research," in *Criticism and the Growth of Knowledge*, p. 6.

20. Thomas Kuhn, *The Structure of Scientific Revolutions*, (Chicago: Phoenix Books, University of Chicago Press, 1962), p. 150.

21. 5.430
22. See 5.358–87.
23. See 5.466
24. 6.104
25. 5.119
26. See, for example, 5.212; 5.536.
27. 6.101
28. 6.295
29. W. B. Gallie, *Peirce and Pragmatism* (New York: Dover Publications, Inc. 1966), p. 216.
30. John E. Smith, *Pupose and Thought: The Meaning of Pragmatism* (New Haven: Yale University Press, 1978), pp. 54–55.
31. Ibid., p. 55.
32. This does not necessarily mean that Smith would accept the position advocated here.

THE LOGIC OF VAGUENESS
AND THE CATEGORY OF SYNECHISM

In his article "Issues of Pragmaticism" published in 1905, in *The Monist* (vol. 15, pp. 481–99), Charles S. Peirce complains that "Logicians have been at fault in giving Vagueness the go-by, so far as not even to analyze it." That same year, occupying himself with the consequences of "Critical commonsensism," he affirmed, "I have worked out the logic of vagueness with something like completeness," a statement that causes the majority of the commentators on his work, including the editors of the *Collected Papers*[1] to ask where this logic is to be found. The fever for finding Peirce's manuscripts is fed by the hope of some researchers of discovering the logic of vagueness, a hope that has grown since Carolyn Eisele's publication of his mathematical works. Others—and I count myself among them—believe that in reality this is a matter of something already known. That is, they interpret the affirmation ending the paragraph of reproach addressed to logicians, "The present writer has done his best to work out the Stechiology (or Stoicheiology), Critic, and Methodeutik of the subject," (i.e., Vagueness) as a tripartite semiotic of the vague, still limited, according to Peirce's older works (1896, "Preface" to *The Simplest Mathematics*), to symbols, that is, to the signs of natural language examined from the perspective of logic.

If Peirce could read how much is written today on the type of problems he had in mind when he used the term "vagueness," he would surely clarify himself. But at the same time, he would observe that in the place of a logic of the vague, more types of semantics of linguistic imprecision have developed that either ignore him as a possible predecessor—and not the least among the reasons for this would be, in addition to the unfortunate manner in which he was published, his vague mode of expression—or cite him inappropriately.

In connection to all these problems, and especially in direct relation to this very theme, I intend the following: 1) to consider vagueness in connection to the general vision of Peirce's philosophy, examining the logic of vagueness a) in the context of the epoch and b) from the perspective of the present; 2) to explain vagueness in the context of the current semiotic tendency, that is, its epistemological and not gnoseological aspects, a problem of pragmatics and not semantics; 3) to attempt to establish the reciprocal relationship between the logic of vagueness and the category of the synechism (the principle of the continuum) and the way in which they lead to fuzzy types of logic.

Historical Remarks

Peirce's standpoint, according to which vagueness is a question of representation and not a peculiarity of the object of the representation is clearly stated: ". . . reality is something entirely definite," (MS 385, p. A). This position is obvious in relation to the representation's nature as process (infinite). Hence, it derives from the gnoseological angle. Later, Russell, from the same angle, stated the same idea: "Apart from representation, whether cognitive or mechanical, there can be no such thing as vagueness or precision,"[2] giving as an outright condition for a perfectly logical language that it should in no way be vague. Insistence on the gnoseological moment in definition of the real as object of representation partially explains the subsequent tendency to explaining vagueness in the terms of the theory of knowledge. Frege, about whom it has been lightly affirmed[3] that he did not understand the need for a special logic of vagueness, has the double merit of having grasped what he called *die Weichheit und Veränderlichkeit der Sprache* (the softness and changeability of language), [4] that is, the determined inner nature of vagueness, which he wanted to limit through the aid of a *Begriffschrift* (ideography) and the fact that these characteristics are a condition for the development of language.

The historical context can be enlarged, especially in view of the need to see to what extent a logic of vagueness is really possible and what accumulations have been made in the meantime accomplishing this. Analytical philosophy, for example, translates the question of vagueness into the space of extension and intension. Carnap[5] even gives a kind of negative definition of the zone of vagueness: 'If an object y has neither the intension F_1 nor F_2 of the predicate Q, then a speaker X cannot even attribute, but neither can he not attribute, the predicate Q to y." Wittgenstein [6] implied the idea of the gradual nature of similarities, hence, the continuity factor, which after Peirce had been lost sight of for a long time. Later developments were more and more specialized and technically refined. To name a few: Montague's meaning function,[7] Quine's idea of vague as a consequence of the mode of learning expressions and meaning,[8] Lewis's pragmatically relevant factors,[9] Lakoff's distinction between vague boundaries and fuzzy hedges,[10] etc. I emphasize, however, that they do not actually attain a logic of vagueness but only a logic of the production and determination of meaning. Vague is therefore considered as a semantic notion, fuzzy semantics attempting to give quantitative rules for specifying vagueness in the particular universe of linguistic discourse. The concentration on natural language as a particular sign system and the stereotyped repetition of the fact that its semantics is inexact still have not led very far, one of the very reasons why, in words different from Peirce's,[11] "the

need for an exact theory of inexactitude" is more and more frequently called
for and attempts are being made in this direction.

Taking the whole evolution into consideration, from the mere intuition
of vagueness to the diverse formalisms, especially semantic, we cannot help
observing that progress in the knowledge of the mechanism of producing
meaning in natural language has been relatively minor and that limiting the
problematic to double articulated language is still a step backward in relation
to Peirce's concept of vagueness. The latter is a general theory concerning the
relation between vague and determined as they appear in thought and communication processes and also in processes of signification viewed from the
most general perspective regarding the sign, hence, without being limited to
the linguistic sign. According to Peirce, thought is semiotic. It is dialogical
and realized through signs. The sign itself cannot be absolutely precise. Its
vague nature (indefiniteness) stems from the relation with the object of the
sign which stands for that object or with its interpretant for which it brings
about meaning (sense, meaning, signification). The first relationship
(between sign and object) is a source of indefiniteness in Breadth; the second
(between sign and interpretant) is the source of indefiniteness in Depth (cf.
4.543, 5.448). Peirce eventually dwells on one of these two types of indefiniteness: "Indefiniteness in depth may be termed vagueness," (MS 283,
141, 138–39, rejected pages). Peirce's early or more recent commentators
(James Feibleman,[12] W. B. Gallie,[13] Ch. K. McKeon,[14] J. L. Cohen,[15] etc.)
did not keep this specification, so definitive of Peirce's concept, in mind. Of
course, it would be advisable to try to find out where the notions *Breadth* and
Depth come from in order to more clearly understand even the abovementioned definition of vagueness. Peirce took over these terms from Hamilton[16]
and initially applied them to the study of terms,[17] for extension and comprehension respectively, proposing new meanings and even defining types
such as informed breadth and depth of a term, essential and substantial
breadth or depth of terms, etc. We can ask which of the types mentioned
above participates in defining vagueness and thus arrive at the semiotic concept, initially presented as a theory of the symbol ("to include both concept
and word," 2.418) even though it is already the outline of the triadic structural model of the sign.[18]

Vagueness concerns the informed depth, hence, "in a supposed state of
information" (2.408). Moreover, according to Peirce, depth may be a certain
or doubtful, actual or potential, which is also reflected by the types of
vagueness (certain, doubtful, actual, or potential vague). The typology of
vagueness was not, however, developed by Peirce and not even by those who
later occupied themselves with it. W. J. Jevons,[19] for whom breadth is extension and depth, intension, bewails, somehow in the same manner Peirce did

when he wrote *Ethics of Terminology*,[20] "the peculiar misfortune of the science of logic to have a superfluity of names or synonyms for the same idea. . . ." Jevons's use of the terms breadth and depth (terms not far in meaning from the same used by Peirce) is peculiar to the *pre*-semiotic period of logic (and of science in general).[21] Attempting to give a logical formulation of his vision of vagueness from the horizon of semiotics, Peirce affirmed that vague "is the antithetical analogue of generality. A sign is objectively *general*, in so far as, leaving to the interpreter the right of completing the determination for himself. A sign is objectively *vague*, in so far, as leaving its interpretation more or less indeterminate, it reserves for some other possible sign or experience the function of completing the determination," (4.505). In his conception, the universal phenomenon of vagueness affects the logic of the non-contradiction, which Russell views differently, that is, that the law of the excluded middle is affected (a negative image, from possible true and false together to no true and no false). Peirce did not discover vagueness but only defined it as an implicit part of any sign process, linguistic or otherwise. Therefore, the consciousness of vagueness is part of semiotic consciousness, reflected by the latter in all of the forms of man's semiotic practice.

Methodological Distinctions

In order to understand the logic of vagueness which Peirce affirmed he had elaborated—an affirmation I believe to be *true* and justified—let us see what are the Stechiology (or Stoicheiology), Critic and Methodeutik of vagueness. They are the general theory of the nature and meaning of signs (viewed as representamina, hence icon, index, and symbol), the classification of arguments and the determination of their validity, and lastly, the study of the methods of investigation, exposition, and application of the truth (cf. 1.192, 2.93, 2.229, 3.430, and 4.9). From the view set forth in 1867—a reference date he himself gives—and until the one sustained in 1905, an evolution took place after which Peirce set up a *triadic-trichotomic semiotic* as a new type of logic of a universal nature. It necessarily derives from his general philosophical system, a system established on the basis of the phaneroscopic categories (Possibility, Reality, Necessity) and that it implies, as its very ordering principle, the law of synechism, that is, the doctrine of the continuum. The latter governs knowledge and implies generality. If all that exists is continuous ("Synechism is the doctrine that all that exists is Continuous," 1.172), and if generality and continuity are the same thing (4.172), then we can also understand why vagueness constitutes a universal principle and is not the result of a "defect in thinking or knowledge" (4.344), hence not a gnoseological accident. Vagueness can neither be eliminated ("vagueness . . .

which is no more to be done away with in the world of logic than friction in mechanics," 4.512) nor reduced to ambiguity, a danger that subsequent research has in fact not avoided.

As a semiotic animal (*zoon semiotikon*), man himself is identified as a sign and participates in the endless process of representing and interpreting reality. The potential infinity of the process of investigation and interpretation causes that only a relatively complete meaning (sense, meaning, signification) be determined at each moment. The *process* nature of knowledge concerns its epistemological condition. Vagueness hence represents a sort of relationship between absolute, final determination, which in fact is not attained (the condition of an ideal, therefore) and actual determination of meaning (again as sense, meaning, signification) in concrete semioses. It can already be seen from the model of the processuality of knowledge outlined above that vagueness and continuity cannot be isolated from each other. On the one hand we have sign processes, within the competence of semiotics (as *System of Logic*) and on the other, continuity as a supreme law in the universe of phaneroscopic categories. Semiotics itself, in its divisions and in the sign operations it defines, is the logic of vagueness, and it is in this sense that Peirce affirmed that he had elaborated such a logic. At the beginning, this logic was limited, as already shown, to the symbol, an unclear concept which was clarified processualy, that is, to the extent to which Peirce arrived at the definition of the sign in its generality (the sign of natural language being only one among the possible signs of the global system of semiotics). Starting out from the particular term-object relationship, term-interpretant in particular, one arrives at the relationship between the sign and the object for which it stands, in particular the relationship between the sign and its interpretant (conceived as an integral part of the sign, united to the sign through the very act of interpretation). Vagueness thus comes about in the domain of the interpretant, a fact that has already led us to affirm that the opinion according to which "vagueness is a semantic notion" (with the addition that "it is deficiency of meaning," as sustained by Kit Fine, for example[22]) does not correspond to the essential determination of vagueness as a semiotic characteristic. It follows from Peirce's analysis that vagueness is situated in the field of pragmatics, part of the generalized semiotic field that I have already defined.[23] The deficiency of meaning to which Fine and others refer to is ambiguity (so often confused with vagueness). The referential aspect (which the indefinite in breadth, hence the denotational aspect of the sign, represents) is not a source of vagueness. The mode in which signs are attached to objects, a mode represented by the referential aspect, is, in the final analysis, characteristic of the gnoseological moment. The structural aspect, stemming directly from the sign's triadic-trichotomic structure (which the indefinite in depth, hence the connotational aspect of the sign, represents) shows both what vagueness is and what its logic is. It is a question of the way in which signs are connected to each other—a sign exists only in connection to another—of the way in which it participates in semioses, of the way they are interpreted, that is, of what characterizes the epistemological moment. This, in way of example, justifies the current discussions on the higher order of vagueness (cf. M. Przelecky[24]), the meaning of which can, I believe, have more light shed upon it, considering the unity between vagueness and the continuum.

Recent theories, in the fields of science and the humanities, are characterized by, among other things, a new epistemological condition, in particular by the integration of semiotic consciousness (hence including vagueness which is part of the latter) into scientific and philosophical practices. The evidencing of the semiotic aspect (of natural or formal languages, of the languages of communication or signification, etc.), that follows the prior event of demonstrating the structural aspect, corresponds to that discovery by the modern epistemology according to which "vagueness is not incompatible with precision" (cf. Quine[25]). The need to reunite vagueness with the continuum is not therefore only the consequence of Peirce's semiotic system—which is far from being universally accepted—but also a directly practical consequence necessitated by progressing from quantitative to qualitative evaluations.

Critical Remarks: Vagueness and Fuzziness

Philosophers of language, logicians, and linguists accept that natural languages are vague. However, those who occupy themselves with general sign systems (in their quality as semioticians, logicians, or mathematicians) or with the study of specialized artificial systems (formal language, symbolic systems, institutionalized systems, etc.) start out from the need to define the source of vagueness and from the question of whether vagueness is an implicit characteristic of any semiotic representation or not. In this case too, opinions obviously do not coincide or even converge towards a commonly acceptable truth.

Two different positions should be considered as characteristic of the current evolution of vagueness. On one hand, the concept of semantic competence, which not only affirms the semantic condition of vagueness—an idea I consider out of harmony with Peirce's fundamental concept of vagueness— but also ignores the referential relationship, eliminates the social aspect of meaning fulfillment in the broad sense. It also postulates (Chomsky, as well as Katz and Fodor) the clear distinction between what we know about the meaning of expressions and what we know about the empirical properties of

things and phenomena. The second direction is represented by the new enun-
ciations of the concept of competence (M. Creswell[26] for instance). The
capacity to decide between the truth or falsity of an expression is placed on
the main level, hence the abstraction of all the aspects of meaning that are not
connected to the expression is made. Putnam's model[27] appeared as an alternative to the extent that it was characterized as an outright "realistic route."
Its argumentation is simple: we live in an epoch and in a society in which the
principle of the division of labor functions, evident especially on the social
and economic levels. The inference to linguistic activity is derived somewhat
intuitively. On the basis of ordinary needs and interests, each person feels the
necessity of learning the basic vocabulary. The necessity of setting up a
method with whose help one can establish the relation between word and object (if the word is in univocal relationship with an object or in equivocal
relationship with a number of objects) appears only to specialists. A
relationship of cooperation (analogous to that in the labor process) is thus set
up between experts and non-experts. Specialization, which corresponds to the
growth of science and technology, brings with it the entrenchment of the division of linguistic activity. The mutual interest in cooperation between experts
and non-experts is pragmatic and implies the social factor in language processes. Extension is socially defined through collective competence (which includes that of the experts). If we extend Putnam's model to signs in general—
and in his case as well as in Peirce's, the beginning is made by considering
natural languages—that is, if we extend the model to semiotic reality in its
generality (which in the case of art, for example, would only be a confirmation, the division of competence and the role of experts having been studied)
we observe that the solution of describing semiotic processes (of language, especially) through formal language—Carnap's line—is not sufficient since it
cannot reflect both vagueness and the division of semiotic activity; a division
that assumes more and more refined forms than Putnam supposes. A theory
that considers both aspects is necessary, and such a theory can be merely contextual. (Putnam believes that the attempts made by D. Lewis[28] approach this
ideal.) Here the problem that appears is one of *pragmatic context*, not semantic context, because, as I already have shown, vagueness, as well as the division of semiotic activity (I extend Putnam's concept from the signs of
language to the general system of signs), is determined on a pragmatic level.
Context is not only semiotic, itself being sometimes vague ("its reference is
often intrinsically vague itself," J. Bar-Hillel[29]). But any context, as I
demonstrated in the definition of the semiotic field, can be represented by
signs.

Let us not dwell on this. I have proposed to show that the logic of
vagueness, as an implicit part of semiotics, is always found in association to
the law of synechism, that is, to the doctrine of continuity. Thus Peirce

becomes—I believe this opinion can be sustained—a predecessor of the view based on the model of fuzzy sets and especially their semiotic application in both analytical and synthesizing processes. Furthermore, the sign implies vagueness and the continuum, and this fact stems from Peirce's general concept. Vagueness is modeled within the theory of fuzzy sets through the membership function that can gradually be brought to a higher degree of precision. This membership function has a certain similarity to the density of probability function when the set to which the latter refers is continuous, although the two are essentially different.

The ordinating concept of Peircean semiotics is the relation, the triadic-trichotomic structure preserving hierarchy from the model of the phaneroscopic categories. The preserving of hierarchy (that is, of a certain order relationship called isotony in mathematical language) makes formalization possible with the aid of the algebraic theory of categories. The objects of the fundamental mathematical category of the sign (see MacLane[30]) are represented by what is called *Firstness, Secondness,* and *Thirdness.* (I use the term "mathematical" in order to avoid confusion with Peirce's metaphysical categories.) The nature of order relationship is expressed even through the names used. The relationship between these objects (classes, in fact) has, due to isotony (that is, due to the preservation of hierarchy indicated by name: Firstness before secondness, secondness before thirdness, etc.), the nature of morphism. Here the structure of the relationship between objects, and not the objects themselves, are characteristic. As a result of this intrinsic condition of Peirce's semiotic, a condition that can be strictly formally expressed through the category of sign classes, an important conclusion results: the infiniteness of interpretability, which stems from the sign's vague condition, and indeterminateness, in connection to continuity, causes Peirce's table of signs to make sense only to the extent it is understood as the structure of a continuously functioning system. Peirce himself did not observe this and consequently ordered the ten sign classes (2.264) according to an affinity criterion based on likeness. Actually, he did not observe that the ten sign classes were in reciprocal relationship, that some could be transformed into the others, nor how these transformations take place, although he defined the concept of semiosis (sign process), degenerative processes (leading to replicas) and generative processes (from a low degree of semioticity to a higher degree of semioticity). The application, in the abovementioned sense, of the mathematical theory of categories also permits the explanation of Peirce's so-called inconsistency which led him to write of ten sign classes on one occasion, then 28 (in his letter to Lady Welby of December 14, 1908[31]) and even 66 classes. The explanation is that the ten classes correspond to the simple triadic structure of the phaneroscopic categories, or more precisely to what he called (also in a letter to Lady Welby, October 12, 1904) cenopythagorean categories. Developing this first model, always under the control of the logic of relations—a logic that demonstrates the irreducibility of the triad into diads or monads but assures the reducibility of higher forms into the triad— Peirce introduced, and explained in his letter to William James (March 14, 1909), the division of the object (immediate and dynamic) as well as of the interpretant (immediate, dynamic, final). Considering the morphisms of this category (with no less than six objects), 28 classes actually result (ordinated independent sextuplets in conformity to the hierarchy given in the phaneroscopic categories). Another four trichotomies that Peirce suggested also explain the 66 classes mentioned, classes considered by the editors of his work as its final expression. So it is in no case a question of inconsistency, but an expression of the gradual perfecting of his typology of signs, to date not satisfactorily explained by anyone. Of course, it is captivating to follow the line of Peirce's reasoning, to reconstitute, by respecting the system's internal logic, some of the results that for a long time have been regarded with suspicion or presented as inconsistent (and discarded as such). I have presented these results however, obviously important from a historical perspective, because they can be obtained only on the basis of the hypothesis I have enunciated: the unity between the logic of vagueness and the law of synechism, a hypothesis I have tried to demonstrate on the historical as well as methodical level. It is not only a problem of confirming Peirce and of consecrating him as one more precursor of the fuzzy set theory, but especially of developing his semiotic and putting it into operation. The definition of the dynamics of the sign table based on the consideration of morphisms from the cenopythagorean categories represents a first aspect. A second aspect is the observation that Peirce, basing himself on the unity of vague and continuous, intuited fuzzy relationships, that is he intuited multivalued relations and opened the way to the application of these relationships, belonging to his semiotics, to the dynamics of signs. The typology of the sign classes (the ten, the 28, the 66), as confirmed by the mathematical theory of categories (cf. Marty,[32] Nadin,[33]) should be understood as a network of fundamental reference points in the generalized semiotic field. Whenever this typology is transformed into an end in itself, it leads only to formalistic semiotics. To give a name to a sign (to identify it) does not solve the problem of the way it functions in the semiotic field. The sign can be conceived and interpreted only within the framework of the logic of vagueness and with the participation of the doctrine of the continuum. Fuzzy categories, the extension of the mathematical concept of category, fulfill this desideratum and perfect Peirce's table of fundamental signs by realizing the image of the continuum, hence also the dynamics of sign processes. It is possible to go on, that is, to consider a suggestion of Peirce's (2.227) concerning the trichotomy of the icon, index and symbol, in which case again, the table of sign classes is continuumized, a result corresponding to the spirit of this semiotics based on the unity between vague and continuous.[34] In connection to this, it should be said that the concept of fuzzy sets, particularly of the *ensemble flou*, as they were introduced by Zadeh[35] and Gentilhomme,[36] correspond to the reunion of borderline cases, as vagueness is sometimes defined, with the doctrine of the continuum (which quantifies transition from one quality to another). To quote Zadeh: "The fundamental concept in mathematics is that of a set— a collection of objects. We have been slow in coming to the realization that much, perhaps most, of human cognition and interaction with the outside world involves constructs which are not sets in the classical sense, but rather 'fuzzy sets' (or subsets), that is, classes with unsharp boundaries in which the transition from membership to nonmembership is gradual rather than abrupt. Indeed, it may be argued that much of the logic of human reasoning is not the classical two-valued or even multivalued logic but a logic with fuzzy truths, fuzzy connectives, and fuzzy rules of inference."[37] The semiotic and dialogic nature of thought in Peirce's conception and the model of multivalued logic demonstrated by Zadeh in his definition of fuzzy sets seem to be outright complementary components. It is clear that by joining all the theses I have presented above one can imagine a next level of fuzzy-fuzzy, etc. corresponding to the advancement from one level (or type) of indeterminacy to a higher one, obviously together with the image of the continuum extended to infinity. The exact treatement of the inexact, which many modern tendencies have programmatically assumed, thus becomes semiotically not only possible but also necessary.

I shall not dwell on the various attempts at fuzzy logic, which implicitly deal with some aspects of vagueness (Reiger,[38] Zadeh,[39] etc.). Not even the reservations made in regard to fuzzy logic (Morgan and Pelletier[40]) will be brought into discussion here, although in enunciating them, one touches upon problems concerning the condition of semiotics itself, hence Peirce's basic doctrine (including the logic of vagueness). Our concern here has been to show the necessary relation between the components of this doctrine, a relation frequently ignored even though the price of this ignoring is the spoiling of the consistency of the semiotic procedure undertaken with the means of Peirce's semiotic. In this study, I did not follow a formal path (although I presented results involving mathematical formalization[41]) not because such a path is impossible or unpractical, nor because I fear instinctive rejection of mathematics or logics by semioticians. Rather, my intention was to suggest how congenial to our natural way of thinking and understanding are the logic of vagueness and the doctrine of continuity, hence how congenial the fuzzy approach is to us. Beyond the nonsystematic and often vague nature of Peirce's formulations, this conclusion stands out with real clarity.

Mihai Nadin

University of Bucharest, Institute of Philosophy
University of Munich, Seminar for Philosophy,
Logics and Science Theory

NOTES

*This work is part of a comprehensive research supported by the Humboldt Foundation and accomplished at the University of Munich, Seminar für Philosophie, Logik und Wissenschaftstheorie.

1. *Collected Papers of Charles Sanders Peirce*, vols. I-VI. Charles Hartshorne and Paul Weiss, eds. (Cambridge, Mass.: The Belknap Press of Harvard University Press, 1960). Vols. VII–VIII, Arthur W. Burks, ed. (Cambridge, Mass.: Harvard University Press, 1958). References to this take the usual volume-paragraph form. As far as manuscripts are concerned, reference is made to *Charles S. Peirce Papers in the Houghton Library* by the numbers assigned in Robin's *Annotated Catalogue of the Papers of Charles S. Peirce*. References to Peirce's *New Elements of Mathematics*, edited by Carolyn Eisele, are by volume and page number.
2. Russell, Bertrand: "Vagueness," in *Australian Journal of Psychology and Philosophy*, 1 (1923): 84–92.
3. Wright, Crispin: "On the Coherence of Vague Predicates," in *Synthèse*, 30 (1975): 325.
4. Frege, Gottlob: "Uber die wissenschaftliche Berechtigung einer Begriffsschrift," in *Zeitschrift für Philosophie und philosophische Kritik*, 81 (1882): 48–56.
5. Carnap, Rudolf: *Meaning and Necessity. A study in Semantics and Modal Logic* (Chicago and London: The University of Chicago Press, 1947). In order to take vagueness into account while giving a formulation of the intension of a predicate, "a pair of intensions F_1, F_2 must be stated: X has the disposition of ascribing affirmatively the predicate 'Q' to an object y if and only if y has F_1; and the disposition of denying 'Q' for y if and only if y has F_2. Thus, if y has neither F_1 nor F_2, X will give neither an affirmative nor a negative response; the property of having neither F_1 nor F_2 constitutes the zone of vagueness, which may be possibly empty." pp. 242–43.
6. Wittgenstein, Ludwig: *Philosophical Investigations/Philosophische Untersuchungen* (Oxford: Blackwell, 1958.)
7. Montague, Richard: "Pragmatics," in *Formal Philosophy. Selected Papers of Richard Montague*. Ed. and with intro. by Richmond H. Thomason (New Haven and London: Yale University Press, 1974), pp. 95–119.
8. Quine, Willard van Orman: *Word and Object* (Cambridge, Mass.: The M.I.T. Press, 1960), pp. 125–29.
9. Lewis, D.: "General Semantics," in *Semantics of Natural Language*, Davidson, D. and Harman, G. eds. (Dordrecht, Holland: D. Reidel, 1972).

10. Lakoff, G.: "A Study in Meaning Criteria and the Logic of Fuzzy Concepts," in *Journal of Philosophical Logic*, 2 (1973): 458–508.

11. Moravcsik, J.M.: "Linguistics and Philosophy," in *Current Trends in Linguistics*, 12 (*Linguistics and Adjacent Arts and Sciences*) (The Hague: Mouton, 1974), p. 15.

12. Feibleman, James: *An Introduction to Peirce's Philosophy Interpreted as a System* (New York and London: Harper & Brother Publishers, 1946). Remarks on vagueness are made in a section devoted to "Critical Common-Sensism", pp. 310–16.

13. Gallie, W.B.: *Peirce and Pragmatism* (Harmondsworth, Middlesex: Penguin Books, 1952 and "Peirce's Pragmaticism," in *Studies in the Philosophy of Charles Sanders Peirce*, Philip P. Wiener and Frederic H. Young, eds. (Cambridge, Mass.: Harvard University Press, 1952), pp. 61–75. Approaching "The Problem of Vague Predicates" Gallie notices that Peirce, "in the Pragmaticism Papers, approaches the subject of vagueness from a number of different sides. He claims, for instance, that all our most deeply grounded and in practice indubitable beliefs are essentially vague (5.446); and this is true, in his opinion, both of particular 'acritical' judgments of perception and of such highly general beliefs as that God (in some sense) is real, and that Nature is (in some sense) uniform. On the 'logic of vagueness' he has some remarkably acute and suggestive things to say, although nothing (as far as the Pragmaticism Papers or any other of his published writings show) that bears out his claim to have 'worked out the logic of vagueness in something like completeness." p. 66.

14. McKeon, K. Charles: "Peirce's Scotistic Realism," in *Studies in the Philosophy of Charles Sanders Peirce*, Philip P. Wiener and Frederic H. Young, eds. (Cambridge, Mass.: Harvard University Press, 1952), pp. 238–51.

15. Cohen, L., Jonathan: *The Diversity of Meaning* (London: Methuen & Co. 1962), chap. IX: "Meaning and Vagueness," pp. 265–77. "On C. S. Peirce's view it had been the law of non-contradiction rather than that of excluded middle which is restricted in scope by the phenomenon of universal vagueness," pp. 265–66. "Peirce seems to have concluded not that formal logic is intrinsically inapplicable to ordinary discourse but rather that a new logic, 'a logic of vagueness,' was required, which he said he had 'worked out with something like completeness'; and though Peirce's logic of vagueness has never been found various attempts have since been made to replace its loss," p. 266.

16. Hamilton, Sir William: *Lectures on Logic*. Edinburgh: H. L. Mansel and J. Veitch edit., 2nd vol.

17. Cf. Peirce, Ch., S.: "Upon Logical Comprehension and Extension," *Proceedings of the American Academy of Arts and Sciences*, vol. 7, Nov. 13, 1867, intended as Essay III of *Search of Method* and as chap. 15 of the *Grand Logic*.

18. "A symbol, in its reference to its object, has a triple reference: First, Its direct reference to its object, or the real things which it represents; Second, Its reference to its ground through its object, or the common characters of those objects; Third, Its reference to its interpretant through its object, or all the facts known about its object, cf. First, The informed breadth of the symbol; Second, The informed depth of the symbol." (2.408).

19. Jevons, W. J.: *Lessons in Logic*, 1870, republished by McMillan, 1965.

20. Peirce, Ch.,S.: "Ethics of Terminology," in *Syllabus of Certain Topics of Logic*. (Boston: Alfred Mudge & Son, 1903).

21. Jevons, W. J.: *Lessons in Logic*, p. 39. "breadth: the individual things to which the name *applies*; depth: the qualities the possession of which by those things is *implied*."

22. Fine, Kit: "Vagueness, Truth and Logic," in *Synthèse*, 30 (1975): pp. 265–300.

23. Nadin, Mihai: "Das semiotische Feld," in *Zeichen und Wert* (Tübingen: Günther Narr Verlag, 1980 [forthcoming].)

24. Przelecky, Marian: "Fuzziness as Multiplicity," in *Synthèse* 30 (1975): 375: "second order vagueness: borderline cases of borderline cases in universe U."

25. Quine, Willard van Orman: *Word and Object*, p. 127.

26. Creswell, M.J.: "Semantic Competence," in *Meaning and Translation. Philosophic and Linguistic Approaches* (London: Duckworth [forthcoming]).

27. Putnam, Hilary: "The Meaning of Meaning," in *Mind, Language and Reality* (Cambridge: Cambridge University Press, 1975). " . . . a 'set,' in the mathematical sense, is a 'yes-no' object; any given object either definitely belongs to S or definitely does not belong to S, if S is a set. But words in a natural language are not generally 'yes-no': there are things of which the description 'tree' is clearly false, to be sure, but there are a host of borderline cases," p. 133.

28. Lewis, D.: "General Semantics."

29. Bar-Hillel, Jehoshua: "Indexical Expressions," in *Universal Semantics and Philosophy of Language* (Jerusalem: The Magnus Press, 1970).

30. MacLane, Saunders: *Categories for the Working Mathematician* (New York, Heidelberg, Berlin: Springer Verlag, 1972).

31. Harwick, C. S. (with the assistance of Cook, James): *Semiotics and Significs. The correspondence between Charles S. Peirce and Victoria Lady Welby* (Bloomington: Indiana: Indiana University Press, 1977).

32. Marty, Robert: "Une formalisation de la sémiotique de C. S. Peirce à l'aide de la théorie des catégories." *Semiosis* [forthcoming].

33. Nadin, Mihai: "Sign and the sign theories. On the Scientific Foundation of Semiotics," in *Versus*, (1980) (forthcoming).

34 Nadin, Mihai: "Sign and Fuzzy Automata," in *Semiosis* 1:5 (1977).

35. Zadeh, L.: "Fuzzy Sets," in *Information and Control*, 8 (1965): pp. 338–53.

36. Gentilhomme, Yves: "Les ensembles flous en linguistique," in *Cahiers de linguistique thé*orique et appliquée. Bucharest, 5:47 (1968).

37. Zadeh, L.: "Foreword" to *Introduction to the Theory of Fuzzy Subsets*, vol. 1, by Kaufman, A. (New York: Academic Press, 1975), p. 5.

38. Rieger, Burghard: "Unscharfe Semantik natürlicher Sprache. Zum Problem der Repräsentation and Analyse vager Bedeutungen." (Aachen: MESY, 1976).

39. Zadeh. L.: "Fuzzy Logic and Approximate Reasoning. (In memory of Grigore Moisil)," in *Synthèse* 30 (1975): pp. 407–28.

40. Morgan, Charles, Grady and Pelletier, Francis, Jeffry: "Some Notes Concerning Fuzzy Logics," in *Linguistics and Philosophy*, 1:1 (1977): pp. 79–97. "The first deficiency with fuzzy semantical systems is the lack of simple algorithmic methods which can be programmed for computers to provide a useful toll for logicians, linguists, or researchers in artificial intelligence and robotics."

41. Nadin, Mihai: "On the Semiotic Nature of Value," in *Ars Semeiotica*, 3:1 (1978), (Boulder: *Ars Semeiotica Press*) pp. 33–48.

PEIRCE'S PHENOMENOLOGICAL DEFENSE OF DEDUCTION

Since the publication of Husserl's *Logische Untersuchungen* at the outset of this century, the notion of phenomenology has had a long and important history on the European continent. Of the many claims made on its behalf perhaps the most interesting is that phenomenology is able to ground philosophical assertions in a manner which is neither purely formal nor purely empirical, i.e., that phenomenology as a method is capable of transcending this very distinction. For example, phenomenologists argue that their reduction of essences provides a way of knowing which is neither analytic nor synthetic but both. Having reached such an eidetic intuition phenomenologists claim to have attained a non-trivial universality and necessity.

The significance of this claim can be readily translated into a specific problematic more familiar to the English speaking tradition. The phenomenologist could be seen as claiming that one need not choose between a purely formal justification of deduction such as that provided by Hume and a purely empirical justification of deduction such as that offered by J. S. Mill. One can have it all if one avails oneself of the phenomenological method.

It will be the task of this paper to argue that the English speaking tradition already has such a method available to it without translation in the later thought of Charles Sanders Peirce and that this American version of phenomenology was used to perform just the synthesis in question: to provide a defense of the validity of deductive logic which is both formal and factual.[1] At once Peirce can claim that ". . . logic contents itself almost entirely, like mathematics, with considering what would be the case in hypothetical states of things." (2.65) and "that a premise should be pertinent to such a conclusion, it is requisite that it should relate, not to how we think, but to the necessary connections of different sorts of fact." (2.52)[2] This prima facie contradiction between a formal, hypothetical justification of deduction and an empirical, factual justification is reconciled by Peirce's phenomenology.

1. Precision and the Triad

Before we turn to a direct consideration of Peirce's phenomenological method two other topics in his thought will need to be addressed. The first is his theory of abstraction. Peirce recognizes two kinds: precision and hypostatic abstraction.[3] Precision is a logical operation based on an insight similar to Duns Scotus' formal distinction. This distinction like a purely logical distinction is introduced by the mind yet like the distinction in fact it is

justified by the reality of the object. Peirce calls this formal distinction precision, the logical distinction discrimination, and the distinction in fact dissociation. Compared to the other distinctions precision is:

> the act of supposing (whether with consciousness of fiction or not) something
> about one element of a percept, upon which our thought dwells, without paying
> any regard to other elements. Precision implies more than discrimination, which
> relates merely to the essence of a term. Thus I can, by an act of discrimination,
> separate color from extension; but I cannot do so by *precision*, since I cannot
> suppose that in any possible universe color . . . exists without extension. So with
> *triangularity* and *trilaterality*. On the other hand, precision implies much less
> than dissociation, which, indeed, is not a term of logic, but of psychology. It is
> doubtful whether a person who is not devoid of the sense of sight can separate
> space from color by dissociation . . . but he can, and indeed does do so, by *preci-
> sion* . . . . (1.549n)

Precision is the selective imaginative attention to one element of experience
without attention to its normal real accompaniments. This does not mean
that that element so selected can or does exist separately, but only that it may
be thought separately. Furthermore, the process of precision is nonreciprocal.[4] One can, for example, prescind shape from color and extension
from shape but not vice versa. We can imaginatively suppose a shape whose
color is too poorly lit to see or an extension whose shape is too amorphous to
discern. We cannot however even imaginatively entertain a color which had
no shape or a shape without extension.

The second type of abstraction is hypostasization. Quite simply it is the
abstraction which allows us to infer that x has sweetness from the claim that x
is sweet. Hypostatic abstraction turns the predicate of a proposition into a
subject itself.[5] Precision may then be applied to the hypostasized predicate.
Thus having abstracted "x is sweet" to "the sweetness of x" one may then
proceed to prescind tastiness from sweetness, quality from tastiness, etc.
Hypostatic abstraction is a way of treating a predicate so as to exhibit its
relationships to other predicates. Its truth consists in the fact that other facts
conform to the relationships they exhibit. The hypostasized predicate is an
ens rationis. Though not itself a fact it is nevertheless real as it is a fact about
facts. Thus sweetness might be called a fictitious thing, in one sense.

> But since the mode of being attributed to it *consists* in no more than the fact that
> some things are sweet, and it is not pretended, or imagined, that it has any other
> mode of being, there is after all, no fiction. The only profession made is that we
> can consider the fact of honey being sweet under the form of a relation; and so we
> really can. (4.235)

The major logical and scientific benefit of hypostasization and precision
is that together they afford a way of drawing necessary consequences. Knowing that honey is sweet we may without fear of self-deception regard the

honey as possessing sweetness. If we also know that sweetness and palatability are related through some meaning connection then we now know with certitude some additional facts about honey.

The second topic that must be touched upon at least in a preliminary fashion is Peirce's well-known triadicism, especially as it surfaces in mathematical logic. In his later writings an architectonic structure comes to take on greater and greater significance for Peirce. According to this scheme the sciences of discovery have three great divisions: mathematics, philosophy and idioscopy or the special sciences. Mathematics, including mathematical logic, is distinguished by virtue of the fact that its discoveries are due to observation of its own ideal creatures and that its conclusions, though purely hypothetical and formal, are drawn with necessity. The special sciences (i.e., physics, chemistry, biology, etc.) by contrast are empirical and probabalistic in character and adopt special instrumentation to discover a world not of its own making. Philosophy stands between mathematics and the special sciences making "discoveries" which . . . "come within the range of every man's normal experience, and for the most part in every waking hour of his life." (1.241) Philosophy itself has three parts: phenomenology, the normative sciences (aesthetics, ethics, logic) and metaphysics. It is Peirce's contention that the more general sciences supply principles or starting assumptions for the less general; thus mathematics supplies an ideal world of which philosophy investigates the most general real properties, the special sciences in turn investigating portions of that philosophically determined reality. Given this view the source of the triad must be sought in mathematics, its reality shown in philosophy and its relevance to specific investigation made apparent in empirical research.

Within the realm of mathematical or formal logic Peirce believed his greatest achievement to have been his development of the logic of relatives.[6] This logic is ". . . nothing but formal logic generalized to the very tiptop." (3.473) Whereas in ordinary formal logic class or kind as a relationship of similarity is taken to be primitive, it is Peirce's insight here to seize upon the notion of relation itself as the most primitive relation. While it is well beyond the scope of our interests here to provide anything like a full treatment of Peirce's views on relation we do need to show the intimacy of the triad to it. Perhaps the clearest most direct statement of this centrality of the triad is Charles Hartshorne's.

The reason is that the idea of combination itself is a triple relative, thus $X = YZ$. But then for YZ we can substitute X, and build up the more complex whole $A = XW$, which is now the same as $A = YZW$. In this way any degree of complexity can be reached.[7]

If it will be admitted that the monadic, single variable relation $(X = X)$ and the dyadic, two variable relation $(X = Y)$ are both degenerate relations (the one only to itself directly, the other only to itself under another name) then the triadic relation $(X = YZ)$ is the lowest level genuine relation. Only here is real combination involved. Furthermore, as Hartshorne has argued, any polyadic relation can be expressed as complexes of triads. The conclusion which Peirce draws is that the triad is both necessary and sufficient to express any genuine relationship.

If the most basic of all relationships is relation itself and all relations can be viewed as possible functions of the triad, there is a mathematical (hence hypothetical) reason to look for a triadic structure in all relationships. It is this anticipation that sets the stage for Peirce's system.

2. Phenomenology

We have seen that mathematical logic provides a priori reason to anticipate triadic structures in all relations. But the reasons of mathematics relate only to the "creatures of the mind" (2.192) and as such need have no bearing on existential truth. It is a study of ideal constructions and we have no right to assume that it applies to matters of fact.[8] To move into the real world of fact, a bridge of some sort is required: phenomenology. Phenomenology will justify the application of the triad to the real world. Peirce confirms this interpretation of phenomenology's role.

> We find then a priori that there are three categories of undecomposable elements to be expected in the Phaneron: those which are simply positive totals, those which involve dependence but not combinations, those which involve combination.

> Now let us turn to the phaneron and see what we find in fact. (1.299)[9]

Phenomenology is the attempt to discern any elements that might be universally present in experience, where 'experience' is most broadly construed.[10] No attempt is made to distinguish reality from illusion.[11] Phenomenology is the study of what appears or what seems.[12] Approaching the phenomena in this fashion, Peirce verifies the findings of mathematical logic. There are three universally present elements in every possible experience. They correspond to the monadic relation, the dyadic relation and the triadic relation. Peirce calls them firstness, secondness and thirdness, respectively.

Firstness is that which is as it is in itself regardless of anything else.[13] It is strictly speaking only possibility but it is best approached in ideas of "freshness, life, freedom" (1.302) and especially quality. The quality of being

red, for example, is what it is irrespective of anything else. Qualities of
firstness are *sui generis*. No pure firsts are ever experienced as such but
aspects of firstness are always present. Every experience imaginable will have
its own quality, its own total felt uniqueness. Red has its unique quality of
feeling, but so does walking, Beethoven's Ninth Symphony, affection for a
friend, etc. These are all firsts.

Secondness is dyadic.[14] It is best captured by effort and resistence. It
represents the otherness of the non-ego resisting the efforts of the ego, the
brute facticity of the world. It is the secondness of the percept which compels
perceptual judgment and demands our conformity with it. It is the secondness
of experience which allows us to use predictive success as a mark of truth,
since brute actuality will confound erroneous theories. Every experience has
its element of secondness, that which demands our attention. It is the constant "jab in the ribs" of experience.

Thirdness is the medium which relates firsts with seconds. It is representation itself.[15] It is generality, mentality, relation, law. All experience for
Peirce, since it is cognitive at the lowest-level (the perceptual judgment) is a
third. We begin with our representations of the world and discover within
them a compulsion of bruteness and a quality of feeling.

Phenomenology is a positive empirical science. These categories are not
in any way deduced from the a priori arguments of mathematical logic. If one
wants to verify such claims one must attend to the phenomena. Doesn't every
experience display a cognitive, a brute and a qualitative element? The
categories thus do not rely on arguments; instead they are empirical. They are
not, however, factual in the sense of an inductive science's facts. These elements of experience are universally present. We know this since they are constantly open to inspection with no special effort needed. The requisite experiments can be performed at will both in imagination and without since
phenomenology knows no such distinction. The phenomena are ever present
for scrutiny. Phenomenological statements when made in the face of the
phenomena are universal and indubitable.[16] No data collection is made. No
probabilities are calculated. Every person may test and confirm them at will
merely by an act of imaginative attention.

It should also be clear that firstness, secondness and thirdness are not
parts of experience. They are rather aspects of one unitary whole.
Phenomenology observes the phenomena and then precinds the categories.
They are then hypostasized into the substantives; firstness, secondness and
thirdness—and precinded again.

> Now the categories cannot be dissociated in imagination from each other, nor
> from other ideas. The category of first can be precinded from second and third
> and second can be precinded from third. But second cannot be precinded from
> first, nor third from second. (1.353)

The phenomenological categories are not factually in the phenomena since dissociation cannot separate them. But precision can. Therefore they are aspects of the phenomena, distinguished by the mind but with a justification in the appearance. This justification can be tested at will by appeal to the universally present phenomena. Furthermore the phenomenological categories reveal the hierarchic, nonreciprocal structure of precision: firstness may be precinded from secondness and thirdness, secondness from thirdness but not from firstness and thirdness not at all. One can imaginatively enter a world of qualities without otherness and a world of otherness without cognition of it but one cannot imagine a world of cognitions without an other to cognize nor a world of otherness having no quality. And no world of pure thirdness is imaginable without the other two.

Now that we have seen Peirce's views on abstraction, the triad, and phenomenology we have all we need to reconcile the prima facie contradiction in his justification of deduction.

3. Icons and Diagrams

We know now that triadic analysis is justified in fact. Let us use it to explore the objects of signs. The sign context is composed of the sign itself, the interpretant of the sign and the sign in relation to its object. This last is ". . . the most fundamental [division of signs] . . . ." (2.275). There are three ways in which a sign relates to its object. The resultant signs are called icon, index and symbol and they represent the firstness, secondness and thirdness of the sign's relationship to its object. Icons are somehow *like* their objects.

> A sign by Firstness is an image of its object, and more strictly speaking, can only be an idea . . . A possibility alone is an Icon purely by virtue of its quality, and its object can only be a Firstness. But a sign may be iconic, that is, may represent its object mainly by its similarity, no matter what its mode of being. (2.276)

Images are icons, as are metaphors and any other sign whose representation depends mainly upon some quality of resemblance. For our purposes the most important icons are predicates.

> Hence, every assertion must contain an icon or set of icons, or else must contain signs whose meaning is only explicable by icons. The idea which the set of icons (or the equivalent of the set of icons) contained in an assertion signifies may be termed the *predicate* of the assertion. (2.278)

Indices somehow point out their objects. A weathervane is the classic example. It is an index of the wind because it points in a rather brute fashion (i.e. directly moved by its referent) to the wind's direction. Any sign that establishes a similar dyadic relation will be an index. A pointing finger, a gesture, a barometer, a call of attention, a knock at the door—all are indices.[17] With relation to the assertion the grammatical subject acts as an index. The 'this' of the assertion "This is red" is an index placing the hearer in the same dyadic relation with the red object as the speaker. Every grammatical subject places the interpretant in a mental relation with the object by drawing one's attention to it.

In our example "This is red," then, 'this' is the index and 'is red' is the predicate. Nevertheless, they do not compose an assertion. "Icons and Indices assert nothing." (2.291) A symbol as a third is needed to mediate the icon and index, to be the law of relation that makes that string of signs truly meaningful.

> A *Symbol* is a Representamen whose Representative character consists precisely in its being a rule that will determine its Interpretant. All words, sentences, books, and other conventional signs are symbols. (2.292)

All signs, all thought, all knowledge is symbolic. 'This' and 'is red' could not fulfill their functions as index and predicate if it were not for the conventional meanings attached to them. Bound together by this convention or law, they compose a complete symbol. Nevertheless we can precind the firstness and the secondness of the meaning and hypostasize them into the icon and the index. The justification, of course, is that every imaginable assertion is so analyzable. Again this claim can be checked against experience at will.

This inner checking is itself experience. One observes the onmipresence of the icon by way of inner experiment. This is true especially regarding mathematics. Peirce holds that mathematics is an observational science, observations being made on our mental creations. The necessary reasoning in mathematics is:

> . . . performed by means of observations and experiment, and its necessary character is due simply to the circumstances that the subject of this observation and experiment is a diagram of our own creation, the condition of whose being we know all about. (3.560)

The validity of mathematical reasoning, therefore, results from mental experimentation on iconic representations or diagrams. These diagrams are constructed by us to resemble their objects. The construction of such diagrams is not restricted to mathematics.

> All necessary reasoning whatsoever proceeds by constructions; and the only difference between mathematical and philosophical necessary deduction is that the latter are so excessively simple that the construction attracts no attention and is overlooked. The construction exists in the simplest syllogism in Barbara. (3.560)

One difference between mathematical and philosophical diagrams, then, is the unobtrusiveness of the syllogistic diagrams.

But there is another much deeper line of demarcation between the two sciences. It is that mathematics studies nothing but pure hypothesis, and is the only science which never inquires what the actual facts are; while philosophy, although it uses no microscopes or other apparatus of special observation, is really an experimental science, resting on that experience which is common to us all; so that its principal reasonings are not mathematically necessary at all, but are only necessary in the sense that all the world knows beyond all doubt those truths of experience upon which philosophy is founded. (3.560)

This necessity of philosophical demonstration relies on the universal availability of the experimental data. Its necessity derives ". . . the moment when experimentation can be multiplied *ad libitum* at no more cost than a summoning before the imagination. (4.531)[18]

Deduction is a diagram, therefore the form of the argument itself is iconic.[19] It is an image of the relationships it embodies. Those relata are themselves icons: predicates or hypostasized predicates. A necessary conclusion is drawn by way of the relationships among the icons (predicates) involved. These icons are ideas, mere possibilities.[20] An icon here is a pure meaning in itself.[21] The point of this ideal experimentation is to display an iconic representation of the relationships among icons of meaning. One manipulates these icons mentally and since meanings have internal laws themselves (viz. their own suchness) they will submit to or resist our manipulation.[22] The point of the experimentation is to allow the experimenter to *see* the necessity of the conclusion by perceiving the diagram and multiplying experiments *ad libitum* to insure its generality.[23]

> We form in the imagination some sort of diagramatic, that is, iconic, representation of the facts, as skeletonized as possible . . . This diagram, which has been constructed to represent intuitively or semi-intuitively the same relations which are abstractly expressed in the premises, is then observed, and a hypothesis suggests itself that there is a certain relation between some of its parts—or perhaps this hypothesis had already been suggested. In order to test this, various experiments are made upon the diagram, which is changed in various ways. This is a proceeding extremely similar to induction, from which, however, it differs widely, in that it does not deal with a course of experience, but with whether or not a certain state of things can be imagined. Now since it is part of the hypothesis that only a very limited kind of condition can affect the result, the necessary experimentation can be very quickly completed; and it is seen that the conclusion is compelled to be true by the conditions of the construction of the diagram. (2.778)

This justification of deduction is both formal and factual. It relies on formal meaning relationships existing between icons and it requires a kind of observation of the *universal* facts. This might suffice to reconcile the apparent contradiction. There is another sense of 'fact', however. Deduction must lead us to the truth, i.e., represent the particular facts to be as they are. Here the reconciliation of the formal and factual takes on transcendental overtones. Deduction as necessary reasoning *must* lead us to the facts. It has to capture "... what *must be* the characters of all signs used by a scientific intelligence, that is to say, by an intelligence capable of learning by experience." (2.227) We are in a position now to attempt this more difficult reconciliation. Here are the steps.

(A) We have seen that Peirce recognized a subtle variety of abstraction which allows for separations not separable in experience yet not purely logical. It is a mental separation which is justified in fact. Further, there is a certain non-reciprocity in this abstractive process.

(B) Through a formal, mathematical analysis of relation itself, Peirce is led to expect the structure of all experience to display a triadic structure. This anticipation being mathematical is related only to a hypothetical, ideal world, the world of possibility. Nevertheless, the architectonic begins at mathematical logic with this expectation.

(C) Taking this a priori expectation and this method of abstraction to the data of experience, Peirce isolates three phenomenological categories present in *all* experience. Phenomenology thus fulfills the anticipation of mathematical logic. A certain ideal triadic structure is revealed to be omnipresent in the real, as well as the ideal.

(D) Since phenomenology has demonstrated the universal applicability of the triad to the real world, Peirce is justified in analyzing the sign as it relates to its objects triadically. By nonreciprocal precision and hypostasization he is able to examine in diagram the icon and its relationships. Their relationships are themselves ideal inasmuch as the icons are ideas in themselves, i.e., meanings or substantivized predicates.

(E) All thought is carried in signs. Part of every sign must be an icon. Therefore any possible sign is bounded by what binds the icon, viz. its relationships to other icons. Any possible thought, then, *must* respect the relationships between icons, icons being necessary parts of every sign and signs being necessary to thought. Unless we are to entertain some unknowable we must hold that what cannot be thought in any way is no part of experience. Every possible experience therefore must conform to the relationships among icons as represented in the diagram, i.e., in deduction. Valid deductions *must* be confirmed in all possible facts.

The centrality of phenomenology here is evident. It has shown the applicability of the ideal triad to the real world. Deduction establishes certain necessary meaning relationships about other ideal entities, the meaning icons. These then are known to be applicable to the real world; they are a part of it as a first is to the whole triad. They are the firstness aspects of all experience.

If this reading of Peirce is at all adequate then his phenomenological method achieves for our understanding of deductive logic a result remarkably similar to that of Husserl. Logic for both thinkers is grounded in a fashion transcending the standard options of certain yet empty and empirical yet probable. Both offer under the same name a philosophical method capable of uncovering an ideal realm of meanings; hence a method of analysis not committed to reduction to the non-significant. Given this similarity it may not be unreasonable to hope that a new look at Peirce's phenomenology might lead to a series of developments of the order of those which have followed from the work of Husserl.

The single greatest difficulty to be overcome in this connection is the widespread impression that Peirce's commitment to triadic analysis is metaphysical in character or that it is sheer numerology. Neither charge is justified. Peirce's architechtonic scheme clearly yields the anticipation of the triad in mathematical logic, finds it omnipresent in experience in phenomenology and employs it to ground the normative sciences. All of this is prior to the metaphysical task of describing the most general features of the real world. The rationale for this ordering is clear. Mathematical logic is purely formal, phenomenology and the normative sciences are purely ideal. These realms must be dealt with before one approaches the real as they are clearly more inclusive. Hence triadic analyses do not depend on metaphysical assumptions. Rather they make metaphysics itself possible.

Finally there is no direct response available to the suspicion that at root Peirce's triad is merely number magic. While it does not seem unreasonable to suggest that cognition in all its various expressions is a mediator of the worlds of ideas and sense, no argument can sustain such a cosmic thesis. The "proof" lies rather in its universal relevance to the philosophical project. If the triad and its phenomenological expressions render the otherwise inexplicable available to understanding it will have passed the final test of all.

Charles J. Dougherty

Creighton University

NOTES

1. The "later thought" of Peirce in this context shall mean post-1890. It is after this date that Peirce most clearly develops his notion of phenomenology within an architectonic scheme of all the sciences.

2. The standard convention for reference to Peirce's works is observed throughout. All references are to the *Collected Papers* vols. I–VI edited by Charles Hartshorne and Paul Weiss, vols. VII–VIII edited by Arthur W. Burks. (Cambridge: Harvard University Press, 1931–1958).

3. Peirce varied his spelling of 'precision' and 'precind' during his career. For simplicity I will use these spellings throughout.

4. 1.549

5. 4.235, 4.323, 5.448, 1.83, 4.549, 3.642.

6. 4.1ff

7. Charles Hartshorne, "Charles Peirce's 'One Contribution to Philosophy' and His Most Serious Mistake," *Studies in the Philosophy of C. S. Peirce,* ed. by Philip Weiner and Frederick Young (Cambridge: Harvard University Press) 1952, p. 455.

8. 1.240, 1.53, 1.184, 2.191, 2.763, 3.558.

9. Peirce sometimes used 'phaneron' for 'phenomenon' and 'phaneroscopy' for 'phenomenology'.

10. 1.186, 1.286, 2.84, 5.37, 5.43, 8.239.

11. 2.120, 2.197, 1.287, 5.37.

12. 5.37, 2.197, 2.84.

13. 1.302ff.

14. 1.322ff.

15. 1.337ff.

16. 1.288, 2.197.

17. 2.283.

18. In that sense deductive certainty is the same as inductive certainty in the final ideal community. The ability to multiply examples *ad libitum* fulfills the function of the "long run" since *all* relevant observations are universally present. See also 4.232, 3.538, 2.778.

19. 4.531, 7.205.

20. 4.531, 3.438.

21. See e.g., 8.119, 1.471.

22. 5.45, 1.322, 1.425, 1.455. This suggests elements of thirdness (law) and secondness (resistance) but we are concerned primarily with the iconic *aspect.*

23. 5.148, 5.164, 4.246, 2.191, 2.120.

THE NATURE AND MODES OF TIME

One of the topics that appears regularly in even the most casual inventories of philosophical problems is the problem of time. Time is such a pervasive, resilient feature of experience that it cannot be ignored. But time is also so vague that almost any analysis or tracking procedure we use to enhance and purify its signals overrides or baffles those signals. We begin a study of the phenomena of temporality and find that our attention is displaced from the temporal continuum to different ways of being seated in it.

Charles Sanders Peirce frequently dealt with the problem of time. He dealt with it in a way of befitting its pervasive but vague character, conducting many sorties into its domain but never a single strategic campaign. His longest passages on time are short in comparison with the discussions of time by many other philosophers. But in the aggregate, there is a wealth of material on the different problems of temporality in Peirce's writings. With occasional exceptions, his different pronouncements fit together effectively. Moreover, his doctrines about time are not peripheral, but clearly go to essentials. For insofar as his philosophy is synechistic, it is also temporalistic.

Time, we shall find Peirce arguing, is a paradigm for all other continua. Their main features are foreshadowed by the structure and modes of time. Since time is the best version of continuity, and since continuity is "the form of forms" in Peirce's philosophy,[1] it follows that his philosophy of time resides with certain other elements at the center of his system, helping determine lines of argument in his metaphysics, in his pragmatism and in his account of the logic of the sciences.

We treat Peirce's philosophy of time under these headings:
1. The Origin of Time
2. The Nature of Time
3. The Reality of Time
4. The Modes of Time

Most of his expositors barely mention his theories of time, if they cite them at all. The only students of Peirce's work who give much attention to his views on time are Murray G. Murphey[2] and James K. Feibleman.[3]

1. The Origin of Time

There are four major alternatives regarding the origin of time: (1) time was created, (2) time has evolved, (3) time was both created and has evolved, and (4) time did not arise in any sense whatever, but always was. Peirce did not think this last alternative, the most Hellenic of them, was a serious option. For it would make the universe eternal and recurrent, and rule out novelty and chance. Peirce rejected the eternity of time in the act of affirming the third alternative above. If time were eternal, it would then be co-eternal with God, and would thus limit or constrain Him. "It is a degraded conception to conceive God as subject to Time, which is rather one of His creatures" (4.67).[4] Making God subject to or limited by time would bind God to the necessary relations that typify time.

For Peirce, then, time is the result of the action of a creative ground. Time is brought about by a creative power that is divine (6.505–6). God created it and is still creating it. But Peirce also thought that time evolved or developed. As a part of a universe which gradually arose, time itself has a beginning. There must have been "a state of things before time was organized" (6.214).[5] There were circumstances and complexes when time was not: that is the assumption that Peirce is making his peace with.[6] And such views are the very stuff of myth.

Peirce's creation story goes about like this. In the beginning was an *arche* that was a zone of power (6.193). But it was not yet a stage of orderedness. Flashes of potentiality illumined the primal condition but had not yet ordered it into a world. As the original zone took on organization, the swarm of disparate potentialities became the universe, and temporal and spatial forms are the raiment in which the universe discloses itself. Time and space are features of all that exists. "Existence is a stage of evolution" (6.195). But existence is neither the first nor the last word about things. It is a species of reality, one which tricks itself out in the modes of space and time.

For Peirce, time is the constancy and the intent of God's creative activity as it is manifested in the existing universe. Time is created but not caused.[7] For cause presupposes a temporal order which the relations of dependence and antecedence have as their locus. Peirce thought that there was a clear connection between the argument from design and the belief that the material universe had an arbitrary beginning (6.419). A meaningful argument from design requires that time and space had a beginning, and that matter began with them. In such a finite, material universe, there can be real reactions. It is the spate of real reactions in a non-eternal material universe that sets real time off from mathematical time. Mathematical time is governed by the principle of non-contradiction, and not by the principle of existential reaction that is typical of real time. Mathematical time, Peirce held, is mere possibleness (6.326). It has no arbitrary beginning. It is time without limits, an endless, abstract, eternal time. A flaw in Hellenic cosmology would be, for Peirce, patterning natural or real time after mathematical time, and concluding that the cosmos is eternal.

2. The Nature of Time

Time, for Peirce, is the prime continuum. As a continuum, it welds the world into a greater unity. Objectively outside of us, time also appears in human experience and welds us to the world. It is important for our knowledge of the continua within the material world, especially as in physics (6.387). Indeed, time is the most excellent kind of continuum (6.86). It provides paradigms for all other kinds of continua.

Peirce believed that continuity is "the leading conception of science" and that it plays a part in all of the laws of physics and psychics (1.62). If we assert that time is the best example of kinds of continuity, and that kinds of continuity provide us the leading conceptions of the various sciences, we can conclude that the temporal continuum gives the sciences the legislative ideas for the organization of their different subject matters. Peirce found the entire topic of continuity entrancing (1.171). Things are awash in continua. Peirce could conceive of his work as a synthesis of the various movements in modern science insofar as they treated continuity under the twin forms of time and space. The doctrine that all that exists is continuous is called synechism by Peirce (1.172). The work of Aristotle, Kant, and Hegel on continuity were important precursors to Peirce's investigations. Continuity is a fundamental idea in philosophy and synechism is the doctrine that says as much (6.103). Peirce emphasized continuity over chance. He called his system synechism, as far as preferred titles go, and not tychism (6.202). Tychism emphasizes Firstness, but synechism stresses Thirdness. Indeed, continuity is Thirdness almost to perfection (1.337).

Time is so pre-eminently a kind of continuum that Peirce thought "we envisage every other continuum" according to its devices (6.86). To support this contention, he defines two other continua, mathematical and spatial, in terms of the time continuum (6.164). The implication is clear: the grammar of temporality provides the structure of all other continua which obtain in the realm of actual reactions. Time gives the reactions in the spatial continuum their unique non-general marks, those of exact location and full concreteness (6.82). Indirectly, in that they embody the conditions of possibility, time and space are together inherent in the continuity of nature (4.172). But they are not the sole grounds for continuity in nature. Others are found in the conditions of generality, such as the manner in which some properties are shared by different natural complexes.

Time may be the most excellent kind of continuum. But it is not perfectly continuous (1.412). For time is also a zone where forceful reactions occur, and these reactions dislocate or interrupt the temporal continuum to a degree. Thus, time seems to be continual rather than continuous, sometimes more intermittent than unremitting. This suggests that Peirce was clearly thinking of time in non-spatial terms. But precisely how could there be a discontinuous continuity? Peirce's view of time seems to require such a condition. We can, in imagination, hit on a continuity of this kind if we move away from the images of time as a flowing stream or as the "time-line" of the classroom. Let us try other images. A rope, for example, is continuous but interrupted. A coil of rope fifty feet long has no fifty-foot fibers in it, but is composed of endless overlappings, side-wise interweavings and braidings. The fibers are like the "topical singularities" that interrupt or divide a continuum at a lower level of generality (4.642). A rope can be a suitable image for a discontinuous continuum, discontinuous as regards its partial singularities but continuous as a complex interacting whole.

Let us call that trait of time in virtue of which it is a discontinuous continuum its Peirce-continuity, and hereafter, its P-continuity. Stated formally, P-continuity is "a discontinuous series with additional possibilities" (1.170). This phrasing is one of the expressions Peirce used to define a continuum. Relating the definition of P-continuity to the rope metaphor, we would say that the individual fibers would make up the discontinuous series," and the overlappings and braidings would be part of the "additional possibilities." Elsewhere (6.168), Peirce held that the parts of a continuum which interrupt its perfect continuity arise out of the act of defining. In our image, the hemp fibers are what the rope resolves into through high definition.

In addition to the formal property of the continuum we have denominated as its P-continuity, Peirce held that continuity had defining features which he called Kanticity and Aristotelicity. The Kanticity of a continuum is its endless divisibility or infinite intermediation (4.121; 6.166). This means that between any two points in a continuous series there are more points. This Kant-continuity or K-continuity means that every part of a true continuum has parts of the same kind (6.168). Between any putative isolates set off against each other, there are new isolates which modulate the original relation between the initial features, and these new bits are like the others in some respects.

The third essential feature of the nature of time as the prime continuum is Aristotelicity. The Aristotle-continuity of a continuum or its A-continuity is the property that any two points of a continuum have a common limit (4.122; 6.164). If we take all of the existing points in a continuous series, at any intensified degree of K-continuity we choose, the last member of one part of the series is also the first member of the next part. A-continuity would signify, taken strictly, that the continuous series is never fully disconnected. A continuous series retains connexity in some sense. Every point can be taken as the limit to an infinite series (6.166). As applied to time, this would mean that every part or element of a temporal continuum can be related to every other part.

K-continuity stresses the sense in which time seems to be composed of intervals or durations. A-continuity stresses the sense in which the temporal continuum is composed of instants or moments. If, in addition, every part of a continuum is composed just of parts like itself, then there is no real novelty in time but only combinatory novelty. It was to insure the feature of real beginnings that Peirce worked with the idea of a discontinuous continuum. This third property of the temporal continuum suggests the way the temporal continuum is open to additional properties, qualities and reactions, to Firsts and Seconds. P-continuity is needed to make sense of the additional possibilities from outside a given continuum. Thus, P-continuity would mean that real time is multiply- or n-tracked. Time has branchings and confluences. There are always, P-continuity reminds us, two or more continua braiding together in the existing world of reactions.

3. The Reality of Time

Time is some sort of objective order which exists independent of any perceiving subject. This view is what Peirce wished to argue against Kant. Cusanus, Bruno and Leibniz had all held that space and time are our creations.[8] Newton's doctrines about the objectivity and absoluteness of space and time not withstanding, Kant had followed them.[9] But according to Peirce, time is not ideal but real (5.458; 6.96). It is the way in which the conditions of objective possibility are displayed in the existing universe.

The laws of continuity must be geared down to become entrained in the world as we know it. Real time is time that is present (6.387; 6.506). The logical laws of being, including the laws of the continuum, take on increasing specificity in becoming first the metaphysical laws of reality and then the physical laws of reality. In discussing this transition from timeless being to temporal reality, Peirce uses the categories of actuality, nascence and possibility. These three categories are, respectively, versions of Firstness, Secondness and Thirdness. Historical influences from Aristotle (the emphasis on actuality) and from Duns Scotus (the idea of haecceity) influence this part of Peirce's theory of time.

For Peirce, to exist is to endure in time or to stand out in time as an actual event. Anything that does not exist for a time does not exist at all (3.93n). Thus, a necessary mark of existence is being in time. Another mark of existence is being general. There is no such thing as a sheer particular (3.93n). For being in general requires endurance through change, with the relations holding between the earlier and later stages of change. In order to speak of the same existent inhering through these changing stages, there must be an underlying relational identity of which the different stages are special cases. This relational identity is general as compared to the different stages in which it is displayed. Thus, Peirce can conclude, only general beings exist. There are qualitative possibilities, such as characteristics or properties, and they have a kind of being as Firsts. But they would not have the change and reaction due to ingredience in time, and Peirce does not speak of them as existing. Existence is a stage of evolution (6.195). It is the stage of evolution where time has arisen and force is exerted. It is the zone where reactions occur and actualities come to be. It is the realm of *faits accomplis*.

The mode of actuality is the mode of being where time really acts upon us (5.459). It acts on us about the same way that existing objects act upon us. It influences us as an existent in its own right. Still, time is not merely an existent. Since all existing things are general in some sense, so is time. Time is a form or a law (6.96). In addition to being a power and a general law, time is also a nascence where form and power blend as contracted possibilities or actual events. The actuality of an event consists in its happening then and there (1.24). It becomes partially arrested in time and space through entering into objective relations with other existents. Actuality is something brute, like the sheriff's hand upon one's shoulder, as Peirce was accustomed to saying. The leading edge of the actual is the nascent state of the present. It is where happenings here and now become impervious to additional influences, and become part of the sum of *faits accomplis*. The here and now fades insensibly by degrees into the there and then. The leading edge of the actual, the *hic et nunc* of things, is an aggressive stubbornness. This stubbornness or obstinacy of things is their *haecceitas* (1.405). Qualitative possibilities are braided together in this nascent state of the actual. Their reactions are limited by what can be according to the laws of logical possibility. Their reactions are also limited by what has already become a *fait accompli*. The *hic et nunc* is where the actual and the possible overlap. The reaction between them is brute, blind force (7.532). Possibilities were really welded together. These welds, which are reactions between qualitative elements like Firsts, have all of the here and nowness of events (6.200). Such events might be called pretemporal or proto-temporal events. Peirce needed to allow for such quasi-temporal happenings in order to underwrite his belief that the entire Platonic set of formal possibilities did in fact evolve.

4. The Modes of Time: Present, Past and Future

The traditional categories of modality are possibility, actuality and necessity. Peirce used these categories to draw distinctions between the three modes of time, present, past and future. To study this side of Peirce's philosophy of time is to realize immediately that the modal categories and the modes of time are not congruent. One of the most interesting sides of Peirce's contributions to the philosophy of time arises from his treatment of the relation between logical modality and temporal modality.

Time is related to objective modality, Peirce believed, as species is related to genus. Time is "a particular variety of objective modality" (5.459). Obvious modes of time are past, present and future. He called these features "general determinations of time" (5.458). These general determinations are grounded in the categories of logical modality in some respects. The past is what is actual. The mode of the past is the mode of actuality (5.459). The future is full of new determinations, as guided by law. But it is also full of potentialities, replete with what may become fact, but also may not. Accordingly, the modes of the future are the modes of necessity and possibility (5.459; 5.461). The three modal categories of actuality, possibility and necessity are assigned as features of the past and the future. What, then, is the mode of the present?

In some places Peirce proceeds as if all three of the modal categories characterize the present. Elsewhere, it appears that none of them typify it, that the present is non-existent and thus cannot be modally designated at all. In the former case, all three categories could apply to the present if the present is where the past and future overlap, and is composed jointly of them. This position is sometimes underwritten by Peirce. The present is half past and half to come (6.126). On this view, the present would be the zone where the actual, the necessary and the possible mingle.

Peirce's more customary doctrine, however, is that the present simply has no independent existence. It is at best something like a point instant. We cannot seize the immediate present (3.343). Indeed, the present seems to be nontemporal. Put flatly, we say it contains no time (1.38). The present is outside of time, cut off from the actual and the possible. Taken as a kind of instant, the present is simply a quale-consciousness, utterly severed from the past and future (6.231). It is where the future flows into the past, and where the past mirrors the destiny of the future to the future. But at the juncture of past and future, there is nothing present. There is no present (1.493). There may be the mere possibility of a conceptual cut across an idealized kind of continuum that mathematics can describe, but there is nothing at the present in a durational sense.

The reason that there is no present is that the flow of time keeps all of time's content in a constant process of relocation. There is no present because the fact that is to be present to us is already past (2.84). One result of this radical effervescence of the present is the interruption of the laws of the conservation of mass and energy. The past is broken off from the future, and there is independence of the actual instant (6.87). The past does not have the future in bondage. The present is a boundary (7.536). It is the boundary beyond which the power of the past cannot reach. There is no sheriff's hand in the future. The claims of the past have no direct agency in the future. Peirce is deeply committed to this break in time's passage. The present represents to him a boundary situation where chance is real and where novelty can arise.

Such a break in time's passage, almost by definition, would defy determination and analysis. The present, Peirce holds, is inscrutable (5.458). It is a zone where strange powers are present. It is occult (2.85). Itself lacking duration, it nevertheless accumulates and endures to become the substance of the past. The present has the peculiar property of being atemporal in the sense of having no time in it, yet it accumulates in wholes of time (7.675). It is a surd, a presence without determinations or modalities. It is a *haecceity* (1.405). It seems to be something only in relation to the other two modes of time, the future and the past. With them, it forms a conventional triad, for time is triadic (6.330-331). But apart from them it is nothing at all.

The following illustrations may help to suggest some of what Peirce said about the modes of time and their relations:

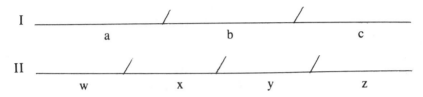

A traditional time line, one which symbolizes that the present has some duration, is illustrated in Case I here. Segment *a* would stand for the past, segment *b* would stand for the present, and segment *c*, the future. But Case I would not be acceptable to Peirce. For he denies that the present, as represented by segment *b*, has any duration. At best, the present *b* is where the past *a* and the future *c* overlap or blend. But Case I does not suggest to intuition that *b* is a power zone without extent in time, and it is just such an idea that is required. Under the double pressure of efficient causation (the force of the past) and final causation (the necessitation of general laws governing the future), the present implodes and becomes occult, effervescent and titanic.

A better representation of Peirce's view would be Case II. There, segments *w* and *x* represent the remote and near past respectively, and segments *y* and *z* represent the near and the remote future, respectively. The segments *x* and *y*, representing the near past and the near future, would be what we by convention call the present. *xy* would have entangling alliances with the efficacy of the past and the potentiality of the future. *xy* is a region of conflicting powers, where the residual malleability from the future suffers contraction so as to be compossible with ineluctable past fact.

Peirce explicitly distinguished between the near and the remote future. The indefinite, more remote future is that part of the future that the modal category of possibility applies to, represented by segment z in the diagram. The indefinite future is truly general, and cannot be fully realized (2.148) But that part of the future that the modal category of necessity applies to is the near future, represented by y. This immediate future, according to Peirce, is inevitable (7.536). In this zone, general laws governing possible relations are becoming more fully operative. This close-up real future is pre-determined (7.666). Given Peirce's application of the modalities of possibility and necessity to the future, and his division of the future into the indefinitely general and the inevitably determined, it is clear that the future is both open (as regards its more distant, general possibilities) and closed (as regards its constraining laws).

The past is also divided into two parts by Peirce, though not as clearly as the future is so divided. The mode of the past is the mode of actuality. Part of the past is still nascent. Segment x in Case II would represent this part of the past. But part of the past is dead, the part symbolized by segment w. The nascent state of the actual he did call the present (5.462). But he also said that there is no present because what is present is already past (2.84). The nascent state of the actual is still alive in some sense, with power and force working there. But the dead, finished part of the past that is no longer open to any kind of modification is the realm of *faits accomplis*. We tend to say that the present is what now is; it is the existential mode of time. But Peirce pushes this sense of time into the close past. For him, the past is the existential mode of time (5.458).

The present, we have seen, does not exist for Peirce except as it is revealed through the interplay of past and future. It is an epiphenomenon of their permutations. They, moreover, do not exist apart from each other. There is no time future by itself, nor a time past by itself. The past-future distinction, he said, is a polar distinction (1.330; 5.450; 5.458). This means that there is a temporal field made of waxing and waning events whose durations overlap and interweave. Any event in the field can be taken as having both antecedents and consequences. If we consider its antecedents, we have an event as the crest or high tide of of other conditions. In relation to the other conditions, the event is their end or telos, the high tide of their range of influence.

These final causes work from the future (6.66). They help to determine what can be. This is the sense in which we say that the future weeds out the past (7.667). But though an event is *in futuro* with respect to some things, it also has the stance *in praeterito* with respect to others. It trails off into other events and helps determine what they are. So taken, the past is an efficient cause working upon the future. Psychologically, for example, the past acts on the future as memory (1.325). To say that the past and future stand in a polar relation is to say that they are concurrent in every event. Trying to think of the future by itself is no help whatever, certainly not if we picture the future as a length of time (5.330). Every event has both past and future aspects, and thus must be understood under the double rubric of final and efficient causes. As half past and half to come, the present or what we take as the present must also be understood in a polar sense.

As half to come, the future is potentiality. Potential being is being *in futuro* (1.218). It is what may come to be in the relations between things. The future acts teleologically upon the past, in terms of thirds (1.325). But it is the more remote future that so acts, that part of the future whose modal character is possibility. Indeed, the future is a world of ideas (6.192). It is the realm of generality that has not yet become fixed in relation to some existing past. As unfixed, the future is undifferentiated (6.191). It is non-ego (7.536). But when the future becomes ours and takes on concreteness, it is then already part of the past (7.531). The analogy Peirce is using is that the non-ego is to the ego as the future is to the past.

In conclusion, it should be pointed out that Peirce's philosophy of time, however powerful in some respects, is limited by its dependence upon mathematical, physicalistic and theological themes. His use of the idea of God in his philosophy of time remains too cloaked in mythological conceptions of traditional theology. His creationist metaphysics does get time on the stage in a cosmogonic prologue. And once on the scene, the role that time plays is largely written for it by the mathematical and natural sciences of his day. Specifically, his account of time and time's domain lacks categories which can make some sense of the poetic, the literary and the social aspects of human creativity. Time does vex the earthbound heart. The world's great literature immerses us in those categories of experience that call us back into ourselves, where we once more meet anxiousness about the future and guilt about the past. No philosophy of time which is not braced by these features of the human condition can be adequate.

Bertrand P. Helm

Southwest Missouri State University

NOTES

1. Charles Hartshorne, "Continuity, The Form of Forms, In Charles Peirce," *The Monist*, 39:521–34. The treatment of time is on pages 530–31.
    2. *The Development of Peirce's Philosophy*, 1961.
    3. *An Introduction To Peirce's Philosophy*, 1946.

4. We use the standard practice for referring to Peirce's *Collected Papers*. Thus, 4.67 means volume 4, paragraph 67 in those papers.

5. The processes and qualities antedating time would be Peirce's Firsts.

6. In Indian philosophy, categories for things antedating time are *prusa* and *praktri*. S.K. Sen, "Time In Sankhya-Yoga," *IPQ*, vol. 8 (1968): pp. 414–15.

7. For Peirce's answer to Kant's fourth antinomy, see Murphey, cited in n2, pp. 45–46.

8. Sir James Jeans *Physics and Philosophy* (New York: The Macmillan Company, 1945), p. 59.

9. Ibid., p. 60.

C. S. PEIRCE AND THE POST-TARSKIAN PROBLEM
OF AN ADEQUATE EXPLICATION
OF THE MEANING OF TRUTH:
TOWARDS A TRANSCENDENTAL – PRAGMATIC
THEORY OF TRUTH

As the title of my paper indicates, I wish to establish a relationship between the problem of an adequate explication of the truth-conception that underlies modern empirical science and the philosophy of C. S. Peirce who is often called the founder of American Pragmatism. In speaking of the truth-conception of modern empirical science, I am thinking of a conception of truth that is necessarily presupposed for an adequate epistemological and methodological understanding of experimental and theoretical natural science and, indeed, for such types of quasi-nomological social science as can be practiced according to the paradigm of natural science. This means that I do not propose directly to thematize the truth-problematics of so called "hermeneutic Geisteswissenschaften" or "critical-reconstructive social sciences" which, in my opinion, transcend the truth-conception as well as the very concept of (natural) science.[1]

But why must we inquire into the relationship between the truth-conception of modern empirical science and the philosophy of C. S. Peirce in view of the fact that modern analytic philosophy has invested so much energy in the logic of modern empirical science and, in that context, into the semantic explication of truth?

I

In order to account for my interest in Peirce's conception of truth and, furthermore (moreover) to introduce my general approach to Peirce's philosophy, I propose to begin by placing my approach in a philosophico-historical context.[2] The context is best explicated in terms of semiotics, especially in terms of the three-dimensional semiotics of the sign-relation or "semiosis," comprehending *syntactics, semantics,* and *pragmatics*, which via C. W. Morris goes back to Peircean ideas and via Morris and R. Carnap has also provided the semiotical background-conception for "logical semantics." With regard to this semiotical setting-story I want to give at least some vague elucidations in the present context.[3]

II

1. For semiotic reasons I do not believe that the concept of truth needed in the philosophy of empirical science can be adequately explicated merely on the basis of logical semantics (i.e., in abstraction from pragmatics) (as little, by the way, as I think that in this way an adequate explication of the concept of *explanation* can be provided[4]).

This means for example that I do not consider Tarski's semantical explication of the meaning of truth for formalized languages as a sufficient basis for a realistic correspondence-theory of truth, as it was considered by Karl Popper and others,[5] but only as an explication of a *necessary* condition for any philosophical theory of truth that is to account for the possibility of logical implication, i.e., of truth-transfer, as it is isolated in formalized semantical systems. Seen in itself, this conception of truth is neutral with regard to different ontological or epistemological positions of philosophy, as Tarski himself emphasized;[6] and this means, I suggest, that it is also neutral with regard to the different classical philosophical conceptions of truth, as, e.g., metaphysical correspondence-theory, evidence-theory, coherence-theory, pragmaticist-theory.

My chief reasons for considering Tarski's semantic conception a formalist minimal conception of truth are semiotic reasons in so far as I reflect upon the fact that, being restricted to formalized languages, this conception must abstract from the pragmatic dimension of actual use or interpretation of language. Thus it must for example abstract from the situation-bound use of objective indexical expressions like "this" and "there" and of subjective indexical expressions in the context of performatives such as "I hereby state that . . .". Now, as C. S. Peirce first made clear in his semiotic logic of inquiry, without the situation-bound function of *indexical* expressions the language of science cannot really grasp (get hold of) reality,[7] and without the later so called performatives (e.g., verbalized acts of "assertion") the human subject of science cannot reflect upon his or her truth-*claim*, in such a way as to take over responsibility for it.[8] This means the following with regard to the problem of a philosophical explication of the meaning of truth:

On the one hand, the equivalence-relation expressed in Tarski's convention T (i.e., "x is true if, and only if, p") cannot pass as an explication of that relation between thought or language and reality that is meant in a realistic correspondence theory of truth. For it only deals with that relation in as far as it tacitly presupposes that the meaning of p can be interpreted—however indirectly—with the aid of a natural language which, as pragmatically ultimate metalanguage of any hierarchy of formalized languages, can, with the aid of indexical expressions, provide a real denotatum for p as a mere designatum of an abstract semantic system. (That the possibility of such an interpretation is not unproblematic may be illustrated with regard to so called "theoretical concepts" of deep theories.)

On the other hand, the abstractive deficiency of the logico-semantical explication of truth is even more radical with regard to its failure to reflect on the truth-claims of the human subjects of knowledge as they are expressed and reflected upon in performative phrases like "I hereby state that . . .". For it is only by reflection on those subjective truth-claims that we can understand the meaning of the strange predicate "is true" whose bearer is sentences, or rather propositions as stated through statements or assertions. For the fact, reflected upon by the so called "redundance"-theory of truth, that the predicate "is true" is implied in the very statement of a proposition simply means that truth is not a strange property of some entities in the world we could get special informations about but rather a claim that human subjects of knowledge connect with propositions by asserting them and which they can make explicit through performative phrases like "I hereby state that . . .". Thus "is true" is in fact redundant as long as our truth-claim is simply implied in our communicative statements, but it is not longer redundant when our implicit truth-claim is called into question and hence has to be made explicit on the level of argumentative discourse.[9]

Against these semiotic arguments for the need of reflection on the pragmatic (i.e., *objective denotative* as well as the *subjective performative*) presuppositions of the semantic explication of truth as predicate of sentences (of formalized languages) there have been directed the following standard semanticist arguments:

With regard to the question of securing real denotata (e.g., identifying real objects to which the predicates of propositions may apply), it has been said that it belongs to the problem of verification and thus has to be solved as a problem of empirical pragmatics which, as a meaningful question, presupposes already the logico-semantical solution of the problem of an explication or definition of the meaning of truth.

Similarly with regard to the question of reflecting on our subjective truth-claims, it has been said that it too constitutes a problem of empirical pragmatics (say, of psycholinguistics),—a problem moreover that should be thematized as a topic of the semantical reference of a metalanguage (say of a behavioristic type of psycholinguistics), in order to avoid the semantical antinomies that are implied in the self-referential language of introspection. In order to show that this problematic has nothing to do with the question of an adequate explication of the meaning of truth, it has been argued that propositions may be true or false quite independently of their being asserted as well as of their being verified.

The plausibility of these semanticist arguments, as far as I can see, rests on a semiotic axiom (or prejudice) that was introduced by C. W. Morris and R. Carnap under the impact of B. Russell's semantic "theory of types" and Tarski's verdict against self-referential use of language. The axiom says that the pragmatic dimension of the triadic sign-relation ("semiosis")—i.e., the dimension of the actual use or interpretation of signs by the human subjects of communication—can only be thematized as a topic of empirical pragmatics (possibly of a behavioristic type), or as a topic of a formal-constructive pragmatics that should provide the theoretical metalanguage for (the semantical thematization of the pragmatical dimension by) empirical pragmatics.[10] From the point of view of this semiotic axiom we cannot conceive of a thematization of the whole actual triadic-relation of semiosis (or eg., sign-mediated cognition) by philosophic reflection on its actual pragmatic dimension. Hence there cannot, it seems, be a semiotical equivalent to transcendental epistemology of a Kantian or Husserlian type. (And this preconception has in fact predetermined the development not only of the Carnapian or Hempelian type of a "logic of Science" but also, I think, the development of Popper's "logic of scientific discovery" up to the late conception of an "epistemology without a knowing subject."[11]) I think, however, that this semiotical axiom—let us call it the axiom of the impossibility of a transcendental pragmatics—is mistaken and, especially is incompatible with Peirce's foundation of semiotics and semiotical logic of inquiry on the basis of the triadic structure of semiosis which was considered by Peirce as a semiotic equivalent of Kant's "synthesis of apperception" and beyond that, of Hegel's concept of "mediation" as structure of the spirit.[12] I shall later come back to this thesis. (See Fig. 1 on next page.)

For the moment let us see in what respect the semanticist arguments in favor of the sufficiency of Tarski's explication of the meaning of truth stand and fall together with (in dependence of) the Morris/Carnap-axiom of semiotics that there cannot be such a thing as a transcendental-reflective pragmatics of the act of sign-interpretation or, for that matter, of sign-mediated cognition.

First it seems plausible that the question of how to settle the problem of verification, or rather confirmation, of scientific hypotheses in one sense might be conceived of as a problem for empirical scientists and in another sense as a problem of an empirical "science of science" (e.g., history of science) and thus far might be subsumed under the topics of empirical pragmatics—although not of a behavioristic type but rather of a hermeneutic-reconstructive type which should be capable of understanding and *evaluating* the good or bad reasons of the empirical scientists in the light

FIG. I.

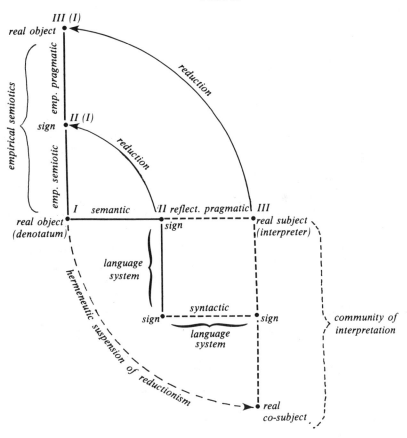

_____ reduction of the Peircean scheme of semiosis within the frame of Logical Empiricism

-------- transcendental-pragmatic supplementation (integration) of the scheme of semiosis within the frame of Transcendental Semiotics

of some normative ideas of what verification or confirmation should be. But then the question arises what kind of explication of the meaning of truth is presupposed by such a type of "empirical" pragmatics: should it be that of logical semantics that cannot even cover the general idea of verification (or confirmation of falsification) and hence is criteriologically irrelevant? Or should it be a type of explication that would be criteriologically relevant by involving some general idea of verification in the broadest sense, i.e., some idea of possible criteria of truth and possibly even of a highest or ultimate criterium of regulative principle, such that in its light the very explication of the meaning of truth could be summed up in terms of a possible integration of possible truth-criteria?

It seems clear to me that under (in terms of) the presupposition of the Morris/Carnap-axiom of semiotics, it must be postulated that the criteriologically irrelevant type of semantical explication of the meaning of truth is not only a necessary but a sufficient presupposition for an empirical pragmatic thematization of the problematic of verification. This postulate is simply enforced by the presupposition that there is no possibility envisaged of conceiving of a reflective-philosophical thematization of the whole triadic relation of semiosis or, for that matter, sign-mediated cognition of the real by a human subject. On the other hand, in terms of (under) the presupposition that there can be a reflective philosophical knowledge a priori of the triadic structure of actual semiosis and of sign-mediated cognition, it seems also clear that the logico-semantical explication of the meaning of truth must tacitly presuppose its possible supplementation by, and possible integration into, a non-empirical pragmatical explication of the very meaning of truth, such that this criteriologically relevant type of meaning-explication must be presupposed by the empirical pragmatics of verification. The standard semanticist argument of a dichotomy of logico-semantical meaning-explication of truth and empirical pragmatics of verification would then amount to an abstractive fallacy, which is based on the non-observance of Peirce's insight into the triadic structure of semiosis.

I shall indeed in the following defend this latter thesis and to that extent heuristically start out from the idea of a transcendental semiotics including a transcendental pragmatics.[13]

With regard to the question whether an adequate explication of the meaning of truth needs to take into account the truth-claims as they may be made explicit by performative phrases, the difference between an abstractive semanticist and a transcendental-pragmatic view of the situation is even more striking and important than with respect to the problem of verification. The difference at stake here may be understood as one between the usual (semanticist) supposition that truth is a matter of propositions and not of speech-acts and the (transcendental-pragmatic) thesis that only by recourse to our subjective *truth-claims* and hence to the meaning of assertions can we understand the (non-redundant) meaning of the predicate 'is true'. For, as the transcendental-pragmatic thesis will claim, we have to understand "is true" as a predicate that within the frame of semantics cannot belong to the level of object-language, and hence of the sentences that express the true or false propositions, but must belong to the level of a metalanguage through which our subjective reflection upon the language of propositions is expressed and objectified so to speak. Now this means that without the possibility of an actual self-reflection of our truth-claims, as it is made possible by performatively expressed assertions, we would be unable philosophically to understand the very difference between object-language and meta-language which is presupposed by the so called semantical explication of truth.

The standard-argument for the semanticist position, viz. the argument that propositions, and thus semantically interpreted sentences, can be true or false quite independently of their being asserted or not asserted, obviously does not really contradict the transcendental-pragmatic thesis; for it only states—correctly of course—that the truth or falsehood of propositions, and hence of sentences, is independent of their being factually asserted. If it were instead to claim that one could conceive of the truth or falsehood of propositions quite independently of the conception of human truth-claims and assertions, as it in fact was claimed by Thomas Aquinas and Bolzano, then transcendental-pragmatical reflection upon the conditions of the possibility of the meaning-claim of phrases like "proposition x is true" must claim that an abstractive fallacy of a semanticist type has been committed. This is indeed a reproach that applies to Popper's conception of an "epistemology without a knowing subject," I suggest.[14] (It does not apply to Thomas Aquinas and to Bolzano only in so far as both of these theologically inspired thinkers could presuppose the divine intellect as transcendental subject of true knowledge in their radical abstraction from human truth-claims.[15])

But the consequences of the difference between the semanticist and the transcendental pragmatic position have not yet been exhausted by what has been pointed out thus far. For if the arguments thus far forwarded are sound, and the meaning of truth cannot be sufficiently explicated merely in terms of a semantical account of propositions but only by recourse to propositions and to performatively expressed assertions as speech-acts through which our propositions are proposed and thus connected with our truth-claims, then there are consequences to be drawn both with regard to the semiotical conception of language that is presupposed by an adequate explication of the meaning of truth and with regard to the subjective-intersubjective dimension of the idea of truth-claims as implied in the meaning of the idea of truth.

In the first respect, we have to take into consideration that it is not the concept of a semantical system of propositional sentences in the sense of Tarski and Carnap that has to be made the basis or framework for an adequate semiotical explication of the concept of truth (and hence of epistemology), but rather a concept of natural language that, from the outset, must account for the twofold (i.e., partly propositional, partly performative) structure[16] of those sentences that can express speech-acts like assertions and thusfar can reflectively (i.e., in a pragmatical sense of self-reference) express human truth-claims. Thereby a critical spotlight is shed on Tarski's conception of natural language as a semantically "closed system" (of propositional sentences) which therefore could not be made the basis or framework for an adequate philosophical explication of the meaning of truth. Looked upon from a transcendental-pragmatical point of view, natural language is not a "semantical system" (of propositional sentences) at all, but rather a (quasi-institutional[17]) system of twofold (propositional-performative) sentence-patterns as possible virtual expressions of human speech-acts which for their part have to integrate the semantical dimension of propositions (abstractively isolated by Tarski and Carnap) into the pragmatical dimension of speech. Due to its twofold sentence-patterns, natural language is indeed pragmatically self-referential; but far from thereby necessarily "implying" semantical antinomies which disqualify natural language as the medium of philosophy, it thereby first of all makes possible human cognitive self-reflection and hence even that type of *philosophical (metalogical) self-reflection of thought* that has to be presupposed by Tarski's postulate of an infinite hierarchy of metalanguages.

(In fact the pragmatically self-referential structure of performative phrases of natural language provides the cognitive basis for those general philosophical insights that must be formulated with the aid of implicitly self-referential universal propositions. But it cannot thereby have become the cause (i.e., sufficient condition) of semantical antinomies; for all philosophical position-sentences, including those of the Scepticists, must take the form of implicitly self-referential universal propositions, and among them also those sentences through which Russell's semantic "theory of types" and Tarski's theory of the necessary splitting of the language (of scientific philosophy) into object-language and metalanguage can be made the object of argumentative discourse. There are in fact good reasons for the view that Russell's and Tarski's verdicts against self-referential language must not be considered as philosophical solutions of the problem of semantical antinomies, but rather as technical devices of avoiding the rise of the very problem by establishing formalized language-systems as "organs" of logico-mathematical ("apodeictic") reasoning which precisely for this reason cannot be substituted for natural language as medium or reflective philosophical rationality.[18] As far as a substantical solution e.g., of the antinomy of the Liar is required, it might rather be reached along the lines of Hegel's verdict against contradicting one's necessary truth-claim. For this verdict seems to represent the most fundamental principle of a transcendental pragmatics of human argumentation.)

In fact, if there must be a theory of truth that may be applied to itself (as, I should think, it must be postulated for an adequate philosophical theory of truth), then the only chance of avoiding an infinite regress in foundation is provided by a transcendental-pragmatic account which should explicate the meaning of truth in terms of the necessity and possibility of redeeming one's own truth-claims.

The talk of redeeming truth-claims, however, besides the general problematic of verification, points to a further dimension of the meaning of truth which may be referred to provisionally by the terms 'intersubjective validity'. And here again our transcendental-semiotical approach opens up a problematic of a possible explication of the meaning of truth that, as far as I know, was seriously taken into account for the first time by C. S. Peirce. What I mean may be systematically reconstructed as follows:

If the human subject of truth-claims is conceived of not only in a Kantian way as subject of the pre-linguistic "synthesis of apperception," but moreover, in a transcendental-semiotical way, as subject of sign-interpretation, then his truth-claims cannot, in principle, be sufficiently redeemed by the evidence of his own synthesis of apperception with regard to data; they have rather to be redeemed by an intersubjectively valid synthesis or unity of sign-interpretation. But this means that the methodical solipsism of modern epistemology from Descartes to Husserl has to be surmounted in favor not only of an a priori warranted intersubjectivity, as it is presupposed in Kant's idea of a "transcendental consciousness," but in favor of the postulate of an indefinite community of sign-interpretation which could reach discursive agreement about the confirmation or falsification of propositions, e.g., of scientific hypotheses and theories, by evidential criteria. And this implies that the old idea of the "consensus omnium," which from Aristotle and the Stoics to Kant was considered rather a common sense index of a merely "subjective criterium of truth,"[19] has to be given the status of a "regulative principle" of redeeming truth-claims that as such is "constitutive" for the meaning of truth qua intersubjective validity.

At this point let us attempt a provisional resumé of the results of our introduction of the transcendental-semiotic or, respectively, transcendental-pragmatic approach: after reducing Tarski's semantical conception of truth—in accordance, I suggest, with its own neutrality-claim—to the status of an abstractive minimal conception which only reclaims a logically indispensable necessary condition of any philosophical explication of the meaning of truth, we have charted in rough outlines the semiotic horizon of a criteriologically relevant explication of the meaning of truth. We have postulated that it should encompass the general idea of possible verification (in a broad sense, i.e., including confirmation or corroboration and hence falsification) as well as that of intersubjective validity to be testified by universal consensus. Now the question may be raised as to the relationship between our semiotically postulated horizon of a criteriologically relevant explication of the meaning of truth and the traditional truth-theories, as e.g., the correspondence-, evidence-, coherence-, and the pragmatist satisfaction-theory of truth. And, in accordance with our own suggestion, we may even supplement this enumeration by the supposition of a consensus-theory of truth.

In this context, it is interesting to observe that in the last decades, partly from the vantage-point of Tarski's semantical theory, partly from the vantage-points that transcend the abstractive semantical, but hardly the semiotical approach, almost all the traditional conceptions have been renewed.

(Thus, e.g., the semantical conception has been widened by integrating pragmatical presuppositions by D. Davidson[20] and in a much more radical sense by E. Tugendhat.[21] Transcending the semantical conception into the direction of an ontological or rather onto-semantical conception by recourse to Wittgenstein's "Tractatus," W. Sellars has developed a theory of "similarity or correspondence or isomorphy between two systems of objects which both belong to the natural order."[22] The coherence-theory of truth which has a neo-Hegelian and a neo-positivist origin was recently revived and elaborated by N. Rescher[23] and L. B. Puntel.[24] Finally different types of a consensus-theory of truth were proposed by the Erlangen-school of dialogical constructivism (W. Kamlah & P. Lorenzen[25] and K. Lorenz[26]) and by J. Habermas[27] in the name of a universal pragmatics.)

Now I think that the horizon of a transcendental semiotics as First Philosophy is suited also to settling the question as to the systematical order of, and hence interrelationship between the different approaches of truth-theories thus far proposed as possible contributions to a full-fledged explication of the meaning of truth. And since I conceive of the philosophy of C. S. Peirce as a first project of a transcendental semiotics including a transcendental pragmatics, I heuristically assume in this essay that it can provide important view-points for settling the question of a systematical integration of the different conceptions of truth.

Thus I shall in the next section try first to outline from a quasi-Peircian point of view the critical (strategical) restrictions that have to be imposed upon the possible configurations of truth-conceptions as ingredients of a transcendental-semiotic explication of the meaning of truth. By this method I hope finally to approach that type of truth-theory that comes closest to Peirce's conception and may both count (figure) as a critical reconstruction of it and be itself most fruitfully reconstructed in the light of Peirce's contributions to a transcendental-semiotic or, respectively, transcendental-pragmatic theory of truth.

III

1. First I suggest that an ontological-metaphysical conception of truth that conceives of correspondence as a relation between entities within the world is ruled out as anachronistic by the critical standards of present philosophy. These standards at least since Kant have been prejudiced by the idea of the uniqueness of the epistemological *subject-object-relation* which cannot in principle be reduced to an *object-object-relation*. Hence any criteriologically relevant attempt to think of an ontological correspondence between thought and reality as though we could conceive of such a relation from a standpoint outside of the epistemological subject-object-relation is confronted with a standard-argument of the post-Kantian (epistemological) paradigm of First Philosophy. The correspondence, the argument runs, can only be verified with respect to the *appearances* of reality by judgments that with respect to *their* correspondence to the *things in themselves* have to be verified on their part which can only be done by judgments about the appearances of reality and so on ad infinitum. (A crosscheck of the validity of this argument seems to be provided on the one hand by those modern versions of the correspondence-theory that avoid the *regressus ad infinitum* by simply talking of a correspondence between propositions and facts which are conceived as existing if and only if the corresponding propositions are true. These theories in order to avoid the *regressus ad infinitum* have to take a *circulus vitiosus* into the bargain; and of course they must be criteriologically irrelevant. Another, even more important, crosscheck of the transcendental-epistemological argument against the metaphysical correspondence-theory is provided, it seems to me, by those biological-evolutionist theories that conceive of correspondence as a relation of real adaption between the cognitive equipments or apparatusses of organisms and their environments.[28] These empirical-scientific theories are, in my opinion, the historically legitimate followers and substitutes for the ontological-metaphysical correspondence-theories of truth; but they testify to their scientific status by loosing direct philosophical relevance, e.g., as possible justifications of their own truth-claims.)

2. Now the aporia of the *infinite regressus* of any attempts of checking the ontological-metaphysical correspondence between thought and reality has often been considered as an argument for the thesis that the truth of propositions can in fact *only* be checked by propositions, and from this it has been concluded that the correspondence-conception of truth has to be abandoned in every respect and to be replaced by a coherence-theory of truth. After O. Neurath and B. Blanshard recently L. B. Puntel has taken this turn;[29] and he has combined it with the other important argument of the

coherence-theory since Hegel viz., that it by definition must be predestined to account for the systematical connection between all conceivable criteria (in a non-definitive sense) of truth and hence, being the ultimate standard or regulative principle of a possible integration of truth-criteria, provides the definitive *explicans* or *definiens* for a philosophical explication of the meaning of truth.[30]

In dealing with this claim from a transcendental-semiotical point of view, I would first concede that the importance of the coherence-conception lies in fact in the circumstance that it provides a criterium for the connection of truth-criteria which must be used by us in the process of redeeming our truth-claims. From this it follows, among other things, that the coherence-theory of truth cannot be refuted alone by the argument that there may be different, i.e., rival, consistent systems of propositions; for, since coherence is more than mere consistency, rival consistent systems may even then be submitted to the criterium of their coherence with other truth-candidates, if they all happen to be coherent in themselves. But the pity is that the criterium or regulative principle of coherence, if it is not supplemented by other independent criteria of truth, applies to too much. It provides no criterium for a distinction between our thoughts about possible worlds and our knowledge about the real world. The reason for this idealistic deficiency of a pure coherence-theory of truth may be exposed, I think, in the light of a transcendental semiotics of Peircean provenience.

First it may be shown that the coherence-theoretician goes too far when from the fact that our experiential data are always language-impregnated or theory-impregnated data he concludes that in testing hypotheses in the last analysis we can only compare propositions with propositions.[31] The crucial semiotic argument against this thesis is provided by Peirce's distinction between three types of signs, viz., icons, indices, and symbols, and his proof that human language, as it is used in "perceptual judgments" and hence in the context of confirmation and innovative discoveries, cannot work alone on the basis of the general conceptual meaning of symbols which are determined merely by the linguistic conventions, as Hegel supposed in his chapter on "sensuous certainty" ("sinnliche Gewissheit") in the "Phenomenology of the Spirit."[32] Against this paradigmatic preconception of an idealistic coherence-theory of truth, Peirce has shown that the situation-bound use of indexical expressions and even of predicates in perceptual judgments must at least participate in the function of "indices" and "icons" which get their meanings immediately within the perceptual situation.

Thus, for example the perceptual statement that is expressed by the sentence "Now I see there a church with two steeples," or rather "This there is a church with two steeples,"[33] gets its immediate meaning not only from the conventional meanings that its components convey as linguistic signs (including e.g., as Hegel rightly noticed (remarked), such general meanings as *nowness, thereness* and *thisness*) but besides that e.g., by the *real causal connection* between language and the *existing reality* in space and time that alone can legitimize my actual use of the indexical expressions 'there' and 'this'. It furthermore gets its immediate meaning also by the perceptual application of the predicate "church with two steeples." This crucial element of perceptual verification is decisively legitimized by the iconic evidence of a qualitative phenomenon that is distinguished as a *real* phenomenon, i.e., beyond its merely possible iconic quality, by its being opened up to our attention by the simultaneous legitimized application of the "indexcal expressions which, so to speak, testify to the clash of our attention with the resistance of the existing reality. Thus the phenomenologically legitimized application of the connection of indexical expressions and predicates whose *symbolic* meaning is satisfied (or fulfilled) by *iconic evidence* within the perceptual situation seems to make up that criterium of truth as evidence for a correspondence between propositions and reality has to be combined in some way with the coherence-criterium, in order to distinguish our well confirmed knowledge of the real world from mere coherent imaginations concerning a possible world.

3. In this context one has to realize, I think, that during the era of the second (epistemological) paradigm of First Philosophy not only the coherence-theory of truth has been proposed as an alternative to the ontological-metaphysical correspondence-theory but also, since Descartes, an evidence-theory of truth. This type of truth-theory reached its most elaborate and argumentatively strongest form in Husserl's phenomenology, where it in fact amounts to an "Aufhebung" (i.e., suspension and preservation) of the idea of correspondence by substituting the idea of a reflective evidence of the correspondence between the meaning-intention of our judgments or propositions and the "self-givenness" of the phenomena that fulfill our meaning-intentions. Now I think that Peirce's semiotical approach, at least as it was developed in his "phenomenological" or "phaneroscopic" period (e.g., in the "Lectures on Pragmatism" of 1903), comes close to reconfirming Husserl's approach up to a certain point.[34]

Thus it seems clear to me that Peirce's analysis of the function of indexical expressions in connection with that of the iconical relationship between perceptual qualities (or relations!) and predicates within the context of actual perceptual statements converges with Husserl's analysis in ascertaining the fact that against this type of evidence (of correspondence) it cannot be objected that it does not provide an additional criterium of truth beyond the symbolic meaning of the proposition that can be inserted (incorporated) into a coherent system of propositions. It is simply implausible that the intuitional evidence of confirming e.g., the truth of the proposition "The church has two steeples" by having a look at the church should add nothing to that proposition than just a subjective evidence-feeling that could only be interesting for the psychologists.[35] (Therefore it is also implausible and even amounts to a "category-mistake" to say that perceptual evidence is just a motive, i.e., a cause, by which the coming about of a "basis-sentence" of empirical science can be explained;[36] for the perceptual evidence is of course a good reason for accepting a perceptual judgment, and it can be understood as such also by the discourse-partners of the human subject of the perception.)

At this point it becomes clear, I suggest, that *language-analytical* philosophy as third paradigm of First Philosophy went too far in its semanticist antipsychologism when it completely banished the achievements of evidence-phenomenology from the business of philosophical "explication" in the so called "context of justificiation." (This is also suggested by the aporetic results of the attempts at explication of the different meanings of "explanation" under abstraction from the pragmatic dimension of explanation as synthetic achievement of cognition.[37]) The philosophical problem today seems to be rather to combine the language-analytical with the phenomenological approach in such a way as to account for the "interwoveness" (Wittgenstein) of language-use and experiential evidence within the frame of a language-game. It is precisely this problem that is taken up and, I think, solved to some extent by Peirce's semiotical analysis of the interaction of the sign-functions of icons, indices and symbols within the actual situation of a perceptual statement. For the special point of this semiotical account is the proof that the very use of the language of perceptual statements cannot be understood in terms of the semanticist presupposition that it conveyes no other meaning besides the *symbolic* meaning of abstract propositions that can be incorporated into a formalized semantical system.

But, as a semiotic approach, the Peircean analysis of the interaction of *icons, indices* and *symbols* within the actual situation of a perceptual statement also has implications that transcend and thereby show up the limits of a phenomenelogical evidence-theory of truth. For the intuitional iconical evidence that legitimizes the application of predicates to existing objects that can be identified with the aid of "indexical expressions" must also for its part be interpreted with the aid of the general meaning that is conveyed by the predicates as symbols that belong to a conventional semantical system. Hence our truth-claims cannot be immediately and definitely grounded on, or redeemed by, intuitional evidence; for all intuitional evidence of perception is always symbolically interpreted evidence, or, in other words, is language-impregnated or even theory-impregnated.

(For Peirce himself, the interdependence, or, respectively, interaction of indexical and iconical evidence, on the one hand, and symbolical interpretation in the light of general meanings, on the other hand, could figure as a *semiotic* equivalent to the Kantian insight that "concepts without intuitions are empty and intuitions without concepts are blind.")

This means, however, that the evidence can change since the iconical data may be re-interpreted in the light of other language-systems, e.g., of more powerful theories. There is no doubt that in this context the function of coherence as a criterium of truth becomes prominent. But this does not mean that the function of evidence (of correspondence) as a truth-criterium becomes dispensable (or even becomes equivalent to the recourse to a dogma, as it has been said.[38]) For again and again the object-relation or the contact with reality of the coherent propositional systems has to be secured by perceptual judgments. It is appropriate, rather, to state that the criterium of evidence as related to a single interpreting consciousness and hence as a matter of "methodical solipsism" (Husserl) has to be distinguished from, and transcended in favor of, the requirement of intersubjective validity which comes into the play by (as) the demand for a consensus about the correct or valid (frame of) interpretation of evident data.

4. At this point we can introduce the last and most important vantage-point of a transcendental-semiotical truth-conception of Peircean inspiration. It could be called the transcendental-pragmatic alternative to the coherence-theory as an account of the systematic interconnection of the different criteria of truth as ingredients (moments) of an integrative explication of the meaning of truth.

We may start out with the thesis that an absolutization of the coherence-theory of truth amounts to a metaphysical hypostatization of language in so far as it absolutizes the abstract unity of propositions as a medium of knowledge without reflection upon the two other places of the triadic relation of language-mediated cognition of something real by an interpreter or subject of cognition. In supposing *coherence of propositions* as ultimate comprehensive criterium and explicans of the meaning of truth, it ignores the fact that coherence of propositions is only then a criterium of truth, if it may be interpreted by a subject of cognition as a coherence of such propositions that may be qualified as vehicle of true knowledge by their logical consequences, i.e., basic propositions that again by a subject of cognition, may be interpreted as being confirmed (or at least being not falsified) by evident data.

The next step then is made possible by the insight that the transcendental subject of a possible unity of sign-interpretation cannot be represented by the consciousness of a single sign-interpreter; although his subjective wittness of the objective evidence (of a correspondence between perceptual judgments and the given phenomena) is indispensable as an ingredient of that progressive process of re-interpretation of evidences in the light of coherent propositional systems that, in principle, can lead to a Unity of interpretation in the long run. On the basis of similar considerations C. S. Peirce as early as 1868 came to state that the conception of true knowledge about the real to be reached by a scientific process of inference and sign-interpretation "involves the notion of a *Community*, without definite limits, and capable of definite increase in knowledge" (5.312).

His point in this context is that the Kantian "thing-in-itself," i.e., the *real*, which in fact can never be "known" by a single consciousness at any stage of the scientific process of sign-interpretation, must nevertheless be conceived as the "knowable" in the long run in relation to the indefinite community of interpreters. (cf. also 5.257, 5.265, 5.275, 5.310) For the distinction between the real and the unreal, as we can learn it only by the occurance of errors, Peirce claims, is equivalent to a distinction between "an *ens* relative to private idiosyncrasy, and an *ens* such as would stand in the long run." The real, then Peirce continues, "is that which, sooner or later, information and reasoning would finally result in, and which is therefore independent of the vagaries of me and you." And since on these presuppositions "a proposition whose falsity can never be discovered, and the error of which therefore is absolutely incognizable, contains . . . absolutely no error," Peirce concludes, rightly I think, that the Kantian idea of an unknowable thing-in-itself dissolves itself in favor of the (regulative) idea of the real as correlate of an ultimate consensus to be reached in the indefinite community of investigators (5.312). Later (especially 1871 and 1878) Peirce explicitly brings together the ideas of *truth, ultimate consensus* and *reality*, e.g., in the following formula:

"The opinion which is fated to be ultimately agreed to by all who investigate is what we mean by the truth, and the object represented in this opinion is the real" (5.408; cf. 8.12).

Thereby, I would suggest, Peirce has provided the basic elements of a transcendental-semiotic, or, respectively, transcendental-pragmatic concensus-theory of truth. For it may be said that the main elements of the Kantian epistemology of "transcendental idealism" are here semiotically transformed, i.e., suspended and preserved, in the following way: The idea of transcendental consciousness as subject and warrant of objectively valid knowledge is replaced by the idea of the indefinite community of sign-interpreters whose consensus is the nontranscendable ultimate criterium, we can conceive of, for the intersubjective validity and thus for the *truth* of our knowledge. Correspondingly, the transcendental unity of objective data in the "synthesis of apperception," which Kant postulated as a transcendental synthesis, so to speak, of the truth-criteria of *evidence* (of phenomenological correspondence) and coherence within, or for, the transcendental consciousness, is replaced by, or transformed into, the postulate or regulative principle of the ultimate unity of sign-interpretation by consensus about the meaning and truth of propositions.[39] Correspondingly, the *real* as transcendental object of knowledge is conceived of not as that which can be factually "known" but as the "knowable," and that means, as that which *would be* the object of the "ultimate opinion" of the indefinite community of investigators.

Thus we have singled out, I think, the core of Peirce's original contribution to a criteriologically relevant explication of the truth-conception of modern empirical science; although we have not yet taken into account the special connection of this early conception with, and its supplementation by, Peirce's famous "pragmatist," or rather "pragmaticist," principle of meaning-explication which, of course, can and must be also applied to the meaning of truth (although not necessarily in the way proposed by W. James). Before continuing with our reconstruction of Peirce's theory of truth, however, let us have a look at a contemporary version of the consensus-theory of truth which in many respects comes close to Peirce's conception. What I have in mind is J. Habermas's outline of a "universal-pragmatic concensus or discourse-theory of truth."[40] Might it be possible, it may be asked, to confront Peirce's and Habermas' conceptions in such a way as to mutually reconstruct their views and thereby supplement and improve them? In the forthcoming continuation of my paper I will try, at least roughly, to sketch some pertinent suggestions from the view-point of a transcendental semiotics and, respectively, transcendental pragmatics.

IV

Let us begin with an attempt to single out the common features or similarities, on the one hand, and the differences, or even contrasts, on the other hand, in comparing the approaches of Peirce and Habermas.

First I must emphasize once more that I consider both philosophies to be a version of what I call "transcendental pragmatics." In doing so, I am aware of the fact that this conjecture can be called into doubt or at least problematized in both cases.[41] My justification for insisting on it must be provided by the consideration that the very strength and significance of both philosophies as theories of truth, i.e., the possibility of transcending and integrating the traditional truth-theories into a *consensus-* or *discourse-theory* of truth depends in my opinion on their *transcendental pragmatic* status. As an illustration of this thesis, I want to immediately introduce what I would consider the most profound common basis of Peirce's and Habermas's truth-conceptions.

In Peirce the point I have in mind is expressed in the following passages which belong to the context of Kant-transformation which I have already brought into focus: "a proposition whose falsity can never be discovered, and the error of which therefore is absolutely incognizable, contains, upon our principle, absolutely no error" (5.311). And ". . . any truth more perfect than this destined conclusion [sc. "which is fated to be ultimately agreed to by all who investigate"] . . . any reality more absolute than what is thought in it, is a fiction of metaphysics" (8.12).

This is what I would call a *sense-critical argument*, since it is apt to show that we cannot meaningfully contrast a transcendent metaphysical ultimate criterium of truth with the regulative idea of an ultimate consensus of the indefinite community of sign-interpretation and hence have to acknowledge that regulative idea as a transcendental-pragmatic presupposition of our enterprise of investigation, if it should make sense at all. This, I think, is the reason why Peirce can postulate that, although, or rather, precisely because, we have no guarantee "that man or the community (which may be wider than mankind) shall ever arrive at a state of information greater than some definite finite information;" since life may be annihilated at some time, the idea of the ultimate consensus "involves itself a transcendent and supreme interest. . . ." that may be, on the one hand, the subject of an "infinite hope," and, on the other hand, "is always a hypothesis uncontradicted by facts and justified by its indispensableness for making any action rational" (5.357).

Now, I think, a connection can be established on this very fundamental level of *sense-critical* or *transcendental-pragmatic* arguments between Peirce's approach and Habermas's "universal-grammatic" doctrine of the four "validity-claims" [i.e., *intelligibility*, *truth*, *rightness*, and *veracity* (sincerity, truthfulness)] that are necessarily connected with human speech-acts inasfar as speech is the vehicle and witness to human *reasonableness* qua *majority* (Mündigkeit"). Given in this context the following passages of Habermas seem to be relevant: "On this view [i.e., according to the thesis that the 'meaning of truth' may be explicated in terms of a possible redemption, i.e., "discursive settlement of experience-based validity claims"] I may ascribe a predicate to an object if and only if every other person who *could* enter into dialogue with me *would* also ascribe the same predicate to the same object. In order to distinguish true from false statements I make reference to the judgments of others—in fact to the judgments of all others with which I could ever hold a dialogue (among whom, contrary to fact, I include all the dialogue-partners I could find if my life-history were coextensive with the history of mankind) . . . . Truth means the promise of attaining a rational consensus.[42]

It is important to note that Habermas here is speaking about a *necessary explication of the meaning* of truth and not about a *sufficient criterium of truth*. The difference between these two aspects of the problem is clarified by the following passage which serves as an answer to the objection that accidently-brought-about agreements cannot serve as truth-criteria: "—. . .

'discursive settlement' is a normative concept: only a *grounded* consensus is a consensus we can reach in discourses. This one alone holds a truth-criterium, but the meaning of truth is not the circumstance that a consensus will in fact be reached, but [the pre-supposition]: that at any time and place, if only we enter into discourse, a consensus can be arrived at under conditions that warrant its being a grounded consensus."[43]

The point that connects this explication of the meaning of truth with Peirce's statements lies in my opinion in the following circumstance: In these statements—as a result of *transcendental-pragmatic* or *sensecritical reflection*, as I would claim—a postulate is exposed the validity of which can be defended quite independently, and hence in advance, of the settlement of the question whether, or, respectively, how, the bringing about of a grounded consensus can be secured; although this question of *the conditions* of a grounded consensus will be the next question to be settled and as such is dealt with in Peirce's as well as in Habermas's approach. Thus the need for explicating the pragmatic meaning of truth—i.e., of what truth *for us can mean*—in terms of an ultimate "consensus omnium" is based on the fact that it, from the outset, is the only alternative to giving up the whole enterprise of cognition or investigation in the sense of arriving at knowledge the truth-claim of which can be justified by arguments. It makes no sense—and testifies to a misunderstanding of *transcendental-pragmatic* arguments—in this situation to first insist on answering the question, whether the transcendental-pragmatic presupposition is true, i.e., can be verified at all as an hypothetic assumption, so to speak.[44]

For this very question of a possible verification of an assumption cannot be meaningfully tackled without presupposing already the adequacy of the initial move of a consensus-theory of truth. We thus far get here a glimpse of what may be called a *transcendental-pragmatic ultimate foundation of philosophy* (and science), which, of course, is very different from a *deductive grounding* by axioms (and hence of axioms) that could be objectified with the aid of a semantical system of sentences or, respectively, propositions.[45]

Now, before trying to settle the question of the ideal conditions of a grounded consensus, we should ask for the relationship between the *consensus*-theory as an explication of the meaning of truth and the above mentioned truth-conceptions, as, e.g., the *correspondence-*, evidence-, *coherence-*, and *pragmatic satisfaction*-theory. With regard to this question there seems to be some central concordance as well as some characteristic difference between Peirce and Habermas.

A fundamental concordance, as far as I can see, exists between both thinkers with respect to the insight that it is not the *real* (in itself), as it is conceived in a *metaphysical correspondence*-theory as independent of our thought in general or, more precisely, of the possible redemption (discursive settlement) of our truth-claims, that can serve as *transcendent* criterium or standard of truth but rather that ultimate "consensus omnium" which would necessarily constitute the correlate of the real as it can be meaningfully thought of as that "which would hold in the long run." From this concordance I would derive the fact that both Peirce and Habermas sometimes quite naturally (without embarrassment) speak of a necessary correspondence between our judgments or propositions and the facts or reality. What is meant in this context, I suggest, is only that correspondence with the correlates of true propositions that is necessarily (and trivally) presupposed by any truth-theory, but cannot without circularity be explicated in a criteriological relevant way.[46] Hence the later Peirce even gives a methodologically relevant definition of truth in terms of "concordance with . . ." that avoids talking of reality; it runs; "Truth is that concordance of an abstract statement with the ideal limit toward which endless investigation would tend to bring scientific belief" (5.565). Peirce adds that such a concordance can of course only be ascribed to an abstract statement together with the concession of its inexactness and its onesidedness.

Yet, besides that, there is also a difference between Peirce's and Habermas's use of the terms "facts" and "correspondence with the facts"; such that one eventually may derive from this difference a distinction between two different types of a *consensus*-theory of truth. Peirce seems to propose a *consensus*-theory that integrates, together with the *coherence* and the *pragmatist*-theory of truth a certain phenomenological account for the *evidence of correspondence*. Habermas, on the other hand, seems to suggest a *consensus*-theory that rather excludes the other truth-conceptions,[47] especially the phenomenological conception of the *evidence of correspondence*; and precisely thereby Habermas's theory seems to come close to a pure *coherence*-conception of truth.[48]

Habermas's truth-conception seems to me to suffer from the following ambiguity: On the one hand, it presupposes that the abstract *facts* which are the correlates of true propositions are asserted by us with respect to *objects* in the world and hence that the meaning of truth must be explicated in terms of a "discursive settlement" of "experience-based validity-claims." He even grants in this context that the *correspondence*-theory of truth rests on a "correct observation" insofar as it insists on the postulate that true propositions must be "supported" or "founded" by "facts" in the sense of something that is "given" in "objects of experience." And thus far he suggests, it might be possible "that we can explicate the pragmatic relation between cognition and objects of experience with the aid of the concept of correspondence."[49] On the other hand, Habermas makes a rigorous distinction between the question of truth about abstract facts, which for him is a question of reflective validity-claims to be settled on the level of argumentative discourse, and the question of evidence about objects of experience, which for him is a question of pre-discursive information within the frame of pre-reflective communicative interaction between people. Thus he concludes: "Questions of truth are consequently raised not so much in reference to the innerworldly correlates of action-related cognition as rather to facts associated with discourses that are experience- and action-free. Whether states of affairs are or are not the case is not decided by experiental evidence, but by the course of argument."[50]

Now I would not dispute the difference stated by Habermas—along with Ramsay and Strawson—between objects of pre-discursive experience and abstract facts as reference-matter of truth-claims and their discursive settlement, since it is only this difference that can explain the *non-redundance* of the predicate "is true" in the case of reflective truth-claims and their discursive settlement (which I think is a fine point of Habermas). But I would emphasize at the same time that the discursive settlement of *empiric-scientific* truth-claims, in contra-distinction say to those of mathematics, does presuppose *as a necessary condition* what Habermas grants as the *possibility* of making use of experience also in the context of discursive argumentation.[51] This means, however, that the discursive settlement of *empiric-scientific* truth-claims by "substantial arguments" must not immediately take recourse to explanatory arguments about facts as explananda, as Habermas suggests,[52] but first of all must take recourse to reports that testify to the existence of the explananda. And these reports have to come down to *perceptual statements*, if the reporter should be pressed by his opponents in the discourse. Now at this point, I think, the superiority of a *transcendental-pragmatical consensus theory* of truth over a *coherence-theory of discourse* rests precisely on the fact that the former can take the evidence-testimonies of the single discourse-partners as criteriological ingredients of the very discourse to be weighed out in connection with the theoretical coherence-criteria. For it is not the case, as it is sometimes suggested today by a logistic type of analytic philosophy, that the ("indexical" and "iconical") evidence of perceptual judgments can only be accounted for as external causes of basic propositions, such that these were by no means distinguished by their *evidence* from other propositions. It rather belongs to the very procedure of consensus-formation, I suggest, to understand the evidence of perceptual judgments as good reasons for the reporter's accepting them, and hence as criteria of possible truth to be discursively mediated with other criteria.

In order now to understand and evaluate the Peircean approach as a possible alternative or supplementation of the contemporary types of consensus-theory of truth, one should start out, I suggest, from facing the problem of how a *grounded* consensus can function and hold as ultimate criterium or regulative principle for an integration of all relevant truth-criteria. The answer to this question that can be found in Peirce is provided in the last analysis by the doctrine of the *three fundamental categories*. It was first developed by Peirce in the "New List of Categories" of 1867, i.e., in the context of a *transcendental-semiotical* transformation of Kant's so-called "metaphysical" and "transcendental deduction of the categories."[53] (Later Peirce has supplemented or even replaced his first transcendental-semiotical derivation of the categories by a derivation of the three fundamental categories from the mathematical logic of relations and a "phenomenological" or "phaneroscopial" illustration of their philosophical applications.[54])

On this doctrine, there are three aspects of reality as well as of its semiotically-mediated cognition that must be taken into account by epistemology: "firstness," i.e., relation-free quality as a pure *possibility* of being; "secondness," i.e., the dyadic relation or "clash" between the *I* as will and *existent* reals as "brute facts" that resist our will; and finally "thirdness," i.e., the triadic relation of *mediation* between possible qualities and existent (dyadic) facts by general meaning, i.e., general laws of nature or general rules of *interpretation* and hence of semiotic *representation* and *continuation* of the structure of reality by human "habits" of action. Now, on these presuppositions, the question as to how a grounded consensus of the community of investigators may be conceived of as the ultimate criterium or regulative principle of integration of all possible truth-criteria may be answered roughly in the following way.

Since truth must take the form of a public *representation* of the structure of reality (and since reality cannot be explicated in a criteriologically-relevant way in terms of a transcendent reality), it must be finally explicated in terms of *sign-interpretation*, e.g., on the level of *argumentative discourse*, as it was first developed by philosophy. On the other hand, the deficiency of the (scholastic and the rationalistic a priori) method of purely philosophical seminar-discussion had consisted in the fact that its way of reaching consent by arguments, if it reached it at all,[55] left out of consideration (ignored) the vote of nature, so to speak. Now this vote can be established, according to Peirce, by experiments, i.e., by the "method of science." This means, according to my interpretation, that the pre-discursive ways of experiential integration of *firstness* and *secondness* into *thirdness*, i.e., data-interpretation by perceptual judgments, are put into the service of scientific discourse by being methodically used as sources of inspiration for setting up innovative hypotheses or as means of experimental confirmation of theoretical hypotheses.

The main problem for Peirce in this context was that of bridging the gap between the *particularity* of our intuitions of perceptual qualities including relations ("firstness") on the occasion of factual confrontations with resistent "brute facts" ("secondness"), and the *universality* of interpretative meaning in arguments. And the answer he had to propose and which he elaborated throughout his life is constituted by his conception of a methodological connection between three types of inference: viz., *deduction* as pure expression (model) of *thirdness*, i.e., mediation without information, and "synthetic" inference in the sense of *induction* and *abduction* or *retroduction*. 'Induction in this context should primarily stand in the service of *confirmation* on the basis of enumerative encounters with brute facts. Thus it would bring home, so to speak, the "thirdness" from "secondness." 'Abduction' or 'retroduction', on the other hand, is supposed to provide the creative synthesis of data experience by interpretative and explanatory hypotheses. Thus it draws, so to speak, conceptual "thirdness" from intuitive "firstness." In this context two of Peirce's theorems are of special importance.

On the one hand, Peirce held that our perceptual judgments are unconscious cases of abductive inference, although he was later prepared to concede that there are limit-cases of perceptual judgments that are beyond the scope of man's control of his logical operations and hence must be taken as practically uncriticizable starting-points of inference and interpretation.[56] In any event for Peirce this theorem had to provide a crucial mediation between firstness and thirdness, and thus between the particularity of our intuitions and the universality of the meaning of our arguments. On the other hand, a second crucial mediation between these poles, viz. thirdness of secondness, is made plausible, on Peirce's account, by a theory of *inductive confirmation*.

As far as I can see, Peirce here proceeded from Kant's suggestion that the universality and necessity of scientific inductions are but the analogues of philosophical universality and necessity (5.223n). From this he drew the conclusion that we can and must postulate that "whenever instances may be had in as large numbers as we please, *ad infinitum*, a truly universal and necessary proposition is inferable" (5.223n). Thus Peirce came to substitute in the place of Kant's "transcendental deduction" of the validity of "synthetic judgments a priori" a transcendental deduction of the validity of inductive inference in the long run (see especially 5.223nn, 5.349–52 and 2.690–93).[57] Later, especially in his "Lectures on Pragmatism" (1903), Peirce was no longer satisfied by this foundation of the validity of induction by a transcendental postulate or regulative principle, because it did not sufficiently show, "why perception should be allowed such authority in regard to what is real" (5.211). He now claimed as an additional criterium for the truth of inductive inferences that, analogous to perception as unconscious abduction, it should be possible to intuitively perceive the generality of a governing law or rule as the *continuity of reality* and thus provide a perceptual evidence-orientation for that process of inductive confirmation that, according to the transcendental postulate, would prove the reality of the universality of a hypothesis in the long run (cf. 5.198ff and 5.209–11).[58] Thus Peirce came to conceive of a "firstness of thirdness" in the case of *inductive evidence-confirmation* as well as in the case of *abductive hypothesis* as a perceptual basis that is supposed by our synthetic inferences as arguments.

In order to present this doctrine of "synthetic inferences" as Peirce's answer to the problem of bridging the gap between the *particularity of sensuous evidence* and the *universality of argumentative truth-claims*, one has, however, to consider—and I would emphasize this—that perceptual judgments as the basis of abductive as well as inductive inference imply always prior *symbolic interpretations* in the light of language-systems. Peirce, it is true, in contradistinction to present philosophy after the so-called "linguistic turn," did not so much stress the somewhat relativistic dependence of sign-interpretation on language-systems (or, for that matter, "language-games" as parts of "forms of life") as he did the indefiniteness of the process of sign-interpretation in the indefinite community of interpretation. For Peirce this latter process seemed to represent something like a normatively postulated universal language-game of progressive science that was credited a priori to make possible an agreement about meaning between scientists even across the different languages, so to speak.[59]

In this context, I think, one should mention an ingenious continuation and supplementation of Peirce's semiotics by the later Josiah Royce, who emphasized that, simultaneously with, and complementarily to, perceptual cognition we have to constantly *re-interpret* the meanings of our words as part of the process of cultural tradition, which even must take place as an internalized process in our tacit use of language.[60] I would suggest it is only by presupposing this supplementation of Peirce's approach, i.e., by taking into consideration the hermeneutic conditions of *communicative understanding* as an at least implicit[61] precondition of scientific-philosophic discourse, that we can adequately assess the preceding suggestions. For the *hermeneutic* account of communicative understanding has to complete the *transcendental-semiotic* account for the possibility and necessity of an integration of perceptual criteria concerning the evidence of correspondence of our thought with brute facts and iconical qualities and relations as well as of *coherence*-criteria of logical inference into a grounded consensus by discursive arguments in the interpretation-community of scientists.

Habermas seems to re-confirm this point in a sense, when he expresses the assumption "that there is a connection between the consensus-producing force of an argument on the one hand and the corresponding conceptual system on the other," such that "an argument is satisfactory only if all its parts belong to the same language."[62] According to modern insights into the significance of language-systems for the formation of theories, Habermas indeed emphasizes that "observation-data . . . which we may want to bring into arguments are, naturally, interpreted experiences and therefore dependent upon the categorial framework of the chosen language-system."[63] But, contrary to certain post-Wittgensteinian tendencies of considering semantical systems as ultimate incommensurable frames of possible understanding, and basing arguments on natural history, Habermas considers it possible that argumentation "is not merely based upon a relation between linguistic system and reality which is 'appropriate' in the sense that it has been antecedently drilled into it by a natural and biological process of cognitive development, but itself sets forth the medium in which that cognitive development can be continued as a conscious learning process."[64] In this sense he considers it a necessary condition of the possibility of a *grounded consensus* that can figure as criterium of truth that "progress in knowledge" can take the "form of a substantial critique of language," such that the "structural possibility exists of inquiring behind, modifying and replacing the warranting language in which experiences at any given time are interpreted."[65]

I think indeed that this reflective explication and reformation of the language of discourse must itself form the *hermeneutic* part of argumentative discourse which must make up a continuum, so to speak, with *hermeneutic-reconstructive sciences* as, e.g., history of science. The latter type of a "science of science" would then, of course, not be just an empirical social science that inquires into the causes of "paradigm-change" but rather a critical mediation of *causal explanations* of *quasi-natural processes* and of *normatively relevant* reconstructions of the good or bad rules and reasons that promoted or blocked the progress of science. And the ultimate guiding norm of this attempt of hermeneutic reconstruction would be provided by the very regulative principle of integrating all possible truth-criteria into a consensus by argumentative discourse. Such a program of a continuation of the quasi-natural process of human cognition by discursive procedures within the interpretation-community of investigators was also the object of Peirce's conception of a "normative" logic of inquiry. He conceived of it as a continuation and supersedure of our first "instinctive" theoretical divinations by methodical "self-control" as part of an anthropological and thereby even cosmological "rationalization"-process.[66]

It is only in connection with this "rationalization" -process that Peirce also applies the "Pragmatical Maxim" of meaning-explication to the concept of truth (see, e.g., 5.375, n2). That is to say, there are two dimensions of an explication of truth in terms of practical corroboration of satisfaction that Peirce would envisage. One of them refers to corroboration *within* the process of experimental science, the other refers to that growth of "concrete reasonableness" by human "habit" -formation which Peirce conceives of as possible consequence of the method of science in society. In this latter context, however, the later Peirce had to face the problem of a certain revision or supplementation of the "Pragmatic Maxim," since he realized that the idea of a "pragmatic" corroboration by experiments always presupposes prior "practical" aims (cf. 5.412). Hence the problem of a practical corroboration of science itself would involve the question of a "summum bonum" which cannot be settled by experimental science. It is in this context that he wrote:

> In order to understand pragmatism, therefore, well enough to subject it to intelligent criticism, it is incumbent upon us to inquire what an ultimate aim, capable of being pursued in an indefinitely prolonged course of action, can be (5.135; cf. also 5.3 and 5.402n).

But I do not think that Peirce became fully aware of those problems of truth and of its relations to social praxis that, so to speak, fell between science and ethics, as, e.g., the problematic of the truth of *communicative understanding* between people as participants of a communication-community.[67]

Our discussion of the linguistic and hermeneutic pre-conditions of the idea of discursive consensus-formation may have shown that a full-fledged explication of the meaning of truth in terms of discursive consensus cannot be provided without answering the question as to the *conditions* of a grounded consensus. In fact I would reckon all epistemologically-relevant devices of integrating relevant truth-criteria into the discursive consensus-formation with the conditions of a grounded consensus. Nevertheless there are still further extra-epistemological conditions of the possibility of a grounded consensus which have been taken into consideration by Peirce as well as by Habermas.

Peirce, as early as 1869 in his essay on "The Grounds of Validity of the Laws of Logic," stipulated that nobody could be logical in his (synthetic) inferences who would not sacrifice his personal interests, including even his interest in the salvation of his soul by a religious belief, to the interest of the indefinite community of investigators in reaching the truth in the long run (cf. 5.354). And from this he concluded that the ideal perfection of knowledge would belong to a community within which that identification by "self-surrender" of every member with the community would be complete (5.356). Later, in his foundation of the "normative sciences," he simply stated that the logic of inquiry, being a normative science of acting for a good purpose, presupposes the "normative science par excellence," viz. "ethics" (cf. 5.130, 5.131, 5.36, 1.573, 1.91, 1.612f, 2.199).

Habermas comes to similar conclusions. Since he traces back the pragmatic meaning of truth to the meaning of just one of the "validity-claims" which are necessarily connected with human consensual speech-acts, viz., *intelligibility*, *truth*, *rightness*, and *veracity* (sincerity); and since he furthermore can state that—for reasons of a *transcendental-pragmatic* character of necessity, I would claim—in our consensual speech-acts we must, more or less counterfactually, anticipate an "ideal speech-situation," by which the necessary conditions of a redemption of all four validity-claims would be fulfilled, he comes to postulate that only the fulfillment of certain ethical requirments of the ideal speech-situation can guarantee that "liberation of discourse from constraints of action" which is a pre-condition for a discursive settlement of validity-claims and, among them, truth-claims.

It is interesting to note in this context one characteristic difference in Peirce's and Habermas's determination of the ethical preconditions of argumentative discourse: Peirce connects his principle of "self-surrender" with a rather negative theory of the individual self,[68] such that for him the suppression of individuality rather than self-expression or self-representation seems to be a requirement of the ethics of argumentative discourse. (In fact Peirce never extends the application of the concept of argumentative discourse beyond the range of scientific discourse.) Habermas, on the other hand, claims "two non-trivial conditions which must be satisfied in ideal speech situations, in order to insure that the participants in the conversation actually can take up a discourse and not merely imagine they are conducting a discourse while in truth they are communicating under pressure of action":[69] The one condition consists in an "equal opportunity" for all discourse-partners "to avail themselves of representative speech-acts—i.e., to bring their attitudes, feelings and intentions to expression." This requirement of a "reciprocal harmonisation of the contexts of individual utterances" has to be fulfilled, on Habermas's account, in order to make possible the veracity (sincerity) of the individual persons as discourse-participants. The other condition consists in an "equal opportunity" for all discourse-partners "to avail themselves of regulative speech-acts—i.e., to command and resist, to permit and to forbid, to make and receive promises, to give and demand accountings, etc." This requirement of "complete reciprocity in regard to expectations of behavior," excluding privileges, has to be fulfilled, in order to guarantee the "suspension of reality-constraints" on the discourse, i.e., its unburdening from action by "the formal equal distribution of opportunity to initiate and continue discourse."[70]

I think in fact that Habermas's postulates are an even more adequate, i.e., more concrete, account of that fundamental requirement of "trans-subjectivity"[71] that makes up the true core of Peirce's idea of "self-surrender," since it does not exclude and condemn as idiosyncratic the possible contributions of individuality to the discourse but rather provides equal chances for them. The background for Habermas's more realistic account of the ethical pre-conditions of a grounded consensus can be found, I suggest, in his more concrete account of the *social*, i.e., communicative-hermeneutic presuppositions of human understanding as a precondition of argumentative discourse, even in the case of natural science. For it is above all the requirement of making transparent and revisable even the pre-reflective quasi-natural pre-conceptions as they are implied in the "language-games" as parts of "forms of life" that motivates Habermas's postulates.

But finally there is again a profound agreement between Habermas and Peirce in regard to the question of the *realisability* of the ethical pre-conditions of a grounded consensus.

As an ideal criterium for our judging, i.e., legitimising or criticising real agreements with regard to their having fulfilled the ethical prerequisite of a genuine consensus, the ideal speech-situation is a *regulative principle* in the Kantian sense; but beyond that, the ideal speech-situation is for Habermas a "constitutive condition of rational discourse," since it is an unavoidable "imputation" of the participants in such a discourse, even if it has at the same time the character of a "counterfactual anticipation" of a "foreshadowing life-form."[72] Now, since we cannot know a priori "whether this preshadowing . . . is . . . a mere deception (subreption) . . . or whether the empirical conditions for the (if only approximate) realization of the supposed life-form can practically be brought into being," but nevertheless *cannot help* making that "imputation" as a "practical hypothesis," as long as we are willing to argue (i.e., to think!), we are again confronted with that structure of a *sense-critical* or *transcendental-pragmatic* argument that I have exposed in the preceding as paradigm of a nondeductive type of ultimate foundation in philosophy.

Precisely this, it seems to me, is the structure of Peirce's principle of "hope" which he calls a "hypothesis uncontradicted by facts and justified by its indispensableness for making any action rational" (5.357; cf. 2.654f; 2.661).

Karl-Otto Apel

Johann Wolfgang Goethe-Universität
Frankfurt-am-Main

NOTES

1. Cf. K.-O. Apel, "The Apriori of Communication and the Foundations of the Humanities," in *Man and World*, 5 (1972): 3–27, and "Types of Social Science in the Light of Human Interests of Knowledge," in *Social Research*, 44 (1977): 425–70.

2. Cf. K.-O. Apel, *Der Denkweg von Charles S. Peirce* (Frankfurt a.M.: Suhrkamp, 1975). Cf. also my German edition of C. S. Peirce, *Schriften I und II* (Frankfurt a.M.: Suhrkamp, 1967 and 1970). (English trans.: *Charles S. Peirce: From Pragmatism to Pragmaticism* [Amherst, MA: The Univ. of Massachusetts Press, forthcoming].)

3. Cf. K.-O. Apel, "Szientismus oder transzendentale Hermeneutik? Zur Frage nach dem Subjekt der Zeicheninterpretation in der Semiotik des Pragmatismus," in R. Bubner, et al., eds., *Hermeneutik und Dialektik*, Festschrift für H.-G. Gadamer (Tübingen: J. C. B. Mohr, 1970), vol. I, pp. 105–45; repr. in K.-O. Apel, *Towards a Transformation in Philosophy* (London: Routledge and Kegan Paul, 1979); K.-O. Apel, "C. W. Morris und das Programm einer pragmatisch integrierten Semiotik," Einführung zu C. W. Morris, *Zeichen, Sprache und Verhalten* (Düsseldorf: Schwann, 1973), pp.9–66; K.-O. Apel, "Transcendental Semiotics and the Paradigms of First Philosophy," in *Philosophic Exchange*, vol. 2, no. 4 (1978), pp. 3–22.

4. For a thorough account of the aporetics of a logico-semantical explication of the concept of *explanation*, see W. Stegmüller, *Wissenschaftliche Erklärung und Begründung*, (Berlin and New York: Springer, 1969); for an alternative approach, see K.-O. Apel, *Die 'Erklären/Verstehen'-Kontroverse in transzendental-pragmatischer Sicht*, (Frankfurt a.M.: Suhrkamp, 1979). Cf. also K.-O. Apel, "The Erklären/Verstehen-Controversy in the Philosophy of the Human and Natural Sciences," in: G. Fløistad, ed., *Chronicles* (of the International Institute for Philosophy), vol. II (forthcoming).

5. Cf. most recently H. Keuth, *Realität und Wahrheit* (Tübingen: J. C. B. Mohr, 1978).

6. Cf. A. Tarski, "Die semantische Konzeption der Wahrheit," in Sinnreich, ed., *Zur Philosophie der idealen Sprache* (München: Deutsches Taschenbuch Verlag, 1972), pp. 77 and especially 87.

7. See, e.g., *Collected Papers*, 4.56: "It seems certainly the truest statement for most languages to say that a *symbol* is a conventional sign which being attached to an object signifies that that object has certain characters. But a symbol, in itself, is a mere dream; it does not show what it is talking about. It needs to be connected with its object. For that purpose, an *index* is indispensable. No other kind of sign will answer the purpose. That a word cannot in strictness of speech be an index is evident from this, that a word is general—it occurs often, and every time it occurs, it is the same word, and if it has any meaning *as a word*, it has the same meaning every time it occurs; while an index is essentially an affair of here and now, its office being to bring the thought to a particular experience, or series of experiences connected by dynamic relations."

"A *meaning* is the associations of word with images, its dream exciting power. An index has nothing to do with meanings; it has to bring the hearer to share the experience by *showing* what he is talking about. The words *this* and *that* are indicative words. They apply to different things every time they occur."

"It is the connection of the indicative word to a symbolic word which makes an assertion."—Cf. 2.335; 3.363; 2.287; 8.41.

8. Cf., e.g., 5.30 and 2.315.

9. As for the "redundance"-theory of truth, cf. F. P. Ramsey, "Facts and Propositions," *Proceedings of the Aristotelian Society*, Supp. vol. 7 (1927); A. J. Ayer, *Language, Truth, and Logic*, London, 1935; P. F. Strawson, "Truth," in *Analysis* 9 (1949); as for the proposed solution of the problem that was exposed by the redundance-theory, see J. Habermas, "Wahrheitstheorien," in Fahrenbach, ed., *Wirklichkeit und Reflexion*, (Pfullingen: Neske, 1974), pp. 211–65, ibid. p. 215.

10. See, e.g., C. W. Morris, *Foundations of the Theory of Signs* (Chicago: International Encyclopedia of Unified Science, 1938), vol. I, 2, pp. 29, 35, 52; R. Carnap, *Testability and Meaning*, in *Philosophy of Science* III (1936) and IV (1937), p. 454; R. Carnap, *Introduction to Semantics*, (Cambridge, MA: Harvard Univ. Press, 1942), §§ 4, 38 [9], 39; R. Carnap, "On Some Concepts of Pragmatics," in *Philosophical Studies VI* (1955), pp. 89–91; R. Martin, *Towards a Systematic Pragmatics* (Amsterdam: North Holland Publishing Co., 1959). For a critical reconstruction of this whole development of Logical Empiricism, see E. Tugendhat, "Tarskis Semantische Definition der Wahrheit und ihre Stellung innerhalb der Geschichte des Wahrheitsproblems im Logischen Positivismus," in *Philos. Rundschau*, 8 (1960): 133–59, repr. in G. Skirbekk, ed., *Wahrheitstheorien* (Frankfurt a.M.: Suhrkamp, 1977), pp. 189–223. Cf. also my papers quoted in nn3 and 13.

11. See K. R. Popper, *Objective Knowledge*, (Oxford: Clarendon Press, 1972), pp. 106–52.

12. See my *Denkweg von Charles S. Peirce*, cited in n2, above, and my paper, "From Kant to Peirce: The Semiotic Transformation of Transcendental Logic," in L. W. Beck, ed., *Proceedings of the Third International Kant Congress*, 1970 (Dordrecht, Holland: Reidel, 1972), pp. 90–104, repr. in L. W. Beck, ed., *Kant's Theory of Knowledge*(Dordrecht, Holland: Reidel, 1974), pp. 23, 37. As for Peirce's relation to Hegel, cf. also Max Fisch, "Hegel and Peirce," in J. J. O'Malley et al., eds., *Hegel and the History of Philosophy* (The Hague: Martinus Nijhoff, 1973).

13. For the development of this idea, cf. the following of my papers: "Programmatische Bemerkungen zur Idee einer transzendentalen Sprachpragmatik," in T. Airaksinen et al., eds., *Studia Philosophica in Honorem Swen Krohn* (Turku: Annales Universitatis Turknensis, 1973), pp. 11–36, repr. in C. H. Heidrich, ed., *Semantics and Communication* (Amsterdam: North Holland Publishing Co. and New York : American Elsevier, 1974), pp. 81–108; "Zur Idee einer transzendentalen Sprachpragmatik," in J. Simon, ed., *Aspekte und Probleme der Sprachphilosophie* (Freiburg/München: Alber, 1977), pp. .83–326; "Transcendental Semiotics and the Paradigms of First Philosophy," in *Philosophic Exchange*, vol. 2, no. 4 (1978): 3–24.

14. Cf. K. R. Popper, *Objective Knowledge* (Oxford: Clarendon Press, 1972), ch. 3. I am, of course, *not* arguing against Popper's distinction between a realm of "objective," i.e., true or false, knowledge and a realm of factual beliefs of real subjects to be thematized in history or in psychology. I am, however, arguing against Popper's, as well as Bolzano's and the Semanticists' overlooking the (transcendental-pragmatic) fact that the concept of propositions of theories that may be conceived as true or false and thus may be called "objective knowledge" as being the topic of a nonpsychologistic *epistemology* must presuppose the concept of a corresponding *subjective truth-claim*. Now in as far as a human subject of knowledge is the carrier of this claim and thereby enters the "indefinite community of investigators" (Peirce), in so far it is not only an "inhabitant of the second world," to use Popper's term, but moreover in charge of the transcendental subject of true knowledge, so to speak. Without this latter presupposition, which re-establishes Kantianism in terms of a *three-dimensional* semiotics, the meaning of "objective knowledge" were bound to dissolve itself. For its meaning cannot be that of an hypostatized *realm of being* in the platonist sense but, I suggest, is rather that of the *correlate of arguing* (i.e., proposing, confirming or refuting) within the frame of argumentative discourse.

It is interesting in this context that G. Frege, who by his strong verdict against psychologism is one of the fathers of modern *semanticism*, was still aware of the fact that the epistemological dimension of the subject of knowledge cannot be simply sur-rendered to psychology. Thus, after having pointed out that the law of gravitation can never be thought of as an association of ideas ("Vorstellungen") in somebody's mind, he continues: "Yet the grasping of this law is a psychic process, after all! Yes, but it is a process that is rather located at the border of the psychic and therefore will not be capable of being completely understood from a purely psychological standpoint; for something must be considered essential in this context that is not psychic in the proper sense, namely the thought ("der Gedanke"); and this process is perhaps the most mysterious ("der geheimnisvollste von allen")." Frege indeed dismisses this question by stating: "Since however it (sc. "the thought") is of a psychic kind, we need not care for it within logic. It is enough that we can grasp thoughts and recognize them to be true. How this might be possible is a question for itself." (G. Frege, *Schriften zur Logik und Sprachphilosophie*, ed. by G. Gabriel [Hamburg: Felix Meiner, 1971], pp. 63f.—trans. K.-O. Apel). This, I think, is *not* a suggestion of an "epistemology without a knowing subject," but only an abstractive isolation of the object of formal logic.

15. Cf., e.g., B. Bolzano, *Wissenschaftslehre*, 1. Band (Sulzbach: 1837), p. 113ff. By postulating a transcendental subject of true knowledge as a presupposition for the meaning of the predicate ' . . . is true', I am not maintaining, as against Bolzano, that truth had to be conceived as being "posed" ("gesetzt") by the divine intellect or a transcendental consciousness. I am in fact maintaining that it cannot be conceived meaningfully without at the same time conceiving in principle of a subject that may claim that its statements (i.e., stated propositions) are valid for, and hence could and should be accepted by, every other possible subject of knowledge irrespective of their being factually asserted. This tenet may figure as an implicit definition of the concept of a *transcendental subject* of true knowledge within the framework of Transcendental Semiotics.

16. The term 'double-structure of speech' ('Doppelstruktur der Rede') was in-troduced by J. Habermas in his essay "Vorbereitende Bemerkungen zu einer Theorie der kommunikativen Kompetenz" in J. Habermas & N. Luhmann, *Theorie der Gesellschaft oder Sozialtechnologie* (Frankfurt a.M.: Suhrkamp, 1971), pp. 104ff., in order to summarize a chief result of Austin's and Searle's speech-act theory to the ef-fect that by the double-structure of speech among other things a self-referential ex-position of the implicit validity-claims (meaning-claims, sincerity-claims, truth-claims, and rightness-claims) of human speech is made possible. (Cf. also n9, above.) I would suggest that by the idea of the "double-structure of speech" a new paradigm is provided for the philosophy of language in view of the fact that the paradigm of the *semanticist* era of language-analysis was rather represented by Karl Bühler's distinc-tion between the "representative" function of language (i.e., of *propositions*!), which alone was considered as constituting the priority of human language, and the com-municative functions (i.e., the functions of "self-expression" and "appealing") which were considered to be common to humans and animals.(Cf. K. Bühler, *Sprachtheorie* (Jena: 1934; Stuttgart: Fischer,[2]1965). The point of the new paradigm is of course com-pletely missed if the pragmatic dimension of performing or understanding il-locutionary acts is itself to be thematized by its objectification as a referential object of the semantical (i.e., representative) dimension of propositions of a metalanguage and thus by ascribing truth-values to performative sentences that, among other things, have the function of a self-referential exposition of truth-claims. Since this latter move constitutes the *semantization*-strategy of the prevailing types of "formal pragmatics" (from R. Carnap and R. Martin to R. Montague and D. Lewis), it is not surprising that Y. Bar-Hillel in his review "On Habermas' Hermeneutic Philosophy of

Language", *Synthese* 23 (1973) should only prove his nonunderstanding of the whole approach. Cf. also K.-O. Apel, "Zwei paradigmatische Antworten auf die Frage nach der Logos-Auszeichnung der menschlichen Sprache," in H. Lützeler, ed, *Kulturwissenschaften* (Bonn: Bouvier, 1980), pp. 13–68.

17. In fact natural language could be called the (transcendental-pragmatic) *meta-institution* with respect to all human institutions. Cf. my argument with A. Gehlen's "philosophy of institutions," in K.-O. Apel, *Transformation der Philosophie* (Frankfurt a.M.: Suhrkamp, 1973), vol. I, pp. 197ff., and my argument with J. R. Searle in my essay "Sprechakttheorie and transzendentale Sprachpragmatik zur Frage ethischer Normen" in K.-O. Apel, ed., *Sprachpragmatik und Philosophie* (Frankfurt a.M.: Suhrkamp, 1976), esp. pp. 104ff.

18. Cf. K.-O. Apel, "Types of Rationality To-day," in Th. Geraets, ed., *Rationality Today* (Ottawa University Press, 1978), pp. 307–40.

19. Cf. I. Kant ("Nachlass," ed. by Preussische Akademie, Nr. 2128): "Das objektive Kriterium der Wahrheit ist die Übereinstimmung der Vorstellungen untereinander nach allgemeinen Gesetzen des Verstandes und der Vernunft, d.i. durch Anschauungen oder Begriffe"; "Das subjektive Kriterium der Wahrheit ist die Übereinstimmung eines Urteils mit anderen sowohl in demselben Subjekt als in verschiedenen."

20. Cf. D. Davidson, "Truth and Meaning," in *Synthese* 17 (1967); "True to the Facts," in *Journal of Philosophy*, 66 (1969); "In Defense of Convention T," in H. Leblanc, ed., *Truth, Syntax and Modality* (Amsterdam: North Holland Publishing Co., 1973).

21. E. Tugendhat, *Vorlesungen zur Einführung in die sprach-analytische Philosophie* (Frankfurt a.M.: Suhrkamp, 1976).

22. Cf., e.g., W. Sellars, *Science, Perception, and Reality*, (New York: The Humanities Press, 1977), p. 219.

23. N. Rescher, *The Coherence Theory of Truth* (Oxford: Clarendon Press, 1973). In fact Rescher does not propose the coherence theory as an explication of the meaning of truth, but only as a theory that provides an "authorizing," but not "guaranteeing" criterium of truth.

24. L. B. Puntel, *Wahrheitstheorien in der Neueren Philosophie* (Darmstadt: Wissenschaftliche Buchgemeinschaft, 1978).

25. W. Kamlah and P. Lorenzen, *Logische Propädeutik* (Mannheim: Bibliographisches Institut, 1967).

26. K. Lorenz, "Der dialogische Wahrheitsbegriff," in *Neue Hefte für Philosophie*, vol. 2, no. 3 (1972): 111–23.

27. See n9, above.

28. Cf., e.g., C. F. von Weizsäcker, *Die Einheit der Natur* (München: Hanser, ⁴1972, pp. 336ff., and K. Lorenz, *Die Rückseite des Spiegels, Versuch einer Naturgeschichte menschlichen Erkennens* (München and Zürich: Pieper, 1973).

29. See n24, above.

30. Puntel, cited in n24, above, p. 215f.

31. This thesis of modern coherence-theory was impressively stated by O. Neurath in connection with the paradoxicality of Wittgenstein's talk about the relationship between language and reality in the "Tractatus" and the search of the Logical Positivists for pre-linguistic "protocol-sentences." Cf. O. Neurath, "Soziologie im Physicalismus," in *Erkenntnis*, 2 (1931): 393–431, esp. p. 396f and p. 403.

32. Cf. G. W. F. Hegel, *Phänomenologie des Geistes*, A, I: "Die sinnliche Gewis-
¹ sheit, das Dieses und das Meinen."

33. The example was used by M. Schlick in his argument with Neurath in "Facts
and Propositions," in *Analysis* 2 (1934/35): 65–70. I believe Schlick was right in considering his "Konstatierungen" to be "the points of contact between knowledge and
reality"; (cf. "Über das Fundament der Erkenntnis" in *Erkenntnis* 4 [1934]: 98); but,
like Husserl, he was not yet prepared to mediate the phenomenological distinction of
perceptual judgments with the acknowledgement of their being nonetheless language-
impregnated (and hence theory-impregnated) and hence open to revision by
reinterpretation. It is precisely this mediation between a phenomenological evidence-
theory of truth and "fallibilism" in the sense of indefiniteness of interpretation that
became possible by Peirce's semiotical account for the interaction of *icons, indices*
and *symbols* in *perceptual judgments* as limit-cases of *hypotheses*.

34. Cf. H. Spiegelberg, "Husserl's and Peirce's Phenomenologies: Coincidence or
Interaction," in *Philos. and Phenom. Research* 17 (1956): 164–85. Regarding the internal tension between Peirce's "phenomenology" or "phaneroscopy" of 1902 ff. and
his semiotical logic of *symbolic mediation* (in the sense of "Thirdness"), cf. my account in *Der Denkweg von C. S. Peirce*, cited in n2, above, pp. 203ff.

35. Thus far also E. Tugendhat (cited in n21, above, pp. 161ff., esp. pp. 182ff. and
205ff.) goes too far, it seems to me, in superseding the *phenomenological* paradigm of
philosophy by that of *language-analysis*.

36. Cf. K. Popper, *Logic of Scientific Discovery* (London: Hutchinson, 1959), pp.
95ff. and p. 105. Popper's logicism in this context comes close to Neurath's position
and amounts to a complete surrender of the phenomenon of *experimental evidence* to
the realm of psychological explanation. I would like to suggest that, under this
epistemological presupposition, the idea of falsification finally can no longer be interpreted as wrecking of theories by reality, since, by abstraction from experiential
evidence as an authorizing, if not sufficient, truth-criterium, the confrontation of
theories with falsifiers amounts to a confrontation between rivaling theories which
then can no longer defend their priority-claim by—among other criteria—recourse to
experiential support. The result of this version of pluralism seems to become visible in
Feyerabend's dissolution of Critical Rationalism.

37. Cf. my book cited in n4, above.

38. Cf., e.g., H. Albert, *Traktat über Kritische Vernunft*, (Tübingen: J. C. B.
Mohr, 1968), pp. 14 and 30.

39. From 1866 Peirce outlined his semiotical transformation of Kant's
"transcendental idealism" in passages like the following: "We find that every judgment is subject to a condition of consistency; its elements must be capable of being
brought to a unity. This consistent unity since it belongs to all our judgments may be
said to belong to us. Or rather since it belongs to the judgments of all mankind, we
may be said to belong to it." (Fragment of 1866, quoted in Murphey, *The Development
of Peirce's Philosophy* [Cambridge, MA: Harvard Univ. Press, 1961], p. 89.) Later
this germinal transcendence of the methodical solipsism of a transcendental
philosophy of the consciousness qua "I think" is continued as follows: " . . . consciousness is a vague term . . . consciousness is sometimes used to signify the *I think*,
or unity in thought; but the unity is nothing but consistency, or the recognition of it.
Consistency belongs to every sign, so far as it is a sign . . . there is no element whatever
of man's consciousness which has not something corresponding to it in the word . . .

the word or sign which man uses is the man himself . . . the organism is only an instrument to thought. But the identity of a man consists in the *consistency* of what he does and thinks . . . . The existence of thought now depends on what is to be hereafter; so that it has a potential existence, dependent on the future thought of the *community*." (5.313–16)

40. See n9, above.

41. For the different possible perspectives of Peirce-interpretation see my *Der Denkweg von Charles S. Peirce* (Frankfurt a. M.: Suhrkamp, 1975), pp. 33f. (Cited hereafter as *DD*.) For Habermas's precautions against the term "transcendental pragmatics" cf. his essay "Was heisst Universal-pragmatik?" cited hereafter as WHU in: K.-O. Apel (ed.) *Sprachpragmatik und Philosophie* (Frankfort a. M.: Suhrkamp, 1976), esp. pp. 201ff.

42. See Habermas, WHU, p. 219 (trans. K.-O. Apel).

43. WHU, p. 239f.

44. This initial move is followed by B. Stroud's famous paper on "Transcendental Arguments" (*Journal of Philosophy*, 65, [1968]: 241–56) which, as far as I can see, was prominent in discouraging the recent discussion of a post-Wittgensteinian version of transcendental philosophy.

45. Cf. K.-O. Apel, "The Problem of Philosophical Fundamental Grounding in Light of a Transcendental Pragmatic of Language," in *Man and World*, 8/3 (1975): 239–75.

46. WHU, p. 215f.

47. Cf. O. Höffe, "Kritische Uberlegungen zur Konsenstheorie der Wahrheit (Habermas)," in: *Philosophisches Jahrbuch*, 83 (1976): 313–32.

48. Thus L. P. Puntel, in *Wahrheitstheorien in der Neueren Philosophie* (Darmstadt: Wissenschaftliche Buchgemeinschaft, 1978) almost claims Habermas's theory as argumentative evidence for his coherence-conception.

49. WHU, pp. 218f.

50. Habermas, WHU, p. 218. Habermas's rigorous distinction between "objects of experience" and "facts" as correlates of propositions seems to me to presuppose a certain nominalism (and a nominalistic understanding of transcendental philosophy) which fits in with orthodox Kantianism and certain strands of modern logic of language, but cannot cope with Peirce's semiotical transformation of the transcendental logic of cognition which I called "sense-critical realism" (cf. *DD*, pp. 41ff.). In his *Knowledge and Human Interests* (Boston: Beacon Press, 1971, II, 5) Habermas found it necessary to refute Peirce's semiotical realism as a relapse into pre-Kantian metaphysics, whereas I would consider it to be an integral part of transcendental semiotics and hence transcendental pragmatics which overcomes the paradoxicalities of Kant's conception of unknowable things in themselves. (Cf. also *DD*, p. 257, n41, and p. 34f., n217).

51. WHU, p. 217f.

52. WHU, 241ff. Here Habermas's discourse-theory of truth in fact seems to collapse into a pure coherence-theory.

53. Cf. C. S. Peirce, "On a New List of Categories," in: *Proceedings of the American Academy of Arts and Sciences*, VII (1967): 287–98. For supplementing materials and a critical interpretation of this early period of Peirce's thought cf. M. C. Murphey, *The Development of Peirce's Philosophy*, (Cambridge, MA: Harvard University Press, 1961), pp. 55ff. For my own interpretation, which sometimes deviates from Murphey's, see *DD*.

54. Cf. Murphey, cited in n53, above, pp. 269ff.

55. Cf. *Collected Papers*, 5.358–87. Cf. my interpretation in *DD*, pp. 115ff.

56. See *Collected Papers*, 5.115ff., 5.142, 5.181ff., 5.194. Cf. my interpretation in *DD*, pp. 297ff.

57. Cf. my interpretation in *DD*, pp. 73ff. and "From Kant to Peirce: The Semiotic Transformation of Transcendental Logic," in: L. W. Beck (ed.), *Kant's Theory of Knowledge* (Dordrecht, Holland: D. Reidel, 1974), pp. 23–37.

58. *DD*, pp. 310–18.

59. Cf. my argument for a "transcendental language-game" of hermeneutic understanding as against the post-Wittgensteinian pluralism-relativism in K. -O. Apel, "The Communication Community as the Transcendental Presupposition for the Social Sciences," in Apel, *Towards a Transformation of Philosophy* (London: Routledge & Kegan Paul, 1980), pp. 136–79.

60. Cf. Josiah Royce, *The Problem of Christianity* (New York: 1913), vol. II, pp. 146, and my interpretation in *Towards a Transformation of Philosophy* (cited in n59, above), pp. 199ff.

61. It becomes explicit when scientific progress faces a crisis as the continuum of a philosophical explication of scientific concepts and an empiric-hermeneutic reconstruction of the history of science.

62. WHU, p. 244.

63. WHU, p. 245.

64. WHU, pp. 249f.

65. WHU, p. 250.

66. C. S. Peirce, *Collected Papers*, 5.4; 5.433; 5.402, nn19 and 20. For the history of (the evolution of) science cf. 6.10, 6.50, 5.47, 5.173, 5.445, 5.498, 5.586, 5.591, 5.603, 1.118. Cf. also my interpretation in *DD*, pp. 196ff. and 268ff.

67. Cf. my critical comments in *DD*, pp. 164ff. and 349ff.; cf. also my "Scientism or Transcendental Hermeneutics?," in Apel, *Towards a Transformation of Philosophy* (cited in n59, above) sec. III.

68. Cf., e.g., *Collected Papers*, 5.235, 5.317, 1.673; for the context and background of Peirce's anti-individualism cf. G. Wartenberg, *Logischer Sozialismus. Die Transformation der Kantschen Transzendentalphilosophie durch C. S. Peirce* (Frankfurt a. M.: Suhrkamp, 1971), esp. pp. 54ff.

69. WHU, p. 255.

70. WHU, p. 256.

71. For this term cf. P. Lorenzen, *Normative Logic and Ethics* (Mannheim/-Zürich: 1969), pp. 73ff.

REFLECTIONS ON PEIRCE'S AESTHETICS*

I

The first thing to note about Peirce's semiotic aesthetics is that Peirce himself had very little to say about it. Two articles published in the *Journal of Asthetics and Art Criticism* are concerned with determining Pierce's views on aesthetic theory. The first was by Max Oliver Hocutt, in 1962, called "The Logical Foundations of Peirce's Aesthetics."[1] This article has something less than an auspicious start, however, since its first sentence reads, "There is a sense in which it might be said that Charles Peirce had no aesthetics."[2] And since that sentence is followed in the next paragraph with one of the flattest— or, if you prefer, deadest of metaphors, to wit:

> Probably the best single explanation of this fact is that Peirce was wedded to logic and knew her to be a satisfying spouse. A contented husband is, like any other husband, frequently distracted by charming young things—but usually only for fleeting moments. Peirce was no exception.[3]

It is nothing less than a miracle that anyone interested in aesthetics would continue reading the article. If one's interest in Peirce is stronger than one's expectation of a graceful style, however, continued reading of the argument will discover the author's opinion that Peirce's few aesthetic fragments may be said to contain three suggestions for an aesthetic theory: first, that the art object is an icon; second, that the aesthetic value of an art icon is the harmony of its intrinsic qualities; and third, that the interpretant by which a viewer responds to the art icon is a feeling or emotion. Peirce's realism is also operative in showing the relationship between these three propositions. The iconicity of the art object establishes only its sign-character; the clue to reading this sign-character is as always in the interpretant, here a feeling (the subjective correlate of "objective" properties and qualities of the work of art); and when these phenomenally objective properties are verified by a continual replication of the emotional interpretant, the object is correctly called "beautiful."

The surprise of this account of Peirce's aesthetic theory is that it recognizes that iconicity does not imply mimesis: i.e., that it does not follow from an artwork's iconic sign-quality that it must represent an object of nature. That, as will be pointed out later, has been the bane of the second generation Peirceans. Since the object referred to by the icon need not exist, a work of art may be an icon without being a realistic rendition of a portion of the natural scene:

> There is nothing in Peirce's view of art to suggest that "realism" is the only legitimate or proper art technique. Since there need be no existential counterpart for the aesthetic icon, invidious comparisons of works of art with actual things are irrelevant. The work of art must be appreciated for the qualities it possesses itself.[4]

At this juncture in the argument, Hocutt finds not *one*, but *two* "objects" that might serve as designata for the iconic art sign: first, the particular set and arrangement of the qualities *intended by the artist*; and second, the essence of beauty, defined in a straightforward Platonic sense and interpreted below as kalos or harmony. If, however, there were only the first object, no viewer other than the painter could ever judge of the artwork's inconicity; and since the second serves as check on the arbitrary subjectivity of the artistic intention, there is hardly any need to refer to the first. Hence Peirce's aesthetic theory comes down to this:

> The aesthetically valuable object is a sign which "means" what it does in virtue of possessing the characteristics of its object. It is, in short, an icon. What the aesthetic icon represents is, speaking generally, an instance of *kalos*, that is, a certain complex of qualities which appears as a simple quality because of the internal relatedness of the members of the complex. The effect on an interpreter of an aesthetic sign is a feeling, or rather, a complex feeling having correspondence to the complex quality which is the object of the aesthetically valuable sign.[5]

As for the supposed relationship between "logic" and aesthetics, in one sense of the term, the narrower, in which "logic" means critical logic, that science depends upon aesthetics as a first to its third (as qualities are primary to facts and laws), while in the most general sense, logic as semiotic, aesthetic theory clearly depends upon it. Or in Peirce's own words, "obsistent logic" depends upon aesthetics, but aesthetics itself depends upon "originalian logic."

Ten years later C. M. Smith in an article entitled "The Aesthetics of C. S. Peirce,"[6] points out that the Peircean aesthetic is not limited to the application of sign-theory as a specialized version of originalian logic, but is rather referred to by Peirce as "an exact science," a "normative science," "a science of ideals of what is objectively admirable," etc. Given its Platonism, however, Peirce's normative science of aesthetics is neither new nor particularly enlightening. And although in his development of the theory of signs Peirce made a number of suggestions relative to aesthetics, that theory contains few explicit references to what a complete aesthetic theory would be like. We read, for example, that an aesthetics would have as its central feature an explicit concentration on the firstness of experience, and that art has a capacity for arresting or fixing qualities and feelings, as it exhibits them for contemplation. The theory of signs merely gives a way of interpreting the sign functions of works of art.

Smith is careful to spell out the relationship of Peirce's categories of experience (firstness, secondness, and thirdness) with respect to the three elements within a sign-function: sign, object, and interpretant. According to the first trichotomous division, a sign is, for the interpretant, either a qualisign, a sinsign, or a legisign, depending upon whether it is a quality, an actual existent, or a law. According to the second trichotomy, the ground of the relation determines signs to be icons (by virtue of a similarity), indices (by virtue of an existential connection), or symbols (as determined by the habit of association, and hence as exhibiting regularity and law). Finally, in the third trichotomy, the object of the sign is, for the interpretant, presented as a rheme (qualitative possibility), a dicisign (a sign of actual existence), or an argument (a sign of law, i.e., understood "to represent its Object in its character of sign"). If aesthetics is bound, as Peirce maintained, to the immediacy of firstness, it might be said that the aesthetic sign is a rhematic iconic qualisign, i.e., a quality, or a work of art under the aspect of its qualitative wholeness, serving as a sign of a distinct qualitative possibility by virtue of a similarity between the two. Such indeed is a simple icon.

But an icon denotes its object, whether that object is known to exist or not: "The mind noting the iconic nature of a sign is stirred to sensations analogous to those that would be the effect of the possible object, but it can become aware of this analogy only through the mediation of another sign, the interpretant or 'significate effect' of a sign."[7] Thus, Hocutt's warning against interpreting the iconicity of artworks as representational of actually existent objects is reinforced by this reading of Peirce's theory. Since, moreover, the significate effects of simple icons are the only vehicles of direct communication through signs [2:279], this claim often made for artworks seems founded in semiotic theory. And, on the other hand, although works of art usually make no truth claims, a close examination of their structures may lead the viewer of art to otherwise ordinarily hidden truths concerning their objects. This is the aspect of the sign-situation that led Suzanne K. Langer to develop her theory of the art object as "a symbol" of a pattern of sentience, a form of insight into man's capacity to feel.[8]

But besides the simple icon, there are other icons, of the second and third categories: iconic sinsigns, or diagrams, having a structural similarity with their objects, e.g., the schematic of an electrical circuit as a diagram of the actual circuit; and iconic legisigns, which function as general laws or types for innumerable tokens, each of which is a sinsign of a particular kind, as, for example, the "model" of a year's production is reproduced in each automobile of a given series. Within aesthetics, the design model of a multiple-original medium like graphic printmaking may also serve as an example here.

According to still another division of icons, Peirce refers to a different triad: hypoicons, i.e., "any material image, such as a painting . . . in itself, without legend or label . . .," [2:276] diagrams, and metaphors. If the hypoicon is the firstness of a first (a simple qualitative similarity), it may be called an image; but those which represent the relations, mainly dyadic, of the parts of a thing by virtue of similar relations in its own structure are *diagrams*, while icons illustrating the thirdness of a first, i.e., those which "represent the representative character of a representamen by representing a parallelism in something else" [2.277] are *metaphors*. Smith points out how a "tension" as the funded quality of two component qualities (let us say, the "pull" felt to exist between adjacent planes of complementary colors) may be considered an example of "the first degree of genuine thirdness" in that one quality mediates between two others. A metaphor may indeed be interpreted as representing this representative character of the tense triad of quality being taken as equivalent to a similar tension observed in another medium; perhaps even, says Smith, in the human psyche.[9]

Can this somewhat dense typological schema be applied to other "aesthetic" phenomena? Surely, claims Smith, it might serve as a guide to understanding the various interpretations given to works of art. For example, if a portrait has a name or a legend attached to it, it is an indexical rather than an iconic sign because it would stand for its object through the nameplate. Without the legend, however, the portrait would serve as an iconic sinsign, referrring to the person represented in the portrait by virtue of similar physiognomic characteristics. Unfortunately for both a coherent aesthetic theory and for the aesthetic interpretation of Peirce's semiotic, the iconicity of the work of art was mostly interpreted to be of this variety. But as Hocutt had already noticed, the object of an icon need not exist, and some "portraits" may be of fictional characters, such as Paul Bunyan or Mary Poppins, whose physical characteristics are known through descriptions in other media. Such icons would still be iconic sinsigns. Next, if the painting is to be reproduced by lithographic or any other means it would then become an iconic legisign, determining what properties the "copies" of the original must possess in order to be replicas of the original.

But that is not all. Everything depends upon how the painting is attended to. If one views the total effect of the component qualities as itself a single quality, and that quality is perceived as, say, "strength," then the emotional interpretant of the image would be the same or similar to the significate effect of any other object exhibiting the same kind of strength. Lastly, if the lines and brush strokes of a given sensuous surface are perceived as "crude," stark, or powerful, they may themselves be taken as metaphors of the crudity, starkness or power of the subject they represent; and if they are, as in the case of Picasso's *Guernica* analyzed below, they are taken as a metaphor.[10] Thus, in Smith's account, there are as many interpretants as there are ways to view the phenomenal structures of a painting, and one would be misadvised to look for a single interpretant which would define necessary and sufficient properties of "works of art."

Between Hocutt, writing in 1962, and Smith, in 1972, for the same journal, the one finding the sketch of an aesthetic theory and the other, only a system for classifying the various ways works of visual art may be interpreted as signs, what is there to be chosen? Perhaps an answer may be found for this question if we consider the aesthetic writings of Peirce's followers and their critics—a task projected for the next section of this article.

II

The first of the second generation Peircean accounts of aesthetic experiences was given by Charles Morris, working, in 1939, within the tradition of the "unified science" movement.[11] The advantage of his application of the Peircean account, he thought, was the possibility of unifying science through the general theory of signs. As phenomena of firstness, and of the immediate communication of feelings, art works would best be interpreted as icons, much as has been explained for Hocutt's and Smith's account of Peirce's own theory. Morris was aware, however, that an icon may have an object that does not necessarily exist, and hence distinguished between the "denotata" and "designata" of the iconic sign; both these terms were applied to the object referred to by the sign. What Morris added to the Peircean account was the notion of a sign-vehicle, to replace Peirce's notion of a representamen. This substitution allowed for the interpretation of a sign or, as Morris said, of sign-situations in terms of a sign-vehicle, that object which served as sign, its designata, and the interpretant.

Since works of art were, for the most part, composite signs made up of other signs, there were three dimensions of sign analysis pertinent to works of art: the relation within the sign vehicle of component signs to each other (syntactics); that between the sign-vehicle and its designatum (semantics); and that between the sign-vehicle and its interpretant (pragmatics). Although these designations are themselves only rough metaphors for various ways of reading the aesthetic sign's significance, they do correspond to three conventional interpretations of an artwork's functioning in human experience; or, if you prefer, to three different putative definitions of the working of a work of art. Formalistic aestheticians emphasize the "syntactical dimension" of an aesthetic sign's constitution; and mimetic aesthetic theorists have always emphasized the "semantic dimensions," while expressionists have found the "pragmatic dimension" the most illuminating of an artwork's characteristics for developing an aesthetic theory.

The difficulty in these analyses was to find a counter or candidate for the "semantic dimension" in obviously nonrepresentational works. This, I take it, was the crux of the debate; and it rests upon a serious mistake. For instead of assuming that nonrepresentational works constitute the limiting or boundary concept of the ideal of mimesis, the debate should have centered around the propriety of considering the iconicity of apparently pictorial art as the end or value of that form of expression. There shall be more about where the debate should have been centered later. It suffices for the moment to consider the way in which nonrepresentational works were interpreted as the limiting cases of an artwork's "iconicity."

The only modification necessary to understand Morris's use of Peircean semiotics is that "sign" has been replaced by "sign-vehicle" and that the object of a sign-vehicle may be either a designatum or a denotatum, the latter being a designatum that actually exists. A realistic scene or portrait would then have both a designatum and denotatum, whereas a scene or portrait of a purely imaginary entity or person would have only a designatum. Whichever, the (artwork) sign would have a "semantic dimension." Other works of art would seem, on the surface of the matter, to lack this dimension entirely, leaving the expressiveness of the work to be determined solely by its "syntactic dimension"; but Morris always refused to make this step with the formalistic aestheticians. His assumption is as follows: "every iconic sign has its own sign-vehicle among its denotata," and "there is sometimes no denotatum other than the aesthetic sign vehicle itself.[12] When this occurs the artwork as sign vehicle may be described as the funded quality of component qualities, and its denotatum would be the "value" of this quality as a possibility (i.e., its rheme is a possible value), actually known by the significate effect in the interpretant. In this way, even so-called nonobjective works of art may fulfill the threefold conditions for being a sign.

Although Morris's account of the semiotics of artworks influenced generations of students at the University of Chicago, it came under the stringent criticism of Richard Rudner (1951) and Charles L. Stevenson (1958).

Rudner's account is the easiest to dispense with.[13] He claimed that any theory of aesthetic value which maintained that it was both immediately experienced and at the same time mediated by a sign was manifestly inconsistent. The argument was general, aimed at Suzanne K. Langer's theory of art symbolism, as well as Morris's and all others that interpreted an artwork to be a sign.

The source of Rudner's confusion was his interpretation of immediacy as the experience of "any object valued in and for itself," which I can only take to mean "valued for its intrinsic properties." The confusion is so simple any reader of Hegel would have caught it straightaway. Immediacy is a predicate applying in the first instance to consciousness intending an object, not to the object or its values. It is only on reflection that consciousness discovers its mediated components, an ego and its objects. If Rudner had attended to the growing development of the Hegelian phenomenology, it would have been no mystery how the object of an immediately-felt consciousness "dirempts" into its two component parts, and then returns to itself in a new state of conscious immediacy following the diremption. Farfetched? Not at all. If one were to look for an historical precedent to Peirce's theory of "transuasion," no clearer model than the Hegelian movement from simple consciousness to consciousness mediated by its object and the return to a more complicated form of immediacy could be found. Indeed any object considered in itself fulfills the role of the sign-vehicle; in relationship to our consciousness of it, it exists for us, as an object of our intending (of a significant function); and the two stages are mediated by our future awareness of them as being a new object for consciousness, now in- and for-itself. When this future awareness has been fulfilled, we will have achieved a new status of immediacy, and the dialectic may continue.

C. M. Smith registers basically the same complaint against Rudner, pointing out that surely Peirce did maintain that artworks were icons, therefore signs and the objects of a mediated experience. What Rudner forgot is that an icon is a degenerate sign; that its meaning is confined to category the first. Such a sign (or an object so interpreted) states no facts, indicates no laws. And since it does not involve any thinking in the ordinary sense of this term, it may be said to have the immediate impact it does.[14] The secret is in the interpretation of the interpretant; and if we refuse Morris's own idiosyncratic interpretation of the iconic sign's denotatum, we should still be able to feel the tension between our perception of the artwork's sensuous surface and the conception of any mimetic elements found in its "depth" when the work is conventionally representational, or to feel the tensions of the component qualities of that surface if it contains no depth. All feelings are immediately felt, and some of them are interpretants.

Smith puts this last point in a slightly different way. He claims that there is only one interpretant for the entire significant relation, whether the sign itself be a quality, an existent entity, or a general law, and whether the object of that sign is a rheme, a dicisign, or argument; and that interpretant is the object of an immediate awareness once the relationship has been established between the sign and its object. Rudner, in a word, was guilty of trying to deduce possible aesthetic responses—or to eliminate impossible ones on the basis of a deduction, instead of reporting on his actual responses one by one, as they occurred.

Charles Stevenson's argument takes Morris to task for a number of reasons, most of which will likewise be found to be irrelevant.[15] Like Rudner, Stevenson throws in Langer's theory as another "symbolic theory" incapable of fulfilling the conditions of symbolism in the nonrepresentational arts. Once again we are faced immediately with the assumption that the iconicity of a representational work is paradigmatic, while nonrepresentational works are the theoretical "hard cases" straining the general theory's credibility. I have already indicated that this assumption is wrongheaded, and shall try to explain myself more fully in the last section of this article.

Stevenson does have the good sense to direct his arguments against the specific theories of Morris and Langer, rather than attempting to refute all aesthetic theories of the semiotic type; and I am still interested in Morris only, as the first and most influential Peircean. Morris, it is alleged by Stevenson, uses the term "sign-situation" so broadly that nothing of which we can become aware can fail to define a sign-situation. This would have come as a surprise to both Morris and Peirce, not because what is alleged is false, but because that is what both of them had precisely maintained. Nothing is brought to awareness without the mediacy of some sign. Why is this stated as a criticism of Peirce's and Morris's aesthetic theories, if indeed it is a fact of consciousness? If we attend to the three specific corollaries of this general remark perhaps we shall be led to understand.

First, Morris had noted that certain parts of largely complex signs set up expectations for a kind of fulfillment in other parts of the same complex sign. Why, asks Stevenson, should the initial perception be said to be a sign of eventual fulfillment? Answer: the phenomenon in question takes place at the level of the "syntactic dimension" of the signifying icon. The allegation is not made that any leading motif must resemble its anticipated resolution, but only that both in their relationship constitute a sign-vehicle whose designatum is a possible feeling (a rheme), and that the connection between this sign-vehicle and this rheme is established by the significate effect of their relationship: it is felt, in the interpretant, as a feeling. Stevenson's remark, that noting the relationship between leading motif and anticipated resolution is so "elementary" that calling it "symbolic" adds nothing to its significance,[16] must be suspect since he does not deny such relationships exist, and whether they may be truly symbolic is precisely the point mooted in his article. This latter point, then, may not be so summarily disregarded without begging the question.

His second specific quarrel is with the possibility of a sign-vehicle's having its own properties as one of its denotata. Morris introduced his notion, we remember, in order to show how a work of nonobjective art may be said to denote its own values, since values (by Morris as well as by Peirce) were thought to be properties of objects. What sticks in Stevenson's craw here is the "oddity" of the claim that something may represent itself. Don't all things resemble themselves? Why are all things then not works of art? The question is ignorant, since it abstracts from the felt qualities of the interpretant, and from the limiting firstness of aesthetic signs. All things that may be contemplated may have their aesthetic qualities, to be sure; but if they do, and there is no element of representation either of an existent thing or of a general law, then the object of that sign-relation will be a rhematic possibility. And there is no absurdity involved in stating that a complex iconic sign denotes the possibility of a subjectively-felt value precisely because the interpretant registers the feeling of that value.

Stevenson's third objection may be answered in the same way. He claims that the Peircean semiotic aesthetic (as worked out by Morris) suffers from a certain lack of specificity in the definition of the "aesthetic" interpretant, since aesthetic signs are all considered icons yet may be considered under specific circumstances as having other signific functions, say as an index or a symbol. It is of course, true that artworks may be both indices and symbols in the Peircean sense (I shall treat of that later), but if it is agreed that aesthetic value is a matter of firstness, and in its paradigmatic form of the firstness of a first, then we need not speak to the question of "the" aesthetic interpretant; any interpretant would be aesthetic which had the requisite sign-status. Certainly there is no implication that all aesthetic signs have the same interpretant; that would be absurd. Interpretants merely follow the properties of the sign. The question, posed by Stevenson, concerning the relation between the icon and its denotatum must be answered by our experiencing some kind of interpretant. The sign-vehicle possesses qualities external to the interpreting mind; its denotatum, as a mere possibility, is likewise external to any particular mind; the interpretant which notes the iconic relation between the two is an internal structure of the mind intending the sign for its values.

From my own reading of all three—Morris, Rudner, and Stevenson—I can only marvel at the effect of the latter two's criticisms. From 1951 (Rudner) and 1958 (Stevenson) to 1962 (Hocutt) and still later to 1972 (Smith), the Peircean semiotic aesthetic was thought to be dead for lack of support. True, there were in the interim few proponents of the theory, but philosophers had by then gotten out of the habit of reading Peirce's seminal work on the subject. In what follows I shall attempt to relate what I have learnt about aesthetics from reading Peirce's semiotics. If Rudner and Stevenson may be fairly said to have forgotten the interpretants of particular works of art, rereading Peirce may help us rediscover them.

III

I have in the foregoing sections of this article been concentrating on the Peircean semiotic theory as itself constituting a phenomenon of recent aesthetics. That it should have been relatively unknown even after the first publication of the *Collected Papers* comes as no surprise: Peirce's early reputation had been made as a scientist, philosopher of science, and logician, and the prejudice had it that such people are not supposed to be interested in aesthetics. Moreover, Peirce's writings contained only the barest suggestions for an aesthetic theory. It was Charles Morris's interest in the unity of science movement that led to the full scale development of a "Peircean" aesthetic, and after its formulation in 1937–38 it enjoyed a considerable vogue before becoming the object of criticism by analytical philosophers.

In the meantime, however, Suzanne K. Langer had developed her special theory of musical expressiveness (1942)[17] and the general theory of aesthetic expressiveness (1953)[18] based upon her interpretation of an artwork's "symbolic" functioning. Although there was a difference in Morris's and Langer's theory of symbolism (in Morris, the sign-vehicle was the physical artifact itself; in Langer's the phenomenal or "virtual" object served as a symbol of human feeling), the ground for the sign (or symbol) relation in both was similarity of structure in the sign and its object.

The widespread popularity of Langer's account led to the conception of "semiotic" theories of aesthetics as those which impute the sign-function to works of art. Rudner's criticism and, seven years later, those of Stevenson succeeded in bringing about the demise of interest in semiotic theory until 1962, when Hocutt in particular pointed out the logical foundations of Peirce's aesthetics. Ten years later C. M. Smith laid the groundwork for evaluating the degree to which Charles Morris had assimilated and that to which he had modified Peirce's original suggestions. In the foregoing I have treated this historical phenomenon as a series of modulations upon the theme of human consciousness intending what Peirce called "the interpretant."

Most recently J. Jay Zeman (1977) took up the theme of the aesthetic sign in Peirce's semiotic,[19] but was inclined to fill in the "missing elements" of the Peircean aesthetics by appealing to analogous structures in the aesthetic theory of John Dewey.

What have I learnt from personally observing this phenomenon? First of all, that semiotic may be used as a tool for interpreting responses to works of art, and that the iconicity of a painting is not the only ground for the relationship of significance between the painting and its denotatum or designatum. Philosophers of art have most often focused on that property of paintings, but not always with an eminent degree of success. Art historians are often prone to accept the artifact as an index, i.e., an existent thing referring to the artist or to the physical process by which the artist made the artifact. The critical term "action painting," introduced into recent art history by Harold Rosenberg, illustrates an indexical reading of painting as a true symbol, as a sign of a general style, of the functioning of socio-economic or political conditions, or the national character of its maker, etc. Indeed, the very same painting may be interpreted in any of these ways.

Picasso's *Guernica*, for example, may be considered aesthetically as an icon, not of the real scene of destruction that took place during that day of the Spanish Civil War (26 April 1937), but the author's vivid imagination of that scene, rendered in stark and forceful clash of broken lines and forms, all enhanced by the extreme contrast of color limited to a single dimension, its value. As such, the painting may be experienced as the rhematic iconic qualisign it is: the object of the sign (its denotatum, per Morris) is a determinate possibility, this feeling of horror and outrage; the sign-vehicle, this organization of visual counters; the interpretant, our feeling the horror. And as Morris had correctly pointed out, there is no oddity in supposing the "same" thing to be a sign of itself in an important way, as long as one distinguishes between the features of the thing qua signifying and those of the thing qua signified.

Aestheticians get themselves in trouble only when a second degree of iconicity is discerned within the same painting, as when they point out that an imagined scene of an actual war is depicted within *Guernica*. There is nothing either wrong or wrongheaded about the same sign's possessing two denotata, even when the ground of the sign-relation is iconicity. Nothing necessitates that the structure of an icon correspond in a one-to-one relationship with the structure of its object. One subset of its properties may be analogous to one kind of object, while another subset may be analogous to still another at the same time. This is what happens in our phenomenal attention to paintings like *Guernica*, containing both "surface" and "depth" elements. The painting may depict a real event, but that event must be reduced to its visual and affective aspects to become a part of a visual work of art. The surface properties govern surface expressiveness; the depth properties (reduced to visual characteristics) govern a similar depth expressiveness. In our experience of such paintings, therefore, one set of expressive qualities reinforces the other:

the work is still a rhematic iconic qualisign, for the harmonious strata of surface and depth expressiveness is itself felt as a quality, the interpretant mediating the painting perceived as a stratified quality and the determinate possibility of this same quality as a constituent feature of a possible world. Plato, of course, would have called this feature an "eidos," and contemporary phenomenologists, a "purely intentional object," but to speak in this way is to open an ontological question too long to be answered here. It is better perhaps to follow the lead of the painter, and to respond to his painting as an "arrangement in grey and black," rather than as a portrait of his mother. He, of course, had a mother; but no one except perhaps Whistler himself and his mother should care how she looked while sitting in her rocking chair.

When it was said in the earlier sections of this article that the question of a painting's representationality or nonrepresentationality has been a red herring in recent aesthetic debate, the reason was this: the problematic case of iconicity is not a nonrepresentational painting (as Stevenson tried to show), but the representational, since the temptation is to interpret such paintings as dicisigns, i.e., as making a statement about an existent object in our actual world. Cultural historians do this all the time, but then no one has ever accused a cultural historian of being an aesthetician; nor an aesthetician of being a cultural historian, although this latter possibility has brighter prospects than the former. And the reason for this is that each treats the same aesthetic objects from the point of view of different interpretants. Let it just be restated that in one of the senses of the terms involved aesthetics is, for Peirce, a necessary condition for a complete logic. Therefore, for a cultural historian to give a complete picture of this or any other epoch, he must refer ultimately to the distinctive qualities of human experience that serve as firsts to the seconds of his observations; and what is true of the objects of his signs is true of the sign-vehicles themselves.

Professor C. M. Smith has already pointed out how the same "sign" could be interpreted as a sinsign of a legisign; and if we relax the criterion of firstness for the designata of aesthetic signs, it is likewise clear that their "object" may be dicisigns or arguments. Literary works, of course, are constructed in part with dicisigns and contain many arguments; but on this matter it is most probably safer to agree with Ingarden that the statements of a literary work comport only "pseudo-judgments" and that any argument composed of pseudo-judgments can only have a pseudo-conclusion: i.e., there is no way to judge of the purported truth of a conclusion if that truth depends upon statements which are themselves not discernably true. It is for this reason that it is logically odd to claim that works of art may bear a truth value or that they demonstrate either probably or conclusively that anything whatever is true in our actually existent world. Nothing will prevent the attempt to treat works of art as a statement or an argument, but it seems apparent that all such attempts in making abstraction of the firstness of experience likewise make abstraction of anything's aesthetic qualities. That in the end is why cultural historians make poor aestheticians.

In summary, although Peirce's semiotic gives a ready system for classifying art objects, it does not give us a single clue as to how an aesthetic sign (either as a quality or an existent object—a qualisign or a sinsign) is to be described in concrete fact. That still depends upon our experience of such signs, our reflections upon them, and our ability to describe the objects of our reflection: in a word, upon a successful application of the phenomenological epoché, wherein the firstness of a first is most clearly apparent to us. Or, as Peirce would put it, we shall have to learn or relearn how to pay closer attention to the *phanerons* of our minds in order reflectively to interpret the interpretants of our aesthetic signs. This latter activity, of course, is the business of aesthetic theory; but the theory of the interpretant had become all but extinct only because aestheticians had in the first instance lost the technique of scanning their phanerons. A thorough dosage of phenomenology may help us to regain this technique. A course in phaneroscopy, anyone?

E. F. Kaelin

Florida State University

NOTES

* Read before the Edgar Henderson Memorial Symposium on The Philosophy of Charles S. Peirce, 17 May, 1980.
N.B.: All references to Peirce's *Collected Papers* are given in the conventional manner, by volume and paragraph, within the text itself.
1. *Journal of Aesthetics and Art Criticism*, 21 (Winter, 1962): 157–66.
2. Ibid., p. 157.
3. Ibid.
4. Ibid., p. 159.
5. Ibid., p. 165.
6. *Journal of Aesthetics and Art Criticism*, 31 (Fall 1972): 21–29.
7. Ibid., p. 25.
8. Cf. her *Philosophy in a New Key* (New York: Penguin Books, 1948), original, 1942; and *Feeling and Form* (New York: Scribner's Sons, 1953).
9. Smith, "The Aesthetics of C. S. Peirce," p. 26.
10. Ibid.
11. See his "Aesthetics and the Theory of Signs," *The Journal of Unified Science*, 8 (June, 1939): 131–50.

12. Ibid., pp. 136, 131.

13. "On Semiotic Aesthetics," reprinted from the *JAAC* in *Aesthetic Inquiry*, ed. Monroe Beardsley and Herbert Schueller (Belmont, CA: Dickenson Publishing Co., 1967), 93–102.

14. Smith, "The Aesthetics of C. S. Peirce," p. 28.

15. "Symbolism in the Nonrepresentational Arts," in *Introductory Readings in Aesthetics*, ed. John Hospers (New York: The Free Press, 1969), 185–210.

16. Ibid., p. 188.

17. See her *Philosophy in a New Key*.

18. See her *Feeling and Form*.

19. J. Jay Zeman, "The Esthetic Sign in Peirce's Semiotic," *Semiotica*, 19 (1977): 241–58.

DESCARTES, PEIRCE
AND THE COGNITIVE COMMUNITY

The pragmatist tradition in epistemology initiated by Peirce has, I believe, proved a particularly fruitful one. And since Peirce's work in the theory of knowledge was motivated, to a considerable extent, by his radical opposition to the Cartesian tradition, a close study of the early papers in which Peirce offers a comprehensive critique of Cartesian epistemology promises to be philosophically as well as historically rewarding.

So one object of the present paper is to get clear exactly what Peirce thought was wrong with the Cartesian theory of knowledge, and to assess the force of his criticisms. Peirce's critique has two themes—that Descartes' method is impossible, and that it is pointless; my argument will be that on the usual interpretation, which makes the first theme dominant, Peirce's criticisms are thoroughly inconclusive, but that on a revised interpretation, which allows the second theme to dominate, Peirce's criticisms turn out to be more effective. On this interpretation, furthermore, it becomes possible to see the full significance of Peirce's concern to shift the focus of epistemological attention from the individual to the cognitive community.

The other object of this paper—more ambitious, and, I fear, less adequately executed—is to bring out what is plausible and attractive about the pragmatist alternative to Cartesianism. And my theme, here, will be intimately connected with my proposed reinterpretation of Peirce's critique of Descartes: how the notion of a cognitive community, as used by Peirce, promises an escape from the Cartesian dilemma of dogmatism *or* scepticism.

I begin though, modestly, with an account of Peirce's objections to Descartes. Understanding these objections requires quite a broad comprehension of Peirce's own epistemological theories; and in view of this the best procedure seems to be to start with Peirce's explicit criticisms of Descartes and then gradually to build up a complete picture by fitting these into the context of Peirce's theory of inquiry, his critical commonsensism, his fallibilism, his idealism, and so on.

I

Peirce's Criticisms of 'the Spirit of Cartesianism'

The strategy of the two early anti-Cartesian papers with which I shall begin is as follows. In the first ("Questions Concerning Certain Faculties

Claimed for Man"[1]) Peirce argues that human beings do not have the powers with which the Cartesian philosophy endows them: we cannot know our own internal states by introspection, but must infer them from our knowledge of external facts; we have no faculty of Intuition, rather all our cognitions are hypothetical and fallible; we cannot think except in signs; and we have no conception of the absolutely incognisable. Then, in the second paper ("Some Consequences of Four Incapacities"[2]) Peirce uses the conclusions of the first to argue that the Method of Doubt is impossible, and we should begin, instead, with the beliefs we actually have; that Descartes' epistemology is viciously individualistic, and we should base epistemology, rather, on the community; that Descartes' procedure relies on a single chain of argumentation, while a more scientific epistemology would trust, rather, to the multiplicity and variety of its arguments; and that Descartes is eventually obliged to rest his case on inexplicable facts ('God made it so'), which, according to Peirce, is never allowable.

We shall need to look at these criticisms more closely.

1. The Method of Doubt urges us to begin philosophy by doubting everything. It is impossible, Peirce urges, to begin with complete doubt. For doubt is not voluntary, and so the attempt to use Descartes' method is bound to be a fraud — we shall at best *pretend* to doubt what, really, we believe. (It is no accident, he remarks, that Descartes ends up reinstating his original beliefs, for 'no one who follows the Cartesian method will ever be satisfied until he has formally recovered all those beliefs which in form he has given up'.[3] Furthermore, genuine doubt requires a specific reason, and this makes complete, systematic doubt impossible, since a reason for doubt is something else one believes. These criticisms of Descartes anticipate important elements in Peirce's own theory of belief and doubt, which I shall discuss in some detail below.

2. Descartes' criterion of certainty is that 'the things that we conceive very clearly and distinctly are all true'.[4] It is pernicious, Peirce argues, to make single individuals absolute judges of truth. Peirce denies the supposedly intuitive character of self-consciousness, arguing that, on the contrary, self-consciousness is a relatively late development arising from the child's acknowledgement, as a result of his interactions with others, of his liability to ignorance and error. Furthermore, Peirce insists that all thought is in signs, and signs are essentially public. Peirce rejects Descartes' radical opposition to tradition and authority. Epistemology should be concerned, not with the individual, but with the community. It should use the methods of science, and science is essentially public, not individualistic.

3. Descartes' procedure is, first, to use the Method of Doubt to isolate a residue of indubitable propositions, and by discerning what it is that makes

them indubitable to discover a criterion of truth which will enable him to reconstruct the rest of his knowledge. But, according to Peirce, the Method of Doubt is impossible, and there *are* no indubitable propositions; so he has small hopes of this enterprise. Descartes tries to reconstruct his *bona fide* knowledge by means of a single chain of inference, and such a chain can be no stronger than its weakest link. Peirce urges, instead, the claims of a cable metaphor, according to which our knowledge rests on many arguments, and derives its strength from their plurality. This, he holds, is the method of science, which philosophy should emulate.

4. Descartes is driven to admit 'inexplicables', premisses for which he has no justification save that 'God made it so'. Peirce will allow no incognizables; instead, he accepts a certain kind of idealism, in which truth and reality, though independent of any individual, are defined in terms of the long-run agreement of the whole community of inquirers. So, unlike Descartes, he cannot admit that there are unknowable truths. There is a clear connection here with his critique of Descartes' pernicious individualism; the individual is now the locus of ignorance and error, the community the locus of knowledge, truth and reality.

The main points of contrast between Descartes' and Peirce's epistemologies are summarised in the table below:

DESCARTES	**PEIRCE**
1. Method of doubt.	Method of doubt impossible: doubt not voluntary, requires specific reason. Must begin with the beliefs we have.
2. Individualism. Certainty of self-consciousness. Rejection of tradition, authority.	Community-oriented. Define truth, reality via intersubjective agreement. Individual as locus of ignorance, error. Self-consciousness learned via interactions with others. All thought in public signs.
3. Dogmatism – quest for certainty. Chain of inference.	Fallibilism. No infallible Intuition. No indubitable first premisses. Cable of many arguments: continuity of knowledge.
4. Inexplicables ('God made it so'). Realism.	No incognizables: idealism.

I shall be largely concerned, in the next part of the paper, to assess the force of Peirce's objections to the Method of Doubt. This, however, requires a preliminary discussion of Peirce's theory of inquiry.

Peirce's Theory of Inquiry: Belief and Doubt.

After the publication of his critique of Descartes' epistemology in the two papers of 1868, Peirce worked out a detailed theory of belief and doubt[5], largely based on ideas due to the Scottish psychologist Alexander Bain.

According to Bain, belief is a disposition to action: 'Preparedness to act on what we affirm is . . . the sole, the genuine, the unmistakable criterion of belief'.[6] This theory is to apply to animal as well as human beliefs. And it is to apply to theoretical as well as practical beliefs, the difference being that in the former case the opportunities for the manifestation of the disposition are rare. Belief comes in degrees, depending, presumably, on the strength of the disposition to act. The 'opposite' of belief is not disbelief (which is belief in the opposite), but *doubt* or *uncertainty,* which results from the 'checking' of a belief by a new experience, and is a disagreeable mental state, closely allied with the emotion of fear. People are subject to two, opposing, cognitive tendencies: the tendency to accept as a general rule what has not yet been contradicted by experience (Bain calls this 'primitive credulity', and sometimes refers to it as a form of induction); and the tendency to be discouraged by 'contradictions', that is, experiences inconsistent with what is already believed (Bain calls this 'acquired scepticism'). Bain suggests that in a sense one can only really be said to have a belief after an unreflective expectation has survived 'checks'; belief is 'innate credulity tempered by checks'.[7] Repeated confirmations of a belief increase our confidence in it, and can secure us from the expectation of future checks to which acquired scepticism inclines us.

It is not surprising that Peirce should have found this strikingly naturalistic theory attractive. It influenced him in a number of ways: (a) He describes the pragmatic maxim of meaning as 'scarcely more than a corollorary'[8] of Bain's theory of belief. The connection is this: if belief is a disposition to act, the criterion of identity of a belief, i.e., of propositional identity, is to be given by specifying the relevant disposition to act; thus, the meaning of a proposition is to be given in terms of its effects on behaviour. (It is worth observing that when Ramsey, in 'Facts and Propositions',[9] describes his account as 'pragmatist' no doubt part of what he has in mind is that he too treats beliefs as dispositions to act—specifically, in order to account for degrees of belief, as dispositions to bet at certain odds—and that he too draws the conclusion that individuation of beliefs must proceed by specification of the relevant dispositions.) (b) Peirce uses Bain's account of belief in his own theory of inquiry. Doubt, according to Bain, is unpleasant; one prefers a stable belief-habit. Inquiry, according to Peirce, begins with the stimulus of doubt, and its object is precisely to move from a state of doubt (which is uncomfortable) to a new belief (which is comfortable):[10]

[Belief] → Interruption by stimulus → doubt → new belief
→ interruption → doubt → new belief . . . etc.

Because doubt consists in the interruption of a belief by some experience, inquiry, which is motivated by doubt, must start in the context of some
problem-situation, i.e., one must have had, consciously or otherwise, some
earlier belief the interruption of which threw one into doubt. Peirce stresses
the continuity of inquiry: the beliefs with interruption of which inquiry begins
shade into unconscious habits of action, not different in kind from animals'
unreflective reactions. (So there are connections here with the thesis of the
continuity of cognition, which plays a role in Peirce's denial of Cartesian 'Intuitions'.) Inquiry aims at stable beliefs, which are safe from doubt. Peirce
argues that the Scientific Method is the only one which meets this requirement, since, being 'constrained by reality', it is able to produce beliefs which
are not liable to be checked by recalcitrant experience—beliefs, in other
words, which are true. (c) Lastly, and most relevantly to my present purpose,
the doubt/belief theory of inquiry seems considerably to strengthen Peirce's
objections to the Method of Doubt. First, doubt, in the theory Peirce derives
from Bain, is characterised by means of its causal origin: doubt is the state
one is in as a result of an external check to a previously-held belief. This underpins Peirce's claim that doubt is not voluntary, so that the recommendation that one try to doubt everything one believes with the object of isolating
the indubitable residue cannot be followed. Peirce's definition makes doubt,
in a certain sense, secondary to belief; and this underpins his insistence that
we must begin, not with a pretended doubt, but with the beliefs we actually
have. 'Many and many a philosopher', Peirce observes, 'seems to think that
taking a piece of paper and writing down 'I doubt that' is doubting it, or that
it is a thing he can do in a minute as soon as he decides what he wants to
doubt'. This is why there are so many 'counterfeit paper doubts' in circula-
tion. 'Genuine doubt', however, 'does not talk of beginning with doubting'.[11]
Third, the theory is that one is thrown into doubt as a result of a specific
check to a belief; and this underpins Peirce's argument that doubt must rest
on a specific reason, and so cannot be generalised as Descartes wanted.

There are, of course, a number of pretty obvious difficulties with the
theory of belief and doubt that Peirce takes from Bain, which I shall mention
but (with one exception) not discuss:
——the connection between belief and action is not direct, but is mediated by
the agent's desires, so that some means of isolating the belief from the desire
component is required (this is achieved in Ramsey's account of belief as disposition to bet by means of the presumption that everyone desires money);
——it must be specified whether unconscious beliefs and desires are to be allowed;

——it must be specified whether dispositions to *verbal* behaviour are to be included—which creates a difficulty, since if verbal behaviour is *not* allowed it is unlikely that the theory will be able to account for highly theoretical beliefs, while if it *is* allowed it is unlikely that the pragmatic maxim can be relied upon, as intended, to rule out metaphysical beliefs;[12]

——an account of dispositions will be needed (Peirce's shift from an early nominalism to a later realism will be relevant here);[13]

——criteria of identity of actions will be needed (and this, since the theory of meaning depends on the theory of belief, may introduce a threat of circularity in view of the intentional character of actions);

——the logical relations between beliefs will have to be explained by means of suitable relations between the dispositions with which the beliefs are identified. This may introduce difficulties: if the belief that p is the disposition D, say to do A in conditions $C1$, B in conditions $C2$, etc., what disposition is to be identified with the belief that *not* p?

This last point introduces an issue which deserves more sustained consideration, *viz.*, the relation between causal and logical elements in the theory.[14] Peirce's (like Bain's) account of doubt is, in part and explicitly, causal: doubt is the state that results from the inhibition of belief by some stimulus. But it is also, more covertly, logical; for Peirce seems to take it for granted that the kind of experience that will interrupt one's belief is a falsifying experience, an experience, that is, which gives one grounds to believe something incompatible with what one already believes. The paradigm would be, say, the inhibition of someone's belief that all swans are white by his seeing a black swan. (There is, I suspect, a similar marriage of causal and logical considerations in the concept of a 'recalcitrant experience' with which Quine operates in 'Two Dogmas'.[15]) Now presumably it is possible that a belief should be inhibited by something other than a falsifying experience (e.g., a bang on the head, a drug, evidence that one wrongly takes to be falsifying, learning that someone else believes differently); and it is also possible that a falsifying experience should fail to inhibit one's belief. (Compare the literature on cognitive consistency[16] for interesting examples of the extent of people's imperviousness to logically pertinent evidence.) It is not necessary to conclude that Peirce's theory depends on a falsely optimistic assumption to the effect that people's beliefs are inhibited always and only by falsifying experiences (though it is perhaps relevant to recall that Peirce does sometimes manifest this kind of optimism, e.g., in offering a theory according to which fallacious inference is always the result of the misapplication of a valid rule[17]). But it is important to recognise that a concept of doubt which requires that one's belief has been checked by an experience which is logically relevant as well as causally effective is very much narrower than the ordinary concept; and that given such a concept it is trivially true that one is genuinely in doubt only if one has a specific reason to doubt. Peirce's objection that Descartes' doubts are a pretence, and his objection that they lack reasons, are logically connected by his definition of doubt.

It is also now evident that one must be wary that no equivocation (as between Peirce's and Descartes' senses of 'doubt') vitiates the assessment of Peirce's critique of Descartes' method.

II

The Method of Doubt Defended

I am now in a position to defend Descartes' method against Peirce's claim that it is impossible; this I shall do by means of arguing that there is evidence that Descartes' method is relevantly different from what Peirce takes it to be, and that it does not require, what Peirce insists is impossible, that one voluntarily set out to doubt what one initially believes.

Descartes describes his procedure thus:

> . . . because I would devote myself solely to the search for truth, I thought it was necessary that I should . . . *reject, just as though it was absolutely false, everything in which I could imagine the slightest doubt,* so as to see whether after that anything remained in my belief that was entirely indubitable.[18] (my italics)

> I shall proceed by *setting aside* all that in which the least doubt could be supposed to exist, *just as if I had discovered that it was absolutely false.*[19] (my italics)

Peirce's assessment of Descartes' method is worth giving in full:

> We cannot begin with complete doubt. We must begin with all the prejudices which we actually have when we enter upon the study of philosophy. These prejudices are not to be dispelled by a maxim, for they are things which it does not occur to us *can* be questioned. Hence this initial scepticism will be a mere self-deception, and not real doubt; and no-one who follows the Cartesian method will ever be satisfied until he has formally recovered all those beliefs which in form he has given up. It is, therefore, as useless a preliminary as going to the North Pole would be in order to get to Constantinople by coming down regularly upon a meridian. A person may, it is true, in the course of his studies, find reason to doubt what he began by believing; but in that case he doubts because he has a positive reason for it, and not on account of the Cartesian maxim. Let us not pretend to doubt in philosophy what we do not doubt in our hearts.[20]

Peirce thinks that Descartes is urging a policy of deliberate, systematic doubt, and that, since doubt is neither voluntary nor generalisable, this is bound to be a fraud. But this misrepresents Descartes' aim.

As I understand it, Descartes' project is this: The aim is to discover which, if any, of the things he believes is certain (no other consideration, such as the need to act even on less than certain beliefs, is to be given any weight, the greatest possible disvalue being placed on error, on believing something false). The method is to begin with the beliefs one actually holds and submit them to a severe test, retaining only those which pass the test (given the importance attached to avoiding error, it is crucial that the test be stringent enough, that it not pass beliefs which are to the slightest degree uncertain). Beliefs which fail the test, which are *not* certain, are to be suspended (*s'-pêcher de donner créance, suspendre son jugement*); though to do this it may, if the beliefs are well-entrenched, be necessary to make the mental effort of pretending to disbelieve them.[21] The place at which doubt enters the procedure is in the test to which Descartes proposes that beliefs be submitted: he will suspend belief in anything which is *dubitable*, anything it is *possible to doubt*.

Does this procedure require deliberate doubt? One might suppose that it does, since the test of whether it is possible to doubt something would be to *try* to doubt it, and see whether one can do so. But this idea rests, I believe, on a misinterpretation of Descartes' conception of dubitability. To say that a proposition is dubitable might mean either of two things: that it is psychologically possible that someone should actually doubt it; or that it is possible that there should be a reason for doubting it.[22] (I'll call these, respectively, the descriptive and the normative interpretations of 'dubitable'.) I think it is clear that Descartes is concerned with dubitability in the normative sense.[23] Unless he is, it would be quite mysterious why he should offer elaborate arguments (the arguments from illusions, dreams, and the possibility of the malicious demon) to show that it *is* possible that there should be reason to doubt (almost) all his beliefs; and quite mysterious what the relevance of the test is to the aim of the enterprise. If 'dubitable' is used normatively, the pertinence of arguments designed to show that there could be reason to doubt this or that belief is obvious; and so is the *rationale* of the test: so long as it is however barely possible that a belief should be mistaken, one should give it up, since the worst outcome, having a false belief, is taken to be much worse than failing to hold a true belief, and the possibility of a mistake, however remote, exposes one, however slightly, to this risk. (It would be natural to wonder, at this point, whether it is the *epistemological* or the *logical* possibility of doubt which Descartes is attempting to exclude; I fear the text offers no answer to this question, though I should, myself, slightly favour the former interpretation.)

Peirce might object that Descartes is concerned with merely theoretical, as opposed to practical, doubt.[24] And since on Peirce's theory one presumably doesn't doubt unless one's disposition to act is genuinely interfered with, for him, in a sense, only practical doubt is genuine doubt. (But this gives Peirce himself problems, as mentioned above, where highly theoretical doubts and beliefs are concerned. In general, it would be fair to say, Peirce is ambivalent about whether he really wants to sustain a serious distinction between theory and practice.) This objection is certainly relevant to Descartes' insistence that any belief that there is even the remotest possibility of a reason to doubt should be suspended. But Descartes has a reply to it: suspension of any belief which is however slightly doubtful is a rational policy given that the object of the enterprise is to avoid at all costs, including failure to believe something true, believing something false. 'As far as practical life is concerned', Descartes concedes, 'it is sometimes necessary to follow opinions which one knows to be very uncertain'.[25]

So Descartes' test, dubitability, does *not* require deliberate doubt. And Descartes, as he says, intends to begin with the beliefs he actually has, which is, according to Peirce, the only place one *can* begin; the puzzle is why Peirce should regard this as an objection to Descartes. But it might be supposed that, even with the ambiguity of 'dubitable' cleared up in favour of the normative interpretation, Descartes' method does still require deliberate doubt, deliberate doubt, namely, of the propositions that fail his test. But Descartes does not propose to doubt any proposition which fails his test, but to suspend belief in it. He observes that it is:

> Not . . . that I imitated the sceptics, who only doubt for the sake of doubting, and pretend to be always uncertain.[26]

But perhaps the objection can be reformulated. Granted that Descartes does not recommend a policy of deliberate doubt, nevertheless he does, as I have stressed, require a deliberate suspension of belief, and is not this vulnerable to the objection that suspension of belief cannot be voluntarily undertaken? To understand what is at issue here, one must first get clear what suspension of belief is, and how it relates to doubt in Peirce's sense. When he proposes to suspend belief in any less than certain proposition, Descartes intends, I take it, at least that he should bring it about that he neither believes nor disbelieves that proposition; suspension of belief and doubt have in common the absence of both belief and disbelief ($-Bp$ & $-B-p$). But it is part of Peirce's definition of doubt that it has come about as a result of the interruption of a previous belief by a falsifying experience. And since it is the causal origin of Peircian doubt which entails its involuntary character, one cannot simply extrapolate Peirce's thesis that doubt is involuntary to conclude that suspension of belief is also involuntary.

Still, even if it doesn't follow from Peirce's theory of doubt, might it not nevertheless be *true* that one cannot voluntarily suspend belief? Sometimes Descartes claims in a pretty unqualified way that suspension of belief is voluntary:

... judging or refraining from judgement is an act of the will ... it is evident that it is under our control ... [27]

But his suggestion that one feign disbelief in order to shake off an obstinate belief indicates that he has some appreciation of the fact that suspending belief is not (to borrow a memorable phrase of Peirce's) *quite* as easy as lying. The idea that one can, in any straightforward way, make oneself start, or stop, believing something is pretty implausible. (I can report that my efforts to stop myself believing that I was sitting at my desk writing this proved unsuccessful!) But it does seem that one can voluntarily exert an *indirect* effect on what one believes – for example, by putting oneself in the way of evidence which supports what one wants to believe, by associating with people who already believe what one wants to believe, and so on. (Compare behaviour therapists' methods of improving one's self-image,[28] or Pascal's prescription for making oneself believe in God.[29] Peirce's theory of belief makes Pascal's prescription very plausible; if the belief that *p* is a disposition to act in a certain way, what could be more natural than that deliberately acting as if *p* should induce one to believe it?) And if this is right, Descartes' proposal to suspend dubitable beliefs is, after all, feasible.

Peirce had, as we saw, two, related objections to the Method of Doubt: that doubt is not voluntary, and that it requires a specific reason. The first objection fails, because the feasibility of Descartes' project does not depend on the possibility of deliberate doubt. But might not the second objection still be sustained? In fact, is it not plausible to suppose that the second objection is made *more* plausible by the normative interpretation of 'dubitable', since this requires a *reason* for doubt?

The objection is that doubt requires a specific reason, so that it cannot be generalised; 'complete' doubt is impossible. Peirce doesn't spell out the argument, but if one considers his opening remark that 'We cannot begin with complete doubt' in the light of his later comment that one doubts only when one has a 'positive reason' to do so, it is plausible to think that he has in mind something like this: that doubt requires a specific reason—the one supplied by the experience which inhibits the earlier belief—which must itself be something one believes, so that one can't doubt *everything*, since doubting anything implies believing something else. (The argument has, of course, strong affinities with considerations repeatedly advanced by Wittgenstein.[30])

This criticism *is* relevant to Descartes' arguments from illusions and dreams. It may indeed be true that whenever in the past Descartes has discovered that his senses have deceived him, he has done so on the basis of other perceptual judgements (how the tower looks from close up, that he just woke., etc.). And it is important that his argument why *any* of his sensory judgements may be mistaken does not show that *all* his sensory judgements might be mistaken. (The difference is that between '(p) it is possible that . . .' and 'It is possible that (p) . . .') But I don't think Descartes ever supposed that he could establish the stronger conclusion by means of the arguments from illusions and dreams.[31] In any case, it can be plausibly argued that the weaker conclusion is itself quite sufficient to support the recommendation that one suspend belief in *all* sensory judgements; for if *any* sensory judgement may be mistaken, and one has no way to know *which* are, nor which are more likely to be, then the objective of avoiding error can only be achieved by the suspension of *all* sensory beliefs. (Cf. Williams's fungus analogy.[32]) It is worth observing that Peirce himself believes that any of our beliefs may be mistaken—this is one of his formulations of fallibilism—and that, though we do have knowledge, we can't be sure *which* of our beliefs *are* knowledge, and which mistaken or ill-founded;[33] it is also worth observing that Peirce himself[34] appeals to the possibility that one is dreaming, or under the influence of a hypnotist, as an argument why any of one's beliefs may be mistaken.

If I am right that the special nature of Descartes' enterprise would motivate suspension of *all* sensory beliefs on the basis of the fact that *any* of them might be mistaken, Peirce's objection to the generalisation of doubt can be deflected.

Peirce, I conclude, does not establish his claim that Descartes' method is impossible. This conclusion enables me to make sense of something otherwise puzzling: that in Peirce's own epistemology there are ideas which seem very close to the Cartesian method. I have already commented on e.g., Peirce's use of the argument from dreams; I want, next, to consider in some detail the affinities between Descartes' method and Peirce's 'critical commonsensism'.

Critical Commonsensism

According to Peirce, though there is a presumption in favour of commonsense beliefs, one should not accept them without question, but should submit them to critical scrutiny.[35] It is not that one should, *per impossibile*, set out to doubt what one initially believes, but rather that one should work out what experiences would constitute counter-evidence to commonsense beliefs, and in what circumstances one would expect such experience to occur if it ever does, and then to *court* that experience by exposing oneself to those circumstances. (This is roughly Popper's recommendation, too:[36] bold conjecture, unflinching exposure to falsification.)

But *why* should or would one first imaginatively work out what would falsify a belief, and then go to the trouble of inviting falsification? Peirce holds that inquiry can only begin with *real* doubt engendered by *real* interruption of *real* belief; the only cognitive motivation he allows is desire to escape the discomfort of doubt.[37] But now it begins to look as if the 'critical' element in 'critical commonsensism' will be as motiveless as Peirce urges, against Descartes, deliberate doubt would be. (Why look for trouble?)

In the papers on critical commonsensism Peirce supplies a motivation for deliberate criticism of commonsense beliefs by acknowledging that doubt may be brought about, not only by recalcitrant experience, but also by reflection on one's beliefs,[38] and by imaginary, rather than actual, experiments.[39] There are precedents for this acknowledgement in the work of Bain, who makes use, implicitly, of a distinction between first- and second-order beliefs; e.g., he observes that, having had some (first-order) beliefs checked by experience, one might generalize to form the (second-order) belief that one's (first-order) beliefs are always liable to recalcitrance: this is 'acquired scepticism'.[40] The second-order belief that first-order beliefs are sometimes subject to check *itself* constitutes a reason for a second-order expectation of further checks of hitherto-surviving first-order beliefs, and hence supplies a motive for anticipating such checks. (If you have reason to expect trouble, it may be better to look for it than to have it catch you unawares.)

But this *rationale* requires one to allow doubts which are, as it were, *indirectly* rather than *directly* caused by experience, and, in consequence, no longer to insist that a doubt must have, so to speak, *its own, specific* reason. (My genuine doubt about whether all crows are black, for example, may arise from my experience of seeing a black swan, which directly inhibited my belief that all swans are white and indirectly inhibited my belief that all crows are black.)

But once one admits indirect causes of doubt, the necessarily involuntary character of doubt is put into question. The cause of my doubt may not be direct and external, but indirect and internal (reflection, imaginary experiments). Peirce (though he continues to inveigh against the Cartesian error of doubt at will[41]) seems to acknowledge this, when he writes that:

> [The Critical Commonsensist] . . . invents a plan for attaining to doubt, elaborates it in detail, and then puts it into practice, although this may involve a solid month of hard work . . . [42]

So this *rationale* for deliberate criticism of beliefs makes Critical Commonsensism feasible, but only at the cost of accentuating its affinities with Descartes' method. For how, now, is Peirce to draw the line between a *specific* reason for doubt, and no reason at all? Descartes, after all, appeals to something like the kind of second-order reason to which Peirce alludes, when he observes, *à propos* of his sensory beliefs' having been mistaken in the past, that he would be imprudent to trust someone he knew had once deceived him.[43]

III

The discussion so far points to the conclusion that Peirce has no really plausible objection to Descartes' method, that he misrepresents what that method is, and that, indeed, he uses something very much like it himself. But this, I think, underestimates Peirce; and I want, in the next part of the paper, to suggest that he really has another, different, and more serious objection to Descartes' procedure, which, however, his—as I have argued—mistaken insistence that the Method of Doubt is impossible leads him to underplay.

Fallibilism

Descartes' procedure has a critical stage, in which he is to seek out and suspend any dubitable beliefs, and a constructive stage, in which he is to investigate how much *bona fide* knowledge can be salvaged. In describing his procedure, Descartes often uses the metaphor of rebuilding on new foundations—the whole town [his original, pre-critical beliefs] is to be razed to the ground [submitted to the Method of Doubt] and then rebuilt on solid, reliable foundations [clarity and distinctness as criteria of truth].[44] There is debate, however, about whether, and if so, in what sense, Descartes is properly described as 'foundationalist'.[45] For present purposes foundationalism can be roughly characterised as the conjunction of two theses:

    (i) that some of our beliefs are epistemologically privileged (certain, indubitable, incorrigible or whatever)—I'll call this 'dogmatism'—

and

    (ii) that any of our other beliefs that are justified, are justified by means of the support of these privileged beliefs—I'll call this 'Euclideanism'.[46]

Descartes holds (a) that at least one belief is indubitable, i.e., survives the test of the Method of Doubt, and (b) that on this basis he can devise a criterion of truth (clearness and distinctness), by means of which he can prove the existence of God, which in turn allows him to acquire 'a perfect knowledge of an infinitude of things'.[47] While it is debatable whether (b) qualifies Descartes as a Euclidean, (a) qualifies him as a dogmatist.

The fallibilist opposes dogmatism, and denies that there are any epistemologically privileged beliefs. Peirce is a fallibilist, and this is where his real, deep objection to Descartes lies. Peirce doesn't believe that any residue of indubitables would be left after Descartes' critical procedure; for he believes that any of our beliefs could be mistaken, and consequently that if we were to suspend those of our beliefs that might be mistaken, we should end up suspending all our beliefs—which would place an immovable obstacle in the road of inquiry; and for Peirce, of course, there is no intellectual sin more heinous than 'blocking the road of inquiry'.

Peirce's fallibilism is explicitly propounded by way of contrast with Descartes' dogmatism—notably, for instance, in his critique of our supposed faculty of Intuition. Here, Peirce's argument is that there is no *reason* to suppose that we have any such faculty, since anything we are supposed to know intuitively is more plausibly explained as inferred belief, that there is no *need* to suppose that we have any such faculty, since the thesis of the continuity of cognition blocks the argument that there must be some uninferred beliefs to serve as first premises, and that there is no *point* in supposing that we have any such faculty, since, even if we did, it could supply no epistemological guarantees unless we also had an infallible faculty for distinguishing the *bona fide* pronouncements of Intuition from impostors, . . . and, of course, so on.[48](Descartes seems to have been fully aware of the third point, and to have acknowledged that, though what we clearly and distinctly perceive to be the case is true, we may be mistaken in thinking that we clearly and distinctly perceive *p* to be the case.[49])

In the two early anti-Cartesian papers, oddly enough, Peirce offers no direct argument against the alleged indubitability of the *cogito*, though there are hints of such an argument in his discussion of the concept of the self, and especially in his claim that self-consciousness is a relatively late development, achieved by the child only after his interactions with others have impressed him with his liability to ignorance and error. These hints are amplified in later writings. In the *Grand Logic* of 1893 Peirce argues that the 'I' of Descartes' 'I think' 'is nothing but a holder together of ideas', that 'there is no warrant for putting it in the first person singular'. He goes on to urge, in a passage strikingly modern in tone, that no single belief could be genuinely clear and evident: 'such clearness and evidentness as a truth can acquire will consist in its appearing to form an integral unbroken part of the great body of truth'. Even if the *cogito* is psychologically irresistible, it leaves logical room for error. 'We can never', Peirce insists, 'attain absolute certainty'.[50] Peirce's argument here is less than conclusive. Even if we were convinced that Descartes was not entitled to conclude '*I* exist', it would not follow that *nothing*—not even a weaker belief framed without the first-person pronoun—is indubitable.

It is true that in the papers on Critical Commonsensism Peirce frequently refers to commonsense beliefs as 'indubitable'; but by this he means that those are beliefs which we do not, perhaps even could not, question, not that they could not be mistaken. 'Indubitable beliefs', he recognises, 'may be proved false'.[51] In Descartes' sense of 'indubitable', Peirce does not believe there are indubitables.

Descartes' method is possible, but pointless; the critical stage couldn't be, as Descartes supposed, a preliminary to the constructive stage, for nothing will remain, if we set our epistemological standards so high, to serve as the basis from which to rebuild. None of our beliefs is certain. So the enterprise of seeking out the certain beliefs on which to base our knowledge is misguided, for it is predictably fruitless.

This already, I think, explains something otherwise puzzling. Peirce's insistence that the Method of Doubt is impossible suggests that his complaint is that Descartes is *too sceptical*; which, in view of the fact that Peirce is a fallibilist who regards Descartes as objectionably dogmatist, has him coming at Descartes from, so to speak, the wrong direction. The suggestion that Peirce's fundamental objection is, rather, that the Method of Doubt is pointless, suggests, on the contrary, that Peirce's complaint is that Descartes is *not sceptical enough*; which has the virtue of having Peirce come at Descartes from the right direction.

But if I was right to suggest that there are affinities between Descartes' method and Peirce's critical approach to commonsense, doesn't this mean that Peirce's own method would be (as possible as, but) no less pointless than, Descartes'? This doesn't follow. For Peirce's recommendation that one subject commonsense beliefs to criticism is not intended as a preliminary to any reconstruction on the basis of the beliefs that survive criticism. As a result of critical scrutiny, we subject our beliefs to test; those that fail, we reject, those that pass, we keep, but only provisionally, until or unless they fail some future test. Beliefs which we *have* reason to doubt are retained, but tentatively, subject to future test. And that, since there *are* no beliefs which it is impossible that we should have reason to doubt, is the best we can do.

There is a connection to be made here with Peirce's objection to the constructive part of Descartes' programme, that it relies on a single chain of inference. *If* one had indubitable premises, exclusive reliance on them would pose no cognitive danger; but since, according to Peirce, one does not, it would be more prudent to rely on numerous arguments, with different premises, so that the failure of one need not be disastrous. There is also a moral to be drawn about Peirce's attitude to the idea that avoiding error at all costs is the appropriate aim of cognitive endeavour. Such a goal, Peirce would hold, could be achieved only by believing nothing at all. *Getting the truth* is no less important than *avoiding error*.

Some comparative remarks seem worth making. Peirce's account is, like Polanyi's, *fallibilist* (we could always be wrong) but *committal* (we believe, and act upon, our hypotheses). Contrast Popper's view, which is not only fallibilist but also noncommittal; according to Popper, scientists do not believe their conjectures. (The comparison is complicated by Popper's tendency to equate 'belief' with 'faith' or 'conviction', whereas Peirce allows that belief comes in degrees.) This comparison raises intriguing questions—which, however, I shan't attempt to answer here—about the relation between *fallibilism* (our liability to mistakes), *revisability* (our readiness to change our beliefs in response to new evidence), and *commitment* (degrees of belief).[52]

Idealism

The main burden of Peirce's objection to Descartes' procedure, I have suggested, should be taken to be that, given that any of our beliefs might be mistaken, it is pointless, since the critical procedure will leave no residue of indubitable beliefs to form the basis of a reconstruction. Descartes is not sceptical enough. But there is another theme in Peirce's critique which seems to be at odds with this. Peirce adopts a quasi-idealist position, according to which reality and truth are, though independent of any individual, logically dependent upon the community of inquirers.[53]

This, I think, has a bearing on an argument of Descartes which I have not so far discussed, namely, the demon argument. Though this interpretation is disputed, I think it is plausible to suppose that Descartes takes the demon argument to show, not just that *any*, but that *all* our sensory beliefs might be mistaken.[54] This interpretation is supported by the distinction Descartes draws, as he introduces the argument, between his being *sometimes* and his being *constantly* deceived, and by his subsequent decision to suspend belief in 'all . . .external things'; as well as by the consideration that whereas the arguments from illusions and dreams rely upon a contrast between veridical and illusory or dream perceptions, the demon argument does not.[55] Peirce doesn't expressly comment on this argument, but it is interesting to speculate what his idealism might have led him to say about it. Though Peirce would presumably not deny that it is possible that an *individual* should be systematically misled, he would be committed to denying that it is possible that the whole *community* should be so misled, since truth is defined in terms of the community. (Remember that Peirce objects to the individualistic character of Descartes' enterprise, so that he would, anyway, want the whole thing recast in the idiom of 'we' rather than 'I'. More about this below.) I observe that Williams—who does not specifically discuss Peirce's critique of Descartes—suggests that hostility to Descartes' enterprise might arise either from a rejection of the whole quest for certainty, or from a rejection of realism;[56] Peirce, as we can now see, opposes Descartes on *both* scores.

Peirce thought of fallibilism as an intermediate epistemological position, less optimistic than dogmatism, but at the same time less pessimistic than scepticism. He would not allow—as Descartes may have supposed—that one can avoid scepticism only by establishing some form of dogmatism, by finding some indubitable basis on which to reconstruct our knowledge; fallibilism avoids scepticism without requiring any indubitables. So it is plausible to think of Peirce as, on the one hand, objecting that Descartes is too optimistic, failing to realize that there are no indubitable beliefs, since *any* of our beliefs could be mistaken; while, on the other hand, objecting that Descartes is too pessimistic, that his pre-emptive argument grants too much to the sceptic, since *all* our beliefs couldn't be mistaken. This view of the matter is supported by Peirce's comment that while the pragmatist would never talk, like Descartes of '*beginning* with doubting', in the end 'his genuine doubts will go much further than those of any Cartesian'.[57] Peirce has something like the following picture

OPTIMISM		**PESSIMISM**
dogmatism	**fallibilism**	**scepticism**
some of our	*any* of our	*all* of our
beliefs could	beliefs could	beliefs could
not be wrong	be wrong	be wrong

Peirce holds than *any* but not *all* of our beliefs could be mistaken, that dogmatism is too optimistic and scepticism too pessimistic. (The modal operators here, of course, cry out for attention: could for all we know? logically could? . . . or what? But my present object is not to offer an unambiguous definition of dogmatism, fallibilism, etc., but only to offer a sketch of the way *Peirce* conceived these positions. And for this purpose, the ambiguity is probably more desirable than not.) The connection with his preference for a 'cable' metaphor is clear: although *any* of the fibres in the cable might break, *all* cannot; since some of its fibres will hold, the cable is safe.

The picture does not yet, however, bring out the full significance of the contrast between Peirce's and Descartes' attitudes to the status of the individual *vis à vis* the cognitive community.

The Individual and the Community

Peirce complains that Descartes makes the acquisition of knowledge an individual venture when really it is a community enterprise. But, one might object, surely Peirce's own theory of inquiry is couched in terms of belief and doubt, and surely Peirce cannot deny that it is the individual who believes and doubts? This point, I think, must be conceded; it is clear that it would be a mistake to interpret Peirce as putting forward some kind of quasi-Hegelian theory according to which a community might—except derivatively from its members—have beliefs or suffer from doubts. Nevertheless, the role that Peirce assigns to the individual cognitive agent is a relatively modest one, for at least four reasons:

(i) Peirce stresses the ways in which individuals learn from each other; and though he rejects the 'Method of Authority' he stresses the role of tradition in science. In a pregnant anti-Cartesian passage of the *Grand Logic* Peirce comments that:

> Descartes marks the period when Philosophy put off childish things and began to be a conceited young man. By the time the young man has grown to be an old man, he will have learned that traditions are precious treasures, while iconoclastic inventions are always cheap and often nasty.[58]

(Cf. Polanyi.)[59]

(ii) In particular, he urges that the individual's consciousness of himself is derived from interactions with others. (Cf. Mead.)[60]—Taking (i) and (ii) together, it is clear that, for Peirce, though it is the individual who has beliefs, interactions between individuals play a crucial role in the genesis and growth of knowledge.

(iii) What the individual believes, according to Peirce, is linguistically expressed ('all thought is in signs'), and language is essentially public. (Cf. Wittgenstein,[61] and Putnam on the role of experts in determining meaning.[62])

(iv) And the criterion of the truth of what the individual believes, according to Peirce, is the long-run agreement of the whole community of inquirers. —Taking (iii) and (iv) together, it is clear that, for Peirce, the *meaning* and *truth* of individuals' beliefs depend upon *public* language and criteria.

Although Descartes allows that others may reconstruct their knowledge by following his method, his enterprise surely is radically individualistic by comparison with Peirce's. He is vehemently opposed to any reliance on tradition or authority. His criteria of certainty are private rather than public. And his reliance on individualistic criteria of certainty raises the problem of other minds in an acute form; whereas Peirce's account of the development of one's concept of oneself from interactions with others avoids the Cartesian contrast between one's infallible, intuitive knowledge of oneself and one's fallible, risky inference to others.

This may suggest that Peirce could be represented as holding that, though *any* of *one's* beliefs could be mistaken, *all* of *our* beliefs could not—a formula which looks as if it brings out the distinction between the individual and the community as well as that between scepticism and dogmatism. But this way of putting it brings some major problems to light. According to Peirce's definition, the truth is that opinion on which users of the Scientific Method will, or perhaps would, agree in the (perhaps infinitely) long run. This use of 'the opinion' reveals that, in the absence of criteria for individuation of beliefs, the distinction between 'any' and 'all' will be problematic. Before agreement is reached, furthermore, it is doubtful that it will make sense to speak of 'the beliefs of the community'. But equally it is clear that, where those beliefs upon which the Scientific Community eventually agrees are concerned, Peirce's position is not just not sceptical, but downright dogmatic: *all* of *their* beliefs—i.e., *all* of the beliefs *of each individual member* of the community—will, when the community reaches agreement, be, by definition, true. Indeed, it begins to look as if Peirce's fallibilism seems an attractive intermediate position only because it, in effect, combines a short-run, individualistic scepticism with a long-run, community-oriented dogmatism. (This isn't quite right, since, if the community does not yet agree, someone must believe p and someone else $-p$, which guarantees that they cannot both of them be wrong; but Peirce would surely take little comfort from the fact that his position avoids out-and-out scepticism only in virtue of *dis*agreement within the community.)

In short, though Peirce's position offers what seems to me a very appealing compromise between our cognitive limitations and our cognitive aspirations—it acknowledges the ubiquity of one's liability to error and the inevitability of one's cognitive dependence on others, but at the same time it offers the prospect of our attaining genuine knowledge—it is also profoundly problematic. The following difficult issues, at least, need to be settled:

(1) how to accommodate the tensions between Peirce's short-run, individual-oriented fallibilism and his long-run, community-oriented infallibilism;[63]

(2) how to accommodate the tensions between Peirce's stress on the cognitive community and his apparently individualist doubt/belief theory of inquiry;

(3) how to acknowledge the importance of Peirce's recognition of the ways in which we learn from each other, without begging the Problem of Other Minds;

(4) what exactly the scope of 'the cognitive community' and 'the long run' is supposed to be; and

(5) how to sustain the distinction between fallibilism and scepticism.

I am not so ambitious as to hope, in what remains of the present paper, to offer serious answers to any of these questions. What, more modestly, I shall try to do is to sketch an analogy which may put the last of the issues raised here—and perhaps some broader, metaphysical issues, too—in a new, and I hope illuminating, perspective.

IV

The Jigsaw of Knowledge

I suggest that we think of our beliefs as like a jigsaw, a picture we put together from various pieces (bits of information).[64]

It is perhaps necessary for me to say, at the outset, that the analogy is of course not perfect—if it were, it would cease to *be* an analogy! An important *prima facie dis*analogy is that a jigsaw is an artifact; whereas what we are doing as we try to figure out what the world is like is not, presumably, putting together a picture previously made by some other agent. This turns out to be important. I should also observe that I regard the role of analogy as rather to *raise* questions than to answer them; and that it is not, of course, suggested that this analogy is incompatible with others—Quine's web metaphor, for example.

I'll begin, in fact, by applying the analogy to Quine's epistemology.[65] Quine's 'whole of science' would be a completed jigsaw, with all the pieces forming a coherent picture. His holistic, neo-verificationist theory of meaning implies that individual pieces have a 'meaning' only in the context of the whole picture—e.g., a blue and white piece is only a 'piece of sky' in the context of a completed jigsaw; before the jigsaw was complete, it was possible that it should have turned out to be, say, a piece of sea. Quine's argument for his holistic theory of verification is to the effect that to test, say, an hypothesis in astronomy you may need to assume some optical theory about the workings of your telescope, and to test the optical theory you may need to assume some psychological theory about visual perception, . . . and so on, with nothing reliably irrelevant; so that *no* statement is immune from revision. That is, any piece of the jigsaw, however apparently securely fitted in place, may have to be moved to make room for another. Two classes of statement, perceptual statements and logical laws, however, turn out to have a rather special status. Observational statements (of which Quine speaks as 'close to the sensory periphery') would be analogous to pieces the place of which is apparently obvious—say a blue piece with clouds, which almost *has* to be sky— but which nevertheless could turn out not to go there after all, but, say, in a picture in the picture. Laws of logic (of which Quine speaks as 'distant from the sensory periphery') would be analogous to, say, right angled pieces, which, apparently, *have* to go at the corners, and without which, apparently, *no* picture could be completed. Is this compatible with Quine's insistence that even logical laws are revisable?—I think it is; for it might turn out that the jigsaw is not, after all, rectangular, but, say, circular, when the 'corner' pieces would, after all, be displaced.

The idea of a circular, or otherwise unconventional, jigsaw, raises a new issue. Need one assume that we are, as it were, supplied only with pieces that fit together in *one* jigsaw, or might it be that we are, rather, in the position of a man with the pieces of several, jumbled-up jigsaws, perhaps with all the pieces of more than one, or perhaps with all the pieces of only one, among them? I shall assume that we should use all the pieces (which needn't mean that we must take all the pieces at 'face value', a point which turns out to be important); but that it could be that the same set of pieces can be put together in different ways to make different jigsaws. (Think of double-sided jigsaws.) The view that there are 'alternative conceptual schemes' would be analogous to the idea that radically different jigsaws, in *some* sense as good as each other, can be made by putting the pieces together in radically different ways, (Cf. Wittgenstein's 'forms of life',[66] Goodman's conceptual pluralism,[67] etc.)

A question that now arises is whether we should think of each of us as having his own collection of pieces, or whether the jigsaw is to be conceived, rather, as the jigsaw 'of *human* knowledge'. This is a good question to have raised, because it makes it apparent that there is a similar issue with respect to Quine's 'web': are the 'beliefs' that are revised and replaced in response to goings on at the sensory periphery *our* beliefs? or *one's* beliefs? or what? And this reveals that Quine has to reconcile the fact that it is *individuals* who have sensory experiences with the *social* character of decisions about what should be revised.

In Pepper's metametaphysics a conceptual scheme ('world hypothesis') may be inadequate either in terms of *precision* (analogue: poor standards of fit—you have to force the pieces), or in terms of *scope*.[68] The idea of scope connects with my presumption that you must use all the pieces—a jigsaw that is coherent only in virtue of not using some pieces is inadequate.

But I suggested that, though one should use all the pieces, one needn't take them all 'at face value'. To explain this, I shall rely on an intuitive, though no doubt vague, distinction between *explaining* something and *explaining it away*. Consider cases where we decide that previously accepted perceptual judgements must have been mistaken. Although we are not always able to explain how the original mistake occurred, ideally we want to have the misleading data explained away. (Example: I think I see a man lurking in the shadows, but it turns out to have been, say, a gatepost. Compare the way we explain away 'sightings' of UFOs, etc.[69]) In terms of the jigsaw analogy, we could describe the process of 'explaining away' as putting the offending piece *in a picture* in the picture (it looked like a piece of sky, but turned out to be a piece of sky in a picture in the picture).

Both a jigsaw that doesn't use all the pieces, and a jigsaw that puts too many pieces into pictures within the picture, would fall under suspicion of inadequate scope. The first doesn't explain enough; the second explains too much away.

Now I want to consider Descartes' 'evil demon' hypothesis in the light of this discussion. To defeat scepticism, Descartes thinks, we must rule out the hypothesis that our beliefs are caused by the efforts of a demon set upon deceiving us. (One might call this kind of scepticism a 'conspiracy theory'. Notice that so, in a sense, is Descartes' 'God made it so'—except that 'God is not a deceiver'.) How does the 'demon' jigsaw relate to the 'external world' jigsaw? I think, like this: the 'demon' jigsaw puts the *whole* of the 'external world' jigsaw into a picture within the picture.[70]

This is like what we do when we 'explain away' mistaken perceptual judgements—only *wholesale*. (This brings out the relation between the [local] argument from illusion and the [global] demon argument.) The demon hypothesis explains everything away. The postulation of the demon, one wants to say, is gratuitous; it *explains away* everything that the external world jigsaw *explains*.

The jigsaw analogy may suggest too *passive* a picture of the cognitive enterprise—for the pieces of a real jigsaw are, of course, all *supplied* to us. It is an important fact about the jigsaw of human knowledge that we may not have all the pieces and that the pieces we are 'supplied' with may require our help to knock them into determinate shape. One might put it this way: we can not only arrange and rearrange the pieces we are 'given', but also, as it were, *make* pieces to fill in gaps, and *reshape* pieces to fit (these would correspond, very roughly, to devising theories and interpreting data, respectively). One reason why one wants to describe the demon hypothesis as 'gratuitous', is that all the pieces of the parts of that jigsaw that aren't in a picture in the picture are made by us.

Peirce might have put the point I have just made by saying that we haven't any 'specific reason' to believe that the demon hypothesis may be true. The demon hypothesis is consistent with all the evidence we have for the existence of the external world, but we have no reason for believing it—no reason, that is, beyond the fact that it may be true for all we know.

Verificationist attempts to refute scepticism by urging that the sceptical hypothesis is unverifiable and therefore meaningless have their attractions; but it is not easy to persuade oneself that such refutations rely on honest toil rather than (verbal) theft.[71] The picture-within-a-picture diagnosis suggested by the jigsaw analogy points to where the work needs to be put in: in explaining why the evidence we have is better evidence for the external world than for the demon (why the fact that it may be true for all we know is *not* a reason for believing the demon hypothesis). This problem, I suggest, is quite analogous to the problem of explaining why the same evidence supports a 'green' hypothesis better than a 'grue' hypothesis;[72] which, if it does nothing else, at least reduces two notorious problems to one!

Susan Haack

University of Warwick

NOTES

1. "Questions Concerning Certain Faculties Claimed for Man," *Journal of Speculative Philosophy*, 2 (1868): 103–14; and in *Collected Papers* (hereafter *CP*), ed. C. Hartshorne, P. Weiss, and A. Burks (Cambridge, MA: Harvard University Press, 1931–58), 5.213–63.

2. "Some Consequences of Four Incapacities," *Journal of Speculative Philosophy*, 2 (1868): 140–57; and in *CP*, 5.264–317.

3. *CP*, 5.264 (1868).

4. R. Descartes, *Discourse on Method* (1637), in E. S. Haldane, and G. R. T. Ross, *Philosophical Works of Descartes* (hereafter *HR*) (Cambridge University Press, 1911), vol. 1, p. 102.

5. See especially "The Fixation of Belief," *Popular Science Monthly*, 12 (1877): 1–15; *CP*, 5.358–87.

6. A. Bain, *The Emotions and the Will* (hereafter *EW*) (New York: Longman's Green, 1859), p. 505 (page references to 3rd, 1875 edition).

7. *EW*, p. 526.

8. *CP*, 5.12 (c. 1906). Cf. M. Fisch, "Alexander Bain and the Genealogy of Pragmatism," *Journal of the History of Ideas* 15 (1954): 413–44.

9. F.P. Ramsey, "Facts and Propositions," (1927), in *The Foundations of Mathematics*, ed. R. B. Braithwaite (London: Routledge and Kegan Paul, 1931), p. 155.

10. *CP*, 5.373–75 (1877).

11. *CP*, 6.499 (c. 1906); cf. *CP* 5.443 (1905), 'genuine doubt always has an external origin'; *CP* 5.509, (c. 1905), 'A true doubt is . . . a doubt which really interferes with the smooth working of the belief-habit'; and *CP* 6.469 (1908).

12. See e.g., *CP* 5.422 (1905), [pragmatism] will serve to show that almost every proposition of ontological metaphysics is either meaningless gibberish . . . or else is downright absurd'.

13. Cf. M. Fisch, "Peirce's Progress from Nominalism Towards Realism," *The Monist*, 11 (1967): 159–78; S. Haack, "Pragmatism and Ontology: Peirce and James," *Revue Internationale de Philosophie*, 121–22 (1977): 377–400.

14. This problem is recognized in Robert G. Meyers' "Peirce on Cartesian Doubt," *Transactions of the Charles S. Peirce Society*, 7 (1967): 13–23; see especially p. 17.

15. W. V. O. Quine, "Two Dogmas of Empiricism," (TD), *Philosophical Review*, 60 (1951): 20–40; and in *From a Logical Point of View* (New York: Harper Torchbooks, 1953), pp. 20–46.

16. See e.g., L. Festinger, *A Theory of Cognitive Dissonance* (Stanford, CA: Stanford University Press, 1957); R. P. Abelson, *et al*, eds, *Theories of Cognitive Consistency* (Chicago), IL: Rand McNally, 1968); and R. Jervis, *Perception and Misperception in International Politics* (Princeton, NJ: Princeton University Press, 1976), ch. 4., for particularly striking examples.

17. *CP*, 5.282 (1868).

18. *Discourse on Method*, *HR*, vol. 1, p. 101.

19. *Meditations II* (164), *HR*, vol. 1, p. 149.

20. *CP*, 5.265 (1868).

21. *Meditations*, *HR*, vol. 1, p. 148. Haldane and Ross translate Descartes as speaking of *abstaining from judgement (HR*, vol. 1, 176) and *witholding assent (HR*, vol. 1, 145), rather than of doubt.

22. In e.g., P. Unger, *Ignorance* (Oxford: Oxford University Press, 1975), ch. 3, it is clearly the former sense of 'doubtful' that is at issue.

23. Contrast Popkin's interpretation of the *cogito* as reporting Descartes' failure to manage to doubt his own existence: *The History of Scepticism from Erasmus to Descartes* (hereafter *HS*) (Atlantic Highlands, NJ: Humanities Press, 1964; New York: Harper Torchbooks, 1968), p. 186 (page references to Harper Torchbook edition).

24. Recall that *CP* 5.265 (1868) urges that we not 'pretend to doubt in philosophy what we do not doubt in our hearts'; see also 5.376 (1877) and 8.108 (c. 1910).

25. *Discourse on Method*, *HR*, vol. 1, p. 100.

26. *Discourse on Method*, *HR*, vol. 1, p. 99.

27. *HR*, vol. 2, p. 126. Cf. H. Frankfurt, *Demons, Dreamers and Madmen* (hereafter *DDM*), (Indianapolis, IN: Bobbs-Merrill, 1970), ch. 2.

28. See e.g., S. A. Rathus, and J. S. Nevid, *Behavior Therapy* (New York: Doubleday, 1977; New York: Signet, 1978), ch. 4.

29. B. Pascal, *Pensées* (1670), Everyman, 1931.

30. L. Wittgenstein, *On Certainty*, trans. G. A. Paul, and G. E. M. Anscombe, (Oxford: Basil Blackwell, 1969).

31. Cf. *Meditations*, *HR*, vol. 1, p. 145; and B. A. O. Williams, *Descartes*, (hereafter *D*) (New York: Penguin, 1978), p. 54.

32. Williams, *D*, p. 54.

33. *CP*, 5.311 (1868).

34. *CP*, 1.150 (c. 1896).

35. See *CP*, 5.438–52 (1905) and 5.497–537 (c. 1905); cf. James E. Broyles, "Charles S. Peirce and the Concept of Indubitable Belief," *Transactions of the C. S. Peirce Society*, 1 (1965): 77–89.

36. See e.g., K. R. Popper, "Science: Conjectures and Refutations," in *Conjectures and Refutations* (London: Routledge and Kegan Paul, 1963); cf. S. Haack, "Two Fallibilists in Search of the Truth," *Proceedings of the Aristotelian Society, Supplement*, 51 (1977): 63–83.

37. Some writers, by contrast, allow an important role to *curiosity*; see e.g., M. Polanyi, *Personal Knowledge*, (*PK*) (London: Routledge and Kegan Paul, 1958), paperback edition, 1973, p. 120 ff.

38. *CP*, 5.510 (c. 1905).

39. *CP*, 5.517 (c. 1905).

40. *EW*, p. 513 ff.

41. *CP*, 5.524 (c. 1905).

42. *CP*, 5.451 (1905).

43. *Meditations, HR* vol. 1, p. 145.

44. *Discourse, HR*, vol. 1, p. 89, for example.

45. Cf. James W. Cornman, "Foundational Versus Nonfoundational Theories of Justification," in G. S. Pappas, and M. Swain, eds. *Essays on Knowledge and Justification* (Ithaca, NY: Cornell University Press, 1978), 229–52; see also Williams, *D*, p. 61 for a discussion of the sense in which Descartes' enterprise is foundationalist.

46. The terminology is Rescher's; see *Cognitive Systematization* (Oxford: Basil Blackwell, 1979), ch. 3.

47. *Meditations, HR*, vol. 1, p. 185.

48. *CP*, 5.214 (1868), 5.391 (1878); cf. 7.108 (c. 1910): 'I will not . . . admit that we know anything whatever with *absolute certainty*'.

49. See e.g., *Discourse, HR*, vol. 1, p. 102; cf. Frankfurt, *DDM*. ch. 13.

50. *CP* 4.77 (1893); see also 7.462 (1893).

51. *CP* 5.451 (1905).

52. See M. Polanyi, *PK*, ch. 10; K. R. Popper, *Objective Knowledge* (Oxford: Oxford University Press, 1972); I. Levi, "Truth, Fallibilism and the Growth of Scientific Knowledge," *Boston Colloquium for the Philosophy of Science*, 1975.

53. Thomson prefers to refer to this as 'Peirce's verificationist realism', stressing the independence of reality from the individual rather than its dependence on the community; see his paper of that title in *Review of Metaphysics*, 33 (1979): 74–98.

54. Cf. Williams, *D*, p. 56, for a defence of the view I am maintaining; W. E. Morris, "The Structure of Cartesian Scepticism," (unpublished), for a rival interpretation.

55. *Meditation* I, *HR* vol. 1, pp. 147, 148 (the italics in the second quotation are mine).

56. *D*, pp. 65–67, 211–12.

57. *CP* 6.499 (c.1906).

58. *CP* 4.71 (1893); for Peirce's attack on the 'Method of Authority', see *CP* 5.380 (1877).

59. M. Polanyi, "The Republic of Science: Its Political and Economic Theory," in *Knowing and Being* (hereafter *KB*), ed. M. Greene (London: Routledge and Kegan Paul, 1969), pp. 49–73. Cf. S. Haack, "Personal or Impersonal Knowledge?—Some Comparative Remarks on Popper's and Polanyi's Epistemologies," unpublished.

60. G. H. Mead, "The Social Self" (1913) and "The Genesis of the Self and Social Control" (1924) in *Selected Writings*, ed. A. J. Reck (Indianapolis, IN: Bobbs-Merrill, 1964).

61. Cf. R. J. Haack, "Wittgenstein's Pragmatism," forthcoming in *American Philosophical Quarterly*.

62. H. Putnam, "Is Semantics Possible?" in *Language, Belief and Metaphysics*, ed. H. E. Kiefer, and M. K. Munitz, (Albany, NY: State University of New York Press, 1970), pp. 50–63, and in S. P. Schwartz, ed., *Naming, Necessity and Natural Kinds* (*NNNK*) (Ithaca, NY: Cornell University Press, 1977), 103–18; "Meaning and Reference" *Journal of Philosophy*, 70 (1973): 699–711, and in *NNNK*, 119–32.

63. See e.g., K. R. Popper, "Truth, Rationality and the Growth of Scientific Knowledge" in *Conjectures and Refutations* (London: Routledge and Kegan Paul, 1963), p. 225; S. Haack, "Fallibilism and Necessity," *Synthese*, 41 (1979): 37–63.

64. The analogy is borrowed from Polanyi, *KB*, p. 50 ff.; Polanyi's concern however, is with a separate issue: how science should be organized so as to maximize its prospects of discovering the truth. Cf. also N. Rescher, "Foundationalism, Coherentism, and the Idea of Cognitive Systematisation," *Journal of Philosophy*, 71 (1974): 695–708.

65. W. V. O. Quine, TD: "Epistemology Naturalized," in *Ontological Relativity*, (New York: Columbia University Press, 1969); "The Nature of Natural Knowledge," in *Mind and Language*, ed. S. Guttenplan (Oxford: Oxford University Press, 1975).

66. L. Wittgenstein, *Philosophical Investigations*, trans. G. E. M. Anscombe (Oxford: Basil Blackwell, 1953).

67. N. Goodman, *Ways of Worldmaking* (Hassocks, England: Harvester Press, 1978).

68. S. Pepper, *World Hypotheses* (Berkeley, CA: University of California Press, 1942).

69. Cf. T. Kuhn, *The Structure of Scientific Revolutions* (Chicago, IL: University of Chicago Press, 1962).

70. There is one feature of Descartes' use of the demon argument, brought to my attention by Tom Baldwin, that this does not capture so well as I would like: that the possibility of the demon is thought to show *mathematical* as well as *sensory* beliefs to be dubitable.

71. It is worth observing the affinities between Peirce's view and that of O. K. Bouwsma, in "Descartes' Evil Genius," *Philosophical Review*, 58 (1949): 141–51; and in *Metameditations*, ed. A. Sesonske, and N. Fleming (Belmont, CA: Wadsworth, 1965).

72. N. Goodman, *Fact, Fiction and Forecast* (Cambridge, MA: Harvard University Press, 1955; Indianapolis, IN: Bobbs-Merrill 1965). I suspect, as Goodman does, that the *temporal* character of the green/grue issue is not fundamental.

*This paper was read, in various versions, to the philosophy departments of Haverford College and the Universities of Guelph, Arizona, Birmingham, East Anglia, and York. Thanks are due for helpful comments made on these occasions. Special thanks to Christine Battersby, Charles Whitely, Paul Humphries and Rita Nolan.

ON C. S. PEIRCE'S THEORY OF THE PROPOSITION: PEIRCE AS A PRECURSOR OF GAME-THEORETICAL SEMANTICS*

I

Peirce discusses the nature and structure of propositions in several manuscripts written in the 1890's and during the first decade of this century. In this paper I shall outline the main features of Peirce's theory of the proposition, especially his account of what may be called *indeterminate indices* in propositions.[1]

Peirce distingushes a *proposition* from an *assertion* or affirmation. He says:

> I grant that the normal use of a proposition is to affirm it; and its chief logical properties relate to what would result in reference to its affirmation. It is, therefore convenient in logic to express propositions in most cases in the indicative mood. But the proposition in the sentence, 'Socrates est sapiens', strictly expressed, is 'Socrates sapientem esse'. The defence of this position is that in this way we distinguish between a proposition and the assertion of it, and without such distinction it is impossible to get a distinct notion of the nature of the proposition. One and the same propositon may be affirmed, denied, judged, doubted, inwardly inquired into, put as a question, wished, asked for, effectively commanded, taught, or merely expressed, and does not thereby become a different proposition. (MS 517; *NE*, vol. 4, p. 248)

This view has later become familiar as the distinction between the content and the force of a sentence, or the sentence radical and the mood of a sentence.[2]

However, as Peirce notes in the above paragraph, he takes the main logical properties of propositions to be dependent on their assertive use and his analysis of the structure of propositions is based on this assumption.

According to Peirce, every assertion involves an utterer and an interpreter, or a speaker and a hearer, even though the latter may have only a "problematical existence" (*CP*, 2.334). Peirce characterizes the act of assertion in three different ways:

(1) First, he says:

> The assertion consists in furnishing of evidence by the speaker to the listener that the speaker believes something, that is, finds a certain idea to be definitively compulsory on a certain occasion. (MS 787; *CP* 2.335)

(2) In MS 284 ("The Basis of Pragmaticism") Peirce says that an assertion "is an endeavour to make the person addressed [*i.e.*, the interpreter] think in a certain way," that is, believe something.

(3) In another MS entitled "The Basis of Pragmaticism" (280), Peirce says that

> to assert a proposition means to accept responsibility for it, so that if it turns out ill, or as Mr. Schiller says (by implication) *unsatisfactory*, in a certain way which we need not define, but which is called proving to be false, he who asserted it regrets having done so.

Elsewhere he notes that an assertion involves (on the utterer's part) "a voluntary self-subjection to penalties" in the event that the proposition turns out to be false, and says that such penalties are comparable to the legal penalties associated with making a false statement under oath. (MS 517; *NE* vol. 4, p. 249)

The last characterization of an assertive act is, from the logical point of view, by far the most important one, and plays an important role in Peirce's analysis of propositions.

II

According to Peirce, every proposition can be analysed as consisting of a subject and a predicate:

> A proposition consists of two parts, the *predicate* which excites something like an image or dream in the mind of the interpreter, and the subject, or subjects, each of which serves to identify something which the predicate represents. (MS 280)

In Peirce's classification of signs, the subject of a proposition is an indexical symbol: its function is to direct the interpreter's attention to a certain object or objects; whereas the predicate is what Peirce calls an iconic symbol: it represents a quality which the proposition in question represents as a quality of the object. (*CP*. 2.312)

The indexical character of the subject is clear enough in the case of proper names; according to Peirce, a (logically) proper name is an expression which "denotes a single individual well known to exist by the utterer and the interpreter" (MS 517; *NE*, vol. 4, p. 243). However, the subject of a proposition may also be a complex expression involving common nouns. According to Peirce, even such complex expressions function in basically the same way as indexical expressions. He says that [the function of a common noun] is the same as that of the Proper Name. That is, it merely draws attention to an object and so puts its interpreter into condition to learn whatever there may be to be learned from such attention. Now attention can only be drawn to what is already in experience. A proper name can only function as such if the utterer and interpreter are already more or less familiar with the object it names. But the peculiarity of a common noun is that it undertakes to draw attention to an object with which the interpreter may have no acquaintance. For this purpose it calls up to his mind such an image as a verb calls up, appeals to his memory that he has seen different objects [as] the subjects of that image, ... and then of those which might be so recollected or imagined, the noun indefinitely names one. (MS. 516)

Peirce is evidently speaking here of the function of a common noun in the subject-position of a sentence.

What does it mean to say that a common noun, when it occurs in the subject of a sentence, names an object "indefinitely"? A name either is or is not a name of a given object; there is no third possibility. "Indefinite name" and "indefinite naming" are clearly elliptical expressions. One of the most interesting features of Peirce's theory of the proposition was his explanation of how these expressions are to be understood.

If the subject of a sentence is not a simple indexical expression, such as a proper name or a pronoun, Peirce calls it a *precept*. (*CP* 2.330) A precept does not denote (or indicate) any definite singular object, but shows how the utterer and the interpreter should act in order to find a singular object or an "occasion of experience" to which the predicate may be regarded as being applicable. (*CP* 2.330, 2.336)

Peirce calls such signs indeterminate signs. An indeterminate indexical symbol can be interpreted, or as Peirce also says, *explicated* as representing more than one singular object. (MS 283) I shall stretch Peirce's use of the word 'index' slightly and call such signs *indeterminate indices*.

Peirce distinguishes between two types of indeterminacy, which he calls *indefiniteness* and *generality* (MS 283, *CP* 5.448n.). An indeterminate subject does not consist of a common noun alone, but of a common noun and a quantifier (or as Peirce also calls it, a *selective*), which indicates the type of indeterminacy exemplified by a given proposition. Indefiniteness is indicated by the existential quantifier *some*, generality by the quantifier *any*. Absence of indefiniteness is called definiteness, and absence of generality, individuality. Every sign is either individual (not general) or definite (not indefinite), and a sign which is both definite and individual is called a *singular* sign. (MS 9, MS 515)

In what sense does a precept, or an indeterminate index, show how the utterer and the interpreter must act in order to find a singular object or an index of a singular object which may be regarded as the subject of the assertion?

Peirce's explanation of the meaning of quantifier phrases is based on his account of the use of a proposition in an assertion, and it resembles the modern game-theoretical interpretation of quantifiers.[3]

By asserting a certain proposition, the utterer accepts responsibility for it and subjects himself to certain penalties in case the proposition turns out to be false. Thus the utterer is essentially a defender of any proposition that he may assert. On the other hand, it is important for the interpreter to detect any falsehood asserted by the utterer, since, as Peirce notes, "the affirmation of a proposition may determine a judgment to the same effect in the mind of the interpreter to his cost" (MS 517; *NE*, vol. 4, p. 249). Hence the utterer and the interpreter have opposite interests and attitudes with respect to the truth of any proposition asserted by the former. Peirce describes the situation as follows:

> The utterer is essentially a defender of his own proposition, and wishes to interpret it so that it will be defensible. The interpreter, not being so interested, and being unable to interpret it fully without considering to what extreme it may reach, is *relatively* in a hostile attitude, and looks for the interpretation least defensible. (MS 9, pp. 3–4)

Peirce occasionally calls the interpreter of a proposition its "opponent" (e.g., in MS 515). Thus the language-game played by the utterer and the interpreter with respect to an indeterminate proposition is, according to Peirce, a zero-sum game.[4]

Given this asymmetry in the roles of the utterer and interpreter, the meaning of different types of indeterminate indices can be explained as follows:

An indeterminate index is indefinite if and only if the utterer of the proposition is free to choose (or select) the object which the index is regarded as representing; that is, the utterer is free to choose the interpretation of the subject-term. An existential quantifier is a sign of the utterer's choice or move in the language-game. In the case of a definite proposition the utterer leaves himself no latitude of interpretation; Peirce notes that

> A definite proposition is one the assertor [i.e., the utterer] of which leaves himself no loop-hole for escape against attack by saying that he did not mean so and so, but something else. (MS 515, p. 25)

However, the utterer may not only not leave himself any such latitude of interpretation, but he may also, as Peirce says,

> [allow] his opponent [i.e., the interpreter] a choice as to what singular object he will instance to refute the proposition, as in "Any man you please is mortal." (MS 515)

In other words, if the proposition has a general index, the interpreter has the right to choose the singular object which the index it regarded as representing: a universal quantifier transfers the choice of the singular to the interpreter.

Peirce observes that

> It seems an odd thing, when one comes to ponder it, that there should be such a mode of signification as the latter [i.e., generality], in which the utterer of a sign transfers to its interpreter the office of determining what that sign is to be apprehended as meaning. Its familiarity blinds us to the wonder of it. (MS 283)

If an indeterminate index is a complex quantifier phrase involving several quantifiers, each existential quantifier indicates the utterer's choice of a singular object and each universal quantifier the interpreter's choice. Peirce observes that

> whichever of the two makes his choice of the object he is to choose, after the other has made his choice, is supposed to know what that choice was. This is an advantage to the defense or attack, as the case may be. (MS 9, §3)

Here Peirce assumes that the semantical game he is describing is a game with perfect information; this amounts to the assumption that the quantifiers in a complex indeterminate index are always ordered and do not branch.[5] This assumption entails that every indeterminate index is either individual (not general) or definite (not indefinite) since the choice of an object cannot simultaneously belong to both parties (both the utterer and the interpreter). (Cf. MS 9, §2)

If the truth of a proposition is defined as the utterer's ability to defend it successfully against the interpreter's attack, as Peirce does, this analysis of quantifier phrases gives quantified sentences correct truth-conditions and is essentially similar to the modern game-theoretical interpretation of quantifiers. Peirce did not possess a well-defined concept of *strategy*, but his concept *defensibility against attack* comes close to the game-theoretical definition of truth. (A sentence is true if and only if its utterer has a winning strategy in the game associated with it.)[6] In Peirce's *Collected Papers*, this game-theoretical account of indeterminate indices is very appropriately called "The Pragmatic Interpretation of the Logical Subject" (*CP*, vol. 2, p. 187)

Above I have discussed only Peirce's game-theoretical interpretation of quantifier phrases (indeterminate indexical symbols). Many other parts of speech can be understood in a similar way. For example, Peirce observes that a necessary proposition is a sort of universally quantified proposition and a statement of possibility can be regarded as an existential proposition (*CP*

2.382). Thus modal expressions can also be understood in terms of the choices made by the utterer and the interpreter in a language-game, but in this case the players do not make choices among the individuals of a given universe, but among possible courses of events.

Peirce often called indefiniteness "vagueness" (*CP* 5.447–5.450, 5.505 –5.506) and referred to the logic of indefinite expressions as "the logic of vagueness" (*CP* 5.506). Many philosophers who have recently been interested in the logic of vagueness have observed that Peirce used this expression, but they have been disappointed at finding out that Peirce's logic of vagueness seems to be just a formulation of the quantification theory. For example, in her recent book *Deviant Logic* Susan Haack notes:

> [Peirce] seems from his examples, to have had a somewhat eccentric conception of vagueness . . . .
> He contrasts vague with general sentences and he gives examples which suggest that he understands by a 'general' sentence, one which is universally quantified, and by a 'vague' sentence, one which is existentially quantified.[7]

These remarks do not give an entirely correct impression of Peirce's theory of vagueness. Peirce's account of vagueness is part of his theory of indeterminacy, and as I tried to show above, the most interesting feature of this theory is not that it was a version of quantification theory, but rather the pragmatic or game-theoretical interpretation of indeterminate indices.

Moreover, the discussion of vagueness and generality to which Haack refers concerns only the indeterminacy of the subject or the indeterminacy of indexical symbols. The contemporary discussion of vagueness in concerned with the indeterminacy of the predicate, not that of the subject. The classical paradox of the sorites (the paradox of the heap) illustrates vagueness of the latter type. Peirce's theory of indeterminacy covers both types of vagueness; he also discusses the indeterminacy of the predicate (e.g., in MS 283). However, I shall leave a discussion of that aspect of Peirce's theory of vagueness for another occasion.

Risto Hilpinen

University of Turku

NOTES

* This is a considerably shortened and condensed version of a paper read in a meeting of the Philosophical Society of Finland in Helsinki, November 1977. More recent ver-

sions of the paper were presented at the Department of Philosophy of Kansas State University, Manhattan, Kansas, on April 29, 1980, and in the Edgar Henderson Memorial Symposium on the Philosophy of Charles S. Peirce at Florida State University, Tallahassee, May 18, 1980.

I am indebted to the American Council of Learned Societies for a fellowship which enabled me to study Peirce's philosophy at Harvard University in 1975–1976, and to Florida State University for support of research during the spring quarter of 1980.

1. I follow the usual method of citing from the *Collected Papers of Charles Sanders Perice*, ed. by Charles Hartshorne and Paul Weiss, vols. 1–6 (Cambridge, MA: Harvard University Press, 1931–1938) (here abbreviated '*CP*') by volume and paragraph number. Carolyn Eisele, ed., *The New Elements of Mathematics of Charles S. Peirce* (The Hague, Netherlands: Mouton Publisher, 1976; Atlantic Highlands, NJ: Humanities Press) will be abbreviated '*NE*', and references to the microfilm edition of Peirce's papers (Widener Library, Harvard University) will be indicated by 'MS', followed by the number of the manuscript.

2. Cf. Erik Stenius, *Wittgenstein's Tractatus: A Critical Exposition of the Main Lines of Thought* (Oxford: Basil Blackwell, 1964), ch. 9 (especially pp. 157–65), and Michael Dummett, *Frege: Philosophy of Language* (London: Duckworth, 1973), ch. 10.

3. For game-theoretical semantics, see the articles included in Esa Saarinen, ed., *Game-Theoretical Semantics* (Dordrecht: D. Reidel Publishing Company, 1979); especially Jaakko Hintikka, "Quantifiers in Logic and Quantifiers in Natural Languages" (pp. 27–47), "Quantifiers vs. Quantification Theory" (pp. 49–79), and "Quantifiers in Natural Languages: Some Logical Problems" (pp. 81–117).

4. The games considered in game-theoretical semantics are zero-sum games; cf. Jaakko Hintikka, "Quantifiers vs. Quantification Theory," in Saarinen, ed., *Game-Theoretical Semantics*, p. 51. (cited in n3, above).

5. If the requirement of perfect information is given up, the quantifiers need not be linearly ordered, but may branch. For the game-theoretical semantics of branching quantifiers, see Jaakko Hintikka, "Quantifiers vs. Quantification Theory" in Saarinen, ed., *Game-Theoretical Semantics*, (cited in n3, above) pp. 59 ff. and in the same work, "Quantifiers in Natural Languages: Some Logical Problems," pp. 88 ff.

6. Cf. Jaakko Hintikka, "Quantifiers in Logic and Quantifiers in Natural Languages," in Esa Saarinen, ed., *Game-Theoretical Semantics* (cited in n3, above) p. 36.

7. Susan Haack, *Deviant Logic: Some Philosophical Issues*, (Cambridge: Cambridge University Press, 1974), p. 109.

PRAGMATISM, SCIENCE, AND METAPHYSICS*

Introduction

In 1934 Charles W. Morris, then a young philosopher at the University of Chicago, visited Rudolf Carnap in Prague, where the latter was teaching on the science faculty of Charles University. Morris, a philosopher familiar with Peirce's work and himself following the traditions of pragmatism, was impressed with the positivist program. Two years later he played an important role in Carnap's move to a professorship at the University of Chicago.[1] In the following year, 1937, Hermann in Paris published a slim but eloquent book by Morris, *Pragmatism, Logical Positivism, and Scientific Empiricism*. Its thesis was that American pragmatism and European positivism were entirely complementary philosophical movements, and that the collaboration of the adherents of the two could lead to a new form of scientific empiricism more fruitful than either.

Carnap did give this suggestion of Morris cautious lip service in "Testability and Meaning,"[2] his first important paper in the United States. But active intellectual collaboration between members of these two philosophical movements did not, in fact, occur. Indeed, as philosophy developed after the disruptions of World War II, relationships between members of the two groups might best be characterized as marked by mutual misunderstandings and distaste. Morris abandoned his hopes for their fusion and turned his attention to other matters, Carnap continued to develop his own views, and only the *International Encyclopedia of the Unified Sciences*, which they founded together, remains to testify to such a vision.

Without commenting further on what might have been, and the social and political reasons why it may have failed to come about, let us look at those aspects of theory and outlook shared by the two movements, as well as those on which they differed, and see what the substantive problems were. For reasons of simplicity and breadth of scope, attention will be focused on the theories of Peirce and Carnap, with special attention to the details of Peirce's views where these are not as widely known.

It is hard to look at the work of Peirce (1839–1914) and Carnap (1891–1970) without being impressed, as Morris was, by the similarity of spirit they seemed to share—in spite of the fifty years that separated their lives.

—Both took science as a source of inspiration for what philosophy could be.

—Both noted that scientists settled their problems, while often philosophers engaged in empty talk.

—Both recognized that the *methods* of science played a key role in this difference, with the disciplined relation of theory and observation being the heart of these methods.

—Both defined cognitive concepts in terms of the sensible or tangible outcomes of their use.

—Both recognized other forms of meaning appropriate in nonscientific contexts.

—Both labelled as 'meaningless' and 'nonsense' those cognitive statements that had no conceivable tangible outcomes of use.

—Both thought that much metaphysics, when examined, proved to be nonsense in just that sense.

—Both took logical analysis to be a key element in the clarification of philosophical problems.

But, in the end, it was the differences that carried the day. I think there were three of major importance.

—Peirce thought metaphysics, properly conducted, an important philosophical enterprise fully consonant with science, and left us volumes of his own writing on the topic. Carnap eschewed such work, leaving such of it as might not be nonsense to be settled as a matter of taste or by convention.

—Carnap chose the path of nominalism with respect to universals; Peirce is an ebullient realist.

—Carnap attempted to draw a sharp line between the language of observation and the language of theory; Peirce vigorously argued that no such attempt was defensible or possible.

These are very large issues, and it is not possible to do them justice within the scope of this essay. Furthermore, both of these traditions are alive, in one form or another, and engaged in current work which departs in a variety of ways from the approaches of Peirce and Carnap while, nevertheless, taking portions of their theories for granted. There will be space to do little more than comment obliquely and occasionally on such contemporary theories. In what follows, I shall attempt to focus on the first of the larger issues sufficiently to see the tantalizing problems of this hoped for merger of pragmatism with positivism into a new scientific empiricism that never came off. Perhaps another generation can do better.

Logical Positivism

Carnap's first major work, *The Logical Structure of the World (Der Logische Aufbau Der Welt)*, originally published in 1928[3], outlines a basic epistemological theory regarding the relationship of general knowledge, especially that of science, to human experience and observation. It was a fusion of classical empirical and rationalistic philosophies, inspired especially by the development of new techniques of logic and their application to the resolution of problems in the foundations of mathematics. The work of his own teacher, Frege, along with that of Russell, Whitehead, and Wittgenstein, provided major elements. While he changed parts of his theory from time to time to meet difficulties as they arose, he remained faithful to the basic plan throughout his life. I might add that it is a plan that has attracted the efforts and loyalty of thousands of philosophers, and a great deal of work is being done in its spirit today.

The *Aufbau* itself is imbued with a tone of reasonableness, respect for scientific professionalism, and appreciation for the advantages of the exactness and clarity that mathematics and logic can provide in the solution of difficult problems—that would have pleased Peirce immensely. He would not have been so pleased with its classical empiricism and rationalism. But setting such considerations aside for now, it will pay us first to sketch that basic plan, for it is so familiar, both to its supporters and its critics, that we run the risk of failing to notice aspects of it that are important in understanding substantive differences between pragmatism and positivism.

The basic plan was to devise a "constructional system" whose undefined elements were what is "given" in experience, and whose method of construction was provided by the tools of modern logic. The style of construction was that used in the foundations of mathematics, where elegance, simplicity, clarity, and economy of materials were important. The end result would be the clarification of our knowledge on a scientific and mathematical basis. In this manner did the demands of classical empiricism fall into harmony with those of classical rationalism. For classical empiricism counted nothing as knowledge that was not derived from experience, and this plan rested on experience as constituting the elements on which the construction was based. At the same time, classical rationalism insisted that we know, through thinking, more than is given in experience. Here the answer is, in effect, to deny that any new *substantive* knowledge is provided by thinking, for the only elements to be admitted in the construction process are those given in experience; while that process itself is given over as the domain of the highest form of rationality: logic.

The ensuing "constructs," "constructions," "reconstructions" or "explications," if properly done, ought to be such as to please both those with empirical and with rationalistic inclinations. For they use only the given data of experience as their raw materials, and proceed with the clarity, elegance, and deductive certainty of logic to their outcomes. Thus, the constructs would be meaningful on the standards set by both schools. Given the construct, one could always follow a clear logical path back to its experiential base, thereby guaranteeing that it would always be empirically verifiable. And the constructs themselves, framed in the language of *Principia*, would display this information in the most simple, elegant, and perspicuous manner. Locke and Descartes would both rejoice.

Putting this powerful tool to work, Carnap began a careful analysis of philosophical problems, including some that were metaphysical, with an eye to their clear resolution along these lines. This project was shortly abandoned, however, when Carnap was convinced by Wittgenstein that the method of construction exemplified the only manner in which a synthetic sentence could have meaning, and that metaphysics was meaningless precisely because its sentences lacked any experiential base. Metaphysics was, therefore, unverifiable in principle because one could not identify the experiences one would expect to have were its sentences true. Carnap writes in his intellectual autobiography:

> The most decisive development in my view of metaphysics occurred . . . in the Vienna period, chiefly under the influence of Wittgenstein. I came to hold that many theses of traditional metaphysics are not only useless, but even devoid of cognitive content . . . . The view . . . was based on Wittgenstein's principle of verifiability. This principle says first, that the meaning of a sentence is given by the conditions of its verification and, second, that a sentence is meaningful if and only if it is in principle verifiable, that is, if there are possible, not necessarily actual, circumstances which, if they did occur, would definitely establish the truth of the sentence. This principle of verifiability was later replaced by the more liberal principle of confirmability.[4]

His long article, "Pseudoproblems in Philosophy"[5] develops this theme in a more popular form, and in another, "The Overthrow of Metaphysics",[6] the technique is applied in a critical attempt to show that Heidegger's celebrated thesis that negation negates itself (*Das Nicht sich nichtet*) is, like the rest of metaphysics, devoid of cognitive content.

With time, Carnap found it necessary to modify parts of this program. He developed doubts about the thesis of extensionality; that is about the universal applicability of extensional languages like those of *Principia*. "Verifiability" was further broadened to "testability," thereby including Popper's "falsifiability." In place of actual constructions, which for both logical and methodological reasons were abandoned, Carnap introduced the notion of "correspondence rules" that would relate "observational terms" to "theoretical terms." Finally, Carnap even spelled out some conditions in which a theoretical term not bound to an observation term by a correspondence rule might yet play a meaningful role in a theory[7]. In place of what was given in experience serving as the elements for the constructions or reconstructions, with Neurath's help he tried to develop a method for working from a physical base. He also used the protocols of intersubjective observation (a "heteropsychological" rather than an "autopsychological" base, he called it), for this seems to avoid the problems of subjectivity and is what scientists rely on in their work. But in the end, he said, he thought sensory elements like those of Mach would be best: sensory qualities such as standard colors, but indexed to individuals and in time and place in a sensory field[8]. And for those metaphysical problems that were not nonsensical but required, at the least, a choice of language or methods, Carnap preferred to tolerate competing choices, or resolve the issue by stipulation or convention.[9] But he saw all these changes as minor adjustments: reconstructionism on an empirical base, and, what amounted to its converse, verifiability, remained his vision to the end, and it is a vision bequeathed to many.

Pragmatism

In sharp contrast to the orderly appearance of Carnap's work, Peirce left us a bewildering variety of writings, only a small portion of which have yet been published, although a major effort to edit and publish them is now underway. In commenting on these, Arthur Burks divides them into an earlier group, in which he thinks Peirce used the pragmatic principle as a verifiability theory of meaning in Carnap's sense, and a later period, in which his philosophy takes a distinctly Kantian tone.[10] While I have no competing view of how we ought to group Peirce's works, I find the differences between the pragmatic maxim and the verifiability principle as tantalizing as their similarities. I think these differences both explain why Peirce thought metaphysics important while Carnap thought it nonsense or to be settled by convention, and why Charles Morris's hopes for a union of effort between pragmatists and positivists went unrealized.

At the same time, I think Burks is right in stressing the importance of Kant's philosophy as an influence on Peirce's work, although it seems to have been a steady one. He arrived at the pragmatic principle itself, he tells us, through profound reflection on Kant, whose work he first studied with his father at an early age. He does not mention what portion of Kant's theories served as his inspiration here,[11] but the earliest passage I can find in which something like the pragmatic principle occurs is from a paper published in 1868 critical of what he calls the Cartesian tradition in philosophy. The passage opens by referring to one of his own principles introduced at the onset of the paper:

> We come now to the consideration of the last of the four principles whose consequences we were to trace: namely that the absolutely incognizable is absolutely inconceivable. That, upon Cartesian principles the very realities of things can never be known, most competent persons must long ago have been convinced. Hence the breaking forth of idealism, which is essentially anti-Cartesian, in every direction, whether among empiricists (Berkeley, Hume) or noologists (Hegel, Fichte). The principle now brought under discussion is directly idealistic; for *since the meaning of a word is the conception it conveys, the absolutely incognizable has no meaning because no conception attaches to it. It is, therefore, a meaningless word: and, consequently, whatever is meant by any term as "the real" is cognizable in some degree.*[12]

Notice that, like the classic verifiability principle of half a century later, Peirce uses his to rule out a metaphysical thesis as meaningless. And, like the verifiability principle, he does so on methodological grounds: that *some* conception must be attached to the words. But he does not have a theory as to how this must be done, least of all that it must be on a sensory or experiential base with an extensional logical structure. The principle serves him well for the extreme case he is dealing with, namely the status of the unknowable and the virtue of any philosophy which hands over a large portion of what we need to know to such a nether region. But its range of application is narrow. Ten years later a fully general pragmatic maxim appears. Following is a translation from the French of its first statement:

> To consider what practical effects we think can be produced by the object of our conception. The conception of all these effects is the complete conception of the object.[13]

Here we move from considering that we know what we know through some conception of it to an analysis of that conception in terms of its practical effects, or, more accurately, *all* of those. He explains further (in French):

> To develop the meaning of a thought, it is simply necessary to determine what habits it produces, because the meaning of a thing consists simply in the habits it implies. The character of a habit depends on the way in which it can make us act not only in a given probable circumstance but in all possible circumstances, however improbable they might be. What is a habit depends on these two points: when and how it causes action. For the first point: when? every stimulus to action arises from a perception; for the second point: how? the purpose of every action is to bring about a sensible result. Thus we reach the tangible and the practical as the base of all differences of thought, however subtle they may be.

Thus "practical effects" are further analyzed in terms of our habits of action, the perceptual stimuli that give rise to them, and their tangible results, but, again, we are to consider these in "all possible circumstances."

His own first English version appeared later the same year in *The Monist* and varied only slightly. As he recounts it in 1905:

> Pragmaticism was originally enounced in the form of a maxim, as follows: Consider what effects that might *conceivably* have practical bearings you *conceive* the objects of your *conception* to have. Then your *conception* of those effects is the whole of your *conception* of the object.
>
> I will restate this in other words . . . .: The entire intellectual purport of any symbol consists in the total of all general modes of rational conduct which, conditionally upon all the possible different circumstances and desires, would ensue upon the acceptance of the symbol.[14]

The only additional element I can find in this version is the requirement that the action be rational.

A version he wrote for the entry for 'pragmaticism' for the 1902 edition of Baldwin's *Dictionary* goes back to the propadeutic function of the 1868 rule, but now puts it in terms of broad scope:

> The opinion that metaphysics is to be largely cleared up by the application of the following maxim for attaining clearness of apprehension: "Consider what effects, that might conceivably have practical bearings, we conceive the object of our conception to have. Then our conception of these effects is the whole of our conception of the object."[15]

Notice that, unlike the verifiability principle, which took the entire enterprise of metaphysics to rest on unverifiable claims, and, thus, to be nonsensical, Peirce sees the function of pragmatism, or pragmaticism, as he called it for awhile, to be to "clear up" metaphysics. He does not talk about its "overthrow."

By this time, Peirce's theory had had a profound impact on the work of William James, whose voluntaristic version of "pragmatism" had been the main reason for Peirce to give up using that word. In the same *Dictionary* article, Peirce wrote that the work of James (*Will to Believe,* 1896, and more):

> pushed this method to such extremes as must give us pause. The doctrine appears to assume that the end of man is action—a stoical axiom which, to the present writer at the age of sixty, does not recommend itself so forcibly as it did at thirty. If it be admitted, on the contrary, that action wants an end, and that that end must be something of a general description, then the spirit of the maxim itself, which is that we must look to the upshot of our concepts in order rightly to apprehend them, would direct us towards something different from practical facts, namely to general ideas, as the true interpreters of our thoughts.[16]

I think it was not the "stoical axiom" so much as the interpretation of practical actions in terms of the *will* to believe that troubled him here. And in fact he does not seem to really withdraw the role of rational action as much as to supplement it with the notion that their desired outcomes can be embodied in

"general ideas." For if we were to take him at his word and leave the actions
out, we would end up with the unenlightening proposal that "conceptions" be
analyzed in terms of "general ideas." Perhaps another fear stemmed from
James's emphasis on some one or another particular outcome of an action.
While Peirce's formulations of the pragmatic maxim had specified that every
possible outcome was a part of the conception being considered, he might
have imagined that the tendency to misinterpret the maxim by focusing on
single practical effects could best be countered in this way. He continues by
saying that, nevertheless, the maxim has been "of great utility in leading to a
relatively high grade of clearness of thought," and suggests that after applying it:

> with conscientious thoroughness . . . a still higher grade of clearness of
> thought can be attained by remembering that the only ultimate good . . . the prac-
> tical facts . . . can subserve is to further the development of concrete
> reasonableness; so that the meaning of the concept does not lie in any *individual*
> reactions at all, but in the manner in which those reactions contribute to that
> development.

Thus he again eschews the notion that the desired outcome of the use of the
pragmatic maxim is a practical fact of an individual reaction. And, in contrast to the verifiability principle, which ought to work by giving us absolute
clarity or the knowledge that our thesis was nonsense, Peirce promises only
that the pragmatic maxim can be useful in leading us to a "relatively high
grade of clearness of thought": a modest, but improvable, goal.

The following year he put the maxim this way during a lecture:

> Pragmatism is the principle that every theoretical judgment expressible in a
> sentence in the indicative mood is a confused form of thought whose only mean-
> ing, if it has any, lies in its tendency to enforce a corresponding practical maxim
> expressible as a conditional sentence having its apodosis in the imperative
> mood.[17]

One can guess that he applied it to *theoretical* judgments because he was
speaking to philosophical audience, and the central role of rational action is
again apparent. On the assumption that a very large number of conditional
sentences are possible, depending on one's circumstances and aims, this version does not differ from the original. And the function of the maxim to ex-
pose meaninglessness remained unchanged. In the same lecture he considered
the suggestion that the choice of words was a "practical" action, and
responded testily:

> But a thinker must be shallow indeed if he does not see that to admit a
> species of practicality that consists in one's conduct about words and modes of
> expression is at once to break down all the bars against the nonsense that
> pragmatism is designed to exclude.

But Peirce did not regard the pragmatic maxim as carving out the entire domain of meaning. In an article in *The Monist* in 1905, which also shows his realism with respect to universals, he writes:

> It would also have been well to show that the pragmaticist does not make forms to be the only realities in the world, any more than he makes the reasonable purport of a word to be the only kind of meaning there is.[18]

This seems to correspond to Carnap's conceding that the verifiability principle applies only to cognitive meanings, and that there are noncognitive meanings as well. An undated manuscript from about this period that Peirce did not publish repeats this point more clearly:

> I understand pragmatism to be a method of ascertaining the meanings not of all ideas, but only of what I call "intellectual concepts," that is to say, of those upon the structure of which arguments concerning objective fact may hinge . . .[19]

In the same manuscript he goes on to make the conventional distinction between primary and secondary qualities, pointing out that the qualities of feeling have no intrinsic significance. But then he writes:

> Intellectual concepts, however . . . carry some implication concerning the general behavior either of some conscious being, or some inanimate object, and so convey more not merely than any feeling, but more, too, than any existential fact, namely the "would acts," "would dos" of habitual behavior; and no agglomeration of actual happenings can ever completely fill up the meaning of a "would-be."

This version, in its reference to habitual behavior, indicates that the form he gave to the original pragmatic maxim in 1878 remains active in his later thinking. And in referring to "would acts" he seems merely to be emphasizing the importance of the universal operator in that first version's statement that the meaning of a concept was comprised by how we might act in "all possible circumstances". Any sum of particular circumstances would fall short of this. The new element is the relegation of experience to the realm of secondary qualities; it has no "intrinsic" significance. The topic is not pursued, but enough is said to prevent us from interpreting the pragmatic maxim as requiring, like the verifiability principle, that the base for the construction of our conceptions be what is given in experience. Yet the main thrust of the passage is not that experience is secondary, but that *particular* experiences or *particular* facts are inadequate to develop the meaning of a conception.

One reason for this is described in the 1868 paper cited above, a portion of which appears again in a manuscript dated about 1905:

> No thought in itself, then, no feeling in itself, contains any others, but is absolutely simple as it is immediately present, a mere sensation without parts . . .

and therefore, in itself, without similarity to any other . . . but absolutely *sui generis* . . . [20]

In a footnote he adds:

> Observe that I say *in itself*. I am not so wild as to deny that my sensation of red today is like my sensation of red yesterday. I only say that the similarity can *consist* only in the physiological force behind consciousness—which leads me to say I recognize this feeling the same as the former one . . .

The passage concludes:

> Finally, no present actual thought . . . has any meaning, any intellectual value; for this lies not in what is actually thought, but in what this thought may be connected with in representation by subsequent thoughts; so that the meaning of a thought is . . . virtual.

To put the matter another way, he takes experiences to be particular in the sense of being unique, unanalyzed, uncategorized, and unrelated as they are "given." Recognition of similarities, categorization, analysis, the study of relationships: all these are the work of the knower. But such work is fallible. Hence we cannot place heavy reliance on the results reached by any individual person. Again, from the same paper of 1868:

> The spirit of Cartesianism . . . teaches . . . . that the ultimate test of certainty is to be found in the individual consciousness; whereas scholasticism had rested on the testimony of sages and of the Catholic Church . . . .

> But thus to make single individuals absolute judges of truth is most pernicious. The result is that metaphysicians will all agree that metaphysics has reached a pitch of certainty far beyond that of the physical sciences;—only they can agree upon nothing else. In sciences in which men come to an agreement, when a theory has been broached it is considered to be on probation until this agreement is reached . . . . We individually cannot reasonably hope to attain the ultimate philosophy which we pursue; we can only seek it, therefore, for the *community* of scholars . . . .

> Philosophy ought to imitate the successful sciences in its methods, so far as to proceed only from *tangible* premises which can be subjected to careful scrutiny . . . . Its reasoning should form not a chain which is no stronger than its weakest link, but a cable whose fibers may be ever so slender, provided they are sufficiently numerous and intimately connected.[21]

Thus, one of the things Peirce has learned by taking science as the model for knowledge is that the process is a social, not an individual one. His famous notion that the truth is that which investigators are ultimately fated to believe arises in this context. Inquirers sharing goals and methods, even though they may not be in a position to meet together—or even be contemporaries in time—may, through the social invention of writing, become members of the same community of scholarship. Within the limits of time, they can share problems, theories, plans for actions to test the theories, and the experienced results of those tests. Their working together increases the liklihood that errors will be detected and the truth determined, but no certainty is provided for this, not even by fate. Indeed, the suggestion, I think, is analogous to that of Weierstrass about infinitesimals, which Peirce greatly admired. For just as the infinitesimal is defined as the limit approached by a ratio as its denominator approaches zero, so truth is defined as the limit approached by generation after generation of relentless investigators, who form a community by communicating their results.

That raises a final issue about Peirce's theory that is pertinent to the problem. He maintains that our experiences, in addition to being unanalyzed as given, do not result in images or determinate perceptions. By 'determinate', here, he means that it can be decided whether every possible predicate or its negation applies, as, for example, would be the case for a physical object, which we could investigate indefinitely. He writes in 1868:

> But the conclusive argument against our having any images, or absolutely determinate representations in perception, is that in that case we have the materials in each such representation for an infinite amount of conscious cognition, which we never yet become aware of. Now there is no meaning in saying that we have something in our minds which never has the least effect on what we are conscious of knowing . . . .[22]

While there is not time to even begin to discuss his theory of signs, (semiotics), like perceptions, they are indeterminate also:

> Notwithstanding their contrariety, generality and vagueness are, from a formal point of view, seen to be on a par . . . . Hence . . . a sign can only escape from being either vague or general by not being indeterminate. But . . . no sign can be absolutely and completely determinate . . . . No communication of one person to another can be entirely definite . . . .[23]

His reasons are interesting. The incomparability of one person's feelings and experiences with another's leads inevitably to misunderstandings, he says, although he thinks an increase in our knowledge of physiology may reduce the problem somewhat. But, however that may work out, no one person's interpretation of words is based on the same set of experiences as another's, he adds. And, finally, he says even our own thinking to ourselves is in dialogue form, and takes on the character of our discourse with another. Quine has explored some of these problems in great detail with similar and well-known results, although that cannot be pursued here.[24]

The important outcome of this issue for the broad structure of Peirce's theory is that our interpretation of our experiences is not only subject to the kinds of errors that can arise from individual knowers applying analytic tools of judgment to the content of the given, but that this content itself is not fully determinate. Further degrees of indeterminacy enter by the very character of the process by which signs are related to experience. This indeterminacy affects the entire process of inquiry, and is especially important to social interchanges between investigators, which, as Peirce sees things, is the very heart of science.

Contrasts

I think we are now at the point where it is possible to understand the chief differences between the pragmatic maxim and the verifiability principle, gain some further insights into the intellectual difficulties that would have attended a marriage of pragmatism and positivism, learn something more about their differing treatment of metaphysics, and, perhaps, look to the future.

To begin with basic principles, both the pragmatic maxim and the verifiability principle remained essentially stable throughout their respective parent's working lifetimes. Peirce's various formulations emphasize now one and now another of the pragmatic maxim's many facets, and he disowns the cousin that was James's offspring. But when all that is taken into account, each version of the pragmatic maxim is compatible with the others, and they seem mutually reinforcing. The verifiability principle, although an adopted child, was brought up and loved as his own by Carnap, and remained central to his thinking to the end. His ideas about it changed only as regards the best way to implement it.

Given this broad stability, and the fact that both forced the test of experience on concepts as the central core of their meaning, what do their differences come to? For Peirce, as we have seen, the beginning of any concept lies in experience. Experiences happen to us, serve as the stimulus to thought and to possible action, and, on the basis of that thinking we eventually do act in the world, thus landing ourselves in more experiences. The content or meaning of our concepts consists not in determinate images nor in empty abstractions, but in thinking general enough to encompass all possible outcomes of our acting on those concepts. Since both the stimulus to thought and its outcome lie in experience, the pragmatic maxim is empirical from start to finish. But it is not empirical in the literal sort of way suggested by the medieval slogan: "Nothing in the mind that is not first in the senses." That is to say, it does not attempt to guarantee empirical content by monitoring the original sensory input, and then following it through the intellectual processes to make sure nothing is added. On Peirce's view a great deal may be added by any person, because the experiences have to be sorted out, categorized, related to other experiences past, present, and possible future ones, and calculations and hypotheses have to be worked out as to possible outcomes. Mistakes may be made all along the line, but they can be corrected; because the anticipated outcomes are in terms of experience, we may eventually find out whether our selections, judgments, and hypotheses were correct or not. And since, within the limits of accuracy of communication, we can share these successes and failures with other inquirers, we are in a position to pool their judgments, successes, and failures in seeking knowledge with ours. So as a result both of individual and social activity, there is, on this view, a great deal in our minds that was not first in our senses, but it has to stand the successive tests of experience that our actions lead us into. We may often be wrong, both as individuals and as groups, but if we persist in our inquiry, since our results with their endless would-acts, would-dos, and would-bes have infinite consequences, our ideas are infinitely corrigible. On this view, the worst sin was to take a step that halts further inquiry, and, indeed, throughout his writings Peirce holds this to be the most blameworthy thing an investigator could do.

But metaphysics could come out in two places upon pragmatic analysis. It might consist in theories so disconnected from experience that they have no bearing on possible human actions and their outcomes in experience. If, upon diligently applying the pragmatic maxim in trying to make our ideas clear we reach this conclusion about some principle of metaphysics, then we can say it is meaningless nonsense. Of course, like all judgments on Pierce's view, this kind is fallible too; another analysis yielding a contrary conclusion might be produced, in which case it would have to be considered on its merits by the scholars concerned. Nevertheless, Peirce was confident that much of what passed for metaphysics in his day would be seen to be meaningless nonsense when analyzed pragmatically. In this, I think, his agreement with Carnap would have been complete.

However, because others severed their theories of metaphysics so sharply from the realm of human experience and action does not mean that the rest of us must follow them in this folly. That brings us to the second place in which metaphysics could appear: in conceptions that pass pragmatic muster as having a bearing on possible experience, but which are methodological in character or otherwise so broad as to overarch whole fields of inquiry. Peirce has offered us volumes of his own disciplined yet sometimes speculative thinking in metaphysics. He has theories about basic categories in nature and in human life, theories about relationships between them, from the role of evolutionary theory to inductive methods, probability theory, and philosophy of logic. But all of these theories arise out of the stimulus of experience and the selection and deliberation that follow, and all have consequences for human action. Likewise, all are fallible, but, by the same token, corrigible, and Peirce offered them in the spirit of an inquirer who hopes others will carry on the investigations he has begun and find his results to be true or false or the basis for something better.

In sharp contrast to this approach, however, the positivist program is an extension of the medieval empirical maxim I cited above.[25] On the version worked out in *The Logical Structure of the World*, Carnap, like Peirce, begins with the given particulars of experience. And, like Peirce, he sees these immediate experiences as unanalyzed and unanalyzable *as given*. But the difference arises here. Carnap, identifying the experiences in terms of place and time, takes them as particulars to serve as the elements in the construction of concepts, using what he calls the "quasi-analysis" of classes and relation extensions, which is "quasi," he says, because, following Frege and Russell, such things as classes are fictions, but convenient to talk about. Thus, in the sentence 'Fido is a dog', 'Fido' is a "proper name," standing for a particular individual, and 'dog' is a class or "quasi object" or "general object." It is called the latter because it, too, can serve as the subject of a sentence, as in 'Dogs are mammals'. Carnap explains:

> In the original usage of signs, the subject position of a sentence must always be occupied by a proper name. However, it proved advantageous to admit into the subject position also signs for general objects and, finally, also other incomplete symbols. This improper use, however, is permissible only when a transformation into proper use is possible, i.e., if the sentence can be translated into one or more sentences which have only proper names in their subject positions. More about this later.

This form of nominalism, he wrote:

> concerns only the problem of the *logical function* of symbols (words) which designate general objects. The question whether these designata have reality (in the metaphysical sense) is not thereby answered in the negative, but is not even posed . . .[26]

And at the end it turns out that a question which cannot be posed "constructively" (that is, using the elements and methods Carnap here proposes), is metaphysical in the sense of not belonging within rational science:

> *The (second) concept of reality cannot be constructed in an experiential constructional system; this characterizes it as a nonrational, metaphysical concept.*[27]

Thus, while the verifiability principle sounds very relaxed about the manner in which a sentence is to be verified: "the meaning of a sentence is given by the conditions of its verification"—in practice I think Carnap regarded statements as verifiable only if they were capable of being constructed or reconstructed (in the above manner or in later analogous ways). For it is only by carrying out the construction that you put yourself in a position to understand the "conditions . . . of verification": namely the way in which the basic elements of the system, immediate experiences in this first version, are embedded in the logical structure.

For our purposes we may ignore the changes that occurred from time to time in Carnap's view of what ought to be taken as the basic elements in the process of construction, and what the details of that process ought to be. For the role of metaphysics here is clear. To the extent that its claims can be analyzed constructively, it is a part of science, and at the end of *The Logical Structure of the World* Carnap spells out some aspects of realism, idealism, and phenomenalism that are entirely consonant with what he there calls "construction theory." And to the extent that its claims cannot be analyzed constructively they can have no rational basis in experience, and we have no alternative but to regard them as nonempirical, meaningless, empty, irrational, and, well, *metaphysical*. For, by dint of much effort, that is what the positivists succeeded in convincing many that the word 'metaphysics' meant.

In spite of that fact, however, a host of questions remain which seem metaphysical in character but not meaningless, for some choice among them is required, and the choices have different consequences. For example, there is the choice of the base used in the construction or reconstruction, and the reasons offered for making that choice. Carnap, after his original choice of immediate personal or "auto-psychological" experience, favored, in turn, a physical object base, a "heteropsychological" base limited to the observations of trained scientists, and sensations treated in Mach's style. I gather Wittgenstein made the same original choice in the first version of the *Tractatus*.[28] Or, to put the question in another way, given the syntax of "protocol sentences," "elementary sentences," or "basic propositions," some decision must be made about their semantic interpretation. While Carnap occasionally said they were equivalent, or that it did not matter what choice one made, or that he favored linguistic tolerance in these matters, he always made a choice, and, once made, generally treated it as a stipulation, convention, or, indeed, a matter of protocols.

The same sort of problem arises with the logic of the construction process. Carnap did not choose his title, *The Logical Structure of the World*, lightly nor as a joke. But is the logic of Frege, Russell and Whitehead, and Hilbert *the* logic of the world? While those, say, of Lewis, are not? Is it the logic of the world in the same sense in which philosophers once took Euclid's geometry to be the geometry of the world? By what considerations is one to defend the thesis of extensionality? Or attack it? And, indeed, within the work of the logical structure many other questions arise, for there are many places where choices may be made. Carnap, as we saw, described these as "framework" questions, and was content to see them settled by convention, by stipulation, or perhaps even by a vote of the scientists concerned. For, like Peirce, he thought of himself as a scientist, and he hated bickering.

But these "framework" questions turn out to be the same sort that Peirce found to remain in metaphysics once it had been purged of those issues in which human experience had no bearing whatever. These are the questions of methodology or of content that overarch entire fields of inquiry: theories about basic catagories in nature and in human life and the relationships between them. Once one has chosen a logical framework, the categories fall out. But has one made the right choice? And how can one tell? The difference in the approach of these two philosophers is that in Carnap's theory no method is provided: the questions are to be settled in some arbitrary or conventional manner; whereas on Peirce's theory they are treated as higher-order scientific theories and must stand or fall on the consequences of our using them. On such matters, Carnap's way brings inquiry to a halt, for there is no way of testing a convention. And for Peirce, one could do nothing worse than to halt inquiry. Likewise he would see no need to do so, for, on his view, concepts have endless consequences for human action. So while no single investigator may hope to be sure he is right on any matter, the community of science, which crosses the borders of generations as well as of nations, can be confident that the widening circle of human action and experience would eventually lead us to sensory outcomes that would bring us to reject or embrace any theory we had come to entertain under the pragmatic maxim, no matter how abstract or metaphysical it might be. Framework questions, like those of basic categories of nature, can be expected to have such consequences also, and even though no quick answer can be expected, they should be asked and inquiry pressed forward.

On this issue I think Peirce is right and on methodological grounds. It cannot be rational to prefer a conventional answer to one resting on the tests of experience where the question is a cognitive one. Conventions are appropriate where it truly makes no difference which choice is made so long as everyone abides by it, as, for example, on which side of the road to drive. An approach which leaves us with major philosophical issues to be settled in this way is seriously lacking. And the result is especially ironic, for the chief aim of the verification principle is to ensure that every substantive cognitive theory be made to stand the test of experience, while the consequence of applying it has been to exempt from this test our most far-reaching theories. On Peirce's approach, no theory is ever exempt, and the processes of testing and recasting theories, even those concerning frameworks, can be continued as long as there are inquirers with imagination, wit, and means to do so and a scholarly community for them to work in.

Closely related to this issue is the manner in which the question of meaningfulness is attacked on the two approaches. If we ask this question for some problematic theory using Carnap's method of construction or any of its kin, we find that a definitive answer is not easy to come by. We are to "analyze" the theory by taking its complex sentences apart into their simpler components until we come to the simplest of all, which will express the empirical content of the theory. For on this approach, empirical meaningfulness is modelled rather closely on deduction. For a sound deduction we must begin with premises that are true, and then proceed with one valid deductive step after another until, if we are able, we reach the desired conclusion. Since deduction is a truth-conserving process and we have begun it from true premises, we can rest assured our conclusion will have that same desirable quality. On the positivist approach, in order to have an empirically meaningful statement one must begin with elementary statements that have empirical content, then proceed step by step in a manner that preserves without adding to this content until, if we are successful, we reach the desired conclusion. Since we started with elements that had empirical content and used a content-conserving method, we cannot fail to have a conclusion with that same desirable quality.

This approach, however, collides directly with Peirce's denial that what is "given" is fully determinate or something that can be symbolized. As I have tried to delineate above, he sees experiences to be complex things that happen to us, so to speak. They impel us to action, and out of this action more experiences arise. From this welter, and on the basis of our needs or inclinations, we select elements to classify, categorize, and express in symbols as may suit our needs or inclinations. It is only in the form of symbols, which are tokens of types, as he put it, that information from experience is available to us intellectually. But in this form they are no longer what is "given," and hence can serve as guarantors of nothing. Their conservation through the constructive process as an attempt to preserve a precious commodity—the information supplied by nature—is pointless. For we may make mistakes in selection and classification, and even more mistakes in communication, both with ourselves and others.

Since selection is already a theoretical activity, on Peirce's view one could not distinguish between theoretical and observation languages; this is a point Dewey, Feyerabend, and Kuhn have made more recently. And to adopt protocols for the expression of observations is as arbitrary as to adopt conventions for the solution of framework questions: both halt the inquiry of testing against experience whether that protocol or convention works best in the long run. Indeed, it is Peirce's view that the only way to reduce the effect of these errors is to join with others in subjecting our theories to the test of future experiences as we act on the basis of them.

Nevertheless, prodigious efforts were made to carry out the constructive program. If we think of the successes of the products of those efforts as tests of the merits of the constructive program, seen as a problem of which framework or metaphysics we ought to adopt, pragmatism would forecast some difficulties. And there have been some. Indeed, if we take the constructive program as a wholesome remedy to be applied to determine whether some problematic theory is verifiable, difficulties at once arise. To begin with, theories in science and practical affairs are not susceptible of such analysis: they are not put together using those components and methods. Although some complained about this, saying that Carnap did not really understand science, the remedy was straightforward. On the one hand, scientist could be encouraged to become methodologically enlightened and adopt these methods of "theory construction" in their new work, and, on the other, philosophers familiar with science could tackle theories already in existence and "reconstruct" them along these lines. And any historian of philosophy looking at the work of the past three decades would have to record the fact that a great deal of both of these activities went on.

But, again, serious difficulties arose. That same historian would have to record that while methodological enlightenment of the positivist kind became widely diffused throughout the sciences, it led to little in the way of the "construction" of new theories. And while a great deal of energy and ingenuity have been focused on the "reconstructive" process, a host of technical difficulties has plagued the effort, with the result that no theory has yet been "reconstructed" in a way to satisfy those working in the field, which, in the end, was Carnap's goal—although much work is still being done. However, it is not my purpose to discuss these difficulties or dwell on the problems with a doleful face, but, rather, to look at a single difference between the pragmatic maxim and the verifiability principle that is significant in this context.

Bearing in mind that we need to determine of some problematic theory whether it is verifiable or not, we can, first, set aside the easy case of a theory that has already been verified. If it has already been verified, it is certainly verifiable, but its verifiability would no longer be of interest. While that would be a fine scientific solution not to be scoffed at, we were promised a method to determine the verifiability of a theory that did not rest on its actual verification. Assuming that successful constructions or reconstructions were available, a theory would be verifiable if, when constructive analysis were applied to it, that analysis would lead us to its empirical base: to the precise experiences we could expect to have if the theory were true and we were in a position to test it. When those experiences have been spelled out explicitly and precisely, then, on the principle of verifiability, we know the theory is verifiable. If they cannot be specified, we are to conclude the theory is meaningless.

But here difficulties of just the sort that would be predicted by the pragmatic maxim begin to arise. They are of two sorts. First, while one can determine a portion of the consequences of a problematic theory in terms of what we ought to be able to observe under specified circumstances should it be true, these will not be all the observational consequences, for new ones are continually discovered as action or inquiry continue. This is as true of practical affairs as of science. There is no shortage of politicians who have been trapped by the unimagined outcomes of their policies. Beck, Feyerabend, Kuhn, and others have shown that it is characteristic of science that new empirical consequences of theories arise unpredictably as research and practice continue.[29] Yet the meaning of the theory, on the constructivist view, consists in just those observational consequences specified. There can be no "surplus" meaning; the discovery of new consequences ought not to be possible.

Second, when a new theory is developed it is often impossible to foresee just what its observational consequences might be. The new theory will have consequences of several kinds, and may have connections with already existing theories. But observational consequences may take some time to develop, and frequently require the corollary invention of new skills and techniques, as well as new intermediary theories. This has been true with the theoretical considerations that led Dirac to the concept of anti-matter, Morgan to genes, and Einstein to the general relativity theory and the unified field theory. At the time these theories were proposed, their authors were not in a position to specify their observational consequences, nor could they have reasonably been in a positon to foresee them. In fact, in the case of unified field theory we are still some distance from being able to specify the exact observations to be expected, for existing equipment is still too inaccurate by an order of magnitude, and the precise form that adequate equipment might take has not yet been envisaged.

In contrast, on the pragmatic maxim, while the meaning lies in the experienced consequences of a theory just as it does on the verifiability principle, these are endless, and there can, thus, be no requirement to spell them all out in advance. Not only are there too many, they also depend on our choosing to act in any of an unknown number of ways, and thus there is room for the development of future knowledge, new skills, and now undreamt of technologies—all being coherently linked with the problematic theory we started with.

While the possibilities for the synthesis of pragmatic and positivistic insights into a truly scientific empiricism were not realized in Carnap's day, they are still in our hands to be used as we and our posterity see fit. If the work of classic positivism has been arbitrary in its treatment of the place of observation in knowledge and in subjecting its own theories to the test of experience, I have tried to show that it shares with classic pragmatism the same attitudes toward science as a model for philosophic work. Carnap wrote in the Preface to the first edition of the *Logical Structure of the World*:

> The basic orientation and line of thought of this book are not property and achievement of the author alone but belong to a certain scientific atmosphere which is neither created nor maintained by any single individual. . . . The new type of philosophy has arisen in close contact with the work of the special sciences, especially mathematics and physics. Consequently they have taken the strict and responsible orientation of the scientific investigator as their guideline for philosophical work . . . . The individual no longer undertakes to erect in one bold stroke an entire system of philosophy. Rather, each works at his special place within the one unified science . . . . If we allot to the individual in philosophical work as in the special sciences only a partial task, then we can look with more confidence into the future: in slow careful construction insight after insight will be won. Each collaborator contributes only what he can endorse and justify before the whole body of his coworkers. Thus stone will be carefully added to stone and a safe building will be erected at which each following generation can continue to work.

And then:

> We feel that there is an inner kinship between the attitude on which our philosophical work is founded and the intellectual attitude which presently manifests itself in entirely different walks of life; we feel this orientation in artistic movements, especially in architecture, and in movements which strive for meaningful forms of external organization in general. We feel all around us the same basic orientation, the same style of thinking and doing. It is an orientation which demands clarity everywhere, but which realizes that the fabric of life can never quite be comprehended. It makes us pay careful attention to detail and at the same time recognizes the great lines which run through the whole. It is an orientation which acknowledges the bonds that tie men together, but at the same time strives for free development of the individual. Our work is carried by the faith that this attitude will win the future.[30]

Thus did Carnap join his high hopes for scientific philosophy with the *Bauhaus* and the *Erklärung*. Much has happened in the half century since this optimistic statement of 1928. Entirely independently, it shares many of the thoughts of Peirce in 1868. And in 1982 philosophy has taken on some of the lineaments both men envisioned. Perhaps Charles Morris was not wrong after all: just too early.

David Gruender

Florida State University

NOTES

*A version of this paper was delivered to the Edgar Henderson Memorial Symposium on the Philosophy of Charles S. Peirce held at Florida State University, May, 1980. I am indebted to its discussants.

1. Charles Morris, "On the History of the International Encyclopedia of Unified Sciences," in *Logic and Language: Studies Dedicated to Professor Rudolf Carnap on the Occasion of His Seventieth Birthday* (Dordrecht: D. Reidel Publishing Co., 1962), p. 242.

2. Rudolf Carnap, "Testability and Meaning," *Philosophy of Science,* 3 (1936): 419–71; 4 (1937): 1–40.

3. Rudolf Carnap, *Der Logische Aufbau der Welt* (Berlin: Weltkreis-Verlag, 1928); *The Logical Structure of the World,* tr. George A. Rolf, (Berkeley: University of California Press, 1967), bound with *Pseudoproblems in Philosophy.*

4. Rudolf Carnap, "Intellectual Autobiography" in Paul Arthur Schilpp, ed. *The Philosophy of Rudolf Carnap*, vol. 11, Library of Living Philosophers (La Salle, IL: Open Court, 1963), p. 45.

5. Rudolf Carnap, *Scheinprobleme in der Philosophie* (Berlin: Weltkreis-Verlag, 1928); *Pseudoproblems in Philosophie,* tr. George A. Rolf, (Berkeley: University of California Press, 1967), bound with *The Logical Structure of the World.*

6. Rudolf Carnap, "Ueberwindung der Metaphysik durch logische Analyse der Sprache" *Erkenntnis,* 2 (1931–32): 219–41; "Elimination of Metaphysics Through Logical Analysis of Language," tr. Arthur Pap in A. J. Ayer, ed., *Logical Positivism* (New York: Macmillan Publishing Co., 1959), pp. 60–81.

7. Rudolf Carnap, "The Methodological Character of Theoretical Concepts" in Herbert Feigl and Michael Scriven, eds., *The Foundations of Science and the Concepts of Psychology and Psychoanalysis,* vol. 1 of the Minnesota Studies in the Philosophy of Science (Minneapolis: University of Minnesota Press, 1956), pp. 38–76.

8. Carnap, *Structure,* p. vii.

9. Rudolf Carnap, "Empiricism, Semantics, and Ontology," *Revue internationale de philosophie,* 4 (1950): 20–40; reprinted in Leonard Linsky, *Semantics and the Philosophy of Language,* (Urbana: University of Illinois Press, 1952), and elsewhere.

10. Elsewhere in this issue.

11. See Immanuel Kant, *Critique of Pure Reason,* ch. 3 of the Transcendental Doctrine of Judgment, beginning about A236, B295.

12. Charles Sanders Peirce, *Collected Papers of Charles Sanders Peirce,* ed. by Charles Hartshorne and Paul Weiss (Cambridge, MA: Harvard University Press, 1931) and later, 5.310 (The first digit refers to the volume number; those after the decimal point refer to the item number).

13. Peirce, *Collected Papers,* 5.18; E. F. Kaelin helped me with the French.

14. 5.438.

15. 5.2

16. 5.3.

17. 5.18.

18. 5.434.

19. 5.467.

20. 5.289.

21. 5.264–5.

22. 5.305.

23. 5.506.

24. Willard Van Orman Quine, *Word and Object* (Cambridge: MIT Press, 1960), ch. 2.

25. The program is pretty well laid out by William of Ockham (c 1280–1349). See *The Philosophical Writings of William of Ockham*, ed. & tr. Theophilous Boehner (Edinburgh: Thomas Nelson & Sons, 1937).

26. *Structure*, pp. 49–50.

27. *Structure*, p. 283.

28. Personal Communication from G. H. Von Wright.

29. Lewis White Beck, "Constructions and Inferred Entities," *Philosophy of Science*, 17 (1950).

30. *Structure*, pp. xvi–xviii.

PEIRCE ON ABSTRACTION

Events in the history of thought have often moved as elements of drama—now tense, now tragic, now triumphant. And, it would appear, sometimes ludicrous. This latter is the thrust of a parody which Molière visited upon the savants of his day; he pictures a candidate for a medical degree being solemnly asked why opium puts people to sleep. Just as solemnly and sagaciously, the candidate replies:

> Quia est in eo,
> Virtus Dormitiva,
> Cujus est natura,
> Sensus assopire.

This incisive and revealing answer—that opium puts people to sleep "because there is in it a dormitive power whose nature it is to lull the senses to sleep"— is greeted by a happy congratulatory chorus: "You have responded well indeed, you are most worthy to join our learned brotherhood!"

Peirce refers explicitly to this scene in one location (5.534),[1] and mentions opium and its "dormitive virtue" *passim*, especially in his later writings. The scene from *Le Malade Imaginaire*, of course, ridicules an affected scholarship which conceals its ignorance even from itself with explanations that don't explain; the implicit argument of the parody is that (1) Opium puts people to sleep; and (2) Opium has dormitive power; are essentially equivalent statements, and that if (2) adds anything to (1), it is the hypostatized fiction of a power which deadens not only the senses of those who actually take the dope, but also the critical abilities of those who speak seriously of such powers. The criticism is not unlike that directed more recently by behaviorists against "mentalism" in psychology, with so-called uncritical hypostatizations such as "mind," "freedom," and even "grammar" taking the place of "dormitive power."

Peirce placed his pragmatist's emphasis on the role of possible observable effects in the explication of concepts (5.402), and he was clear in his opposition to what might be called "Cartesian mentalism" (see, e.g., 5.264 ff.); we might expect him, then, to jeer with Molière at the perversion of explanation expressed in this burlesque of an oral exam. Interestingly and emphatically, however, he does not jeer; he writes that this scene

> is a poignant satire, because everybody is supposed to know well enough that the transformation from a *concrete predicate* to an abstract noun in an oblique case,

> is a mere transformation of language that leaves the thought absolutely un-
> touched. I knew this as well as everybody else until I had arrived at that point in
> my analysis of mathematics where I found that this despised juggle of abstraction
> is an essential part of almost every really helpful part of mathematics; and since
> then, what I used to know so very clearly does not appear to be at all so.[2]

This is the mature Peirce speaking, and most of the material we will draw upon is from his later work. Before we get into a detailed study of that, however, we shall look briefly at some of his early mentions of abstraction, and will make clear which of the different historical concepts of abstraction is of concern to him. The detailed study of his treatment of the topic will begin by examining the way abstraction interacts in his thought with his concept of "theorematic reasoning"; we then consider abstraction and "contextualism" or "perspectivalism" in Peirce's thought. After looking briefly at the relationship of abstraction to *entia rationis*, we move through the contrast between the abstract and the concrete to an examination of abstraction and Peircean thirdness; this includes an indication of how the concept fits into Peirce's semiotic.

Possibility is also associated with abstraction in Peirce's writing; I sketch the outlines of a fit between these concepts. Finally, as a link to more recent thought and a further elucidation of Peircean abstraction, I examine abstraction in connection with some topics from recent linguistic theory and from Gestalt theory.

Peirce mentions abstraction at least as early as the 1867 "On a New List of Categories" (see 1.549); another early reference (1868) is given in 2.422. In these locations, he apparently fails to make an important distinction which he is clear about in his later writings, as for example, about 1901:

> A decrease in supposed information may have the effect of diminishing the depth
> of a term without increasing its information. This is often called *abstraction*; but
> it is far better to call it *prescission*; for the word *abstraction* is wanted as the
> designation of an even far more important procedure, whereby a transitive ele-
> ment of thought is made substantive, as in the grammatical change of an adjec-
> tive into an abstract noun. This may be called the chief engine of mathematical
> thought. (2.364)

Prescission is the process in which blue, green, and red balls are all recognized as spherical, and German Shepherds and Chihuahuas are both recognized as dogs. We *prescind from* the color, say, and, considering only the shapes, recognize the sameness of all balls in this regard. Peirce suggests in this passage that we *not* think of this process as abstraction, but reserve *that* term for the process which enables us to speak of the "dormitive virtue" of opium.

The 1867 and 1868 locations (1.549, 2.422) appear to ignore the abstraction/prescission distinction. It might be tempting to see this as evidence of an essential difference in treatment of this topic from the early to the late Peirce. The early Peirce recognized the distinction, however, at least so far as the *products* of the two processes are concerned; in an 1868 letter to the editor of the *Journal of Speculative Philosophy* he writes:

> You have apparently understood me as applying the term "abstract" to any concept the result of abstraction. But as I intimated [see 6.620], I adopt that acceptation in which "whiteness" is said to be abstract and "white" concrete. (6.627)

It would seem that Peirce here is following the historical and ambiguous tradition of calling both prescission and the transformation from "white" to "whiteness" abstraction, while being clear about the difference between the results of the processes, and so between the equivocally named processes themselves.

Peirce was later to become very clear about naming the processes; I note one other passage, from a 1904 letter to E. H. Moore:

> There are two entirely different things that are often confused from no cause that I can see except that the words *abstract* and *abstraction* are applied to both. One is αφαιρεσις leaving something out of account in order to attend to something else. That is *precisive* abstraction. The other consists in making a subject out of a predicate. Instead of saying, Opium puts people to sleep, you say it has dormitive virtue. This is an important proceeding in mathematics. For example, take all "symbolic" methods, in which operations are operated upon. This may be called *subjectal abstraction.*[3]

Peirce also (and more frequently) calls that process "hypostatic abstraction." It is hypostatic or subjectal abstraction that Peirce is interested in; a hint as to *why* he is interested in it is given in his allusions in these passages to mathematical reasoning; we shall develop this aspect of abstraction at length.

Jaakko Hintikka has done us the great service of bringing to our attention[4] and tying to contemporary experience one of Pierce's central observations about necessary—which is to say mathematical—reasoning: this is that nontrivial deductive reasoning, even in areas where explicit postulates are employed, always

> considers something not implied in the conceptions so far gained [in the particular course of reasoning in question], which neither the definition of the object of research nor anything yet known about could of themselves suggest, although they give room for it.[5]

Such "theorematic reasoning," to use Peirce's term, introduces its novel elements into the reasoning process in the form of icons, which are then "experimented upon in imagination." That "all necessary reasoning is diagrammatic"[6] is a refrain of which the later Peirce seems not to tire; "theorematic reasoning," with its introduction of novelty in diagram, or icon, he contrasts with "corollarial reasoning," which requires the introduction of no *new* icon or construction (the last word suggests, and is intended to suggest, the constructions employed in the proof of the propositions of Euclidian geometry).[7]

Hintikka suggests that "Peirce himself seems to have considered a vindication of the concept of abstraction as the most important application of his discovery [of the theorematic/corollarial distinction]."[8] Peirce would indeed have agreed that the light shed on necessary reasoning by this distinction helps greatly to illuminate the role of abstraction;[9] in fact, so far as the interaction of abstraction and theorematic reasoning is concerned, he remarks that

> the operation of abstraction, in the proper sense of the term . . . turns out to be so essential to the greater strides of mathematical demonstration that it is proper to divide all theorematic reasoning into the Non-abstractional and the abstractional. I am able to prove that the most practically important results of mathematics could not in any way be attained without this operation of abstraction.[10]

For Peirce, as we have noted, all necessary reasoning is diagrammatic, where "a diagram is a representamen which is predominantly an icon of relations" (4.418) and

> one can make exact experiments upon uniform diagrams; and when one does so, one must keep a bright lookout for unintended and unexpected changes thereby brought about in the relations of different significant parts of the diagram to one another. Such operations upon diagrams, whether external or imaginary, take the place of the experiments upon real things that are performed in chemical and physical research . . . . experiments upon diagrams are questions put to the nature of the relations concerned. (4.530)

To recast some of our remarks in language that Dewey, say, might have used: where the diagrams involved are already apart of the unproblematic in inquiry, the reasoning involving them is corollarial; where the synthetic reconstruction or generation[11] of the needed diagrams is *itself* part of the problematic, the reasoning is theorematic. The diagrams or icons so supplied and employed are, of course, signs, and so have objects.[12] Now, these objects might be abstract, but let us examine a case in which the objects have a non-abstract character. I have a little 3-D puzzle; the assembly steps for for it must be executed in a given order. To get it together, I must assemble in my head a model—an icon or related set of icons—of the spatial and temporal relations involved in the assembly. My production of these icons and my experimentation on them are aided by the ongoing assembly of the puzzle itself, but the icons involved are unquestionably distinct from the puzzle, as signs are distinct from their objects. The object of the icons here is the puzzle-in-assembly. Insofar as the icons are novel, the necessary reasoning based on them is theorematic, on my analysis. But it seems reasonable to think of that reasoning as what Peirce calls "Non-abstractional" theorematic reasoning, because, in this case, of the actual existent nature of the object.[13] Comparable "abstractional reasoning" might involve an investigation of the relations between properties of puzzles, using statements like "The difficulty of a puzzle is proportional to its complexity," or some such; note, for future reference, the generality of this last statement compared to those about a concrete puzzle. I note, by the way, that the puzzle-in-assembly itself is not "non-abstract" in some absolute sense; more on this anon.

Let us look now at some more of Peirce's remarks:

> An abstraction is something denoted by a noun substantive, something having a name; and therefore, whether it be a reality or whether it be a figment, it belongs to the category of *substance*, and is in proper philosophical terminology to be called a *substance*, or thing.[14]

However, we might expect that abstractions will differ somewhat from "ordinary things"; after all, "You couldn't load a pistol with dormitive virtue and shoot it into a breakfast roll."[15] So, further,

> An abstraction is a substance whose being consists in the truth of some propositions concerning a more primary substance.
> By a primary substance I mean one whose being is independent of what may be true of anything else. Whether there is any primary substance in this sense or not we may leave to the metaphysicians to wrangle about.[16]

Peirce, I believe, presents the concept of *absolutely* primary substance as a logical "limit point," as a regulative ideal; we need not commit ourselves to a search for such substances[17]—it is enough, I would suggest, that we recognize primacy here as *relative*; from the perspective of ordinary common sense experience, for example, something I can shoot into a breakfast roll has a primacy that "dormitive virtue" does not; speaking relatively,

> By a *more* primary substance I mean one whose being does not depend on all that the being of the less primary substance does, but only on a part thereof.[18]

As a mathematical example, Peirce suggests the relationship between a point and a line;[19] if we think of lines, or filaments, as *loci* of moving points, or particles, then

> if the particles be conceived as primary substances, the filaments are abstractions, that is, they are substances the being of any one of which consists in something being true of some more primary substance or substances none of them identical with this filament.[20]

It is obvious that what Peirce is calling abstraction figures in a most fundamental way in the definition of mathematical concepts. Note that in a mathematical discipline there is often considerable freedom as to which con-

cepts are considered "primitive"—thus what is considered "primary substance" in the above sense is really a matter of *perspective* or *context*. We
may contrast this with the absolutistic reductionism of, for example, *Principia Mathematica*.

What we are saying applies as well in the physical sciences. Classical
mechanics nowadays is commonly taught as a meter/kilogram/second
system; length, mass, and time are primitives from this viewpoint, and force
(as well as other relevant concepts) is defined in terms of them. But I learned
theoretical engineering mechanics in a foot/pound/second format; English
vs. metric is not at issue in this case. What *is* is that "pound" here is a unit of
force rather than mass. There is no problem: the unit of mass (a "slug,"
which weighs about 32.2 pounds on the surface of the earth) is defined in
terms of length, *force*, and time, and we are in business. These examples fit
well with Peirce's desire to leave absolutely primary substance "for the
metaphysicians to wrangle about." This suggests that implicit in Peirce's
theory of abstraction is a perspectival approach to reality akin to that made
explicit by, say, Charles Morris in his "Objective Relativism."[21]* Indeed,
Peirce carries his theory beyond mathematics or theoretical physics:

> Atoms are supposed to have existences independent of one another. But in
> that case according to our definition of an *abstraction*, a collection of atoms, such
> as are all the things we see and handle are [*sic*] *abstractions*.[22]

So it would be wrong to think of abstractions as purely and always fictions:

> to deny every mode of being to anything whose being consists in some other fact
> would be to deny every mode of being to tables and chairs, since the being of a
> table depends on the being of the atoms of which it is composed, and not *vice-
> versa*. (4.463)

I wish to emphasize that Peirce is not advocating the naive reductionism
which claims that what a table *really* is is mostly empty space with appropriate molecules at strategic locations; he refuses to "deny every mode of
being" to macro-physical objects, and the passage just quoted may be taken
as a defense of the reality of at least certain "abstractions." Also, I note that
Peirce is not here "arguing to" the existence of tables and chairs. This is a
matter of brute secondness, which sets the boundaries within which a theory
of abstraction must operate, rather than *vice-versa*. I would suggest even
further that since the evidence for and about atoms is secured and processed
mediately compared to the evidence for and about tables and chairs, there are
perspectives from which the atoms may be considered the abstractions and
the tables and chairs the "primary substances." That that which is considered
primary substance in this theory of abstraction is a matter of perspective or

* Editor's Note: the term "Objective Relativism" was coined by Arthur E. Murphy in 1927, in an article Entitled "Objective
Relativism in Dewey and Whitehead." *Philosophical Review*, 36 (1927), pp. 121–44.

context rather than an absolute stance for Peirce finds support in another passage—I note that this passage and the associated preceding ones were written very close together (about 1903). In discussing collections, which he sees as an important class of abstraction, Peirce remarks that

> According to the definition [of collection], there must be a collection of luminaries of the day. But there happens to be only one luminary of the day; namely, the Sun. Here, then, is a collection having but one member. Is not that collection the Sun itself? I reply, certainly not. For a collection is an *ens rationis*. Its being consists in the truth of something. But the Sun is not an *ens rationis* and its being does not consist in the truth of any proposition. It consists in the act of brute force in which it reacts with everything in its neighborhood.[23]

Here the sun—which is as much a matter of atoms as is my table—is placed in the position of "primary substance"—primary with respect to the abstraction which is its singleton set. In the context of the previous passages, I take this as strong evidence that at least implicit in Peirce's theory of abstraction is a "radical perspectivalism." This is hardly the most thoroughly examined aspect of Peirce's philosophy, but it fits well with the broader context of his work as well as with the empirical methodology of pragmatism in general.

Note that the above quoted passage speaks of *entia rationis*; I will mention that Peirce in this period uses the terms 'ens rationis' and 'abstraction' (the product of the process) virtually synonymosly; 4.463 (earlier quoted) also uses 'ens rationis'; there he speaks of an *ens rationis* as having "its being [consist] in some other fact." In 4.463 he clearly speaks of *entia rationis* as the end products of abstraction. In the lecture just before quoted[24] he relates 'collection' and 'abstraction'; in 5.534 he reminds us that "a collection is an hypostatic abstraction, or *ens rationis*"[25]; similar juxtapositions and interchangable usages occur *passim*. It is clear that the product of hypostatic abstraction is, for Peirce, an *ens rationis* (see 3.642 for another example); whether he recognized other *entia rationis* than abstractions might possibly be considered an open question; my present belief, however, is that it is safe to identify the Peircian *ens rationis* with the product of his hypostatic abstraction, which emerges as a process of exceptionally broad applicability; the nature of this broad applicability will, I think begin to emerge in what follows.

It is very common to contrast the *abstract* with the *concrete*; you have perhaps noted that so far, very little has been explicitly said about this; although Peirce often speaks of abstraction, he less often places it explicitly in contrast with the concrete. When he does, he is most likely to refer to the predicate which enters into the definition of the abstraction as concrete—he notes that "*hard* is concrete and *hardness* is abstract"[26]; in the first quoted passage of this paper, he speaks of hypostatic abstraction as "the transformation of a *concrete predicate* into an abstract noun."[27] The relationship of the abstract to the concrete is closely connected to that between the abstraction and the "more primary substances" or namable things upon which the abstraction's "being" depends, in that the concrete predication contrasted with a given abstraction is applied to the more primary substances upon which the abstraction in question depends. Although Peirce felt that abstraction was of vital importance in reasoning, he insisted, consistent with the pragmatic maxim (5.402), that the being of abstractions—their semantic meaning—swings on possible effects in the domains where are made the concrete predications associated with those abstractions. Peirce tells us that according to the definition of a proposition,

> the Interpretant of it . . . represents the proposition to be a genuine index of a Real Object, independent of the representation . . . . the definition adds that this Object is a Secondness or real fact. (2.315)

"Real fact" here should not be construed too narrowly; Peirce was always most emphatic about not limiting the real to the actual existent—remember, for example, that we are interested here in the truths of mathematics as well as those of the world of actual existents. Later in the paragraph above cited, Peirce connects experience in a very broad sense "—whether outward experience, or experience of fancies—" with real facts; *possible experience* is the key to the meaningfulness of propositions; that paragraph goes on:

> every kind of proposition is either meaningless or has a Real Secondness as its object. This is a fact that every reader of philosophy should carefully bear in mind, translating every abstractly expressed proposition into its precise meaning in reference to an individual experience. (2.315)

I would suggest that the "Real Seconds" associated with the "meaning in reference to an individual experience" of an abstract proposition are found among the more primary substances upon which the being of the abstraction depends; "real seconds," then, are such relative to appropriate perspectives. Consistent with what I am here suggesting, we find Peirce praising certain pragmatists of his day for

> their insistence upon interpreting all hypostatic abstractions in terms of what they *would* or *might* (not acutally *will*) come to in the concrete. (6.485)

Abstractly stated propositions must be connected with individual experiences. But as the citations above indicate, each abstraction is interpreted in terms of the whole range of possible events or occurrences associated with the concrete predications on which the abstraction is based, from which it is "necessarily inferred" (see 4.463). An abstraction from this viewpoint is a unification of or a continuum between possible occurrences, and so is a thirdness, a generality, a habit; the being of the abstraction is dependent upon concrete occurrences, but *they* are dependent on *it* for their intelligible ordering. Let us look further; discussing symbols, Peirce remarks that

> Every symbol is an *ens rationis*, because it consists in a habit, a regularity; now, every regularity consists in the future conditional occurrence of facts not themselves that regularity. (4.464)

In other words, the being of a habit or regularity consists in the truth of propositions concerning facts, whose being is, in turn, a matter of secondness. Each habit or regularity is, then, an abstraction in the sense we have been developing. But we have already noted that each abstraction may be reasonably considered to be a habit or regularity. This all has the rather remarkable effect of identifying Peirce's theory of abstraction as *a theory of thirdness in general*, which goes a long way toward explaining the extreme broadness of applicability of abstraction in Peirce's view.

Notice that I have not said "*the* theory of thirdness." The intelligible wholes which are thirds present us with a variety of aspects from which we may study and theorize about them; the aspects are related, but emphasize different features of the thirdness in question. As an example, consider mathematical functions. A function may be studied as itself an object with its own structure, composition, relatedness to other functions, etc.; from this point of view, it is an abstraction in Peirce's sense. Secondly, it may be studied in terms of its domain and codomain, as a mapping which involves the possible arguments and values of the function. Thirdly, the function may be considered a *set of instructions* for effecting certain outcomes. This third point of view mediates between that of function as abstract structure and function as a set of domain/codomain ordered pairs. This triadic view, then, considers a thirdness X (in this example, a mathematical function) *first*, from the point of view in which it is an intelligible body of interconnected relations, capable of being represented by icons and fruitfully studied by experimentation on those icons. As such, it is an *abstraction*, whose "being" resides in the concrete events whose conditional possibility is predicted by it. X may, then, also be viewed *concretely*, as the set of those possible events. From this point of view a mathematical function is a set of domain/codomain ordered pairs, and a habit in general is a "bundle" of possible conditioned outcomes or "behaviors." Finally, X may be considered a *regularity*; in the case of the mathematical function, this was the function considered as a set of instructions for effecting certain outcomes; in case the abstraction connected with X is the dormitive power of opium, the regularity connected with X would emphasize that, in general, when opium is administered under given conditions, the subjects predictably tend to go to sleep.

I feel that Peirce's thought considers thirdness from all of these aspects, and that an adequate overall analysis of thirdness demands that all these aspects be appropriately examined; the theory of abstraction focuses primarily on the first of these perspectives.

It seems to me that the analysis in terms of Peirce's categories I have just suggested is very much like that implicit in one of Peirce's own analyses: this is that of his "third trichotomy of signs"—the third, that is, of the ten trichotomies he discusses in his correspondence with Lady Welby.[28] The third trichotomy is a classification of signs based on "The Nature of Their Dynamical Objects" (8.366); I let Peirce comment:

> It is usual and proper to distinguish two Objects of a sign, the Mediate without and the Immediate within the sign. The interpretant is all that the sign conveys: acquaintence with its Object must be gained by collateral experience. The Mediate object is the Object outside the sign; I call it the *Dynamoid*[29] Object. The Sign must indicate it by a hint; and this hint, or its substance, is the *Immediate* Object. Each of these two objects may be said to be capable of either of the three Modalities [possibility, acutality, or necessity], although in the case of the Immediate Object, this is not quite literally true. Accordingly, the Dynamoid Object may be a Possible; when I term the sign an *Abstractive*; such as the word Beauty; and it will be none the less an abstractive if I speak of "the Beautiful," since it is the ultimate reference, and not the grammatical form, that makes the sign an *Abstractive*. When the Dynamoid object is an Occurrence (Existent thing or actual fact of past or future), I term the sign a *Concretive*. . . . For a sign whose Dynamoid Object is a Necessitant, I have no better designation than a "*Collective*," which is not quite so bad a name as it sounds to be until one studies the matter . . . .[30]

It is not surprising that Peirce would have difficulties with the word 'collective' here; he regularly emphasizes that "a collection is an hypostatic abstraction, or *ens rationis*"(5.534), and here he is contrasting "collectives" with "abstractives." Although in his treatment of existential graphs he experiments with notations which distinguish collections from abstractions in general,[31] it is not at all clear that these notational differences correspond to the third trichotomy in any way. I would suggest that Peirce's placement of "collective" in the mediating position in that trichotomy has much the same function as viewing thirdness as regulative has in the analysis I have proposed; taking an object as a collective might—from the viewpoint of the third trichotomy—help me to see it as constituted both *by* ordering principle and *of* individual seconds, and so this view would have the collective mediating between the abstractive and the concretive. Perhaps "Regulative" would be preferable to "Collective" as a name for the third in this trichotomy; this would also tend to reflect the connection with necessity which Peirce wishes to make here.

I would like simply to point out that there is another important Peircean triad which is very closely related to those we are examining: this is his classification of logic as abductive, inductive, and deductive; discussion of this must wait till another time.

The theory of abstraction is a theory of thirdness, but as the above analyses suggest, the thirdness of abstraction is a *first* with respect to certain other viewpoints on thirdness. The "being" of abstractions consists, Peirce tells us, in "what they *would* or *might* (not actually will) come to in the concrete."(6.485) This and the analysis of the third trichotomy point to an element of possibility involved in abstractions; in fact, we find Peirce speaking of "an essential part of the doctrine of Existential Graphs [which] treats of the general properties of qualities and relations."[32] This doctrine, Peirce tells us, is

> the doctrine of *substantive possibility*, because qualities and relations are possibilities of a peculiar kind. In a secondary sense a quality may be said to exist when it has, as it were, a replica in an existing thing. But strictly speaking, a quality does not exist. For to *exist* is to be a subject of blind compulsion. A quality not only neither exerts nor suffers such force, but it cannot even be called an *idea* of the mind. For things possess their qualities just the same, whether anybody thinks so or not. The being of a quality consists in the fact that a thing *might* be such or such like.[33]

We are here reexamining some of the ground we have covered before, but from a slightly different viewpoint. The "doctrine of substantive possibility" which Peirce is discussing is pretty clearly the theory of hypostatic abstraction, with emphasis on the *entia rationis* involved as *possibilities*. It is not uncommon for Peirce to associate quality with possibility (see, for example, 1.304); we find this emphasis explicit in the notion of substantive possibility. I would suggest that this notion of possibility is—like 'abstraction' itself—a touching point between Peirce and the Scholastic tradition with which he sometimes associates his thought; "possibility" in this sense is *potentia esse*, potency to existence. I think that this is clear from the way that Peirce relates the abstract with the concrete; another example, employing language even more scholastic in tone than heretofore, supports this:

> A quality is an *ens rationis*, of course. That is, it consists in a certain proposition having a meaning. The term *essence* means being such as the subject of the essence necessarily is. Quality then has *essence*. But it has no *existence*, because it neither exercises nor suffers brute compulsion.[34]

So quality and hypostatic abstractions are involved with possibility. But we must not assume that all of Peirce's uses of 'possibility' are reducible to, or even similar to this one. We get a monition of this in 4.549, where Peirce mentions sequences of abstractive operations, and seems to imply that based on such sequences may be divisions of the subject matter of logic; he warns us, however,

> that the divisions so obtained must not be confounded with the different Modes of Being: Actuality, Possibility, and Destiny (or Freedom from Destiny). On the contrary, the succession of Predicates of Predicates [and so of hypostatic abstractions] is different in the different Modes of Being. (4.549)

The comment of the editors of vol. 4 that the "Modes of Being" are "usually called categories by Peirce" is only partly to the point; the Modes of Being are specifically the "Universes" represented by the "tinctures" in the 1906 "Prolegomenon to an apology for Pragmaticism"—of which 4.549 is a part—and several other contemporary manuscripts by Peirce. In one such manuscript, Peirce has characterized these "Universes of modes of reality" as the Universe of Real Capacities, the Universe of Actual Fact, and the Universe of tendencies (which he explicitly associates with destiny), and comments that

> the imperative need of the further manifold differentiation of each of them [the three universes] is . . . . apparent. It is clear that the differences are not differences of the *predicates* or *significations* of the graphs, but of the predetermined objects to which the graphs are intended to refer. Consequently, the Iconic idea of the System requires that they should be represented not by differentiations of the Graphs themselves, but by appropriate visible characters of the surfaces upon which the Graphs are recorded.[35]

He then goes on to discuss how to go about varying the characters of the surfaces; the tentative result is his "tinctured existential graphs." The point of this is that tinctured existential graphs is, essentially, one of Peirce's attempts—half a century before Kripke and Prior succeeded—to set up what we recognize as a "possible-world semantics" for the existential graphs.[36] The "predetermined objects" in the above passage, then, will differ not as dormitive virtue differs from opium and breakfast rolls—since dormitive virtue pertains to the same universes as does opium—but as the namable individuals in one possible world in quantified modal logic differ from those in another. In terms of *possibility*, this means that we cannot expect the concept of possibility associated with qualities as "substantive possibility" (i.e., hypostatic abstractions) to automatically coincide with that developed via the possible-worlds approach of the "tinctures."

From my last remarks, it should be clear that Peirce saw the existential graphs as having an important role in the study of hypostatic abstraction; unfortunately, space will not permit a detailed development of this intersection of two of the important areas of the late work of Peirce. Don Roberts has discussed many of the aspects of Peirce's "gamma system of graphs" as they affect the theory of abstraction;[37] I feel that there is room for considerable study in this area, and Roberts's work gives us a good start on this. One aspect of Peirce's gamma graphs that deserves mention here is his use of (implicitly quantified) "lines of identity" to represent qualities and relations (4.470 ff.); this makes the *entia rationis* involved the values of quantified variables, and represents a logical step which reasonably follows the naming of those abstractions. This constitutes another link to the earlier-mentioned work of Hintikka, who employs "higher level" quantification in his explication of Peirce's concept of theorematic reasoning.[38] There are here strong suggestions of the intimacy of the link between theorematic reasoning and abstraction; there remains, I believe, valuable work to be done in this connection.

As I approach the conclusion of this effort, I would like to comment on some connections between the material I have been investigating and some other matters of contemporary interest, and in the process, cast more light upon hypostatic abstraction itself. First of all, we have seen Peirce both explicitly and implicitly treat the process of abstraction as a grammatical transformation. In contemporary language popular in some circles and controversial in many (but of indubitable import), the movement to an abstraction is like the mapping from a "deep" to a "surface" structure in transformational grammar; indeed, we might consider it an *example* of such a transformation. Whatever the flux and controversy surrounding transformational grammars, it is clear that in the transformations therein considered, there must be a continuity of *meaning* in some sense of the term between the "deep" structures and the structures on which they are mapped. (I might insert that for such a theory to make sense, it must also account for differences in use—and so, some of us would say, meaning—between such structures.) The simplest kind of situation here is that in which the deep and the surface structures are both assertions; in many important cases we would expect such assertions to be true and false under the same conditions, that is, to be semantically equivalent. This is so of the active to passive transformation of

(1) Opium puts people to sleep.

to

(3) People are put to sleep by opium.

It is also true of the kind of transformation central to this paper, from (1) to

(2) Opium has dormitive power.

If anything is clear about Peirce's view of the relationship of (1) to (2), it is that there is a difference between them; that the difference is not semantic we have indicated. To give the question a Jamesian twist: "What, then, is the difference that *makes* the difference?" It seems to me that the answer to this would be relevant not only to Peirce's theory of abstraction, but to contemporary discussions of language in general.

Actually, for all the head-scratching that this kind of question has caused, the answer, from an authentic Peircean point of view, is close at hand: "Consider what effects . . . ," says the pragmatic maxim (5.402 again). Specifically, consider the effects of a sign insofar as it paricipates in semiosis—consider its *interpretants*. Peirce's repeated insistence that the "being" of an abstraction consists in the truth of statements about "more primary substances" is a recognition that semantically—so far as their objects[39] are concerned—(1) and (2) are equivalent. But he also insists that we *gain* something by use of the abstraction—our reasoning about the relations involved in the object of our study is facilitated, sometimes dramatically. This is an effect of the use of the abstractive signs; it is an effect arising in the use of these signs as signs, and so is among their interpretants. The effect is a disposition, a *habit* regulative of reasoning behavior, and so is a final logical interpretant.(5.491) Here is a point at which it is useful to draw on some Morrisian terminology, specifically, Morris's distinction between the syntactic, semantic, and pragmatic dimensions of semiotic.[40] While the abstractive and nonabstractive assertions have the same meaning on the semantic dimension, they differ, often considerably, on the pragmatic dimention, which depends on the relation of the sign to its interpretants. One of the advantages of introducing Morris's terminology is that it is in fairly general use, and so gives us continuity with terminology likely to be employed in the continuing dialogue on language. In fact, we now find Chomsky commenting that

> It makes sense, I think, to distinguish what is sometimes called "grammatical competence" from "pragmatic competence." . . . Pragmatic competence underlies our ability to use [knowledge of form and meaning in language] along with the conceptual system to achieve certain ends or purposes. It might be that pragmatic competence is characterized by a certain system of constitutive rules represented in the mind, as has been suggested in a number of studies.[41]

Chomsky uses 'meaning' here in the sense of semantic meaning. The uses to which signs are put are directly correlative with the effects these signs have when used as signs—their interpretants; Chomsky and I are then talking about the same things. That consideration of pragmatic competence is essential for Chomsky in 1980 is indicated by his remark that

> I assume that it is possible in principle for a person to have full grammatical competence and no pragmatic competence, hence no ability to use a language appropriately, though its syntax and semantics are intact.[42]

Whether or not one can have grammatical competence without any pragmatic competence might be argued; nevertheless, it is clear that in any case, without pragmatic competence the language could not be used, and so would be effectively "absent." So my suggestion that the difference made by hypostatic abstraction is a component of meaning on the pragmatic dimension isn't only reasonable in relation to Peirce scholarship, but in the context as well of the most recent thought in the contemporary theory of linguistics.

We have seen Peirce state that "An abstraction is something denoted by a noun substantive, something having a name."[43] All of Peirce's talk of substance in this context, in fact, is talk of *namable* things, insofar as they are namable. Naming, as part of language, is a human process whose peduncles merge in prehistory with the mythically expressed efforts of humans to understand and control their environment. Cassirer, commenting on these mythic roots of culture, observes that "He who knows the true name of a god or demon has unlimited power over the bearer of the name."[44] So we name *entia rationis*, and gain power over the intelligibilities implicated in them. Of course, we do not see the bare naming as constitutive of that power; Cassirer again remarks that

> It is the name which introduces the first factor of constancy and permanence into this manifold; the identity of the name is the preliminary step, an anticipation of the identity of the logical concept.[45]

Naming is one aspect of a larger process, that of *attending* to significant organizations of data in our interactions with our environment; for Peirce,

> Attention is a certain modification of the contents of consciousness with respect to a centre. This centre is where there is a strong sense-will reaction, which imparts to the idea the nature of an index (weathercock, sign-post, or other blind, forcible connection between thought and thing). Now, the subject of a proposition is just such an index. Hence the real phenomenon of attending to a quality, say white, or making it the centre of thought, consists in thinking of it as the subject to which the other elements of thought are attributes.(2.428)

He goes on to point out that attention is associated with hypostatic abstraction (rather than with prescission). Peirce's terminology here suggests a way of looking at abstraction which has great import not only for the matter of this paper, but also, I beleive, for philosophical work in general.

Organisms deal adaptively with their environments in cycles involving perception, manipulation of the environment, and consummation;[46] it is typical of Dewey and Morris, for example, to emphasize in their thought our ties with these natural movements. This adapative integration with the environment demands the selection of relevant materials and the creative structuring of these materials into new integral wholes ordering the organism/environment field. That Gestalt psychologists such as Köhler, Wertheimer, and Koffka emphasized the role of such organismic integrations of material in *perception* is well-known; that the concept of gestalt formation extends well beyond organization of the perceptual field is emphasized by contemporary Gestalt therapists[47] and has received careful and articulate—if not well-known—philosophical study.[48]

The pragmatists have not dealt with the gestalt *by name* as a philosophical concept, but it is implicit and close to the surface in much of their work; the ending of the irritation of doubt by belief in Pierce's theory (5.358 ff.), for example, is the completion of a gestalt; another example close to the matter of this paper is the creative construction of the icons of theorematic reasoning. In Dewey, whose work is, in many ways, complementary to that of Peirce, we see the gestalt figuring centrally in esthetics and ethics as well as in logic; we have the *type* of esthetic experience when "An experience has a unity that gives it its name, *that* meal, *that* storm, *that* rupture of friendship."[49] In ethics,

> Good consists in the meaning that is experienced to belong to an activity when conflict and entanglement of various incompatible impulses and habits terminate in a unified orderly release in action.[50]

And in logic, Dewey defines *inquiry* as

> the controlled or directed transformation of an indeterminate situation into one that is so determinate in its constituent distinctions and relations as to convert the elements of the original situation into a unified whole.[51]

This is strongly consonant with Peirce's theory of inquiry, and the examples from esthetic and ethical theory likewise fit with Peircean pragmatism.[52]

So the concept of the gestalt—under other names—is no stranger to pragmatic thought; nor are other concepts associated with gestalt theory: the ubiquitous pragmatic insistence that the problematic emerges within a largely unproblematic situation, for example, is an important case of the gestaltists' figure/ground polarity. I would suggest that the theory of abstraction is quite susceptible of analysis in gestalt terms; Peirce's association of "attention with respect to a centre"(2.428) with abstraction is directly suggestive of the process which chooses elements from the manifold and organizes them into *figure*—the process of gestalt formation. The integrative activity of most organisms, including a lot of human activity, involves the structuring of concrete materials in the environment. But in the course of human evolution, we learned that "things" other than actual existents can be named, can be made centers of attention. Peirce's theory of abstraction is an explicit taking-in-account of this fact, and an attempt to locate it in our overall dealings with reality.

Abstraction occurs in specific contexts, relative to perspectives, and so does gestalt formation; both provide unified manipulable wholes as part of the resolution of problematic situations. The wholes are structurings of existent facts, be they about the observed positions of Mars or the anxieties and excitements of human contact. Perls, Hefferline, and Goodman, commenting on the contextual nature of Gestalt Therapy, remark that

> as treatment progresses it is frequently necessary to change the emphasis of approach, from the character to the muscle-tension to the habit of rapport to the dream and back again. We believe that it is possible to avoid circling aimlessly if, precisely by accepting all these to give a variety of contexts, one concentrates on the structure of the figure/background, and provides free occasions for the self progressively to integrate the self.[53]

The employment of abstractions here speaks for itself; the recognition and use in concrete situations of such abstractions is integral to this method, which I see as having vital connections to the theory of abstractions we have been examining.

The material on abstraction and gestalt formation as well as that relating to transformational grammar is, because of space limitations, merely suggestion. Similarly, in what I have done here, I see many suggestions for further work in Peirce scholarship as well as mathematical logic; one Peircean topic that suggests itself to me is that scantily-explored Peircean "methodeutic."[54] There is much fruitful work to be done in connection with what Peirce calls abstraction. I can see a number of paths in my own work associated with these matters, and hope that others in the community of "all who inquire" (5.407) will find fruitful fields here as well.

J. Jay Zeman

University of Florida

NOTES

1. *The Collected Papers of C. S. Peirce*, vols. 1–6, ed. Charles Hartshorne and Paul Weiss, 1931–35; vols. 7–8, ed. A. W. Burks, 1958 (Cambridge MA: Harvard University Press). Citations from the *Collected Papers* are as usual in Peirce scholarship; the first numeral is the volume, and the rest is the paragraph; thus 5.534 is paragraph 534 of volume 5.

2. Charles S. Peirce, *The New Elements of Mathematics*, vols. 1–4, ed. Carolyn Eisele (The Hague: Mouton, 1976). Citations from this series will be marked by 'Eisele', followed by volume number and page number. The present citation is Eisele 4, p. 160.

3. Eisele 3/2, p. 917 (volume 3 is bound in two parts). Other relevant statements by Peirce are at 2.428, 4.235, 4.463, 4.332.

4. Jaakko Hintikka, "C. S. Peirce's 'First Real Discovery' and its Contemporary Relevance," *Monist* 63:3 (July, 1980): 304–13.

5. Eisele 4, p. 49.

6. Ibid., but see also 1.162, 4.430 ff., and many other locations in the later work of Peirce; the concept is expressed as early as 1885, in 3.363.

7. See Hintikka for details. (cited in n4, above).

8. Ibid., p. 13.

9. It seems to me that the passages cited by Hintikka on this point (Eisele 4, pp. 49–50, 159–60) are really just indirect evidence for the statement that "Peirce himself seems to have . . . ."; this does not, however, weaken the argument that abstraction was of key importance to Peirce, and that abstraction and theorematic reasoning work together in the most important kinds of mathematical reasoning.

10. Eisele 4, p. 49.

11. This "generation" is *gestalt formation*, to use more recent terminology; more on this later.

12. My personal preference in terminology for the second semiosical *relatum* is for Morris's 'signification'; see Charles Morris, *Signification and Significance* (Cambridge: MIT Press, 1964). Since we are dealing with Peirce here, I will, however, use 'object', understanding the word in the very broad sense of Peirce's semiotic.

13. There may also, of course, be nonabstractional corollarial reasoning.

14. Eisele 4, p. 161.

15. Ibid., p. 162.

16. Ibid.

17. That this is also Peirce's view is suggested by Eisele 4, p. 164, where, having argued for the reality of abstractions, Peirce states that they "may be real—indeed, a good deal less open to suspicion than are the primary substances." On absolutely primary substance as a "regulative ideal," compare Peirce's concept of truth and the real (5.407).

18. Eisele 4, p. 162.

19. Ibid., pp. 162–63.

20. Ibid., p. 163; see also 4.235.

21. Charles Morris, *The Open Self* (New York: Prentice-Hall, 1948), p. 129 ff.

22. Eisele 4, p. 163.

23. Eisele 3/1, p. 354.

24. Ibid., p. 353.

25. Eisele 4, p. 164.

26. Ibid., p. 160.

27. Ibid.

28. See 8.344 ff. and 8.366; also, see Charles S. Peirce and Victoria Lady Welby, *Semiotic and Significs*, ed. Charles S. Hardwick (Bloomington: Indiana University Press, 1977), pp. 83–84.

29. Elsewhere, Peirce uses 'dynamic' or 'dynamical'.

30. Peirce and Welby, pp. 83–84.

31. See, for example, 4.411–13; for some discussion of abstraction and the existential graphs, see Don Roberts, *The Existential Graphs of C. S. Peirce* (= *Approaches to Semiotics* 27 (The Hague: Mouton, 1974), p. 64ff.

32. Eisele 3/1, p. 350.

33. Ibid., pp. 350–51.

34. Ibid., p. 353.

35. Ms. 300 in the Peirce Microfilms and in Richard Robin, *Annotated Catalogue of the Papers of C. S. Peirce* (Amherst MA: University of Massachusetts Press, 1967); the quoted passage is on pp. "Bed 38" and "Bed 39" of Ms. 300.

36. See J. Jay Zeman, "Peirce's Logical Graphs," *Semiotica* 12:3 (1974): 251ff; For considerable detail on tinctured existential graphs, see Roberts, p. 87ff.

37. Roberts, p. 64ff.

38. Hintikka, pp. 6–7, 11–13.

39. Once again, I confess to being more comfortable, personally, with Morris's 'signification' than with Peirce's 'object'.

40. Charles Morris, *Foundations of the Theory of Signs* (Chicago, IL: University of Chicago Press, 1938), p. 6ff.

41. Noam Chomsky, *Rules and Representations* (New York: Columbia University Press, 1980), p. 59.

42. Ibid.

43. Eisele 4, p. 161.

44. Ernst Cassirer, *The Philosophy of Symbolic Forms*, vol. 2, tr. Ralph Manheim, (New Haven, CT: Yale University Press, 1955), p. 41.

45. Ibid., vol. 3, p. 14.

46. See Morris, *Signification and Significance*, p. 3ff. for connections between this and semiotic.

47. A basic document is Frederick Perls, Ralph Hefferline, and Paul Goodman, *Gestalt Therapy* (New York: Dell, 1951).

48. See, for example, Aron Gurwitsch, *The Field of Consciousness* (Pittsburgh, PA: Duquesne University Press, 1964).

49. John Dewey, *Art as Experience* (New York: Capricorn, 1958 [orig. 1934]), p. 37.

50. John Dewey, *Human Nature and Conduct* (New York: Modern Library, 1957), p. 196.

51. John Dewey, *Logic: The Theory of Inquiry* (New York: Holt, 1938), pp. 104–05.

52. For expansion here, see J. Jay Zeman, "The esthetic sign in Peirce's semiotic," *Semiotica*, 19:3/4 (1977): 241–58.

53. Perls, Hefferline, and Goodman, p. 245.

54. Methodeutic is a projected but undeveloped part of Peirce's semiotic which fits approximately where pragmatics does in the Morrisian terminology; he sometimes calls it "speculative rhetoric"; see 2.93, 2.229. For mention of a "method to discover methods" in deductive reasoning, see 3.364, 3.454.

MEANING AS HABIT:
SOME SYSTEMATIC IMPLICATIONS OF PEIRCE'S
PRAGMATISM

Peirce's pragmatic stress on meaning in terms of habits of response is, of course, well known.[1] However, the language in which it is usually expressed tends too often to conflate its epistemic and ontological dimensions,[2] thereby hiding from view its full systematic significance. The following discussion will focus on the emergence of such meanings as epistemic relational structures which embody the characteristics of the dynamics of organism-environment interaction in their very internal structure and which lead outward toward the universe, providing an experienced content which is at once epistemic and ontological.

For Peirce, meanings are to be understood as logical structures,[3] not as psychological or biological facts. Peirce does not want to give meaning an existence independent of purpose, yet he does not want to reduce meaning to the categories of psychology or biology.[4] Meanings are to be understood, for Peirce, as relational structures emerging from behavioral patterns, as emerging from the lived through response of the human organism to that universe with which it is in interaction. Or, in other terms, human behavior is meaningful behavior, and it is in behavior that the relational patterns which constitute conceptual meaning are rooted. What, however, is meaning as a relational pattern? A purely relational pattern devoid of sensuous criteria of recognition would be a pattern of relationships relating nothing that had reference to the world, while a pure datum, devoid of the relational pattern, could not be an object of thought. Indeed, for Peirce, sensuous recognition and conceptual interpretation represent two ends of a continuum rather than an absolute difference in kind. His view that sensuous recognition involves interpretive aspects, in some yet to be determined sense, is fairly clear cut and can be found in his view that there are no first impressions of sense.[5] However, Peirce's view that conceptualization requires imagery is open to some confusion. He states that "I will go so far as to say that we have no images even in actual perception." Yet, he objects to Kant, not because Kant requires a schema for the application of a concept to experience, but because he separates the schema from the concept, failing to recognize that a schema for the application of a concept to the data of experience is as general as the concept.[6] And, if the schema is to allow for the application of a concept to sense experience, then imagery, in some sense at least, would seem to be required.

The resolution of this difficulty lies in the definition of image which Peirce so emphatically rejects in the former statement, that is, the definition of image as an absolutely singular representation, a representation absolutely determinate in all respects.[7] Thus, Peirce accepts imagery as part of conceptual meaning, but refuses to equate such imagery with determinate, singular, representation. In the schematic aspects of conceptual meaning, then, there would seem to be found the inseparable mingling of the sensuous and the relational as the vehicle by which we think about and recognize objects in the world. It is to the relation between habit and schematic structure that the ensuing discussion will turn.

Such a relation emerges only in unifying Peirce's unsystematic analyses found scattered throughout his writings, for Peirce did not explicitly recognize until late in his career that in addition to his carefully worked out logical analysis of the sign process, or relation between representamen, interpretant, and object, his philosophy required a similarly worked out logical analysis of the internal structure of the concept or logical interpretant.[8] Peirce thus came to recognize that conceptual meaning must include within itself the emotional, energetic and logical interpretants. Or, in other terms, it must include the elements of Firstness, Secondness, and Thirdness found, in some form, in all analyses, in this case: Firstness as feeling core or sensuous content; Secondness as response or set of acts; and Thirdness as structure or resultant image.[9] Imagery, then, as part of the internal structure of meaning, is inseparably connected with sense content as Firstness and pattern of reaction as Secondness. As Peirce observes, "To predicate a concept of a real or imaginary object is equivalent to declaring that a certain operation, corresponding to the concept, if performed upon that object would . . . be followed by a result of a definite general description."[10] Or, in other terms, "How otherwise can a habit be described than by a description of the kind of action to which it gives rise, with the specification of the conditions and the motive?"[11]

Here it should be noted that it is habit which gives rise to certain kinds of action in the presence of certain kinds of conditions to yield certain kinds of results. And, if the act is dependent upon the condition or sensory content, then different sensory cues will give rise to different acts. Thus, there is not one act but an indefinite number of acts corresponding to an indefinite number of possible sensory conditions. For example, varying perspectives yield varying appearances and hence varying resulting acts. Indeed, even if one considers only one essential property, so that the application of a physical object meaning is determined solely by the presence of one property, there is the possibility of an unlimited number of possible conditions and resultant acts. Yet, this indefinite number radiates from one intended objectivity. Precisely what it means to apprehend an object or objective structure rather than an appearance only is to have "filled in" the result of a particular act with the results of other possible acts given other possible cues. Thus, in a sense there are an indefinite number of cues, acts, and resulting appearances. Yet, in another sense, though there are an indefinite number of possibilities they are all "part of" the one result, an objectivity having certain characteristics. The difference between an apprehended appearance and an apprehended object for Peirce is precisely this difference in levels of meaning organization.[12]

Thus, if we are to meaningfully assert the existence of physical objects, or in other terms, to perceive a world of objectivities, then there must be, in addition to sensory cue, act, and further sensory appearance, that which binds into a system the set of possibilities which as a system give rise to the resultant objective structure. Here it is necessary to distinguish between the logical interpretant or resultant structure, and the ultimate logical interpretant as the living habit which binds together into a systematic unity the various possibilities, thus making the logical interpretant possible. It is habit which binds into a system the set of possible conditions and possible acts which as a system gives rise to the objective structure. As Peirce states, "to say that mental phenomena are governed by law" means that "there is a living idea" which pervades mental phenomena.[13] Further, habit does more than unify three pre-existent elements. Only as habit performs its function of unifying sensory conditions and reactions does structure emerge at all. As Peirce notes, "the general idea is the *mark* of the habit."[14] And, perhaps even more significant, it is habit which determines reaction, and it is reaction which partially determines the nature of the sensory cue. Thus, it is habit, ultimately, which partially determines the nature of the sensory cue. As Peirce stresses, "Feeling which has not yet emerged into immediate consciousness is already affectible and already affected. In fact, this is habit . . . "[15] Or, in other terms, "Thus, the sensation, so far as it represents something, is determined, according to logical law, by previous cognitions; that is to say, these cognitions determine that there shall be a sensation."[16]

Peirce's position can perhaps best be clarified by taking the term 'image' as 'aspect'. For example, one may say, quite correctly, that an ocean presents a turbulent image or aspect. And, while the specific empirical content of experience is best understood as one particular among many, the image of the schema for the application of a living habit to experience is best understood as the one which determines the many. Indeed, the importance of the content of the image of the schema lies in the way in which it comes into being. Such an image represents an aspect of the dispositional structural order by which it is regulated, whether the resultant image is taken at the level of appearance or of objectivity. Such an image as representing an aspect of an ordering cannot be reduced to the content of any experience, whether imagined or actual. Rather, it represents principles or possibilities in terms of which sensory content can emerge within experience.

An examination of the internal dynamics of the meanings by which objects come to conscious awareness indicates that habits are partially constitutive of immediate perceptual experience. Pure "feeling core" or pure Firstness or pure "sense content" is "there" in experience as the logically or epistemically final basis and ultimate referent for all cognitive activity. In this sense it is epistemically primitive. Further, such a "feeling core" held apart from particular experiences must be "there" as part of the image if concepts are to be applicable to experience. But, such a core is precisely the sensuous core of the schematic image, and as such partakes of the generality of the image. Neither the image nor its sensuous core can be apprehended independently of the structural orderings of habit, for their character is partially determined by the generative functioning of habit. Habit is thus the living meaning which generates acts of response in relation to criteria for grasping the situations in terms of which such activity is appropriate. And, since these meanings are constitutive of perceptual experience, both the world of perceptual objectivities and the supposed "immediate" grasp of "pure" appearance is shot through with the structural orderings of habitual modes of response. In brief, all perceptual experience is shot through with the relationship between human action and apprehended content, for such felt dispositions and tendencies to act enter into the very tone and structure of any experienced content. Thus, meanings emerge from organism-environment interaction as precise relational structures unified by habit as a rule of generation and organization, and they contain activity and temporal reference in the very heart of their logical structure. Such meanings are not reducible to the biological only, for what habit binds together into a unity is a triadic relation of factors emerging from organism-environment interaction, a triadic sign relation through which a perceptual world gives itself to conscious awaremess.

Because of the epistemic dimensions of habit, then, the grasp of experienced "immediacies" cannot be divorced from the structures of objectivity, for the character of the immediacies is generated by the dispositional structural orderings which yield objectivities. "We are, of course directly aware of positive sense qualities in the percept (although in the percept they are in no wise separate from the whole object)."[17] And, just as it can be said that habit yields qualities as appearances of objectivities, "So when feeling emerges into immediate consciousness, it always appears as a modification of a more or less general object already in the mind."[18] Because of the function of habit, appearances emerge for conscious awareness only within a world of appearing objects. They are not the historic originals for the contruction of objects.

The apprehension of appearance, obtained by reflective abstraction from the world of perceptual objects, is important within Peirce's pragmatic understanding of verification, for verification is not just a temporal linear affair but rather includes logical or epistemic levels. Grasp of appearance is the most fundamental level for verification in experience in the sense that it is that level most devoid of interpretive elements and, as indicating the way a thing appears as opposed to the way a thing is, is itself devoid of future reference. Indeed, this level is most devoid of interpretive elements precisely in the sense that reference to future experience contained in assertions of objectivity is withheld. In a certain sense, however, interpretation is very much in evidence, since the appearance obtained by a change of focus or abstractive attention reflects, in the very structure of its appearance, that context of objectivity which one is attempting to withhold. In this way, the appearances of the intended object serve as the verification of what is meant. Thus, while the ontological dimensions of habit lead to the expression of the validity or appropriateness of meanings in terms of the ongoing conduct of the biological organism emersed in a natural world, the epistemic dimensions of habit lead to their expression in terms of the phenomenological description of the appearance of what is meant.

It is the epistemic dimension of meaning in terms of habit which provides, further, the source of a sense of the concrete unity of objectivity as more than a collection of appearances. Just as a continuum may generate an unlimited number of cuts within itself, so a disposition as a rule of organization and generation contains within itself an unlimited number of possibilities of specific acts to be generated. As Peirce states, "a true continuum is something whose possibilities of determination no multitude of individuals can exhaust," while a habit or general idea is a living feeling, infinitesimal in duration and immediately present, but still embracing innumerable parts.[19] That such an objective concreteness which transcends any indefinite number of appearances is built into our very sense of objectivity is evinced in Peirce's description of habit as the "living continuum" indicated above. In such an "absence of boundedness a vague possibility of more than is present is directly felt."[20] Or, as he emphasizes, a pragmatist must subscribe to the doctrine of real possibility because nothing other than this can be so much as meant by saying that an object possesses a character.[21] Habit, then, is the source of our sense of a reality of physical objectivities whose possibilities of being experienced transcend, in their very nature, the experiences in which they appear.

Thus, the conceiving mind cannot, by the very nature of meaning, be tied down to a consciousness which apprehends actualities only, for the implicit content of our concepts includes meaningful assertions about potentialities which reach out beyond that which will ever be actualized. Embodied in the actuality of our conceptual structures as dispositional, then, is a sense of a reality which transcends actual occasions of experience.

Such an understanding of meaning leads directly to process, for if one tries to reduce the process of lived time to a series of knife-edged moments, one has taken away the basis for the primitive epistemological "feel" of continuity. And, in doing this, one has ruled out of court the very possibility of the functioning of meaning as dispositional, and hence has ruled out of court the basis for a primitive epistemological "feel" of real potentialities. "There is no span of present time so short as not to contain . . . something for the confirmation of which we are waiting."[22] But this "peculiar element of the present, that it confronts us with ideas which it forces upon us . . . is something which accumulates in wholes of time and dissipates the more minutely the course of time is scrutinized."[23] Thus, such a structure of meaning grounds in lived experience a primordial grasp of time as process. What occurs within the present awareness is not the apprehension of a discrete datum in a moment of time, but rather the time-extended experiential "feel" within the passing present of a readiness to respond to more than can ever be specified. This "feel" provides the experiential basis for the meaningfulness of a process metaphysics.

Further, the dispositional theory of meaning leads to a metaphysics of realism as opposed to a nominalism, a realism not of eternal essences but a "process realism" in which there are real modes of behavior which govern what occurs. Laws cannot be understood as some shorthand for what occurs. Laws, which outrun any number of actualities are, as modes of behavior, the source of the structures emerging in what occurs. Man's habits of response are precisely lawful modes of behavior structuring emerging activities. Here, in Peirce's pragmatic understanding of meaning in terms of habit, the answer to the problem of the meaningfulness of his realism is to be found, for a disposition or habit as a rule of generation is something whose possibilities of determination no multitude of actually generated instances can exhaust. It is the awareness of habit as a disposition or readiness to respond to more than can be specified which gives a concrete meaning to the concept of a "process realism," of a real lawfulness which governs unactualized possibilities. Thus, the meaning of the potentialities or dynamic tendencies which are held to characterize the real is to be found in the awareness of the actuality of habit as that which can never be exhausted by any number of exemplifications.

Finally, the sense of unactualized possibilities embedded in meaning as dispositional brings a sense of real alternatives—they could do otherwise—into the very heart of perceptual awareness, providing an experientially meaningful basis for the rejection of deterministic hypotheses, and a directly felt sense of the spontaneous, of the pure possibilities of a nondeterministic universe. Thus, the pervasive features of the epistemic dimension of meaning as habit lead to a sense of the pervasive textures of the independently real. As Peirce observes:

> Suffice it to say once more that pragmatism is, in itself, no doctrine of metaphysics, no attempt to determine any truth of things. It is merely a method of ascertaining the meanings of hard words and of abstract concepts. All pragmatists of whatever stripe will cordially assent to that statement. *As to the ulterior and indirect effects of practising the pragmatistic method, that is quite another affair . . .*[24]

Such effects are well evidenced in Peirce's claim that:

> There are certain questions commonly reckoned as metaphysical, and which certainly are so, if by metaphysics we mean ontology, which as soon as pragmatism is once sincerely accepted, cannot logically resist settlement. These are for example, What is reality? Are necessity and contingency real modes of being? Are the laws of nature real? Can they be assumed to be immutable or are they presumably results of evolution? Is there any real chance or departure from real law?[25]

Pragmatism, then, is far more than a tool for clarifying the meanings of terms. Rather, the very tool leads to a particular ontological content. Indeed, such a content belongs not only to ontology, but also "to 'epistemology,' an atrocious translation of *Erkenntnislehre*."[26]

At this point it may be objected that though these subtle tones of experiencing within the internal structure of meaning provide a phenomenological sense of an anti-deterministic yet lawfully processive universe, there is no basis for the claim that they in fact are features of the metaphysically or ontologically real.[27] It is to this issue that the remaining discussion will turn.

For Peirce, as for all the pragmatists, man is a natural organism in interaction with a natural environment. One of the most distinctive and most crucial aspects of pragmatism is its concept of experience as having the character of an interaction or transaction between man and his environment. Experience is that rich ongoing transactional unity between man and his environment, and only within the context of meanings which reflect such an interactional unity does what is given emerge for conscious awareness. Indeed, such a transactional unity itself has epistemic or phenomenological dimensions, for that which intrudes itself inexplicably into experience is not bare datum, but rather evidences itself as the over-againstness of a thick world "there" for my activity. "Deceive yourself as you may, you have a direct ex-

perience of something reacting against you."[28] And, if experience is an interactional unity of man's responses to the ontologically real, then the nature
of experience reflects both the responses man brings and the pervasive textures of that independent reality or surrounding natural environment.[29] There
is thus, for the pragmatist in general, and for Peirce in particular, a "two
directional openness" within experience. What appears opens in one direction
toward the structures of the independently real or the surrounding natural environment and in the other direction toward the structures of man's modes of
grasping that independently real, for what is experienced is in fact a unity
formed by each in interaction with the other. The pervasive textures of experience, which are exemplified in every experience and embedded within the
meanings by which we respond to the world, are at the same time indications
of the pervasive textures of the independent universe which, in every experience, gives itself for our responses and which provides the touchstone for
the workability of our meanings. The basic textures of experience thus lead to
the outlines of the categories of metaphysics.[30] As Peirce so well states this
transition from the pervasive features of meaning and experience to the pervasive features of the independently real, "that time and space are innate
ideas, so far from proving that they have merely a mental existence, as Kant
thought, ought to be regarded as evidence of their reality. For the constitution
of the mind is the result of evolution under the influence of experience."[31]
And, time as process brings with it a processive content, for "Time with its
continuity logically involves some other kind of continuity than its own.
Time, as the universal form of change cannot exist unless there is something
to undergo change and to undergo a change continuous in time there must be
a continuity of changeable qualities."[32] That such qualities cannot be taken as
subjective is evidenced through the bringing together of two claims by Peirce.
"Not only is consciousness continuous in a subjective sense . . . its object is
ipso facto continuous. In fact, this infinitesimally spread out consciousness is
a direct feeling of its contents as spread out."[33] Further, though "Everything
which is present to us is a phenomenal manifestation of ourselves," this "does
not prevent its being a phenomenon of something without us, just as a rain-
bow is at once a manifestation both of the sun and of the rain."[34]

Such phenomenal manifestations cannot be understood in terms of a
dichotomy between appearance and reality, for Peirce stresses that his
philosophy "will not admit a sharp sundering of phenomena and substrates.
That which underlies a phenomenon and determines it thereby is, itself, in a
measure, a phenomenon."[35] What appears within experience, then, is also the
appearance of the independently real; there is no ontological gap between appearance and reality. Further, it is at the same time "to me" to whom it appears and reflects my intentional link with the externally real. Thus, Peirce

can say that "Perhaps it may reconcile the psychologist to the admission of perceptual judgments involving generality to be told that they are perceptual judgments concerning our own purposes."[36] Yet, "since no cognition of ours is absolutely determinate, generals must have a real existence."[37] What appears, then, opens in one direction toward the structures of the independently real and in the other direction toward the structures of our mode of grasping the independently real. Or, in other terms, what appears within experience is a function of both in interaction and thus "mirrors" neither exactly, though it reflects characteristics of each. Man's link with his world includes, for Peirce, a vital intentionality at the level of sensibility. The externally real from a certain particular place does not, at any level of awareness, cause a reaction as does a stimulus. Rather, it has a significance, and is a being which is acted upon even as it acts upon us. The structures which come to awareness in experience are an interactional unity of such activities.

Precisely because all contents of awareness are an intentional unity of meaning and being, of knower and known, the continuity of changeable qualities which reflects both the immediacy of conscious experience and the character of the independently real is a limiting concept within experience, for "the development of mind has practically extinguished all feeling."[38] Indeed, as indicated above, though meaning contains a core of felt content, such a core is not experienceable apart from the dispositionally generated structures which present the possibilities in terms of which the sensory may appear. Thus, the grasp of experience as containing repeatable, recognizable qualities "which have been seen before and may be seen again" is a product of the vital intentionality of meaning as habit. Pure Firstness, on the other hand "is predominant, not necessarily on account of the abstractness of that idea, but on account of its self-containedness. It is not in being separated from qualities that Firstness is most predominant, but in being something peculiar and idiosyncratic."[39] Such a characterization leads Peirce to speak of Firstness in terms of qualities of feeling,[40] for what are the characteristics of feeling according to Peirce? "There is no resemblance at all in feeling, since feeling is whatever it is, positively and regardless of anything else, while the resemblance of anything lies in the comparison of that thing with something else."[41]

Pure feeling, then, as a limiting concept within experience, would seem to indicate the boundary of consciousness, the idealized moment of organism-environment interaction, and the pure concrete having, within such a moment, of the indefinitely rich universe within or upon which meaning as habit operates to create a world of perceived objects. The brute meaningless feel of qualitative immediacy is a philosophic abstraction or limiting concept analogous to that of a moment within process or a point on a line. Brute having or brute qualitative feel, devoid of the meanings implicit in dispositional modes of response, would be brute interaction at an instant. But, the concept of interaction at an instant is an abstraction from the reality of process, and brute activity is an abstraction from the continuity of a dispositional mode of response. Such pure feeling is a philosophic idealization, but not an unreal one. The felt concreteness of the continuum of changeable qualities is "there"; it is that which we always experience, but which we always experience through the web of meanings our habits have woven into it. This level of unique qualitative immediacies is important in understanding the ontological categories as they emerge from Peirce's pragmatic understanding of meaning as habit, for it indicates that Firstness in its metaphysical aspect does not indicate any sort of determinate repeatables. To allow the repeatability of appearing qualities to lead to a metaphysics which gives an independent ontological status in any sense to qualities as determinate repeatables is completely to ignore this most basic mode of Firstness,[42] and to lose a crucial key to understanding his metaphysics.

That Firstness is the most elusive and ignored of Peirce's categories has been repeatedly noted.[43] As one commentator has summarized the problem of Firstness, both "abstract qualities" and "chance variations" belong to the category of Firstness, and they seem to have in common only the fact that they are neither Seconds nor Thirds and therefore are relegated to the category of Firsts.[44] As he continues, it may well be asked why chance variations should not be assigned to some new fourth category.[45] On this view, Firstness seems to have become the systematic dump-heap for that which will not fit into the categories of Secondness and Thirdness. Yet, if Firstness is indeed first, one would expect it to provide the significant starting point for the metaphysical functions assigned to the other categories. If, as indicated by approaching Firstness through Peirce's pragmatic theory of meaning, qualitative immediacy and chance variation are intimately related, then the need for some "new fourth category" dissolves and Firstness does indeed become the significant starting point of Peirce's metaphysics, for it indicates the infinitely varied, concrete qualitative richness of a universe in process, the substratum of pure chance diversity within which random activities occur and begin to take on habits. It is this interrelationship which will be explored in the ensuing discussion.

Peirce observes that "Generality is either of that negative sort which belongs to the merely potential, as such, and this is peculiar to the category of Firstness, or it is of the positive kind which belongs to conditional necessity, and this is peculiar to the category of law."[46] Further, "The general is seen to be precisely the continuous."[47] Generality, then, must involve continuity; hence the generality of Firstness can only be fully understood when this category is viewed from the aspect of the continuity which pervades it. Here it may be objected that continuity belongs to the category of Thirdness. However, if the general is the continuous, then the negative generality of Firstness must imply a negative continuity which belongs to the category of Firstness rather than Thirdness. This negative continuity or negative generality of Firstness indicates a negative possibility or mere "may-be" which contains no positive possibility or "would-be" and which thus provides no positive range for further determinations. As Peirce states the position, "Firstness is essentially indifferent to continuity."[48] Indeed, just as feeling was seen above to refer to that qualitative element which in its purity can be related to nothing beyond itself, so the negative generality and continuity of Firstness, which forms the cosmological basis for our experience of Firstness, can be related neither to what has been nor to what will be; it has no relatedness; it contains no "would-be"; in short, it is a qualitative continuum of negative possibilities, a "substratum" of pure chance.[49]

How, then, does this view of Firstness relate to the other categories? The intimate interrelation of Secondness and Thirdness for Peirce is indicated to some extent in his statement that

> The court cannot be imagined without a sheriff. Final causality cannot be imagined without efficient causality, but no whit the less on that account are their modes of action polar contraries. The sheriff would still have his fist, even if there were no court; but an efficient cause, detached from a final cause in the form of a law would not even possess efficiency; it might exert itself, and something might follow post hoc, but not propter hoc; for propter implies potential regularity. Now without law there is no regularity; and without the influence of ideas there is no potentiality.[50]

Again, Peirce writes that the court, or the category of Thirdness, "can have no concrete being without action, as a separate object on which to work its government."[51] Thus, it can be seen that efficient causation, in the sense of actualization of a possibility, requires the rational or "ideal causality"[52] of Thirdness to provide the positive potentialities, while Thirdness, apart from its relation to Secondness is not real. Because Peirce's category of Firstness is considered confused, or, at best, elusive, the interrelation of Secondness and Thirdness is usually discussed in isolation from Firstness. This fact, combined with Peirce's emphasis on his Scholastic Realism, leads too often to an understanding of the interrelation of Secondness and Thirdness in terms of relationships appropriate to a static, substantive universe. However, when Firstness is integrated with Secondness and Thirdness from the backdrop of Peirce's pragmatic focus on habit, a different type of relationship comes to light. Such an integration can best be approached by way of Peirce's cosmology, for his cosmological account, in which the random actions and reactions of the substratum of pure chance gradually tend to take on habits which in turn limit future interactions, will lead to an interrelation of the categories in terms of processive emergence.

It may be held that to view the ontological problem of the relationship of the categories in terms of the cosmological problem of the origin of the categories is to commit a sort of genetic fallacy at the metaphysical level. However, only if the emergence of Thirdness from Secondness and Firstness is recognized can the status of Thirdness be adequateldy understood. Furthermore, as has been so aptly noted, the sequence to be traced is not, in the initial stages, a temporal one at all. It is an objective logical sequence.[53]

At first sight there seems to be an ambivalence in Peirce's cosmological categorization of the primordial state. On the one hand, he seems to establish a type of situation which represents Firstness alone. On the other hand, he attempts to show that such a primordial state contains the germ of a generalizing tendency. The ensuing discussion will attempt to indicate the manner in which the primordial state does suggest a representation of the First category alone, yet nonetheless contains the germ of a generalizing tendency. This generalizing tendency lies in Peirce's First Category in the form of a qualitative continuum. It has been seen that Firstness is a negative generality or negative continuity in that it does not limit the future as does law. Further, Firstness is also a pure possibility in relation to Secondness, for its being as possibility is not dependent upon its actualization.[54] From the indeterminate qualitative continuum which is logically prior to both Secondness and Thirdness, anything can occur in that any two parts can interact. These random reactions occur from the brute blind force of Secondness or efficient causation acting on the substratum of pure spontaneity. And, though Firstness is essentially indifferent to its continuity, when interaction of two parts of the continuum occurs, that which interacts is continuous and provides a positive possibility of future interactions by excluding certain possibilities in its very occurrence. As Peirce illustrates:

> Let the clean blackboard be a sort of diagram of the original vague potentiality . . . I draw a chalk line on the board. This discontinuity is one of these brute acts by which alone the original vagueness could have made a step toward definiteness. There is a certain element of continuity in this line. Where did this continuity come from? It is nothing but the original continuity of the blackboard which makes everything upon it continuous.[55]

Again, as Peirce notes, the discontinuity can be produced upon that blackboard only by the reaction between two continuous surfaces into which it is separated. Thus, what is a singularity or discreteness in the containing continuum is itself a positive generality in relation to the discrete cuts potentially "in" it. In brief, Secondness, or bare brute action and reaction, is a distinct analytic element within the ongoing process or evolving qualitative continuum. However, there is no such thing as disembodied interaction, and actuality as it contextually occurs in the passing present is characterized by the brute hereness and nowness of the shock of interaction or efficient causation "acting upon" the substratum of pure chance or "negative continuity" in accordance with the limitations placed upon it by the positive possibilities of Thirdness.

Here we see the manner in which acts or Secondness can be characterized both as privative, brute, blind or unintelligible, and as that which gives reality to laws and general types. Secondness, as distinct from Firstness or Thirdness, is a brute action and reaction. In this sense it is the acting compulsion of efficient causation. Secondness is a mode of behavior of the concrete qualitative continuum—the mode of behavior which is characterized by efficient causation. It is the bruteness of interaction of two parts of a qualitative process. Thus, existence is a mode of behavior of the general; it is the mode of behavior characterized by interaction. And, it is the interaction, not that which interacts, which is individual, brute, and blind. But, this brute, blind interaction of the general qualitative continuum is precisely what turns negative possibility into positive possibility, mere "maybe" into "would-be." Thus, Secondness is that which makes possible the very reality of Thirdness.

We can see now why Peirce insists that Thirdness does not contract into Secondness—Thirdness is not the kind of 'thing' that can be in Secondness. Indeed, if one insists on using spatial language, it is more accurate to say that Secondness is in Thirdness than that Thirdness is in Secondness, for a continuum may be said to contain its cuts, potential or actual, but the cuts do not contain the continuum.[56] Thus, Peirce can say that Secondness does not contain any Thirdness at all, for an "*existing* thing is simply a blind reacting thing" though "existing *things* do not need reasons; they are reasons."[57] Here, then, can be found the significance of Peirce's view that synechism and realism are intimately linked.[58] Their linkage is to be found in Peirce's process realism as it develops from his pragmatic understanding of meaning as habit.

Peirce's pragmatism thus leads to the metaphysical vision of an infinitely rich evolving universe in process, a universe which has emergence and novelty built into the very core of its being, and through any and every cross-section of which run two modes of behavior. Such a process does not contain the hard discrete exactitudes of repeatable qualities or universal classes, for such a reality is a continuum which "swims in indeterminacy."[59] For this reason, the principle of continuity, which pervades the independently real, is "fallibilism objectified."[60] Indeed, in such a processive universe, "Truly natural classes may, and undoubtedly often do, merge into one another inextricably,"[61] and thus boundary lines must be imposed, although the classes are natural.[62]

Thus, our lived perceptual experience is an intentional unity of knower and known which emerges through our modes of grasping the independently real continuum of qualitative events which "swims" in indeterminacy. The internal structure of meaning as habit both provides the tool for "cutting the edges" of such a processive continuum and allows for a primordial experiential grasp of its continuities, real relations and real potentialities; for a sense of an anti-deterministic world in which one grasps real alternative possibilities; for the "feel" of the surd, brute, otherness of the environment to which one must successfully respond. Peirce's pragmatic understanding of meaning as habit, then, incorporates the textures of the ontologically real within the very heart of the structure of meaningful experience, bringing to a unity the knowing by man of the world and the being of man in the world.

Sandra B. Rosenthal

Loyola University,
New Orleans

NOTES

1. See, for example, Charles Sanders Peirce, *Collected Papers,* vol. 1–4, ed. Hartshorne and Weiss (Cambridge, MA: The Belknap Press of Harvard University, 1931–1935); vol. 7, 8 ed. Burks (Cambridge, MA: Harvard University Press, 1958), 5.491 and 5.486. (Hereafter cited using only conventional two-part number).

2. This distinction refers to the epistemic and ontological dimensions of *meaning* in terms of habit. There is intended at this point no reference to "habit-takings" of the universe.

3. 4.9

4. 8.326; 8.332. It must be emphasized that purposive biological activity, as the foundation of meaning, cannot be understood in terms of scientific contents. Rather, it is the "lived through" biological activity of the human organism and, as such, is capable of phenomenological description.

5. 5.416, 5.213; 7.465.

6. 5.531 (See also 7.407 for a discussion of Kant's schema in relation to Peirce's position.)

7. 5.298–99.

8. 8.305.

9. Peirce refers to such an analysis both as logical and as "phaneroscopic."

10. 6.132.

11. 5.491. (The use of 'motive' here seems analogous to 'anticipated result'.)

12. These two levels correspond respectively to the content of the perceptual judgment in its narrow and wide senses. These two senses of the perceptual judgment are developed by me in some detail in "Peirce's Theory of the Perceptual Judgment: An Ambiguity," *Journal of the History of Philosophy,* 7 (1969).

13. 6.152.
14. 7.498.
15. 6.141.
16. 5.291.
17. 7.624.
18. 6.142.
19. 6.170, 6.138.
20. 6.138.
21. 5.457.
22. 7.675.
23. Ibid.
24. 5.464. (Italics not in text.)
25. 5.496.
26. Ibid.
27. The terms 'ontological' and 'metaphysical' are used interchangeably in this essay, although Peirce at times makes a distinction, seeming to label as 'metaphysical' issues which are pragmatically "meaningless gibberish" or at best unsolvable.
28. 2.139.
29. More precisely stated, the surrounding natural environment *is* the independently real as it enters into the field of interest of an active organism.
30. Thus, Peirce's phenomenology, in providing categories as "classifications of all that is in any way present to mind in experience" provides as well the epistemic categories for analyzing the structures of meaning and the metaphysical or ontological categories for delineating "modes of being."
31. Section 14, Article 23, p. 33 of *The Microfilm Edition of the Peirce Papers.*
32. 6.132.
33. 6.111.
34. 5.283.
35. 7.629.
36. 5.166. Peirce's use of the term 'judgment' is of course not intended to indicate a highly intellectualized process but to emphasize that perception is not the "passive receiving" of a spectator theory of knowledge.
37. 5.312.
38. 6.132.
39. 1.302.
40. 5.444.
41. 1.310. To think of feeling as used by Peirce in terms of psychology is to be misled by a word, for as Peirce himself emphatically states, "If by psychology we mean the positive observation science of the mind or consciousness . . . psychology can teach us nothing of the nature of feeling, nor can we gain knowledge of any feeling by introspection, for the very reason that it is our immediate consciousness." 1.308.
42. See, for example, John Boler, *Charles Peirce and Scholastic Realism* (Seattle: University of Washington Press, 1963). Although recognizing the significance of Peirce's switch from substance to process in most areas, Boler finds that at one point at least there is for Peirce "real commonness," or repetition of form in some sense (p. 158); Boler's argument seems to hinge on the unstated assumption that Peirce's ontological category of Firstness implies repeatable, fully structured qualities.
43. See, for example, Isabel Stearns, "Firstness, Secondness, and Thirdness," *Studies in the Philosophy of Charles Sanders Peirce*, ed. Wiener and Young

(Cambridge, MA: Harvard University Press, 1952), pp. 196–97; John Boler, *Charles Peirce and Scholastic Realism,* pp. 122–23.

44. Douglas Greenlee, "Peirce's Hypostatic and Factorial Categories," *Transactions of the Charles S. Peirce Society: A Quarterly Journal in American Philosophy,* 4 (1968): 55, 58.

45. Ibid., p. 58.

46. 1.427.

47. 8, p. 279.

48. 6.205.

49. Perhaps this clarifies the meaning of Peirce's statement, usually interpreted as indicating an idealistic metaphysics, that "wherever chance spontaneity is found, there in the same proportion feeling exists. In fact, chance is but the outward aspect of that which within itself is feeling." 6.265.

50. 1.213.

51. 5.436.

52. 1.212.

53. Thomas Goudge, *The Thought of C. S. Peirce* (Toronto: University of Toronto Press, 1950), p. 144.

54. 1.531.

55. 6.203.

56. 1.478, 5.107 (continuity); 8.208 (contraction)

For Peirce, "A true continuum is something whose possibilities of determination no multitude of individuals can exhaust" (6.170). (It may be objected that there is a sense in which the cuts do contain the continuum, since the possibilities inherent in the continuum cut are partially dependent upon the possibilities inherent in the continuum from which it is cut. However, this objection depends upon viewing the cut not in its aspect of discreteness or Secondness, but in its aspect of continuity or Thirdness.)

57. 4.36; 5.107. (Italics added.)

58. 6.169 ff.

59. 1.171–1.172.

60. 1.171.

61. 1.209.

62. Section 427, pp. 40–41 of *The Microfilm Edition of the Peirce Papers.*

PEIRCE ON MEANING*

1. Introduction

More often than not, the attractive features of Peirce's theory of meaning have been overlooked because of the temptation on the part of many philosophers to dismiss Peirce as a benighted forerunner of a narrow form of verificationism frequently identified with the view of the early Vienna Positivists. The ontological upshot of this narrow form of verficationism is the thesis that sentences are empirically meaningful only if belief in them would not commit us to belief in the existence of any abstract or nonphysical entities. Verificationism, as so construed, renders empirically meaningless all sentences which are not reducible by way of suitable paraphrase to sentences about physical objects either directly or indirectly observable. And, from a logical point of view, it is difficult to see how this form of verificationsim could attain any measure of plausibility independently of a justification rooted ultimately in a Humean reduction of ideas to impressions of sense and the consequent insistence that the truth (and hence the meaning) of empirical sentences is a function of whether or not they originate from, and are reducible to, sensory impressions.

In examining the rudiments of Peirce's theory of meaning, I shall argue that any temptation to read Peirce as a narrow verificationist is unfortunate because his naturalism holds out for a form of verificationism that allows for verifying belief in the existence of abstract entities. Indeed, I shall argue that, generally considered, Peirce's theory of meaning provides for a considerably more ideal form of empiricism than does the theory of meaning proposed by one of Peirce's chief critics, namely, Professor Quine, who in fact does endorse the narrow form of verificationism.

2. The Pragmatic Maxim

Peirce claimed that before we can employ the method of science to determine the truth of any given proposition, we must first know what that proposition means; and to that end he provided a criterion for meaning, the pragmatic maxim, as early as 1878:

> Consider what effects, that might conceivably have practical bearings, we conceive the object of our conception to have. Then our conception of these effects is the whole of our conception of the object.[1]

Peirce understood this maxim to imply that the meaning of any proposition is itself given in another proposition which is simply a general description of all the conceivable experimental phenomena which the assertion of the original proposition predicts. (5.427; 5.412; MS 618 (p. 1); MS 619 (p. 2); MS 289 (p. 8ff); MS 292 (p. 11); MS 290 (p. 33ff)). In short, the meaning of any 'intellectual concept' or proposition is to be conveyed by another expression or proposition which mentions only the observable properties that one would expect under certain circumstances if the original proposition were true. This latter expression Peirce dubbed the "logical interpretant." (5.480ff). Thus, for example, the meaning of the term 'hard', or the proposition "This is hard," is expressed by "Not scratchable by many other substances;" or "This will not be scratched by many other substances" respectively. (5.403; 5.483; 8.176; 8.195).

More specifically, however, the meaning of any given expression is obtained by translating that expression into a set of conditional statements, the antecedents of which prescribe certain operations to be performed, while the consequents of which specify certain observable phenomena which should and would occur as the result of performing those operations if the proposition were true.[2] For example, consider again the expression 'hard'. As just noted, the expression means "not scratchable by many other substances;" but, given that the *logical interpretant* is also equivalent to a set of conditionals, the expression "not scratchable by many other substances" means more properly "*If* you *were* to take some object which is said to be hard, and if you *were* to scratch it with many substances, *then* it would not be scratched.[3] In short, for Peirce, the meaning of what he calls "intellectual concept" or proposition is simply the conditions of its verification. (5.412; MS 327).

Moreover, in spite of the unfortunate phraseology, the pragmatic maxim, as stated, is not so much a criterion for the meaning of concepts or words as it is a criterion for the meaning of certain propositions or sentences. Even though Peirce frequently slips into talking about the meaning of a concept or word, generally he talks about the meaning of a concept in terms of the meaning of a sentence such as "This is lithium," "This diamond is hard," or "The sun is blue." (8.183ff). And apart from the fact that Peirce frequently claimed it is not words or concepts, but rather *sentences* that are meaningful (MS 316 (p. 44); 8.184; 8.178; 8.195; 2.296), the fact that the meaning of a concept or term is construed by Peirce in terms of the conditions of its verification, suggests that for Peirce, talking about the meaning of a concept or a word is in fact talking about the meaning of a sentence or proposition; for only sentences and propositions (and not concepts or words) can be verified.[4] So, while Peirce's unfortunate phrasing of the pragmatic maxim would appear to suggest the opposite, it would be a mistake to urge that Peirce's theory of meaning takes concepts or words as the primary vehicle of semantic focus or significance. More on this shortly.

In further probing the import of the pragmatic maxim, we can note that the conditional statements which express the meaning of any concept or proposition state, in effect, the law governing the object of the proposition or conception. For example, the above cited conditionals which express the meaning of the proposition "This is lithium" imply the law-like generalization "All lithium is translucent vitreous, insoluble, etc." And this is what Peirce meant when he claimed that the meaning of any concept or proposition is a general description of all the experimental phenomena which the assertion of the proposition virtually predicts. (5.427: 8.195; MS 327). It is also what he meant when he said:

> To say that a body is hard, or red, or heavy, or of a given weight, or has any other property, is to say that it is subject to law and therefore is a statement referring to the future. (5.450)

The law (or habit)[5] which is tacitly expressed in the meaning of a concept or proposition and which accounts for the meaning of our propositions, is what Peirce called *Thirdness*, or the element of generality, continuity, or mediation in our experience. Hence it is the lawlike character of our experience which accounts for the meaning of our concepts and propositions; for it is the lawlike character of our experience which accounts for the properties, a description of which constitutes meaning. Indeed, Peirce claimed that, in the end, it is the law itself which is expressed in the conditionals, which constitutes the ultimate meaning of a proposition. (5.491). His reason for saying as much is that the *logical interpretant* is itself meaningful in virtue of another *logical interpretant*. And if we are to avoid an infinite regress of *logical interpretants*, we must maintain in the last analysis that the ultimate meaning (*ultimate* logical interpretant) is the very law which the logical interpretants (conditionals) express.[6]

In addition to all this, Peirce effectively argued for the view that the conditional statements which express, or give, the meaning of a proposition are nonterminating or open-ended, as it were. No set of conditional statements can ever logically exhaust the meaning of the original statement. And this is because the generalization of the conditionals is, as a general description, incapable of fully identifying an object. The meaning of any sentence is exhausted by its sensory implications, but the sensory implications are unlimited. In other words, the meaning of any given proposition can only be partially specified in terms of an antecedently understood empirical vocabulary. This aspect of Peirce's theory of meaning (an aspect generally overlooked although essential for understanding his fallibilism) derives in part from his claim that, strictly speaking, all utterances are in some significant respect indeterminate in meaning, and hence to a certain degree vague or imprecise. Of course, for the purposes of ordinary discourse, this is not much of a problem since we can generally render our utterances sufficiently precise to avoid being misunderstood. But, still, the meaning of any given proposition can never be fully specified because the generalization of the conditionals which express the meaning is of the nature of general sign which, in being general, cannot completely identify the object of which it is a sign. (5.447 note). Sometimes Peirce claims that the reason for this natural indeterminacy of propositional meaning, or the reason why no general description (or sign) can identify an object, derives from the fact that all propositions are hypothetical assertions about the nature of our perceptual experiences which are always, in some sense, imprecise due to the action of the universe upon the perceiver. (5.540n; 3.93).[7] More frequently than not, however, he professed that the indeterminacy of all propositions is fundamentally rooted in the natural indeterminacy of the objects of perception or the objects which the sign is supposed to represent. Indeed, when talking about the indeterminacy of meaning, Peirce invariably located the source of that belief in his contention that there is no object which is absolutely determinate with respect to its having or not having every known property:

> The absolute individual can not only not be realized in sense or thought, but can not exist, properly speaking. For whatever lasts for any time, however short, is capable of logical division, because in that time it will undergo some change in its relations. But what does not exist for any time, however short, does not exist at all. All, therefore, that we perceive or think, or that exists, is general. So far there is truth in the doctrine of scholastic realism. But all that exists is infinitely determinate, and the infinitely determinate is the absolutely individual. This seems paradoxical, but the contradiction is easily resolved. That which exists is the object of a true conception. This conception may be made more determinate than any assignable conception; and therefore it is never so determinate that it is capable of no further determination. (3.93 nl).

Thus Peirce's denial of the existence of absolute individuals provided the logical foundation for his doctrine on the indeterminacy of meaning. Since no object in the universe can ever be fully determinate with respect to its having or not having every known property, it follows that any proposition about the universe is vague in the sense that it cannot hope to fully specify a determinate set of properties. I believe that it is for this reason also that, for Peirce, the meaning of any proposition is always open to further specification by the utterer, although an exhaustive specification cannot be given.[8]

If only for the sake of future discussion, it should be pointed out that Peirce came to designate his denial of the existence of absolute individuals as

the doctrine of *synechism* (all that is, is general) and he insisted that the
doctrine could be established in at least two ways. First of all, the doctrine
recommends itself as the only one consistent with an evolutionary cosmology.
Secondly (as is hinted at in the last quoted text), the doctrine can be independently established in virtue of the infinite divisibility of the continuum
as soon as it is shown that all things exist in the continuum of time and space.[9]
It is because all things swim in the continuum of space and time that it is
theoretically impossible for us to specify all their properties and hence render
our propositions fully determinate with respect to meaning. This second argument convinced Peirce that the mathematics of the continuum would provide
a logic for the universe and, in effect, the key that would open the door of his
cosmology; but it also furnished the logical foundation for a most distinctive
characteristic of his theory of meaning.

Before turning to other aspects of Peirce's theory of meaning in the context of assessing Quine's evaluation of it, we can reflect on the scope and ontological implications of the pragmatic maxim.

Peirce said that his primary motivation in enunciating the pragmatic
maxim was to do away with, as cognitively meaningless, all those propositions that could not be verified in accordance with the method of the physical
sciences. (5.6; 5.423). But this should not be taken to imply that the adoption
of the pragmatic maxim entails the view that all and only those sentences are
meaningful which are empirically verifiable. Indeed, for Peirce, there are a
host of propositions that are meaningful but not empirically verifiable.
Imperatives, explicatives, and interrogatives, for example, are meaningful;
they have what Peirce calls "emotive" or "energetic" interpretants (and not
'logical' interpretants) and this is to say that they are meaningful, but not
'cognitively' meaningful because they cannot be either true or false. (5.480ff).
Similarly, propositions of mathematics and logic are meaningful, but since
they deal exclusively with hypothetical states of things, and assert no matter
of fact about anything actual, they are not empirically verifiable. (See
4.189–203). Accordingly, it seems safer to say that Peirce enunciated the
pragmatic maxim not to brand as meaningless all propositions in principle
unverifiable by the method of the natural sciences, but rather to specify a
criterion of meaning suitable for purportedly factual assertions (assertions
about what there is) which he believed necessary for the purpose of
theoretical inquiry. Recall that, for Peirce, philosophy is a branch of
theoretical science. It is concerned with the conditions for the ascertainment
of what is fact and hence, has nothing to do (*qua philosophy*) with propositions which are not in principle verifiable. (3.560; 1.659; 5.432; 5.107; 5.14nl;
5.61).

But even when we grant that the pragmatic maxim, as thus far explicated, was intended as a criterion of meaning for factual propositions, it

should not be thought that its adoption proscribes as meaningless any statements trafficking in assertions about abstract entities—as though it could not be a fact that there are nonhypothetical abstract entities. Because Peirce once claimed that pragmaticism is a species of prope-positivism, and because of his insistence upon the method of the natural sciences as the only method for the ascertainment of truth, there has been, I think, a strong tendency to suppose that the pragmatic maxim is an early statement of that narrow form of verificationism generally identified with the Early Vienna Positivist who urged that factual assertions about abstract entities are meaningless because in principle not verifiable. I submit, however, that Peirce did not think that the concpet of verification (or verifiability) should be so narrowly construed as to render belief in all abstract entities meaningless. Nowhere does he say that a belief in abstract entities is a meaningless belief. And there is nothing in his empirical criterion of meaning that implies it. What the pragmatic maxim asserts is that the meaning of any proposition is nothing more than the conceivable practical effects which the assertion would imply—if the proposition were true. Our conception of these effects, which might conceivable have practical bearing, just is our conception of the object. The word 'practical' of course, is ambiguous and has been variously construed by different philosophers. But, given what has been argued above, I think it should be construed to refer to those conceivable effects which, in terms of scientific practice, would count for verifying the proposition if it were asserted. This does not imply that one cannot verify belief in the existence of abstract entities. Unless one holds that belief in the existence of abstract entities has no observational results that could count for verifying the belief, there is nothing in the pargmatic maxim which implies that statements about abstract entities are meaningless.

Moreover, the plausibility of this line of reasoning is further enhanced when we consider that Peirce argued for the existence of certain abstract entities and never even considered whether it was inconsistent with his commitment to naturalism. After all, he argued for what he called his "Neglected Argument for the Existence of God". (MS 841 (p. 1); 6.496ff). And he spent a good deal of ink commenting on the existence and nature of the Absolute Mind. Indeed, when he argued that matter is effete mind because the phenomena of consciousness cannot be accounted for under mechanistic laws (1.162) he was, whether we agree with the argument or not, arguing for the existence of an abstract entity on the ground that such a belief leads to certain observable effects which cannot be explained by appealing to any purely materialistic alternative. And when he took a dim view of Telepathy it was not because belief in such a phenomenon was a matter of believing in an abstract entity, but rather because belief in the thesis did not, at the time, allow for observable, predictable and controllable effects that would count for verifying the phenomenon. (MS 881; 1.115). For similar reasons he also argued for the existence of real modalities, possibilities. (4.547).[10] So, even though Peirce's pragmatic maxim sustains a verificationist interpretation, its adoption does not render meaningless statements about abstract entities. Peirce's naturalism implies a concept of verification which extends beyond the view that only sentences about physical objects, defined in sensory terms, can be verified. And in every case where Peirce committed himself to belief in the existence of an abstract entity, it was simply because he felt that the purposes of an adequate explanation required it, that proceeding on purely physicalistic assumptions did not in fact succeed, and, moreover, that what exists is what is asserted to exist in an adequate explanation. Naturally, all this raises the question as to what, for Peirce, is an adequate explanation; but it seems clear that, however he construed it, an adequate explanation need not require appeal to only physical objects. And all this is further evidenced not only by Peirce's criticism of Comte for construing verification in such a way that only those hypotheses are verifiable which contain reference to only directly observable facts (7.91; 2.511 note; MS 475 (p. 58); MS 318 (Prag. 21)) but also by his explicit claim that "science is approaching a critical point; its old and purely materialistic conceptions will no longer suffice." (7.158 note 5).

Finally, as noted in the introduction above, it is difficult to see how the narrow form of verificationism can be defended independently of the view that the truth of empirical sentences is a function of whether or not they originate from, and are reducible to, sentences descriptive of sensory impressions. It is well known, however, that, for Peirce, the truth of a sentence or belief is not a matter of how it originates, but rather a matter of whether or not what the sentence predicts will continue to be confirmed by the scientific community. And this seems to be another reason for disparaging the narrow verificationist's interpretation of the Pragmatic Maxim, since such an interpretation would require of Peirce a certain view on the nature of truth which he clearly did not endorse.

All the above considerations reflect rudimentary characteristics of Peirce's theory of meaning; and, in evaluating it more fully, which I shall now do, certain other aspects of the theory will come to light, aspects which are crucial but which can best be fleshed out in the course of some critical reflection.

3. Assessment of Peirce's Theory of Meaning

In reflecting on the merits of Peirce's theory of meaning as thus far stated, we can underscore its attractiveness by reflecting on Quine's recent assessment of Pragmatism in general and on Peirce's pragmaticism in particular.[11]

Quine argues that although all classical pragmatists belong to the empiricist's tradition, pragmatism followed, rather than led, empiricism in its five most interesting turns for the better. (p. 1). He describes these five turning points and then examines the professing (classical) pragmatists with respect to them in an attempt to determine the extent to which these pragmatists either fostered or favored the most important developments in empiricism. Roughly, Quine concludes that the classical pragmatists, including Peirce, were not very impressive empiricists since the five distinctively important advances in the history of post-Humean empiricism were not either fostered or abetted by the classical pragmatists in any clear way. They were in fact followers at best and not leaders in the empiricist tradition.

As Quine lists them, the first of the five turning points in the advancement of post-Humean empiricism was the shift of semantic focus from ideas to words, a shift Quine credits to John Horne Tooke. The second turning point was the shift of semantic focus from terms to sentences, and this, Quine says, is to be credited to Bentham. The third is the shift of semantic focus from sentences to systems of sentences; and on this point Duhem made the contribution. The fourth is methodological monism which is simply the abandonment of the synthetic-analytic dualism. Quine is characteristically modest in not ascribing this development to his own efforts. And finally, the fifth major advance in the empiricist's tradition is the commitment to Naturalism which bespeaks abandonment of first philosophy prior to science. (pp. 2–9).

In confronting Peirce's empiricism in the light of these turns for the better, Quine urges that, perversity of expression aside, Peirce's pragmatic maxim is implicitly a criterion of meaning for sentences and is, in short, the verification theory of meaning echoed in the Vienna Circle. (p. 11). But Quine hastens to add that it is difficult to regard the verification theory of meaning as distinctive of pragmatism. The verification theory of meaning is, he says, what any empiricist could be expected to come out with when asked the meaning of sentences. (p. 11).

According to Quine, however, acceptance by both Peirce and the Vienna Circle of the verification theory of sentence meaning does not go far enough. For Quine, an adequate empiricist theory of meaning must hold out for a holistic or system-centered semantics, which is the third important turning point for the better in post-Humean empiricism. As Quine construes it, holism is the view that the meaning of any empirically significant statement is not always to be specified in terms of any unique set of sensory experiences whose occurence would uniquely confirm the sentence. Any theoretical sentence can be held as true if we are willing to make drastic enough adjustments in the theory. The truth of the theoretic sentence (as opposed to the observational sentence) is a function of the truth of the theory as a whole; and since the meaning of the sentence is the conditions of its verification, it is the theory as a whole which provides the meaning of the theoretical sentence. On this score, Quine agrees that there are many passages in Peirce which could be cited to show that Peirce was aware that scientific theory confronts its evidence holistically. But, Quine adds, Peirce's awareness here is "hard to reconcile with his facile account of pragmatic meaning, or of one's conception of an object." (p. 12). Besides, on Quine's view we cannot derive semantic holism from Peirce's limit theory of truth because that theory of truth is unacceptable.[12] So, for these reasons Quine claims that, unfortunately, Peirce was by no means clearly committed to a holistic or system-centered semantics.

On Quine's reckoning, semantic holism carries with it a repudiation of the analytic-synthetic distinction; and repudiating that distinction makes Fallibilism come easy if we also repudiate first philosophy as an ideal. Repudiating the analytic-synthetic distinction is the fourth turning point which bettered empiricism after Hume. Curiously enough, however, Quine does not make any attempt to determine whether or not Peirce also repudiated the distinction and if so, for what reasons. In short, as Quine sees it, Peirce's theory of meaning did not clearly embrace either semantic holism or the repudiation of the analytic-synthetic distinction.

Quine does grant, however, that Peirce scored a major point for Naturalism, the fifth step in the evolution of empiricism, in envisaging behavioristic semantics, a semantics which defines belief in terms or dispositions to act. But even here it is a matter of damning with fainting praise; for, on Quine's view, Peirce's behavioral account of belief is not one to rest with. (p. 19). And this is because there is no hope of carrying it out sentence by sentence. Dispositions to behave are bad criteria for determining beliefs. What is laudable, then, about Peirce's contribution here is simply that it is behavioristic in spirit. (p. 19). In spite of its apparent limitations in the hands of Peirce, behaviorist semantics, Quine says, might well be considered the sixth great step in post-Humean empiricism; and Quine grants that it is a distinctively pragmatic (and Peircean) contribution to empiricism.

In summarizing his analysis of the pragmatist's place in empiricism Quine says:

> The professing pragmatists do not relate significantly to what I took to be the five turning points in post-Humean empiricism. Tooke's shift from ideas to words, and Bentham's from words to sentences, were not detectable in Peirce's pragmatic maxim, but we found that Peirce's further semantic discussions to be sentence oriented in implicit ways. Peirce seemed at odds with Duhem's system centered view, until we got to Peirce's theory of truth; but this we found unacceptable. Other pragmatists were sentence oriented in an implicit way, but still at odds with the system centered view, until we made hypothetical-deductive sense of Schiller's humanism. On the analytic-synthetic distinction and on naturalism, the pragmatists blew hot and cold.

Thayer tried to formulate the distinctive tenets of pragmatism, but the result was complex, and to make it come out right he had to pad his roster with some honorary pragmatists. In limiting my attention to the card carriers, I have found little in the way of shared and distinctive tenets. The two best guesses seemed to be behavioristic semantics, which I so heartily approve, and the doctrine of man as truth-maker, which I share in large measure. (p. 20).

So much for Quine's assessment of Peirce's theory of meaning. The question now is whether or not this assessment is right, and I shall argue that it is not.

Given our earlier reflections on the pragmatic maxim, and Peirce's explication of its meaning and intent, we can agree with Quine that, infelicitous phrasing aside, the pragmatic maxim was offered as a criterion for the meaning of sentences. For the reasons mentioned earlier, however, Peirce's provision of the pragmatic maxim as a criterion for the meaning of sentences is quite explicit in the various ways he explicated the import of the maxim. Secondly, and for reasons also noted above, it is wrong to suggest without qualification that the pragmatic maxim is simply the expression of the verificationist theory of meaning "echoed in the Vienna Circle." To do so is misleading and represents a fundamental misconstrual of pragmaticism because it tends to suggest (given the fairly common reading of Vienna positivism in terms of narrow verificationism) that, for Peirce, sentences asserting the existence of abstract entities are meaningless because not verifiable. This may well have been part and parcel of the early positivist's theory of meaning but, as we have seen, the adoption of the pragmatic maxim does not carry in its train a repudiation of abstract entities, just as it does not carry with it the view that only those sentences are meaningful which are either analytic or empirically verifiable. The most that can be said here is that Peirce, like the positivists, held that the meaning of a descriptive proposition is the conditions of its verification; but that does not imply repudiating abstract entities, and it does not require that only those sentences are meaningful which have truth conditions.[13]

Quine applauds the shift of semantic focus from terms to sentences but sees nothing very distinctive in the pragmatist's endorsement of the view. (p. 11). This predictable criticism derives from his mistaken belief that the pragmatic maxim amounts to nothing more than an early statement of the verification theory of meaning, echoed in the Vienna Circle, and his identification of the shift with the adoption of the verificationist's theory of sentence meaning. At any rate, and for the reasons noted above, it is distinctive of Peirce's pragmaticism that, in providing for the shift, it did not thereby imply a commitment to narrow verificationism. On Quine's view, however, the shift of semantic focus from terms to sentences was especially welcome because it allowed for paraphrase and the elimination of reference to abstract entities. (p. 4). It is important, I think, to note that this virtue, which Quine now attributes to the shift, can obtain only if verificationism is understood to imply a complete repudiation of abstract entities. After all, the shift of semantic focus from terms to sentences could hardly have had the effect of supporting the nominalist's reservations unless the nominalist had assumed (as the early Quine certainly did) that *any* meaningful sentence utilizing abstract terms can, without losss of meaning, be paraphrased into a sentence committing us to the existence of physical objects only. Certainly, verificationism, as Quine here construes it, could not have been (and cannot be) the view that *some*, but not *all*, empirically meaningful statements utilizing abstract terms admit of physicalistic paraphrase; for, if that were the case, distinguishing between those meaningful statements that *do*, and those that *do not*, admit of physicalist paraphrase would be arbitrary. How could we distinguish between sentences which are meaningful but not capable of physicalist paraphrase, and sentences which are meaningless because not capable of physicalistic paraphrase? In short, there is a contradiction involved in saying that verificationism had (or has) the virtue of purging some but not all abstract entities; for if it succeeds in purging *any* at all, it could only do so under the assumption that *any* sentence not capable of physicalistic paraphrase is meaningless. In other words, if verificationism has any virtue at all by way of purging reference to abstract entities, it can only succeed in doing that on the condition that any sentence not so paraphrasable is meaningless. Quine, of course, says that although we cannot purge all reference to abstract entities in science, still, the virtue of the shift of semantic focus from terms to sentences was that it allowed the nominalist to pursue his reservations more fully than was previously possible. (p. 4). And, for the reasons mentioned, I am arguing that it could not have had that virtue and still allow for belief in some abstract entities. In sum, Quine urges that, from an empiricist's viewpoint, what was distinctive and important about the shift was that it abetted the nominalist's program; and this, I submit, it could not have done unless we assume that the shift carried with it a commitment to narrow verificationism. Peirce's verificationism, however, does not principally seek to sustain nominalism. And how Quine can consistently urge that abstract entities in science cannot be wholly eliminated and yet, at the same time, claim that the virtue of verificationism is that it allowed us to pursue our nominalistic reservations more fully is, I have argued, quite quiestionable.[14] Peirce's verificationism, and hence his naturalism, is distinctive in that, unlike Quine's, it *consistently* allows for belief in abstract entities and its importance is underscored by the fact that such a form of verificationism would appear to be a necessity, given that science cannot dispense with reference to abstract entities.

Secondly, and more interestingly, Quine claims that although we can doubtlessly find texts which show that Peirce was unquestionably aware that scientific theory confronts its evidence holistically; still, such awareness is hard to reconcile with Peirce's facile account of pragmatic meaning, or of one's conception of an object. (p. 12). And if we are tempted to think that holism is implied by Peirce's theory of truth, then Quine argues that Peirce's theory of truth is all wrong. So, for these reasons Quine asserts that Peirce cannot be thought to have successfully endorsed semantic holism, the third important turning point in post-Humean empiricism. Moreover, Quine does not stand alone on this point. Føllesdal, for example, has argued that Quine's thesis on the indeterminacy of translation is nothing more than the combination of Duhem's holism and Peirce's verificationism.[15] Bypassing momentarily the discussion of whether or not Peirce's verificationism is the same as the verificationism Quine has in mind in the thesis on the indeterminacy of translation, Føllesdal's equation implies, or at least strongly suggest, that semantic holism is not a thesis we can attribute to Peirce. And there are probably a good many others who might agree.

In replying to this line of reasoning, the first thing to note is that there are a number of texts which indicate that Peirce was unquestionably aware that scientific theory confronts its evidence holistically.[16] On Peirce's view, for example, we will always find discrepancies between theory and observation (1.132); and when we seek to verify a law, the discrepancies between theory and observation can either be written off to errors in observation (1.3-32) or can be used to modify the theory to fit the observations. (1.74; 2.771). And this reflects what he elsewhere argued, namely, that any sentence can be held in the face of disconfirming evidence by adjusting other sentences in the theory. (MS 290 pp. 2–3). He even suggests that we keep our theories as flexible as possible to accomodate wayward data. (5.376 no. 2 note no. 1). Moreover, for Peirce, verification is ultimately a matter of finding out how much like the truth our hypothesis is, that is, what proportion of its anticipations or predictions will be verified. (2.775). So, predictions need not *always* come out for the law to be true; for, what we are seeking is a matter of statistical corroboration. (8.194).

To suggest that these texts are not to be taken seriously because they are hard to reconcile with Peirce's "facile account of pragmatic meaning or of one's conception of an object" seems too enigmatic as a reason for disparaging the holistic dimensions of Peirce's semantics. Moreover, were we to urge that Peirce's holism is readily implied by his frequent endorsement of the view that the truth of any descriptive proposition is a function of whether or not it would be endorsed by the scientific community in the idealized long-run, then Quine would remind us that such a theory of truth is unacceptable. Although considerations of space do not here permit it, I would argue that Quine's criticism of Peirce's theory of truth is itself unacceptable because Quine's criticism is predicated on the false but generally accepted contention that Peirce has a limit theory of truth.[17] And if this is so, it would appear that Quine's strongest reason for rejecting the view that Peirce favored holism is deficient. For the moment, however, I think we can conclude that there is ample textual evidence favoring the position that Peirce was committed to holism.

The last two turning point in post-Humean empiricism are (a) the shift to methodological monism (which implies, and is implied by, the repudiation of the analytic-synthetic distinction) and (b) the move to Naturalism. With respect to (b), Peirce was an undaunted naturalist simply because he never tired of insisting upon the exclusive use of the method of the natural sciences for the ascertainment of truth. (1.128; 5.6). Moreover, it is interesting to note that with regard to (a), Peirce's reasons for rejecting the analytic-synthetic distinction do not feed on nominalistic scruples; and since this is a pointed consideration in his naturalism, we can reflect briefly on it now.

Traditionally understood, analytic propositions are propositions that are so true that it is inconceivable that they should ever be false in any universe of discourse. But, for Peirce, what we cannot conceive today, we may be able to conceive tomorrow. (8.191), and so 'inconceivability of the opposite' is by no means an index of absolute certainty in the sense of 'true in all possible universes of discourse'. (2.29). Moreover, apart from the liability of error in all forms of reasoning, and part from the history of science which teaches us that even our most exact theories are only rough approximations subject to continual revision, Peirce claimed that all reasoning is fundamentally synthetic (based ultimately upon observation and inductive inference) and hence a matter of probability and not certainty. (3.528; 2.693; 2.685; 8.83; 2.778). Just as Peirce's espousal of *synechism* provided him with the logical foundation for this thesis on the inherent indeterminacy (vagueness) of all propositions, the inherent indeterminacy of all our propositions accounts for their being not exactly true.[18] And he clearly extended this view to include the propositions of mathematics and logic. His reasoned acceptance of a thoroughgoing synechism especially convinced him of the fallible nature of mathematics.[19] And on this latter score, he argued that the apparently necessary character of mathematical and logical reasoning is obtained by means of observation and 'experimentation' upon the objects of our own creation, diagrams. In short, the apparently necessary character of mathematical and logical reasoning is due simply to the circumstance that the subject of the observation is a diagram of our own creation, a hypothetical state of affairs the conditions of whose being we know all about since we create it. (3.560; 2.778).[20] Because the propositions of mathematics and logic are about hypothetical states, the reasoning can be necessary, that is, not subject to empirical falsification; but since the same propositions are dependent upon diagrammatic observation, they are as fallible as any conclusion based upon observation.[21] These are dark sayings, of course, but the fact that Peirce construes the subject matter of math and logic in terms of hypothetical entities created by us and whose properties are inferred by us from diagrammatic observations of them, speaks in favor of the view that, for Peirce, while mathematics and logic may make use of abstractions, mathematical entities are not real platonic abstract entities since they don't exist independently of minds. Mathematical and logical truths are truths about hypothetical entities, entities which exist only conceptually; but even then, the truths about such entities are only *apparently* necessary because the truths proceed by way of inference from diagrammatic observation which is subject to error. Or so it would seem.

Whether or not Peirce is right in all this is a long story which we cannot enter into here. But even if he were wrong in claiming that the propositions of mathematics and logic are dependent, to some relevantly important degree, upon observation and experiment, still, it would certainly seem that the fallible nature of *all* propositions follows from a thoroughgoing synechism, a synechism which he quite clearly extended, by way of its fallibilistic implications, into a domain of mathematical and logical reasoning. However rough and ready these reasons may appear, it is significant that Peirce did not eschew analyticity, either directly or by way of implication, for the reason that failure to do so would have committed him to belief in the existence of abstract entities.[22] More on this shortly.

In the light of the above considerations, we can conclude that, Quine's assessment notwithstanding, Peirce espoused the five turning points which have doctrinally advanced empiricism since Hume. But the resulting empiricism is radically non-Humean owing to the broad verificationism implied by the adoption of the pragmatic maxim. More importantly, however, Peirce's theory of meaning would appear to advance the empiricist enterprise in at least two ways heretofore not noted.

In the first place, because the pragmatic maxim does not rule against belief in abstract entities, it provides a solid intuitive base for an empiricism which cannot quite swallow the view that science can effectively dispense with all reference to abstract entities. It is because Quine does not see this as part of Peirce's theory of meaning that he fails to see this as something distinctive and important by way of providing comfort for a naturalism which, like Quine's, cannot effectively jettison belief in abstract entities. In this regard Peirce's theory of meaning is not so much an extension of post-Humean empiricism as it is a repudiation in favor of an idealized empiricism.

Quine, of course, has most recently come out in favor of an ontology of real platonic abstract entities, numbers.[23] It is, however, difficult to see how this ontological turn is consistent with the narrow verificationism Quine endorses. After all, if, as Quine claims, the virtue of verificationism is that it allows us to pursue our nominalistic aims (a virtue which I have argued above is inconsistent with belief in the existence of *any* abstract entities and which Quine wrongly supposes to be implied by Peirce's endorsement of the shift of semantic focus from terms to sentences), then holding on to the verificationist theory of meaning, as so construed, would seem to be inconsistent with, because rendering meaningless, an ontology of abstract entities. Peirce's verificationism, however, is not at odds with such an ontology and hence furthers the ends of an idealized empiricism; whereas Quine's verificationism undermines his idealized empiricism by rendering its ontology meaningless. It is only by returning to a Peircean verificationism that Quine could justify his ontology of abstract entities.

In the second place, methodological monism, identified with the rejection of the analytic-synthetic distinction, seems more plausible in Peirce's hands than it does in Quine's. This is because Quine's rejection of analyticity ultimately rests on nominalistic scruples and is thus inconsistent with his ontological turn to abstract entities, whereas Peirce's rejection of that distinction does not feed on such scruples and hence is not at all inconsistent with such an idealized empiricism. Let me explain.

Schuldenfrei has argued, convincingly I believe, that Quine is a radical positivist whose attack on analyticity in "Two Dogmas of Empiricism" is best viewed as an attempt to purify positivism by moving against an aspect of positivism which he sees as inconsistent with a purified naturalism, that is, a naturalism that can have no truck with modalities necessary for explaining analyticity,[24] and Quine himself has said that in "Two Dogmas of Empiricism" he was not arguing for pragmatism but rather seeking to repair empiricism.[25] We now know, of course that the repair job consisted in scotching the analytic-synthetic distinction and urging the doctrine of holism. On Quine's view, if we take verificationism seriously, something which even the positivists themselves did not do,[26] then we must rule against analyticity since analyticity involves a commitment to belief in modalities the existence of which, since they are abstract entities, cannot be verified. Accordingly, it seems reasonable to view Quine's attack on analyticity as motivated by the belief that a purified naturalism requires a verificationism that is inconsistent with belief in abstract entities. And if this is so, how can Quine's abandonment of analyticity be consistent with his liberalized ontology? Boorse has argued that Quine's liberalized epistemology is inconsistent with his semantic positivism, that sustaining the former implies abandoning the latter, and that with the abandonment go all the arguments for indeterminacy of translation.[27] I am further suggesting that Quine's rejection of the analytic-synthetic distinction is inconsistent with his liberalized ontology since that rejection is also based upon radical semantic positivism, or, as I have called it above, a narrow verificationism. Keeping the ontology implies abandoning the semantic positivism, and, with that, Quine's attack on the analytic-synthetic distinction falls to the ground carrying with it his defense of methodological monism. Peirce's defense of methodological monism does not suffer such criticism because his rejection of the analytic-synthetic distinction is not rooted in semantic positivism or a narrow verificationism. These considerations also seem to suggest that an idealized or liberal cmpiricism can undermine the analytic-synthetic distinction only if it repudiates nominalism; and in that case, the rejection of the distinction (which rejection is essential for methodological monism) would require a theory of meaning consistent with a commitment to abstract entities. For this reason Peirce's assault on the analytic-synthetic distinction provides a more coherent empiricist foundation for methodological monism than does Quine's assault on the same distinction. And all this should lend force to the view that there is something distinctively important to be learned from Peirce's theory of meaning if an adequate empiricism is to sustain methodological monism.

In sum, I have been arguing that Quine has misconstrued Peirce's verificationism, overlooked Peirce's rejection of the analytic-synthetic distinction and has unjustifiably slighted Peirce's espousal of holism. Moreover, for all the reasons mentioned above, Peirce's theory of meaning represents a naturalism consistent with an idealized empiricism, an empiricism which Quine adopts but which, owing to his narrow verificationism, he cannot justify.

Finally, something should be said briefly about Peirce's empiricism as it relates to Quine's doctrine on the indeterminacy of translation. As noted above, Føllesdal has urged that the doctrine on the indeterminacy of translation is nothing more than the combination of Peircean verificationism and Duhemian holism. Since I have argued that Peirce was clearly committed to the doctrine of holism, it might be tempting to suggest that, in the end, Peirce too would adopt the doctrine on the indeterminacy of translation. But nothing could be further from the truth because Peirce's verificationism is not at all the same form of verificationism that Quine adopts; and Hintikka has been quick to note that Føllesdal's equation is guilty of conflating the two without careful examination.[28] Hintikka claims that Føllesdal's equation hides the extraordinarily narrow interpretation Quine puts on notions like observability and possible observation, notions which are presupposed in any concept of verificationism. For Quine, possible observations do not include observations that would have been made had another possible course of events been realized. (p. 7). Hintikka, I think, is right; but I would add that the reason why Quine does not do as much is because it would ential a commitment to modalities which his narrow verificationism does not allow. Peirce is not at all committed to such a narrow interpretation of possible observations because he does not espouse such a narrow verificationism. Not only is Quine not close to the pragmaticism of Peirce, he is, unfortunately for his liberalized ontology, at odds with it. From an ontological viewpoint, Peirce is just not in the Humean tradition and Quine is trapped there with an ontology that won't fit it.

Moreover, bypassing Boorse's argument that the indeterminacy of translation falls to the ground with a theory of meaning that would be consistent with Quine's liberalized ontology, the ontological upshot of the indeterminacy thesis is something that Peirce would not endorse. Without caring to argue the details here (because this paper is already too long) I think we can grant that Peirce was well aware that physical theory is underdetermined by observational data. (7.117). But that there could be *unto eternity* mutually incompatible, but empirically equivalent, translation manuals for current theory is something he could not endorse because it would be inconsistent with his view that science, unto eternity, is progressive and that, given time, we shall find out the ways things substantially are. Defending this latter claim, however, involves defending Peirce's theory of truth, a theory which I also believe is sorely misunderstood but capable of strenuous defense.[29]

Robert Almeder

Georgia State University

NOTES

*I would like to thank R. L. Arrington, M. Snoeyenbos, R. Ketchum and P. Hare for their comments on an earlier draft.

1. 5.402 (revised for publication in 1902). See also 5.2; 5.9; 5.18; 5.427; MS 327. I follow the standard method for citing from *The Collected Papers of Charles Sanders Peirce* (vols. 1–6, eds. Charles Hartshorne and Paul Weiss, Harvard University Press, Cambridge: 1936, and vols. 7–8, ed. Arthur Burks, Harvard University Press, Cambridge: 1959). For example, volume 5, section 322, would be cited as 5.322. Reference to the unpublished papers are preceded by an MS followed by the appropriate number of the MS. For example MS 233 would refer to the unpublished manuscript numbered 233. The microfilm edition of the unpublished papers can be obtained from the Widener Library, Harvard University, Cambridge, Mass.

2. See 5.18; 4.453; 5.480–83; 3.440; 3.472; 4.572; 8.194–5; 8.359–61; 2.330; 3.440; MS 817 (p. 3).

3. It is important to note that initially (as noted in 5.18 and suggested in 2.330), Peirce had insisted that the meaning of any positive assertion consisted in a corresponding conditional, the antecedent of which is of the form 'If you do *x*, then etc.' rather than "If you *were* to do *x*, then etc." The initial formulation led Peirce to the

following question: suppose a diamond crystallized in the middle of the earth and was accidently consumed by fire before one could verify that it was hard. Was that diamond *really* hard? Peirce initially answered the question by saying that it was simply a matter of linguistic convenience to say that the diamond was really hard. (5.403). Much later, however, he changed his mind on this question and argued that the hardness of the diamond does not accrue to it in virtue of the actual employment of the experimental method. Indeed, to say that a diamond is hard, is to say that if one *were* to perform certain operations, then certain sensible results *would* ensue. (5.457). See also 5.480–482; 5.457; 8.380–4; 1.420; 6.327; 8.216; 4.546; 4.580ff; 8.208; 5.453; 8.359–61; MS 289 (p. 11); 2.330; 5.529.

4. 5.553. See also 5.467; 2.407 nl; 5.412.

5. Peirce identified the concept of law with the concept of habit. The laws of the universe are the habits which the universe takes on. Hence if the meaning of any proposition is fundamentally a statement of the laws which govern and account for the properties of objects, then it would follow that what a proposition means is simply what habits it involves (5.400). See also 5.18; 2.148; MS 289 (p. 4).

6. See 5.491 and MS 318. In his book, *The Development of Peirce's Philosophy*, Professor Murphey argues (as against Buchler and Gentry), that the logical interpretant *cannot* be the meaning of any proposition; rather the meaning of any proposition is what the logical interpretant expresses, namely, the law or habit which the adoption of the given statement as a belief would imply (p. 315ff). Actually, however, the truth of the matter seems to be that for Peirce, the meaning of a proposition is expressed by a set of conditional statements which express a law so that ultimately the meaning of a proposition derives from the existence of laws (habits). Meaning for Peirce is not law; rather law is the foundation of meaning or accounts for the existence of meaningful propositions. 'Meaning' is a property of utterances. (5.427).

7. On the indeterminacy of meaning see also 2.428; 1.549; 2.357; 5.569; 6.494; 5.505–6; 1.339; 2.646; 8.208; 6.496; 5.157; 5.183; 5.480; 5.447–8; 5.554; MS 432 (Logic IV p. 193); MS 9 (p. 5).

8. For a defense of the view that conceptual inexactness is a necessary feature of empirical concepts, see R. G. Swinburne's 'Vagueness, Inexactness and Imprecision', in *The British Journal for the Philosophy of Science* 29, No. 4. See also the opposing view as expressed by Marvin Kohl in "Bertrand Russell on Vagueness," *Australasian Journal of Philosophy* (May, 1969), pp. 31ff. In this latter regard, it should be noted that, for Peirce, it is not the case that a term is vague because the *extent* of its application is essentially doubtful. Finally, for a fuller treatment of Peirce's views on individuals and for a defense of the view that Peirce, both early and late, consistently denied the existence of individuals, see my 'Peirce's Pragmatism and Scotistic Realism' in *The Transactions of the Charles S. Peirce Society: A Quarterly Journal in American Philosophy* (Spring 1973) pp. 3–23.

9. 1.175; 3.93ff; MS 886; MS 949 (p. 2ff); MS 950. See also M. G. Murphey's *The Development of Peirce's Philosophy* (Cambridge: Harvard University Press, 1963), last chapter.

10. For reasons which cannot be discussed here, I would add, however, that Peirce's views on the nature of universals and numbers did not incline him to construing either as real platonic abstract entities.

Incidentally, it has been argued that Peirce's commitment to a belief in abstract entities is inconsistent with his obvious espousal of naturalism, and that this bespeaks an unfortunate inconsistency which runs throughout his philosophical world-view.

(See T. Goudge's *The Thought of Charles Sanders Peirce*. Toronto: University of Toronto Press, 1950). It can be argued, however, that this criticism assumes that naturalism, by definition, is a doctrine which asserts that only physical objects exist; and while this may be true for many naturalists, it seems clear that Peirce's naturalism is not to be construed in this way. Rather it is the thesis that only with the employment of the method of the natural sciences can we determine the truth of what is asserted to exist. On this latter construal of naturalism, if it can be argued, as Peirce did, that belief in the existence of abstract entities can have conceivable practical or observable effects which would verify the belief, then there is no reason to assume that naturalism implies repudiating an ontology of abstract entities.

11. 'The Pragmatist's Place in Empiricism'. At present this paper is unpublished but was read at a Symposium on Pragmatism at the University of South Carolina in 1975. In referring to this essay I am referring to a copy of the paper obtained at the Colloquium. The proceedings of the Symposium will soon be published by the University of South Carolina Press and will include Quine's paper.

12. p. 12. Quine also argues that that the limit theory of truth is distinctive of Peirce and could perhaps best be construed anthropocentrically as a sort of idealism or social Protagoreanism, representing scientific method as dictating to reality.

13. See 2.511 n. 1; 2.639; 2.640; 2.511 n; 5.203; 5.198; 5.402 n. 2 and 5.423.

14. Curiously enough, Quine frequently identifies *verificationism* as a view about the meaning of sentences, a view which he contrasts with *holism*. So construed, of course, *verificationism* is a doctrine Quine rejects in favor of *holism*. But when he identifies it as a theory about sentence meaning, a theory which allows one to purge some (but not all) reference to abstract entities, it is not a doctrine which he rejects; and I am arguing that if, as Quine urges, *verificationism* has the virtue of supporting the nominalist's stance, it could only achieve that end only if *narrow verificationism*, as I have construed it, is true. And this is to say that Quine's endorsement of the virtue of verificationism is inconsistent with his adopting an ontology that allows for belief in *any* abstract entities. Presumably, these considerations will dispel the charitable suggestion that there is nothing at all inconsistent with adopting verificationism as a technique for purging reference to some abstract entities and countenacing an ontology that allows for belief in abstract entities.

15. 'Indeterminacy of Translation and the Underdetermination of the Theory of Nature', *Dialectica* 27 (1973), 289–301.

16. 5.426; 5.467; 7.78; 5.424; 5.506; 2.762; 2.407ff; 2.637; 2.709; 2.717; 2.732. In arguing, as we have, that the pragmatic maxim is a criterion for the meaning of sentences, it need not be thought that the adoption of the pragmatic maxim is inconsistent with the adoption of holism. Holism, I take it, is *not* the view that *sentences* do not have meaning; rather, it is the view that the meaning of the sentence is issued in terms of the conditions for the whole theory in which the sentence is embedded.

17. For a detailed examination of Peirce's theory of truth and various objections against it, see my 'Fallibilism and the Ultimate Irreversible Opinion' *The American Philosophical Quarterly Monograph* vol. 9, 1975, pp. 33–54 and 'Science and Idealism', *Philosophy of Science* 40 (1973), 242–254.

18. 7.419; 1.171–2; 7.566ff; 6.13; 6.553ff; 5.296ff; 1.103ff and 7.95.

19. See 2.77; MS 334 E2; 5.567–9; 7.566.

20. See also 2.81; 1.145; 1.149; MS 334 E2; MS 426 (Logic II p. 71); MS 425 (Logic 86).

21. 2.447; 1.140; 2.693; 4.237; 4.478; 4.531; 5.376 n2 n1; 1.630; 7.108; 1.248; 2.216; 2.30; MS 16 (p. 7); MS 334 E2; MS 606 (Li6 28).

22. For other texts bearing on Peirce's rejection of the analytic-synthetic distinction see 5.187; 2.192; 2.176; 2.162; 2.171ff; 3.527; 4.71; 2.173; 2.158; 1.633; 1.661; 2.151; 2.192; 5.506; 5.560; 5.183; 5.480; 4.447; 6.496; 5.554; 4.487; 1.441ff MS 955 (p. 4); MS 200 (MME 82); MS 200 (MME 96); MS 1 (p. 4); MS 355.

23. 'Whither Physical Objects?', in *Essays in Memory of Imre Lakatos*, ed. by R. S. Cohen, P. K. Feyerabend, and M. W. Wartofsky, D. Reidel, Dordrecht, 1976, pp. 497–504.

24. 'Quine in Perspective', *The Journal of Philosophy* 69 (1972), 5–14.

25. "The Pragmatist's Place in Empiricism," p. 21.

26. 'Epistemology Naturalized', in *Empirical Knowledge*, edited by R. Chisholm and R. Schwarz (New York: Prentice-Hall, 1972).

27. 'The Origins of the Indeterminacy Thesis', *The Journal of Philosophy*. 62 (1975), p. 370.

28. 'Quine vs Peirce', *Dialectica*, 30 (1976) pp. 7–8.

29. See my *The Philosophy of Charles Peirce: A Critical Introduction* (Oxford: Basil Blackwell, 1980) Chapter one.

C. S. PEIRCE ON BIOLOGICAL EVOLUTION
AND SCIENTIFIC PROGRESS*

In the distant future I see open fields for far more important researches. Psychology will be based on a new foundation, that of the necessary acquirement of each mental power and capacity by gradation. Light will be thrown on the origin of man and his history.

—Charles Darwin

The evolutionary theory in general throws great light upon history and especially on the history of science—both its public history and the account of its development in an individual intellect. As great a light is thrown upon the theory of evolution in general by the evolution of history, especially that of science—whether public or private.

—Charles S. Peirce

1. Introduction

Charles Sanders Peirce (1839–1914) has gradually gained recognition as a precursor of a wide variety of important intellectual developments of our own century. He was a pioneer of symbolic logic, set theory, probability theory, semantics, and semiotics. He was an indeterminist in physics a generation before the advent of the quantum theory. In philosophy, he formulated a great many of those ideas which have later become associated with the names of Karl Popper, W. V. O. Quine, and the later Wittgenstein. In almost all areas of his thought, Peirce was what one calls 'ahead of his times', a thinker more properly belonging to the mid-twentieth than to the late nineteenth century.

Yet on the subject of biological evolution this otherwise seminal thinker appears strangely dated, at times reactionary and obscurantist, and always confusing. Peirce's chief philosophical concerns were the logic and history of science; and his writings on these subjects abound with physiological analogies to individual thought-processes, and evolutionary analogies to the historical growth of scientific knowledge. At times he clearly goes beyond mere analogy and attempts straightforward biological and evolutionary *explanations* of intellectual phenomena. At the same time, his attitude towards the theory of natural selection was always ambiguous, and at times outright hostile. As Philip P. Wiener puts it in an oft-quoted passage, "Peirce was less than lukewarm toward Darwin's theory of natural selection as a scientific hypothesis."[2] Against Darwin's theory he opposed a speculative theory of cosmic evolution, incorporating, besides natural selection, elements of

Lamarckism, catastrophism, Schelling's idealism, and St. John's Gospel. Wiener suggests that Peirce's attitude towards Darwinism was shaped partly by a priori metaphysical biasses, partly by personal loyalty towards his teacher Louis Agassiz, a catastrophist who opposed Darwin throughout his life.[2] Peirce, then, picked and chose from biology whatever could be made to fit his own preconceived metaphysics and cosmology, no matter if the "fit" took the shape only of far-flung analogies. On this interpretation, which has become something lide the received view, Peirce's views on biological evolution are not wholly rational and cannot be rationally reconstructed— except, perhaps, to the extent that his evolutionary cosmology can be so reconstructed. As for his cosmology, few have been able to make head or tail of it, and it is generally regarded as "the black sheep or white elephant of his philosophical progeny," as W. B. Gallie aptly puts it.[3]

The interpretation which will be advanced in this paper, is that Peirce's criticisms of Darwinism can be seen as rational, interesting, and not obvious-ly invalid, quite apart from any consideration of his highly speculative evolutionary cosmology. They should not, however, be viewed as serious con-tributions to biological theory, which was not Peirce's field, but as contribu-tions to epistemology and to the philosophy and history of science, which were Peirce's fields par excellence. Put briefly, the incongruities which the received view, following Wiener, dismisses as irrational, can be seen as a perfectly rational attempt to solve a twofold problem in epistemology. On the one hand, Peirce opposed a whole host of traditional dualisms, between life and non-life, between man and nature, and between mind and matter, dualisms which prescribed absolute boundaries to the problems which could be investigated by the methods of empirical science. On the other hand, he opposed the in his day fashionable "positivistic" suppression of genuine problems of logic, epistemology and metaphysics, a suppression frequently motivated or rationalized by biological reductionism. On both hands, Peirce was concerned to uphold the freedom of inquiry and remove barriers to further scientific progress. The focal point for understanding Peirce's attitude towards Darwinism is to be found in his own motto: "Do not block the way of inquiry!" (*Collected Papers*, I.135)

In venturing into the rarefied air of technical Peirce-scholarship, I am aware of treading on ground which has been trodden before by people more knowledgeable than I, and I am conscious of an obligation to specify what sort of interpretative principles I shall employ, and what sort of claims I am making for my own interpretation. Briefly, the history of Peirce-scholarship may be divided into two major phases. The first phase, which is represented i.a., by Justus Buchler,[4] J. K. Feibleman,[5] and W. B. Gallie, comprised "rational reconstructions," or attempts at presenting Peirce's thought as a systematic unity. This approach was challenged around 1950 by Wiener and by T. A. Goudge,[6] and the first phase was definitively buried in 1961, with the appearance of Murray G. Murphey's monumental work,[7] which pushed the attempt at rational reconstruction to its limit, and gave a prima facie irrefutable demonstration that no systematic unity is to be found in Peirce's thought. Anyone who wishes today to uphold the interpretations of Buchler or Feibleman, will have to meet Murphey's formidable challenge. Until that challenge has been met, Peirce-scholarship is in its second phase of meticulous biographical scholarship, elucidating the development of Peirce's thought. Outstanding names in this enterprise are Murphey himself, Philip P. Wiener, and Max Fisch.[8]

In taking exception to Wiener's interpretation of Peirce's evolutionism, I do not wish to challenge him in the field of biographical scholarship. Nor do I wish to take up Murphey's challenge against the "systematic" tradition. There remains a third option, exemplified i.e., by John F. Boler's work on Peirce's scholastic realism.[9] The renunciation of attempts to find a systematic *unity* in Peirce's thought does not entail a renunciation of all attempts at rational reconstruction. Aspects of Peirce's thought may be rationally reconstructed, even though it is admitted that the whole cannot be. Evidently, the whole range of rational reconstructions which may be so produced, will never fit together like a jigsaw-puzzle into one comprehensive interpretation of Peirce's thought. It follows that the motivation for so limiting one's perspective cannot be *merely* to advance our understanding of Peirce; rather, that understanding is to some extent renounced on for the sake of other benefits, specifically a better understanding of the particular problems with which Peirce at various times dealt, and which are presumed to hold an independent interest.

The point of departure for this paper, then, is that the problems which occupied Peirce are of interest in their own right, and that Peirce has interesting and worthwhile things to say about them. The relationship between our knowledge of man as an animal and our knowledge of man as a knower is a subject of controversy today, as it was in Peirce's day. The extension of the model of natural selection to the explanation of all spheres of human activity is still advocated, in different ways, by e.g., Edward O. Wilson,[10] Stephen Toulmin,[11] and Donald T. Campbell.[12] Among these, at least Wilson is currently sufficiently influential to motivate an interest in arguments to the contrary. At the same time, it is not in the end all that satisfactory simply to conclude that man's intellectual evolution is "different from" biological evolution. We cannot, except at the risk of obscurantism, draw an absolute boundary to the sphere of application of evolutionary biology. What wants explaining, is how come evolution through natural selection has produced a new and different mode of evolution which does *not* operate through natural selection? Peirce was, to my knowledge, one of the first who seriously tackled this problem,[13] and later discussions do not seem to me to have advanced much beyond the solution which he proposed.[14]

It should be added that Peirce's discussion has even wider ramifications than those indicated. One corollary of extending the natural-selection model to the evolution of science is that scientific theories come to be viewed as instruments of organic adaptation. Since Peirce attacks this extended application of Darwinism primarily by attacking its instrumentalist corollary, his discussion remains a profound and powerful critique of instrumentalism, independently of the issue of the evolutionary origins of science.

In this paper, I shall first sketch Peirce's response to Darwin's theory of evolution. I shall then indicate the broader implications of this response, by placing it in relation to Peirce's twofold opposition both to traditional dualism and to the reductionistic instrumentalism fashionable in his day.

2. Peirce's Response to Darwin

It has become a commonplace to describe pragmatism as part of the intellectual response to Darwinism,[15] and, on the whole, as a favorable response. The chief forerunner of pragmatism, Chauncey Wright, was one of Darwin's earliest and most orthodox defenders in America. William James, with Peirce the co-founder of pragmatism, gained his intellectual reputation by extending Darwinian theory to psychology. John Dewey, perhaps the most influential of the pragmatists, never tired of claiming his intellectual descent from Darwin. And, no matter what philosophical differences there were between the three great pragmatists, they fully shared the conception of human knowledge, not as something either static or disembodied, but as essentially a human activity, with historical antecedents, and capable of indefinite future growth.

This conception was not unique to the pragmatists, nor was it unique to the post-Darwinian era. The conception of culture as a process of growth had long been emphasized by a variety of thinkers, including Comte, Schelling, Hegel, Spencer, and Buckle. Clausius and Maxwell had shaken the faith (epitomized in Kant) in the finality and completeness of Newtonian mechanics. Still, within the Anglo-Saxon tradition, Peirce was well-nigh alone[16] in drawing the daring conclusion that science was not the sort of thing that ever *could* be finished. The most striking feature of nineteenth-century science, in Peirce's view, was the increasing role of statistics, not only in the kinetic theory of gases, but, more importantly, in the theory of measurement, in which he himself was one of the pioneers. From the ubiquity of probable errors in scientific measurements, Peirce concluded, firstly, to the inherent inexactitude of all scientific measurements, and hence to the existence of real chance in nature, and, secondly, to the radical fallibility and improvability of all scientific predictions. Science was not in the process of becoming more certain; it was in the process of growing *less* certain, and its uncertainty was becoming progressively more obvious as statistical explanations gradually replaced deterministic ones.

One would expect this conception of science to predispose Peirce favorably towards Darwinism; and so it did, up to a point. What particularly appealed to Peirce in Darwin's theory was an aspect which Darwin himself tried to conceal in embarrassment, namely the employment of chance as a mode of explanation. Peirce was, to my knowledge, the first thinker who explicitly recognized the statistical character of Darwin's theory, and recognized this as a scientifically respectable mode of explanation. Time and again he returns to this theme, praising Darwin for his application of statistical methods to biology, and referring to the Darwinian theory of evolution as an application to the animal realm of a general theorem of probability. For instance, in 1877, Peirce wrote: "The Darwinian controversy is, in large part, a question of logic. Mr. Darwin proposed to apply the statistical method to biology. The same thing has been done in a widely different branch of science, the theory of gases." (CP, V.364) Again, in 1891, he explicitly compared Darwinian evolution with what goes on in a gambling saloon:

> This Darwinian principle is plainly capable of great generalization. Wherever there are large numbers of objects having a tendency to retain certain characters unaltered, this tendency, however, not being absolute but giving room for chance variations; then, if the amount of variation is absolutely limited in certain directions by the destruction of everything which reaches those limits, there will be a gradual tendency to change in directions of departure from them. Thus, if a million players sit down to bet at an even game, since one after another will get ruined, the average wealth of those who remain will perpetually increase. (CP, VI.15)

This analogy with a betting-game may be strained; for instance, it seems to link increase in fitness with decrease in numbers. Still, the mathematics of natural selection could not be satisfactorily worked out until the advent of the particulate inheritance theory. It is no less than remarkable that, even without an inkling of particulate inheritance, Peirce was able to such an extent to anticipate the kind of mathematical formulation of the theory of natural selection which was only worked out forty years later by R. A. Fisher.[17]

Yet Peirce's admiration for Darwin was limited to his method; it did not extend to the substance of his theory. In 1869, Peirce praised Darwin for his meticulous observations, while dismissing his theories as "theories which in themselves would barely command scientific respect." (CP, I.33) And, as late as 1893, he wrote that Darwin's hypothesis

> did not appear, at first, at all near to being proved; and to a sober mind its case looks less hopeful now than it did twenty years ago; but the extraordinarily favorable reception it met with was plainly owing, in large measure, to its ideas being those toward which the age was favorably disposed, especially, because of the encouragement it gave to the greed-philosophy. (CP, VI.297)

The latter statement may, of course, be taken as a factual statement, and, to some extent, a true one: the case for Darwinism did not, in fact, look all that hopeful in 1893, and it was not to improve until three decades later. The association of Darwin's scientific hypothesis with the greed-philosophy is clearly disparaging in intent. Still, this statement occurs in a context where Peirce attacks the Social Darwinism of a popular economics text; in his serious discussions of evolution his attitude towards Darwinism is not that of simple rejection. Towards natural selection as an explanation of biological evolution, Peirce maintained a scientifically healthy skepticism; what he outright rejected, was the application of Darwin's theory outside the field of biology. And, as we shall see, he fully recognized that even this rejection stood in need of explanation and argument.

Most of Peirce's remarks on Darwin's theory appear in the context of discussions of the origin and growth of intellectual activities in general, and of science in particular. Peirce never doubted that science has originated from instinctive beliefs, which were originally naturally selected because of their adaptive value. The reasons for this belief were two. On the one hand, he believed that science progresses towards the truth, and that it had, in fact, attained a number of truths, although one could not with certainty identify these. On the other hand, he had learnt from De Morgan that the choice between rival theories is always underdetermined by the data, and that, given any finite body of data, there will always be an infinite number of theories which will account for them.[18] How, then, can we have arrived at any true theories? The observed data do not force any theories on us; we cannot arrive at them by blind guesses, since the law of chances is overwhelmingly against the guess being right. But it is precisely the merit of natural selection that it has the power to overcome such adverse odds, by operating on large numbers over long stretches of time. We may therefore have evolved true rudimentary ideas of e.g., force and matter, because it is of adaptive value to have true ideas of such things. And, once we have attained some rudimentary truths of great generality, these will limit the scope for further guessing, confining the range of possible hypotheses to a finite and manageable number. So Peirce concluded in 1903:

> If you carefully consider with an unbiassed mind all the circumstances of the ear-
> ly history of science and all the other facts bearing on the question, . . . I am quite
> sure that you must be brought to acknowledge that man's mind has a natural
> adaptation to imagining correct theories of some kind, and in particular to cor-
> rect theories about forces, without some glimmer of which he could not form
> social ties and consequently could not reproduce his kind. (CP, V.591)

Earlier, in 1898, Peirce traced all scientific knowledge back to the two instincts of *feeding* and *breeding*:

> The instincts connected with the need of nutrition have furnished all animals with
> some virtual knowledge of space and of force, and made them applied physicists.
> The instincts connected with sexual reproduction have furnished all animals at all
> like ourselves with some virtual comprehension of the minds of other animals of
> their kind, so that they are applied psychists. Now not only our accomplished
> science, but even our scientific questions have been pretty exclusively limited to
> the development of those two branches of natural knowledge. (CP, V.586)

Science, it would seem, not only has originated in instinctual knowledge
resulting from biological adaptation, but is preserved as a human activity by
virtue of its adaptive value.

The only biological notion that is here explicitly invoked, is that of adaptation; on the role of natural selection in such adaptation, we shall for the moment note that Peirce seems to have been undecided. In 1877, Peirce expressed these doubts as to whether the rational habits of scientific thought could
have been naturally selected:

> Logicality in regard to practical matters . . . is the most useful quality an animal
> can possess, and might, therefore, result from natural selection; but outside of
> these . . . upon unpractical subjects, natural selection might occasion a fallacious
> tendency of thought. (CP, V.366)

Then, in 1902, he had turned about-face and wrote as follows, regarding the
pre-scientific, dogmatic attitude of mind:

> As civilization and enlightenment advance, however, this style of thought tends
> to weaken. Natural selection is against it; and it breaks down. (CP, II.149)

Next year, he was again skeptical of natural selection, and added this footnote to the above-quoted passage from 1877:

> Let us not, however, be cocksure that natural selection is the only factor of evolu-
> tion; and until this momentous proposition has been much better proved than as
> yet it has been, let it not blind us to the force of very sound reasoning. (CP,
> V.366n)

As I do not wish to create more problems of textual interpretation than
necessary, I may perhaps be permitted to dismiss the expression "natural
selection" in the second quotation as probably a metaphor. As for the

remaining two quotations, the first one, from 1877, expresses doubt whether the scientific *habits of mind* could have been naturally selected; and this, indeed, is a frequently recurring doctrine of Peirce's. What is not, however, denied, is that our rudimentary *world-view*, which limits the range of scientific guessing, may have been naturally selected; and this, indeed, is a frequently recurring doctrine of Peirce's. What is not, however, denied, is that our rudimentary *world-view*, which limits the range of scientific guessing, may have been naturally selected. There is thus nothing to prevent us from taking the notion of adaptation, in Peirce's account of the origin of science, in the sense of adaptation by natural selection. What the footnote from 1903 adds, is only a doubt, and in fact a justified doubt, that natural selection is the *only* factor in evolution. This doubt opens the door for the speculation that the scientific attitude may yet have evolved biologically, though through some other agency than natural selection. But this speculation is by the way, and seems to me peripheral to Peirce's account of the origin of science.

Peirce, then, not only does not rule out the possibility that the scientific activity is a product of natural selection; he even makes the rationality—i.e., the truth-producing capacity—of science *depend* on the formation of rudimentary cosmological beliefs through biological adaptation, carefully making room for the occurrence of such adaptation by natural selection— should that turn out to be the correct theory. What Peirce does, however, deny, is that natural selection can play any significant part in the internal development of science. As to the question of why it should be thought to play any part at all, I must beg the reader's patience; for the moment I only wish to sketch Peirce's main conclusions on the subject.

To start with, Peirce already held the modern, "Popperian" view of science as a process of trial and error, where experiment and observation only enter the process at the stage of testing preconceived, conjectural hypotheses, which are neither forced on us by observations, nor definitively proved by observations. The only definitive test-results are refutations; confirmations can never be more than tentative. When we 'accept' a highly confirmed hypothesis, the only rationale is that of the economy of research. This view of science had been advocated earlier (in the 1830's) by William Whewell, who was greatly admired both by Peirce and Darwin.[19] Whether Whewell in any way influenced Darwin in the direction of looking for trial-and-error processes in nature, remains an interesting subject of speculation; what is clear, is that both Peirce and a number of his contemporaries recognized the obvious *analogy* between the process of scientific growth and that of biological evolution. So, for instance, in 1902 Peirce wrote:

> We here proceed by experimentation. That is to say, we guess out the laws bit by bit. We ask, What if we were to vary our procedure a little? Would the result be the same? We try it. If we are on the wrong track, an emphatic negative soon gets

put upon the guess, and so our conceptions get nearer and nearer right. The improvement of our inventions are made in the same manner. The theory of natural selection is that nature proceeds by similar experimentation to adapt a stock of animals or plants precisely to its environment, and to keep it in adaptation to a slowly changing environment. (CP, II.86)

All that is here asserted, is a structural analogy between the two processes. Earlier, in 1896, Peirce had gone further and claimed that Darwinian evolution literally takes place in the evolution of science:

But another sort of Darwinian evolution undoubtedly does take place. We are studying over phenomena of which we have been unable to acquire any satisfactory account. Various tentative explanations recur to our minds from time to time, and at each occurrence are modified by omission, insertion, or change in the point of view, in an almost fortuitous way. Finally, one of these takes such an aspect that we are led to dismiss it as impossible. Then, all the energy of thought which had previously gone to the consideration of that becomes distributed among the other explanations, until finally one of them becomes greatly strengthened in our minds. (CP, I.107)

The kind of "Darwinian" evolution of science that Peirce contemplated, was an evolution where *theories* compete for our scarce mental resources, and where we ourselves operate as the agency of selection. It is debatable whether this attempted application of Darwinism to the growth of science is really more than another analogy. A literal application, it seems to me, would have to hold that theories are selected because they help *us* survive; this possibility Peirce did not seriously contemplate.

These analogies are not all that remarkable; they are fairly obvious, and they were recognized by many of Peirce's contemporaries, such as e.g., James, Mach, Boltzmann, Simmel, and Le Roy. What is Peirce's almost unique merit, is that he did not get dazzled by such analogies. In the passage from 1896, quoted above, he emphasizes that Darwinian evolution is only one—and even the least important one—among several modes of scientific evolution. Science also progresses in a Lamarckian fashion, through purposive efforts at modifying old theories to make them fit new observations. (CP, I.108.) (He might have added that it also depends on "Lamarckian" inheritance of acquired knowledge, a feature lately stressed by P. B. Medawar.[20]) Lastly, science also progresses in a catastrophic, or cataclysmic, fashion, conformable to the theory of Cuvier and Agassiz; i.e., it progresses through spectacular revolutions in theories or experimental techniques. Peirce anticipates Kuhn in claiming that this "certainly has been the chief factor in the historical evolution of institutions as in that of ideas." (CP, VI.17)

Peirce's arguments for Lamarckism and catastrophism are directed against an uncritical and exaggerated use of the Darwinian *analogy* in describing the growth of science. As such, they are not without interest; more interesting, however, are his arguments against the *literal* use of Darwinian theory in explaining the growth of science. These arguments are based on the recognition of the (relative) accuracy, uncertainty, and generality of scientific knowledge, as opposed to the vagueness, reliability, and particularity of natural, instinctual beliefs. The latter may have been naturally selected (and must have resulted from adaptation through *some* biological agency); the former cannot have been.

In 1878, Peirce described how true conceptions of time, space, and force may have resulted from natural selection, and how science may thus have got off the ground to start with (cf. also pp. 335–36, above); and he concludes:

> Such a hypothesis naturally suggests itself, but it must be admitted that it does not seem sufficient to account for the extraordinary accuracy with which these conceptions apply to the phenomena of Nature, and it is probable that there is some secret here which remains to be discovered. (CP, VI.418)

In 1892, Peirce is more categorical in drawing the distinction between natural beliefs and scientific propositions:

> The general approximation to truth in natural beliefs is, in fact, a case of the general adaptation of genetic products to recognizable utilities or ends. Now, the adaptations of nature, beautiful and often marvellous as they verily are, are never found to be quite perfect; so that the argument is quite *against* the absolute exactitude of any natural belief . . . (CP, VI.50)

Peirce may have forgotten that he has elsewhere denied the "absolute exactitude" of scientific beliefs as well; still, the argument holds: the relative exactitude of science goes far beyond what is needed for purposes of *immediate* survival; hence, it cannot have been naturally selected.

Furthermore, instinctual beliefs are both extremely *reliable* within their field of application, and *limited* in their field of application to the primitive conditions under which they have been formed. By contrast, rational beliefs, including the propositions of science, are never as reliable as natural beliefs, but they are much more general, so that the reliability that they do have pertains to highly complex and changing conditions:

> The great facts have always been known; such as that instinct seldom errs, while reason goes wrong nearly half the time, if not more frequently. But . . . the original beliefs only remain indubitable in their application to affairs that resemble those of a primitive mode of live. (CP, V.445 [1905])

And again Peirce writes, in 1905:

> as we develop *degrees of self-control* . . . occasions of action arise in relation to which the original beliefs, if stretched to cover them, have no sufficient authority. In other words, we outgrow the applicability of instinct—not altogether, by any manner of means, but in our highest activities. (CP, V.511)

In short, quite apart from any analogy there might or might not be between biological evolution and the growth of science, at least the literal application of evolutionary biology runs up against a boundary. Peirce does not draw the boundary between man and nature, or between consciousness and matter; rather, the line is drawn between man's highest mental activities, primarily science, and his natural, common-sense beliefs which govern everyday thought and action. The difference between the two, to borrow a later terminology from Jon Elster,[21] is that the former is a "globally maximizing" activity, while the latter is a "locally maximizing" one. Local maximization is immediately adaptive, and can therefore be picked out by natural selection; global maximization is not, and cannot be.

This completes our survey of Peirce's response to Darwin's theory of natural selection. We shall look, next, at some of the reasons for this response, as well as at some of its broader implications, by placing Peirce's evolutionism in the context of his broader epistemological concerns, as well as those of some of his contemporaries.

3. Peirce's Conception of Science

I have already referred to Peirce's fallibilistic conception of science as a process of trial and error, a conception originally propounded by Whewell and handed down to our own age chiefly through Karl Popper.[22] According to this conception, science follows a "hypothetico-deductive" method. Theories are not "based on," or "derived from," observations; they are preconceived hypotheses, or guesses, which we afterwards subject to the test of experiment or observation. More importantly, hypotheses *remain* hypotheses, no matter how many tests we perform. A scientific hypothesis is a universal statement, which remains underdetermined by any finite number of observations. There never is any logical or empirical reason why the *next* observation should not contradict the hypothesis. Logically, therefore, the experimental confirmation of a hypothesis is an endless process. The reason why we in fact rest satisfied with a finite (and often small) number of confirming tests is an economic one: research is expensive, and so we give priority to those tasks which promise to give the highest return. The same rationale dictates that we prefer those hypotheses which, if false, can be falsified with the smallest expenditure of time, energy, and other resources. The best scientific hypothesis, all other things being equal, is the one which lends itself most readily to experimental falsification:

> It is a great mistake to suppose that the mind of the active scientist is filled with propositions which, if not proved beyond reasonable cavil, are at least extremely probable. On the contrary, he entertains hypotheses which are almost wildly incredible, and treats them with respect for the time being. Why does he do this?

> Simply because any scientific proposition whatever is always liable to be refuted and dropped at short notice . . . . The best hypothesis, in the sense of the one most recommending itself to the inquirer, is the one which can be the most readily refuted if it is false. (CP, I.120 [1896])

It was Peirce's conviction that the goal of science is truth, in the absolute sense of that which "does not depend on what you or I or any man thinks" (CP, V.408 [1878]), and also that the method of hypothesis and experiment is such that it will inevitably converge on the truth in the indefinite long run: "It is true that agreement [i.e., with observation] does not show the guess is right; but if it is wrong it must ultimately get found out." (CP, I.121 [1896]) It is essential, however, that the virtue of the method consists only in its tendency to produce truth *in the long run*. In the short run, hypotheses are selected on the ground of falsifiability, and there is no reason why a hypothesis so selected should be true. Hence, in the short run, the method must be expected to lead us wrong more often than right. Scientific hypotheses, therefore, are not appropriate candidates for *belief*, and still less do they form any suitable basis for rational action. These conclusions were drawn with especial clarity in a lecture in 1898:

> Nothing is *vital* for science; nothing can be. Its accepted propositions, therefore, are opinions at most; and the whole list is provisional. The scientific man is not in the least wedded to his conclusions. He risks nothing upon them. He stands ready to abandon one or all as soon as experience opposes them . . . . There is thus no proposition at all in science which answers to the conception of belief. But in vital matters, it is quite otherwise. We must act in such matters; and the principle upon which we are willing to act is a *belief*. (CP, I.635–636)

One often hears it claimed today that the hypothetico-deductive method rationally presupposes an interest in technical control over material things and processes.[23] It is of some interest, therefore, that Peirce, who was one of the earliest proponents of this method, drew the exactly opposite conclusion: just because scientific theories are in the nature of hypotheses, subject to empirical falsification, it follows that science is not essentially a tool for action, and that the rationalty of science must be sought elsewhere than in its potential usefulness—technical or otherwise. In 1898, Peirce went so far as to *define* science by its uselessness:

> A useless inquiry, provided it is a systematic one, is pretty much the same thing as a scientific inquiry. Or at any rate if a scientific inquiry becomes by any mischance useful, that aspect of it has to be kept sedulously out of sight during the investigation or else . . . its hopes of success are fatally crushed. (CP, I.668)

The scientist must not concern himself with the technical or practical[24] uses of science, since such concerns would require him to *believe* in certain hypotheses, and would thereby undermine his scientific attitude. There can be no direct correlation, therefore, between the scientists' choice of hypotheses and society's choice of technological innovations; the two proceed from different and incompatible criteria. The rationality of the scientific method cannot, therefore, be found in its usefulness for the survival of the species, but, according to Peirce, only in its truth-producing capacity:

> [Science] does not consist so much in *knowing*, nor even in "organized knowledge," as it does in diligent inquiry into truth for truth's sake, without any sort of axe to grind, nor for the sake of the delight in contemplating it, but from an impulse to penetrate into the reason of things. (CP, 1.44 [1896])

Peirce, then, opposed the *instrumentalist* view of scientific theories as tools for technical application, and advocated a *realist* conception of science as an activity aiming at objective truth as its long-run goal. Since the words 'pragmatism' and 'instrumentalism' are today used well-nigh interchangeably, it is worth pointing out, in passing, that there is no tension between *Peirce's* pragmatism and his anti-instrumentalism. The gist of Peirce's pragmatism is that a scientific hypothesis must have conceivable practical, i.e., *testable*, consequences, and, more generally, that any meaningful statement must have such consequences. This doctrine might perhaps be more happily termed 'experimentalism': there is an intimate connection between knowledge and action, but that connection consists in the usefulness of certain actions—namely, experimental actions—for the advance of knowledge. Actions are instruments of knowledge, not the other way around. So Peirce could write without any real contradiction:

> Indeed, we may go so far as to say that the scientist cares for nothing which could not conceivably come to have a bearing on some practical question. Whether a magnitude is commensurable or not has a practical bearing on the mathematician's action. On the other hand, it cannot be said that there is any kind of proportion between the scientific interest of a fact and its probability of becoming practically interesting. (CP, VII.186 [1901])

In its first two occurrences, the word 'practical' clearly means that which has a bearing on actions, including the laboratory actions of scientists, and even the actions performed on paper by mathematicians. In its third occurrence, the word must rather be taken in the sense of 'extra-scientific'; clearly, questions which are practical enough for a scientist designing an experiment may have no extra-scientific interest whatever.

To conclude this brief aside on Peirce's pragmatism, it should be added that the stress he always placed on the word 'conceivable' and its cognates, saved him from the rather common experimentalist error of restricting the field of scientifically interesting questions to whatever was testable by *ex-*

isting experimental techniques.[25] Peirce's version of experimentalism does not make the limits of speculation coincide with the limits of available technology. But for this emphasis on conceivable, rather than actual, testability, Peirce's experimentalism might well have been thought to let instrumentalism in through the back-door.

When a man goes out of his way to contest such obvious facts as the practical usefulness of science, one is curious to know what, concretely, is the point of this assertion. It is probably worth bearing in mind that Peirce's chief intellectual preoccupations were mathematics and symbolic logic, and that his contributions in those fields were of such a path-breaking and fundamental kind that they could have no practical application in his lifetime—nor could any such application have been predicted.[26] In his lifetime Peirce had scant success in gaining a hearing for his logical theories. In 1898, when he was invited to give a series of guest-lectures at Harvard, he intended to devote these lectures to mathematical logic, but his sponsor William James dissuaded him and urged him to speak instead on "vitally important topics."[27] For Peirce, nothing was more important than logic, and it is hardly surprising that he used these lectures to defend pure, disinterested research, and deride the whole notion of "vital importance."

It would nonetheless be unfair to conclude that Peirce's anti-instrumentalism is merely a case of special pleading. Peirce had a genuine and general concern, both for the freedom of science from political intervention, and for the integrity of non-scientific modes of cognition, exemplified by i.a., common-sense knowledge and religious belief. When Peirce denies that science is, or should be, useful, he is not in the silly position of either denying or deploring the existence of technology. On the one hand, he is warning against the threat to scientific progress of placing science under externally imposed social and political goals, a threat implicit in Karl Pearson's pronouncement that the goal of science is to "strengthen social stability." (CP, 8.133 [1901])[28] On the other hand, he is arguing against the intrusion of provisional and tentative scientific conclusions, such as those of the higher historical criticism, into practical affairs, such as those of religion. (CP, 1.617–620 [1898]) Peirce makes both these points by claiming that the internal growth of scientific knowledge cannot be reconstructed with reference to any extra-scientific goal, but only with reference to truth, and to the approximation towards truth through hypothesis and experimentation.

This sketch of Peirce's conception of science should suffice to explain part of his ambiguous attitude towards Darwin's theory of evolution. Note that there is nothing in this conception which denies that science is, in the long run, useful, or that the scientific activity is adaptive and is maintained only so long as it remains adaptive. What is denied, is that each individual move in the game of science necessarily is adaptive, and, hence, that the rationality of scientific decisions can be explained or justified on the grounds of the adaptive trend of scientific progress. Now Darwin, to my knowledge, did not assert anything of this kind. Nonetheless, this was rather commonly assumed by Peirce's contemporaries to be a corollary of Darwin's theory. It does not seem unreasonable, therefore, given Peirce's pronounced anti-instrumentalism and his primary concern with the methods and history of science, to interpret his criticisms of Darwin's theory as really part of a polemic against the "Darwinian" instrumentalists of his time. This interpretation seems all the more justified as almost all of Peirce's criticisms of Darwin, as we have seen, occur in the context of discussions of scientific progress, a discussion to which Darwin himself contributed little, if anything.

Who, then, were these instrumentalists? One particularly frequent target of Peirce's criticisms was the above-mentioned statistician Karl Pearson. In *The Grammar of Science*, originally published in 1892, Pearson opens by claiming:[29]

> The insight which the investigations of Darwin, seconded by the suggestive but far less permanent work of Spencer, have given us into the development of both individual and social life, has compelled us to remodel our historical ideas and is slowly widening and consolidating our moral standards.

Noting that his age is a time of maladaptive instability and social disintegration, Pearson goes on to conclude:[30]

> The sole reason that can be given for any social institution or form of human activity . . . lies in this: their existence tends to promote the welfare of human society, to increase social happiness, or to strengthen social stability . . . . I assert that the encouragement of scientific investigation and the spread of scientific knowledge by largely inculcating scientific habits of mind will lead to more efficient citizenship and so to increase social stability.

Pearson's Darwinism is of a rather general kind, confined as it is to the ethos of science. He does not go on to apply it to the *method* of science, nor does he draw the parellel between Darwinian evolution and the method of conjectures and refutations. Curiously enough, he fails to draw this parallel precisely because he is overimpressed by Darwin's claim that he himself followed a strictly "Baconian," inductive method; and Pearson even cites Darwin's autobiographical statements as a refutation of Stanley Jevons's exposition of the hypothetico-deductive method.[31]

A more explicit attempt at using Darwin's theory of evolution to buttress an instrumentalist conception of scientific method was made by Ernst Mach, who wrote, for instance, in *The Analysis of Sensations* in 1906:[32]

The biological task of science is to provide the fully developed human individual with as perfect a means of orientating himself as possible. No other scientific ideal can be realized, and any other must be meaningless.

This perspective is developed in further detail in his *Popular Scientific Lectures* in 1910. Here, Mach declares as his aim:[33]

Here I wish simply to consider the growth of natural *knowledge* in the light of the theory of evolution. For knowledge, too, is a product of organic nature . . . . . If Darwin reasoned rightly, the general imprint of evolution and transformation must be noticeable in ideas also.

Mach then proceeds to draw a parallel between scientific hypotheses and animal organs, pointing out that neither spring up fully developed, but that both grow by a process of adaptation to a changing environment:[34]

When a vertebrate animal chances into an environment where it must learn to fly or to swim, an additional pair of extremities is not grown for the purpose. On the contrary, the animal must adapt and transform a pair that it already has. The construction of hypotheses, therefore, is not the production of artificial scientific method. This process is unconsciously carried on in the very infancy of science.

Finally, in his brief intellectual autobiography in 1919, Mach employs this biological analogy to justify his own criterion of scientific rationality, namely, the criterion of economy or simplicity in the adaptation of theories to facts:[35]

Expressed very briefly, the task of scientific knowledge now appears as: *the adaptation of ideas to facts and the adaptation of ideas to one another.* Every favorable biological process is an event of self-preservation, and as such is also a process of adaptation, more economical than an event detrimental to the individual. All favorable cognitive processes are special cases, or parts, of biologically advantageous processes.

In Peirce's own circle of acquaintances, the evolutionary analogy was drawn with even greater explicitness by William James, in a lecture in 1880, published in 1897 in *The Will To Believe*. Citing Jevons with approval, James claims that "The conceiving of the law is a spontaneous variation in the strictest sense of the term," and he continues the analogy as follows:[36]

The scientific hypothesis arouses in me a fever of desire for verification. I read, write, experiment, consult experts. Everything corroborates my notion, which being then published in a book spreads from review to review and from mouth to mouth, till at last there is no doubt I am enshrined in the Pantheon of the great diviners of nature's ways. The environment *preserves* the conception which it was unable to *produce* in any brain less idiosyncratic than my own.

Like Mach, James completes the anology by proposing an instrumentalist criterion of rationality, by which ideas are regarded as organs or instruments of adaptation, to be judged solely on the ground of their economy in action. "Truth," says James in his *Pragmatism* (1907), means nothing but this:[37]

> that ideas (which themselves are but part of our experience) become true just in so far as they help us to get into satisfactory relation with other parts of our experience, to summarize them and get about among them by conceptual short-cuts instead of following the interminable succession of particular phenomena. Any idea upon which we can ride, so to speak; any idea that will carry us prosperously from any one part of our experience to any other part, linking things satisfactorily, working securely, simplifying, saving labor; is true for just so much, true in so far forth, true *instrumentally*.

James may have been only a part-time instrumentalist; but his ideas were developed more consistently by his less erratic younger contemporary John Dewey, who is the last among the instrumentalists we shall look at. Dewey's understanding of Darwin's theory is a matter of dispute; what is beyond dispute is that he regarded himself as preëminently a Darwinist, and that he explicitly drew instrumentalist conclusions from his Darwinism, by construing the progress of science as a process of organic adaptation. His earliest comprehensive statement of this position is found in his *Studies in Logical Theory* from 1903, a work which was cited with approval by James, in his *Pragmatism*. Dewey here proposes the replacement of formal logic with psychology, understood as a "natural history of thought." The parallel between this natural history and the evolutionary history of the species is made abundantly clear:[38]

> The significance of the evolutionary method in bilogy and social history is that every distinct organ, structure, or formation, every grouping of cells or elements, is to be treated as an instrument of adjustment or adaptation to a particular environing situation . . . . Psychology as the natural history of the various attitudes and structures through which experiencing passes . . . is indispensable to logical evaluation the moment we treat logical theory as an account of thinking as a response to its own generating conditions, and consequently judge its validity by reference to its validity in meeting its problems.

From this perspective, logical validity becomes an empirical matter, a matter of the economy and efficiency with which a thought-process helps us adjust to an external situation:[39]

> From this point of view the various types and modes of conceiving, judging, and inference are treated, not as qualifications of thought *per se* or at large, but of reflection engaged in its specific, most economic, effective response to its own particular occasion; they are adaptations for control of stimuli.

In his essay 'The Intellectualist Criterion for Truth' in 1907, Dewey extends this notion of validity to cover truth in general; the measure of truth is simply the utility or efficiency of an idea in fulfilling an external purpose:[40]

> The criterion of the worth of an idea is thus the capacity of the idea . . . to operate in fulfilling the object for the sake of which it was projected. Capacity of operation in this sense is the test, measure, or criterion of truth.

Finally, in *The Quest For Certainty* in 1929, Dewey extends his instrumentalism to the analysis of scientific method, explicitly equating the method of science with the method of technology:[41]

> The progress of inquiry is identical with advance in the invention and construction of physical instrumentalities for producing, registering, and measuring changes.
> Moreover, there is no difference in logical principle between the method of science and the method pursued in technologies.

I have chosen to focus on these four instrumentalists—Pearson, Mach, James, and Dewey—not only because of their intrinsic importance in our intellectual history, but also because we are in the fortunate position of knowing Peirce's reactions to all four of them. Pearson's book was in 1901 subjected to a scathing review by Peirce, who objected to Pearson's central doctrine "first, that it is historically false . . . , second, that it is bad ethics; and, third, that its propagation would retard the progress of science." (CP, VIII.135) We have already seen Peirce's reasons for the first and third objection. What is of especial interest in the second objection, is that Peirce does not rest his anti-instrumentalism on a claim for the ethical neutrality of science. On the contrary, by attacking utilitarianism in ethics, and upholding a kind of Kantianism, he is in a position to defend the detachment and disinterestedness of science precisely on ethical grounds:

> The only ethically sound motive is the most general one; and the motive that actually inspires the man of science, if not quite that, is very near to it—nearer, I venture to believe, than that of any other equally common type of humanity. On the other hand, Professor Pearson's aim, "the stability of society," which is nothing but a narrow British patriotism, prompts the *cui bono* at once. (CP, VIII.141)

If this reads like a naive glorification of the disinterested scientist, there are two observations to be made: first, that Peirce himself came close to exemplifying this ideal; second, that, if one is to formulate an ethics of science, it is precisely ideals one is interested in.

Most of Peirce's scattered remarks on Mach pertain to his positivism, which Peirce dismissed as a pierce of a priori metaphysics of the most pernicious kind. While he grudgingly concedes to Mach the importance of his recognition of the role of economy in research, he rejects the instrumentalism implicit in Mach's principle of economy:

> But Mach goes altogether too far. For he allows thought no other value than that of economizing experiences. This cannot for an instance be admitted. Sensation, to my thinking, has no value whatever except as a vehicle of thought. (CP, V.601 [1903]. Cf. also VII.220n18)

Peirce's reaction to James is almost infuratingly ambivalent. James was probably Peirce's closest friend, as well as one of the very few contemporaries who took Peirce's philosophy seriously. It is understandable that in his published writings Peirce tried to minimize their differences. Still, in his private letters Peirce was free with admonitions and criticisms, as e.g., in this letter from 1909, in response to the MS of James's *A Pluralistic Universe*:[42]

> I thought your *Will to Believe* was a very exaggerated utterance, such as injures a serious man very much, but to say what you now do is far more suicidal. I have lain awake several nights in succession in grief that you should be so careless of what you say.

Time and again, Peirce apparently attempted to convince himself that he and James really agreed; only, James expressed himself sloppily. In the end, this attempt was not successful. In his *Pragmatism* and earlier, James had propounded a clearly instrumentalist version of pragmatism, and had saddled Peirce with the authorship of the doctrine. Peirce was thereby placed under the responsibility of disassociating himself from James's pragmatism—if he were to defend his own doctrine. The line of demarcation was drawn in 1902, when Peirce wrote, in the article "Pragmatic and Pragmatism" in Baldwin's *Dictionary*:

> In 1896 William James published his *Will to Believe*, and later his *Philosophical Conceptions and Practical Results*, which pushed this method to such extremes as must tend to give us pause. The doctrine appears to assume that the end of man is action—a stoical axiom which, to the present writer at the age of sixty, does not recommend itself so forcibly as it did at thirty. If it be admitted, on the contrary, that action wants an end, and that that end must be something of a general description, then the spirit of the [pragmatic] maxim itself, which is that we must look to the upshot of our concepts in order rightly to comprehend them, would direct us towards something different from practical facts, namely, to general ideas, as the true interpreters of our thought. (CP, V.3)

As Peirce was reluctant to polemicize publicly against James, so he was cautious in his public criticisms of Dewey. His review of the latter's *Studies in Logical Theory* in 1904 is on the whole favorable; still, it ends by issuing a warning against "prejudging the question of whether or not there be a logic which is more than a mere natural history." (CP, VIII.190) In a letter to Dewey the same year, Peirce employs less circumspection in castigating his relativization of the concept of "truth":

> Chicago hasn't the reputation of being a moral place; but I should think that the effect of living there upon a man like you would be to make you feel all the more the necessity for Dyadic distinctions,—Right and Wrong, Truth and Falsity.

By 1905, through the work of James, Dewey, and F. C. S. Schiller, the word 'pragmatism' had become practically synonymous with 'instrumentalism', and Peirce found it necessary to complete the break by abandoning the term 'pragmatism' and announcing the birth of 'pragmaticism'—"which is ugly enough to be safe from kidnappers." (CP, V.414)

We have seen, then, the pervasive influence of Darwinism among Peirce's contemporaries, we have seen that a number of these derived an instrumentalist conception of science from a generalized version of Darwin's theory of evolution, and we have seen that Peirce strenuously opposed this instrumentalism, taking his stand on a realist interpretation of the hypothetico-deductive model of science. These considerations explain and render rational Peirce's criticisms of Darwin's theory—*on the assumption that a theory of biological evolution should apply to human cultural evolution*, including the evolution of science. This is an assumption which Peirce shared with Pearson, Mach, James, and Dewey. Indeed, on this count he had preceded them all, in his two 1868-articles "Questions Concerning Certain Faculties Claimed For Man" and "Some Consequences of Four Incapacities," where he delivered a shattering blow at Cartesian dualism and placed man's knowledge of himself squarely within the category of natural, empirical knowledge. Given this assumption, Peirce could not consistently reject instrumentalism as an account of scientific method without rejecting, at the same time, Darwinism as an account of biological evolution. Or, at the very least, he could not consistently accept Darwin's theory as the *whole* story concerning biological evolution.

What must be our present-day judgement on the issue? In Peirce's time, it was defensible to take a wait-and-see attitude towards Darwinism; today, we are stuck with the "synthetic" (sometimes called "neo-Darwinian") theory of evolution, and philosophers who question this theory have scant hope of being taken seriously by the academic community. Still, it can hardly be seriously maintained any longer that science progresses by the literal action of natural selection; even a self-styled "natural-selection epistemologist" such as D. T. Campbell does not claim any more than a structural analogy between the two processes.[43] Even this is too strong a claim if one is to explain the provisional retention of hypotheses on the ground of their fruitfulness for further research (e.g., because of high falsifiability), in disregard of the possibility that they may turn out false, and therefore useless for technology. Natural selection knows no analogy to this feature of scientific method. At the same time, it seems undeniable, and has indeed been emphasized by biologists such as J. S. Huxley[44] and P. B. Medawar,[45] that human *biological* evolution has been, and is, profoundly affected by the evolution of culture, including that of science. What still needs explaining, therefore, is how evolution through natural selection can have given rise to a different mode of evolution, *not* acting through natural selection.

By relegating natural selection to a subsidiary role in the process of cosmic evolution, Peirce was compelled to confront just this question. In the lower stages of his mental activity, man, according to Peirce, evolves through organic adaptation (by natural selection or by some other means); in the higher stages, he evolves through a process where each individual step may be counter-adaptive (although all of them cannot be). The question is, by what agency can we account for the transition from the lower to the higher stages? Peirce's answer, proposed in "The Fixation of Belief" in 1877, seems to me still to merit serious attention. Since this is one of Peirce's most widely read articles, I shall not give a detailed exposition of it, but confine myself to indicating what I take to be the point of the article.

Science, in this article, is treated as a particular form of the general activity of "inquiry," which Peirce defines as the struggle to escape *doubt* and attain a state of *belief*. (CP, V.373) Belief, in its turn, is equated with a stable condition of fixed habits of action, while doubt is equated with the irritating and dissatisfied state of hesitancy between different courses of action. It is clear without further ado why this activity of inquiry may arise by a process of organic adaptations: habits of action are adaptive, in so far as they enable us to act with a maximum of economy and efficiency; the disruption of habits is correspondingly maladaptive, or counter-adaptive. The problem of the article is the question of how the method of science could be picked out by natural selection as the favored method of inquiry. Natural selection can pick out methods only on the ground of their effectiveness in settling belief; on this count, the scientific method has no obvious superiority over a number of pre-scientific, irrational methods. Its sole claim to superiority lies in its capacity in the long run to bring about *true* belief, at the expense of constant unsettlement of belief in the short run. Since natural selection knows nothing of the truth of beliefs, and has no truck with the long run, it seems prima facie impossible that it can ever have generated such a thing as the scientific method.

Peirce approaches the problem by enumerating three pre-scientific methods of inquiry and considering how they would fare by the criterion of effectiveness in settling belief. The first and simplest is the method of tenacity, which consists in simply continuing to believe that which one already believes. But this method, simple and beautiful though it is, can never be effective within a community of several individuals:

> The social impulse is against it. The man who adopts it will find that other men think differently from him, and it will be apt to occur to him, in some saner moment, that their opinions are quite as good as his own, and this will shake his confidence in his belief. (CP, V.378)

The obvious next step is to impose one opinion on the entire community, by the method of authority. This method, which has been practised with fair success both by oriental despots and by the medieval church, can maintain settled belief for a while, but it, too, will break down in the long run. One reason is that, as different nations come into contact with one another, people will realize that the same method in different places generates opposite beliefs, and that the method is therefore arbitrary and irrelevant to the content of their beliefs. Hence:

> A different new method of settling opinions must be adopted, that shall not only produce an impulse to believe, but shall also decide what proposition it is which is to be believed. (CP, V.382)

This is achieved by the a priori method, as practised by the rationalist philosophers. This method, which consists in believing that which is agreeable to reason, fails, however, in that it makes belief a matter of changing fashions, and it has historically resulted in a succession of mutually incompatible systems of thought. Reason, therefore, does not suffice to establish firm beliefs:

> To satisfy our doubts, therefore, it is necessary that a method should be found by which our beliefs may be determined by nothing human, but by some external permanency—something on which our thinking has no effect. (CP, V.384)

Such a method, of course, is, in Peirce's view, the method of science, where belief is determined by experience. Peirce's conception of scientific method is by now familiar to us, and I shall not repeat what Peirce has to say about it in "The Fixation of Belief." At this point, I merely wish to draw attention to the progression in the above discussion. The settlement of belief is thwarted, successively, by the lack of consensus within the community, the lack of consensus across communities, and the lack of conformity to external facts. The first two shortcomings are remedied by successively adaptive steps: the method of authority is more effective than that of tenacity, and the a priori method is more effective than the method of authority. The next step, to the scientific method, is not adaptive; but, by the time we have adopted the a priori method, we have thereby already developed rationality, and so we are in a position to analyze the failure of the previous methods, and to see that they broke down because they did not lead to *true* beliefs, which alone can be stable in the long run. And *this* stage has been reached by purely adaptive steps.

So understood, what Peirce is saying is that rationality is "pleiotropic"—i.e., it comes in a package-deal, like the gene which protects against malaria, but causes sickle-cell anemia. The evolution of rationality is itself an adaptive step in the process of developing fixed belief; but, once rationality has evolved, it may act through counter-adaptive intermediate steps, thereby generating its own, novel mode of evolution. Hence one may consistently view science as an animal activity, which has originated from, and is maintained by, natural selection, but whose internal growth is yet governed by its own, nonnatural mechanisms of variation and selection.

4. Conclusion

It has been shown that Peirce's ambiguous attitude towards Darwin is most properly understood as part of a polemic against those contemporary instrumentalists who reached their conclusions by applying Darwin's theory to the evolution of science, an application which Darwin did not himself make. Peirce was barking up the wrong tree in blaming Darwin and his theory for the illegtimate extension of that theory beyond the realm of its applicability. Still, so far from being a reactionary and obscurantist opponent of the progress of biological science, Peirce in fact anticipated questions which are still in the fore of the discussion, and proposed answers which are at least not outdated by the subsequent progress of biology. His arguments remain a powerful challenge to the recent trends of sociobiology and evolutionary epistemology.

Peter Skagestad

University of Oslo

NOTES

* This paper was prepared as part of the project "Research and Ideology," financed by a grant from The Norwegian Research Council for Science and the Humanities (NAVF). For assistance, encouragement, comments, and criticisms, the author wishes to thank Professor Israel Scheffler of Harvard University, Professor Donald T. Campbell of Northwestern University, and Professor Abner Shimony of Boston University.

1. Philip P. Wiener, *Evolution and the Founders of Pragmatism* (Cambridge, MA: Harvard University Press, 1949) p. 77.

2. Ibid., p. 78, e.g., : "Peirce's preference for the Lamarckian and cataclysmic views was based not on the scientific evidence of biology, but on the neat ways in which they fitted into his metaphysical and theistic evolutionism."

3. W. B. Gallie, *Peirce and Pragmatism* (New York: Dover Publications, 1966) p. 216.

4. Justus Buchler, *Charles Peirce's Empiricism* (New York: Harcourt-Brace, 1939).

5. James K. Feibleman, *An Introduction to Peirce's Philosophy, Interpreted as a System* (Cambridge, MA: MIT Press, 1969).

6. Thomas A. Goudge, *The Thought of C. S. Peirce* (New York: Dover Publications, 1969).

7. Murray G. Murphey, *The Development of Peirce's Philosophy* (Cambridge, MA: Harvard University Press, 1961).

8. Max H. Fisch, "Alexander Bain and the Genealogy of Pragmatism," *Journal of the History of Ideas* 15 (1954).

9. John F. Boler, *Charles Peirce and Scholastic Realism* (Seattle, WA: University of Washington Press, 1963).

10. Edward O. Wilson, *Sociobiology: The New Synthesis* (Cambridge, MA: Harvard University Press, 1975).

11. Stephen Toulmin, *Human Understanding*, vol. I (Princeton, NJ: Princeton University Press, 1972).

12. Donald T. Campbell, "Evolutionary Epistemology," in P. A. Schilpp, ed., *The Philosophy of Karl Popper*, The Library of Living Philosophers (La Salle, IL: Open Court, 1974), pp. 413–63.

13. Another pioneer was Thomas H. Huxley, whose remarkable essay *Evolution and Ethics* (New York: Appleton & Co., 1898) in many ways parallels Peirce's argumentation.

14. I should note here Jon Elster's MS "Beyond Gradient-Climbing: Some Critical Notes on Biological Evolution and Social Change," which, however, came into my hands too late to be fully taken account of in the present paper. (Now forthcoming as Chapter 1 in his *Ulysses and the Sirens* [Cambridge: Cambridge University Press, 1979]).

15. Cf. e.g., Cynthia Eagle Russett, *Darwin in America: The Intellectual Response 1865–1912*, (San Francisco: W. H. Freeman, 1976).

16. He was preceded by William Whewell, as he himself frequently acknowledged, cf. e.g., CP, I.404 and VI.604.

17. Cf. R. A. Fisher, *The Genetical Theory of Natural Selection* (Oxford: Oxford University Press, 1930).

18. Cf. Cp, I.450 on de Morgan.

19. On Whewell's impression on Darwin, cf. the motto for *The Origin of Species*, as well as *The Autobiography of Charles Darwin* (New York: W. W. Norton, 1969), pp. 66, 104.

20. P. B. Medawar, "Unnatural Science," in *The New York Review of Books* 24 (1977): 14.

21. Cf. Elster, cited in n14, above.

22. Cf. Karl R. Popper, *The Logic of Scientific Discovery* (New York: Harper & Row, 1959).

23. E.g., Jürgen Habermas, "Dogmatism, Reason, and Decision," in *Theory and Practice* (Boston: Beacon Press, 1973), esp. pp. 263–64.

24. Peirce did not make this distinction, and so I shall make no use of it in what follows.

25. On the baneful influence of this error, cf. Nils Roll-Hansen, "Critical Teleology: Immanuel Kant and Claude Bernard on the Limitations of Experimental Biology," in *Journal of the History of Biology* 9 (1976): 59–91.

26. Turing's application of mathematical logic to the construction of computers was foreseen by no-one—least of all by Turing himself. On Turing, cf. Howard De Long, *A Profile of Mathematical Logic* (London: Addison-Wesley, 1971), pp. 197–99.

27. Ralph Barton Perry, *The Thought and Character of William James*, briefer version (Cambridge, MA: Harvard University Press, 1948), p. 285.

28. Karl Pearson, *The Grammar of Science*, third edition (London: Adam and Charles Black, 1911), p. 8.

29. Ibid., p. 1.

30. Ibid., pp. 8–9.

31. Ibid., p. 34: "Here, as elsewhere, the reader will find that I differ very widely from Stanley Jevons' views as developed in *The Principles of Science*. I cannot but feel that chapter xxvi of that work would have been recast had the author been acquainted with Darwin's method of procedure."

32. Ernst Mach, *The Analysis of Sensations* (New York: Dover Publications, 1959), p. 37.

33. Mach, *Popular Scientific Lectures* (Chicago: The Open Court Publishing Co., 1910), pp. 217–18.

34. Ibid., p. 229.

35. Mach, *Die Leitgedanken meiner naturwissenschaftlichen Erkenntnislehre und ihre Aufnahme durch die Zeitgenossen* (Leipzig: Verlag von Ambrosius, 1919), p. 4. English translation in Toulmin, ed., *Physical Reality* (New York: Harper & Row, 1970), pp. 30–31.

36. William James, *The Will To Believe* (New York: Longmans, Green & Co., 1902), pp. 249–50.

37. James, *Pragmatism: A New Name For Some Old Ways of Thinking* (New York: Longmans, Green & Co., 1908), p. 58.

38. John Dewey, *Essays in Experimental Logic* (New York: Dover Publications, 1953), pp. 93–94.

39. Ibid., p. 84.

40. Reprinted in Dewey, *The Influence of Darwin on Philosophy* (New York: Peter Smith, 1951), pp. 150–51.

41. Dewey, *The Quest For Certainty* (New York: Capricorn Books, 1960), p. 84.

42. Perry, cited in n27, above, p. 29.

43. Campbell, cited in n12, above.

44. J. S. Huxley, *Evolution in Action* (New York: The New American Library, 1953), p. 14.

45. Medawar, cited in n20, above.

BIBLIOGRAPHY OF CHARLES PEIRCE
1976 THROUGH 1981

INTRODUCTION

Serious study of Peirce began some fifty years ago, in 1931, with the publication of the first of six volumes of the *Collected Papers of Charles Sanders Peirce,* edited by Charles Hartshorne and Paul Weiss (Cambridge, MA: Harvard University Press, 1931–1935). Arthur Burks added two volumes to that collection in 1958. In the meantime there had appeared, and continued to appear, several one-volume editions, namely those by Morris R. Cohen, Justus Buchler, Vincent Tomas, Philip P. Wiener, and Edward C. Moore. A new era in Peirce scholarship began in 1975 with the appearance of the first of three important multi-volume editions: *Charles Sanders Peirce: Contributions to "The Nation,"* edited by Kenneth L. Ketner and James E. Cook (Lubbock: Texas Tech Press, 1975–1979); *The New Elements of Mathematics by Charles S. Peirce,* edited by Carolyn Eisele (The Hague: Mouton, 1976); and *Charles Sanders Peirce: Complete Published Works, Including Selected Secondary Materials,* the 149-microfiche collection edited by members of the Texas Tech University Institute for Studies in Pragmaticism (Greenwich, CT: Johnson Associates, 1977).

The increase in Peirce scholarship marked by these three editions is even more marked in the number of secondary studies on Peirce—which increase is clearly reflected in the pages that follow. It will no doubt continue as the volumes of the most recent and ambitious edition begin to appear. This is the twenty-volume *Writings of Charles S. Peirce: A Chronological Edition,* in preparation at the Peirce Edition Project at Indiana University/Purdue University at Indianapolis. Volume 1, which largely consists of hitherto unpublished materials, is scheduled for early 1982, and two or three volumes annually thereafter. There will be a complete bibliography, both primary and secondary, in a supplementary volume to that edition.

The present bibliography is intended to supplement and update the secondary bibliography in *A Comprehensive Bibliography and Index of the Published Works of Charles Sanders Peirce,* the companion volume to the microfiche edition, which itself was a supplement to and revision and updating of Max H. Fisch's three earlier compilations. The chronological boundaries of my bibliography are not rigid. I have, on the one hand, included such 1982 publications as I could locate; on the other, I have added a number of items omitted in the earlier bibliography and have repeated some that appear there in incomplete form. Still, my bibliography is not a systematical and complete revision of its predecessor. My primary responsibility was to examine and gather materials published from 1976 through 1981.

I have done my best to give accurate and complete information for each entry. Most items were verified from the originals; some were verified in the standard reference tools; a few, not yet published, came to me by personal communication. Inevitably, human frailty causes errors and omissions. In addition, circumstances often conspire against the makers of bibliographies. Particularly troublesome are library binding schedules as well as the slow arrival and processing of very recent books and journals, all of which have made this bibliography less accurate and complete than it might have been. Consequently, I would appreciate notice of errors and omissions so that they may be corrected and included in future supplements and revisions.

The present bibliography departs in several ways from the format and practices of its predecessor. There the arrangement was alphabetical by author and chronological within the author entry, and all entry numbers were preceded by capital S (for Secondary). Here the arrangement is alphabetical by author and title, and each entry is identified by a bracketed number. These numbers are consecutive from the first entry in section I to the last in section VI, except that multiple-author entries are unnumbered after the first citation. In these and other cases, bracketed numbers are used for cross-referencing; numbers preceded by S refer to the earlier bibliography. All essays contained in the collections listed in section II appear separately in section III. Reviews are given under the monographs or collections they review, not as separate items; a few review articles are listed in section III. Items not yet published are identified as "forthcoming," or when the exact volume or issue in which they are scheduled to appear is known, they are given without page numbers.

I have abbreviated journal names. These abbreviations, always without a period, include the following words: Academy (Acad), American (Am), Association (Assoc), Bulletin (Bull), College (Coll), Department (Dept), Education (Educ), History (Hist), Humanities (Hum), International (Intl), Journal (J), Language (Lang), Literature (Lit), Modern (Mod), National (Natl), Philosophical (Philos), Philosophy (Phil), Proceedings (Proc), Quarterly (Q), Research (Res), Review (R), Society (Soc), Studies (Stud), Supplementary (Suppl), University (Univ), Volume (Vol), and Transactions (Trans). The word *Transactions* refers to the *Transactions of the Charles S. Peirce Society*.

I thank Professor Yuji Yonemori of the University of the Ryukyus for sending me an English version of "A List of the Articles on Peirce: Japan" (compiled by Akira Ohara of Waseda University), and my dear colleague Max H. Fisch for providing me with items in his files that might otherwise have escaped my notice. I hope, finally, that the present bibliography will prove helpful and will lead both the beginning student and the seasoned scholar to a fuller and better understanding of the relevance of Charles Peirce.

Christian J. W. Kloesel

Peirce Edition Project,
Indiana University/Purdue University
at Indianapolis

I. MONOGRAPHS AND DISSERTATIONS

[1] Almeder, Robert F. *The Philosophy of Charles S. Peirce: A Critical Introduction.* Totowa, NJ: Rowman & Littlefield, 1980.
Review: Delaney, C. F. *Transactions* 18 (1982), 195–197.

[2] Altshuler, Bruce J. "The Pragmatic Maxim of C. S. Peirce: A Study of Its Origin and Development." Diss. Harvard 1977.

[3] Anding, James Eugene. "Peirce's Defense of Scientific Method." Diss. Waterloo (Canada) 1979. *DAI* 40:9A (1980), 5079.

[4] Apel, Karl-Otto. *Charles Sanders Peirce: From Pragmatism to Pragmaticism.* Tr. John Michael Krois, with a Foreword by Richard J. Bernstein. Amherst: University of Massachusetts Press, 1981. (Translation of S 43.)

[5] Bertilsson, Margareta. *Towards a Social Reconstruction of Science Theory: Peirce's Theory of Inquiry and Beyond.* Lund: Bokcafeet, 1978.

[6] Bosco, Nynfa. *Studio sul pragmatismo di C. S. Peirce.* Turin: Giappichelli, 1977. (Vol. 1 of *Dalla scienza alla metafisica.* See [619].)

[7] Boytor, Zigmond. "The Persistence of Pragmatism: A New Interpretation of Peirce's Concept of Abduction and Its Relevance to Dewey's and Piaget's Systems of Thought." Diss. Wayne State 1976. *DAI* 37:11A (1976), 7018.

[8] Brown, Robert Allen. "Peirce's Normative Conception of Truth." Diss. Brandeis 1979. *DAI* 40:5A (1979), 2728.

[9] Brunning, Jacqueline. "Peirce's Development of the Algebra of Relations." Diss. Toronto (Canada) 1981. *DAI* 42:10A (1982), 4473.

[10] Calvet, Theresa. *Signe ou symbole: introduction à la théorie sémiotique de C. S. Peirce.* Louvain-la-Neuve and Madrid: Cabay, 1981. (Revised version of her 1977 dissertation at the Catholic University of Louvain. Introduction and Chapter 3 also published separately as *Un, deux, trois: catégories fondamentales,* same publisher.)

[11] Cater, R. M. "The Unity of Peirce's Thought: The Function of Continuity and Complementarity in the Theory of Abstraction." Diss. Pennsylvania State 1977. *DAI* 38:5A (1977), 2842–2843.

[12] Christopherson, Rose. "The Categories of Logic and Experience in Kant and Peirce." Diss. Pennsylvania State 1978. *DAI* 39:8A (1979), 4976–4977.

[13] Cook, James Edward. "Chance and Rationality in the Philosophy of Charles S. Peirce." Diss. Kansas 1978. *DAI* 39:7A (1979), 4319–4320.

[14] Davis, William H. *Peirce's Epistemology.* The Hague: Martinus Nijhoff, 1972.

[15] Deledalle, Gérard. *Théorie et pratique du signe: introduction à la sémiotique de Charles S. Peirce.* Paris: Payot, 1979.

Review: Kloesel, C. J. W. *Transactions* 17 (1981), 70–77.

[16] Dipert, Randall Roy. "Development and Crisis in Late Boolean Logic: The Deductive Logics of Peirce, Jevons, and Schröder." Diss. Indiana 1978. *DAI* 39:5A (1978), 2976.

[17] Dozoretz, Jerry. "Indubitability and Truth in Peirce's Epistemic Methodology." Diss. California at Santa Barbara 1977. *DAI* 38:7A (1978), 4209.

[18] Dudik, Evan Matthew. "Peirce: The Argument for Realism and the Efficacy of Law." Diss. Texas at Austin 1977. *DAI* 38:5A (1977), 2844–2845.

[19] Esposito, Joseph L. *Evolutionary Metaphysics: The Development of Peirce's Theory of Categories.* Athens: Ohio University Press, 1980.
Review: Michael, F. *Transactions* 17 (1981), 279–283.

[20] Frederick, John Norris, Jr. "Chance, Causality, and Freedom in the Writings of C. S. Peirce." Diss. Georgia 1977. *DAI* 38:8A (1978), 4881–4882.

[21] Keiner, Mechtild. "Untersuchungen zur Entwicklung des 'icon'- Begriffes bei Charles S. Peirce." Diss. Stuttgart (Germany) 1978.

[22] Lewis, James David. "The Pragmatic Foundation of Symbolic Interactionism," Part 1. Diss. Illinois at Urbana-Champaign 1976. *DAI* 37:1A (1976), 650–651.

[23] Lyne, John Russell. "C. S. Peirce on Rhetoric and Communication." Diss. Wisconsin at Madison 1978. *DAI* 39:4A (1978), 1926–1927.

[24] McCarthy, Jeremiah Edward. "Peirce's Normative Science." Diss. North Carolina at Chapel Hill 1980. *DAI* 41:4A (1980), 1640.

[25] McNeal, Barbara Lynn. "Semiosis as a Theory of Aesthetics." Diss. Florida 1977. *DAI* 38:11A (1978), 6771.

[26] Mandell, Daniel Neil. "Charles S. Peirce's Critique of Foundationalism." Diss. Notre Dame 1979. *DAI* 40:7A (1979), 4086.

[27] Maroosis, James. "Further Consequences of Human Embodiment: A Description of Time and Human Existence as Disclosed at the Origin of Peirce's Philosophy of Community." Diss. Toronto (Canada) 1981. *DAI* 42:10A (1982), 4476.

[28] Mohr, Knut. "Der amerikanische Pragmatismus als Grundlage der Werttheorie John Deweys," pp. 1–51. Diss. Mainz (Germany) 1968.

[29] Noble, N. A. Brian. "The Architectonic Method of Charles S. Peirce." Diss. Waterloo (Canada) 1981.

[30] Ochs, Peter Warren. "Charles Peirce's Metaphysical Conviction." Diss. Yale 1979. *DAI* 40:11A (1980), 5902.

[31] Orange, Donna Marie. "The Development of Peirce's Theism." Diss. Fordham 1980. *DAI* 40:12A (1980), 6312.

[32] Pape, Helmut. "Die Perspektivität der natürlichen Sprachen und die Ontologie der Zeichen: Eine Untersuchung zu Philosophie und Semiotik des C. S. Peirce." Diss. Hamburg (Germany) 1981.

[33] Purcell, Frank Palmer. "The Prehistory of Pragmatism: Critical Commonsense and Scholastic Realism in the Education of Charles Sanders Peirce." Diss. Columbia University Teachers College 1979. *DAI* 40:9A (1980), 5087.

[34] Rescher, Nicholas. *Peirce's Philosophy of Science: Critical Studies in His Theory of Induction and Scientific Method.* Notre Dame, IN: University of Notre Dame Press, 1978.
Reviews: Altshuler, B. *Philos R* 90 (1981), 138–143.
Fellows, R. *Philos Books* 22 (1981), 17–20.

Goudge, T. A. *Transactions* 15 (1979), 176–179. (See also [213].)

Haack, S. *Metaphilosophy* 11 (1980), 295–297.

Potter, V. G. *Thought* 54 (1979), 215–217.

Rosenthal, S. B. *R of Metaphysics* 32 (1979), 565–566.

Strong, J. V. *Phil of Science* 46 (1979), 655–657.

[35] Rochefort, Jean-Claude. "La réception de Charles S. Peirce en Allemagne: période 1960–1980." Diss. Montréal (Canada) 1981.

[36] Rodgers, William Joseph. "Charles S. Peirce's Theistic Metaphysics." Diss. St. John's 1978. *DAI* 39:7A (1979), 4328.

[37] Schmitt, Sister Rosina. "The End of Evolution in Peirce's Cosmology." Diss. St. Louis 1978. *DAI* 39:3A (1978), 1642.

[38] Sebeok, Thomas A., and Jean Umiker-Sebeok. *"You Know My Method": A Juxtaposition of Chrales S. Peirce and Sherlock Holmes*. Foreword by Max H. Fisch. Bloomington, IN: Gaslight Publications, 1980. (Earlier version, without Foreword, in *Semiotica* 26 [1979], 203–250.)
Review: Ayim, M. *Transactions* 17 (1981), 182–185.

[39] Shields, Paul Bartram. "Charles S. Peirce on the Logic of Number." Diss. Fordham 1981. *DAI* 41:12A (1981), 5134.

[40] Sini, Carlo. *L'etica e il problema delle scienze normative in Peirce*. L'Aquila: Centro Tecnico, Culturale ed Assistenziale, 1974.

[41] ——. *La semiotica di Peirce: anno academico 1974–75*. L'Aquila: Centro Tecnico, Culturale ed Assistenziale, 1975.

[42] ——. *Semiotica e filosofia: segno e linguaggio in Peirce, Nietzsche, Heidegger e Foucault*. Bologna: Mulino, 1978.

[43] Skagestad, Peter. *The Road of Inquiry: Charles Peirce's Pragmatic Realism*. New York: Columbia University Press, 1981.
Review: Haack, S. *Transactions* 18 (1982), 197–201.

[44] ——. *Vitenskap og menneskebilde: Charles Peirce og amerikansk pragmatisme*. Oslo: Universitetsforlaget, 1978.

[45] Stephens, Gayle Lynn. "Peirce's Critique of Introspection." Diss. Massachusetts 1978. *DAI* 39:5A (1978), 2983.

[46] Thibaud, Pierre. *La logique de Charles Sanders Peirce: de l'algèbre aux graphes*. Aix-en-Provence: Editions de l'Université de Provence, 1975. (See S 1408.)
Review: Gauthier, Y. *Dialogue* (Canada) 16 (1977), 746–748.

[47] Tierney, William F., II. "Charles S. Peirce on the Grounds for Religious Belief." Diss. Catholic University of America 1979.

[48] Toben, G. F. "Die Fallibilismusthese von Ch. S. Peirce und die Falsificationsthese von K. R. Popper: Untersuchung ihres Zusammenhangs." Diss. Stuttgart (Germany) 1977.

[49] Turley, Peter T. *Peirce's Cosmology*. New York: Philosophical Books, 1977.
Review: Dipert, R. R. *Nature and System* 1 (1979), 134–141.

[50] Twaddell, G. E. "Peirce's Relationship with Hegel." 2 vols. Diss. Universitas Catholica Parisiensis 1976.

[ ] Umiker-Sebeok, Jean. See [38].

[51] Vigener, Gerhard. *Die zeichentheoretischen Entwürfe von F. de Saussure und Ch. S. Peirce als Grundlagen einer linguistischen Pragmatik*. Tübingen: Gunter Narr, 1979.

[52] Yonemori, Yuji. *Peirce's Semiotic*. Tokyo: Keiso-Shobo, 1981. (In Japanese.)

II. COLLECTIONS

[53] "Au-delà de la sémiolinguistique: la sémiotique de C. S. Peirce." *Langages* 14:58 (June 1980). See [111, 145, 167, 357, 389, 408, 430, 508].
[54] "Essays on the Philosophy of Charles Peirce." *Synthese* 41:1 (May 1979). See [68, 142, 215, 347, 459].
  Review: Savan, D. *Transactions* 17 (1981), 62–65.
[55] "Giovanni Vailati, Charles Sanders Peirce." *Nominazione: Collana-Rivista Internazionale di Logica* No. 3 (1982).
[56] [The Hunter College Peirce Colloquium, 8 May 1981] *Historia Mathematica* 9:3 (August 1982). See [138, 175, 197, 266, 355, 397].
[57] *Peirce's Logic of Relations and Other Studies.* By R. M. Martin. Dordrecht-Holland; Cinnaminson, NJ: Foris Publications, 1980. See [311–314, 316–320].
[58] *Proceedings of the C. S. Peirce Bicentennial International Congress.* Ed. Kenneth L. Ketner et al. Graduate Studies 23. Lubbock: Texas Tech Press, 1981.
[59] "The Relevance of Charles Peirce." *The Monist* 63:3 (July 1980). See [74, 97, 163, 200, 208, 222, 225, 230, 235, 354, 448].
[60] "The Relevance of Charles Peirce: Part II." *The Monist* 65:2 (April 1982). See [200, 214, 217, 234, 253, 419, 540].
[61] *The Relevance of Charles Peirce.* Ed. Eugene Freeman. La Salle, IL: The Hegeler Institute, 1982. Combines [59] and [60] and further contains [68, 459, 651, 671, 681] and a Preface by John E. Smith.
[62] *Studies in Peirce's Semiotic: A Symposium by Members of the Institute for Studies in Pragmaticism.* Ed. Kenneth L. Ketner and Joseph M. Ransdell. Peirce Studies 1. Lubbock, TX: Institute for Studies in Pragmaticism, 1979. See [108, 164, 171, 185, 203, 221, 376, 392, 401].
  Review: Johnstone, H. W. *Transactions* 16 (1980), 357–360. See also [542]. Skagestad, P. *Am J of Semiotics* 1:3 (1982), 107–111.
[63] *Studies in the Scientific and Mathematical Philosophy of Charles S. Peirce: Essays by Carolyn Eisele.* Ed. Richard M. Martin. The Hague: Mouton, 1979. See [171, 173, 174, 177–180].
[64] "The Thought of C. S. Peirce." Part 1 of *Pragmatism and Purpose: Essays Presented to Thomas A. Goudge.* Ed. L. W. Sumner, John G. Slater, and Fred Wilson. Toronto: University of Toronto Press, 1981. See [123, 199, 309, 413, 431, 433, 465, 484, 488].
[65] "A Tribute to C. S. Peirce and In Memory of Jan Mukarovský." *Semiotica* 19:3–4 (1977). See [184, 188, 189, 272, 380, 405, 429, 464, 515, 539].
[66] *Versus: Quaderni di Studi Semiotici* No. 15 (September-December 1976). See [99, 128, 167, 458].

III. ESSAYS AND ARTICLES

[67] Aiken, Henry David. "Contra—The Moral Point of View." *Philosophic Exchange* 3 (1980), 57–79.
[68] Almeder, Robert. "Peirce on Meaning." *Synthese* 41 (1979), 1–24.
[69] Almeida, J. "Trois cas de rapports intratextuels: la citation, la parabolisation, le commentaire." *Sémiotique et Bible* 15 (1979), 23–42.
[70] Altshuler, Bruce. "The Nature of Peirce's Pragmatism." *Transactions* 14 (1978), 147–175.
[71] ———. "Peirce's Theory of Truth and His Early Idealism." *Transactions* 16 (1980), 118–140.

[72] Ames, Van Meter. "Zen to Mead." *Proc and Addresses of the Am Philos Assoc* 33 (1960), 27–42, at 33–37.

[73] Anttila, Raimo. "Child Language, Abduction and the Acquisition of Linguistic Theory by Linguists." *Neurolinguistics* 5 (1976), 24–37.

[74] Apel, Karl-Otto. "C. S. Peirce and the Post-Tarskian Problem of an Adequate Explication of the Meaning of Truth: Towards a Transcendental-Pragmatic Theory of Truth, Part 1." *Monist* 63 (1980), 386–407. Part 2 in *Transactions* 18 (1982), 3–17; both parts in [61].

[75] ____. "Einführende Bemerkungen zur Idee einer 'transzendentalen Sprachpragmatik'." In *Semantics and Communication*, ed. Carl H. Heidrich, pp. 81–108, at 82–93. Amsterdam: North-Holland; New York: Elsevier, 1974.

[76] ____. "Zur Idee einer transzendentalen Sprach-Pragmatik: Die Dreistelligkeit der Zeichenrelation und die 'abstractive fallacy' in den Grundlagen der klassischen Transzendentalphilosophie und der sprachanalytischen Wissenschaftslogik." In *Aspekte und Probleme der Sprachphilosophie*, ed. Josef Simon, pp. 282–326. Freiburg: Karl Alber, 1974.

[77] Asawa, Sachio. "C. S. Peirce's Tychism: Even God Plays with Dice." *Shiso* No. 670 (April 1980). (In Japanese.)

[78] Ayers, Robert H. "C. S. Peirce on Miracles." *Transactions* 16 (1980), 242–254.

[79] Ayim, Maryann. "Language Universals and Scientific Hypotheses: The Children of a Retroduction." *Canadian J of Res in Semiotics* 7:2 (1979–80), 89–100 and 107–108. See also [409].

[80] ____. "Theory and Practice at the Crossroads: A Peircean Perspective on Political Signs." In [602], pp. 13–26.

[81] ____, and Goldwin Emerson. "Dewey and Peirce on Curriculum and the Three R's." *J of Educational Thought* 14:1 (1980), 23–37.

[82] Baer, Eugen. "Semiosis as Dialogue." *Phil Today* 25 (1981), 3–11.

[83] Basin, E. "Sign, Representation, Art: On the Semiotic Concept of C. S. Peirce." *Voprosy Literatury* No. 4 (1974), 166–187. (In Russian.)

[84] Batts, Vincent, Thomas Cook, and John Lincourt. "Hypothetical Fallibilism in Peirce and Jevons." *Transactions* 15 (1979), 132–157.

[85] Beckmann, Jan P. "Realismus und Pragmatismus: Zum Möglichkeitsbegriff bei Duns Scotus und Peirce." In *Regnum hominis et regnum dei: Acta quarti congressus scotistici internationalis*, ed. Camille Bérubé, I: 333–345. Rome: Societas Internationalis Scotistica, 1978.

[86] Beckmann, Peter. "Definierende Eigenschaften für Zeichenklassen." *Semiosis* No. 14 (1979), 48–60.

[87] ____. "Semiotische Analyse einiger Grundbegriffe der intuitionistischen sowie der formalistischen Mathematik." *Semiosis* No. 17–18 (1980), 79–90.

[88] Bedell, Gary. "Has Peirce Refuted Egoism?" *Transactions* 16 (1980), 255–275.

[89] Bense, Max. "The Abstract Conception of the 'Sign'." In [601], pp. 52–54.

[90] ____. "L'essai de Max Bill 'La pensée mathématique dans l'art de notre temps'." *Semiosis* No. 19 (1980), 29–36.

[91] ____. "Präsemiotische Triaden der Peirceschen Semiotik." *Semiosis* No. 12 (1978), 46–56.

[92] ____. "Die semiotische Konzeption der Ästhetik." *LiLi* 7 (1977), 188–201.

[93] ____. "Das Zeichenklassen-System der Bourbakischen Strukturtheorie der Mathematik." *Semiosis* No. 21 (1981), 19–28.

[94] Berger, Wolfgang. "Über Iconizität." *Semiosis* No. 17–18 (1980), 19–22.

[95] Bhattacharya, A. K. "C. S. Peirce's Theory of Signs and Their Interpretants." *Indian Phil and Culture* 11 (1966), 41–45.

[96] Biggs, Norman L., E. Keith Lloyd, and Robin J. Wilson. "C. S. Peirce and De Morgan on the Four-Colour Conjecture." *Historia Mathematica* 4 (1977), 215–216.

[97] Boler, John. "Peirce, Ockham and Scholastic Realism." *Monist* 63 (1980), 290–303.

[98] Bonfantini, Massimo A. "Verso una comune comprensione e definizione die termini de Peirce." *Scienze Umane* 3 (1979), 171–179.

[99] ____, and Roberto Grazia. "Teoria della conoscenza e funzione dell'icona in Peirce." *Versus* No. 15 (1976), 1–15.

[100] van den Boom, Holger. "Der Ursprung der Peirceschen Zeichentheorie: Eine logisch-phänomenologische Rekonstruktion." *Zeitschrift für Semiotik* 3 (1981), 23–39.

[101] Boon, James A. "Saussure/Peirce à propos Language, Society and Culture." *Semiotica* 27 (1979), 83–101.

[ ] Bourgeois, Patrick L. See [423].

[102] Braun, John E. "The 'Speculative Rhetoric' of Charles Sanders Peirce." *Phil and Rhetoric* 14 (1981), 1–15.

[103] Brink, Chris. "On Peirce's Notation for the Logic of Relatives." *Transactions* 14 (1978), 285–304.

[104] Broadbent, Geoffrey. "Building Design as an Iconic Sign System." In *Signs, Symbols, and Architecture*, ed. Broadbent et al, pp. 311–331. New York: Wiley, 1979. Shorter version in [601], pp. 904–908.

[105] Brock, Jarrett E. "An Introduction to Peirce's Theory of Speech Acts." *Transactions* 17 (1981), 319–326.

[106] ____. "The Origin and Structure of Peirce's Logic of Vagueness." In [618], I: 133–138.

[107] ____. "Peirce's Anticipation of Game-Theoretical Logic." In [602], pp. 55–64.

[108] ____. "Principal Themes in Peirce's Logic of Vagueness." In [62], pp. 41–49.

[109] Brown, Richard H. "The Emergence of Existential Thought: Philosophical Perspectives on Positivist and Humanist Forms of Social Theory." In *Existential Sociology*, ed. Jack D. Douglas and John M. Johnson, pp. 77–100, at 89–91. Cambridge: Cambridge University Press, 1977.

[110] Bruss, Elizabeth W. "Peirce and Jakobson on the Nature of the Sign." In *The Sign: Semiotics Around the World*, ed. R. W. Bailey et al., pp. 81–98. Ann Arbor: Michigan Slavic Publications, 1978.

[111] Bruzy, Claude, Werner Burzlaff, Robert Marty, and Joëlle Réthoré. "La sémiotique phanéroscopique de Charles S. Peirce." *Langages* 14:58 (1980), 29–59.

[112] Buczyńska-Garewicz, Hanna. "The Degenerate Sign." *Semiosis* No. 13 (1979), 5–15.

[113] ____. "The Meaning of *Interpretant*." *Semiosis* No. 21 (1981), 10–14.

[114] ____. "Mediation and the Problem of Beginnings." *Archiwum Historii Filozofii* 25 (1979), 275–301. (In Polish.)

[115] ____. "Peirce's Criticism of Cartesian Epistemology." *Semiosis* No. 11 (1978), 21–32.

[116] ____. "Peirce's Method of Triadic Analysis of Signs." *Semiotica* 26 (1979), 251–259.

[117] ——. "Semiotics and the Newspeak." *Semiosis* No. 17–18 (1980), 91–99.
[118] ——. "Semiotics and the Philosophy of Signs." Introduction to translation of [548], pp. 5–39. Warsaw, 1980. (In Polish.)
[119] ——. "Sign and Continuity." *Ars Semeiotica* No. 2 (1978), 3–15.
[120] ——. "Studies in the Meaning of Semiotics." *Teksty* 2:50 (1980), 183–187. (In Polish.)
[121] ——. "The Theory of Signs and Cartesian Doubt." *Studia Filozoficzne* No. 4 (1979), 113–125. (In Polish.)
[122] ——. "The Transcendental and Objective Character of the Object of Signs." *Studia Filozoficzne* No. 6 (1977), 101–113. (In Polish.)
[123] Burbidge, J. W. "Peirce on Historical Explanation." In [64], pp. 15–27.
[124] Burks, Arthur W. "Logic, Biology and Automata: Some Historical Reflections." *Intl J of Man-Machine Stud* 7 (1975), 297–312.
[125] ——. "Man: Sign or Algorithm? A Rhetorical Analysis of Peirce's Semiotics." *Transactions* 16 (1980), 279–292.
[   ] Burzlaff, Werner. See [111].
[126] Calvet, Theresa. "Semiótica e pragmática." In [543], pp. 107–112.
[127] Campbell, Donald T. "Evolutionary Epistemology." In *The Philosophy of Karl Popper*, ed. Paul Arthur Schilpp, I:413–463, at 437–440. La Salle, IL: Open Court, 1974.
[128] Caprettini, Gian Paolo. "Sulla semiotica di Ch. S. Peirce: il 'nuovo elenco di categorie'." *Versus* No. 15 (1976), 29–48.
[   ] Caramella, Elaine. See [132].
[129] Caspar, Ruth. "The 'Neglected Argument' Revisited: From C. S. Peirce to Peter Berger." *Thomist* 44 (1980), 94–116.
[130] Chauviré, Christiane. "Peirce, le langage et l'action: sur la théorie peircienne de l'assertion." *Etudes Philosophiques* 1979, 3–17.
[131] ——. "Pragmatisme et nécessité logique." *Revue de Métaphysique et de Morale* 84 (1979), 536–551.
[132] Chnaiderman, Miriam, Francisco Ivan da Silva, and Elaine Caramella. "A práxis da semiótica ou a semiótica da práxis." In [543], pp. 127–133.
[133] Christopherson, Rosemarie, and Henry W. Johnstone, Jr. "Triadicity and Thirdness." *Transactions* 17 (1981), 241–246.
[134] Clarke, Bowman L. "Peirce's Neglected Argument." *Transactions* 13 (1977), 277–287.
[   ] Cook, Thomas. See [84].
[135] Crombie, E. James. "Peirce on Our Knowledge of Mind: A Neglected Third Approach." In [614], pp. 77–85. (See S 299.)
[136] Curd, Martin V. "The Logic of Discovery: An Analysis of Three Approaches." In *Scientific Discovery, Logic, and Rationality*, ed. Thomas Nickles, pp. 201–219. Dordrecht-Holland: D. Reidel, 1980.
[137] Dauben, Joseph W. "C. S. Peirce's Philosophy of Infinite Sets: A Study of Peirce's Interest in the Infinite Related to the Birth of American Mathematics and Contemporary Work of Cantor and Dedekind." *Mathematics Magazine* 50:3 (1977), 123–135.
[138] ——. "Peirce's Place in Mathematics." *Historia Mathematica* 9 (1982), 311–325.
[139] Davis, William H. "Do Instinctive Truths Incline Us Toward the Truth?" *Phil Today* 22 (1978), 307–318.
[140] Deely, John N. "Historical Antecedents to Peirce's Notion of Iconic Signs." In [602], pp. 109–120.

[141] ———. "'Semiotic' as the Doctrine of Signs." *Ars Semeiotica* No. 1 (1977), 41–68.

[142] Delaney, C. F. "Peirce's Account of Mental Activity." *Synthese* 41 (1979), 25–36.

[143] Deledalle, Gérard. "Les articles pragmatistes de Charles S. Peirce." *Revue Philosophique de la France et de l'Etranger* 170 (1980), 17–29.

[144] ———. "Un aspect méconnu de l'influence de Peirce sur la 'phénomenologie' de James." *Semiosis* No. 17–18 (1980), 59–61.

[145] ———. "Avertissement aux lecteurs de Peirce." *Langages* 14:58 (1980), 25–27.

[146] ———. "English and French Versions of C. S. Peirce's 'The Fixation of Belief' and 'How To Make Our Ideas Clear'." *Transactions* 17 (1981), 141–152.

[147] ———. "L'idéologie de la critique leninienne de l'empiriocriticisme. I: sémiotique de l'idéologie." *Semiosis* No. 14 (1979), 34–47.

[148] ———. "La métaphysique du signe." *Semiosis* No. 11 (1978), 39–43.

[149] ———. "Pour lire la théorie des signes de Charles S. Peirce." *Semiosis* No. 6 (1977), 29–36; and No. 9 (1978), 29–44.

[150] ———. "Pour une lecture sémiotique de la sémiotique de Peirce." *Kodikas/Code* 1 (1979), 5–8.

[151] ———. "Les pragmatistes et la nature du pragmatisme." *Revue Philosophique de Louvain* 77 (1979), 471–486.

[152] ———. "Le representamen et l'objet dans la *semiosis* de Charles S. Peirce." *Semiotica* 33 (1981), 195–200.

[153] Dipert, Randall R. "Peirce's Propositional Logic." *R of Metaphysics* 34 (1981), 569–595.

[154] ———. "Peirce's Theory of the Dimensionality of Physical Space." *J of the Hist of Phil* 16 (1978), 61–70.

[155] ———. "Peirce's Theory of the Geometrical Structure of Physical Space." *Isis* 68 (1977), 404–413.

[156] ———. "Schröders Beitrag zur Logik und den Grundlagen der Mathematik." *Fridericiana* 27 (1981), 23–44.

[157] ———. "Set-Theoretical Representations of Ordered Pairs and Their Adequacy for the Logic of Relations." *Canadian J of Phil* 12 (1982), 353–374.

[158] ———. "Types and Tokens: A Reply to Sharpe." *Mind* 89 (1980), 587–588. See [446].

[159] Dobrosielski, Marian. "C. S. Peirce on the Impossibility of Intuitive Knowledge." *Dialectics and Humanism* 4 (1977), 121–134.

[160] Dougherty, Charles J. "C. S. Peirce's Critique of Psychologism." In [614], pp. 86–93. (See S 370.)

[161] ———. "The Common Root of Husserl's and Peirce's Phenomenologies." *New Scholasticism* 54 (1980), 305–325.

[162] ———. "How To Make Our Ideas Safe." *New Scholasticism* 52 (1978), 202–213.

[163] ———. "Peirce's Phenomenological Defense of Deduction." *Monist* 63 (1980), 364–374.

[164] Dozoretz, Jerry. "The Internally Real, the Fictitious, and the Indubitable." In [62], pp. 77–87.

[165] Duchesneau, François. "La philosophie anglo-saxonne de Bentham à William James." In *La philosophie du monde scientifique et industriel (1860–1940)*, pp. 123–150, at 143–150. Paris: Hachette, 1973. (Vol. 6 of *Histoire de la philosophie: idées, doctrines*.)

[166] Dusek, Val. "Geodesy and the Earth Sciences in the Philosophy of C. S. Peirce." In *Two Hundred Years of Geology in America*, ed. Cecil J. Schneer, pp. 265–275. Hanover, NH: University Press of New England, 1979.

[167] Eco, Umberto. "Peirce and Contemporary Semantics." *Versus* No. 15 (1976), 49–72. French version in *Langages* 14:58 (1980), 75–91.

[168] ____. "Peirce's Notion of Interpretant." *Mod Lang Notes* 91 (1976), 1457–1472.

[169] ____. "Pour une reformulation du concept de signe iconique: les modes de production sémiotique." *Communications* 29 (1978), 141–191.

[170] ____. "The Theory of Signs and the Role of the Reader." *Bull of the Midwest Mod Lang Assoc* 14:1 (1981), 35–45.

[171] Eisele, Carolyn. "Charles S. Peirce: Semiotician in Mathematics and the History of Science." In [62], pp. 31–39; with slight changes also in [63], pp. 300–307.

[172] ____. "A Comment on C. V. Jones' Review of *The New Elements*." *Historia Mathematica* 5 (1978), 91–92. (See [252].)

[173] ____. "The Four-Color Problem." In [63], pp. 216–222.

[174] ____. "The Mathematical Foundations of Peirce's Philosophy." In [63], pp. 237–244.

[175] ____. "Mathematical Methodology in the Thought of Peirce." *Historia Mathematica* 9 (1982), 333–341.

[176] ____. "Mathematics as a Key to Peirce's Semiotics." In [618], I: 123–128.

[177] ____. "Peirce as a Precursor in Mathematics and Science." In [63], pp. 292–299.

[178] ____. "Probability in Logic and the History of Science." In [63], pp. 108–114.

[179] ____. "The Problem of Mathematical Continuity." In [63], pp. 208–215.

[180] ____. "The Role of Modern Geometry in Peirce's Philosophical Thought." In [63], pp. 245–250.

[181] Elling, Elmar. "Zum Begriff des ikonischen Zeichens bei Charles Sanders Peirce." *Papiere des Münsteraner Arbeitskreises für Semiotik* 7 (1978), 21–36.

[   ] Emerson, Goldwin. See [81].

[   ] Espe, Hartmut. See [285].

[182] Esposito, Joseph L. "The Development of Peirce's Categories." *Transactions* 15 (1979), 51–60.

[183] ____. "Invention, Convention, and Necessity." *Dialectica*, forthcoming.

[184] ____. "Is there a Semiocentric Predicament?" *Semiotica* 19 (1977), 259–270.

[185] ____. "On the Origins and Foundations of Peirce's Semiotic." In [62], pp. 19–24.

[186] ____. "On the Question of the Foundation of Pragmaticism." *Transactions* 17 (1981), 259–268.

[187] ____. "Sellars and Scientific Idealism." *Idealistic Stud* 8 (1978), 40–61.

[188] ____. "Semiotics and Philosophy at the International Peirce Congress." *Semiotica* 19 (1977), 355–366.

[189] Fairbanks, Matthew J. "Reality as Language in the Peircean Semiotic." *Semiotica* 19 (1977), 233–239.

[190] Faris, J. A. "Charles Sanders Peirce, Philosopher and Logician (1839–1914)." *Proc of the Royal Irish Acad*, Section C, 77:11 (1977), 279–300.

[191] ____. "C. S. Peirce's Existential Graphs." *Bull of the Institute of Mathematics and Its Applications* 17 (1981), 226–233.

[192] Feibleman, James K. "Activity as a Source of Knowledge in American Pragmatism." *Tulane Stud in Phil* 12 (1963), 91–105, at 95–97.
[193] Ferrara, Lucrecia d'Alessio, and Decio Pignatari. "Signe verbal, signe non-verbal." In [601], pp. 269–273.
[194] Feuer, Lewis S. "God, Guilt, and Logic: The Psychological Basis of the Ontological Argument." *Inquiry* 11 (1968), 257–281, at 266 and 279n34.
[195] Fisch, Max H. Foreword to [38].
[196] _____. "Peirce's General Theory of Signs." In [605], pp. 31–70.
[197] _____. "Peirce's Place in American Life." *Historia Mathematica* 9 (1982), 265–287.
[198] _____. "Peirce's Place in American Thought." *Ars Semeiotica* No. 1 (1977), 21–37.
[199] _____. "The 'Proof' of Pragmatism." In [64], pp. 28–40.
[200] _____. "The Range of Peirce's Relevance." *Monist* 63 (1980), 269–276; and 65 (1982), 123–141.
[201] _____. "Was There a Metaphysical Club in Cambridge?—A Postscript." *Transactions* 17 (1981), 128–130.
[202] _____, and Christian J. W. Kloesel. "Peirce and the Florentine Pragmatists: His Letter to Calderoni and a New Edition of His Writings." *Topoi* 1:2 (1982).
[203] _____, Kenneth Laine Ketner, and Christian J. W. Kloesel. "The New Tools of Peirce Scholarship, with Particular Reference to Semiotic." In [62], pp. 1–17.
[204] Fox, June T. "Peirce and the Pragmatists: A Study in Contrasts." *Educational Theory* 16 (1966), 262–270.
[205] Frederick, J. Norris. "The Structure of Metaphor." In [602], pp. 143–154.
[206] Gardner, Martin. "On Charles Sanders Peirce: Philosopher and Gamesman." *Scientific Am* 239:1 (1978), 18, 23–24, 26.
[207] Garvin, Paul L. "Linguistics and Semiotics." *Semiotica* 20 (1977), 101–110.
[208] Gavin, William J. "Peirce and 'The Will to Believe'." *Monist* 63 (1980), 342–350.
[209] _____. "Pragmatism and the Classical Definition of Truth: A Re-Specification of the Context of American Philosophy." *Intl Philos Q* 19 (1979), 473–483. (Review article of [608].)
[210] Godfrey-Smith, William. "The Generality of Predictions." *Am Philos Q* 15 (1978), 15–25.
[211] _____. "Names, Indices and Individuals." *Analysis* 37 (1976), 1–10.
[212] Götz, Matthias. "Buridans Esel: Zur Semiotizität von Marken." *Semiosis* No. 19 (1980), 57–67.
[213] Goudge, Thomas A. "Peirce and Rescher on Scientific Progress and Economy of Research." *Dialogue* (Canada) 20 (1981), 357–365. (Review article of [34].)
[   ] Grazia, Roberto. See [99].
[214] Gruender, David. "Pragmatism, Science, and Metaphysics." *Monist* 65 (1982), 189–210.
[215] Haack, Susan. "Fallibilism and Necessity." *Synthese* 41 (1979), 37–63.
[216] _____. "'Is It True What They Say About Tarski?'" *Phil* 51 (1976), 323–336, at 328–330.
[217] _____. "Peirce, Descartes and the Cognitive Community." *Monist* 65 (1982), 156–181.
[218] _____. "Pragmatism and Ontology: Peirce and James." *Revue Internationale de Philosophie* 31 (1977), 377–400.

[219] ——. "Two Fallibilists in Search of the Truth." *Proc of the Aristotelian Soc, Suppl Vol* 51 (1977), 63–84. (See [282].)

[220] Hacking, Ian. "The Theory of Probable Inference: Neyman, Peirce and Braithwaite." In [596], pp. 141–160.

[221] Hardwick, Charles S. "Peirce's Influence on Some British Philosophers: A Guess at the Riddle." In [62], pp. 25–30.

[222] Harris, James F., and Kevin Hoover. "Abduction and the New Riddle of Induction." *Monist* 63 (1980), 329–341.

[223] Harrison, Stanley M. "Charles S. Peirce: Reflections on Being a Man-Sign." *Proc of the Am Catholic Philos Assoc* 53 (1979), 98–106.

[224] Hartshorne, Charles. "The Neglect of Relative Predicates in Modern Philosophy." *Am Philos Q* 14 (1977), 309–318.

[225] ——. "A Revision of Peirce's Categories." *Monist* 63 (1980), 277–289.

[226] Hatta, Yoshio.."Peirce's Abduction." *Riso* No. 506 (July 1975). (In Japanese.)

[227] Hausman, Carl R. "Value and the Peircean Categories." *Transactions* 15 (1979), 203–223.

[228] Hawkins, Benjamin S., Jr. "A Reassessment of Augustus de Morgan's Logic of Relations: A Documentary Reconstruction." *Intl Logic R* 10 (1979), 32–61.

[229] Hebb, D. O. "To Know Your Own Mind." In *Images, Perception, and Knowledge*, ed. John M. Nicholas, pp. 213–219. Dordrecht-Holland: D. Reidel, 1977.

[230] Helm, Bertrand P. "The Nature and Modes of Time." *Monist* 63 (1980), 375–385.

[231] Herbenick, Raymond M. "Peirce on Systems Theory." *Transactions* 6 (1970), 84–98.

[232] Herzberger, Hans G. "Peirce's Remarkable Theorem." In [64], pp. 41–58.

[233] Hester, William. "A Note on Existence." *Phil and Phenomenological Res* 2 (1941), 101–103.

[234] Hilpinen, Risto. "On C. S. Peirce's Theory of the Proposition: Peirce as a Precursor of Game-Theoretical Semantics." *Monist* 65 (1982), 182–188.

[235] Hintikka, Jaakko. "C. S. Peirce's 'First Real Discovery' and Its Contemporary Relevance." *Monist* 63 (1980), 304–315.

[236] Hiro, Mutsuo. "On the Mediation between Common-Sensism and Criticism: The Philosophy of C. S. Peirce." *Bull of the Coll of the Hum of Hiroshima Univ* No. 36 (1976), 69–89. (In Japanese.)

[237] Hiroike, Saburo. "Peirce and James: A Way to Dewey." *Bull of Tokyo Univ* No. 13 (1956). (In Japanese.)

[238] Holenstein, Elmar. "Zur semiotischen Funktion der Euler-Kreise und ihrer historischen Alternativen." *Zeitschrift für Semiotik* 2 (1980), 397–402. (See [241].)

[239] Hooker, Michael. "Peirce's Conception of Truth." In *The Philosophy of Wilfrid Sellars: Queries and Extensions*, ed. Joseph C. Pitt, pp. 129–133. Dordrecht-Holland: D. Reidel, 1978.

[   ] Hoover, Kevin. See [222].

[240] Howells, Edmund G. "Hume, Shaftesbury, and the Peirce-James Controversy." *J of the Hist of Phil* 15 (1977), 449–462.

[241] Hubig, Christoph. "Zu Holensteins Bemerkungen über die semiotische Funktion der Euler-Kreise." *Zeitschrift für Semiotik* 2 (1980), 403–409. (See [238].)

[242] Hunt, W. Murray. "Some Observations on Peirce's Theory of the Categories." *Susquehanna Univ Stud* 10 (1977), 119–130.

[243] Ichii, Saburo. "Peirce's Views on Science." *Riso* No. 193 (May 1949). (In Japanese.)

[244] Ichiyanagi, Tomio. "C. S. Peirce's Semiotic: The Problem of Intersubjectivity." *Senshu-Jinbun-Ronshu* No. 13 (April 1974). (In Japanese.)

[245] Inagaki, Ryosuke. "Peirce's Theory of Habit." *Shiso* No. 678 (December 1980). (In Japanese.)

[246] Ito, Kunitake. "The Foundations of Scientific Inquiry in Peirce." *Shiso* No. 683 (May 1981). (In Japanese.)

[247] Jakobson, Roman. "A Few Remarks on Peirce, Pathfinder in the Science of Language." In [570], pp. 31–38. (Two earlier versions, the former entitled "A Few Remarks on Structuralism," in *Mod Lang Notes* 91 [1976], 1534–1539; 92 [1977], 1026–1032.)

[248] ——. "A Glance at the Development of Semiotics." In [570], pp. 1–29, at 7–12. (Patricia Baudoin's translation of *Coup d'oeil sur le développement de la sémiotique.* See S 715.)

[249] ——. "Quest for the Essence of Language." *Diogenes* 51 (1965), 21–37. Also in *Roman Jakobson: Selected Writings*, II: 345–359. The Hague: Mouton, 1971.

[250] Johansen, Jørgen Dines. "Sémiotique et pragmatique universelle." *Degrés* 8:21 (1980), bl–33.

[251] ——. "Sign Concepts/Semiosis/Meaning." In *Danish Semiotics*, ed. Johansen and Morten Nøjgaard, pp. 123–176, at 151–176. Copenhagen: Munksgaard, 1979.

[ ] Johnstone, Henry W., Jr. See [133].

[252] Jones, Charles V. "A Missing Table in C. S. Peirce's *New Elements of Mathematics*, Vol. 1." *Historia Mathematica* 4 (1977), 441–442. (See [172].)

[253] Kaelin, E. F. "Reflections on Peirce's Aesthetics" *Monist* 65 (1982), 142–155.

[254] Kainz, H. P. "Pragmatism, Pragmatic Ethics, and Reconstructed Philosophy: Some Metaphilosophical Considerations." *Divus Thomas* 78 (1975), 254–272.

[255] Kamidera, Tsunekazu. "The Theory of Inquiry in Pragmatism, with Special Reference to C. S. Peirce's Logic of Inquiry." *Bull of the Coll of Educ of Hiroshima Univ* No. 24 (December 1975). (In Japanese.)

[256] Kaminker, J. P. "Objets et interprétants dans la lecture de la presse." *Semiosis* No. 8 (1977), 17–30.

[257] Kasamatsu, Koichi. "The Method of Inquiry in Peirce." *Mental Science* (Japan) No. 13 (March 1974). (In Japanese.)

[258] Kawamura, Jinya. "The Early Peirce." *Bull of the Coll of the Hum of Yokohama Natl Univ* No. 7 (March 1962). (In Japanese.)

[259] ——. "Recent Studies on Peirce, with Special Reference to Boler's Interpretation." *Bull of the Coll of the Hum of Yokohama Natl Univ* No. 11 (1965). (In Japanese.)

[260] Keiner, Mechtild. " 'Likeness or Copy' im Frühwerk von C. S. Peirce." *Semiosis* No. 11 (1978), 45–53.

[261] ——. "Über den Icon-Begriff und seine Einführung in die Semiotik bei Peirce." *Semiosis* No. 7 (1977), 35–43.

[262] ——. "Zur Bezeichnungs- und Bedeutungsfunktion des Zeichens." *Semiosis* No. 17–18 (1980), 34–40.

[263] Kelly, Derek A. "Architecture as Philosophical Paradigm." *Metaphilosophy* 7 (1976), 173–190.

[264] ——. "Peirce, Hartshorne and Weiss." *Indian Philos Q* 4 (1976), 41–58.

[265] Kemp-Pritchard, Ilona. "Peirce on Individuation." *Transactions* 14 (1978), 83–100.

[266] Ketner, Kenneth L. "Carolyn Eisele's Place in Peirce Studies." *Historia Mathematica* 9 (1982), 326–332.

[267] ——. "Peirce's Ethics of Terminology." *Transactions* 17 (1981), 327–347.

[268] ——. "Peirce's Existential Graphs as the Basis for an Introduction to Logic: Semiosis in the Logic Classroom." In [602], pp. 231–240.

[269] ——. "Semiotic and Folkloristics." In [618], I: 129–132.

[   ] ——. See [203].

[270] Kevelson, Roberta. "Charles S. Peirce's 'Dialogism', 'Continuous Predicate', and Legal Reasoning." *Transactions* 18 (1982), 159–176.

[271] ——. "Peirce's Semiotics as Catalyst in Legal Science: Consequences." In [602], pp. 241–254.

[272] ——. "Reversals and Recognitions: Peirce and Mukarovsky on the Art of Conversation." *Semiotica* 19 (1977), 281–320.

[273] ——. "Riddles, Legal Reasoning, and Charles S. Peirce's Existential Graphs." *Semiotica*, forthcoming.

[274] Kisiel, Theodore. "The Rationality of Scientific Discovery." In *Rationality To-Day/La rationalité aujourd'hui*, ed. Theodore F. Geraets, pp. 401–411. Ottawa: Editions de l'Université d'Ottawa, 1979.

[275] Klein, William F. "Ransom and Semiotics." *Critical Inquiry*, forthcoming.

[276] Kloesel, Christian J. W. "Charles Peirce and the Secret of the Harvard O.K." *New England Q* 52 (1979), 55–67.

[277] ——. " 'Peirce Project' Aims to Rectify 'Neglect' of Philosopher." *Convergence: Bull of the IUPUI Center for Am Stud* 1:1 (1980), 4.

[   ] ——. See [202] and [203].

[278] Kojima, Masaharu. "The Background of Peirce's Phenomenology." *Bull of the John Dewey Soc of Japan* No. 20 (1976).

[279] ——. "On Peirce's Existential Graphs." *Phil of Science* (Japan), No. 12 (1979). (In Japanese.)

[280] Kolenda, Konstantin. "Peirce on Person and Community." *Rice Univ Stud in Phil* 66:4 (1980), 15–32.

[281] ——. "Truth and Fallibilism." *Transactions* 15 (1979), 251–258.

[282] ——. "Two Fallibilists in Search of the Truth." *Proc of the Aristotelian Soc, Suppl Vol* 51 (1977), 85–104. (See [219].)

[283] Köller, Wilhelm. "Das dreistellige Zeichenmodell von Peirce." In *Zeichen, Text, Sinn: Zur Semiotik des literarischen Verstehens*, ed. Kaspar H. Spinner, pp. 33–74. Göttingen: Vandenhoeck & Ruprecht, 1977.

[284] Krampen, Martin. "Perfusion of Signs Without Confusion." *Ars Semeiotica* 2 (1979), 327–359. (Review article of [583].)

[285] ——, Hartmut Espe, and Klaus Schreiber. "Zur Mehrdimensionalität ikonischer Zeichen: Varianzanalytische Untersuchungen." *Zeitschrift für Semiotik* 2 (1980), 95–103. (Revised version in [618], II: 18–25.)

[286] Krausser, Peter. "The Three Fundamental Structural Categories of Charles S. Peirce." *Transactions* 13 (1977), 189–215.

[287] Krois, John Michael. "Peirce's Speculative Rhetoric and the Problem of Natural Law." *Phil and Rhetoric* 14 (1981), 16–30.

[288] Lachs, John. "Peirce, Santayana and the Large Facts." *Transactions* 16 (1980), 3–13.

[289] Laferrière, Daniel. "Making Room for Semiotics." *Academe: Bull of the AAUP* 66 (1979), 434–440.

[290] Landsberg, Marge E. "The Icon in Semiotic Theory." *Current Anthropology* 21 (1980), 93–95.

[291] Larsen, Svend Erik. "La structure productrice du mot d'esprit et de la semiosis: essai sur Freud et Peirce." *Degrés* 8:21 (1980), dl–18.

[292] Lee, Donald S. "Pragmatic Ultimates: Contexts and Common Sense." *Southern J of Phil* 15 (1977), 493–503.

[293] Lee, Harold N. "Royce as Logician." *Tulane Stud in Phil* 4 (1955), 61–74, at 66–68.

[294] Levi, Isaac. "Incognizables." *Synthese* 45 (1980), 413–426.

[295] ———. "Induction as Self Correcting according to Peirce." In [596], pp. 127–140.

[296] Levy, Ronald. "Peirce's Theory of Learning." *Educational Theory* 2 (1952), 151–157, 176.

[297] Lewis, J. David. "The Classic American Pragmatists as Forerunners to Symbolic Interactionism." *Sociological Q* 17 (1976), 347–359.

[298] Lincourt, John M. "Communication as Semiotic." *Communication* 3 (1978), 3–20.

[   ] ———. See [84].

[299] ———, and Paul V. Olczak. "C. S. Peirce and H. S. Sullivan on the Human Self." *Psychiatry* 37 (1974), 78–87.

[300] ———. "H. S. Sullivan and the Phenomenology of Human Cognition." *Intl J of Social Psychiatry* 25 (1979), 10–16.

[301] Liszka, Jakob. "Community in C. S. Peirce: Science as a Means and as an End." *Transactions* 14 (1978), 305–321.

[302] ———. "Peirce and Jakobson: Towards a Structuralist Reconstruction of Peirce." *Transactions* 17 (1981), 41–61.

[   ] Lloyd, E. Keith. See [96].

[303] Lyne, John R. "Rhetoric and Semiotic in C. S. Peirce." *Q J of Speech* 66 (1980), 155–168.

[304] McGrath, Michael. "Peirce and James: Epistemological Perspectives." *Educational Theory* 18 (1968), 376–379.

[305] Machan, Tibor. "C. S. Peirce and Absolute Truth." *Transactions* 16 (1980), 153–161.

[306] Macksey, Richard. "Lions and Squares: Opening Remarks." In *The Structuralist Controversy: The Languages of Criticism and the Sciences of Man*, ed. Macksey and Eugenio Donato, pp. 1–14, at 3–7. Baltimore: Johns Hopkins Press, 1972.

[307] McNeill, John W. "Peirce on the Possibility of a Chance World." *Transactions* 16 (1980), 49–58.

[308] Madden, Edward H. "Methodological Pragmatism Appraised." *Metaphilosophy* 11 (1980), 76–94. (Review article of [589].)

[309] ———. "Scientific Inference: Peirce and the Humean Tradition." In [64], pp. 59–74.

[310] Marra, William A. "The Five-Sided Pragmatism of William James." *Mod Schoolman* 41 (1963), 45–61.

[311] Martin, R. M. "De Morgan and the Logic of Relations." In [57], pp. 46–53. (See S 906.)

[312] ———. "Individuality and Quantification." In [57], pp. 11–24. (See S 907.)

[313] ———. "Of Servants, Lovers, and Benefactors: Peirce's Algebra of Relatives of 1870." *J of Philos Logic* 7 (1978), 27–48. Also in [57], pp. 25–45.

[314] ———. "On Peirce, Bradley, and the Doctrine of Continuous Relations." *Idealistic Stud* 7 (1977), 291–304. Also in [57], pp. 98–109.

[315] ———. "On Peirce's Analysis of Events." In [578], pp. 275–285.

[316] ———. "On Peirce's Anticipation of the Semantic Notion of Truth: A Dialogue with Velian." *Transactions* 13 (1977), 241–252. Also in [57], pp. 87–97.

[317] ———. "On the Logic of Idealism and Peirce's Neglected Argument." *Idealistic Stud* 9 (1979), 22–32. Also in [57], pp. 110–120.

[318] ———. "The Relation of Representation." In [57], pp. 67–79. (See S 904.)

[319] ———. "The Relational Formulae of 1883." In [57], pp. 54–61.

[320] ———. "Some Icons of Second Intention." In [57], pp. 62–66. (See S 903.)

[321] ———. "The Strange Costume of Peirce's Hegelism: A Dialogue." In [578], pp. 286–305.

[322] Marty, Robert. "Une formalisation de la sémiotique de C. S. Peirce à l'aide de la théorie des catégories." *Ars Semeiotica* 2 (1979), 275–294.

[323] ———. "Semiotik der Epistemologie." In *Die Einheit der semiotischen Dimensionen*, pp. 233–250. Tübingen: Gunter Narr, 1978. Also, in French, in *Semiosis* No. 10 (1978), 24–37.

[324] ———. "Signe et phanéron." *Semiosis* No. 20 (1980), 31–44.

[325] ———. "Sur la reduction triadique." *Semiosis* No. 17–18 (1980), 5–9.

[326] ———. "Trichotomies de l'icône, de l'indice et du symbole." *Semiosis* No. 15 (1979), 5–18.

[   ] ———. See [111].

[327] Menne, Albert. "Peirce-Kongress in den Niederlanden 1976." *Allgemeine Zeitschrift für Philosophie* 1:3 (1976), 75–77.

[328] Merrell, Floyd. "Carlos Fuentes and C. S. Peirce: At the Edge of Semiotic Activity." *Punto de Contacto/Point of Contact* 1:4 (1977), 69–77.

[329] ———. "Some Signs that Preceded Their Times: Or, Are We Really Ready for Peirce?" *Ars Semeiotica* 2 (1979), 149–172.

[330] Merrill, Daniel D. "De Morgan, Peirce and the Logic of Relations." *Transactions* 14 (1978), 247–284.

[331] Mertz, Donald W. "Peirce: Logic, Categories, and Triads." *Transactions* 15 (1979), 158–175.

[332] Meschonnic, H. "Le langage est une maladie." *Cahiers du Chemin* 23 (1975), 74–134.

[333] Meyers, Robert G. "Skepticism and the Criterion in Peirce." *Transactions* 14 (1978), 3–17.

[334] Miccoli, Paolo. "Logica, verità e realtà nel pensiero di Charles Sanders Peirce." *Aquinas* 19 (1976), 3–24.

[335] Michael, Emily. "An Examination of the Influence of Boole's Algebra on Peirce's Developments in Logic." *Notre Dame J of Formal Logic* 20 (1979), 801–806.

[336] ———. "A Note on Peirce on Boole's Algebra of Logic." *Notre Dame J of Formal Logic* 20 (1979), 636–638.

[337] ———. "A Note on the Roots of Peirce's Division of Logic into Three Branches." *Notre Dame J of Formal Logic* 18 (1977), 639–640.

[338] ———. "Peirce's Adaptation of Kant's Definition of Logic: The Early Manuscripts." *Transactions* 14 (1978), 176–183.

[   ] ——. See [340].

[339] Michael, Fred. "The Deduction of Categories in Peirce's 'New List'." *Transactions* 16 (1980), 179–211.

[340] ——, and Emily Michael. "Peirce on the Nature of Logic." *Notre Dame J of Formal Logic* 20 (1979), 84–88.

[341] Michaels, Walter Benn. "Interpreter's Self: Peirce on the Cartesian 'Subject'." *Georgia R* 31 (1977), 383–402. Also in *Reader-Response Criticism: From Formalism to Post-Structuralism*, ed. Jane P. Tompkins, pp. 185–200. Baltimore: Johns Hopkins University Press, 1980.

[342] Miller, James D. "Holmes, Peirce and Legal Pragmatism." *Yale Law J* 84 (1975), 1123–1140.

[343] Miller, John F., III. "The Role of Habits in Peirce's Metaphysics." *Southwestern J of Phil* 9:1 (1978), 77–85.

[344] Miller, Willard M. "Peirce on Pragmaticism and History." *Transactions* 14 (1978), 42–52.

[345] Moore, Edward C. "Actuality and Potentiality." Forthcoming in a Festschrift for Arthur Burks, Dordrecht-Holland: D. Reidel, 1982.

[346] Moreno, Jonathan D. "The Pragmatic 'We' Reconsidered." *Southern J of Phil* 17 (1979), 95–105.

[347] Morgan, Charles G. "Modality, Analogy, and Ideal Experiments according to C. S. Peirce." *Synthese* 41 (1979), 65–83.

[348] Morpurgo-Tagliabue, Guido. "I paralogismi della pansemiotica (e Ch. S. Peirce e J. Locke)." *Giornale Critico della Filosofia Italiana* 55 (1976), 396–415.

[349] Moseley, Jeannine. "Peirce and Perceptual Judgments." *Dialogue* (J of Phi Sigma Tau) 7:1 (1965), 1–12.

[350] Mott, Peter L. "Haack on Fallibilism." *Analysis* 40 (1980), 177–183. (See [219].)

[351] Murphey, Murray G. "Toward a Historicist History of American Philosophy." *Transactions* 15 (1979), 3–18.

[352] Murphree, Idus. "Peirce: The Experimental Nature of Belief." *J of Phil* 60 (1963), 309–316.

[353] Nadin, Mihai. "Aesthetic Sign Processes." *Kodikas/Code* 2 (1980), 337–349.

[354] ——. "The Logic of Vagueness and the Category of Synechism." *Monist* 63 (1980), 351–363.

[355] Nagel, Ernest. "Peirce's Place in Philosophy." *Historia Mathematica* 9 (1982), 302–310.

[356] Nattiez, Jean-Jacques. "Les fondements théoriques de la notion d'interprétant en sémiologie musicale." *Canadian J of Res in Semiotics* 7:2 (1979–80), 1–19.

[357] Nef, Frédéric. "Note sur une argumentation de Peirce (à propos de la valence verbale)." *Langages* 14:58 (1980), 93–102.

[358] Niiniluoto, Ilkka. "Notes on Popper as Follower of Whewell and Peirce." *Ajatus* 37 (1978), 272–327.

[359] ——. "On the Realist Theory of Scientific Progress." In *16th World Congress in Philosophy 1978*, Section Papers, pp. 463–466. Düsseldorf, 1978.

[360] ——. "Scientific Progress." *Synthese* 45 (1980), 427–462.

[361] ——. "Statistical Explanation Reconsidered." *Synthese* 48 (1981), 437–472, at 442–445.

[362] ——. "Verisimilitude, Theory-Change, and Scientific Progress." *Acta Philosophica Fennica* 30:2–4 (1979), 243–264.

[363] Nishikatsu, Tadao. "The Autonomy of Logic: A Study of Peirce (7)." *Josei J of Hum* No. 4 (1977). (In Japanese.)

[364] ———. "Chance and Law: A Study of Peirce (3)." *Josei J of Economics* 7:1 (July 1971). (In Japanese.)

[365] ———. "Consciousness and Cognition: A Study of Peirce (4)." *Josei J of Hum* No. 1 (December 1973). (In Japanese.)

[366] ———. "The Logical in Peirce: A Study of Peirce (1)." *Josei J of Economics* 5:1 (April 1969). (In Japanese.)

[367] ———. "On the Rationality of Science: A Study of Peirce (5)." *Phil of Science* (Japan) No. 7 (November 1974). (In Japanese.)

[368] ———. "Peirce's Concept of Probability: A Study of Peirce (2)." *Phil* (Japanese Philos Assoc) No. 20 (October 1970). (In Japanese.)

[369] ———. "Philosophy of Discovery: A Study of Peirce (6)." *Josei J of Economics* 11:1–3 (November 1975). (In Japanese.)

[370] Ochs, Peter. "Peirce's Metaphysical Equivalent of War." *Transactions* 17 (1981), 247–258.

[371] O'Connell, James. "C. S. Peirce and the Problem of God." *Philos Stud* (Ireland) 8 (1958), 24–45.

[372] O'Dowd, Sarah C. "Semiotic Perspectives on Comparative Language." In [602], pp. 355–364.

[373] Oehler, Klaus. "Idee und Grundriss der Peirceschen Semiotik." *Zeitschrift für Semiotik* 1 (1979), 9–22. A revised and expanded version in *Die Welt als Zeichen: Klassiker der modernen Semiotik*, ed. Martin Krampen et al., pp. 15–49. Berlin: Severin & Siedler, 1981.

[374] ———. "A New Tool for Peirce Research." *Semiotica* 25 (1979), 161–165. (Review article of S 753.)

[375] ———. "Notes on the Reception of American Pragmatism in Germany, 1899–1952." *Transactions* 17 (1981), 25–35.

[376] ———. "Peirce's Foundation of a Semiotic Theory of Cognition." In [62], pp. 67–76.

[377] ———. "The Significance of Peirce's Ethics of Terminology for Contemporary Lexicography in Semiotics." *Transactions* 17 (1981), 348–357.

[ ] Olczak, Paul V. See [299] and [300].

[378] Oliva, Joseph. "Interpretant and Interpretation." In [602], pp. 365–372.

[379] Olson, Raymond E. "Knowing What We Mean." *J of Phil* 56 (1959), 473–485.

[380] Ormiston, Gayle L. "Peirce's Categories: Structure of Semiotic." *Semiotica* 19 (1977), 209–231.

[381] Pape, Helmut. "Peirce und Russell über die Funktion von Logik und Deixis in der Identifikation singulärer Objekte." *Kodikas/Code* 2 (1980), 145–154.

[382] ———. "A Peircean Theory of Indexical Signs and Individuation." *Semiotica* 31 (1980), 215–244.

[383] ———. "Zeichen und Existenz: Ein ontologisches Problem der Peirceschen Zeichentheorie und Metaphysik." In [618], I: 139–145.

[384] Parret, Herman. "Principes de la déduction pragmatique." *Revue Internationale de Philosophie* 30 (1976), 486–510.

[385] Pavis, Patrice. "Fondements d'une sémiologie du théâtre sur la distinction de Peirce entre icônes, index et symboles." In [601], pp. 885–890.

[386] ———. "Représentation, mise en scène, mise en signe." *Canadian J of Res in Semiotics* 4:1 (1976), 63–86.

[387] Pearson, Charls, and Vladimir Slamecka. "A Theory of Sign Structure." *Semiotic Scene* 1:2 (1977), 1–22.

[388] Pelc, Jerzy. "Prolegomena zu einer Definition des Zeichenbegriffs." *Zeitschrift für Semiotik* 3 (1981), 1–9. (English version in [618], I: 45–52.)

[389] Peraldi, François. "Présentation" to [53]. *Langages* 14:58 (1980), 5–7.

[390] ——. "Why Did Peirce Terrorize Benveniste?" *Semiotica* 1981 Special Supplement, 169–180.

[391] Pfeifer, David E. "George Berkeley: Precursor of Peircean Semiotic." In [618], I: 67–74.

[392] ——. "Peirce's Application of Semiotic to God." In [62], pp. 89–100.

[393] Pignatari, Decio. "The Contiguity Illusion." In [605], pp. 84–97.

[   ] ——. See [193].

[394] Podlewski, Regina. "Theorie der Rhetorik aus semiotischer Praxis bei Ch. S. Peirce." *Semiosis* No. 22 (1981), 28–39.

[395] Potter, Vincent G. "C. S. Peirce's Argument for God's Reality: A Pragmatist's View." In *The Papin Festschrift: Essays in Honor of Joseph Papin*, ed. Joseph Armenti, pp. 224–244. Villanova, PA: Villanova University Press, 1976.

[396] Prendergast, Thomas L. "The Structure of the Argument in Peirce's 'Questions concerning Certain Faculties Claimed for Man'." *Transactions* 13 (1977), 288–305.

[397] Putnam, Hilary. "Peirce the Logician." *Historia Mathematica* 9 (1982), 290–301.

[398] Pycior, Helena M. "Benjamin Peirce's *Linear Associative Algebra*." *Isis* 70 (1979), 537–551, at 545–547.

[399] Quine, W. V. "The Pragmatists' Place in Empiricism." In [584], pp. 21–39, at 29–32.

[400] Randall, John Herman, Jr. "Josiah Royce and American Idealism." *J of Phil* 63 (1966), 57–83, at 60–65.

[401] Ransdell, Joseph M. "The Epistemic Function of Iconicity in Perception." In [62], pp. 51–66.

[402] ——. "A Misunderstanding of Peirce's Phenomenology." *Phil and Phenomenological Res* 38 (1978), 550–553. (See [490].)

[403] ——. "Semiotic and Linguistics." In [606], pp. 135–185.

[404] ——. "Semiotic Objectivity." *Semiotica* 26 (1979), 261–288.

[405] ——. "Some Leading Ideas of Peirce's Semiotic." *Semiotica* 19 (1977), 157–178.

[406] Rector, Monica. "Glossário de semiótica ou semiológia." *Vozes* 68:8 (1974), 5–17.

[407] Reiss, Timothy J. "Peirce and Frege: In the Matter of Truth." *Canadian J of Res in Semiotics* 4:2 (1976–77), 5–39.

[408] ——. "Peirce, Frege, la vérité, le tiers inclus et le champ pratique." *Langages* 14:58 (1980), 103–127.

[409] ——. "Peirce vs. Chomsky: A Reply to [79]." *Canadian J of Res in Semiotics* 7:2 (1979–80), 101–106.

[   ] Réthoré, Joëlle. See [111].

[410] Rey, Alain. "'Abstraction' et représentation (iconologie et sémiotique picturale)." In [601], pp. 812–814.

[411] Rhodes, Janice Deledalle. "Charles S. Peirce's *Arabic Grammar*." *Ars Semeiotica* 2 (1979), 365–368.

[412] Roberts, Don D. "An Introduction to Peirce's Proof of Pragmaticism." *Transactions* 14 (1978), 120–131.

[413] ——. "The Labeling Problem." In [64], pp. 75–87.

[414] Romeo, Luigi. "The Bivium Syndrome in the History of Semiotics." *Colorado Res in Linguistics* 7 (1977), 55–83.

[415] ——. "Charles S. Peirce in the History of Linguistics: An Outline for Research." *Ars Semeiotica* 2 (1979), 247–252.

[416] ——. "Of Signs and Seeds: Danté in Arisbe and Bloomington." *Canadian J of Res in Semiotics* 5:3 (1978), 25–30.

[417] Rosenthal, Sandra B. "Activity and the Structure of Perceptual Experience: Mead and Peirce Revisited." *Southern J of Phil* 15 (1977), 207–214.

[418] ——. "C. S. Peirce: Pragmatism, Semiotic Structure, and Lived Perceptual Experience." *J of the Hist of Phil* 17 (1979), 285–290.

[419] ——. "Meaning as Habit: Some Systematic Implications of Peirce's Pragmatism." *Monist* 65 (1982), 230–245.

[420] ——. "On the Epistemological Significance of What Peirce Is Not." *Transactions* 15 (1979), 19–27.

[421] ——. "The Philosophical Contributions of Douglas Greenlee (1935–1979): An Appreciative Survey." *Transactions* 15 (1979), 243–250.

[422] ——. "Pragmatism, Phenomenology and the World of Appearing Objects." *Intl Philos Q* 17 (1977), 285–291.

[423] ——, and Patrick L. Bourgeois. "Pragmatism, Scientific Method, and the Phenomenological Return to Lived Experience." *Phil and Phenomenological Res* 38 (1977), 56–65.

[424] Rostankowski, Cynthia. "Semiotic and Creativity." In [602], pp. 439–444.

[425] Sagal, P. T. "Peirce on Infinitesimals." *Transactions* 14 (1978), 132–135.

[426] Sakiyama, Katsuhiro. "Peirce's Logic." *Bull of Phil and Psychology* (Rissho Univ.) No. 2 (1969). (In Japanese.)

[427] ——. "Peirce's Views of Science and Religion." *Bull of the Coll of Lit of Rissho Univ* No. 21 (March 1965). (In Japanese.)

[428] Savan, David. "Abduction and Semiotics." In [606], pp. 252–262.

[429] ——. "Questions Concerning Certain Classifications Claimed for Signs." *Semiotica* 19 (1977), 171–195.

[430] ——. "La séméiotique de Charles S. Peirce." *Langages* 14:58 (1980), 9–23.

[431] ——. "The Unity of Peirce's Thought." In [64], pp. 3–14.

[432] Schneider, Herbert W. "The Pragmatic Movement in Historical Perspective." In *Something of Great Constancy: Essays in Honor of the Memory of J. Glenn Gray, 1913–1977*, ed. Timothy Fuller, pp. 102–109. Colorado Springs: The Colorado College, 1979.

[433] Schouls, Peter A. "Peirce and Descartes: Doubt and the Logic of Discovery." In [64], pp. 88–104.

[   ] Schreiber, Klaus. See [285].

[434] Scott, Frances W. "Art and Objectivity." In [602], pp. 475–484.

[435] Sendaydiego, Henry B. "Charles Sanders Peirce on God." *J of the West Virginia Philos Soc* 12 (1977), 24–26.

[436] Settle, Tom. "Induction and Probability Unfused." In *The Philosophy of Karl Popper*, ed. Paul Arthur Schilpp, II: 697–749, at 724–732 and 737–740. La Salle, IL: Open Court, 1974.

[437] ——. "Popper versus Peirce on the Probability of Single Cases." *British J for the Phil of Science* 28 (1977), 177–180.

[438] Sezai, Yoshio. "C. S. Peirce's Behavioristic Theory of Signs." *Annual R of Phil of Science* (Japan) No. 4 (1964). (In Japanese.)

[439] Shapiro, Gary. "Intention and Interpretation in Art: A Semiotic Analysis." *J of Aesthetics and Art Criticism* 33 (1974), 33–42.

[440] _____. "Peirce's Critique of Hegel's Phenomenology and Dialectic." *Transactions* 17 (1981), 269–275.

[441] Shapiro, Michael. "Poetry and Language, 'Considered as Semeiotic'." *Transactions* 16 (1980), 97–117.

[442] _____. "Russian Conjugation: Theory and Hermeneutic." *Language* 56 (1980), 67–93.

[443] _____. "Sémiotique de la rime." *Poétique* 20 (1974), 501–519.

[444] _____. "The Structure of Meaning in Semiotic Perspective." In *Papers from the Fourth International Conference on Historical Linguistics*, ed. Elizabeth C. Traugott et al., pp. 53–59. Amsterdam: Benjamins, 1980.

[445] _____. "Toward a Global Theory of Style: A Peircean Exposé." *Ars Semeiotica* 3 (1980), 241–247.

[446] Sharpe, R. A. "Type, Token, Interpretation and Performance." *Mind* 88 (1979), 437–440. (See [158].)

[447] Shinbara, Osamu. "C. S. Peirce's Pragmaticism: From a Linguistic Point of View." *Annual Res Report of Doshisha Women's Coll* 28:1 (November 1977). (In Japanese.)

[448] Short, T. L. "Peirce and the Incommensurability of Theories." *Monist* 63 (1980), 316–328.

[449] _____. "Peirce's Concept of Final Causation." *Transactions* 17 (1981), 369–382.

[450] _____. "Semeiosis and Intentionality." *Transactions* 17 (1981), 197–223.

[451] "Signs and Their Users: The Interrelations of Logic, Life, and Computing Machines." *Res News* (University of Michigan) 31:1–2 (1980), 8–15.

[ ] da Silva, Francisco Ivan. See [132].

[452] Singer, Beth J. "John E. Smith on Pragmatism." *Transactions* 16 (1980), 14–25. (Review article of [608]. See also [462].)

[453] Singer, Marcus G. "Peirce: Not 'But' But 'Not'." *Transactions* 17 (1981), 36–40.

[454] Singer, Milton. "For a Semiotic Anthropology." In [605], pp. 202–231, at 211–225.

[455] _____. "Personal and Social Identity in Dialogue." In *New Approaches to the Self*, ed. Benjamin Lee. New York: Plenum, 1981.

[456] _____. "Signs of the Self: An Exploration in Semiotic Anthropology." *Am Anthropologist* 82 (1980), 485–507.

[457] Sini, Carlo. "Il problema del segno in Husserl e in Peirce." *Filosofia* 29 (1978), 543–558.

[458] _____. "Le relazioni triadiche dei segni e le categorie faneroscopiche di Peirce." *Versus* No. 15 (1976), 17–27.

[459] Skagestad, Peter. "C. S. Peirce on Biological Evolution and Scientific Progress." *Synthese* 41 (1979), 85–114.

[460] _____. "Pragmatic Realism: The Peircean Argument Reexamined." *R of Metaphysics* 33 (1980), 527–540.

[ ] Slamecka, Vladimir. See [387].

[461] Smith, John Clark. "Peirce's Religious Metaphysics." *Intl Philos Q* 19 (1979), 407–425.

[462] Smith, John E. "Comments on Beth J. Singer's [452]." *Transactions* 16 (1980), 26–33. (See also [608].)

[463] ———. "Receptivity, Change and Relevance: Some Hallmarks of Philosophy in America." In [614], pp. 185–198.

[464] Smith, Michael D. "Peirce and Piaget: A Commentary on Signs of a Common Ground." *Semiotica* 19 (1977), 271–279.

[465] Sprigge, T. L. S. "James, Santayana, Tarski, and Pragmatism." In [64], pp. 105–120.

[466] Stack, George J. "Peirce: pragmatismo, positivismo y metafísica científica." *Folia Humanística* 16 (1978), 369–381.

[467] Stanley, William A. "An American Philosopher: Charles Peirce—Scholar, Cartographer, Mathematician and Metrologist." *NOAA Magazine* 8:2 (1978), 16–19.

[468] Stephens, G. Lynn. "Cognition and Emotion in Peirce's Theory of Mental Activity." *Transactions* 17 (1981), 131–140.

[469] ———. "Peirce on Psychological Self-Knowledge." *Transactions* 16 (1980), 212–224.

[470] Stern, Kenneth. "A Defence of Cartesian Doubt." *Dialogue* (Canada) 17 (1978), 480–489.

[471] Stetter, Christian. "Peirce und Saussure." *Kodikas/Code* 1 (1979), 124–149.

[472] ———. "Semiose als kontinuierlicher Prozess." In *Die Einheit der semiotischen Dimensionen*, pp. 155–170. Tübingen: Gunter Narr, 1978.

[473] ———. "Zum Problem 'ästhetischer' Zeichen bei Charles S. Peirce." In [618], I: 253–260.

[474] Stigler, Stephen M. "Mathematical Statistics in the Early States." *Annals of Statistics* 6 (1978), 239–265, at 246–251.

[475] Suits, Bernard. "Doubts About Peirce's Cosmology." *Transactions* 15 (1979), 311–321.

[476] Sullivan, Denis F. "Instinct and Dogmatism." *Transactions* 15 (1979), 61–67.

[477] ———. "Peirce and the Possibility of Metaphysics." *New Scholasticism* 51 (1977), 38–61.

[478] ———. "Peirce and the Truth of Moral Propositions." *Proc of the Am Catholic Philos Assoc* 51 (1977), 183–192.

[479] Takemoto, Masahiro. "Sentimentalism in Peirce." *Res Bull of Koka Women's Junior Coll* No. 16 (1978). (In Japanese.)

[480] Taranto, Robert E. "The Mechanics of Semiotics and of the 'Human Mind'." *Semiosis* No. 15 (1979), 19–29; and No. 17–18 (1980), 41–52.

[481] Tarasti, Eero. "Peirce and Greimas from the Viewpoint of Musical Semiotics: An Outline for a Comparative Semiotics." In [602], pp. 503–512.

[482] Telotte, J. P. "Charles Peirce and Walker Percy: From Semiotic to Narrative." In *Walker Percy: Art and Ethics*, ed. Jac Tharpe, pp. 65–79. Jackson: University Press of Mississippi, 1980.

[483] Thagard, Paul R. "Semiotics and Hypothetic Inference in C. S. Peirce." *Versus* No. 19–20 (1978), 163–172.

[484] Thayer, H. S. "Peirce on Truth." In [64], pp. 121–132. Earlier version in [614], pp. 63–76.

[485] ———. "Pragmatism: A Reinterpretation of the Origins and Consequences." In [584], pp. 1–20.

[486] ———. "The Revolution in Empiricism: Peirce on Scientific Knowledge and Truth." *Southern J of Phil* 17 (1979), 531–545.

[487] Thibaud, Pierre. "Un système peircèen des modalités." In *Systèmes symboliques, science et philosophie: travaux du séminaire d'epistémologie comparative d'Aix-en-Provence*, pp. 71–79. Paris: Editions du Centre National de la Recherche Scientifique, 1978.

[488] Thompson, Manley. "Peirce's Conception of an Individual." In [64], pp.133–148.

[489] ——. "Peirce's Verificationist Realism." *R of Metaphysics* 32 (1978), 74–98.

[490] Tibbetts, Paul. "Peirce's Phenomenology: A Reply to Professor Ransdell." *Phil and Phenomenological Res* 38 (1978), 554–556. (See [402].)

[491] Toyama, Tomonori. "A Reappraisal of Peirce's Semiotic." *Contemporary Thought* (Japan) 4:10 (October 1976). (In Japanese.)

[492] Tsurumi, Shunske. "The Meaning of Peirce." *Shiso* No. 289 (1948). (In Japanese.)

[493] Turquette, Atwell R. "Alternative Axioms for Peirce's Triadic Logic." *Zeitschrift für mathematische Logik und Grundlagen der Mathematik* 24 (1978), 443–444.

[494] ——. "Minimal Axioms for Peirce's Triadic Logic." *Zeitschrift für mathematische Logik und Grundlagen der Mathematik* 22 (1976), 169–176.

[495] ——. "Minimal Quantification Axioms for Peirce's Triadic Logics." In *Abstracts of Short Communications and Poster Sessions*, p. 5. Helsinki: International Congress of Mathematicians, 1978.

[496] Uchida, Kohei. "Charles S. Peirce's Philosophy, with Special Reference to His Realism." *Annual Res Bull of Gakushuin Univ* No. 14 (1967). (In Japanese.)

[497] ——. "On the Nature of C. S. Peirce's Philosophy: A Survey of His Early Thought." *Annual Res Bull of Gakushuin Univ* No. 23 (1976). (In Japanese.)

[498] ——. "The Various Aspects of Pragmatism in Peirce." *Annual Res Bull of Gakushuin Univ* No. 17 (1970). (In Japanese.)

[499] Ueda, Seiji. "From Peirce to Dewey." *Riso* No. 252 (May 1954). (In Japanese.)

[500] Ueyama, Shunpei. "Development of Peirce's Theory of Logic." *Science of Thought* (Japan) 1 (1954). (In Japanese.)

[501] ——. "The Logical Thought of Charles Peirce." In *Essays in Commemoration of the 25th Anniversary of the Research Institute of Humanities of Kyoto University*, November 1954. (In Japanese.)

[502] ——. "Peirce's Philosophy of History." *Shiso* No. 335 (May 1952). (In Japanese.)

[503] ——. "The Pragmatistic Theory of Truth." *Riso* No. 260 (1955). (In Japanese.)

[504] ——. "The Theory of Abduction." *Bull of Hum* (Res Institute of Hum of Kyoto Univ) 1978. (In Japanese.)

[505] Uozu, Kunio. "Peirce's Theory of Perception." *Bull of the Coll of Law and Hum of Kumamoto Univ* No. 19 (December 1965). (In Japanese.)

[506] van Zoest, Aart J. A. "Eine semiotische Analyse von Morgenstern's Gedicht 'Fisches Nachtgesang'." *LiLi* 4 (1974), 49–67.

[507] Vandamme, Fernand. "Peirce, Action and Semantics." *Philosophica* 19 (1977), 111–117.

[508] Verón, Eliseo. "La sémiosis et son monde." *Langages* 14:58 (1980), 61–74.

[509] Vianu, Ion. "Sémiotique de la folie." *Semiosis* No. 16 (1979), 36–44.

[510] Vickers, John M. "On the Reality of Chance." In *PSA 1978*, vol. 2. East Lansing, MI: Philosophy of Science Association, 1979.

[511] ____. "Truth, Consensus, and Probability: On Peirce's Definition of Scientific Truth." *Pacific Philos Q* 61 (1980), 183–203.

[512] Vitali, Theodore R. "The Peirceian Influence on Hartshorne's Subjectivism." *Process Stud* 7 (1977), 238–249.

[513] Walther, Elisabeth. "Ergänzende Bemerkungen zur Differenzierung der Subzeichen." *Semiosis* No. 17–18 (1980), 30–33.

[514] ____. "Vorläufige Bemerkungen zu trichotomischen Triaden." *Semiosis* No. 21 (1981), 29–39.

[515] Wells, Rulon S. "Peirce's Notion of the Symbol." *Semiotica* 19 (1977), 197–208.

[516] ____. "Thirdness and Linguistics." In [606], pp. 186–200.

[517] Wheeler, Clementine. "Centennial of an American Philosophy." *Humanist* 38 (September/October 1978), 51.

[   ] Wilson, Robin J. See [96].

[518] Witschel, Günter. "Die beiden Funktionen der 'pragmatischen Maximen' und der Begriff der 'Überzeugung'." *Semiosis* No. 11 (1978), 5–19.

[519] Wolter, Allan B. "An Oxford Dialogue on Language and Metaphysics." *R of Metaphysics* 31 (1978), 615–648; and 32 (1978), 323–348. Revised and shorter version, entitled "A 'Reportatio' of Duns Scotus' Merton College Dialogue on Language and Metaphysics," in [609], I:179–191.

[520] Yamashita, Masao. "The Semiotic Theories of St. Augustine and Peirce." *Jinbun-Ronkyu* (Kansai Gakuin Univ) 14:3 (1963). (In Japanese.)

[521] Yonemori, Yuji. "Peirce's Concept of Sign." In *Essays Presented to Prof. Genshu Asato, LL.D., in Honor of His Retirement from the University of the Ryukyus*, pp. 321–356. Tokyo: Eihosha, 1972. (In Japanese.)

[522] ____. "Peirce's Phenomenology." *Bull of the Coll of Educ of the Univ of the Ryukyus* No. 15 (March 1972), 1–15. (In Japanese.)

[523] ____. "Pragmaticism: A Study of Peirce." In *Essays Presented to Prof. Asao Maedomari in Honor of His Retirement from the University of the Ryukyus*, pp. 151–165. Tokyo: San Printing Co., 1976. (In Japanese.)

[524] ____. "A Study of Peirce's Semiotic (I): The Structure of Peirce's Semiotic and the Classification of Signs." *Bull of the Coll of Educ of the Univ of the Ryukyus* No. 9 (June 1966), 1–15. (In Japanese.)

[525] ____. "A Study of Peirce's Semiotic (II): Signs." *Bull of the Coll of Educ of the Univ of the Ryukyus* No. 10 (March 1967), 1–12. (In Japanese.)

[526] ____. "A Study of Peirce's Semiotic (III): Interpretant, Meaning, and Habit." *Bull of the Coll of Educ of the Univ of the Ryukyus* No. 13 (June 1970), 1–16. (In Japanese.)

[527] Yoshinami, Eiji. "C. S. Peirce's Theory of Categories (I)." *Bull of the Okayama Univ of Commerce* 11:3 (October 1976); and 11:4 (December 1976). (In Japanese.)

[528] ____. "C. S. Peirce's Theory of Categories (II)." *Bull of the Okayama Univ of Commerce* 15:1–2 (September 1979); and 15:3 (January 1980). (In Japanese.)

[529] ____. "The Existence of an External World: 'Reality' and 'Existence' in Peirce." *Bull of the Okayama Univ of Commerce* 5:1 (December 1969). (In Japanese.)

[530] ____. "A Glance at C. S. Peirce's Theory of Categories." *Bull of the John Dewey Soc of Japan* No. 18 (October 1976). (In Japanese.)

[531] ____. "On Quality: J. Dewey and C. S. Peirce." *Bull of the Okayama Univ of Commerce* 3:2 (August 1968). (In Japanese.)

[532] ——. "Paradoxes in the Theory of Time: 'Perception' and 'Time' in Peirce." *Bull of the Okayama Univ of Commerce* 2:1 (September 1966). (In Japanese.)

[533] ——. "Peirce's Concept of Probability." *Bull of the Okayama Univ of Commerce* 8:1 (November 1972). (In Japanese.)

[534] ——. "Peirce's Theory of Abduction: His Early and Later Views." *Bull of the Okayama Univ of Commerce* 9:1 (November 1973). (In Japanese.)

[535] ——. "Some Issues Concerning the Interpretation of C. S. Peirce's Pragmatism." *Bull of the Okayama Univ of Commerce* 2:2 (June 1967). (In Japanese.)

[536] ——. "Some Issues in C. S. Peirce's Theory of Categories." *Bull of the Okayama Univ of Commerce* 3:2 (August 1968). (In Japanese.)

[537] Zanoni, C. P. "Development of Logical Pragmatism in Italy." *J of the Hist of Ideas* 40 (1979), 603–619.

[538] Zellweger, Shea. "Sign-Creation and Man-Sign Engineering." *Semiotica* 38 (1982), 17–54.

[539] Zeman, J. Jay. "The Esthetic Sign in Peirce's Semiotic." *Semiotica* 19 (1977), 241–258.

[540] ——. "Peirce on Abstraction." *Monist* 65 (1982), 211–229.

[541] ——. "Peirce's Theory of Signs." In [583], pp. 22–39.

[542] ——. "Pragmaticism and Semiotic." *Semiotica*, 36 (1981), 309–327. (Review article of [62].)

IV. GENERAL WORKS AND PROCEEDINGS

[543] *Anais do primeiro colóquio de semiótica* (6–8 November 1978). Rio de Janeiro: Edições Loyola—Pontifícia Universidade Católica, 1980. (See [126] and [132].)

[544] Armstrong, D. M. *Universals and Scientific Realism.* 2 vols. Cambridge: Cambridge University Press, 1978.

[545] Aune, Bruce. *Rationalism, Empiricism, and Pragmatism: An Introduction.* New York: Random House, 1970.

[546] Beckman, Frank S. *Mathematical Foundations of Programming*, pp. 69ff. Reading, MA: Addison-Wesley, 1980.

[547] Bense, Max. *Die Unwahrscheinlichkeit des Ästhetischen und die semiotische Konzeption der Kunst.* Baden-Baden: Agis-Verlag, 1979.

[548] ——. *Vermittlung der Realitäten: Semiotische Erkenntnistheorie.* Baden-Baden: Agis-Verlag, 1976.

[549] Bentele, Günter, and Ivan Bystřina. *Semiotik: Grundlagen und Probleme*, pp. 20–29. Stuttgart: Kohlhammer, 1978.

[550] Biggs, Norman L., E. Keith Lloyd, and Robin J. Wilson. *Graph Theory: 1736–1936.* Oxford: Clarendon, 1976.

[ ] Bourgeois, Patrick L. See [593].

[551] Boyer, Merle W. *Language and Religion in the Light of the Analysis of Signs.* Chicago: University of Chicago Press, 1946.

[ ] Brandom, Robert. See [590].

[552] Buczyńska-Garewicz, Hanna. *Sign, Meaning, Value: Essays in American Philosophy*, pp. 5–50. Warsaw: Ksiazka i Wiedza, 1975. (In Polish.)

[553] Burks, Arthur W. *Chance, Cause, Reason: An Inquiry into the Nature of Scientific Evidence.* Chicago: University of Chicago Press, 1977.

[554] Busse, Klaus-Peter, and Hartmut Riemenschneider. *Grundlagen semiotischer Ästhetik*, pp. 55–83. Düsseldorf: Schwann, 1979.

[   ] Bystřina, Ivan. See [549].

[555] Caprettini, Gian Paolo. *Aspetti della semiotica: principi e storia*, pp. 49–57, 117–145. Turin: Einaudi, 1980.

[556] ——. *La semiologia: elementi per un'introduzione*, pp. 77–106. Turin: Giappichelli, 1976.

[   ] Courtés, Joseph. See [564].

[557] Den Ouden, Bernard. *The Fusion of Naturalism and Humanism.* Washington, DC: University Press of America, 1979.

[558] Dubarle, Dominique. *Logos et formalisation du langage*, pp. 127–150. Paris: Klincksieck, 1977.

[559] Dumitriu, Anton. *History of Logic*, III:335–336 and IV:48–49. Tunbridge Wells: Abacus Press, 1977.

[560] Eames, S. Morris. *Pragmatic Naturalism: An Introduction.* Carbondale and Edwardsville: Southern Illinois University Press, 1977.
  Review: Deledalle, G. *Transactions* 14 (1978), 136–138.
  Koch, D. F. *J of the Hist of Phil* 18 (1980), 368–371.

[561] Eco, Umberto. *The Role of the Reader: Explorations in the Semiotics of Texts*, pp. 175–199. Bloomington: Indiana University Press, 1979.

[   ] Edwards, Herbert W. See [568].

[562] Flower, Elizabeth, and Murray G. Murphey. *A History of Philosophy in America*, II:567–631. New York: Capricorn Books, 1977.
  Review: Reck, A. J. *Transactions* 14 (1978), 322–326 (I).
  Wiener, P. P. *Transactions* 14 (1978), 327–333 (II).

[563] Friedrich, Paul. *Language, Context, and the Imagination: Essays by Paul Friedrich*, ed. Anwar S. Dil, pp. 1–18. Stanford, CA: Stanford University Press, 1979.

[564] Greimas, Algirdas Julien, and Joseph Courtés. *Sémiotique: dictionnaire raisonné de la théorie du langage.* Paris: Hachette, 1979.

[565] Haack, Susan. *Philosophy of Logics*, pp. 97–99, 238–242. Cambridge: Cambridge University Press, 1978.

[566] Hawkes, Terence. *Structuralism and Semiotics*, pp. 123–130. Berkeley and Los Angeles: University of California Press, 1977.

[567] Holenstein, Elmar. *Linguistik, Semiotik, Hermeneutik: Plädoyers für eine strukturale Phänomenologie.* Frankfurt: Suhrkamp, 1976.

[568] Horton, Rod W., and Herbert W. Edwards. *Backgrounds of American Literary Thought*, pp. 159–168. New York: Appleton-Century-Crofts, 1952.

[569] Imhasly, Bernard, Bernhard Marfurt, and Paul Portmann. *Konzepte der Linguistik: Eine Einführung*, pp. 63–75. Wiesbaden: Athenaion, 1979.

[570] Jakobson, Roman. *The Framework of Language.* Michigan Studies in the Humanities 1. Ann Arbor: Horace H. Rackham School of Graduate Studies, 1980. (See [247] and [248].)

[571] Kockelmans, Joseph J. *Philosophy of Science: The Historical Background*, pp. 281–294. New York: Free Press, 1968.

[572] Kuklick, Bruce. *The Rise of American Philosophy: Cambridge, Massachusetts, 1860–1930*, pp. 104–126. New Haven: Yale University Press, 1977.
  Reviews: Madden, E. H., and P. H. Hare. *Transactions* 14 (1978), 53–72.
  Michalos, A. C. *Dialogue* (Canada) 19 (1980), 175–177.

Sessions, W. L. *Process Stud* 8 (1978), 56–60.

[573] Laferrière, Daniel. *Sign and Subject: Semiotic and Psychonalytic Investigations into Poetry*, pp. 9–15. Lisse: Peter de Ridder Press, 1978.

[574] Lewis, J. David, and Richard L. Smith. *American Sociology and Pragmatism: Mead, Chicago Sociology, and Symbolic Interaction*, pp. 27–58, 79–86. Chicago: University of Chicago Press, 1980.

[   ] Lloyd, E. Keith. See [550].

[575] Lyons, John. *Semantics*, I:95–119. Cambridge: Cambridge University Press, 1977.

[576] McNeill, David. *The Conceptual Basis of Language*, pp. 39–54. Hillsdale, NJ: Lawrence Erlbaum Associates, 1979.

[577] Malmberg, Bertil. *Signes et symboles: les bases du langage humain*, pp. 93–130. Paris: Picard, 1977.

[   ] Marfurt, Bernhard. See [569].

[578] Martin, R. M. *Primordiality, Science, and Value*. Albany: State University of New York Press, 1980. (See [315] and [321].)

[579] Mayer, Frederick. *A History of American Thought: An Introduction*, pp. 248–258. Dubuque, IA: Wm. C. Brown, 1951.

[   ] Murphey, Murray G. See [562].

[580] Nadin, Mihai. *Zeichen und Wert*. Tübingen: Gunter Narr, 1981.

[581] Nöth, Winfried. *Dynamik semiotischer Systeme: Vom altenglischen Zauberspruch zum illustrierten Werbetext*, pp. 12–18. Stuttgart: J. B. Metzler, 1977.

[582] Percy, Walker. *The Message in the Bottle: How Queer Man Is, How Queer Language Is, and What One Has to Do with the Other*, pp. 298–327. New York: Farrar, Straus and Giroux, 1975.

[583] *A Perfusion of Signs*. Ed. Thomas A. Sebeok. Bloomington: Indiana University Press, 1978. (See [284] and [541].)

[   ] Portmann, Paul. See [569].

[584] *Pragmatism: Its Sources and Prospects*. Ed. Robert J. Mulvaney and Philip M. Zeltner. Columbia: University of South Carolina Press, 1981. (See [399] and [485].)

[585] Prior, A. N. *The Doctrine of Propositions and Terms*, ed. P. T. Geach and A. J. P. Kenny, pp. 88–90, 118–119. London: Duckworth, 1976.

[586] ——. *Papers in Logic and Ethics*, ed. P. T. Geach and A. J. P. Kenny, pp. 126–129, 141–142, 157. London: Duckworth, 1976.

[587] Proudfoot, Wayne. *God and the Self: Three Types of Philosophy of Religion*. London: Associated University Press, 1976.

[588] Quinton, Anthony. *The Nature of Things*, pp. 218–223. London: Routledge & Kegan Paul, 1973.

[589] Rescher, Nicholas. *Methodological Pragmatism: A Systems-Theoretic Approach to the Theory of Knowledge*, pp. 57–62, 123–125. Oxford: Blackwell, 1977. (See [308].)

   Reviews: Almeder, R. F. *Transactions* 15 (1979), 83–87.
   Altshuler, B. *Philos R* 88 (1979), 490–496.
   Yolton, J. W. *Idealistic Stud* 6 (1976), 218–238.

[590] ——, and Robert Brandom. *The Logic of Inconsistency: A Study in Non-Standard Possible-World Semantics and Ontology*, pp. 106–117, 124–126. Oxford: Blackwell, 1980.

[　] Riemenschneider, Hartmut. See [554].

[591] Rohatyn, Dennis A. *Two Dogmas of Philosophy and Other Essays in the Philosophy of Philosophy*, pp. 174–176. Rutherford, NJ: Fairleigh Dickinson University Press, 1977.

[592] Rollin, Bernard E. *Natural and Conventional Meaning: An Examination of the Distinction*, pp. 54–59. The Hague: Mouton, 1976..

[593] Rosenthal, Sandra B., and Patrick L. Bourgeois. *Pragmatism and Phenomenology: A Philosophic Encounter*, pp. 40–44, 61–65, 77–81. Amsterdam: B. R. Gruner, 1980.

[594] Roth, Robert J. *American Religious Philosophy*. New York: New York University Press, 1967.

[595] Schneider, Reinhard. *Semiotik der Musik: Darstellung und Kritik*. Munich: Fink, 1980.

[596] *Science, Belief and Behaviour: Essays in Honour of R. B. Braithwaite*. Ed. D. H. Mellor. Cambridge: Cambridge University Press, 1980. (See [220] and [295].)

[597] Sebeok, Thomas A. *The Play of Musement*. Bloomington: Indiana University Press, 1981.

[598] ――――. *The Sign & Its Masters*, pp. 107–122. Austin: University of Texas Press, 1978.

[599] Sefler, George F. *Language and the World*, pp. 84–88. Atlantic Highlands, NJ: Humanities Press, 1974.

[600] Sellars, Roy Wood. *Reflections on American Philosophy from Within*, pp. 27–32. Notre Dame, IN: University of Notre Dame Press, 1969.

[601] *A Semiotic Landscape/Panorama sémiotique*. Ed. Seymour Chatman, Umberto Eco, and Jean-Marie Klinkenberg. The Hague: Mouton, 1979. (See [89, 104, 193, 385, 410].)

[602] *Semiotics 1980* (Proceedings of the Fifth Annual Meeting of the Semiotic Society of America, Lubbock, Texas, October 1980). Ed. Michael F. Herzfeld and Margot D. Lenhart. New York: Plenum, 1981. (See [80, 107, 140, 205, 268, 271, 372, 378, 424, 434, 481].)

[603] Shapiro, Michael. *Asymmetry: An Inquiry into the Linguistic Structure of Poetry*. Amsterdam: North-Holland, 1976.

[604] Sherover, Charles M. *The Human Experience of Time: The Development of Its Philosophic Meaning*, pp. 384–394. New York: New York University Press, 1975.

[605] *Sight, Sound, and Sense*. Ed. Thomas A. Sebeok. Bloomington: Indiana University Press, 1978. (See [196, 393, 454].)

[606] *The Signifying Animal: The Grammar of Language and Experience*. Ed. Irmengard Rauch and Gerald F. Carr. Bloomington: Indiana University Press, 1980. (See [403, 428, 516].)

[607] Singer, Milton. *Man's Glassy Essence: Explorations in Semiotic Anthropology*. Bloomington: Indiana University Press, 1982.

[608] Smith, John E. *Purpose and Thought: The Meaning of Pragmatism*. New Haven: Yale University Press, 1978. (See [209, 452, 462].)

[　] Smith, Richard L. See [574].

[609] *Sprache und Erkenntnis im Mittelalter: Akten des VI. Internationalen Kongresses für mittelalterliche Philosophie der Société Internationale pour l'Etude de la Philosophie Médiévale, 29. August–3. September 1977 in Bonn.* 2

vols. Miscellanea Mediaevalia 13. Ed. Jan P. Beckmann et al. Berlin: de Gruyter, 1981. (See [519] and [650].)

[610] Stevens, Edward. *The Religion Game, American Style.* New York: Paulist Press, 1976.

[611] Stroh, Guy W. *American Ethical Thought.* Chicago: Nelson-Hall, 1979.

[612] ——. *American Philosophy from Edwards to Dewey: An Introduction,* pp. 77–119. Princeton, NJ: Van Nostrand, 1968.

[613] Trigg, Roger. *Reality at Risk.* London: Sussex Harvester Press, 1980.

[614] *Two Centuries of Philosophy in America.* Ed. Peter Caws. Totowa, NJ: Rowman and Littlefield, 1980. (See [135, 160, 463].)

[615] Vickers, John M. *Belief and Probability,* chapter 3. Dordrecht-Holland: D. Reidel, 1976.

[616] *Die Welt als Zeichen: Klassiker der modernen Semiotik.* Ed. Martin Krampen, Klaus Oehler, Roland Posner, and Thure von Uexküll. Berlin: Severin and Siedler, 1981. (See [373].)

[617] Wilson, R. Jackson. *In Quest of Community: Social Philosophy in the United States, 1860–1920,* pp. 32–59. New York: Wiley, 1968.

[   ] Wilson, Robin J. See [550].

[618] *Zeichenkonstitution: Akten des 2. Semiotischen Kolloquiums Regensburg 1978.* 2 vols. Ed. Annemarie Lange-Seidl. Berlin: de Gruyter, 1981. (See [106, 176, 269, 285, 383, 388, 391, 473].)

V. TRANSLATIONS

[619] *Antologia degli scritti di C. S. Peirce.* Ed. Nynfa Bosco. Turin: Giappichelli, 1977. (Vol. 2 of *Dalla scienza alla metafisica.* See [6].)

[620] *Charles S. Peirce: écrits sur le signe.* Ed. Gérard Deledalle. Paris: Editions du Seuil, 1978.
    Reviews: Stetter, C. *Transactions* 16 (1980), 169–174.
    Walther, E. *Semiosis* No. 13 (1979), 65.

[621] *Charles S. Peirce: scritti di filosofia.* Ed. William J. Callaghan, tr. Luciano M. Leone. Bologna: Cappelli, 1978.

[622] *Charles S. Peirce: semiotica—i fondamenti della semiotica cognitiva.* Ed. Massimo A. Bonfantini, Letizia Grassi, and Roberto Grazia. Turin: Einaudi, 1980.

[623] *Charles Sanders Peirce: la ciencia de la semiotica.* Ed. Armando Sercovich, tr. Beatriz Bugni. Buenos Aires: Nueva Visión, 1974.

[624] *Charles Sanders Peirce: escritos coligidos.* Ed. Armando Mora d'Oliveira and Sergio Pomeraugblum. São Paulo: Abril Cultural, 1974.

[625] *Charles Sanders Peirce: lecciones sobre el pragmatismo.* Ed. Dalmacio Negro Pavón. Buenos Aires: Aguilar, 1978.

[626] *Charles Sanders Peirce: pragmatismo e pragmaticismo—saggi scelti.* Ed. G. Gilardoni. Padua: Liviana, 1966.

[627] *Charles Sanders Peirce: Schriften zum Pragmatismus und Pragmatizismus.* 2nd ed. Ed. Karl-Otto Apel, tr. Gert Wartenberg. Frankfurt: Suhrkamp, 1976. (See S 33–34.)

[628] *Charles Sanders Peirce: scienza e pragmatismo.* Ed. Piero Bairati. Turin: G. B. Paravia, 1972.

[629] *Charles Sanders Peirce: semiótica.* Ed. José T. Coelho Netto. São Paulo: Perspectiva, 1977.

[630] *Charles Sanders Peirce: semiótica e filosofia.* Ed. Octanny Silveira da Mota and Leonidas Hegenberg. São Paulo: Cultrix, 1972.

[631] *Peirce, James, and Dewey.* Ed. Shumpei Ueyama and Masao Yamashita. Tokyo: Chuokoronsha, 1968. (Vol. 48 of *Great Books of the World.* In Japanese.)

VI. ADDENDA

[632] Almeder, Robert. "Peircean Fallibilism." *Transactions* 18 (1982), 57–65.

[633] Altshuler, Bruce. "Peirce's Theory of Truth and the Revolt Against Realism." *Transactions* 18 (1982), 34–56.

[634] Apel, Karl-Otto. "C. S. Peirce's and Jürgen Habermas' Consensus Theory of Truth." *Transactions,* forthcoming.

[635] Bambrough, Renford. "Peirce, Wittgenstein, and Systematic Philosophy." *Midwest Stud in Phil* 6 (1981), 263–273.

[636] Beckman, Frank S. "The Identity of Professor James Moriarty." *Baker Street J* 31 (1981), 207–212.

[637] Black, Walter R. "The Unity of the Epistemology of C. S. Peirce." Diss. Rice 1982. *DAI* 43:2A (1982), 469.

[638] Brunning, Jacqueline. "A Brief Account of Peirce's Development of the Algebra of Relations." *Am J of Semiotics* 2:1–2 (1983).

[639] Buczyńska-Garewicz, Hanna. "Husserl and Peirce." *Phenomenology Information Bull* 5 (October 1981), 105–110.

[640] ____. "On the Concept of the Degenerate Sign." *Studia Semiotyczne* 11 (1981), 121–140. (Revised version of [112], in Polish.)

[641] ____. "Sign and Dialogue." *Am J of Semiotics* 2:1–2 (1983).

[642] ____. "The Sign: Its Past and Future." *Semiosis* No. 25–26 (1982), 111–118.

[643] Bybee, Michael David. "Peirce's and James's Theories of Truth: A Critical Reformulation and Evaluation." Diss. Hawaii 1981. *DAI* 42:12A (1982), 5146.

[644] Chauviré, Christiane. "Peirce, Popper et l'abduction." *Revue Philosophique de la France et de l'Etranger* 171 (1981), 441–459.

[645] Clark, Romane. "When is a Fallacy Valid? Reflections on Backward Reasoning." *Notre Dame J of Formal Logic* 23 (1982), 1–13.

[646] Deledalle, Gérard. "Les grands thèmes de la philosophie de Charles S. Peirce." *Semiotica* 32 (1980), 329–337. (Review article of S 753, Part 2.)

[647] Eco, Umberto. "Grandi riscoperte: Charles Sanders Peirce—professione: genio; nazionalità: americana." *L'Espresso* No. 28 (11 July 1976), 52–56.

[648] Eisele, Carolyn. "An Introduction to Peirce's Mathematical Semiotic." *Am J of Semiotics* 2:1–2 (1983).

[649] Fisch, Max H. "Just *How* General is Peirce's General Theory of Signs?" *Am J of Semiotics* 2:1–2 (1983).

[650] Floss, Karel. "Die Sprachphilosophie und die Triaden." In [609], vol. 2.

[651] Freeman, Eugene. "The Search for Objectivity in Peirce and Popper." In [61]. (See also S 523 and [671].)

[652] Hantzis, Catharine Wells. "Peirce on Logic: Phenomenology as the Basis for Normative Science." Diss. California at Berkeley 1981. *DAI* 42:12A (1982), 5148.

[654] Karger, Angelika H. "Das Peircesche Bewusstseinskonzept." *Semiosis* No. 27 (1982).

[654] Keiner, Mechtild. "Peirce und Husserl: Zu einer Gegenüberstellung von Hanna Buczyńska-Garewicz [639]." *Semiosis* No. 27 (1982).

[655] Kemp-Pritchard, Ilona. "Peirce on Philosophical Hope and Logical Sentiment." *Phil and Phenomenological Res* 42 (1981), 75–90.

[656] Kepchar, John Howard, Jr. "Kant, Peirce, and the Transcendental Method." Diss. North Carolina at Chapel Hill 1981. *DAI* 42:6A (1981), 2716.

[657] Ketner, Kenneth L. "The Best Example of Semiosis and Its Use in Teaching Semiotics." *Am J of Semiotics* 1:1–2 (1981), 47–83.

[658] Kevelson, Roberta. "Time as Method in Charles Sanders Peirce." *Am J of Semiotics* 2:1–2 (1983).

[659] Kloesel, Christian J. W. "The First Barrier: Peirce's Early Theory of Signs (1863–1885)." *Am J of Semiotics* 2:1–2 (1983).

[660] Krois, John Michael. "Vico's and Peirce's 'Sensus Communis'." In *Vico: Past and Present*, ed. Giorgio Tagliacozzo, II:58–71. Atlantic Highlands, NJ: Humanities Press, 1981.

[661] Laudan, Larry. *Science and Hypothesis: Historical Essays on Scientific Methodology.* Dordrecht-Holland: D. Reidel, 1981.

[662] Levy, Stephen Harry. "A Comparative Analysis of Charles S. Peirce's Philosophy of Mathematics." Diss. Fordham 1982. *DAI* 43:1A (1982), 185.

[663] Liszka, Jakob. "Peirce and Lévi-Strauss: The Metaphysics of Semiotic and the Semiosis of Metaphysics." *Idealistic Stud* 12 (1982), 103–134.

[664] Magdum, Dinkar. "The Relation Between Peirce and Kant with Respect to the Fundamentals of Mechanics." *Semiosis* No. 24 (1981), 5–13.

[665] Martins, António. "De Peirce a Habermas: sobre a(s) teoria(s) intersubjectiva(s) da verdade." *Biblos*, January 1980, 425–455.

[666] Morier, Claude. "L'apport de Leibniz à la sémiotique." *Semiotica* 32 (1980), 339–355. (Review article of Marcello Dascal, *La sémiologie de Leibniz*.)

[667] ———. "Le père oublié de la sémiotique moderne: C. S. Peirce." *Semiotica* 39:3–4 (1982). (Review article of [10].)

[668] Nesher, Dan. "Remarks on Peirce's Pragmatic Theory of Meaning." *Transactions* 18 (1982), 75–90.

[669] Orange, Donna. "Peirce's Falsifiable Theism." *Am J of Semiotics* 2:1–2 (1983).

[670] "Peirce's Semiotic and Its Audiences." *Am J of Semiotics* 2:1–2 (January 1983). Special Peirce issue edited by Kenneth L. Ketner; besides the thirteen articles listed in the present section, it contains "A Brief Intellectual Autobiography by Charles Sanders Peirce" edited by Ketner.

[671] Popper, Karl. "Reply to Eugene Freeman [651]." In [61].

[672] Rochberg-Halton, Eugene, and Kevin McMurtrey. "The Foundations of Modern Semiotic: Charles Peirce and Charles Morris." *Am J of Semiotics* 2:1–2 (1983).

[673] Rohatyn, Dennis. "Resurrecting Peirce's 'Neglected Argument' for God." *Transactions* 18 (1982), 66–74.

[674] Rothenberg, Kenneth H. "Peircean Principles and Disenchantment with the Social Sciences." Diss. Wayne State 1981. *DAI* 42:2A (1981), 737.

[675] Schlossberger, Eugene. "Fallibilism and the Ideal Scientific Community." *Transactions* 18 (1982), 230–231.

[676] Schönenberg, Michael. "Die Entwicklung der Fundamentalkategorien von C. S. Peirce: Eine historisch-systematische Untersuchung." Diss. Stuttgart (Germany) 1979.

[677] Scott, Frances W. "Process from the Peircean Point of View: Some Applications to Art." *Am J of Semiotics* 2:1–2 (1983).

[678] Sheriff, John K. "Charles S. Peirce and the Semiotics of Literature." In *Semiotic Themes*, ed. Richard T. De George, pp. 51–74. Lawrence: University of Kansas Publications, 1981.

[679] Singer, Marcus G. "Not 'But' But 'Not': A Note." *Transactions* 18 (1982), 227–229.

[680] Skidmore, Arthur. "Peirce and Semiotics: An Introduction to Peirce's Theory of Signs." In *Semiotic Themes*, ed. Richard T. De George, pp. 33–50. Lawrence: University of Kansas Publications, 1981.

[681] Smith, John E. "Community and Reality." In [61]. (See S 1358.)

[682] ____. "The Tension Between Direct Experience and Argument in Religion." *Religious Stud* 17 (1981), 487–498.

[683] Smith, Kim. "Peirce and the Prague School on the Foundational Role of the 'Aesthetic' Sign." *Am J of Semiotics* 2:1–2 (1983).

[684] Spinks, C. W. "Peirce's Demon Abduction: Or How to Charm the Truth out of a Quark." *Am J of Semiotics* 2:1–2 (1983).

[685] Stetter, Christian. "Das Wahrnehmungsurteil bei Kant und Peirce." In *Ästhetik und Umwelt*, ed. Hermann Sturm, pp. 47–62. Tübingen: Gunter Narr, 1979.

[686] Thayer, H. S. *Meaning and Action: A Critical History of Pragmatism*. Second edition. Indianapolis: Hackett, 1981
  Review: Altshuler, B. *Transactions* 18 (1982), 255–265.

[687] Ueding, Wolfgang M. "A German Supplement to the Secondary Peirce Bibliographies." *Am J of Semiotics* 2:1–2 (1983).

[688] Walther, Elisabeth. "Common-Sense bei Kant und Peirce." *Semiosis* No. 23 (1981), 58–66.

[689] Weinsheimer, Joel. "The Realism of C. S. Peirce, or How Homer and Nature Can Be the Same." *Am J of Semiotics* 2:1–2 (1983).

INDEX

Abailard (Abelard), Peter, 99
Abelson, R. P., 263n
Achinstein, Peter, 132n
Adams, John Couch, 72
Adams, M. M., 96, 107n
Adler, Mortimer, 28
Agassiz, Louis, 13, 352, 358
Airaksinen, T., 220n
Albrechts-Tyteca, L., 28
Albert, H., 223n
Almeder, Robert, 347n, 348n, 349n.
Altshuler, B., 105, 107n
Andersen, Henning, 20
Anscombe, G. E. M., 263n, 265n
Anselm, Saint, 99
Apel, Karl-Otto, 26, 218n, 219n, 220n, 221n,
   222n, 223n, 224n, 225n
Aquinas, Saint Thomas, 99, 100, 102, 103,
   104, 197
Aristotelians, medieval, 98, 99, 104, 130, 131,
   183
Aristotle, 15, 20, 28, 31, 85, 89, 90, 92, 93,
   103, 111, 116, 119n, 182, 199
Arrington, R. L., 346n
Augustine, Saint, 96
Austin, John L., 221n
Ayer, A. J. (Sir Alfred), 14, 219n, 293n

Bacon, Francis, 28, 364
Bain, Alexander, 243, 244, 245, 251, 262n
Baldwin, James M., 279, 368
Baldwin, Tom, 265n
Bar-Hillel, J., 162, 168n, 221n
Bartlett, John, 29
Battersby, Christine, 265n
Baumol, W. J., 14
Beardsley, Monroe, 239n
Beck, L. W., 220n, 225n, 291, 294n
Becker, 13
Beethoven, Ludwig Van, 173
Bentham, Jeremy, 337
Bergson, Henri, 75, 85
Bernard, Claude, 374n

Bernstein, Richard J., 35n, 132n
Berkeley, George, 80, 88, 95, 101, 105, 277,
   278
Beth, E. W., 117, 119n
Black, Max, 133n
Blackwell, 37n
Blanshard, Brand, 87, 201
Blumer, Herbert, 21, 22
Bochenski, Joseph M., 92, 93
Boehner, Theophilous, 294n
Boler, John, 95, 97, 107n, 328n, 329n, 352,
   373n
Boltzmann, Ludwig, 358
Bolzano, Bernard, 197, 220n, 221n
Boole, George, 26, 113, 117
Boorse, 346
Bourgeois, Patrick, 26
Boutroux, Emile, 75
Bowditch, Nathaniel, 29
Bowsma, O. K., 265n
Bradley, Francis Herbert, 90
Braithwaite, R. B., 262n
Brock, Jarrett, 133n
Brouwer, L. E. J., 12
Broyles, James E., 263n
Bruno, Giordano, 184
Brutus, Marcus Junius, 100
Bubner, R., 219n
Buckle, Henry Thomas, 353
Buchler, J., 347n, 351, 352, 373n, 375
Bühler, Karl, 221n
Bunyan, Paul (fictional), 229
Burks, Arthur W., 9, 15, 94n, 119n, 132n,
   145n, 149, 154n, 166n, 178n, 262n, 277,
   311n, 327n, 346n, 375
Butts, Robert, 94n

Cadwallader, Joyce V., 14
Cadwallader, Thomas C., 14
Caesar, Julius, 100
Calvin, John, 49
Campbell, Donald T., 352, 369, 372n, 373n,
   374n

407

Campbell, Lewis, 30
Carmichael, R. D., 28, 36n
Carnap, Rudolf, 77, 154n, 157, 162, 166n, 191,
    194, 196, 197, 198, 220n, 221n, 273, 274,
    275, 276, 277, 281, 284, 285, 286, 287, 288,
    289, 290, 291, 293n
Carus, M. Blouke, 8
Carus, Paul, 76
Cassirer, E., 309, 313n
Chisholm, R., 349n
Chomsky, Noam, 19, 35n, 161, 308, 313n
Clausius, Rudolf Julius Emanuel, 353
Cohen, Bernard I., 34n
Cohen, J. L., 158, 167n
Cohen, Morris R., 9, 16, 17, 375
Cohen, R. S., 349n
Colodny, Robert G., 132n
Columbus, Christopher, 74
Compton, Arthur Holly, 14, 15
Comte, August, 336, 353
Cook, James E., 168n, 375
Copernicus, 144
Cornman, James W., 264n
Cotton, J. H., 35n
Creswell, M. J., 162, 168n
Curd, 28
Curtis, Charles P., 29
Cusanus, Nicolaus, 184
Cuvier (Baron), 358

Davidson, D., 166n, 200, 222n
Darwin, Charles, 144, 350, 351, 353, 354, 355,
    357, 358, 359, 360, 364, 366, 369, 372, 373,
    374n
Dedekind, Richard, 12
De Long, Howard, 374n
DeMorgan, Augustus, 355, 373n
Democritus, 85
Descartes, Renee, 49, 68, 145n, 148, 199, 203,
    240, 241, 242, 243, 244, 246, 247, 248, 249,
    250, 251, 252, 253, 254, 255, 256, 257, 261,
    262n, 263n, 264n, 265n, 276, 277, 278, 282,
    295
Dewey, John, 16, 17, 21, 22, 235, 289, 298,
    309, 310, 313n, 353, 366, 367, 368, 369,
    374n
Dirac, Paul Adrien Maurice, 291
Dougherty, Charles J., 26
Duhem, Pierre M. M., 337, 338, 341, 345
Dummett, Michael, 272n
Dunham, Albert M., 22
Dusek, Val, 13

Eames, Charles, 34n
Eames, Ray, 34

Eco, Umberto, 13
Einstein, Albert, 15, 80, 92, 144
Eisele, Carolyn, 11, 14, 15, 34n, 109, 110, 111,
    113, 114, 115, 116, 117, 119n, 155n, 166n,
    272n, 311n, 312n, 313n, 375
Elster, Jon, 360, 373n
Euclid, 112, 113, 114, 287, 298
Erasmus, 263n
Euler, Leonhard, 72

Fann, K. T., 27, 28, 145n
Faris, J. A., 30
Fa Tsang, 86, 87
Faye, 12
Feibleman, James, 158, 167n, 180, 351, 352,
    273n
Feigl H., 132n, 154n, 293n
Festinger, L., 263n
Feyerabend, P. K., 121, 122, 123, 124, 125,
    132n, 223n, 289, 291, 349n
Fichte, Johann Gottlieb, 278
Fisch, Max H., 9, 55n, 76, 154n, 220n, 262n,
    352, 373n, 375, 376
Fisher, R. A., 354, 373n
Fine, Kit, 160, 168n
Fodor, Jerry A., 161
Fleming, N. 265n
Fløistad, G., 219n
Føllesdal, D., 106, 107n, 341, 345
Frankfurt, Harry, 145n
Freeman, Eugene, 10, 13, 14, 25, 33, 80, 81
Frege, G., 26, 115, 117, 118, 157, 166n, 220n,
    221n, 272n, 275, 286, 287
Freud, Sigmund, 23

Gabriel, G., 221n
Gadamer, H.-G., 219n
Galileo, 130
Gallie, W. B., 155n, 158, 167n, 351, 373n
Gehlen, A., 222n
Gentry, George V., 347n
Geraets, Th., 222n
Gilman, Daniel Coit, 9
God, (the Deity), 77, 84, 86, 152, 180, 189,
    242, 249, 335
Goldfeld, S. M., 14
Good, I. J., 26
Goodman, Nelson, 135, 137, 138, 139, 140,
    141, 142, 143, 144, 145n, 146n, 260, 265n,
    311
Goodman, Paul, 213n
Gore, 28
Goudge, Thomas A., 36n, 329n, 348n, 352,
    373n
Grajewski, M., 100, 107n

Gray, J. Glenn, 36n
Green, Maurice R., 22
Greene, M., 264n
Greenlee, Douglas, 329n
Greenslet, Ferris, 29
Gurwitsch, Aron, 313n
Guttenplan, S., 265n
Gutting, Gary, 28, 37n

Haack, R. J., 264n
Haack, Susan, 262n, 263n, 264n, 271, 272n
Habermas, J., 200, 207, 208, 209, 210, 211, 214, 215, 216, 217, 218, 219n, 221n, 224n, 373n
Hall, G. Stanley, 23
Haldane, E. S., 262n
Hamilton, Sir William, 158, 167n
Hanson, Norwood Russell, 15, 28, 121, 123, 132n
Hardwick, Charles S., 35n, 168n, 312n
Hare, Peter H., 21, 346n
Harman, G., 166n
Hartshorne, Charles, 9, 18, 22, 33, 64, 75, 94n, 119n, 132n, 145n, 154n, 166n, 171, 172, 178n, 179n, 189n, 262n, 272n, 293n, 311n, 327n, 346n, 375
Hefferline, Ralph, 311, 313n
Hegel, 25, 38, 41, 43, 46, 67, 87, 88, 102, 182, 194, 198, 202, 203, 220n, 223n, 232, 257, 278, 353
Hegeler, Edward C., 7
Heidegger, Martin, 26, 276
Heidrich, C. H., 220n
Hempel, Carl, 154n, 194
Henderson, Edgar, 8
Henle, Paul, 20, 35n
Henry, D. P., 99, 107n
Herbrand, Jacques, 117
Herzberger, Hans G., 25
Hilbert, David, 118, 287
Hilpenen, Risto, 119n
Hintikka, Jaakko, 94n., 106, 107n, 115, 116, 117, 119n, 120n, 272n, 297, 298, 307, 312n, 313n, 345
Hintikka, Merril, 119n
Hocutt, Max Oliver, 226, 227, 228, 229, 230, 234
Höffe, O., 224n
Hoijer, Harry, 36n
Holmes, Sherlock, 12, 119n
Hospers, John, 239n
Horowitz, Irving Louis, 21
Hume, David, 88, 90, 137, 138, 141, 144, 145, 169, 277, 330, 337, 338, 341, 342, 343
Humphries, Paul, 265n

Husserl, 19, 25, 26, 36n, 82, 86, 89, 169, 178, 194, 199, 203, 205, 223n
Huxley, J. S., 370, 374n
Huxley, Thomas H., 373n

Jackson, Frank, 145n
Jakobson, Roman, 13, 19, 20, 21
James, Wm., 9, 21, 22, 43, 56, 75, 92, 147, 150, 151, 154, 164, 207, 262n, 279, 280, 284, 308, 353, 358, 363, 364, 366, 367, 368, 369, 374n
Jastrow, Joseph, 17, 22
Jeans, Sir James, 190n
Jervis, R., 263n
Jevons, Stanley, 364, 374n
Jevons, W. J., 158, 159, 167n, 168n, 365
Johnstone, Henry W., 28
Jones, Wm. B., 94n

Kaelin, E. F., 293n
Kamlah, W., 200, 222n
Kant, Immanuel, 32, 33, 58n, 67, 82, 101, 117, 119n, 182, 183, 184, 194, 199, 201, 205, 206, 212, 213, 218, 220n, 222n, 223n, 224n, 277, 293n, 314, 321, 327n, 353, 367, 374n
Katz, J., 161
Keisler, H., Jerome, 11
Kepler, 136
Kernan, 16
Ketchum, R., 346n
Ketner, Kenneth, 26, 375
Keuth, H., 219n
Kevelson, Roberta, 26
Kiefer, H. E., 264n
Kisiel, 37n
Koffka, Kurt, 310
Kohl, Marvin, 347n
Köhler, W., 310
Kripke, Saul A., 306
Krohn, Swen, 220n
Krois, Michael, 37n
Kuhn, T. S., 123, 124, 133n, 150, 151, 154n, 265n, 289, 291, 358
Kloesel, Christian J. W., 375

Ladd-Franklin, Christine, 17, 27
Lakatos, Imre, 154n, 349n
Lakoff, G., 157, 167n
Lamarck, 351, 358, 373n
Langer, Suzanne K., 228, 231, 235, 238n, 239n
Larsen, Svend Erik, 23
Laudan, 28
Le blanc, H., 222n
Lee, Benjamin, 35n
Leibniz G., 85, 86, 87, 92, 93, 109, 184

Le Roy, 358
Leverrier, Urbain J. J., 72
Levi, I., 264n
Lévi-Strauss, Claude, 20
Lewis, C. I., 157, 287
Lewis, J. David, 21, 162, 166n, 168n, 221n
Lincourt, John M., 21, 22, 36n, 47
Linsky, Leonard, 293n
Locke, John, 24, 276
Lutoslawski, Wincenty, 30, 31
Lonergan, B., 102, 107n
Lorenz, K., 200, 222n
Lorenzen, P., 200, 222n, 225n
Luhmann, N., 221n
Lützeler, H., 222n

MacLane, Saunders, 163, 168n
Mach, Ernst, 80, 277, 287, 358, 364, 365, 366, 367, 368, 369, 374n
Mansel, H. L., 167n
Maquet, Jaques, 36n
Mannoury, Gerrit, 12
Marquand, Allan, 14
Martin, R. M., 34n, 220n, 221n
Marty, Robert, 164, 168n
Maxwell, Grover, 132n, 154n
Maxwell, James Clerk, 353
McCulloch, Warren, 27
McKeon, Ch. K., 158, 167n
Mead, George Herbert, 21, 22, 257, 264n
Mead, Margaret, 19
Medawar, P. B. (Sir Peter), 358, 370, 373n, 374n
Medusa, 68
Meinesz, Vening, 12
Menger, Karl, 74
Meyers, Robert G., 262n
Michael, Frederick, 36n
Mill, John Stuart, 53, 141, 169
Mills, C. Wright, 21, 22
Mitchell, 24
Molière, 295
Montague, Richard, 157, 166n, 221n
Moody, E. A., 99, 107n
Moore, Edward C., 36n, 94n, 133n, 375
Moore, E. H., 297
Moravcsik, J. M., 167n
Morgan, Thomas Hunt, 291
Morgan, Charles, 165, 168n
Morris, Charles, 18, 191, 194, 196, 219n, 220n, 230, 231, 232, 233, 234, 235, 236, 238n, 239n, 273, 277, 292, 293n, 300, 308, 309, 312n, 313n
Morris, W. E., 264n
Munitz, M. K., 264n

Murphey, Murray, 66, 180, 190n, 223n, 224n, 225n, 347n, 352, 373n
Murphy, Arthur E., 300
Murphy, Edward F., 29
Musgrave, A., 154n
Meyers, Robert G., 145n
Michael, Emily, 36n

Nadin, Mihai, 164, 168n
Neptune, 72
Neurath, O., 201, 222n, 223n, 277
Nevid, S. J., 263n
Newman, James R., 29
Newton, Isaac, 15, 80, 122, 131, 144, 184, 353
Newcomb, Simon, 14
Nickles, Thomas, 28
Nolan, Rita, 265n
Nott, Kathleen, 14

Occam or Ockham, 74, 95, 96, 97, 98, 99, 101, 102, 294n
Ogden, C. K., 16, 17
Ohara, Akira, 376
Olczak, Paul V., 22, 36n, 47
Olson, Richard, 35n
O'Malley, J. J., 220n

Pap, Arthur, 77, 293n
Pappas, G. S., 264n
Paul, G. A., 263n
Pascal, Blaise, 249, 263n
Peano, Giuseppe, 26
Pearson, Karl, 363, 364, 367, 369, 374n
Peirce, Benjamin, 13, 91
Peirce, Juliette Froissy, 17
Pelletier, Francis J., 165, 168n
Pepper, Stephen, 260, 265n
Percy, Walker, 22
Perelman, Ch., 28
Perls, Frederick, 311, 313n
Perry, Ralph Barton, 374n
Perseus, 68
Picasso, Pablo, 230, 236
Plato, 31, 77, 227, 237
Poe, Edgar Allan, 19
Polanyi, M., 254, 257, 263n, 264n, 265n
Popper, Karl, 13, 14, 15, 34n, 64, 65, 74, 76, 80, 150, 151, 154n, 192, 194, 197, 220n, 223n, 250, 254, 255, 263n, 264n, 276, 350, 357, 360, 373n
Poppins, Mary (fictional), 229
Popkin, Richard, 263n
Prawitz, Dag, 119n
Prior, Arthur N., 306
Przelicky, Marian, 161, 168n

Puntel, L. B., 200, 201, 222n, 224n
Putnam, Hilary, 26, 96, 106, 108n, 133n, 162, 168n, 257, 264n
Pythagoras, 31, 82, 348n

Quine, W. V. O., 106, 112, 119n, 133n, 157, 161, 166n, 168n, 245, 259, 260, 263n, 265n, 283, 294n, 330, 334, 336, 337, 338, 339, 340, 341, 342, 343, 344, 345, 346, 348n, 349n, 350

Ramsay, F. P., 211, 219n, 243, 244, 262n
Rantala, Veikko, 115, 117, 118, 119n
Rathus, S. A., 263n
Reck, Andrew, 93, 264n
Remes, Unto, 119n
Rescher, N., 23, 222n, 264n, 265n
Richards, I. A., 16
Rieger, Burghard, 168n
Robin, Richard S., 36n, 94n, 133n, 166n, 313n
Robinson, Abraham, 11
Roberts, Don, 26, 306, 307, 312n, 313n
Rolf, George A., 293n
Roll-Hansen, Nils, 374n
Ronat, Mitsou, 19
Rorty, R., 106, 108n
Rosenberg, Harold, 236
Rosenthal, Sandra, 26, 327n
Ross, G. R. T., 262n
Rosser, J. Barkley, 14
Royce, Josiah, 16, 17, 21, 39, 42, 43, 44, 45, 52, 55, 56, 57, 58n, 214, 225n
Rudner, R., 231, 232, 233, 234, 235
Ruskin, John, 37n
Russell, Bertrand, 16, 26, 88, 89, 90, 94, 112, 133n, 157, 159, 166n, 198, 275, 276, 286, 287, 300, 347n
Russett, Cynthia Eagle, 373n

Saarinen, Esa, 272n
Śankara, 90
Santayana, George, 22
Saussure (De Saussure) F., 18, 19, 20
Schaffner, 28
Scheffler, Israel, 146n, 372n
Schelling, Friedrich W. J. von, 351, 353
Schiller, F. C. S., 15, 33, 267, 369
Schiller, Friedrick, 37n
Schilpp, Paul A., 34n, 77, 293n, 373n
Schlick, M., 223n
Schmidt, Emerson P., 21
Schneer, Cecil, J., 34n
Schneider, Herbert, 33
Schuldenfrei, 344
Schueller, Herbert, 239n

Schwartz, Robert, 146n, 349n
Schwartz, S. P., 264n
St. John, 351
Schröder, E., 12, 26
Scott, T. K., 97, 108n
Scotus, Duns, 42, 43, 54, 56, 58n, 71, 95, 98, 99, 100, 101, 102, 105, 167n, 169, 184, 347n
Scriven, M., 132n, 154n, 293n
Searle, J. R., 221n, 222n
Sebeok, Jean Umiker, 12, 16
Sebeok, Thomas A., 12, 13, 16, 34n, 35n
Sellars, Wilfrid, 23, 121, 123, 132n, 200, 222n
Sen, S. K., 190n
Sesonske, A., 265n
Shapere, Dudley, 132n
Shapiro, Marianne, 20
Shapiro, Herman, 98, 108n
Shapiro, Michael, 20
Sheffer, Henry M., 16
Shimony, Abner, 372n
Shorey, Paul, 30
Short, T. L., 133n
Simmel, Georg, 358
Simon, J., 220n
Singer, Milton, 20, 21
Skirbekk, G., 220n
Skolimowski, Henryk, 14, 74
Smith, C. M., 227, 228, 229, 230, 232, 234, 235, 237, 238n, 239n
Smith, John E., 153, 154n, 155n
Smith, Richard L., 21
Snoeyenbos, M., 346n
Socrates, 29, 30, 31
Spencer, Herbert, 353
Spiegelberg, Herbert, 26, 223n
Stanley, Albert A., 35n
Stapp, Henry P., 94n
Stearns, Isabel, 328n
Stegmüller, W., 219n
Stenius, Erik, 117, 119n, 272n
Stevenson, Charles L., 231, 233, 234, 235, 237
Strawson, Sir Peter, 211, 219n
Stroud, B., 224n
Sullivan, Harry Stack, 22, 36n
Swain, M., 264n
Swinburne, R. G., 347n

Tarski, Alfred, 192, 194, 197, 198, 199, 200, 219n, 220n
Thayer, 339
Thomson, 264n
Tomas, Vincent, 19, 375
Tooke, John Horne, 337
Toulmin, Stephen, 352, 373n

Tugendhat, E., 200, 220n, 222n, 223n
Turing, A. M., 374n
Turquette, A. R., 14, 26
Tuttle, Preston, 14

Uhr, Leonard, 23
Unger, P., 263n

Van Hise, 13
Veitch, J., 167n
Venn, John, 72

Walsh, F. Michael, 27
Wartenberg, Gerd, 26, 225n
Wartofsky, M. W., 349n
Weiss, Paul, 9, 25, 94n, 119n, 132n, 145n,
    154n, 166n, 178n, 262n, 272n, 293n, 311n,
    327n, 346n, 375
Weizsäcker, C. F. von, 222n
Welby, Victoria (Lady), 16, 17, 35n, 163, 164,
    304, 312n
Wertheimer, Max, 310
Whately, Richard, 32
Wheeler, John Archibald, 94n
Whewell, William, 15, 28, 357, 360, 373n
Whistler, James (Abbott) McNeill, 237

Whitehead, Alfred North, 16, 22, 26, 75, 82,
    83, 84, 85, 86, 87, 88, 89, 92, 93, 94, 275,
    276, 287, 300
Whitely, Charles, 265n
Wiener, Philip P., 9
Wiener, Philip P., 9, 36n, 57n, 94n, 167n,
    179n, 328n, 350, 351, 352, 372n, 375
Wilkinson, Elizabeth M., 37n
Wilson, Edward O., 352, 373n
Williams, B. A. O., 263n
Williams, D., 250, 255, 264n
Willoughby, L. A., 37n
Wittgenstein, Ludwig, 118, 157, 166n, 200,
    204, 215, 222n, 224n, 249, 257, 260, 263n,
    264n, 265n, 272n, 275, 276, 287, 350
Wright, Chauncey, 21, 353
Wright, Crispin, 166n
Wright, Georg Henrik von, 88, 94n, 294n

Yonemori, Yuji, 376
Young, Frederic H., 9, 36n, 57n, 94n, 167n,
    179n, 328n

Zadeh, I., 165, 168n
Zellweger, Shea, 26, 27, 36n
Zeman, Jay, 119n, 235, 239n, 313n